Financial Management
Principles and Practice

Timothy J. Gallagher
Professor of Finance
Colorado State University

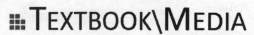

■▪ TEXTBOOK\MEDIA

The Quality Instructors Expect.
At Prices Students Can Afford.

Replacing Oligarch Textbooks since 2004

To my family—Susan, Emily, Ellie, and Zach

FINANCIAL MANAGEMENT: PRINCIPLES AND PRACTICE, 8th Edition

Cover credits:
  Top left: RawPixel.com/Shutterstock.com
  Top right: everything possible/Shutterstock.com
  Middle left: Who is Danny/Shutterstock.com
  Middle right: RawPixel.com/Shutterstock.com
  Lower middle left: Morguefile.com
  Lower middle right: nopporn/Shutterstock.com
  Bottom left: everything possible/Shutterstock.com
  Bottom right: Dean Drobot/Shutterstock.com

ISBN-13: 978-1-7322425-0-0
ISBN-10: 1-7322425-0-X

Library of Congress Cataloging-in-Publication Data
Gallagher, Timothy James, 1952–

Financial Management: Principles and Practice/Timothy J. Gallagher— 8th ed.
p. cm.

Includes bibliographical references and index.
1. Corporation—Finance.   I. Andrew, Joseph D.   II. Title

HG4026. G348 2006
658.15—dc21   2002074888

This book was previously published by: Pearson Education, Inc.

Brief Contents

Preface xiv
About the Author xix

PART 1 THE WORLD OF FINANCE 1

1 Finance and the Firm 3

2 Financial Markets and Interest Rates 23

3 Financial Institutions 41

PART 2 ESSENTIAL CONCEPTS IN FINANCE 59

4 Review of Accounting 61

5 Analysis of Financial Statements 81

6 Forecasting for Financial Planning 113

7 Risk and Return 135

8 The Time Value of Money 163

PART 3 CAPITAL BUDGETING AND BUSINESS VALUATION 209

9 The Cost of Capital 211

10 Capital Budgeting Decision Methods 239

11 Estimating Incremental Cash Flows 277

12 Business Valuation 297

PART 4 LONG-TERM FINANCING DECISIONS 331

13 Capital Structure Basics 333

14 Corporate Bonds, Preferred Stock, and Leasing 359

15 Common Stock 383

16 Dividend Policy 403

PART 5 SHORT-TERM FINANCING DECISIONS 419

17 Working Capital Policy 421

18 Managing Cash 437

19 Accounts Receivable and Inventory 457

20 Short-Term Financing 485

PART 6 FINANCE IN THE GLOBAL ECONOMY 505

21 International Finance 507

Appendix A-1
Glossary G-1
Index I-1

Contents

Preface xiv
About the Author xix

PART 1 THE WORLD OF FINANCE   1

1 Finance and the Firm 3
Learning Objectives 3

When Finance Goes Wrong 3

The 2008 Financial Crisis—Its History and Reverberations Today 4

Chapter Overview 6

The Field of Finance 6

Finance Career Paths 7

Financial Management 7

The Role of the Financial Manager 7

Finance in the Organization of the Firm 8

The Organization of the Finance Team 8

The Basic Financial Goal of the Firm 8

In Search of Value 9

The Importance of Cash Flow 10

The Effect of Timing on Cash Flow Valuation 10

The Influence of Risk 10

Profits versus Company Value 11

Legal and Ethical Challenges in Financial Management 11

Agency Issues 12

The Agency Problem 12

Agency Costs 13

The Interests of Other Groups 13

The Interests of Society as a Whole 13

Forms of Business Organization 14

The Proprietorship 14

The Partnership 15

Special Kinds of Partnerships 15

The Corporation 15

Public and Private Corporations 16

Benefit Corporations 17

Limited Liability Companies (LLCs) 17

What's Next 18

Summary 18 • Key Terms 19 • Self-Test 20 • Review Questions 20 • Build Your Communication Skills 20 • Problems 20 • Answers to Self-Test 21

2 Financial Markets and Interest Rates 23
Learning Objectives 23

Interest Rates Can't Be Negative, Can They? 23

Chapter Overview 24

The Financial System 24

Securities 24

Financial Intermediaries 25

Investment Bankers 25

Brokers 25

Dealers 25

Financial Markets 25

The Primary Market 26

The Secondary Market 26

The Money Market 26

The Capital Market 26

Security Exchanges 26

The Over-the-Counter (OTC) Market 27

Market Efficiency 27

Securities in the Financial Marketplace 27

Securities in the Money Market 27

Treasury Bills 28

Negotiable Certificates of Deposit 28

Commercial Paper 28

Banker's Acceptances 28

Securities in the Capital Market 28

Bonds 28

Bond Terminology and Types 29

Treasury Notes and Bonds 29

Municipal Bonds 30

Corporate Bonds 30

Corporate Stock 30

Common Stock 30

Preferred Stock 31

Interest 31

Determinants of Interest Rates 31

The Real Rate of Interest 31

The Inflation Premium 32

The Default Risk Premium 32

The Illiquidity Risk Premium 32

The Maturity Risk Premium 33

Safe Storage Premium 33

The Yield Curve 34

Making Use of the Yield Curve 35

What's Next 35

Summary 36 • Key Terms 36 • Self-Test 37 • Review Questions 38 • Build Your Communication Skills 38 • Problems 38 • Answers to Self-Test 39

3 Financial Institutions 41

Learning Objectives 41

Too Big to Fail? 41

Chapter Overview 42

Financial Intermediation 42

Denomination Matching 42

Maturity Matching 42

Absorbing Credit Risk 43

Commercial Banks 43

Bank Regulation 44

Commercial Bank Operations 44

Commercial Bank Reserves 45

The Federal Reserve System 45

Organization of the Fed 45

Controlling the Money Supply 46

The Discount Window 47

Government-Sponsored Enterprises (GSEs) and the Mortgage Market 48

Savings and Loan Associations 48

Regulation of S&Ls 49

Mutual Companies versus Stockholder-Owned Companies 49

The Problem of Matching Loan and Deposit Maturities 49

S&Ls' Real Assets 50

Credit Unions 50

The Common Bond Requirement 50

Members as Shareholders 51

Credit Unions Compared with Banks 51

Credit Union Regulation 51

Finance Companies, Insurance Companies, and Pension Funds 51

Types of Finance Companies 51

Consumer Finance Companies 51

Commercial Finance Companies 52

Sales Finance Companies 52

Insurance Companies 52

Life Insurance Companies 52

Property and Casualty Insurance Companies 52

Retirement Plans 53

Annuities 54

Legislation after the Financial Crisis of 2008 54

What's Next 55

Summary 55 • Key Terms 56 • Self-Test 56 • Review Questions 56 • Build Your Communication Skills 57 • Problems 57 • Answers to Self-Test 58

PART 2 ESSENTIAL CONCEPTS IN FINANCE 59

4 Review of Accounting 61

Learning Objectives 61

A Big Shake-up for Accountants and Businesses 61

Chapter Overview 62

Review of Accounting Fundamentals 62

Basic Accounting Financial Statements 63

The Income Statement 63

Revenues 63

Expenses 64

Cost of Goods Sold 64

Selling and Administrative Expenses 64

Depreciation Expense 64

Operating Income and Interest Expense 64

Net Income 65

Earnings per Share (EPS) 65

Common Stock Dividends and Retained Earnings 65

The Balance Sheet 66

The Asset Accounts 66

Current Assets 66

Fixed Assets 67

The Liabilities and Equity Accounts 67

Liabilities 67

Common Stock and Retained Earnings 68

Contents   v

The Statement of Cash Flows 68
  Operating Activities 69
  Adjustment for Depreciation Expense 69
  Changes in Balance Sheet Accounts 69
  Operating Activities 70
  Investment Activities 71
  Financing Activities 71
  Net Cash Flow during the Period 71
Depreciation 71
  Calculating the Amount
    of Depreciation Expense 72
  Depreciation Methods 72
Income Taxes 73
What's Next 74

*Summary 74 • Key Terms 74 • Self-Test 74 • Review
Questions 75 • Build Your Communication Skills 75
• Problems 76 • Answers to Self-Test 80*

5 Analysis of Financial Statements 81

Learning Objectives 81

Apple Earnings Break Records for Q1 2015 81
Chapter Overview 82
Assessing Financial Health 82
  Misleading Numbers 82
  Financial Ratios 83
The Basic Financial Ratios 83
  Calculating the Ratios 84
  Profitability Ratios 84
    Gross Profit Margin 84
    Operating Profit Margin 85
    Net Profit Margin 86
    Return on Assets 86
    Return on Equity 86
    Mixing Numbers from Income Statements
      and Balance Sheets 87
  Liquidity Ratios 87
    The Current Ratio 87
    The Quick Ratio 88
  Debt Ratios 88
    Debt to Total Assets 88
    Times Interest Earned 89
  Asset Activity Ratios 89
    Average Collection Period 89
    Inventory Turnover 90
    Total Asset Turnover 90
  Market Value Ratios 90
    Price to Earnings Ratio 91
    Market to Book Value 91

Economic Value Added and Market Value
    Added 92
  Economic Value Added (EVA) 92
  Market Value Added (MVA) 93
Relationships among Ratios: The Du Pont
    System 94
Trend Analysis and Industry Comparisons 96
  Trend Analysis 96
  Industry Comparisons 96
Summary Analysis: Trend and Industry
    Comparisons Together 97
Locating Information about Financial Ratios 99
What's Next 99

*Summary 100 • Key Terms 100 • Equations Introduced
in This Chapter 100 • Self-Test 101 • Review Questions 102
• Build Your Communication Skills 102 • Problems 102
• Answers to Self-Test 112*

6 Forecasting for Financial Planning 113

Learning Objectives 113

What's Up with Amazon? 113
Chapter Overview 114
Why Forecasting Is Important 114
  Forecasting Approaches 115
    Experience 115
    Probability 115
    Correlation 115
  Why Forecasts Are Sometimes Wrong 115
Forecasting Sales 115
Forecasting Financial Statements 116
  Budgets 116
  Producing *Pro Forma* Financial Statements 117
    Choosing the Forecasting Basis 117
    The *Pro Forma* Income Statement 118
    The Sales Projection 118
    Cost of Goods Sold (COGS) and Selling
      and Marketing Expenses 118
    General and Administrative Expenses 118
    Depreciation Expense 119
    Interest Expense 119
    Income Taxes 120
    Dividends Paid and Additions to Retained
      Earnings 120
    The *Pro Forma* Balance Sheet 120
    Cash and Marketable Securities 120
    Accounts Receivable and Inventory 121
    Property, Plant, and Equipment 121
    Accounts Payable 121

Notes Payable 121

Long-Term Debt 122

Common Stock and Capital in Excess of Par 122

Retained Earnings 122

Additional Funds Needed 122

A Note on Interest Expense 122

Analyzing Forecasts for Financial Planning 123

What's Next 125

Summary 125 • Key Terms 126 • Self-Test 126 • Review Questions 126 • Build Your Communication Skills 126 • Problems 127 • Answers to Self-Test 133

7 Risk and Return 135

Learning Objectives 135

Are You the "Go-for-It" Type? 135

Chapter Overview 136

Risk 136

Risk Aversion 136

The Risk-Return Relationship 136

Measuring Risk 137

Using Standard Deviation to Measure Risk 137

Calculating the Standard Deviation 138

Interpreting the Standard Deviation 140

Using the Coefficient of Variation to Measure Risk 140

The Types of Risks Firms Encounter 142

Business Risk 142

Measuring Business Risk 142

The Influence of Sales Volatility 143

The Influence of Fixed Operating Costs 143

Financial Risk 144

Measuring Financial Risk 144

Portfolio Risk 146

Correlation 147

Calculating the Correlation Coefficient 147

Calculating the Standard Deviation of a Two-Asset Portfolio 148

Nondiversifiable Risk 148

Measuring Nondiversifiable Risk 149

Dealing with Risk 150

Risk-Reduction Methods 151

Reducing Sales Volatility and Fixed Costs 151

Reducing Sales Volatility 151

Insurance 151

Diversification 151

Compensating for the Presence of Risk 151

Adjusting the Required Rate of Return 151

Relating Return and Risk: The Capital Asset Pricing Model 152

What's Next 153

Summary 154 • Key Terms 155 • Equations Introduced in This Chapter 155 • Self-Test 156 • Review Questions 157 • Build Your Communication Skills 157 • Problems 157 • Answers to Self-Test 162

8 The Time Value of Money 163

Learning Objectives 163

Get a Free $1,000 Bond with Every Car Bought This Week! 163

Chapter Overview 164

Why Money Has Time Value 164

Measuring the Time Value of Money 164

The Future Value of a Single Amount 165

The Sensitivity of Future Values to Changes in Interest Rate or the Number of Compounding Periods 168

The Present Value of a Single Amount 168

The Sensitivity of Present Values to Changes in the Interest Rate or the Number of Compounding Periods 171

Working with Annuities 173

Future Value of an Ordinary Annuity 173

The Present Value of an Ordinary Annuity 176

Future Value of an Annuity Due 178

Present Value of an Annuity Due 181

Perpetuities 184

Present Value of an Investment with Uneven Cash Flows 184

Special Time Value of Money Problems 186

Finding the Interest Rate 186

Finding k of a Single-Amount Investment 186

Finding k for an Annuity Investment 188

Finding the Number of Periods 189

Solving for the Payment 191

Loan Amortization 192

Compounding More Than Once per Year 192

Annuity Compounding Periods 195

Continuous Compounding 196

What's Next 197

Summary 198 • Key Terms 198 • Equations Introduced in This Chapter 199 • Self-Test 201 • Review Questions 202 • Build Your Communication Skills 202 • Problems 202 • Answers to Self-Test 208

PART 3 CAPITAL BUDGETING AND BUSINESS VALUATION 209

9 The Cost of Capital 211

Learning Objectives 211

You Can Almost Always Get Capital If Your Idea Is Good Enough 211

Chapter Overview 212

The Cost of Capital 212

Sources of Capital 212

The Cost of Debt 212

The After-Tax Cost of Debt (AT k_d) 213

The Cost of Preferred and Common Stock 215

The Cost of Preferred Stock (k_p) 216

The Cost of Internal Common Equity (k_s) 217

Using the Dividend Growth Model to Estimate k_s 217

The CAPM Approach to Estimating k_s 218

Deciding How to Estimate k_s 219

The Cost of Equity from New Common Stock (k_n) 219

The Weighted Average Cost of Capital (WACC) 220

The Marginal Cost of Capital (MCC) 222

The Firm's MCC Schedule 222

Finding the Break Points in the MCC Schedule 222

Debt Break Points 222

The Equity Break Point 223

Calculating the Amount the MCC Changes 225

The MCC Up to the First Break Point 225

The MCC Schedule and Capital Budgeting Decisions 227

The Optimal Capital Budget 228

The Importance of MCC to Capital Budgeting Decisions 228

Crowdfunding 229

What's Next 229

Summary 230 • Key Terms 230 • Equations Introduced in This Chapter 231 • Self-Test 232 • Review Questions 232 • Build Your Communication Skills 233 • Problems 263 • Answers to Self-Test 237

10 Capital Budgeting Decision Methods 239

Learning Objectives 239

Apple Investments 239

Chapter Overview 240

The Capital Budgeting Process 240

Decision Practices 240

Types of Projects 241

Capital Budgeting Cash Flows 241

Stages in the Capital Budgeting Process 241

Capital Budgeting Decision Methods 241

The Payback Method 241

How to Calculate the Payback Period 242

Payback Method Decision Rule 242

Problems with the Payback Method 242

The Net Present Value (NPV) Method 243

Calculating NPV 243

NPV Decision Rules 246

The NPV Profile 246

Problems with the NPV Method 248

The Internal Rate of Return (IRR) Method 248

Calculating Internal Rate of Return: Trial-and-Error Method 248

Calculating Internal Rate of Return: Financial Calculator 250

IRR and the NPV Profile 251

IRR Decision Rule 251

Benefits of the IRR Method 251

Problems with the IRR Method 251

Conflicting Rankings between the NPV and IRR Methods 251

The Modified Internal Rate of Return (MIRR) Method 252

Capital Rationing 254

Risk and Capital Budgeting 255

Measuring Risk in Capital Budgeting 256

Computing Changes in the Coefficient of Variation 256

Adjusting for Risk 257

Risk-Adjusted Discount Rates (RADRs) 257

What's Next 258

Summary 258 • Key Terms 259 • Equations Introduced in This Chapter 260 • Self-Test 260 • Review Questions 261 • Build Your Communication Skills 261 • Problems 261 • Answers to Self-Test 270

Appendix 10A:

Wrinkles in Capital Budgeting 272

Nonsimple Projects 272

Multiple IRRs 272

Mutually Exclusive Projects with Unequal Project Lives 273

Comparing Projects with Unequal Lives 275
   The Replacement Chain Approach 275
   The Equivalent Annual Annuity (EAA) 275
Equations Introduced in This Appendix 276

11 Estimating Incremental Cash Flows 277

Learning Objectives 277

Saving Money? 277
Chapter Overview 278
Incremental Cash Flows 278
Types of Incremental Cash Flows 278
   Initial Investment Cash Flows 279
      Purchase Price, Installation, and Delivery 279
      Changes in Net Working Capital 279
   Operating Cash Flows 280
      Taxes 280
      Depreciation and Taxes 280
      Opportunity Costs 281
      Externalities 281
   Shutdown Cash Flows 281
   Financing Cash Flows 282
   Incremental Cash Flows of an Expansion Project 282
      Initial Investment Cash Flows 283
      Operating Cash Flows 284
      Shutdown Cash Flows 284
      Cash Flow Summary and Valuation 285
   Asset Replacement Decisions 287
Real Options 287
What's Next 291

Summary 291 • Self-Test 291 • Review Questions 291 • Build Your Communication Skills 292 • Problems 292 • Answers to Self-Test 296

12 Business Valuation 297

Learning Objectives 297

Valuing the M&M Mushroom Company 297
Chapter Overview 298
The Importance of Business Valuation 298
   A General Valuation Model 299
   Applying the General Valuation Model to Businesses 300
   Valuing Current Liabilities and Long-Term Debt 300
   Long-Term Debt 300

Bond Valuation 301
   Semiannual Coupon Interest Payments 303
   The Yield to Maturity of a Bond 304
      Calculating a Bond's Yield to Maturity 304
   The Relationship between Bond YTM and Price 304
Preferred Stock Valuation 305
   Finding the Present Value of Preferred Stock Dividends 305
   The Yield on Preferred Stock 306
Common Stock Valuation 307
   Valuing Individual Shares of Common Stock 307
      The Constant Growth Dividend Model 308
      The Nonconstant, or Supernormal, Growth Model 308
      The P/E Model 310
   Valuing Total Common Stockholders' Equity 310
      Book Value 311
      Liquidation Value 311
   The Free Cash Flow DCF Model 311
      Free Cash Flows 311
      A Real World Example 312
   The Yield on Common Stock 316
Valuing Complete Businesses 317
   The Free Cash Flow DCF Model Applied to a Complete Business 317
   The Replacement Value of Assets Method 318
What's Next 318

Summary 319 • Key Terms 320 • Equations Introduced in This Chapter 320 • Self-Test 322 • Review Questions 322 • Build Your Communication Skills 322 • Problems 323 • Answers to Self-Test 329

PART 4 LONG-TERM FINANCING DECISIONS 331

13 Capital Structure Basics 333

Learning Objectives 333

A Popcorn Venture 333
Chapter Overview 334
Capital Structure 334
   Operating Leverage 334
      Calculating the Degree of Operating Leverage 334
      The Effect of Fixed Costs on DOL 335

The Alternate Method of Calculating DOL 336

The Risk of Operating Leverage 337

Financial Leverage 337

Calculating the Degree of Financial Leverage (DFL) 337

Another Method of Calculating Financial Leverage 338

How Interest Expense Affects Financial Leverage 339

The Risk of Financial Leverage 339

Combined Leverage 339

Fixed Costs and Combined Leverage 340

Breakeven Analysis and Leverage 341

Constructing a Sales Breakeven Chart 341

Revenue Data 343

Cost Data 343

Plotting Data on the Breakeven Chart 343

Applying Breakeven Analysis 344

LBOs 346

Capital Structure Theory 347

Tax Deductibility of Interest 347

Modigliani and Miller 348

Toward an Optimal Capital Structure 348

The Lower Cost of Debt 348

How Capital Costs Change as Debt Is Added 349

The Effect of Risk 349

Establishing the Optimal Capital Structure in Practice 349

What's Next 350

Summary 350 • Key Terms 351 • Equations Introduced in This Chapter 351 • Self-Test 353 • Review Questions 353 • Build Your Communication Skills 353 • Problems 354 • Answers to Self-Test 358

14 Corporate Bonds, Preferred Stock, and Leasing 359

Learning Objectives 359

Negative Interest Rates? 359

Chapter Overview 360

Bond Basics 360

Features of Bond Indentures 360

Security 361

Plans for Paying Off Bond Issues 361

Staggered Maturities 361

Sinking Funds 362

Call Provisions 362

A Sample Bond Refunding Problem 362

Restrictive Covenants 365

Limitations on Future Borrowings 365

Restrictions on Dividends 365

Minimum Levels of Working Capital 365

The Independent Trustee of the Bond Issue 365

Types of Bonds 366

Secured Bonds 366

Mortgage Bonds 366

Unsecured Bonds (Debentures) 366

Convertible Bonds 367

Features of Convertible Bonds 367

The Conversion Ratio 367

The Conversion Value 367

The Straight Bond Value 368

Variable-Rate Bonds 369

Putable Bonds 369

Junk Bonds 369

International Bonds 370

Super Long-Term Bonds 370

Preferred Stock 370

Preferred Stock Dividends 370

Preferred Stock Investors 371

Convertible Preferred Stock 371

Leasing 371

Genuine Leases versus Fakes 371

Operating and Financial (Capital) Leases 372

Accounting Treatment of Leases 372

Lease or Buy? 373

A Lease or Buy Decision Example 373

What's Next 375

Summary 376 • Key Terms 376 • Equations Introduced in This Chapter 377 • Self-Test 377 • Review Questions 377 • Build Your Communication Skills 377 • Problems 378 • Answers to Self-Test 381

15 Common Stock 383

Learning Objectives 383

GoPro Goes Public 383

Chapter Overview 384

The Characteristics of Common Stock 384

Stock Issued by Private Corporations 385

Stock Issued by Publicly Traded Corporations 385

Institutional Investors, Proxy Advisory Firms, and Activist Investors 385

Voting Rights of Common Stockholders 386

    Board of Directors Elections 386

The Pros and Cons of Equity Financing 388

    Disadvantages of Equity Financing 388

    Advantages of Equity Financing 389

Issuing Common Stock 389

    The Function of Investment Bankers 390

        Underwriting versus Best Efforts 390

    Pricing New Issues of Stock 390

        Valuing the Stock of a Company That Is Not
Publicly Traded 392

Rights and Warrants 392

    Preemptive Rights 392

        The Number of Rights Required to Buy
a New Share 392

        The Value of a Right 393

    Warrants 394

        Warrant Valuation 395

What's Next 397

*Summary 397 • Key Terms 397 • Equations Introduced
in This Chapter 398 • Self-Test 399 • Review Questions
399 • Build Your Communication Skills 399 • Problems 399
• Answers to Self-Test 402*

16 Dividend Policy 403

Learning Objectives 403

GE Cuts Its Dividend 403

Chapter Overview 404

Dividends 404

Why a Dividend Policy Is Necessary 404

Factors Affecting Dividend Policy 404

    Need for Funds 404

    Management Expectations and Dividend
Policy 404

    Stockholders' Preferences 405

    Restrictions on Dividend Payments 405

Cash versus Earnings 405

Leading Dividend Theories 406

    The Residual Theory of Dividends 407

    The Clientele Dividend Theory 407

    The Signaling Dividend Theory 408

    The Bird-in-the-Hand Theory 408

    Modigliani and Miller's Dividend Theory 408

The Mechanics of Paying Dividends 408

    Dividend Reinvestment Plans 409

Alternatives to Cash Dividends 409

    Stock Dividends and Stock Splits 410

        Stock Dividends 410

        Adjustment of a Stock's Market Price
after a Stock Dividend 411

        Stock Splits 412

        Adjustment of a Stock's Market Price
after a Stock Split 413

        The Rationale for Stock Splits 413

What's Next 413

*Summary 414 • Key Terms 414 • Equations Introduced
in This Chapter 415 • Self-Test 415 • Review
Questions 415 • Build Your Communication Skills 415
• Problems 415 • Answers to Self-Test 418*

**PART 5 SHORT-TERM FINANCING
DECISIONS 419**

17 Working Capital Policy 421

Learning Objectives 421

The Importance of Liquidity 421

Chapter Overview 422

Managing Working Capital 422

Why Businesses Accumulate Working
Capital 422

    Fluctuating Current Assets 422

    Permanent and Temporary Current Assets 423

Liquidity versus Profitability 424

Establishing the Optimal Level of Current
Assets 425

Managing Current Liabilities:
Risk and Return 425

Three Working Capital Financing
Approaches 425

    The Aggressive Approach 426

    The Conservative Approach 426

    The Moderate Approach 427

Working Capital Financing and Financial
Ratios 428

What's Next 428

*Summary 429 • Key Terms 430 • Self-Test 430 • Review
Questions 430 • Build Your Communication Skills 431
• Problems 431 • Answers to Self-Test 436*

18 Managing Cash 437

Learning Objectives 437

The Importance of Cash 437

Chapter Overview 438

Cash Management Concepts 438

Determining the Optimal Cash Balance 438

　The Desired Minimum Cash Balance 438

　Raising Cash Quickly When Needed 439

　　Predicting Cash Needs 439

　　Coping with Emergencies 439

　The Desired Maximum Cash Balance 439

　Available Investment Opportunities 439

　　Expected Return on Investments 440

　　Transaction Cost of Making Investments 440

　The Optimal Cash Balance 440

　　The Miller–Orr Cash Management Model 440

Forecasting Cash Needs 442

　Developing a Cash Budget 442

Managing the Cash Flowing In and Out
　of the Firm 449

　Increasing Cash Inflows 449

　Decreasing Cash Outflows 449

　Speeding Up Cash Inflows 450

　Slowing Down Cash Outflows 450

What's Next 450

*Summary 451 • Key Terms 451 • Equations Introduced
in This Chapter 451 • Self-Test 452• Review Questions 452
• Build Your Communication Skills 452 • Problems 452
• Answers to Self-Test 456*

19 Accounts Receivable and Inventory 457

Learning Objectives 457

Accounts Receivable and Inventory:
　Necessary Evils? 457

Chapter Overview 458

Why Firms Accumulate Accounts Receivable
　and Inventory 458

How Accounts Receivable and Inventory Affect
　Profitability and Liquidity 459

Finding Optimal Levels of Accounts Receivable
　and Inventory 460

　The Optimal Level of Accounts Receivable 460

　　Credit Policy 460

　　Analyzing Accounts Receivable Levels 461

　The Optimal Level of Inventory 465

　　The Costs of Maintaining Inventory 465

　　Analyzing Inventory Levels 465

Inventory Management Approaches 470

　The ABC Inventory Classification System 470

　Just-in-Time Inventory Control (JIT) 471

Making Credit Decisions 471

Collection Policies to Handle Bad Debts 472

What's Next 474

*Summary 474 • Key Term 474 • Equations Introduced in This
Chapter 475 • Self-Test 475 • Review Questions 475 • Build
Your Communication Skills 476 • Problems 476 • Answers
to Self-Test 481*

20 Short-Term Financing 485

Learning Objectives 485

Cash 'Til Payday 485

Chapter Overview 486

The Need for Short-Term Financing 486

Short-Term Financing versus Long-Term
　Financing 486

Short-Term Financing Alternatives 487

　Short-Term Loans from Banks and Other
　　Institutions 487

　　Self-Liquidating Loans 487

　　The Line of Credit 488

　Trade Credit 488

　　Computing the Cost of Trade Credit 488

　Commercial Paper 489

　　Calculating the Cost of Commercial Paper 489

How Loan Terms Affect the Effective Interest
　Rate of a Loan 491

　The Effective Interest Rate 491

　Discount Loans 492

　Compensating Balances 492

　Loan Maturities Shorter Than One Year 493

　　Annualizing Interest Rates 493

　A Comprehensive Example 495

　　Computing the Interest Cost in Dollars 495

　Computing the Net Amount Received 495

　　Computing the Effective Annual Interest
　　Rate 495

　Computing the Amount to Borrow 496

Collateral for Short-Term Loans 496

　Accounts Receivable as Collateral 497

　Inventory as Collateral 497

What's Next 498

*Summary 498 • Key Terms 499 • Equations Introduced
in This Chapter 499 • Self-Test 500 • Review
Questions 500 • Build Your Communication Skills 500
• Problems 501 • Answers to Self-Test 503*

Contents

PART 6 FINANCE IN THE GLOBAL ECONOMY 505

21 International Finance 507

Learning Objectives 507

Cheering for a Weak Dollar—
Is It Un-American? 507

Chapter Overview 508

Multinational Corporations 508

Financial Advantages of Foreign Operations 508

Ethical Issues Facing Multinational
Corporations 508

Comparative Advantage 509

Exchange Rates and Their Effects 509

Fluctuating Exchange Rates 510

Cross Rates 511

Exchange Rate Effects on MNCS 512

Exchange Rate Effects on Foreign Stock
and Bond Investments 513

Managing Risk 513

Hedging 513

Diversification Benefits of Foreign
Investments 514

American Depository Receipts 514

Exchange Rate Theories 515

Purchasing Power Parity Theory 515

International Fisher Effect 516

Interest Rate Parity Theory 516

Other Factors Affecting Exchange Rates 516

Government Intervention in Foreign Exchange
Markets 517

Political and Cultural Risks Facing MNCs 517

Political Risk 517

Cultural Risk 518

International Trade Agreements 518

NAFTA 518

GATT and WTO 519

European Union and the Euro 519

Free Trade versus Fair Trade 520

*Summary 520 • Key Terms 521 • Equations Introduced
in This Chapter 522 • Self-Test 522 • Review
Questions 522 • Build Your Communication Skills 522
• Problems 522 • Answers to Self-Test 524*

Appendix A-1

Glossary G-1

Index I-1

Preface

The Challenge

The eighth edition of *Financial Management: Principles and Practice* contains many changes and improvements. The 2017 Tax Cuts and Jobs Act, that mostly went into effect in 2018, created drastic changes in what needs to be included in a textbook of this type. The corporate income tax is no longer progressive. It is a flat rate of 21 percent. The alternative minimum tax for corporations has been eliminated. There are new rules for depreciation. There are new rules for taxing dividend income received by a corporation. Business interest expense is not automatically tax deductible as it has been for many years. The new rules are complex and important. All the essential elements are explained and incorporated throughout this eight edition.

The after tax cost of debt is no longer equal to the before tax cost times one minus the marginal tax rate of the firm. This has carry though effects on the weighted average cost of capital, WACC. Beginning in 2018, many corporations will run into limits on the amount of interest expense they can deduct on their tax returns. For many corporations with lots of debt, only a small percentage of their interest expense will be tax deductible. There are interest expense carry forward rules to consider in the new tax law. There are also many important carry through effects from one topic to another. The amount of debt that is part of a firm's optimal capital structure must be reexamined in light of the new tax law. Capital budgeting problems, including those related to lease-buy analysis and credit policy changes, must be redone to reflect the new tax rules for business interest expense.

There are significant improvements in how material presented in earlier editions is covered. Chapter 8, covering time value of money, has received a significant upgrade. Better terminology is used. Detailed step-by-step presentation of the different types of time value of money problems is provided so that a learner can absorb this important material at his or her own pace. There are new timelines so that the learner can picture what type of time value of money problem is being addressed. This will help visual learners. The material on annuities due has been significantly expanded so that it is clear how such problems differ from ordinary annuity problems. Table, algebraic, financial calculator, and Excel® spreadsheet approaches are shown for every type of time value of money problem. Tables may not be used as much as they used to, but they still provide a pedagogic value. The preference for how to address time value of money problems can be customized according to the preferences of the instructor and student. All the options are provided here.

Detailed graphics describing keystroke sequences for solving different types of time value of money problems with a financial calculator are shown. So too are screen captures of Excel spreadsheets, along with embedded explanations, so time value of money problems can be solved with this tool. This time value of money coverage focuses equally on explaining the nature of each type of time value of money problem one may face, in addition to helping the learner to apply the techniques that will get to the correct answer. Understanding the underlying phenomenon and getting the answer correct are both important.

This book continues to be one of the few in this market to give attention to benefit corporations. This includes both those given benefit corporation status granted by the state of incorporation and included in the corporate charter and the certification a corporation may seek from the nonprofit organization B Lab. Corporations that obtain the designation offered by some states, and by B Lab, allows corporations to expand their goals so that the interests of a wide range of stakeholders can be considered, not just the stockholders. Such a designation is, of course, optional. Those corporations seeking only to maximize shareholder wealth are free to do so. The number of corporations seeking to consider the so-called triple bottom line has been growing, however. The triple bottom line includes social responsibility, economic value, and environmental impact. Some refer to this as people, profits, and planet.

There are three sets of optional materials available to those students and instructors who wish to incorporate Excel spreadsheets into financial problem solving. One is called Spreadsheet Tutorpak™. The other is called Spreadsheet Templates. 8e Spreadsheet Tutorpak™, prepared by my friend and colleague Professor Hong Miao in close collaboration with me, is both a tutorial and a set of applications for solving financial management problems with Excel spreadsheets. Students will learn the basics of Excel spreadsheet creation and manipulation with powerful macros behind the scenes such that the student experience is straight forward. Another part of this package contains demonstration spreadsheets, which present key concepts in an easier to understand way than what would be possible on a two-dimensional page. Examples include distribution graphs showing diversification benefits, loan amortization tables, and break-even graphs. Input values can be changed by the student and the resulting changes on output variables can be seen in a dynamic visual way. Also, every time a new type of time value of money or capital budgeting concept is presented, there is a spreadsheet solution the student will create with prompting from the material in the Spreadsheet Tutorpak™ package.

8e Spreadsheet Templates are available for selected end-of-chapter problems. This will reduce the data entry burden for students as they apply their Excel skills to solve these problems. A full solution set of Excel spreadsheets is available to the faculty member using this book. These materials are available in the instructor supplements pack. End-of-chapter problems for which these spreadsheet templates are available are marked with this Spreadsheet Template icon.

> For more, see 8e Spreadsheet Templates for *Microsoft Excel*.

Finance scares some students. There is the fear of numbers that some students have and the mistaken belief that the introductory finance course requires high-level mathematics. Also, some students mistakenly believe finance is an area in which they will not need competency. Finance concepts often seem far removed from daily life. In spite of this, almost every major in a college of business, and many majors in other colleges, require the "Principles of Finance" course. As a result, many of the students who find themselves sitting in finance class on the first day of the semester do not want to be there.

This does not need to be the case. Finance is important, dynamic, interesting, and fun. The challenge to *Financial Management: Principles and Practice* is to convince students of this. In order to learn, students must want to learn. If they can see the usefulness of what is presented to them, they will work hard and they will learn. Students also demand relevancy. This eighth edition tackles head on the changes we must face in the financial world and the new information that must be digested before making financial decisions in the new world we find ourselves in. There are also mistakes made by financial decision makers and government officials from which we must learn.

Many years of teaching experience has taught me that the introductory financial management course can be one that students enjoy and that they see as having added considerable value to their educational experiences. Finance is, after all, central to any business entity. More CEOs have come up through the finance ranks than any other discipline. Students need to know that the principles and practices of financial management apply to any business unit—from the very large multinational corporation to the very smallest proprietorship, including the family. Financial ratios tell a story; they are not numbers to be calculated as an end unto itself. Risk is important and can be managed. Time value of money has meaning and is understood as the central tool of valuation. Funds have a cost and different sources of funds have different costs. Financial performance and condition can be assessed. Amortized loan payments, rates of return on investment, future value of investment programs, and present value of payments to be received from bonds and stocks can be calculated. The opportunities and special challenges of international operations can be understood.

This Approach

Students should walk out of the room after taking the final exam for a finance course believing that they have learned something useful. They should see a direct benefit to themselves personally, rather than just the belief that some set of necessary job skills has been mastered, although the latter will be true if the material is mastered.

Financial Management: Principles and Practice, starts with the student in mind and then packages the finance material so that the students (1) want to learn and (2) learn the necessary material. Finance is not medicine, and it cannot be administered as such. Instead, we believe students must be engaged in such a way that they develop the desire to learn. There are those who approach the task of teaching finance with the philosophy, "Here is the finance knowledge you need. Learn it!" This is not the approach taken by this book.

Distinctive Focus

Although there are many other introductory financial management books on the market, none contains the unique style and content of *Financial Management: Principles and Practice*, eighth edition. Many texts focus mostly on accounting with little presentation of the economic theory that underlies the financial techniques presented. Others assume that the students remember all that was learned in the accounting course that is usually a prerequisite for this course. Still others claim to take a "valuation approach" but present their topics in a straight accounting framework. In this book, we are serious about focusing on what creates value. We are consistent in this approach throughout the book, addressing issues such as what creates value, what destroys it, how value is measured, and how value and risk are related. In so doing, we maximize the value of the finance course to the student.

Organization of the Text

The book is organized into six major parts as follows:

Part 1. *The World of Finance* contains chapters on the structure and goals of the firm, the role of financial managers, and an examination of the financial environment. Special attention is given to how the Financial Crisis of 2008 and the Tax Cuts and Jobs Act of 2017 have affected companies.

Part 2. *Essential Concepts in Finance* presents chapters on accounting statements and their interpretation, forecasting, risk and return, the time value of money, and security valuation. Special attention is given to systematic risk and its role in the Financial Crisis.

Part 3. *Capital Budgeting and Business Valuation* contains chapters on measuring a firm's cost of capital, capital budgeting decision methods, incremental cash flow estimation, and business valuation.

Part 4. *Long-Term Financing Decisions* contains chapters on capital structure basics, corporate bonds, preferred stock, leasing, common stock, and dividend policy. The turmoil in the stock and bond markets during the Financial Crisis is examined.

Part 5. *Short-Term Financial Management Decisions* includes chapters on working capital policy, cash and marketable securities, accounts receivable and inventory, and short-term financing.

Part 6. *Finance in a Global Economy* is where international finance topics are covered, in addition to those international topics that are woven throughout the book. The contagion of the Financial Crisis around the world is examined.

Special Features in the Text

- *Financial Calculator Solutions*—Financial calculator solutions to general time value of money, capital budgeting, and specific security valuation problems are included.
- *Excel® Solution Screen Captures*—The eighth edition presents screen captures that show and describe how a particular finance problem would be solved using Excel. Everywhere a financial keystroke solutions is provided, as was done in previous editions, the Excel solution now also appears. These screen captures not only show how the finance function is set up, but they also describe what is happening within that specific spreadsheet. All input parameters for a particular function, including those that are optional, are shown.
- *Real-World Examples*—Throughout *Financial Management: Principles and Practice* real-world examples are provided, such as the major expansion plan announced in 2017 by Apple Computer and the disruptions to many industries created by Amazon's continuing expansion. Learning objectives are clear.

- *Summaries*—The summary for each chapter specifically describes how the learning objectives have been achieved, and it also provides a bridge to the next chapter.
- *Key Terms*—Each chapter has bolded key terms that are defined in the chapter and repeated in page margins. There are self-test questions and problems at the end of chapters, along with their solutions, so that students can check their grasp of the material presented.
- *Practice Questions and Problems*—Study questions and an abundant number of end-of-chapter problems are included in the appropriate chapters. Many problems from the seventh edition have been redone in the eighth.
- *Computer Spreadsheet Supported Problems*—A number of end-of-chapter problems are marked with the special computer problem logo shown here. This indicates that a downloadable Excel® spreadsheet template is available at *www. textbookmedia.com*. This template contains data for the designated end-of-chapter problem that can then be solved in Excel by the student. This streamlines the use of Excel by students wishing to solve the designated end-of-chapter problems using that tool.
- *Communication Skills*—Suggested assignments to build students' written and oral communication skills are for *Microsoft Excel* included in each chapter.
- *Color*—Color is used for pedagogic effect, not just for looks.

Changes in the Eighth Edition

- The few errors in the seventh edition have been corrected.
- The impact of the Tax Cut and Jobs Act of 2017 on businesses is described in detail and the impact on corporate decision making is incorporated throughout this edition.
- There are updates to the implications of the 2008 Financial Crisis.
- It has been said that textbooks will have to be rewritten if we observe negative interest rates in the market. We have. The material in the determination of the level of interest rates has been rewritten in the 8th edition to explain how market interest rates can become negative.
- There is new material on problems facing public pension funds.
- The material on progressive tax rates for corporations has been deleted. It no longer applies. Full coverage of the new corporate tax laws is provided.
- The accounting treatment for issuing new common stock in the primary market has been expanded.

- Coverage of time value of money has been significantly expanded and improved.
- The impact of the new tax law on cost of capital estimation has been added. The implications of the new tax law here are significant.
- The impact of the new tax law on determining the optimal capital structure for a firm is presented.
- The new timeline for determining and paying dividends is shown along with the new tax treatment of dividend income by corporate investors.
- Many of the end-of-chapter problems have been improved. The new tax law has affected many of these end-of-chapter problems.
- Multiple new chapter openers and real-world examples are found in this new edition reflecting recent real-world developments.

Features Retained from the Eighth Edition

- The book is still written in the student-friendly style that was extremely popular in the first and second editions. The concise, easy-to-understand presentation loved by student users is maintained.
- The book provides the level of rigor professors demand. When professors get past the friendly style, they find all the rigor and all the mainstream topics they expect in a book of this type.

Why Choose Gallagher Eighth Edition?

If you are not already a *Financial Management: Principles and Practice* user, does your book:

- Include comprehensive coverage of the Tax Cut and Jobs Act of 2017 and incorporate throughout the extensive ramifications of this new tax law for a book in this market? The odds are that your current book does not and as such is extremely out of date.
- Describe "benefit corporations" and discuss the issues related to the stakeholders a corporation should consider when making decisions? This is a growing phenomenon that most books in this market ignore.
- Show and describe in detail how financial problems are solved with tables, algebra, financial calculators, and with Excel spreadsheets? This allows the instructor to choose his/her preferred approach.
- Describe crowdfunding as one of the potential sources of capital for a firm?
- Cover real options?
- Cover EVA, MVA, and EBITDA?
- Use a value-added (NPV) approach to the inventory and accounts receivable investment coverage rather than the outmoded return on investment ratio approach?

- Include Excel templates for students and full solutions spreadsheets for instructors for designated problems, along with an available tutorial product that teaches key Excel skills needed by finance students?

The topics that professors actually teach are here. Those that are most likely to be taught in the second course in financial management are left out. Students don't have to buy more than what they need.

The Learning Package

Financial Management: Principles and Practice is one component of a complete learning package carefully put together by the Textbook Media team. This package includes a computerized test bank, a study guide/workbook, an instructor's manual, solutions manual to end-of-chapter material, PowerPoint slides, and downloadable Excel® spreadsheets.

For the Student

- *Downloadable Material*—Companion downloadable material is available at *www.textbookmedia.com*. There are two different Excel® spreadsheet products available. The first is called "8e Spreadsheet Tutorpak™". The second Excel® spreadsheet downloadable product is called Excel Templates. It provides Excel® spreadsheet files containing templates that facilitate solving computer icon designated end-of-chapter problems. Such templates are provided for those selected end-of-chapter problems designated with this icon.
- *Lecture Notes*—PowerPoint files may be downloaded from *www.textbookmedia.com* and used as lecture notes so that students can focus on what their professor is saying without having to simultaneously take copious notes.

For the Professor

Each of the following supplements has been updated by the author to reflect eighth edition changes to the book.

- *Instructor's Manual*—This provides the professor with chapter outlines and suggestions for alternative ways to present the material. Key points are identified, and a variety of types of assistance for class preparation are presented.
- *Solutions Manual*—Detailed solutions, not just final answers, are presented for each end-of-chapter question and problem. These have all been personally checked by the author for accuracy.
- *Complete Excel® Solutions to Designated End-of-Chapter Problems*—Selected end-of-chapter problems are marked throughout the book with an "8e Spreadsheet Template" icon. Adopting professors are provided with the full Excel® solutions for these problems.

- *Spreadsheet Solutions*—Selected end-of-chapter problems, indicated in the textbook with a 8e Spreadsheet Template icon, are solved completely in Excel for the instructor's use. Students are provided with templates that they can use when applying their Excel skills in solving these problems.
- *Test Item File in Word and also compatible with all major LMS vendors*—Multiple-choice, short-answer, and essay questions reflect all the material in the chapter. ExamView allows for complete customization of an exam according to chapters covered, type of problem, and level of difficulty. It allows for integration with all major LMS software. New exam questions have been added to the database.
- *PowerPoint Slides*—Animated slides covering all main topic areas in the text are available to assist the professor during class.

In Conclusion

Don't let your students use a textbook that does not include coverage of the many ways the Tax Cuts and Jobs Act of 2017 has changed the landscape in financial management. Students will understand the very important finance concepts, and master necessary problem-solving skills, when they complete the course in which this text is used. "Students first" is our philosophy at Textbook Media, and this belief shows up throughout the text. Professors who have more enthusiastic students and who grasp the important content, both conceptual and problem solving, will find their classroom experiences more rewarding too. If we have helped to make this happen, we have succeeded in achieving our vision for *Financial Management: Principles and Practice*, eighth edition.

Author Access—The author is accessible to respond to individual questions that may come up. Tim Gallagher may be reached at tim.gallagher@colostate.edu.

Acknowledgments

The author gratefully acknowledges the contributions of the many people who contributed to this endeavor. Without their expertise and talent, this book and the supplemental materials would not have been possible.

I send my thanks to a number of colleagues and key reviewers who contributed to this and previous editions. They are Dianne Morrison (University of Wisconsin–LaCrosse), Zhenhu Jin (Illinois Wesleyan University), Denise Letterman (Robert Morris College), Gary Greene (Manatee Community College), John Armstrong (Dominican College), Atul K. Saxena (Mercer University), William Hudson (St. Cloud State University), Charles W. Strang (Western New Mexico University), James D. Keys (Florida International University), Vickie Bajtelsmit (Colorado State University), John Elder (Colorado State University), Sue Hine (Colorado State University), Hong Miao (Colorado State University), Rob Schwebach (Colorado State University), Chris Stein (Colorado State University), Kent Zumwalt (Colorado State University), Joe Brocato (Tarleton State University), Susan Myrick (Allegheny County Community College), Clark Maxam (Montana State University), Gary Walker (Myers University), Ron Filante (Pace University), Andrew Adkinson (University of Nebraska–Kearney), Mark Sunderman (University of Wyoming), Wendy Pirie (Wesleyan University), Fernando Arellano (University of Dallas), S. R. Das Gupta, Stephen Borde (University of Central Florida) Jimmy Lockwood (Colorado State University) wrote most of the material on American Depository Receipts (ADRs). I am very grateful to him for this important contribution.

I am indebted to my nieces and nephews for providing me with contemporary names to use in end-of-chapter material to make the book more current. They are Mo Gallagher, Jack Gallagher, Bridget Gallagher, Max Abouchar, Ben Abouchar, Charley Abouchar, Mike Gallagher, Ellen Gallagher, and Joe Gallagher.

For this eighth edition, I am indebted to my editor, Ed Laube, of Textbook Media. Ed and his partners Tom Doran and Peggy Morgan had the courage to start a company that redefines textbook publishing. I am excited to be a part of it. This is the future of college textbook publishing. The old model doesn't work anymore, and these people and the others who have created Textbook Media are doing something about it. I'd also like to thank Victoria Putman and Daphne Loecke for their excellent work on the production side of this project. Joe Andrew, my former co-author, has left an indelible mark on this book. My colleague Hong Miao did an outstanding job with the new Excel® material available with this eighth edition from the Publisher. Chris Stein provided extremely valuable feedback as the manuscript was prepared.

Last, but not least, I am most especially grateful for the assistance and support of family members:

Susan, Emily, Ellie, and Zach.

About the Author

Timothy J. Gallagher (Tim) holds the rank of professor in the Department of Finance and Real Estate at Colorado State University. He currently serves as Chair of its Faculty Council. He previously served as Vice Chair and Faculty Representative to the Board of Governors of Colorado State University. Tim served as Chair of the Department of Finance & Real Estate for ten years. He believes strongly in shared governance at universities, and he has been an active member of the American Association of University Professors (AAUP). Tim received his Ph.D. in finance from the University of Illinois at Urbana–Champaign.

PART 1

The World of Finance

Source: Sergey Nivens/Shutterstock

Chapter 1
Finance and the Firm

Chapter 2
Financial Markets
and Interest Rates

Chapter 3
Financial Institutions

We begin our study of financial management with a look at what the field of finance is all about and the environment in which financial managers operate. Chapter 1 introduces you to finance, explains what financial managers do, states the objective of financial management, and describes the four basic forms of business commonly encountered in the U.S. Chapter 2 introduces you to the financial environment in which the firm operates. The financial system is explained, along with the various financial markets and the securities that are bought and sold there. The importance of financial markets to the firm is emphasized. Chapter 2 finishes with a discussion of interest rates, which represent the price of credit in the financial markets. Chapter 3 continues with descriptions of the various types of financial institutions through which buyers, sellers, borrowers, and lenders gain access to the financial markets. These three chapters set the stage for your study of the principles and practice of managing an individual company's finances.

Finance and the Firm

"An investment in knowledge pays the best interest."
—Benjamin Franklin

CHAPTER 1

Source: Maxxigo/Shutterstock

Learning Objectives

After reading this chapter, you should be able to:

1. Describe the field of finance.
2. Discuss the duties of financial managers.
3. Identify the basic goal of a business firm.
4. List factors that affect the value of a firm.
5. Discuss the legal and ethical challenges financial managers face.
6. Identify the different forms of business organization.

When Finance Goes Wrong

If there were any question about the importance of finance in business and for the entire economy one need only look back at the 2008 Financial Crisis. The world is a different place since those dramatic events unfolded and the subsequent moves by legislators and regulators seeking to prevent such a crisis from reoccurring.

In 2007, Bear Sterns had two hedge funds with billions of dollars in assets connected to subprime mortgages. These mortgage loans went to borrowers with low credit ratings and when market interest rates increased in 2006, the interest rates on variable rate mortgages reset upward, thus increasing monthly payments for these borrowers. Defaults on these mortgages soared. Bear Sterns was one of the early casualties of the Financial Crisis. There were many more to come.

In early 2008, the huge mortgage lender Countrywide sold itself to Bank of America at a bargain price to avoid bankruptcy. Later that year, Lehman Brothers, one of the oldest, largest, and most prestigious Wall Street firms did file for bankruptcy. The U.S. government took over the insurance giant AIG and government-sponsored mortgage giants Fannie Mae and Freddie Mac. Other companies that were acquired at bargain basement prices, given federal government bailouts, or that went through a bankruptcy include Merrill Lynch, Bear Sterns, Washington Mutual, Countrywide Mortgage.

The S&P500 Stock Market Index generated a return of –37% in 2008. As stock prices plunged, prices of U.S. Treasury securities soared as investors sought safety. The stock market made up all its 2008 losses, and then some in the years that followed. The memory of these 2008 events linger, however, for those old enough to have seen them. Congress passed the Dodd-Frank Act with its primary purpose being to avoid another such financial and economic train wreck.

The Dodd-Frank Act created the Financial Stability Oversight Council to oversee financial markets, financial institutions, and some non-financial institutions in an attempt to identify new problems before they become a threat to the entire financial system. This created the Federal Insurance Office (FIO) to identify institutions deemed too big to fail, systematically important financial institutions (SIFI) in the language of the law, and create extra regulatory requirements for them. Every liability defaulted upon by one entity creates, by definition, a write-down of an asset by the party holding that claim on the asset side of its balance sheet. When the holder of that asset writes down its value reduces the equity of the holder of that asset and puts the holders of its liability claims in greater danger. When the financial problems are severe, the risk of cascading failures becomes real. JPMorgan/Chase had $2.6 trillion dollars in assets and $2.3 trillion in liabilities in 2017. Clearly, being too big to fail is not a relic of the past.

The Dodd-Frank law also created the Office of Credit Ratings (OCR) to oversee companies such as Moody's and Standard & Poor's that has given very high ratings to mortgage-backed securities that defaulted during the Financial Crisis creating a myriad of problems for the financial system.

Dodd-Frank has its supporters and its detractors. The fact that it became law, and the scope of that law, is a testament to the scope of the damage done to the financial system, and to families, by the 2008 Financial Crisis. Finance is important because when it goes wrong the harm can be very great.

The 2008 Financial Crisis— Its History and Reverberations Today

Huge government-sponsored enterprise (GSE) companies with private sector stockholders, with names such as Fannie Mae and Freddie Mac, bought large amounts of mortgages and bundled them into mortgage-backed securities. Fannie Mae and Freddie Mac lowered the standards for the types of mortgages they would buy. Fannie Mae and Freddie Mac were effectively nationalized in late 2008 when they went broke. Fannie Mae and Freddie Mac have returned to significant profitability in recent years. This profit is going directly to the U.S. Treasury since it received warrants (options to buy) close to 80% of the company's stock plus preferred stock with a 10% dividend yield.[1] The private sector shareholders have been receiving nothing and they are not too happy about it. Legal battles are ongoing. There were insurance companies such as AIG that sold an insurance-like product called a credit default swap to protect those holding these mortgage-backed securities in the event of defaulting mortgages. The fees were collected by AIG, and it sold way more credit default swaps than it could pay off on. AIG was effectively nationalized in early 2009. Today AIG is largely free of those government reins.[2] Everything would have been great if only housing prices had continued to go up as they had for about twenty-five years. General Motors (GM) filed for bankruptcy in June of 2009. It received a large infusion of cash from the federal government. It emerged from bankruptcy and had an initial public offering (IPO) of $20.1 billion in November of 2010. The U.S. Treasury was the largest single stockholder of GM at the time of the IPO. The U.S. Treasury sold the last of its GM stock in 2013.

---

1. https://www.wsj.com/articles/fannie-mae-freddie-mac-shareholders-argue-against-governments-profit-sweep-1460757430.
2. https://www.fool.com/investing/2017/02/22/fannie-mae-and-freddie-mac-earned-20-billion-in-20.aspx.

Executives at big financial firms received big bonuses if they could report big profits. It didn't matter if the profits were really there, as long as the accountants signed off on the numbers. The Sarbanes-Oxley Act of 2002 (aka SOX) was supposed to prevent companies from reporting phony profits, but it wasn't entirely effective. A company had the potential to make much higher profits if it borrowed a lot of money (*leverage* is the polite financial term) to invest more than what its money would allow. Lehman Brothers, a very old and prestigious firm, did this. It went bankrupt in late 2008 and doesn't exist anymore. Also in 2008 venerable Merrill Lynch sold itself to Bank of America at a bargain basement price so as to avoid collapse. Bear Sterns did the same as Merrill Lynch when it sold itself to JPMorgan.

Housing prices had been going up much more quickly than personal income for several decades. If you didn't buy that house soon, it would just be more expensive later. The people on the selling side were only too happy to encourage you to jump in and buy before it was too late and that house went beyond what your income could support. Even those mortgage-backed securities, including those with lots of sub-prime mortgages in them, had been given very high ratings by firms with venerable names such as Moody's, Standard and Poor's, and Fitch. Surely, there was no reason to worry.

Then the unthinkable happened. Housing prices started to go down. Many of these houses had been purchased with little or no money down. This meant that small decreases in the price of the home could create an "under water" situation where the amount of the mortgage balance was greater than the value of the home. This happened to millions of homeowners, both high income and low income. By 2012 many homes in high-income neighborhoods had recaptured much of the lost value. Home values in low-income neighborhoods continued to see values languish near peak financial crisis levels at this time. When some homeowners defaulted, those holding the mortgages lost money. The people holding the mortgages were not, of course, the people who had originally lent the money. Those mortgages had been sold to others, and these mortgages were now held by the "smart guys" who had bought them as part of the mortgage-backed securities that had become so popular, complete with a high credit rating and insurance. It's interesting that the Main Street mortgage brokers, real estate agents, appraisers, and home inspectors already had their money. These defaults did not directly affect the "hicks" who lived outside the hallowed halls of giant Wall Street firms. Who were the real dumb guys here?

What happens when you buy a billion dollars of mortgage-backed securities using five percent of your own money and ninety-five percent borrowed money and then have those mortgages go down in value more than five percent? The answer is you are in big trouble. What happens if the insurance company that sold you the insurance that would pay off if your mortgage-backed securities were to default, doesn't have enough resources to pay off the claims? The answer is both you and the insurance company are in big trouble. What if lots of big "sophisticated" firms did this all at the same time? Nothing would go wrong unless lots of these assets dropped significantly in value at the same time.

Such a thing was thought to be impossible. This was called "systematic risk." Systematic risk is covered in detail in Chapter 7. If you put all your eggs into a hundred different baskets, you are well diversified, unless the baskets are defective and their bottoms all break at the same time. We will weave throughout this book what finance can bring to the table to help us understand what went wrong and how optimal financial decision making can take place. This is only possible if we make an attempt to understand what went so wrong during the 2008 Financial Crisis.

What do all these stories have in common? They deal with finance. Finance has been the focus of the world's attention over the past several years. Not all this attention has been welcome by people in this field. Finance helps us solve problems. If done poorly finance can become the problem. The part of finance known as Wall Street has been the object of much scorn and criticism due to the spread of the problems of major Wall Street firms to banks and insurance companies around the world, in addition to the economic problems that some blame Wall Street for. Companies cutting costs, companies reporting profits or losses, governments concerned about interest rates—this is just a sampling of business stories involving finance that appear every day in the press. Finance is at the heart of business management. No business firm—or government, for that matter—can exist for long without following at least the basic principles of financial management. Was the Financial Crisis the result of greedy bankers trying to line their own pockets at the expense of their stockholders, employees, customers or clients, and taxpayers? Was it the result of government officials who encouraged government-sponsored entities to buy mortgages in the open market from loan originators to facilitate home ownership even if some of those mortgages would never have been made without the opportunity to sell them and the accompanying risk to a government entity? Will Dodd-Frank help to prevent a reoccurrence of such financial crises?

There is much disagreement as to what steps should be taken to strengthen our financial system. This book will address many of the financial principles that underpin this conversation. You will learn how companies are organized and how decisions at those companies are made. Markets are driven by participants with different incentives and views. Financial institutions provide certain benefits to those seeking funds and those looking to invest them. Risk can be assessed and managed, including so-called systematic risk. Valuation is central to the operations of any company, and this requires an understanding of the time value of money and best capital budgeting practices. Different sources of funding, the capital structure of the firm, have different risk and return implications. Firms need liquidity so they have the cash to pay their bills and stay solvent. All these issues have important implications for companies having operations around the world, not just in the company where the corporate headquarters happens to be located. This book is about financial management, not blame and politics. It is designed to introduce you to basic financial management principles and skills. Some of these concepts and skills are surprisingly straightforward; others are quite challenging. All, however, will help you in the business world, no matter what career you choose.

Chapter Overview

In this chapter we introduce financial management basics that provide a foundation for the rest of the course. First, we describe the field of finance and examine the role of financial management within a business organization. Then we investigate the financial goal of a business firm and the legal and ethical challenges financial managers face. We end with a description of four forms of business in the U.S. economy: sole proprietorship, partnership, corporation, and limited liability company.[3]

The Field of Finance

In business, financial guidelines determine how money is raised and spent. Although raising and spending money may sound simple, financial decisions affect every aspect of a business—from how many people a manager can hire, to what products a company can produce, to what investments a company can make.

initial public offering (IPO) The process whereby a private corporation issues new common stock to the general public, thus becoming a publicly traded corporation.

For example, after the close of trading on November 6, 2013, Twitter sold 70 million shares of its stock to the general public for the first time at a price of $26 per share. This is called an **initial public offering (IPO)**. November 7 of that year was the first day of trading for these shares. The closing market price to Twitter on November 7, 2013 was $44.90 per share. On the first day of public trading of these shares the price at the opening bell was $45.10 per share. This means that anyone who bought the Twitter shares at the opening price had seen this investment fall in value by $0.20 that first day. The lucky few on the list to receive the shares on November 6 at the $26 IPO price had seen appreciation at the end of trading on November 7. Twitter stock got into the low 70s toward the end of 2013 but had settled back to the mid-twenties in early 2018. You may wish to look up its stock price after reading this to see how it is doing.

Money continually flows through businesses. It may flow in from banks, from the government, from the sale of stock, and so on; and it may flow out for a variety of reasons—to invest in bonds, to buy new equipment, or to hire top-notch employees. Businesses must pay constant attention to ensure that the right amount of money is available at the right time for the right use.

In large firms it may take a whole team of financial experts to track the firm's cash flows and to develop financial strategies. For instance, when Bank of America acquired Merrill

---

3. Hersh Shefrin, "Why Twitter's IPO Was Really a Failure," *Forbes* (November 8, 2013).

Lynch on January 1, 2009, teams of financial analysts had to work on every detail of the federally assisted deal that involved Bank of America offering its shares to acquire the shares of Merrill Lynch. There were fears that Merrill Lynch would go under, as did Lehman Brothers, if this acquisition of Merrill Lynch by Bank of America had not been executed.[4]

Finance Career Paths

Finance has three main career paths: financial management, financial markets and institutions, and investments. Financial management, the focus of this text, involves managing the finances of a business. Financial managers—people who manage a business firm's finances—perform a number of tasks. They analyze and forecast a firm's finances, assess risk, evaluate investment opportunities, decide when and where to find money sources and how much money to raise, and decide how much money to return to the firm's investors.

Bankers, stockbrokers, and others who work in financial markets and institutions focus on the flow of money through financial institutions and the markets in which financial assets are exchanged. They track the impact of interest rates on the flow of that money. People who work in the field of investments locate, select, and manage income-producing assets. For instance, security analysts and mutual fund managers both operate in the investment field.

Table 1-1 summarizes the three main finance career paths.

Financial Management

Financial management is essentially a combination of accounting and economics. First, financial managers use accounting information—balance sheets, income statements, and statements of cash flows—to analyze, plan, and allocate financial resources for business firms. Second, financial managers use economic principles to guide them in making financial decisions that are in the best interest of the firm. In other words, finance is an applied area of economics that relies on accounting for input.

Because finance looks closely at the question of what adds value to a business, financial managers are central to most businesses. Let's take a look at what financial managers do.

The Role of the Financial Manager

Financial managers measure the firm's performance, determine what the financial consequences will be if the firm maintains its present course or changes it, and recommend how the firm should use its assets. Financial managers also locate external financing sources

TABLE 1-1 Careers in the Field of Finance

Career Area	Function
Financial management	Manage the finances of a business firm. Analyze, forecast, and plan a firm's finances; assess risk; evaluate and select investments; decide where and when to find money sources, and how much money to raise; and determine how much money to return to investors in the business
Financial markets and institutions	Handle the flow of money in financial markets and institutions, and focus on the impact of interest rates on the flow of that money
Investments	Locate, select, and manage money-producing assets for individuals and groups

---

4. "Bank of America to Acquire Merrill as Crisis Deepens," by David Mildenberg and Bradley Keoun, September 15, 2008, Bloomberg. http://www.bloomberg.com/apps/news?pid=newsarchive&sid=a9O9JGOLdI_U.

and recommend the most beneficial mix of financing sources while focusing on the financial expectations and risk tolerances of the firm's owners.

All financial managers must be able to communicate, analyze, and make decisions based on information from many sources. To do this, they need to be able to analyze financial statements, forecast and plan, and determine the effect of size, risk, and timing of cash flows. We'll cover all of these skills in this text.

Finance in the Organization of the Firm

Financial managers work closely with other types of managers. For instance, they rely on accountants for raw financial data and on marketing managers for information about products and sales. Financial managers coordinate with technology experts to determine how to communicate financial information to others in the firm. Management experts in the area of supply chain work are also part of this team. Financial managers provide advice and recommendations to top management.

Figure 1-1 shows how finance fits into a typical business firm's organization.

The Organization of the Finance Team

In most medium-to-large businesses, a chief financial officer (CFO) supervises a team of employees who manage the financial activities of the firm. One common way to organize a finance team in a medium-to-large business is shown in Figure 1-2.

In Figure 1-2 we see that the **chief financial officer** (CFO) directs and coordinates the financial activities of the firm. The CFO supervises a treasurer and a controller. The **treasurer** generally is responsible for cash management, credit management, and financial planning activities, whereas the **controller** is responsible for cost accounting, financial accounting, and information system activities. The treasurer and the controller of a large corporation are both likely to have a group of junior financial managers reporting to them.

At a small firm, one or two people may perform all the duties of the treasurer and controller. In very small firms, one person may perform all functions, including finance.

The Basic Financial Goal of the Firm

The financial manager's basic job is to make decisions that add value to the firm. When asked what the basic goal of a firm is, many people will answer, "to make a lot of money"

Take Note
The point about cash received sooner being better than cash received later works in reverse too. It is better to pay out cash later rather than sooner (all other factors being equal, of course).

---

chief financial officer
The manager who directs and coordinates the financial activities of the firm.

treasurer The manager responsible for financial planning, fund-raising, and allocation of money in a business.

controller The manager who is responsible for the financial and cost accounting activities of a firm.

FIGURE 1-1
The Organization of a Typical Corporation

Figure 1-1 shows how finance fits into a typical business organization. The vice president for finance, or chief financial officer, operates with the vice presidents of the other business teams.

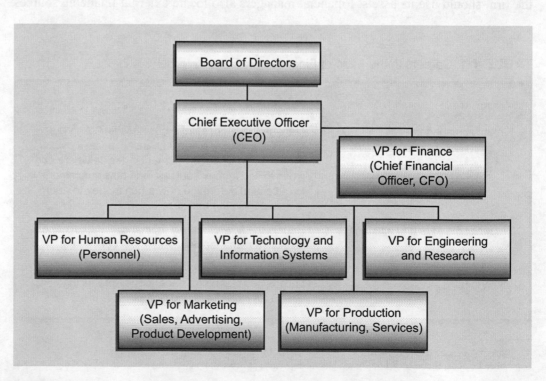

FIGURE 1-2

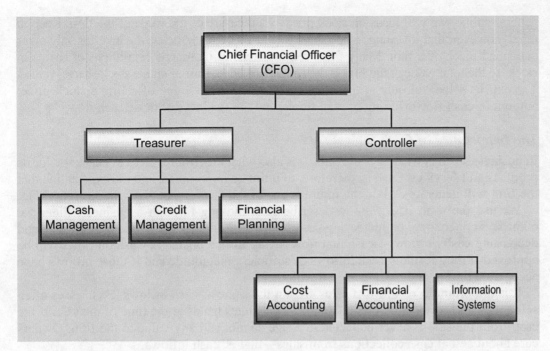

FIGURE 1-2
An Example of How to
Organize a Finance Team

This chart shows how to
organize a finance team in a
medium-to-large business.
Most teams include both
a finance function (on the
left) and an accounting
function (on the right). The
chief financial officer usually
reports to the CEO, as shown
in Figure 1-1.

or "to maximize profits." Although no one would argue that profits aren't important, the single-minded pursuit of profits is not necessarily good for the firm and its owners. We will explain why this is so in the sections that follow. For now, let's say that a better way to express the primary financial goal of a business firm is to "maximize the wealth of the firm's owners." This is an extremely important, even crucial, point, so we will say it again: *The primary financial goal of the business firm is to maximize the wealth of the firm's owners*.

Everything the financial manager does—indeed, all the actions of everyone in the firm—should be directed toward this goal, subject to legal and ethical considerations that we will discuss in this chapter and throughout the book.

Now, what do we mean by wealth? **Wealth** refers to value. If a group of people owns a business firm, the contribution that firm makes to that group's wealth is determined by the market value of that firm.

wealth Assets minus liabilities.

This is a very important point: We have defined wealth in terms of *value*. The concept of value, then, is of fundamental importance in finance. Financial managers and researchers spend a lot of time measuring value and figuring out what causes it to increase or decrease.

In Search of Value

We have said that the basic goal of the business firm is to maximize the wealth of the firm's owners—that is, to maximize the value of the firm. The next question, then, is how to measure the value of the firm.

The value of a firm is determined by whatever people are willing to pay for it. The more valuable people think a firm is, the more they will pay to own it. Then the existing owners can sell it to investors for more than the amount of their investment, thereby increasing current owner wealth. The financial manager's job is to make decisions that will cause people to think more favorably about the firm and, in turn, to be willing to pay more to purchase the business.

For companies that sell stock to the general public, stock price can indicate the value of a business because *stockholders*—people who purchase corporate shares of stock—become part owners of the corporation. (We will discuss stock in greater detail in Chapter 2.) People will pay a higher price for stock—that is, part ownership of a business—if they believe the company will perform well in the future. For example, adjusting historic stock prices for stock splits, Apple began trading at $0.44 per share when it went public in late 1980 and was selling for $170 in early 2018.

For businesses that sell stock publicly, then, the financial manager's basic role is to help make the firm's stock more valuable. Although some businesses do not sell stock to the

Take Note
If the company is
organized in the form
of a corporation then
the company's value is
determined by the value
of the corporation's
common stock and the
focus of the company's
managers is on
maximizing the value
of that stock.

general public, we will focus on stock price as a measure of the value of the firm. Keep in mind, however, that investing in one share (one unit) of stock means the investor only owns one small piece of a firm. Many firms sell hundreds of thousands or millions of shares of stock, so the total value of the firm is the equivalent of the sum of all the stock shares' values.

Next, let's look closely at three factors that affect the value of a firm's stock price: amount of cash flows, timing of cash flows, and the riskiness of those cash flows.

The Importance of Cash Flow

In business, cash is what pays the bills. It is also what the firm receives in exchange for its products and services. Cash is, therefore, of ultimate importance, and the expectation that the firm will generate cash in the future is one of the factors that gives the firm its value.

We use the term *cash flow* to describe cash moving through a business. Financial managers concentrate on increasing cash *in*flows—cash that flows into a business—and decreasing cash *out*flows—cash that flows away from a business. Cash outflows will be approved if they result in cash inflows of sufficient magnitude and if those inflows have acceptable timing and risk associated with them.

It is important to realize that sales are not the same as cash inflows. Businesses often sell goods and services on credit, so no cash changes hands at the time of the sale. If the cash from the sale is never collected, the sale cannot add any value to the firm. Owners care about actual cash collections from sales—that is, cash inflows.

Likewise, businesses may buy goods and services to keep firms running but may make the purchases on credit, so no cash changes hands at that time. However, bills always come due sooner or later, so owners care about cash expenditures for purchases—cash outflows. For any business firm (assuming other factors remain constant), the higher the expected cash inflows and the lower the expected cash outflows, the higher the firm's stock price will be.

The Effect of Timing on Cash Flow Valuation

The timing of cash flows also affects a firm's value. To illustrate, consider this: Would you rather receive $100 cash today and $0 one year from now, or would you rather receive $0 cash today and $100 one year from now? The two alternatives follow:

	Today	One Year from Today
Alternative A	+$ 100	$ 0
Alternative B	$ 0	+$ 100

Both alternatives promise the same total amount of cash, but most people would choose Alternative A, because they realize they could invest the $100 received today and earn interest on it during the year. By doing so they would end up with more money than $100 at the end of the year. For this reason we say that—all other factors being equal—cash received sooner is better than cash received later.

Owners and potential investors look at when firms can expect to receive cash and when they can expect to pay out cash. All other factors being equal, the sooner a company expects to receive cash and the later it expects to pay out cash, the more valuable the firm and the higher its stock price will be.

The Influence of Risk

We have seen that the size of a firm's expected cash inflows and outflows and the timing of those cash flows influence the value of the firm and its stock price. Now let us consider how risk affects the firm's value and its stock price.

Risk affects value because the less certain owners and investors are about a firm's expected cash inflows, the lower they will value the company. The more certain owners and investors are about a firm's expected cash inflows, the higher they will value the company. In short, companies whose expected future cash flows are doubtful will have lower values than companies whose expected future cash flows are virtually certain.

What isn't nearly as clear as the way risk affects value is *how much* it affects it. For example, if one company's cash inflows are twice as risky as another company's cash inflows, is its stock worth half as much? We can't say. In fact, we have a tough time quantifying just how risky the companies are in the first place.

We will examine the issue of risk in some detail in Chapter 7. For now, it is sufficient to remember that risk affects the stock price—as risk increases, the stock price goes down; and conversely, as risk decreases, the stock price goes up.

Table 1-2 summarizes the influences of cash flow size, timing, and risk on stock prices.

Profits versus Company Value

Earlier in the chapter, we said that the single-minded pursuit of profits is not necessarily good for the firm's owners. Indeed, the firm's owners view company value, not profit, as the appropriate measure of wealth. Company value depends on future cash flows, their timing, and their riskiness. Profit calculations do not consider these three factors. Profit, as defined in accounting, is simply the difference between sales revenue and expenses. If all we were interested in were profits, we could simply start using high-pressure sales techniques, cut all expenses to the bone, and then point proudly to the resulting increase in profits. For the moment, anyway. In all probability, managers practicing such techniques would find their firm out of business later, when the quality of the firm's products, services, and workforce dropped, eventually leading to declining sales and market share.

It is true that more profits are generally better than less profits. But when the pursuit of short-term profits adversely affects the size of future cash flows, their timing, or their riskiness, then these profit maximization efforts are detrimental to the firm. Concentrating on company value, not profits, is a better measure of financial success.

Legal and Ethical Challenges in Financial Management

Several legal and ethical challenges influence financial managers as they pursue the goal of wealth maximization for the firm's owners. Examples of legal considerations include environmental statutes mandating pollution control equipment, workplace safety standards that must be met, civil rights laws that must be obeyed, and intellectual property laws that regulate the use of others' ideas.

TABLE 1-2 Accomplishing the Primary Financial Goal of the Firm

The Goal: Maximize the wealth of the firm's owners
Measure of the Goal: Value of the firm
(measured by the price of the stock on the open market for corporations)

Factor	Effect on Stock Price
Size of expected future cash flows	Larger future cash inflows raise the stock price. Larger future cash outflows lower the stock price. Smaller future cash inflows lower the stock price. Smaller future cash outflows raise the stock price.
Timing of future cash flows	Cash inflows expected sooner result in a higher stock price. Cash inflows expected later result in a lower stock price. *(The opposite effect occurs for future cash outflows.)*
Riskiness of future cash flows	When the degree of risk associated with future cash flows goes down, the stock price goes up. When the degree of risk associated with future cash flows goes up, the stock price goes down.

Ethical concerns include fair treatment of employees, customers, the community, and society as a whole. Indeed, many businesses have written ethics codes that articulate the ethical values of the business organization.

Three legal and ethical influences of special note include the agency problem, the interests of non-owner stakeholders, and the interests of society as a whole. We will turn to these issues next.

Agency Issues

agent A person who has the implied or actual authority to act on behalf of another.

principal A person who authorizes an agent to act for him or her.

The financial manager, and the other managers of a business firm, are agents for the owners of the firm. An **agent** is a person who has the implied or actual authority to act on behalf of another. The owners whom the agents represent are the principals. For example, the board of directors and senior management of IBM are agents for the IBM stockholders, the **principals**. Agents have a legal and ethical responsibility to make decisions that further the interests of the principals.

The interests of the principals are supposed to be paramount when agents make decisions, but this is often easier said than done. For example, the managing director of a corporation might like the convenience of a private jet on call 24 hours a day, but do the common stockholder owners of the corporation receive enough value to justify the cost of a jet? It looks like the interests of the managing director (the agent) and the interests of the common stockholder owners (the principals) of the corporation are in conflict in this case.

Executive compensation has also become a lightning rod issue due to the large bonuses paid by some large companies receiving government bailouts in 2009. Some AIG executives had been promised large bonuses before this huge insurance company ran into financial trouble and required federal government assistance to stay in business. Should there be limits on bonuses given to executives of companies receiving federal financial aid? Is it right to abrogate signed employment contracts that had been entered into before the company accepted federal financial aid? What should be the guidelines for determining executive salaries and bonuses at private sector companies that do not receive government money? General Motors and Chrysler took federal money during the 2008 Financial Crisis. Ford did not. Were the decisions made by the Board of Directors of General Motors influenced by the U.S. Treasury when it was a major shareholder immediately after the bailout up to the time it liquidated its holdings in 2013? Are these decisions different than what the Ford Motor Company Board of Directors would make? These issues relate to the agency problem addressed in the next section. Whose interests should company decision makers consider?

The Agency Problem

agency problem
The possibility of conflict between the interests of a firm's managers and those of the firm's owners.

When the interests of the agents and principals conflict, an **agency problem** results. In our jet example, an agency problem occurs if the managing director buys the jet, even though he knows the benefits to the stockholders do not justify the cost.

Another example of an agency problem occurs when managers must decide whether to undertake a project with a high potential payoff but high risk. Even if the project is more likely than not to be successful, managers may not want to take a risk that owners would be willing to take. Why? An unsuccessful project may result in such significant financial loss that the managers who approved the project lose their jobs—and all the income from their paychecks. The stockholder owners, however, may have a much smaller risk because their investment in company stock represents only a small fraction of their financial investment portfolio. Because the risk is so much larger to the manager as compared to the stockholder, a promising but somewhat risky project may be rejected even though it is likely to benefit the firm's owners.

There can also be an agency problem if the non-owner, or small stake owner managers, have an incentive to take too much risk. A manager may qualify for a huge bonus if a large return is earned on a company investment. This manager may borrow lots of money, leverage the company to high levels, in an attempt to achieve this big payoff. If this big gamble with the owners' funds pays off the manager can take the big bonus and retire. If the big gamble doesn't pay off the manager can leave for another job and leave the owners holding the bag for the losses.

The agency problem can be lessened by tying the managers' compensation to the performance of the company and its stock price. This tie brings the interests of the managers and those of the firm's owners closer together. That is why companies often make shares of stock a part of the compensation package offered to managers, especially top executives. If managers are also stockholders, then the agency problem should be reduced.

It is clear that the agency problem has been grossly underestimated and that it is a big part of the reason we experienced the economic and financial crises of 2007 through 2009 and beyond. These issues continued well into 2012. Many big risks were assumed by managers and many of these risks didn't pay off. JPMorgan Chase took some big risks in 2012 by taking positions with the firm's own money that had been designed to reduce risk. These trades ended creating billions of dollars in losses for the company. At least taxpayers didn't end up holding the bag for any of these losses. It was the shareholders who absorbed the brunt of the downside. Board members and the stockholders who elected them, mainly large institutional investors, failed to properly monitor these executives and to give them incentives that were aligned with shareholder interests. It is clear that these issues will be closely examined to reduce the chances of another crisis of this magnitude.

Agency Costs

Sometimes firms spend time and money to monitor and reduce agency problems. These outlays of time and money are **agency costs**. One common example of an agency cost is an accounting audit of a corporation's financial statements. If a business is owned and operated by the same person, the owner does not need an audit—she can trust herself to report her finances accurately. Most companies of any size, however, have agency costs because managers, not owners, report the finances. Owners audit the company financial statements to see whether the agents have acted in the owners' interests by reporting finances accurately.

agency costs Costs incurred to monitor agents to reduce the conflict of interest between agents and principals.

The Interests of Other Groups

Stockholders and managers are not the only groups that have a stake in a business firm. There are also non-manager workers, creditors, suppliers, customers, and members of the community where the business is located. These groups are also **stakeholders**—people who have a "stake" in the business. Although the primary financial goal of the firm is to maximize the wealth of the owners, the interests of these other stakeholders can influence business decisions. Some corporations have organized themselves as "benefit corporations." Such firms are allowed to consider a wider range of stakeholders, not just the owners, when making company decisions. More about that later in this chapter.

stakeholder A party having an interest in a firm (for example, owners, workers, management, creditors, suppliers, customers, and the community as a whole).

As the federal government took ownership interest in companies such as GM, AIG, Fannie Mae, Freddie Mac, and Citigroup, the interests of taxpayers were given weight when executives of these companies made decisions. Taxpayers were effectively part owners of those companies that have received financial bailouts in return for government ownership interests. In effect there are no "other interest groups" for those companies with government investments that were the result of government aid to failing companies. When almost everyone has a stake in a company, how do you decide whose interests receive priority?

The Interests of Society as a Whole

Sometimes the interests of a business firm's owners are not the same as the interests of society. For instance, the cost of properly disposing of toxic waste can be so high that companies may be tempted to simply dump their waste in nearby rivers. In so doing, the companies can keep costs low and profits high, and drive their stock prices higher (if they are not caught). However, many people suffer from the polluted environment. This is why we have environmental and other similar laws—so that society's best interests take precedence over the interests of individual company owners.

When businesses take a long-term view, the interests of the owners and society often (but not always) coincide. When companies encourage recycling, sponsor programs for disadvantaged young people, run media campaigns promoting the responsible use of alcohol, and contribute money to worthwhile civic causes, the goodwill generated as a result of these activities causes long-term increases in the firm's sales and cash flows, which can translate into additional wealth for the firm's owners.

Although the traditional primary economic goal of the firm is to maximize shareholder wealth, the unbridled pursuit of value is too simplistic a view of this goal. Firms often take into account ethical factors, the interests of other stakeholders, and the long-term interests of society.[5]

Figure 1-3 summarizes the various influences that financial managers may consider in their pursuit of value.

Forms of Business Organization

Businesses can be organized in a variety of ways. The four most common types of organization are proprietorships, partnerships, corporations, and limited liability companies (LLCs). The distinguishing characteristics give each form its own advantages and disadvantages.

The Proprietorship

proprietorship A business that is not incorporated and is owned by one person.

The simplest way to organize a business is to form a **proprietorship**, a business owned by one person. An individual raises some money, finds a location from which to operate, and starts selling a product or service. The profits or losses generated are reported on a form called Schedule C of the individual's Form 1040 income tax return. The sole proprietor is responsible for any tax liability generated by the business, and the tax rates are those that apply to an individual.

The sole proprietor has *unlimited liability* for matters relating to the business. This means that the sole proprietor is responsible for all the obligations of the business, even if those obligations exceed the amount the proprietor has invested in the business. If a customer is injured on the company premises and sues for $1 million, the sole proprietor must pay that amount if the court awards it to the plaintiff customer. This is true even if the total amount invested by the sole proprietor in the business is only $10,000.

Although unlimited liability is a major disadvantage of a proprietorship, liability insurance is often available to reduce the risk of losing business and non-business assets. However, the

FIGURE 1-3
Influences on Financial Managers

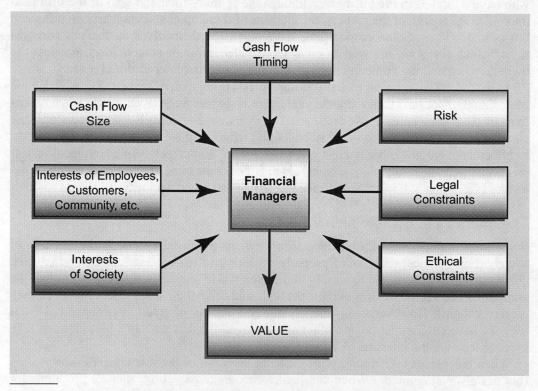

---

5. Not everyone agrees with this approach. The late Milton Friedman, Nobel laureate in economics, claimed that any action taken by a manager that is not legally mandated and that reduces the value available to the owners, is theft.

risk always remains that the business will be unsuccessful and that the losses incurred will exceed the amount of the proprietor's money invested. The other assets owned by the proprietor will then be at risk.

The Partnership

Two or more people may join together to form a business as a **partnership**. This can be done on an informal basis without a written partnership agreement, or a contract can spell out the rights and responsibilities of each partner. This written contract is called the *articles of partnership* and is strongly recommended to lessen the likelihood of disputes between partners.

The articles of partnership contract generally spells out how much money each partner will contribute, what the ownership share of each partner will be, how profits and losses will be allocated among partners, who will perform what work for the business, and other matters of concern to the partners. The percent of ownership for each partner does not have to be the same as the percent each partner invests in the partnership.

Each partner in a partnership is usually liable for the activities of the partnership as a whole.[6] This is an important point. Even if there are 100 partners, each one is technically responsible for all the debts of the partnership.[7] If 99 partners declare personal bankruptcy, the hundredth partner still is responsible for all the partnership's debts.

Special Kinds of Partnerships

Some partnerships contain two different classes of partners, general partners and limited partners. These are called **limited partnerships**, or **LPs**. In a limited partnership, the general partners usually participate actively in the management of the business, whereas limited partners usually do not. Limited partners usually contribute capital and share in the profits but take no part in running the business. As a result, general partners usually contract for a more favorable allocation of ownership, profits, and losses compared with limited partners. General partners have unlimited liability for the partnership's activities. Limited partners are only liable for the amount they invest in the partnership. If you are a limited partner who invests $5,000 in the business, then $5,000 is the most you can lose. For this reason, every partnership must have at least one general partner (a partnership could have all general partners, but it could not have all limited partners).

In some states, attorneys and accountants organize their businesses into what is called a **limited liability partnership**, or **LLP**. This is simply a general partnership that is allowed to operate like a corporation, with limited liability features much like those of a corporation (more about limited liability in the next section).

A partner's profits and losses are reported on Schedule K-1. The dollar figure from Schedule K-1 is entered on the appropriate line of each partner's individual 1040 income tax return. The partners pay any taxes owed. The partnership itself is not taxed because the income merely passes through the partnership to the partners, where it is taxed.

The Corporation

The third major form of business organization is the **corporation**. Unlike proprietorships and partnerships, corporations are legal entities separate from their owners. To form a corporation, the owners specify the governing rules for the running of the business in a contract known as the *articles of incorporation*. They submit the articles to the government of the state in which the corporation is formed, and the state issues a charter that creates the separate legal entity.

Corporations, specifically C corporations described below, are taxed as separate legal entities. That is, corporations must pay their own income tax just as if they were individuals.[8] This is where the often-discussed "double taxation" of corporate profits comes into play. First, a corporation pays income tax on the profit it earns. Then the corporation may distribute to the owners the profits that are left after paying taxes. These distributions,

partnership An unincorporated business owned by two or more people.

limited partnerships (LPs) Partnerships that include at least one partner whose liability is limited to the amount invested. They usually take a less active role in the running of the business than do general partners.

limited liability partnership (LLPs) Business entities that are usually formed by professionals such as doctors, lawyers, or accountants and that provide limited liability for the partners.

corporation A business chartered by the state that is a separate legal entity having some, but not all, of the rights and responsibilities of a natural person.

---

6. But see the discussion that follows on general and limited partners.
7. In legal terms, this concept is called "joint and several liability."
8. Corporations file their income tax returns using Form 1041.

called dividends, count as income for the owners and are taxed on the individual owners' income tax returns. Thus, the IRS collects taxes twice on the same income.

Double taxation of dividends is bad news for the owners of corporations, but there is good news as well. Stockholders, the corporation's owners, have limited liability for the corporation's activities. They cannot lose more than the amount they paid to buy the stock. This makes the corporate form of organization very attractive for owners who desire to shelter their personal assets from creditors of the business.

Corporations have other benefits too. For example, because they exist separately from their owners, they can "live" beyond the death of their original owners. Another benefit of the corporate form of business is that corporations generally have a professional management team and board of directors, elected by the owners. It is the board's job to look out for the interests of the owners (the stockholders). Stockholders, especially in the case of large corporations, usually do not take an active role in the management of the business, so it is the board of directors' job to represent them.

Public and Private Corporations

private corporation
A corporation that does not offer its shares to the general public and that can keep its financial statements confidential.

Some corporations are owned by a small number of stockholders and do now extend ownership opportunities to the general public. These are called **private corporations**. Often these corporations are family owned. Some are owned by a small group of investors who intend to sell the shares to the public at some future time. Private companies are usually, but not always, small. Cargill and Koch Industries are examples of large private companies. Since corporations are created by the various states the rules for forming a private corporation vary. The shares are not traded on organized exchanges or on an organized over-the-counter market such as Nasdaq. Shares of private corporations are usually sold informally on a person-to-person basis. Usually corporate rules require approval of other shareholders before a current shareholder of a private corporation sells shares to a new investor. Frequently, existing shareholders are given a right of first refusal if one among their ranks wishes to sell shares.

public corporations
Corporations that make their shares available to the general public and that have reporting and disclosure requirements private corporations do not.

In contrast to private corporations there are **public corporations**. These are generally large companies that offer their shares to anyone wishing to buy them on an exchange or over the counter market. Public corporations can raise capital by issuing new shares of common stock to the public. Since shares are made available to the general public, there are reporting and disclosure requirements imposed on publicly traded corporations that are not imposed on private corporations. These requirements include releasing annual audited financial statements. These are included in what is called a 10-K report submitted to the Securities and Exchange Commission (SEC). In addition to audited financial statements, 10-K reports contain a wealth of additional information about the company. 10-K reports can be found on the Web at www.sec.gov/edgar.shtml.

C corporations Subchapter C corporations are large corporations that are taxed separately, via the corporate income tax, from their owners.

S corporation A corporation so designated with income that passes through the entity that is subsequently taxed to the owners, with no separate corporate income tax assessed to the company itself.

C corporations, as they are defined in the United States tax code, are separately taxable entities.[9] Another classification in the code is called the **S corporation** (after subChapter S in the code). S corporations do not pay income tax themselves; instead, they pass their income through to the owners, who report it on their individual tax returns. S corporations are generally very small; in fact, this form of business ownership was created to relieve small businesses from some of the rules that large Subchapter C corporations must follow. S corporations can have no more than 100 shareholders, and the shareholders must be individuals (rather than organizations such as other corporations). The stockholders of S corporations also have limited liability.

Professional corporations (PCs) Special corporations for businesses that provide professional services.

Professional corporations, or **PCs**, are special corporations for businesses that provide "professional services," such as medical, legal, accounting, or architectural services. Only members of the profession may be shareholders in the corporation. As with any other corporation, shareholders share limited liability for the corporation's debts. Note, however, that PC status does not protect the firm from malpractice claims.

---

9. The complete reference is Title 26—Internal Revenue Code, Subtitle A—Income Taxes, Chapter 1, Normal Taxes and Surtaxes, Subchapter S—Tax treatment of S corporations and their shareholders. Oddly enough, C corporations are defined in Subchapter S.

Benefit Corporations

Benefit Corporations

The **benefit corporation** is a relatively new type of corporation that is designed to expand the duty of the directors such that the company's impact on society and the environment are considered, along with the interests of the shareholders, when decisions are made. Because corporations are created by a state, it is state law that governs the rules that would apply to a benefit corporation. Not all states allow for the creation of a benefit corporation, but more states appear to be providing for such entities each year.

There is a nonprofit organization called **B Lab** that offers certification for companies that wish to pursue social and environmental goals in addition to the pursuit of profit. This certification is separate from the laws that have been passed in some states that allow for a company to be legally organized as a benefit corporation. B Lab provides certification and verifies that a corporation with this certification is meeting certain standards related to social and environmental practices. A Certified B Corporation is a company that has voluntarily agreed to meet the requirements of B Lab. Since it is voluntary, a corporation in any state may apply for such certification. Only those corporations in states that provide for a corporation to be designated as benefit corporations will have corporate charters that provide for the social and environmental goals such firms pursue. Benefit corporations that have obtained this status from one of the states that allow it are frequently called B Corps for short. This opens up the possibility of confusion with "Certified B Corps," which receive their designation from the nonprofit B Lab. A benefit corporation created by the state is a different entity from a Certified B Corp that has been granted certification from B Lab.

It is less likely that a publicly traded corporation would seek benefit corporation or Certified B Corp status. A growing number of privately held corporations are seeking one of these designations, however. The shareholders, mainly large institutional investors, in publicly traded corporations are less likely to approve any proposal that would diminish the role of seeking to maximize the interests of the common stock shareholders when conducting company policy. If a corporation seeks to achieve benefit corporation status as part of its charter as provided by state law, almost always a super majority of voting shares must approve. To give just two examples, Colorado requires the approval of at least two-thirds of shareholders and Delaware requires approval of at least sixty-six percent of shareholders. This is a high bar. Privately held corporations, on the other hand, have more freedom to pursue the goals of the relatively small number of owners controlling such firms. If such owners place a high value on furthering societal and environmental goals, while also pursuing profits, these owners have every right to do so and now have a way to declare such goals as a matter of company policy.

Etsy, the peer-to-peer e-commerce company is a publicly traded B Corp. It will be interesting to see how popular benefit corporation or Certified B Corp designation becomes with other publicly traded companies. In 2017 Etsy was having financial difficulties, having experienced several consecutive years of net losses, and was contemplating dropping its Certified B Corp status. The CEO of Etsy was removed in 2017. After you read this you might wish to check to see if Etsy still has Certified B Corp status.

Limited Liability Companies (LLCs)

Limited liability companies, or **LLCs,** are hybrids between partnerships and corporations. LLCs pass their profits and losses through to their owners, without taxation of the LLC itself, as partnerships do. They also provide limited liability for their owners, like corporations. S corporations and limited partnerships share these characteristics, but unlike S corporations, LLCs are actually non-corporate entities. The owners of LLCs are called members and they can be individuals or organizations (corporations, other LLCs, trusts, pension plans, and so on). LLCs can also have more than 75 owners. LLCs are popular because they provide the "best of both worlds" between partnerships and corporations. That is, they avoid the double taxation C corporations face while shielding the owners from personal liability.

Table 1-3 summarizes the advantages and disadvantages of the various forms of business ownership.

benefit corporation
A corporation with a charter that allows the board of directors to take into account the interests of a wider range of stakeholders, not just the common stock shareholders, when making corporate decisions. Some states allow such a designation so that workers, suppliers, customers, and community members' interests are considered.

B Lab A non-profit organization that offers certification to companies that meet the organizations' standards for social and environmental activities.

limited liability companies (LLCs) Hybrids between partnerships and corporations that are taxed like the former and have limited liability for the owners like the latter.

TABLE 1-3 Characteristics of Business Ownership Forms

	Proprietorship	Partnership	Corporation	LLC
Ease of formation	Very easy	Relatively easy	More difficult	Relatively easy
Owners' liability	Unlimited	Unlimited for general partners	Limited	Limited
Life of firm	Dies with owner, unless heirs continue operating or sell the business	Surviving partners must deal with the deceased partner's heirs	Can live beyond owners' lifetimes	Dies with owner, heirs may continue operating the business
Separate legal entity?	No	No	Yes	Yes
Degree of control by owners	Complete	May be limited for individual partner	May be very limited for individual stockholder	Depends on the number of owners

What's Next

In this book we will look at how firms raise and allocate funds, and how firms invest in assets that generate returns at a reasonable risk. In Part 1 of the text, we discuss the environment in which financial managers make decisions. In Chapter 2, we will examine how funds are raised in the financial marketplace. In Chapter 3, we'll explore how financial institutions and interest rates affect financial decisions.

Summary

1. *Describe the field of finance.*
   Finance is important to business people. Financial decisions about how to raise, spend, and allocate money can affect every aspect of a business—from personnel to products. Finance also offers career opportunities in three main areas: financial management, financial markets and institutions, and investments. Financial management focuses on managing the finances of a business.

2. *Discuss the duties of financial managers.*
   Financial managers use accounting information and economic principles to guide their financial decisions. They measure the firm's financial condition, forecast, budget, raise funds, and determine the financial goals of the firm's owners. They also work closely with other managers to further the firm's goals.

   At medium and large firms, more than one person usually handles the financial management duties. In some firms a chief financial officer (CFO) supervises the financial activities, including cash and credit management, financial planning, and accounting.

3. *Identify the basic goal of a business firm.*
   The basic goal of the business firm is to maximize the wealth of the firm's owners by adding value; it is not to maximize profits. The value of a firm is measured by the price investors are willing to pay to own the firm. For businesses that sell stock to the general public, stock price indicates the firm's value because shares of stock are units of ownership. So the basic financial goal of such firms is to maximize the price of the firm's stock.

4. *List factors that affect the value of a firm.*
   The value of a firm is affected by the size of future cash flows, their timing, and their riskiness.
   • Cash inflows increase a firm's value, whereas cash outflows decrease it.
   • The sooner cash flows are expected to be received, the greater the value. The later those cash flows are expected, the less the value.
   • The less risk associated with future cash flows, the higher the value. The more risk, the lower the value.

5. *Discuss the legal and ethical challenges financial managers face.*
- Legal and ethical considerations include the agency problem, the interests of other stakeholders, and the interests of society as a whole.
- The agency problem exists when the interests of a firm's managers (the agents) are in conflict with those of the firm's owners (the principals).
- Other stakeholders whose interests are often considered in financial decisions include employees, customers, and members of the communities in which the firm's plants are located.
- Concerns of society as a whole—such as environmental or health problems—often influence business financial decisions.

6. *Identify the different forms of business organization.*
- Proprietorships are businesses owned by one person. The owner is exposed to unlimited liability for the firm's debts.
- Partnerships are businesses owned by two or more people, each of whom is responsible for the firm's debts. The exception is a limited partner, a partner who contracts for limited liability.
- Corporations are separate legal entities. They are owned by stockholders, who are responsible for the firm's debts only to the extent of their investment.
- Limited liability companies are hybrids between partnerships and corporations.

Key Terms

agency costs Costs incurred to monitor agents to reduce the conflict of interest between agents and principals.

agency problem The possibility of conflict between the interests of a firm's managers and those of the firm's owners.

agent A person who has the implied or actual authority to act on behalf of another.

B Lab A non-profit organization that offers certification to companies that meet the organizations' standards for social and environmental activities.

benefit corporation A corporation with a charter that allows the board of directors to take into account the interests of a wider range of stakeholders, not just the common stock shareholders, when making corporate decisions. Some states allow such a designation so that workers, suppliers, customers, and community members' interests are considered. Some corporations seek certification from B Lab, a nonprofit organization not affiliated with any state, that recognizes companies that have met its criteria for considering a similarly broad range of stakeholders when making company decisions.

C corporations Subchapter C corporations are large corporations that are taxed separately, via the corporate payment income tax, from their owners.

chief financial officer The manager who directs and coordinates the financial activities of the firm.

controller The manager who is responsible for the financial and cost accounting activities of a firm.

corporation A business chartered by the state that is a separate legal entity having some, but not all, of the rights and responsibilities of a natural person.

initial public offering (IPO) The process whereby a private corporation issues new common stock to the general public, thus becoming a publicly traded corporation.

limited liability companies (LLCs) Hybrids between partnerships and corporations that are taxed like the former and have limited liability for the owners like the latter.

limited liability partnership (LLPs) Business entities that are usually formed by professionals such as doctors, lawyers, or accountants and that provide limited liability for the partners.

limited partnerships (LPs) Partnerships that include at least one partner whose liability is limited to the amount invested. They usually take a less active role in the running of the business than do general partners.

partnership An unincorporated business owned by two or more people.

principal A person who authorizes an agent to act for him or her.

private corporation A corporation that does not offer its shares to the general public and that can keep its financial statements confidential.

Professional corporations (PCs) Special corporations for businesses that provide professional services.

proprietorship A business that is not incorporated and is owned by one person.

public corporations Corporations that make their shares available to the general public and that have reporting and disclosure requirements private corporations do not.

S corporation A corporation so designated with income that passes through the entity that is subsequently taxed to the owners, with no separate corporate income tax assessed to the company itself.

stakeholder A party having an interest in a firm (for example, owners, workers, management, creditors, suppliers, customers, and the community as a whole).

treasurer The manager responsible for financial planning, fund-raising, and allocation of money in a business.

wealth Assets minus liabilities.

Self-Test

ST-1. What are the three main areas of career opportunities in finance?

ST-2. What are the primary responsibilities of a person holding the title of treasurer at a large corporation?

ST-3. Who is a "principal" in an agent–principal relationship?

ST-4. What legal and ethical factors may influence a firm's financial decisions?

ST-5. What is a Subchapter S corporation?

ST-6. What is an LLC?

ST-7. What is a benefit corporation?

Review Questions

1. How is finance related to the disciplines of accounting and economics?

2. List and describe the three career opportunities in the field of finance.

3. Describe the duties of the financial manager in a business firm.

4. What is the basic goal of a business?

5. List and explain the three financial factors that influence the value of a business.

6. Explain why striving to achieve accounting profits and maximizing stock value are not the same.

7. What is an agent? What are the responsibilities of an agent?

8. Describe how society's interests can influence financial managers.

9. Briefly define the terms *proprietorship*, *partnership*, *LLC*, and *corporation*.

10. Compare and contrast the potential liability of owners of proprietorships, partnerships (general partners), and corporations.

Build Your Communication Skills

CS-1. Divide into small groups. Each small group should then divide in half. The first group should defend the idea that managers of a firm should consider only the interests of stockholders, subject to legal constraints. The other group should argue that businesses should consider the interests of other stakeholders of the firm and society at large.

CS-2. Assume you work for WealthMax Corporation in New York City. You've noticed that managers who work late charge the corporation for their dinners and transportation home. You've also noticed that almost all employees from these managers' departments take office supplies, ranging from pens to computer software, for personal use at home. You estimate the costs of this pilfering at a shocking $150,000 a year. Your boss, the chief financial officer for WealthMax, asks you to write a memo to the offending managers describing why their actions and those of their employees violate their duties and conflict with the goal of the firm. Write this memo.

Problems

The Field of Finance **1-1.** Explain the difference between what an accountant does and what a financial analyst does.

The Basic Financial Goal of a Firm **1-2.** Describe the basic role of a financial manager in a firm that sells stock publicly.

Factors Affecting the Value of a Firm **1-3.** How would the value of a firm be affected by the following events?

    a. The introduction of a new product designed to increase the firm's cash inflows is delayed by one year. The size of the expected cash flows is not affected.

    b. A firm announces to the press that its cash earnings for the coming year will be 10 percent higher than previously forecast.

    c. A utility company acquires a natural gas exploration company. After the acquisition, 50 percent of the new company's assets are from the original utility company and 50 percent from the new exploration company.

1-4. According to federal law, federally chartered banks are permitted to bypass state usury and other laws that would hamper their ability to do business. This makes it possible for loan outlets in some states to offer "quickie" loans of $300 that must be paid back in two weeks with the principal plus $51, which is equivalent to an annual interest rate of over 400 percent. Banks engaged in this practice say they are merely giving people access to emergency credit. Others say the practice is unethical. State your opinion on this issue and justify it.

◀ **Legal and Ethical Challenges**

1-5. Limited liability companies are said to be hybrids between partnerships and corporations. Explain why.

◀ **Forms of Business Organization**

Answers to Self-Test

ST-1. Financial management, financial markets and institutions, and investments.

ST-2. The treasurer of a large corporation is responsible for cash management, credit management, and financial planning.

ST-3. A principal in an agent–principal relationship is the person who hires the agent to act on the principal's behalf. The principal is the person to whom the agent owes a duty.

ST-4. Legal and ethical factors influence businesses. Examples of legal constraints include environmental, safety, and civil rights laws. Examples of ethical considerations include fair treatment of workers, environmental sensitivity, and support for the community.

ST-5. A Subchapter S corporation is a small corporation that is taxed as if it were a partnership. As a result, the owners of a Subchapter S corporation avoid double taxation of corporate income paid to stockholders.

ST-6. LLCs, or limited liability companies, are hybrids between partnerships and corporations. LLCs pass their profits and losses through to their owners, as partnerships do, without taxation of the LLC itself, and they provide limited liability for their owners, as corporations do.

ST-7. A benefit corporation is a corporation organized under state law such that it declares that it has goals related to social and environmental values in addition to the pursuit of profit for its owners.

Financial Markets and Interest Rates

"So everybody has some information. The function of the markets is to aggregate that information, evaluate it, and get it incorporated into prices."
—Merton Miller

Source: ymgerman/Shutterstock

Learning Objectives

After reading this chapter, you should be able to:

1. Describe how the U.S. financial system works.
2. Define *financial securities*.
3. Explain the function of financial intermediaries.
4. Identify the different financial markets
5. Describe the securities traded in the money and capital markets.
6. Identify the determinants of the nominal interest rate.
7. Construct and analyze a yield curve.

Interest Rates Can't Be Negative, Can They?

The Great Recession of 2008 put central banks around the world in major expansionary mode. The traditional remedy for faltering economies would be to lower interest rates to encourage business activity and spending. How low can interest rates go? Surely, zero is a lower bound, is it not?

It turns out that interest rates can be negative. That's right; a lender pays someone to hold his or her money. In early 2016, the Bank of Japan, that country's central bank, began charging commercial banks to hold their reserves, rather than paying interest on such deposits as had been the practice. The European Central Bank took a similar approach a little later that year. Although the U.S. Treasury has never issued government securities with a negative interest rate (although it has issued some with a zero interest rate), the prices of some Treasury bills were bid up in the secondary market to a level above the face value. This created a negative interest rate for the secondary market buyer who held that security until it matured. This happened in September of 2015.

In this chapter, we examine determinants of the level of interest rates, along with the markets where securities trade. In normal times, the preference to have a given amount of money now rather than later still prevails. So too does an aversion on the part of lenders to inflation and default risk. Holding a readily marketable security is preferable to holding one that is difficult to sell at a good price. Long-term interest rates are usually, but not always, higher than short-term interest rates.

These factors result in positive interest rates most of the time. In this chapter, we examine both the normal state of affairs and the unusual state where negative interest rates exist.

Chapter Overview

One of the central duties of a financial manager is to acquire capital—that is, to raise funds. Few companies are able to fund all their activities solely with funds from internal sources. Most find it necessary at times to seek funding from outside sources. For this reason, all business people need to know about financial markets.

As we see in this chapter, there are a number of financial markets, and each offers a different kind of financial product. In this chapter we discuss the relationship between firms and the financial markets and briefly explain how the financial system works, including the role of *financial intermediaries*—investment bankers, brokers, and dealers. Next, we explore the markets themselves and describe financial products ranging from government bonds to corporate stocks. Finally, we examine interest rates.

The Financial System

In the U.S. economy, several types of individuals or entities generate and spend money. We call these *economic units*. The main types of economic units include governments, businesses, and households (households may be one person or more than one person). Some economic units generate more income than they spend and have funds left over. These are called **surplus economic units**. Other economic units generate less income than they spend and need to acquire additional funds in order to sustain their operations. These are called **deficit economic units**.

The purpose of the financial system is to bring the two groups—surplus economic units and deficit economic units—together for their mutual benefit.

The financial system also makes it possible for participants to adjust their holdings of financial assets as their needs change. This is the *liquidity function* of the financial system—that is, the system allows funds to flow with ease.

To enable funds to move through the financial system, funds are exchanged for financial products called *securities*. A clear understanding of securities is essential to understanding the financial system, so before we go further, let's examine what securities are and how they are used.

Securities

Securities are documents that represent the right to receive funds in the future. The person or organization that holds a security is called a **bearer**. A security certifies that the bearer has a *claim* to future funds. For example, if you lend $100 to someone and the person gives you an IOU, you have a security. The IOU is your "claim check" for the $100 you are owed. The IOU may also state *when* you are to be paid, which is referred to as the **maturity date** of the security. When the date of payment occurs, we say the security matures.

Securities have value because the bearer has the right to be paid the amount specified, so a bearer who wanted some money right away could sell the security to someone else for cash. Of course, the new bearer could sell the security to someone else too, and so on down the line. When a security is sold to someone else, the security is being *traded*.

Business firms, as well as local, state, and national governments, sell securities to the public to raise money. After the initial sale, investors may sell the securities to other

surplus economic unit A business, household, or government unit with income greater than its expenditures.

deficit economic unit A government, business, or household unit with expenditures greater than its income.

security A document that establishes the bearer's claim to receive funds in the future.

bearer The holder of a security.

maturity date The date the bearer of a security is to be paid the principal, or face value, of a security.

investors. As you might suspect, this can get to be a complicated business. **Financial intermediaries** facilitate this process. Markets are available for the subsequent traders to execute their transactions.

Financial Intermediaries

Financial intermediaries act as the grease that enables the machinery of the financial system to work smoothly. They specialize in certain services that would be difficult for individual participants to perform, such as matching buyers and sellers of securities. Three types of financial intermediaries are investment bankers, brokers, and dealers.

Investment Bankers

Institutions called **investment banking firms** exist to help businesses and state and local governments sell their securities to the public.

Investment bankers arrange securities sales on either an *underwriting basis* or a *best efforts basis*. The term **underwriting** refers to the process by which an investment banker (usually in cooperation with other investment banking firms) purchases all the new securities from the issuing company and then resells them to the public.

Investment bankers who underwrite securities face some risk because occasionally an issue is overpriced and can't be sold to the public for the price anticipated by the investment banker. The investment banker has already paid the issuing company or municipality its money up front, and so it must absorb the difference between what it paid the issuer and what the security actually sold for. To alleviate this risk, investment bankers sometimes sell securities on a **best efforts basis**. This means the investment banker will try its best to sell the securities for the desired price, but there are no guarantees. If the securities must be sold for a lower price, the issuer collects less money.

Brokers

Brokers—often account representatives for an investment banking firm—handle orders to buy or sell securities. **Brokers** are agents who work on behalf of an investor. When investors call with orders, brokers work on their behalf to find someone to take the other side of the proposed trades. If investors want to buy, brokers find sellers. If investors want to sell, brokers find buyers. Brokers are compensated for their services when the person whom they represent—the investor—pays them a commission on the sale or purchase of securities. Brokers are obligated to find "suitable investments" for their clients. They do not generally have the higher duty that comes when one is acting as a fiduciary. A fiduciary is obligated to put the interests of the principal ahead of all others, including the interests of the fiduciary herself.

Dealers

Dealers make their living buying securities and reselling them to others. They operate just like car dealers who buy cars from manufacturers for resale to others. Dealers make money by buying securities for one price, called the *bid price,* and selling them for a higher price, called the *ask (or offer) price*. The difference, or spread, between the bid price and the ask price represents the dealer's fee.

Financial Markets

As we have pointed out, the financial system allows surplus economic units to trade with deficit economic units. The trades are carried out in the **financial markets**.

Financial markets are categorized according to the characteristics of the participants and the securities involved. In the *primary market,* for instance, deficit economic units sell new securities directly to surplus economic units and to financial institutions. In the *secondary market,* investors trade previously issued securities among themselves. Primary and secondary markets can be further categorized as to the maturity of the securities traded. Short-term securities—securities with a maturity of one year or less—are traded in the *money market;* and long-term securities—securities with a maturity of more than

financial intermediaries Institutions that take in funds from surplus economic units and make those funds available to deficit economic units.

investment banking firm A firm that helps issuers sell their securities and that provides other financial services.

underwriting The process by which investment banking firms purchase a new security issue in its entirety and resell it to investors. The risk of the new issue is transferred from the issuing company to the investment bankers.

best efforts basis An arrangement in which the investment banking firm tries its best to sell a firm's securities for the desired price, without guarantees. If the securities must be sold for a lower price, the issuer collects less money.

broker A person who brings buyers and sellers together.

dealer A person who makes his or her living buying and selling assets.

financial markets Exchanges or over-the-counter mechanisms where securities are traded.

one year[1]—are traded in the *capital market*. A number of other financial markets exist, but we are mainly concerned with these four. In the following sections, we examine each of these markets in turn.

The Primary Market

primary market The market in which newly issued securities are sold to the public.

When a security is created and sold for the first time in the financial marketplace, this transaction takes place in the **primary market**. In January 2015, Wells Fargo Securities helped Regency Centers Corporation sell 2,500,000 shares of common stock to the public, raising about $168.5 million in new equity capital.[2] This was a primary market transaction. In this market the issuing business or entity sells its securities to investors (the investment banker simply assists with the transaction).

The Secondary Market

secondary market The market in which previously issued securities are traded from one investor to another.

Once a security has been issued, it may be traded from one investor to another. The **secondary market** is where previously issued securities—or "used" securities—are traded among investors. Suppose you called your stockbroker to request that she buy 100 shares of stock for you. The shares would usually be purchased from another investor in the secondary market. Secondary market transactions occur thousands of times daily as investors trade securities among themselves. These transactions may occur on an exchange or on the over-the-counter market.

The Money Market

money market The market where short-term securities are traded.

Short-term securities (a maturity of one year or less) are traded in the **money market**. Networks of dealers operate in this market. They use phones and computers to make trades rapidly among themselves and with the issuing entities. The specific securities traded in the money market include Treasury bills, negotiable certificates of deposit, commercial paper, and other short-term debt instruments.

The Capital Market

capital market The market where long-term securities are traded.

Long-term securities (maturities over one year) trade in the **capital market**. Federal, state, and local governments, as well as large corporations, raise long-term funds in the capital market. Firms usually invest proceeds from capital market securities sales in long-term assets such as buildings, production equipment, and so on. Initial offerings of securities in the capital market are usually large deals put together by investment bankers, although after the original issue, the securities may be traded quickly and easily among investors. The two most widely recognized securities in the capital market are bonds and stocks.

Take Note
Do not confuse financial markets with financial institutions. A financial market is a forum in which financial securities are traded (it may or may not have a physical location). A financial institution is an organization that takes in funds from some economic units and makes them available to others.

Security Exchanges

Security exchanges, such as the New York Stock Exchange (NYSE), are organizations that facilitate trading of stocks and bonds among investors. Corporations arrange for their stocks or bonds to be *listed* on an exchange so that investors may trade the company's stocks and bonds at an organized trading location. Corporations list their securities on exchanges because they believe that having their securities traded at such a location will make them easier to trade and, therefore, boost the price. Exchanges accept listings because they earn a fee for their services.

Each exchange-listed stock is traded at a specified location on the trading floor called *the post*. The trading is supervised by specialists who act either as brokers (bringing together buyers and sellers) or as dealers (buying or selling the stock themselves). Promi-

---

1. The distinction between "short term" and "long term" is arbitrarily set at one year or less for the former and more than one year for the latter.

2. http://markets.on.nytimes.com/research/stocks/news/press_release.asp?docTag=201501150846BIZWIRE_USPRX____BW5510&feedID=600&press_symbol=240658"

nent international securities exchanges include the NYSE and major exchanges in Tokyo, London, Amsterdam, Frankfurt, Paris, Hong Kong, and Mexico.

The Over-the-Counter (OTC) Market

In contrast to the organized exchanges, which have physical locations, the **over-the-counter** market has no fixed location—or, more correctly, it is everywhere. The over-the-counter market, or OTC, is a network of dealers around the world who maintain inventories of securities for sale and cash for purchasing. Say you wanted to buy a security that is traded OTC. You would call your broker, who would then shop among competing dealers who have the security in their inventory. After locating the dealer with the best price, your broker would buy the security on your behalf.

The largest and best-known OTC market for common stock is called Nasdaq. Nasdaq dealers enter their bid and ask prices in a worldwide computer network. Many securities issued by very small companies are simply bought and sold over the telephone.

over-the-counter market
A network of dealers around the world who purchase securities and maintain inventories of securities for sale.

Market Efficiency

The term **market efficiency** refers to the ease, speed, and cost of trading securities. In an efficient market, securities can be traded easily, quickly, and at low cost. Markets lacking these qualities are considered inefficient.

The major stock markets are generally efficient because investors can trade thousands of dollars' worth of shares in minutes simply by making a phone call or hitting a few computer keys and paying a relatively small commission. In contrast, the real estate market is relatively inefficient because it might take you months to sell a house and you would probably have to pay a real estate agent a large commission to handle the deal.

The more efficient the market, the easier it is for excess funds in the hands of surplus economic units to make their way into the hands of deficit economic units. In an inefficient market, surplus economic units may end up with excess funds that are idle while deficit economic units may not get the funds they need. When this happens, economic activity and job creation will be lower than it could be, and deficit economic units may not be able to achieve their goals because they could not obtain needed funds.

Financial markets help firms and individual investors buy and sell securities efficiently. So far, we have discussed the various markets in which securities are traded. Now let's turn to the securities themselves.

market efficiency
The relative ease, speed, and cost of trading securities. In an efficient market, securities can be traded easily, quickly, and at low cost. In an inefficient market, one or more of these qualities is missing.

Securities in the Financial Marketplace

Securities are traded in both the money and capital markets. Money market securities include Treasury bills, negotiable certificates of deposit, commercial paper, Eurodollars, and banker's acceptances. Capital market securities include bonds and stock. We describe each of these securities briefly in the following discussion.

Securities in the Money Market

Governments, corporations, and financial institutions that want to raise money for a short time issue money market securities. Buyers of money market securities include governments, corporations, and financial institutions that want to park surplus cash for a short time and other investors who want the ability to alter or cash in their investments quickly.

Money market securities are very liquid; that is, they mature quickly and can be sold for cash quickly and easily. Money market securities also have a low degree of risk because purchasers will only buy them from large, reputable issuers (investors don't want to spend a long time checking the issuers' credit for an investment that may only last a few days). These two characteristics, liquidity and low risk, make money market securities the ideal parking place for temporary excess cash.

Let's take a closer look at the main money market securities.

Treasury Bills

Every week the United States Treasury issues billions of dollars of **Treasury bills** (T-bills). These money market securities are issued to finance the federal budget deficit (if any) and to refinance the billions of dollars of previously issued government securities that come due each week. After the T-bills are initially sold by the U.S. government, they are traded actively in the secondary market. At maturity, the government pays the face value of the T-bill.

Treasury bills are considered the benchmark of safety because they have essentially no risk. This is because obligations of the U.S. government are payable in U.S. dollars—and, theoretically, the U.S. government could print up all the dollars it needs to pay off its obligations. Treasury bills are issued in one-month, three-month, six-month, and one-year maturities.

Negotiable Certificates of Deposit

You may already be familiar with the certificates of deposit (CDs) that you can purchase from your local bank. They are simply pieces of paper that certify that you have deposited a certain amount of money in the bank, to be paid back on a certain date with interest. Small-denomination consumer CDs are very safe investments and they tend to have low interest rates.

Large-denomination CDs (of $100,000 to $1 million or more), with maturities of two weeks to a year, are **negotiable CDs** because they can be traded in the secondary market after they are initially issued by a financial institution. Large corporations and other institutions buy negotiable CDs when they have cash they wish to invest for a short period of time; they sell negotiable CDs when they want to raise cash quickly.

Commercial Paper

Commercial paper is a type of short-term promissory note—similar to an IOU—issued by large corporations with strong credit ratings. Commercial paper is *unsecured*. This means the issuing corporation does not pledge any specific assets as collateral that the lender (the one who buys the commercial paper note) can take on a priority basis if the issuing corporation defaults on the note. That is why commercial paper is only issued by financially strong, reliable firms.

Commercial paper is considered to be a safe place to put money for a short period of time. The notes themselves are issued and traded through a network of commercial paper dealers. Most of the buyers are large institutions.

Banker's Acceptances

A **banker's acceptance** is a short-term debt instrument that is guaranteed for payment by a commercial bank (the bank "accepts" the responsibility to pay). Banker's acceptances, thus, allow businesses to avoid problems associated with collecting payment from reluctant debtors. They are often used when firms are doing business internationally because they eliminate the worry that the lender will have to travel to a foreign country to collect on a debt.

Securities in the Capital Market

When governments, corporations, and financial institutions want to raise money for a long period of time, they issue capital market securities. In contrast to money market securities, capital market securities are often not as liquid or safe. They are not generally suitable for short-term investments.

The two most prominent capital market securities are bonds and stocks. We'll examine these two securities in some depth now.

Bonds

Bonds are essentially IOUs that promise to pay their owners a certain amount of money on some specified date in the future—and in most cases, interest payments at regular intervals until maturity. When companies want to borrow money (usually a fairly large amount for a long period of time), they arrange for their investment bankers to print up the IOUs and sell them to the public at whatever price they can get. In essence, a firm that issues a bond is borrowing the amount that the bond sells for on the open market.

Bond Terminology and Types

Although many types of bonds exist, most bonds have three special features: face value, maturity date, and coupon interest.

- *Face value:* The amount that the bond promises to pay its owner at some date in the future is called the bond's **face value**, or **par value**, or **principal**. Bond face values range in multiples of $1,000 all the way up to more than $1 million. Unless otherwise noted, assume that all bonds we discuss from this point forward have a face value of $1,000.

- *Maturity date*: The date on which the issuer is obligated to pay the bondholder the bond's face value.

- *Coupon interest*: The interest payments made to the bond owner during the life of the bond. Some bonds pay coupon interest once a year; many pay it twice a year. Some bonds don't pay any interest at all. These bonds are called **zero-coupon bonds**.

The percentage of face value that the coupon interest payment represents is called the *coupon interest rate*. For example, assuming the face value of the bond was $1,000, a bond owner who received $80 interest payments each year would own a bond paying an 8 percent coupon interest rate:

$$\$80 \;/\; \$1{,}000 = .08, \text{ or } 8\%$$

The major types of bonds include Treasury bonds and notes, issued by the federal government; municipal bonds, issued by state and local governments; and corporate bonds, issued by corporations. The significant differences among these types of bonds are described in the following sections.

Treasury Notes and Bonds

When the federal government wants to borrow money for periods of more than a year, it issues Treasury notes or Treasury bonds. T-notes have initial maturities from 2, 3, 5, 7, or 10 years. Treasury bonds have maturities greater than 10 years. Both T-notes and T-bonds pay interest semiannually, in addition to the principal, which is paid at maturity. T-notes are auctioned by the Treasury every three months to pay off old maturing securities and to raise additional funds to finance the federal government's new deficit spending.

The name originated decades ago when holders of bearer bonds would actually tear off coupons from their bond certificates and mail them to the bond issuer to get their interest payments, hence, the name *coupon interest*. Today, bonds are sold on a "registered" basis, which means the bonds come with the owner's name printed on them. Interest payments are sent directly to the owner.

Although Treasury securities, such as T-notes and T-bonds, are extremely low risk, they are not risk free. Without the congressional authority to print money, the U.S. Treasury cannot legally pay its obligations, including the interest and principal on Treasury securities. In late 2017 the federal debt ceiling was raised to $19.8 trillion. The national debt had grown to about that same amount as this new debt ceiling figure.[3] The federal government's fiscal policy, designed to get us out of the financial crisis, will surely further increase the amount of the federal debt.

The U.S. Treasury sells securities to the public at its website. www.treasurydirect.gov/.

face value, or par value, or principal The amount the bond issuer promises to pay to the investor when the bond matures. The terms *face value, par value,* and *principal* are often used interchangeably.

zero-coupon bonds Bonds that pay face value at maturity and that pay no coupon interest.

---

3. https://www.washingtonpost.com/graphics/2017/national/debt-ceiling/?utm_term=.adb123d4f9f1

Municipal Bonds

The bonds issued by state and local governments are known as **municipal bonds** or "munis." Many investors like municipal bonds because their coupon interest payments are free of federal income tax.

Municipal bonds come in two types: general obligation bonds (GOs) and revenue bonds. They differ in where the money comes from to pay them off. General obligation bonds are supposed to be paid off with money raised by the issuer from a variety of different tax revenue sources. Revenue bonds are supposed to be paid off with money generated by the project the bonds were issued to finance—such as using toll bridge fees to pay off the bonds to finance the toll bridge.

Corporate Bonds

Corporate bonds are similar to T-bonds and T-notes except they are issued by corporations. Like T-bonds and T-notes, they pay their owner interest during the life of the bond and repay principal at maturity. Unlike T-bonds and T-notes, however, corporate bonds sometimes carry substantial risk of default. As a last resort, the U.S. government can print money to pay off its Treasury bill, note, and bond obligations; but when private corporations run into trouble, they have no such latitude. Corporations' creditors may get paid late or not at all.

Relatively safe bonds are called *investment-grade bonds*. Many financial institutions and money management firms are required to invest only in those corporate bonds that are investment grade. Relatively risky bonds are called *junk bonds*.[4] Junk bonds are generally issued by troubled companies, but they may be issued by financially strong companies that later run into trouble.

This completes our introduction to bonds. Now let's turn our attention to the other major security in the capital market, corporate stock.

Corporate Stock

Rather than borrowing money by issuing bonds, a corporation may choose to raise money by selling shares of ownership interest in the company. Those shares of ownership are **stock**. Investors who buy stock are called stockholders.

As a source of funds, stock has an advantage over bonds: The money raised from the sale of stock doesn't ever have to be paid back, and the company doesn't have to make interest payments to the stockholders.

A corporation may issue two types of corporate stock: *common stock* and *preferred stock*. Let's look at their characteristics.

Common Stock

Common stock is so called because there is nothing special about it. The holders of a company's common stock are simply the owners of the company. Their ownership entitles them to the firm's earnings that remain after all other groups having a claim on the firm (such as bondholders) have been paid.

Each common stockholder owns a portion of the company represented by the fraction of the whole that the stockholder's shares represent. Thus, if a company issued 1 million shares of common stock, a person who holds one share owns one-millionth of the company.

Common stockholders receive a return on their investment in the form of common stock **dividends**, distributed from the firm's profits, and **capital gains**, realized when they sell the shares.[5]

---

4. The term *junk bond* is a slang term that is now widely accepted. Firms trying to sell junk bonds often dislike the term, of course. They would prefer such bonds be referred to as high yield securities.

5. Of course, there is no guarantee that a common stockholder's stock will increase in price. If the price goes down, the stockholder will experience a capital loss.

Preferred Stock

Preferred stock is so called because if dividends are declared by the board of directors of a business, they are paid to preferred stockholders first. If any funds are left over, they may be paid to the common stockholders. Preferred stockholders are not owners and normally don't get to vote on how the firm is run as do common stockholders. Also, holders of preferred stock have a lower expected return than do holders of common stock because preferred stock is a less risky investment. The party that is paid last, the common stockholder, is taking a greater risk since funds may run out before getting to the end of the line.

Of course, there is no guarantee that a common stockholder's stock will increase in price. If the price goes down, the stockholder will experience a capital loss.

Interest

Loans usually mean interest paid by the borrower to the lender in addition to the repayment of the principal amount of the loan. When people lend money to other people, a number of things could happen that might prevent them from getting all their money back. Whenever people agree to take risk, compensation is required before they will voluntarily enter into an agreement. In financial activities, we refer to this compensation as **interest**. Interest represents the return, or compensation, a lender demands before agreeing to lend money. When we refer to interest, we normally express it in percentage terms, called the *interest rate*. Thus, if you lend a person $100 for one year, and the return you require for doing so is $10, we would say that the interest rate you are charging for the loan is $10/$100 = .10, or 10 percent.

interest The compensation lenders demand and borrowers pay when money is lent.

Determinants of Interest Rates

The prevailing rate of interest in any situation is called the **nominal interest rate**. In the preceding example, the nominal interest rate for the one-year $100 loan is 10 percent. The nominal interest rate is actually the total of a number of separate components, as shown in Figure 2-1. We will explore each of these components in the following sections.

nominal interest rate The rate observed in the financial marketplace that includes the real rate of interest and various premiums.

The Real Rate of Interest

Lenders of money must postpone spending during the time the money is loaned. Lenders, then, lose the opportunity to invest their money for that period of time. To compensate for the burden of losing investment opportunities while they postpone their spending, lenders demand, and borrowers pay, a basic rate of return—**the real rate of interest**. The real rate

real rate of interest The rate that the market offers to lenders to compensate for postponing consumption.

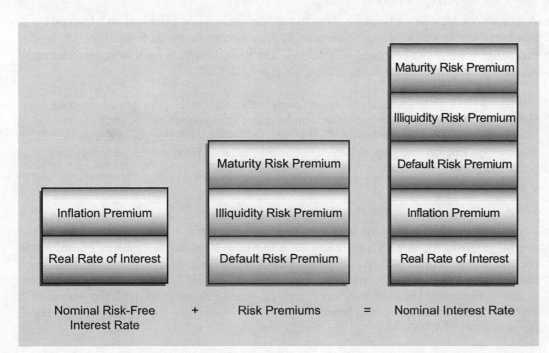

FIGURE 2-1
Components of the Nominal Interest Rate

The nominal interest rate is composed of the real interest rate plus a number of premiums. The nominal risk-free interest rate is the real rate plus an inflation premium. When risk premiums are added, the result is the total nominal interest rate. The adjustment for safe storage, a negative interest premium, is described below.

of interest does not include adjustments for any other factors, such as the risk of not being paid back. We'll describe this in a moment.

Let's continue with the example on page 31, in which you lent a person $100. The total interest rate that you charged was 10 percent (the nominal interest rate). The portion of the total nominal rate that represents the return you demand for forgoing the opportunity to spend your money now is the real rate of interest. In our example, assume the real rate of interest is 2 percent.

Additions to the real rate of interest are called *premiums*. The major premiums are the inflation premium, the default risk premium, the liquidity risk premium, and the maturity risk premium.

The Inflation Premium

Inflation erodes the purchasing power of money. If inflation is present, the dollars that lenders get when their loans are repaid may not buy as much as the dollars that they lent to start with. Therefore, lenders who anticipate inflation during the term of a loan will demand additional interest to compensate for it. This additional required interest is the **inflation premium.**

inflation premium The extra interest that compensates lenders for the expected erosion of purchasing power of funds due to inflation over the life of the loan.

If, when you lent $100, you thought that the rate of inflation was going to be 4 percent a year during the life of the loan, you would add 4 percent to the 2 percent real rate of interest you charged for postponing your spending. The total interest rate charge—so far—would be 6 percent.

The interest rate that we have built so far, containing the real rate of interest and a premium to cover expected inflation, is often called the **nominal risk-free rate of interest**, as shown earlier in Figure 2-1. It is called this because it does not include any premiums for the uncertainties associated with borrowing or lending. The yield on short-term U.S. Treasury bills is often used as a proxy for the risk-free rate because the degree of uncertainty associated with these securities is very small.

nominal risk-free rate of interest The interest rate without any premiums for the uncertainties associated with lending.

The remaining determinants of the nominal interest rate represent extra charges to compensate lenders for taking risk. Risks in lending come in a number of forms. The most common are default risk, illiquidity risk, and maturity risk.

The Default Risk Premium

A *default* occurs when a borrower fails to pay the interest and principal on a loan on time. If a borrower has a questionable reputation or is having financial difficulties, the lender faces the risk that the borrower will default. The **default risk premium** is the extra compensation lenders demand for assuming the risk of default.

default risk premium The extra interest lenders demand to compensate for assuming the risk that promised interest and principal payments may be made late or not at all.

In our $100 loan example, if you weren't completely sure that the person to whom you had lent $100 would pay it back, you would demand extra compensation—let's say, two percentage points—to compensate for that risk. The total interest rate demanded so far would be 2 percent real rate of interest + 4 percent inflation premium + 2 percent default risk premium = 8 percent.

The Illiquidity Risk Premium

Sometimes lenders sell loans to others after making them. (This happens often in the mortgage business, in which investors trade mortgages among themselves.) Some loans are easily sold to other parties and others are not. Those that are easily sold are *liquid*, and those that aren't sold easily are considered *illiquid*. Illiquid loans have a higher interest rate to compensate the lender for the inconvenience of being stuck with the loan until it matures. The extra interest that lenders demand to compensate for the lack of liquidity is the illiquidity risk premium.

You will probably not be able to sell your $100 loan to anyone else and will have to hold it until maturity. Therefore, you require another 1 percent to compensate for the lack of liquidity. The total interest rate demanded so far is 2 percent real rate of interest + 4 percent inflation premium + 2 percent default risk premium + 1 percent illiquidity risk premium = 9 percent.

The Maturity Risk Premium

If interest rates rise, lenders may find themselves stuck with long-term loans paying the original rate prevailing at the time the loans were made, whereas other lenders are able to make new loans at higher rates. On the other hand, if interest rates go down, the same lenders will be pleased to find themselves receiving higher interest rates on their existing long-term loans than the rate at which other lenders must make new loans. Lenders respond to this risk that interest rates may change in the future in two ways:

- If lenders think interest rates might rise in the future, they may increase the rate they charge on their long-term loans now and decrease the rate they charge on their short-term loans now to encourage borrowers to borrow short term.

- Conversely, if lenders think interest rates might fall in the future, they may decrease the rate they charge on their long-term loans now and increase the rate they charge on their short-term loans now to encourage borrowers to borrow long term (locking in the current rate).

This up or down adjustment that lenders make to their current interest rates to compensate for the uncertainty about future changes in rates is called the **maturity risk premium**. The maturity risk premium can be either positive or negative.

maturity risk premium The extra (or sometimes lesser) interest that lenders demand on longer-term securities.

In our example, if you thought interest rates would probably rise before you were repaid the $100 you lent, you might demand an extra percentage point to compensate for the risk that you would be unable to take advantage of the new higher rates. The total rate demanded is now 10 percent (2 percent real rate of interest + 4 percent inflation premium + 2 percent default risk premium + 1 percent illiquidity risk premium + 1 percent maturity risk premium = 10 percent, the nominal interest rate).

The total of the real rate of interest, the inflation premium, and the risk premiums (the default, illiquidity, and maturity risk premiums) is the nominal interest rate, the compensation lenders demand from those who want to borrow money.

Next, we will consider the yield curve—a graph of a security's interest rates depending on the time remaining to maturity.

Safe Storage Premium

In 2015 and 2016, it was not unusual to see bonds issued by governments around the world with negative interest rates. Even some private sector entities had bonds trading at prices that gave negative interest rates. The amount the issuer promised to pay to the investor was less than the amount taken in by the issuer at the time the bond was first sold. The price of a given bond trading in the secondary market was sometimes greater than the amount of cash promised by the issuer of the bond, to be received by the secondary market purchaser. The market interest rate was negative for some U.S. Treasury bills trading in the secondary market in late 2015. This means that the price of a $1,000 face value Treasury bill was greater than $1,000.

Why would a bond investor agree to such a deal? It used to be said that if we ever saw negative interest rates in the marketplace that textbooks would have to be rewritten. Here is that rewrite. Many large institutional investors need a safe investment and may be willing to pay for that safety in the form of a lower acceptable rate of return. If you ran a pension fund or large insurance company, and needed to know a certain amount of funds would be available at a given future time for pension benefits of insurance claims, your options would be limited. When interest rates get very low as they were in 2016, for the reasons described above, these rates may turn negative if those seeking safety are willing to pay extra (and get a lower rate or return) on their investment. Small investors can turn to a deposit insured by the Federal Deposit Insurance Corporation (FDIC) and that FDIC guarantee of $250,000 in insurance will probably be sufficient for that investor. What if you were managing a $10 billion portfolio? Having the first $250,000 of your $10 billion investment portfolio would provide small comfort.

The large institutional investor might be willing to pay extra for safe storage, just as you might be willing to pay for safe storage for your motorcycle or boat if you live in a place with cold winters. The higher price paid by the institutional investor for that safe storage of the investor's cash results in a lower market interest rate. This number could even go negative if the factors above would otherwise dictate an interest rate around zero. The safe storage premium is therefore negative. The investor accepts a lower rate of return, even if the overall interest rate is negative. If you had $10 billion dollars to invest, the U.S. Treasury would be happy to take your money and deliver the promised payments of the government security you chose. Your entire investment would be backed by the full faith and credit of the United States.

Let's say there is a negative interest rate premium in the amount of 1% offered by the lender for this safe storage. The borrower, the U.S. Treasury in this case, would have a clear incentive to agree to the lower interest rate. The total interest rate would reflect the real rate of interest, inflation premium, default risk premium, illiquidity risk premium, maturity risk premium, and this safe storage premium. The inflation risk premium could be negative or positive depending on whether investors believed the general level of prices would decrease or increase. The maturity risk premium could be negative or positive depending on whether there were a downward or upward sloping yield curve. The safe storage premium would always be negative.

Using different numbers than above when the other interest rate elements were examined there might be a +1 percent real rate of interest − 2 percent inflation premium + 1 percent default risk premium + 1 percent illiquidity risk premium + 1 percent maturity premium − 3 percent safety premium = −1 percent nominal interest rate.

The Yield Curve

A yield curve is a graphical depiction of interest rates for securities that differ only in the time remaining until their maturity. Yield curves are drawn by plotting the interest rates of one kind of security with various maturity dates. The curve depicts the interest rates of these securities at a given point in time.

Yield curves of U.S. Treasury securities are most common because with Treasury securities it is easiest to hold constant the factors other than maturity. All Treasury securities have essentially the same default risk (almost none) and about the same degree of liquidity (excellent). Any differences in interest rates observed in the yield curve, then, can be attributed to the maturity differences among the securities because other factors have essentially been held constant. Figure 2-2 shows a Treasury securities yield curve for January 3, 2018.

Beginning in September 2011 and continuing well into 2012, the Federal Reserve was pursuing a monetary policy strategy known as Operation Twist. The objective was to use open market operations, described in Chapter 3, to drive down interest rates on long-term U.S. Treasury securities (10 and 30 year maturities) while pushing up interest rates on short-term U.S. Treasury securities (1 year and less maturities). This would cause the yield curve to "twist." The reason the Federal Reserve was pursuing this strategy is that business investment is more a function of long-term interest rates than short-term. To get the economy going the Federal Reserve wanted to influence long-term rates down to stimulate real investment, plant expansion, and job creation.

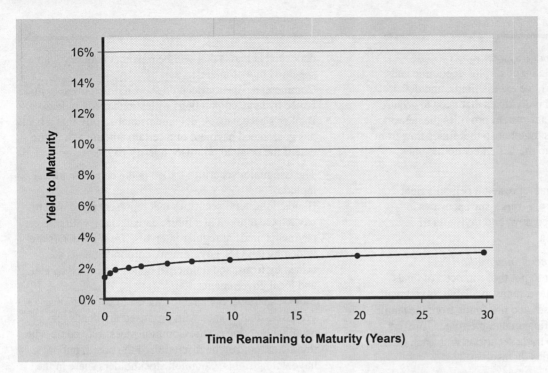

FIGURE 2-2

The Yield Curve as of January 3, 2018

Market interest rates are shown for U.S. Treasury securities, on this date, for various maturities.

Source: https://www.treasury.gov/resource-center/data-chart-center/interest-rates/Pages/TextView.aspx?data=yield

Making Use of the Yield Curve

The shape of the yield curve gives borrowers and lenders useful information for financial decisions. Borrowers, for example, tend to look for the low point of the curve, which indicates the least expensive loan maturity. Lenders tend to look for the highest point on the curve, which indicates the most expensive loan maturity.

Finding the most advantageous maturity is not quite as simple as it sounds because it depends on more factors than cost. For instance, the least expensive maturity is not always the most advantageous for borrowers. If a firm borrows short term, for example, it may obtain the lowest interest rate, but the loan will mature in a short time and may have to be renewed at a higher rate if interest rates have risen in the interim. Borrowing for a longer term may cost a borrower more at the outset but less in the long run because the interest rate is locked in.

Lenders face the opposite situation. Granting long-term loans at relatively high interest rates may look attractive now; but if short-term rates rise, the lenders may miss profitable opportunities because their funds have already been invested. Both borrowers and lenders must balance their desire for return with their tolerance for risk.

What's Next

In this chapter we investigated financial markets, securities, and interest rates. In the next chapter, we will look at another part of the financial environment, financial institutions.

Summary

1. *Describe how the U.S. financial system works.*
   The financial system is made up of surplus economic units, entities and individuals that have excess funds, and deficit economic units, entities and individuals that need to acquire additional funds. The financial system provides the network that brings these two groups together so that funds flow from the surplus economic units to the deficit economic units.

2. *Define financial securities.*
   Securities are documents that represent a person's right to receive funds in the future. Firms issue securities in exchange for funds they need now, and investors trade securities among themselves.

3. *Explain the function of financial intermediaries.*
   Financial intermediaries act to put those in need of funds in contact with those who have funds available. Investment banking firms help businesses acquire funds from the public by issuing securities in the financial marketplace. Brokers help members of the public trade securities with each other. Dealers buy and sell securities themselves.

4. *Identify the different financial markets.*
   Financial markets are forums in the financial system that allow surplus economic units to transact with deficit economic units and for portfolio adjustments to be made. Securities change hands in financial markets. The financial markets include the primary market, in which new securities are issued for the first time; the secondary market, in which previously issued securities are traded among investors; the money market, in which securities with maturities of less than one year are traded; and the capital market, in which securities with maturities longer than one year are traded. Some securities are traded on organized exchanges, such as the New York Stock Exchange, and others are traded over the counter (OTC) in a network of securities dealers.

5. *Describe the securities traded in the money and capital markets.*
   Securities traded in the money market include:
   - Treasury bills: short-term debt instruments issued by the U.S. Treasury that are sold at a discount and pay face value at maturity.
   - Negotiable certificates of deposit (CDs): certificates that can be traded in financial markets and represent amounts deposited at banks that will be repaid at maturity with a specified rate of interest.
   - Commercial paper: unsecured short-term promissory notes issued by large corporations with strong credit ratings.
   - Banker's acceptances: documents that signify that a bank has guaranteed payment of a certain amount at a future date if the original promisor doesn't pay.

   The two major securities traded in the capital market include:
   - Bonds: long-term securities that represent a promise to pay a fixed amount at a future date, usually with interest payments made at regular intervals. Treasury bonds are issued by the U.S. government, corporate bonds are issued by firms, and municipal bonds are issued by state and local governments.
   - Stocks: shares of ownership interest in corporations. Preferred stock comes with promised dividends but usually no voting rights. Common stock may come with dividends, paid at the discretion of the board, but does have voting rights. Common stockholders share in the residual profits of the firm.

6. *Identify the determinants of the nominal interest rate.*
   The nominal interest rate has three main determinants:
   - The real rate of interest: the basic rate lenders require to compensate for forgoing the opportunity to spend money during the term of the loan.
   - An inflation premium: a premium that compensates for the expected erosion of purchasing power due to inflation over the life of the loan.
   - Risk premiums: premiums that compensate for the risks of default (the risk that the lender won't be paid back), illiquidity (the risk that the lender won't be able to sell the security in a reasonable time at a fair price), and maturity (the risk that interest rates may change adversely during the life of the security).

7. *Construct and analyze a yield curve.*
   A yield curve is a graphical depiction of interest rates on securities that differ only in the time remaining until their maturity. Lenders and borrowers may use a yield curve to determine the most advantageous loan maturity.

Key Terms

banker's acceptance A security that represents a promise by a bank to pay a certain amount of money, if the original note maker doesn't pay.

bearer The holder of a security.

best efforts basis An arrangement in which the investment banking firm tries its best to sell a firm's securities for the desired price, without guarantees. If the securities must be sold for a lower price, the issuer collects less money.

bonds Securities that promise to pay the bearer a certain amount at a time in the future and may pay interest at regular intervals over the life of the security.

broker A person who brings buyers and sellers together.

capital gains The profit made when an asset is sold at a price higher than the price paid at the time of purchase.

capital market The market where long-term securities are traded.

commercial paper A short-term, unsecured debt instrument issued by a large corporation or financial institution.

dealer A person who makes his or her living buying and selling assets.

default risk premium The extra interest lenders demand to compensate for assuming the risk that promised interest and principal payments may be made late or not at all.

deficit economic unit A government, business, or household unit with expenditures greater than its income.

dividends Payments made to stockholders at the discretion of the board of directors of the corporation.

face value, or par value, or principal The amount the bond issuer promises to pay to the investor when the bond matures. The terms *face value, par value,* and *principal* are often used interchangeably.

financial intermediaries Institutions that take in funds from surplus economic units and make those funds available to deficit economic units.

financial markets Exchanges or over-the-counter mechanisms where securities are traded.

inflation premium The extra interest that compensates lenders for the expected erosion of purchasing power of funds due to inflation over the life of the loan.

interest The compensation lenders demand and borrowers pay when money is lent.

investment banking firm A firm that helps issuers sell their securities and that provides other financial services.

market efficiency The relative ease, speed, and cost of trading securities. In an efficient market, securities can be traded easily, quickly, and at low cost. In an inefficient market, one or more of these qualities is missing.

maturity date The date the bearer of a security is to be paid the principal, or face value, of a security.

maturity risk premium The extra (or sometimes lesser) interest that lenders demand on longer-term securities.

money market The market where short-term securities are traded.

municipal bonds Bonds issued by a state, city, county, or other nonfederal government authority, including specially created municipal authorities such as a toll road or industrial development authority.

negotiable CDs A deposit security issued by financial institutions that comes in minimum denominations of $100,000 and can be traded in the money market.

nominal interest rate The rate observed in the financial marketplace that includes the real rate of interest and various premiums.

nominal risk-free rate of interest The interest rate without any premiums for the uncertainties associated with lending.

over-the-counter market A network of dealers around the world who purchase securities and maintain inventories of securities for sale.

primary market The market in which newly issued securities are sold to the public.

real rate of interest The rate that the market offers to lenders to compensate for postponing consumption.

secondary market The market in which previously issued securities are traded from one investor to another.

security A document that establishes the bearer's claim to receive funds in the future.

stock Certificates of ownership interest in a corporation.

surplus economic unit A business, household, or government unit with income greater than its expenditures.

Treasury bills Securities issued by the federal government in minimum denominations of $100 in maturities of 4, 13, 26, and 52 weeks.

underwriting The process by which investment banking firms purchase a new security issue in its entirety and resell it to investors. The risk of the new issue is transferred from the issuing company to the investment bankers.

zero-coupon bonds Bonds that pay face value at maturity and that pay no coupon interest.

Self-Test

ST-1. To minimize risk, why don't most firms simply finance their growth from the profits they earn?

ST-2. What market would a firm most probably go to if it needed cash for 90 days? If it needed cash for 10 years?

ST-3. If your company's stock were not listed on the New York Stock Exchange, how could investors purchase the shares?

ST-4. What alternatives does Microsoft, a very large and secure firm, have for obtaining $3 million for 60 days?

ST-5. Assume Treasury security yields for today are as follows:
- One-year T-notes, .25%
- Two-year T-notes, .67%
- Three-year T-notes, 1.07%
- Five-year T-notes, 1.62%
- Ten-year T-notes, 2.20%
- Twenty-year, T-bonds 2.40%
- Thirty-year, T-bonds 2.70%

Draw a yield curve based on these data.

Review Questions

1. What are financial markets? Why do they exist?

2. What is a security?

3. What are the characteristics of an efficient market?

4. How are financial trades made on an organized exchange?

5. How are financial trades made in an over-the-counter market? Discuss the role of a dealer in the OTC market.

6. What is the role of a broker in security transactions? How are brokers compensated?

7. What is a Treasury bill? How risky is it?

8. Would there be positive interest rates on bonds in a world with absolutely no risk (no default risk, maturity risk, and so on)? Why would a lender demand, and a borrower be willing to pay, a positive interest rate in such a no-risk world?

Build Your Communication Skills

CS-1. Imagine the following scenario:

Your firm has decided to build a new plant in South America this year. The plant will cost $10 million and all the money must be paid up front. Your boss has asked you to brief the board of directors on the options the firm has for raising the $10 million.

Prepare a memo for the board members outlining the pros and cons of the various financing options open to the firm. Divide into small groups. Each group member should spend five minutes presenting his or her financing option suggestions to the rest of the group members, who should act as the board members.

CS-2. Prepare an IOU, or "note," that promises to pay $100 one year from today to the holder of the note.
   a. Auction this note off to someone else in the class, having the buyer pay for it with a piece of scratch-paper play money.
   b. Compute the note buyer's percent rate of return if he or she holds the note for a year and cashes it in.
   c. Ask the new owner of the note to auction it off to someone else. Note the new buyer's rate of return based on his or her purchase price.
   d. Discuss the operation of the market the class has created. Note the similarities between it and the bond market in the real world.

Problems

The Financial System 2-1.
   a. What are "surplus economic units"? Give two examples of entities in the financial system that typically would be classified as surplus economic units.
   b. What are "deficit economic units"? Give two examples of entities in the financial system that typically would be classified as deficit economic units.

Financial Markets 2-2. Answer the following, true or false:
   a. Trades among investors at the New York Stock Exchange are primary market transactions.
   b. The money market is where firms go to obtain funding for long-term projects.
   c. Your firm has $2,000,000 of excess funds that will not be needed for one month. You would most likely go to the capital market to invest the money until needed.
   d. Gold and international currencies are traded in the money market.

Financial Markets 2-3.
   a. Arrange the following markets in order from most efficient to least efficient.
      1. The real estate market
      2. The money market
      3. The secondary market (New York Stock Exchange)
      4. The over-the-counter market
   b. Explain the rationale you used to order the markets the way you did in part *a*.

Securities in the Financial Market 2-4.
   a. What characteristics must a security have to be traded in the money market?
   b. Give two examples of securities that are traded in the money market.

Securities in the Financial Market 2-5. Public Service Company of North Carolina issued $150 million worth of bonds this year. The bonds had a face value of $1,000 each, and each came with a promise to pay the bearer $66.25 a year in interest during the life of the bond. What is the coupon interest rate of these bonds?

2-6. If the real rate of interest is 2 percent, inflation is expected to be 3 percent during the coming year, and the default risk premium, illiquidity risk premium, and maturity risk premium for the Bonds-R-Us Corporation are all 1 percent each, what would be the yield on a Bonds-R-Us bond?

Nominal Interest Rate

2-7. Assume Treasury security yields for today are as follows:

Yield Curve

- Three-month T-bills, 4.50%
- Six-month T-bills, 4.75%
- One-year T-notes, 5.00%
- Two-year T-notes, 5.25%
- Three-year T-bonds, 5.50%
- Five-year T-bonds, 5.75%
- Ten-year T-bonds, 6.00%
- Thirty-year T-bonds, 6.50%

Draw a yield curve based on these data. Discuss the implications if you are:

a. a borrower

b. a lender

Answers to Self-Test

ST-1. In most cases, profits are insufficient to provide the funds needed, especially with large projects. Financial markets provide access to external sources of funds.

ST-2. To obtain cash for 90 days, a business firm would most probably go to the money market, in which it would sell a 90-day security. To obtain cash for 10 years, a firm would sell a security in the capital market.

ST-3. Investors would simply purchase the shares on another exchange, or over the counter from a dealer. (Investors simply call their brokers to purchase stock. Brokers decide where to get it.)

ST-4. Microsoft could
- obtain a 60-day loan from a financial institution
- delay payments to its suppliers
- sell commercial paper notes in the money market

ST-5. The yield curve follows:

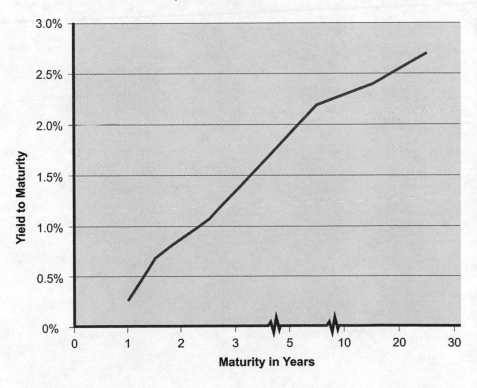

Financial Institutions

"If you owe the bank $100 that is your problem. If you owe the bank $100 million, that's the bank's problem."
—Jean Paul Getty

CHAPTER 3

Source: Frontpage/Shutterstock

Learning Objectives

After reading this chapter, you should be able to:

1. Explain the process of financial intermediation and the role of financial institutions in that process.

2. Define *commercial banks* and explain how reserve requirements influence their operations.

3. Describe how the Federal Reserve regulates financial institutions.

4. Explain how savings and loan associations differ from commercial banks.

5. Describe how credit unions operate.

6. Identify the major characteristics of finance companies, insurance companies, and pension funds.

Too Big to Fail?

Fannie Mae, Freddie Mac, Lehman Brothers, AIG, Bear Stearns, Countrywide Financial, and Washington Mutual were huge financial institutions. Each of these had names that signaled financial strength. All had been around for many years. They all failed in 2008.

Financial institutions are essential to the financial system. We rely on them to make business and mortgage loans, to stand behind the insurance policies issued, and to stand behind promises made in financial instruments. When promises are broken, businesses can fail, state governments can have financial crises, and the whole economy can tank resulting in millions of lost jobs.

Financial institutions take in funds from some while providing funds to others. Promises are made to those who put their funds into a financial institution. The promise may be to pay interest and principal according to specified terms. It may be to insure a house, boat, or life. It may be to provide retirement income according to a specified formula. Promises are also made by some financial institutions via "credit default swaps" to some bond investors to pay scheduled interest and principal if the issuer of the bond defaults.

Sometimes financial institutions make promises to each other. When large amounts of money are at stake the breaking of a promise by one large financial institution can cause the failure of another large financial institution that was relying on that promise. This has the potential to cause a chain reaction of failures by financial institutions.

Most financial institutions are regulated by the federal, state, and local governments in a variety of ways. These regulations are being rethought in light of our Financial Crisis. The public needs to be protected while not unduly intruding on the rights of private sector owners. The Dodd-Frank Act, described in Chapter 1, is an example of government action designed to reduce the likelihood of another major financial crisis. There will be legislative and regulatory options considered in the future in an attempt to prevent another such crisis.

Chapter Overview

In the preceding chapter we discussed how the financial system makes it possible for deficit and surplus economic units to come together, exchanging funds for securities to their mutual benefit. In this chapter we will examine how financial institutions help channel available funds to those who need them. We will also see the important role the Federal Reserve plays in regulating the financial system, protecting both deficit and surplus economic units.

Financial Intermediation

The financial system makes it possible for surplus and deficit economic units to come together, exchanging funds for securities, to their mutual benefit. When funds flow from surplus economic units to a financial institution to a deficit economic unit, the process is known as **intermediation**. The financial institution acts as an intermediary between the two economic units.

intermediation The process by which funds are channeled from surplus to deficit economic units through a financial institution.

Surplus economic units can channel their funds into financial institutions by purchasing savings accounts, checking accounts, life insurance policies, casualty insurance policies, or claims on a pension fund. The financial institutions can then pool the funds received and use them to purchase claims issued by deficit economic units, such as Treasury, municipal, or corporate bonds; and common or preferred stock. (The institutions may purchase real assets too, such as real estate or gold.)

At first glance it might seem that intermediation complicates things unnecessarily. Why do the surplus and deficit economic units need a middle person? The answer is that financial institutions can do things for both that they often can't do for themselves. Here are some examples of the services that financial institutions provide.

Denomination Matching

Members of the household sector (net surplus economic units) often have only a small amount of funds available to invest in securities. Although, as a group, they are net suppliers of funds and have a large amount of funds available, this is often not the case for given individuals or families. Businesses and government entities (net deficit economic units) usually need large amounts of funds. Thus, it is often difficult for these surplus and deficit economic units to come together on their own to arrange a mutually beneficial exchange of funds for securities. The surplus economic units typically want to supply a small amount of funds, whereas the deficit economic units typically want to obtain a large amount of funds.

A financial institution can step in and save the day. A bank, savings and loan, or insurance company can take in small amounts of funds from many individuals, form a large pool of funds, and then use that large pool to purchase securities from individual businesses and governments. This pooling of funds is depicted in Figure 3-1.

Maturity Matching

The typical surplus economic unit likes to make funds available to others for a short period of time. Most people, for example, would like to get their money back on short notice if

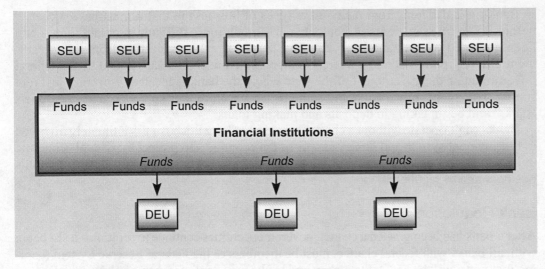

FIGURE 3-1
Pooling

Figure 3-1 shows how small amounts of funds from many small surplus economic units (SEUs) can be pooled and channeled into the hands of a relatively small number of deficit economic units (DEUs). SEUs can also get the short-term securities they usually prefer, while DEUs can issue the long-term securities they usually prefer. The financial institution can also manage and absorb risk better than an SEU typically could. The financial institution provides both SEUs and DEUs what each needs.

the need were to arise. They would prefer to buy securities that have a short maturity. Most businesses and government entities, on the other hand, want to make use of funds for a long period of time. The new plants, roads, airports, and the like that businesses and governments buy and build are long-term projects that often require long-term financing. They would prefer to sell securities that have a long maturity.

Here's the problem: How can exchanges agreeable to both sides be arranged when the surplus economic units want the right to get their funds back quickly and the deficit economic units want to keep the funds for a long time? Remember, a financial institution has many different surplus economic units buying its securities (savings accounts, checking accounts, insurance policies, and so on). The number that will want their funds back on any given day is likely to be small, and they will probably withdraw only a very small percentage of the total funds held in the financial institution. So a large percentage of the funds held by the financial institution can be invested in the long-term securities of deficit economic units, with little danger of running out of funds. The pooling depicted in Figure 3-1 makes this possible.

Absorbing Credit Risk

Credit risk is the risk that the issuer of a security may fail to make promised payments to the investor at the times specified. When surplus and deficit economic units try to arrange for a direct transfer of funds for securities, this problem is often a large one. Surplus economic units do not usually have the expertise to determine whether deficit economic units can and will make good on their obligations, so it is difficult for them to predict when a would-be deficit economic unit will fail to pay what it owes. Such a failure is likely to be devastating to a surplus economic unit that has lent a relatively large amount of money. In contrast, a financial institution is in a better position to predict who will pay and who won't. It is also in a better position, having greater financial resources, to occasionally absorb a loss when someone fails to pay.

Now let us turn to the various types of financial institutions. We'll start with commercial banks, which are regulated by various government entities. We'll also discuss the Federal Reserve System, which plays a major role in bank regulation and in overseeing the financial system.

Commercial Banks

Commercial banks are financial institutions that exist primarily to lend money to businesses. Banks also lend to individuals, governments, and other entities, but the bulk of their profits typically come from business loans. Commercial banks make money by charging a higher interest rate on the money they lend than the rate they pay on money lent to them in the form of deposits. This rate charged to borrowers minus the rate paid to depositors is known as the **interest rate spread**.

interest rate spread The rate a bank charges for loans minus the rate it pays for deposits.

Banking is different from many other types of business in that it must have a charter before it can open its doors. A bank charter—much more difficult to obtain than a city license needed to open another type of business—is an authorization from the government granting permission to operate. Commercial bank charters are issued by the federal government or the government of the state where the bank is located. You can't just rent some office space, buy a vault and some office furniture, put up a sign that says "Joe's Bank," and begin taking in deposits and making loans.

Banks can't operate without a charter because banking is a business intimately involved in the payment system and money supply of the economy. To protect individual economic units and the economy as a whole, the government has decided to control entry into this business and to regulate it, too.

Bank Regulation

After a bank has been granted a charter, government entities continue to scrutinize it. To begin with, all banks with federal charters must be members of the Federal Reserve System (commonly known as "the Fed"). State-chartered banks may apply for membership in the Federal Reserve System but are not required to do so. All members of the Federal Reserve System must also belong to the Federal Deposit Insurance Corporation (FDIC), which insures customer deposits at participating institutions for up to $250,000. Nonmember banks, along with other types of financial institutions, may belong to the FDIC also. Almost all banks—whether federally or state chartered, members of the Fed or not—have FDIC insurance for their depositors.

So many agencies regulate banks that it can be difficult to sort them out. To lessen the potentially extensive overlap of authority, bank-regulating entities have worked out an agreement. The Office of the Comptroller of the Currency (OCC) has primary responsibility for examining national banks, ensuring that they meet accepted standards. The Fed has primary responsibility for examining state-chartered member banks. The FDIC assumes primary responsibility for examining state nonmember banks having FDIC insurance. State banking authorities have primary examining authority over state nonmember banks with no FDIC coverage for their depositors. Figure 3-2 shows the main examination authority structure for commercial banks.

Commercial Bank Operations

Commercial banks operate with more government oversight than most businesses, but they are managed just like other companies. Commercial banks have stockholders, employees, managers, equipment, and facilities, and the primary financial goal of such banks is to maximize value for their stockholders. The banks do most of their business by receiving funds from depositors

FIGURE 3-2
The Commercial Bank Examination System

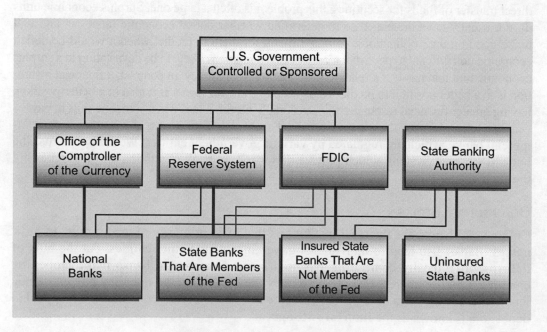

and lending the funds to those who need them. Commercial banks also occasionally issue long-term bonds to raise funds, borrow from the Federal Reserve, or borrow deposits kept by other financial institutions in Federal Reserve banks in what is known as the federal funds market.

Commercial Bank Reserves

Commercial banks are not allowed to lend all the funds they get from depositors. The Federal Reserve requires all commercial banks to keep a minimum amount of reserves on hand. Reserves are cash assets: vault cash, and deposits at the Fed that are available to a bank to meet the withdrawal demands of its depositors and to pay other obligations as they come due. Actually, the reserve requirement is set more with monetary policy in mind than to ensure that banks meet their depositors' withdrawal requests. Bank deposits at the Fed earn interest.

The required level of reserves a bank must hold is determined by applying a certain percentage to the average weekly deposits held by the bank. The exact percentage of deposits a bank must hold in reserve, called the **required reserve ratio**, depends on the type of deposit and the size of the bank. It varies from time to time as determined by the Federal Reserve, subject to certain statutory limits (see Table 3-1).

Table 3-1 shows the amount of reserves financial institutions are required to keep beginning in 2015, depending on the amount of different kinds of deposits. Vault cash and deposits in the bank's account at the Fed are used to satisfy these reserve requirements; they are called **primary reserves**.

In addition to primary reserves, commercial banks generally hold some secondary reserves—assets that can be quickly and easily sold and converted into cash. Secondary reserves consist of short-term securities such as Treasury bills or commercial paper. They serve as a buffer between the very liquid primary reserves and the rest of the assets (mostly loans), which are generally less liquid.

required reserve ratio
The percentage of deposits that determines the amount of reserves a financial institution is required to hold.

primary reserves Vault cash and deposits at the Fed that go toward meeting a bank's reserve requirements.

The Federal Reserve System

The **Federal Reserve System** serves as the central bank of the United States. It regulates the nation's money supply, makes loans to member banks and other financial institutions, and regulates the financial system, as described in the previous section.

Open-market purchases of government securities, making loans to financial institutions, and decreasing reserve requirements all lead to an increase in the money supply. Open-market sales of government securities, receiving payments on loans made to financial institutions, and increasing reserve requirements all lead to a decrease in the money supply.

Federal Reserve System
The central bank of the United States that examines and regulates banks and other financial institutions and that conducts monetary policy.

Organization of the Fed

The Fed is made up of twelve district Federal Reserve banks spread throughout the country, as shown in Figure 3-3, along with a seven-member Board of Governors and a Federal Open Market Committee (FOMC) that has twelve voting members. Both the Board of Governors and the Federal Open Market Committee are located in Washington, D.C. They hold most of the power of the Fed.

The seven members of the Board of Governors are appointed by the president of the United States, subject to confirmation by the United States Senate. The governors serve staggered 14-year terms, partly to insulate them from political influences. It would be

TABLE 3-1 Reserve Requirements as of January 2018

0 percent on net transaction accounts $0 to $16 million
3 percent on net transaction accounts $16 to $122.3 million
10 percent on net transaction accounts over $122.3 million
0 percent on nonpersonal time deposits
0 percent on Eurocurrency liabilities
Source: http://www.federalreserve.gov/monetarypolicy/reservereq.htm

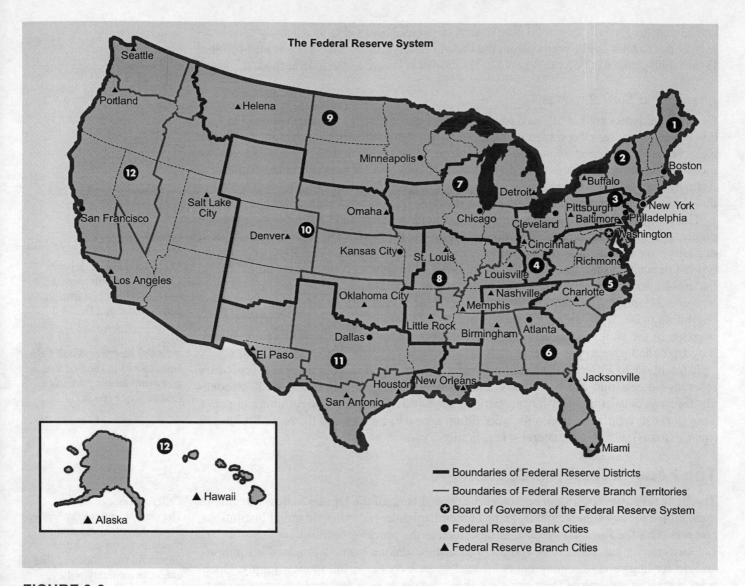

The Federal Reserve System

Boundaries of Federal Reserve Districts
Boundaries of Federal Reserve Branch Territories
❂ Board of Governors of the Federal Reserve System
● Federal Reserve Bank Cities
▲ Federal Reserve Branch Cities

FIGURE 3-3
The 12 Fed Districts in the United States

naive to believe that these members are not subject to some political influences, but a president would normally have to be well into a second (and final) term before successfully replacing a majority of the Fed members.

The twelve voting members of the FOMC are the seven members of the Board of Governors plus five of the twelve presidents of the district Federal Reserve banks. The district bank presidents take turns serving as voting members of the FOMC, although the president of the Federal Reserve Bank of New York is always one of the five. The nonvoting presidents of the district Federal Reserve banks usually attend the FOMC meetings and participate in discussions.

Controlling the Money Supply

open-market operations
The buying and selling of U.S. Treasury securities or foreign currencies to achieve some economic objective.

The main focus of the FOMC is to recommend **open-market operations** that the Fed should implement to increase or decrease the money supply. Open-market operations are purchases and sales of government securities and foreign currencies conducted in the Federal Reserve Bank of New York at a trading desk that exists for this purpose.

When the Fed buys government securities or currencies, it increases bank reserves and the money supply. When the Fed sells government securities or currencies, it decreases bank reserves and the money supply.

When the Fed wishes to increase the money supply, it instructs its traders at the Federal Reserve Bank of New York to buy government securities (primarily T-bills) on the open market. The traders contact government securities dealers (that are mostly commercial banks) around the country and buy the required amount of securities. These dealers have accounts at the Fed. When the Fed buys government securities from a dealer, it credits that dealer's account at the Fed. This action increases the amount of funds held by the dealer banks and enables them to make additional loans and investments. When the additional loans and investments are made, the supply of money in circulation increases, thus accomplishing the Fed's objective.

The exact opposite occurs when the Fed wishes to decrease the money supply. The Fed calls its traders at the Federal Reserve Bank of New York and instructs them to sell government securities on the open market. The traders contact government securities dealers around the country and sell the required amount of securities to them. When the dealers receive their securities, their accounts are debited and the amount of funds held by these banks decreases. The amount of loans and investments then, that these banks can support, also decreases. Some maturing loans are not renewed and some marketable security investments are not replaced because of the loss of funds. The result is a decrease in the supply of money in circulation.

Why, you might ask, would the Fed want to increase or decrease the money supply? The answer is simple: to influence economic activity. When the members of the FOMC feel that the economy is growing too slowly, the Fed increases the money supply, thus increasing liquidity in the economy and stimulating growth. When the economy is growing too fast and inflation seems imminent, the Fed decreases the money supply (or slows down its growth). This causes the economy to "cool off" because liquidity has decreased.

Although the government securities and currency markets are very large and efficient, the Fed is like a large elephant: People notice when it enters the market. It buys and sells in huge amounts, so when the Fed buys or sells securities, its actions can't help but affect prices (and interest rates) across the whole market.

In 2009 the Fed announced a new open market policy called quantitative easing (QE). This first departure from traditional open market operations was called QE1. Federal agency securities and mortgage-backed securities were purchased at the trading desk of the Federal Reserve. This created a demand for these securities that the private sector markets had in large measure abandoned. QE1 was a departure from the Fed's usual practice of trading only U.S. Treasury securities, primarily short-term bills.

In 2010 a second round of quantitative easing, QE2, was announced. The Fed moved into the long-term U.S. Treasury securities markets buying large amounts of these securities. This heavy buying of long-term U.S. Treasury securities by the Fed drove up the prices of these securities. This pushed the interest rates on these long-term securities down. This was the Fed's intent. Real economic activity is spurred more when long-term interest rates move down than when short-term interest rates move down. See Chapter 12 for more information on the inverse relationship between bond prices and interest rates.

In 2012 the Fed announced QE3. This was a new initiative that involved its purchase of large amounts of mortgage-backed securities (MBS). In October of 2014 the Federal Reserve announced it was ending QE3. The Fed has left the door open, however, for reinstituting some form of quantitative easing again if economic conditions call for it.

The Discount Window

The 12 district Federal Reserve banks lend money to financial institutions at the discount window. Originally, only member banks in a Federal Reserve bank's district came to the discount window for loans. Since 1980, however, the district Federal Reserve banks have extended loans to nonmember banks and to nonbank financial institutions, too.

The district Federal Reserve banks also provide clearing services—collecting and paying for checks written on and deposited in banks. The Fed charges fees for the services it provides. The fees collected, interest earned on government securities held, and other sources of income provide the funds the Fed needs to operate. The Fed does not require appropriations from Congress. In fact, if excess profits are left over, as is usually the case, they are turned over to the U.S. Treasury. There are not many federal government entities that turn money over to the Treasury.

Government-Sponsored Enterprises (GSEs) and the Mortgage Market

Fannie Mae (also known as Federal National Mortgage Association) and Freddie Mac (formerly known as Federal Home Loan Mortgage Corporation) were created by Congress to help people obtain financing for home purchases. Both institutions are government-chartered entities that purchase mortgages in the secondary market and either hold these mortgages or bundle them into mortgage-backed securities. Their functions are similar. Fannie Mae was founded in 1938 after the Great Depression while Freddie Mac was founded in 1968. The mortgage backed securities issued by Fannie Mae or Freddie Mac can be bought by investors around the world. In September 2008 Fannie Mae and Freddie Mac were taken over by the U.S. government to avoid the total collapse of these institutions and the ripple effects this would have created for the financial system and for the economy. At the time of the federal takeover these two institutions held or guaranteed about one-half of the approximately $5 trillion dollars' worth of mortgages in the United States.

Both Fannie Mae and Freddie Mac are government-sponsored enterprises (GSEs). They have private sector stockholders (stock prices have dropped to close to $0 with the crisis) but have had access to a line of credit at the U.S. Treasury that other stockholder-owned companies have not. Fannie Mae and Freddie Mac are hybrid private-public entities. Unlike Ginnie Mae (Government National Mortgage Association) the obligations of Fannie Mae and Freddie Mac do not have the explicit backing of the full faith and credit of the United States. Ginnie Mae is a government entity without private sector shareholders. It provides guarantees for some mortgages, primarily those made through the FHA (Federal Housing Administration) or VA (Veterans Administration). The obligations of Ginnie Mae are backed by the full faith and credit of the United States. Ginnie Mae does not buy or sell mortgages nor does it issue mortgage-backed securities. Such distinctions relating to government guarantees may be moot, however, if the United States government finds itself unable to even consider allowing Fannie Mae and Freddie Mac to default on their obligations.

Mortgages eligible for purchase by Fannie Mae and Freddie Mac are known as "conforming mortgages." Mortgages of up to $453,100 were eligible for purchase by Fannie Mae and Freddie Mac in 2018. Interest rates on larger dollar amount loans are usually higher than interest rates on conforming mortgages because those originating these nonconforming loans do not have the opportunity to sell such loans to Fannie Mae or Freddie Mac. The size of the loan is not the only criterion for a mortgage loan to be considered conforming. Such a loan must also meet certain requirements regarding credit quality and the house payment to income ratio of the borrower. There are also requirements regarding the quality and condition of the property being financed with the mortgage.

Fannie Mae and Freddie Mac each received approximately $100 billion from the U.S. Treasury. Treasury received senior preferred stock and warrants (options to buy the stock of these entities) for this government capital infusion. Taxpayers can only hope that Fannie Mae and Freddie Mac recover sufficiently to recover some of the government funds provided to these GSEs. It was believed by the government officials who designed this conservatorship arrangement that the consequences of letting Fannie Mae and Freddie Mac default on their obligations were worse than the cost of this conservatorship. The Federal Housing Finance Agency (FHFA) has been serving as the Conservator for Fannie Mae and Freddie Mac since 2008. This places FHFA in the unusual position of both regulating and running these two mortgage giants. There has been talk of finding a way for Fannie Mae and Freddie Mac to exit conservatorship, but this relationship was still in effect in 2018.

Savings and Loan Associations

savings and loan associations (S&Ls) Financial institutions that take in deposits and make loans (primarily mortgage loans).

Like commercial banks, **savings and loan associations (S&Ls)** are in business to take in deposits and lend money, primarily in the form of mortgage loans. Mortgage loans are loans that are secured by real property such as real estate. If a borrower defaults on a mortgage loan, the lender can take legal possession of the property. The property can then be sold and the lender keeps the proceeds from the sale up to the amount owed. S&Ls make a profit by charging a higher interest rate on the money they lend than the rate paid on deposits they take in.

Like banks, S&Ls can borrow from the Federal Reserve and from other financial institutions. S&Ls can also borrow from one of the 12 Federal Home Loan banks to meet some of their funding needs. The Office of Thrift Supervision (OTS) is the primary regulator of federally chartered S&Ls.

Regulation of S&Ls

Like commercial banks, savings and loan associations must apply for either a federal or a state charter that authorizes them to operate. All federally chartered S&Ls are regulated by the Office of Thrift Supervision (OTS), and almost all S&Ls have their deposits insured by the Savings Association Insurance Fund (SAIF), which is part of the FDIC. Savings and loan associations also have to keep reserves based on their size and the amount and type of deposit.

Mutual Companies versus Stockholder-Owned Companies

Some savings and loan associations are owned by stockholders, just as commercial banks and other corporations are owned by their stockholders. Other S&Ls, called **mutuals**, are owned by their depositors. In other words, when a person deposits money in an account at a mutual S&L, that person becomes a part owner of the firm. The mutual S&L's profits (if any) are put into a special reserve account from which dividends are paid from time to time to the owner/depositors.

mutuals Institutions (e.g., savings and loans or insurance companies) that are owned by their depositors or policy holders.

On the one hand, mutual S&L owner/depositors do not face as much risk as regular stockholder owners: If the mutual S&L loses money, the loss isn't taken out of the owner/depositors' accounts. (Regular stockholder owners, of course, may well see the value of their holdings decline in bad times.) On the other hand, mutual S&L owner/depositors do not enjoy as much reward potential as regular stockholder owners. For example, unlike regular stockholders, who might be able to sell their stock for a profit, mutual S&L owner/depositors can't sell their deposits to other investors at all.

The Problem of Matching Loan and Deposit Maturities

Most of the mortgage loans made by S&Ls have very long maturities (the 30-year mortgage is most common, although 15-year mortgages are becoming increasingly popular). However, most of the deposits that provide the money for these loans have zero or short maturities (passbook savings accounts have zero maturity because the depositor can withdraw at any time; CDs come in maturities of up to five years). This gap between the 15- to 30-year maturity of the S&Ls' major assets and the zero-to five-year maturity of their deposits creates a problem if market interest rates rise. Consider the following example.

Suppose an S&L wanted to make a 30-year, fixed-rate mortgage loan for $100,000 at 7 percent interest. To raise cash for the loan, the S&L sells a one-year $100,000 CD at 3 percent interest. This creates a favorable spread (7% − 3% = +4%) as long as interest rates stay where they are. Table 3-2 shows the S&L's profit during the first year of the loan.

TABLE 3-2 First-Year Profit for an S&L with a 7% Loan Financed by a 3% CD

Interest received from the loan	$100,000 × .07 = $7,000
Interest paid out to the CD holder	$100,000 × .03 = $3,000
	Net Income: $4,000

Note: For simplicity in this example, we assume the loan's terms allow the borrower to make only interest payments each year, deferring payment of the principal until the end of the loan's term.

At the end of the first year, the CD matures and the S&L must pay the CD holder $100,000 plus 3 percent interest ($3,000). So the S&L sells another one-year CD for $100,000, giving the proceeds to the first CD holder. Then it uses $3,000 of its interest income from the loan to pay the interest due on the first CD. At the end of the second year and thereafter, the cycle repeats itself with the S&L selling a new one-year CD each year and using the profits from the loan to pay the interest due on the old CDs. You can see that as long as each new CD is issued for 3 percent interest, the S&L will net a yearly profit of $4,000 ($7,000 income from the loan minus $3,000 paid to the CD holder).

What happens, however, if interest rates rise during the first year, such that at the end of the year the S&L must pay 9 percent to get anyone to buy a new one-year CD? Now the S&L is in trouble. It has to sell a new CD to pay the $100,000 owed to the holder of the first CD, but it can only do so by offering an interest rate two points higher than its mortgage loan is paying. So at the end of the second year, when the S&L must pay the interest to the CD holder, it must pay $9,000 instead of $3,000 and suffers a $2,000 loss for the year. Table 3-3 summarizes the situation.

Of course, market interest rates can go down too, creating extra profits for the S&L, but S&Ls face a risk of loss when market interest rates move against them.

S&Ls' Real Assets

S&Ls also own buildings and equipment that are needed to conduct business. These assets, which do not earn an explicit rate of return, are supposed to be kept to a low level subject to the needs of the institution. As the fraud of the 1980s showed, however, that has not always been the case. Many S&L executives spent much of their companies' money on private business jets, luxurious offices, and even vacation retreats—a clear example of the agency problem discussed in Chapter 1.

Credit Unions

credit unions Financial institutions owned by members who receive interest on shares purchased and who obtain loans.

Credit unions are member-owned financial institutions. They pay interest on shares bought by, and collect interest on loans made to, the members. Members are individuals rather than businesses or government units.

Credit unions are able to make relatively low interest loans to their members because they are cooperative organizations. They don't have to charge extra to make a profit, and they don't pay federal income taxes. Also, they make loans *only* to members, who are presumed to be somewhat better credit risks than the general population.

The Common Bond Requirement

To help ensure that credit union members actually are better credit risks than the general population, credit union members must have a *common bond* with one another. This could mean that all members work for the same company, belong to the same labor union, or perhaps just live in the same town as the other members. The theory is that people who belong to the same group, sharing common values, will be less likely to default on loans supported by money from their fellow group members.

TABLE 3-3 Second-Year Loss for an S&L with a 7% Loan Financed by a 9% CD

Interest received from the loan	$100,000 × .07 = $ 7,000
Interest paid out to the CD holder	$100,000 × .09 = $ 9,000
	Net Income: ($ 2,000)

Members as Shareholders

Credit unions are owned by their members, so when credit union members put money in their credit union, they are not technically "depositing" the money. Instead, they are purchasing *shares* of the credit union.

Like owners of other businesses, credit union members are entitled to any income the credit union has after debts and expenses have been paid. This residual income may be distributed in the form of extra dividends paid on the members' shares or by a rebate on interest paid on loans.

Credit Unions Compared with Banks

Traditionally, credit unions were small institutions that did not compete much with banks. However, they have grown rapidly in recent years and now provide most of the same services as commercial banks. Because banks now see credit unions as more of a threat, the banking lobby is pressuring Congress to treat credit unions more like banks, including the way they are taxed.

Credit Union Regulation

Credit unions must have charters giving them authority to operate, just like banks and S&Ls. They obtain these charters either from the state where they are located or from the federal government. The federal chartering and regulatory body for credit unions is the National Credit Union Administration (NCUA). The NCUA also oversees the National Credit Union Share Insurance Fund (NCUSIF). This fund insures share accounts up to $250,000. All federally chartered credit unions have NCUSIF insurance. State-chartered credit unions may also apply for NCUSIF insurance for the share accounts of their members.

If credit unions have emergency borrowing needs, they can turn to the Central Liquidity Facility (CLF), which was created by Congress in 1978 and is administered by the National Credit Union Administration. Credit unions can also turn to the Federal Reserve Bank in the district where they are located.

Finance Companies, Insurance Companies, and Pension Funds

Finance companies are nonbank firms that make short-term and medium-term loans to consumers and businesses. They often serve those customers who don't qualify for loans at other financial institutions.

Like banks and S&Ls, finance companies operate by taking in money and lending it out to their customers at a higher interest rate. A major difference between finance companies and other financial institutions, however, lies in the source of finance company funds. Banks and S&Ls receive most of their funds from individuals and businesses that deposit money in accounts at the institutions. Finance companies generally get their funds by borrowing from banks or by selling commercial paper.

Types of Finance Companies

There are three main types of finance companies: consumer, commercial, and sales. In the following sections, we will explain the characteristics and functions of each type.

Consumer Finance Companies

Consumer finance companies, sometimes known as small-loan companies, make small loans to consumers for car purchases, recreational vehicles, medical expenses, vacations, and the like. Consumer finance companies often make loans to customers with less than perfect credit. Because the customers are a higher risk, the interest rates charged on loans are usually a little higher to compensate for the greater risk.

Commercial Finance Companies

These firms concentrate on providing credit to other business firms. A special type of commercial finance company is called a factor. Factoring is the buying of a business firm's accounts receivable, thus supplying needed funds to the selling firm. Commercial finance companies also make loans to businesses, usually with accounts receivable or inventory pledged as collateral. This type of financing will be examined in detail in Chapter 20.

Sales Finance Companies

The mission of sales finance companies is to help the sales of some corporation (indeed, many are subsidiaries of the corporation whose sales they are promoting). In the automotive industry, for example, customers are more likely to buy cars from dealers that offer financing on the spot than from dealers who have no financing programs.

A finance company generally gives its retail dealers a supply of loan contract forms, which the dealers fill out at the time of sale. The contract is immediately sold to the finance company (at a slightly reduced price, of course, to allow for the finance company's profit). Ally Financial Inc., formerly GMAC, and the Ford Motor Credit Company are prominent examples of sales finance companies.

Insurance Companies

Insurance companies are firms that, for a fee, will assume risks for their customers. They collect fees, called premiums, from a large number of customers. Then they draw on the pool of funds collected to pay those customers who suffer damages from the perils they have insured against.

There are two main types of insurance companies: life insurance companies, and property and casualty insurance companies.

Life Insurance Companies

Life insurance companies sell policies that pay the beneficiaries of the insured when the insured person dies. You might ask how life insurance companies make any money because everybody dies sooner or later. If the risk life insurance companies were taking in return for the premium received were the risk of their customers dying, it is true that none of them would make any money. The real risk they are taking, however, is that the insured person will die *sooner than expected*.

actuaries People who use applied mathematics and statistics to predict claims on insurance companies and pension funds.

To help assess this risk, insurance companies employ **actuaries**. Actuaries help calculate the premium for a life insurance policy for a person of a given age, gender, and state of health, so that the insurance company can pay the insurance benefit, cover expenses, and make a profit. Actuaries cannot tell specifically *who* is going to die when; but they can predict, with a high degree of accuracy, *how many* in a group of 100,000 healthy 40-year-old males will die during the coming year.

Life insurance companies function as financial intermediaries essentially the same way as commercial banks or savings and loan associations. They take money in from surplus economic units in the form of policy premiums and channel it to deficit economic units in the form of investments in common stock, corporate bonds, mortgages, and real estate. Their payout can be predicted with a high degree of accuracy, so they need only a small amount of liquid assets.

Property and Casualty Insurance Companies

Property and casualty insurance companies insure against a wide range of hazards associated with person and property. These include theft; weather damage from hurricanes, tornadoes, and floods; fire; and earthquakes. Two close relatives of property and casualty companies are health insurance companies, which insure people against injuries and illnesses, and disability insurance companies, which insure people against loss of income from being unable to work.

liability insurance Insurance that pays obligations that may be incurred by the insured as a result of negligence, slander, malpractice, and similar actions.

One special hazard that these companies insure against is a policyholder's own negligence. This kind of insurance is called **liability insurance**. Most people are familiar with automobile liability insurance, but liability coverage can also be purchased for such things as medical malpractice, dog bites, and falls by visitors on your property.

The risks protected against by property and casualty companies are much less predictable than the risks insured by life insurance companies. Hurricanes, fires, floods, and trial judgments are all much more difficult to predict than the number of 60-year-old females who will die this year among a large number in this risk class. This means that property and casualty insurance companies must keep more liquid assets than life insurance companies.

Retirement Plans

Retirement plans are set up by companies, governments, and unions to pay retirement benefits for their employees. Most retirement plans are set up by employers. Employees and employers generally contribute money for the benefit of employees upon an employee's retirement. Some plans are set up in such a way that the employer is legally obligated to pay specified benefits to retired employees. Other plans are set up such that funds are contributed and invested for the benefit of employees but no specific promise is made by the employer to the employee as to the amount of benefits that may be available after retirement.

A retirement plan that obligates the employer to make specified payments to retired employees is called a defined benefit plan (DBP). In a defined benefit plan, contributions are made to a common fund to be drawn upon for the benefit of workers after retirement. This fund is called a **pension fund**. Retirement benefits for retired workers are determined by a formula that usually considers the worker's age, salary, and years of service. The employer is legally responsible for paying the promised benefits to the employee in much the same way a bond issuer is responsible for making promised interest and principal payments to a bond investor. Just as a company occasionally defaults on its bonds when it goes bankrupt, there is a similar risk that in a bankruptcy a company could default on its pension obligations. The **Pension Benefit Guaranty Corporation (PBGC)** insures many private sector pension funds. PBGC is a federal agency that collects premiums from healthy participating pension funds and pays benefits to workers with claims on a pension plan that has been terminated. The maximum annual guaranteed benefit guaranteed by PBGC for a participant age 65 in a single-employer plan in 2018 was $65,045.[1] This would cover the entire benefit owed to most employees whose private sector pension fund had been terminated, but it would cover only a fraction of what would be owed to higher-paid workers with higher promised pension benefits. There have been some airline company bankruptcies that led to pension fund terminations, which resulted in some highly paid pilots receiving a small fraction of what had been promised to them.

A retirement plan that specifies how contributions go into a fund set up for use by an employee upon the employee's retirement is called a defined contribution plan (DCP). These funds are invested for the benefit of the employee. The contributions to be made by the employee and/or employer are spelled out, but no specific retirement benefit is promised by the employer to the employee. Upon retirement the investment assets accumulated on behalf of the employee are simply turned over to that employee to be used to generate income for the employee after retirement. The funds contributed by the employee and/or employer while the employee is working are paid into segregated accounts (not a common fund) for each employee. These individual accounts, set up for each worker, are held by a financial services firm hired to perform this function. Fidelity Investments and TIAA–CREF are examples of financial services firms that perform this function. The funds in each of these accounts belong to the employee, not the employer or the financial services firm holding the investment assets. These assets are not generally available to be taken by creditors of the employer or the financial services firm if either were to go bankrupt. These funds are invested for the benefit of the employee, usually through mutual funds or other investment instruments made available by the financial services firm selected to perform this function.

retirement plans Entities that are set up to provide financial benefits to employees after those employees retire.

pension fund A financial institution that takes in funds for workers, invests those funds, and then provides a retirement benefit based on the worker's age, salary, and years of service.

Pension Benefit Guaranty Corporation (PBGC) A federal agency that collects premiums from pension funds and pays benefits, subject to limitations, to workers with claims on pension funds that have failed.

---

1. https://www.pbgc.gov/wr/benefits/guaranteed-benefits/maximum-guarantee.

Defined benefit plans are relatively rare in the private sector. Private companies are increasingly turning to defined contribution plans for their employees, placing the risk of inadequate investment returns on those employees. Defined benefit plans are more common among government employees, including federal, state, and municipal workers. Many states and municipalities are facing financial crises due in large measure to the fact that many of these plans are grossly underfunded. Promises have been made to these public workers but the assets held by the pension funds are not at a sufficient level to honor those promises. States and municipalities can't create their own money to pay these obligations. The taxpayers are probably going to have to foot the bill. In July of 2013 the city of Detroit declared bankruptcy because of its financial problems, including its large pension obligations. Detroit emerged from bankruptcy in December of 2014. In 2017 Illinois reported that it had unfunded pension liabilities of $185 billion. Moody's estimated that the correct figure is $251 billion.[2] No state has ever declared bankruptcy.

Annuities

An annuity is a series of equal payments made at regular time intervals, such as monthly payments, for a specified period of time. Pension fund benefits are often paid out in the form of annuities. Sometimes the sponsor of a pension fund will use the funds accumulated during the retiring person's working years to purchase an annuity from an insurance company. This provides the retired person's benefits. Insurance companies also sell annuities to investors. In return for the amount paid to the insurance company, the investor receives payments (usually monthly) for the remainder of his or her life. A person who receives annuity payments is called an annuitant. The size of the payments depends on how much money is paid to the insurance company at the time of the employee's retirement, along with factors such as the age, gender (if allowed by law), and state of health of the annuitant. If the pension fund investments made on behalf of a given employee earned a high return, a large amount of money will be available to purchase a large annuity. If the defined contribution pension fund investments performed poorly, the retired employee will be able to purchase only a small annuity.

Sometimes the investments made on an employee's behalf will be paid out in a lump sum at retirement. It is then up to the retired employee to invest this money wisely to generate the needed income during retirement.

Legislation after the Financial Crisis of 2008

The Dodd-Frank Wall Street Reform and Consumer Protection Act was signed into law by President Obama on July 21, 2010. It is named after Senator Christopher Dodd and Representative Barney Frank. This law was passed in reaction to the Financial Crisis of 2008.

The law creates a new consumer protection entity within the Federal Reserve called the Consumer Financial Protection Bureau. It has the authority to require clear and accurate information for consumers from credit providers. The law seeks to avoid a repeat of the bailouts of individual firms that had been deemed too big to be allowed to fail during the Financial Crisis. The new law seeks to provide a means to orderly liquidate financial firms that fail in the future. The Financial Stability Oversight Council is created that is supposed to anticipate emerging systematic risk factors that threaten the entire financial system. There are new transparency requirements for sophisticated positions created by financial firms using derivative securities. Common stockholders now have more say on company affairs including pay for senior executives and golden parachute contracts offered to such executives. There are new transparency requirements for credit rating agencies. Oversight powers for financial regulators are strengthened to reduce fraud, conflict of interest, and manipulation of the financial system.[3]

---

2. https://www.ilnews.org/news/state_politics/illinois-pension-debt-grew-more-in-one-year-than-half/article_1e9b33b4-aea8-11e7-b903-9bcca6639e34.html.

3. http://banking.senate.gov/public/_files/070110_Dodd_Frank_Wall_Street_Reform_comprehensive_summary_Final.pdf.

Also embedded in this law is the so-called Volcker Rule named after former Federal Reserve Chairman Paul Volcker. It restricts certain types of speculative positions by financial firms, the kind that got many such firms into trouble during the Financial Crisis. What is included in the prohibition is not clear, however. Federal regulators were given authority to delay the implementation of certain aspects of the Volcker Rule. They did so in December of 2014.[4] When JPMorgan Chase lost billions of dollars while engaging in this type of activity, frequently referred to as "proprietary trading," many claimed that this trading would not have been banned had the Volcker Rule been in effect in May 2012 when JPMorgan Chase sustained these large losses. This is because the positions being created by JPMorgan Chase had been designed to create risk-reducing hedges, which are allowed under the Volcker Rule. The hedge failed and the bank lost billions. Exactly what is covered by the Volcker Rule continues to be a source of dispute between banks and regulators. Proposed changes to the Dodd-Frank law, including the Volcker Rule, continue to be debated among members of Congress and officials in the White House.

What's Next

In this chapter we have seen how financial institutions help to bring together suppliers and users of funds to the benefit of both and to the economy. Commercial banks, savings and loan associations, credit unions, finance companies, insurance companies, and pension funds do this in different ways and have different constituents, but all assist in this efficient flow of funds.

In the following two chapters we will review financial statements and learn how to analyze them from the perspective of a financial manager.

Summary

1. *Explain the process of financial intermediation and the role of financial institutions in that process.*
   Financial institutions act as intermediaries between surplus and deficit economic units. They coordinate the flow of funds, absorbing differences between the amount of funds offered and needed, between the length of time funds are offered and needed, and between the risk that surplus economic units are willing to bear and the risk that is inherent in the securities offered by the deficit economic units.

2. *Define commercial banks and explain how reserve requirements influence their operations.*
   Commercial banks are financial institutions that are owned by stockholders, that take in deposits, and that make loans (primarily to businesses). Reserve requirements force banks to maintain minimum levels of reserves (vault cash and deposits at the Fed) based on the level and type of deposits they have. Reserves at the Fed pay modest interest so, although they provide liquidity for the bank, the profit potential is limited.

3. *Describe how the Federal Reserve regulates financial institutions.*
   The Federal Reserve is the central bank of the United States. It has seven members on its Board of Governors and a 12 voting-member Federal Open Market Committee.

The 12 district Federal Reserve banks make loans to financial institutions and perform other functions to assist member banks and other financial institutions. The Federal Reserve sets reserve requirements and influences the money supply through its open-market purchases and sales of government securities and foreign currencies. The Fed regulates financial institutions and uses its powers to try to maintain stability in the financial system.

4. *Explain how savings and loan associations differ from commercial banks.*
   Savings and loan associations (S&Ls) are financial institutions that take in deposits and mainly make mortgage loans. The Office of Thrift Supervision is the primary authority for overseeing S&Ls. S&Ls primarily make mortgage loans (to consumers). Banks primarily make commercial loans to businesses.

5. *Describe how credit unions operate.*
   Credit unions are financial institutions that take in funds by selling shares to members and make loans to those members. People are eligible for membership in a credit union if they meet the requirement of having a common bond with the other members. This might be working for a given company, belonging to a certain union, or living in a specified area.

---

4. http://www.americanbanker.com/news/law-regulation/regulators-delay-key-volcker-implementation-date-until-2017-1071746-1.html.

6. *Identify the major characteristics of finance companies, insurance companies, and pension funds.*
Finance companies take in funds, primarily by selling commercial paper, and make personal loans. Insurance companies sell policies, collecting premiums and paying beneficiaries if the insured-against event the insurance covers occurs. Retirement plans take in funds, usually contributed by both the employer and the employee, and invest those funds for future payment to the worker when he or she retires. This retirement benefit may be determined by a formula (a defined benefit plan) or by how much is in the investment fund at the time of retirement (a defined contribution plan).

Key terms

actuaries People who use applied mathematics and statistics to predict claims on insurance companies and pension funds.

credit unions Financial institutions owned by members who receive interest on shares purchased and who obtain loans.

Federal Reserve System The central bank of the United States that examines and regulates banks and other financial institutions and that conducts monetary policy.

interest rate spread The rate a bank charges for loans minus the rate it pays for deposits.

intermediation The process by which funds are channeled from surplus to deficit economic units through a financial institution.

liability insurance Insurance that pays obligations that may be incurred by the insured as a result of negligence, slander, malpractice, and similar actions.

mutuals Institutions (e.g., savings and loans or insurance companies) that are owned by their depositors or policy holders.

open-market operations The buying and selling of U.S. Treasury securities or foreign currencies to achieve some economic objective.

Pension Benefit Guaranty Corporation (PBGC) A federal agency that collects premiums from pension funds and pays benefits, subject to limitations, to workers with claims on pension funds that have failed.

pension fund A financial institution that takes in funds for workers, invests those funds, and then provides a retirement benefit based on the worker's age, salary, and years of service.

primary reserves Vault cash and deposits at the Fed that go toward meeting a bank's reserve requirements.

required reserve ratio The percentage of deposits that determines the amount of reserves a financial institution is required to hold.

retirement plans Entities that are set up to provide financial benefits to employees after those employees retire.

savings and loan associations (S&Ls) Financial institutions that take in deposits and make loans (primarily mortgage loans).

Self-Test

ST-1. Why is intermediation sometimes needed to bring together surplus and deficit economic units?

ST-2. Is it better to be a surplus economic unit or a deficit economic unit? Explain.

ST-3. Define secondary reserves that are held by a bank.

ST-4. What is the difference, if any, between the way commercial banks and credit unions are taxed?

ST-5. What is the common bond requirement that credit union members must have to be eligible for membership?

ST-6. What is a Federal Reserve discount window loan?

ST-7. What are Federal Reserve open-market operations?

Review Questions

1. Define *intermediation*.

2. What can a financial institution often do for a surplus economic unit (SEU) that the SEU would have difficulty doing for itself if the SEU were to deal directly with a deficit economic unit (DEU)?

3. What can a financial institution often do for a deficit economic unit (DEU) that the DEU would have difficulty doing for itself if the DEU were to deal directly with an SEU?

4. What are a bank's primary reserves? When the Fed sets reserve requirements, what is its primary goal?

5. Compare and contrast mutual and stockholder-owned savings and loan associations.

6. Who owns a credit union? Explain.

7. Which type of insurance company generally takes on the greater risks: a life insurance company or a property and casualty insurance company?

8. Compare and contrast a defined benefit and a defined contribution pension plan.

9. What tools are used in online banking to ensure the security of transactions?

Build Your Communication Skills

CS-1. Women live longer than men, on average, but some insurance regulators are forcing insurance companies to ignore this fact when setting rates. Do you think it is ethical to charge women and men, who are otherwise similar in age and other risk factors, different amounts for life insurance? Have two groups of students debate this issue.

CS-2. Read three articles about the Federal Reserve's current monetary policy. Use sources such as *The Wall Street Journal, Fortune* magazine, the *Federal Reserve Bulletin*. Write a brief report (two or three pages) summarizing the Fed's current monetary policy. What issues seem to be influencing the Fed's actions the most? What actions are being taken by the Fed to achieve the goals it has defined for itself?

Problems

3-1. Assume that society is made up of 100 surplus economic units (SEUs) that have $10 each and three deficit economic units (DEUs) that need $100 each. With that in mind, describe (a) how the society would have to operate if there were no financial institutions present to perform financial intermediation, and (b) how financial institutions help overcome the problems you described.

Financial Intermediation Commercial Banks

3-2. a. Assume that the Goodfellows National Bank pays 5 percent interest on depositors' accounts and charges 10 percent interest on loans it makes to businesses. What is Goodfellows' interest rate spread?

Commercial Banks (interest rate spread)

   b. Perhaps that was too simple. To make it a little more challenging, assume that Goodfellows pays 5 percent interest on depositors' passbook savings accounts, which make up 50 percent of all funds on hand, and 7 percent interest on depositors' Certificates of Deposit, which make up the other 50 percent of funds received. Next, assume that Goodfellows charges 10 percent interest on short-term loans, which make up 50 percent of all loans outstanding, and 12 percent interest on long-term loans, which make up the other 50 percent of all loans outstanding. Now what is Goodfellows' interest rate spread?

3-3. Assume that Goodfellows National Bank has $60 million in transaction accounts, $20 million in nonpersonal time deposits, and $10 million in Eurocurrency liabilities. Given the reserve requirements shown in Table 3-1, how much must Goodfellows keep on hand in reserve funds?

Commercial Banks (required reserve ratio)

3-4. Assume that you are attending a meeting of the Federal Reserve's Open Market Committee (FOMC). There is great concern among the members present that the economy is in a recessionary trend.

The Federal Reserve System

   a. What would you recommend that the FOMC do to stimulate the economy?

   b. Explain the chain of events that occurs when the FOMC takes the action that you recommended in part *a*?

3-5. Goodfellows National Bank has decided to compete with savings and loan associations (S&Ls) by offering 30-year fixed-rate mortgage loans at 8 percent annual interest. It plans to obtain the money for the loans by selling one-year 6 percent CDs to its depositors. During the first year of operation, Goodfellows sells its depositors $1,000,000 worth of 7 percent one-year CDs, and homebuyers take out $1,000,000 worth of 8 percent 30-year fixed-rate mortgages.

Matching Loan and Deposit Maturities

   a. Considering only the information above, what is Goodfellows' gross profit for the first year of operation?

   In Goodfellows' second year of operation, Goodfellows must sell $1,000,000 worth of new CDs to replace the ones that mature. However, interest rates have gone up during the year, and now the rate the bank must pay to get people to buy new CDs is 9 percent.

   b. Assuming that Goodfellows does sell $1,000,000 worth of new CDs at 9 percent interest in the second year, and assuming the $1,000,000 worth of 8 percent mortgage loans are still outstanding, what is Goodfellows' gross profit during the second year?

   (*Note:* For the purposes of this problem, assume that the mortgage holders make only interest payments each year.)

Answers to Self-Test

ST-1. Intermediation is sometimes needed when surplus and deficit economic units cannot agree about the denomination, maturity, and risk of the security offered and bought. Financial intermediaries can often give each side what it needs by stepping into the middle of the exchange of funds for securities.

ST-2. There is nothing inherently good or bad in the classification of either a surplus economic unit or a deficit economic unit.

ST-3. Secondary reserves are short-term liquid securities that a bank can sell quickly and easily to obtain cash that can be used to satisfy primary reserve requirements.

ST-4. Commercial banks pay federal income taxes on their profits, whereas credit unions do not.

ST-5. Credit union members are required to have some common bond with the other members before the request for membership is approved. Examples of common bonds required by various credit unions include working for a given company, belonging to a certain union, or living in a certain area.

ST-6. A Federal Reserve discount window loan is a loan made by one of the 12 district Federal Reserve banks to a financial institution from that district.

ST-7. Federal Reserve open-market operations are the purchasing and selling of U.S. government securities and foreign currencies by the Federal Reserve. This is done to affect the amount of reserves in the banking system.

Essential Concepts in Finance

Source: articular/Shutterstock

Chapter 4
Review of Accounting

Chapter 5
Analysis of Financial
Statements

Chapter 6
Forecasting for Financial
Planning

Chapter 7
Risk and Return

Chapter 8
The Time Value of Money

Essential concepts in finance are those subjects that you need to understand in order for the financial management lessons to make sense. They are the "floor on which the furniture sits" so to speak. Chapter 4, Review of Accounting, reintroduces you to accounting, which is the "language" of finance. Chapter 5, Analysis of Financial Statements, illustrates how to read the "story" that the accounting financial statements have to tell. Chapter 6, Forecasting for Financial Planning, takes you one step further by addressing the question: Now that you know the story, what is likely to happen in the future? You can never be sure about what will happen in the future, of course, so Chapter 7, Risk and Return, explains the nature of the risks that financial mangers face, and describes some of the measures that can be taken to deal with risk. Chapter 7 also explores what has been called "the iron law of finance": Increasing reward comes only with increasing risk. Chapter 8, The Time Value of Money, contains what is perhaps the most important topic in the book. This chapter introduces you to the concept that the value of a dollar received today is not the same as the value of a dollar to be received tomorrow. This seemingly simple issue has profound implications that reach throughout the entire field of finance.

Review of Accounting

"Never call an accountant a credit to his profession. A good accountant is a debit to his profession."
—Charles J.C. Lyall

Source: ra2studio/Shutterstock

Learning Objectives

After reading this chapter, you should be able to:

1. Explain how financial managers use the three basic accounting financial statements: the income statement, the balance sheet, and the statement of cash flows.
2. Discuss how depreciation affects cash flow and compute depreciation expense.
3. Explain how the TCJA of 2017 affected the way corporations are taxed.

A Big Shake-up for Accountants and Businesses

In December of 2017 Congress passed the first major revision to the federal tax code since 1986. Called the Tax Cuts and Jobs Act of 2017 (TCJA) it made significant changes to the tax laws for individuals and for corporations. Almost all the changes went into effect for tax year 2018 and later. The greater changes were to corporate tax law.

The Tax Reform Act of 1986 created a progressive income tax system for corporations with the first rate applied to taxable income being 15% and the rate applied to subsequent brackets of income going as high as 39%. Under the 1986 law, only the first $50,000 of corporate taxable income was taxed at 15%. All taxable corporate income above that was taxed at a rate of 25% or higher. Taxable corporate income above $75,000 was taxed at a rate of 34% or higher. This means that the flat 21% tax rate specified by the 2017 TCJA for all corporate taxable income is much lower than what all but the tiniest corporations had been used to paying.

The 2017 TCJA made other changes that are having a significant effect on corporations. Business interest expenses are no longer tax deductible without limit. More on this later in the chapter. Some assets held by corporations that had to be depreciated under the old law can now be fully expensed in the year the asset is acquired. Again, more on this to come.

The 2017 law repealed the alternative minimum tax (AMT) for corporations. It reduced the AMT for individuals but did not repeal it. The tax cuts for corporations are permanent for corporations while those for individuals will expire in 2025 unless new legislation extends them.

Chapter Overview

Accounting plays an important role in a firm's financial success. Accountants prepare financial statements that financial managers use to analyze the condition of a firm and to plan for its future. Financial managers must understand, then, how to analyze and interpret financial statements as they make decisions. The financial manager who knows how to use financial statements can help create value for the firm's owners.

In this chapter, we will review the three major financial statements: the income statement, the balance sheet, and the statement of cash flows. We will also study how depreciation and taxes affect a firm's cash flows.

Review of Accounting Fundamentals

All public corporations in the United States must follow certain accounting guidelines known as Generally Accepted Accounting Principles (GAAP), which require that public corporations prepare financial statements that comply with GAAP rules. The Financial Accounting Standards Board (abbreviated FASB and pronounced Fahz-bee), a private, professional accounting body, publishes these rules governing how public corporations must account for their business activities.

FASB prides itself on its independence. The Securities and Exchange Commission has deferred to FASB with regard to accounting rules publicly traded companies must follow. In April 2012, FASB found itself under a lot of political pressure regarding the valuation of what had come to be called troubled assets.

mark-to-market Recording an asset or liability according to its recent market price.

FASB rules had followed a **mark-to-market** (also known as fair-value) approach to how companies would report the value of certain financial assets. Mark-to-market accounting calls for certain types of assets to be valued for accounting purposes according to what that asset, or a similar asset, trades for between a willing buyer and a willing seller entering into an arm's length transaction. Some argue that this is not a good approach when the markets are in great disarray as they were in 2011 and 2012. FASB must have agreed since it issued a ruling in April 2012 that gave companies permission to exercise significant judgment in placing a value on certain assets. The FASB rule says that when valuing these assets, including mortgage-backed securities, more weight should be placed on transactions that occur when a market is operating in an orderly manner and less when the market is less active. This ruling will allow many financial firms to avoid having to take write-downs on certain assets. Whether FASB exercised prudent judgment in this ruling or caved into political pressure is a matter of much debate.

10-K reports An audited set of financial statements submitted annually by all public corporations to the Securities and Exchange Commission (SEC).

10-Q reports An unaudited set of financial statements submitted quarterly by all public corporations to the Securities and Exchange Commission (SEC).

The Securities and Exchange Commission (SEC) requires all public corporations to file financial statements, and make them available to the public, on 10-K and 10-Q reports. The **10-K reports** contain audited financial statements submitted annually to the SEC for distribution to the public. The **10-Q reports** contain unaudited financial statements submitted quarterly, also for public distribution.

The following basic accounting equation is central to understanding the financial condition of a firm:

$$\text{Assets} = \text{Liabilities} + \text{Equity}$$

Assets are the items of value a business owns. Liabilities are claims on the business by nonowners, and equity is the owners' claim on the business. The sum of the liabilities and equity is the total **capital** contributed to the business. Capital contributions come from two main sources: creditors (including bondholders and banks) and common stockholders. Some firms also have preferred stock that has a claim on the firm after creditors but before common stockholders.

capital Funds supplied to a firm.

Basic Accounting Financial Statements

You can get a good picture of how a firm is doing by looking at its financial statements. The three basic financial statements are the *income statement,* the *balance sheet,* and the *statement of cash flows.* Each of these statements gives a slightly different view of the firm. Let's look at these financial statements and how they interrelate.

The Income Statement

We can compare the **income statement** to a video: It measures a firm's profitability over a period of time. The firm can choose the length of the reporting time period. It can be a month, a quarter, or a year. (By law, a publicly traded corporation must report its activities at least quarterly but may report more frequently.)

income statement A financial statement that presents the revenues, expenses, and income of a business over a specific time period.

The income statement shows *revenues, expenses,* and *income.* Revenues represent gross income the firm earned during a particular period of time (usually from sales). Expenses represent the cost of providing goods and services during a given period of time. Net income is what is left after expenses are subtracted from revenues.

Figure 4-1 shows an income statement for Acme Corporation, a firm that manufactures birdseed, anvils, rockets, explosives, and giant springs. Acme Corporation is primarily a mail-order company, with many customers in the southwestern United States. The income statement is for the year ended December 31, 2018. This income statement describes sales, expenses, and net income for Acme Company from the beginning of the business day on January 1, 2018, until the end of the business day on December 31, 2018.

Revenues

As Figure 4-1 shows, Acme's sales totaled $15 million during 2018. Generally, the income statement does not distinguish between cash and credit sales. As a result, we are not sure how much actual cash came into the firm from the $15 million in reported sales.

Net Sales	$ 15,000,000
Cost of Goods Sold	5,000,000
Gross Profit	10,000,000
Depreciation Expense	2,000,000
S&A Expenses	800,000
Operating Income (EBIT)	7,200,000
Interest Expense	1,710,000
Income before Taxes	5,490,000
Income Taxes (25%) Combined Federal and State	1,373,000
Net Income	$ 4,117,000
'Earnings per Share (4,117,000 shares)	$ 1.00
Common Stock Dividends Paid	$ 400,000
Change in Retained Earnings	$ 3,717,000

FIGURE 4-1
Acme Corporation Income Statement for the Year Ended December 31, 2018

Expenses

Expenses include costs incurred while conducting the operations of the firm and financial expenses, such as interest on debt and taxes owed. These items are matched to the revenues that were generated as the expenses were incurred.

Cost of Goods Sold

The first expense subtracted from sales is *cost of goods sold,* which consists of the labor, materials, and overhead expenses allocated to those goods and services sold during the year.

Subtracting cost of goods sold of $5 million from sales of $15 million gives Acme's *gross profit,* which equals $10 million.

Selling and Administrative Expenses

From gross profit, we next subtract Acme's selling and administrative expenses ($800,000). Selling expenses include marketing and salespeople's salaries. Administrative expenses are for expenses that are difficult to associate directly with sales for a specified time period. These would include office support, insurance, and security.

Depreciation Expense

Depreciation expense is subtracted next—$2 million for Acme in 2018. Depreciation expense is the year's allocation of the cost of plant and equipment that have been purchased this year and in previous years. Because assets provide their benefits to the firm over several years, accountants subtract the cost of long-lived assets a little at a time over a number of years. The allocated portion of the cost of a firm's assets for the income statement's period of time is the depreciation expense.[1] Depreciation expense is a noncash expense. However, because it is a tax-deductible expense, it increases the cash flows of the firm.

Operating Income and Interest Expense

When we subtract selling and administrative expenses and depreciation expense from gross profit, we are left with Acme's *earnings before interest and taxes (EBIT),* also known as operating income. This figure is $7,200,000.

Gross Profit	=	10,000,000
Selling and Administrative Expenses	–	800,000
Depreciation Expense	–	2,000,000
Earnings before Interest and Taxes (EBIT, or Operating Income)	=	7,200,000

EBIT is the profit that the firm receives from its business operations before subtracting any financing expenses. From EBIT, we then subtract *interest expense* associated with any debts of the company to arrive at Acme's *earnings before taxes (EBT).* Acme has $1,710,000 in interest expense. When we subtract this figure from the $7,200,000 EBIT figure, we find Acme had earnings before taxes (EBT) of $5,490,000.

The Tax Cuts and Jobs Act of 2017 (TCJA) for the first time placed a limit on deductions of interest expense for businesses. Before this law was passed business interest paid was fully tax deductible. Now only business interest expenses up to 30% of "adjusted taxable income" are deductible. Adjusted taxable income adds back depreciation, amortization, and depletion expenses to taxable income through 2021. From 2022 on those items cannot be added back, thus placing a stricter limit on what interest expense can be deducted on a business tax return. There is no limit on interest expense deductions by businesses with $25 million or less of annual sales revenue. Since Acme Company has sales revenue of $15 million in 2018, a number less than $25 million, it can subtract all its business interest expenses on its tax return. For those companies that do run into the limit,

---

1. We will discuss further the role of depreciation, and depreciation rules, later in this chapter.

A Special Earnings Category: EBITDA

Financial analysts often make use of another measure of a company's earnings called earnings before interest, taxes, depreciation, and amortization, or EBITDA (pronounced "ee'-bid-dah"). EBITDA is found by adding depreciation expense and amortization expense back to EBIT. Because depreciation and amortizations are noncash expenses, which will be discussed later in this chapter, the result of adding depreciation and amortization back into EBIT is a figure that represents revenues minus cash expenses, or approximately the amount of cash earned by the daily operations of a business.

Although EBITDA is of great interest to financial analysts, it is not required to be reported by the Financial Accounting Standards Board and, thus, is not usually shown as a specific line item on most income statements. As a result, it usually must be calculated manually. Acme's EBITDA for 2018 is

Operating Income (EBIT)	$ 7,200,000
+ Depreciation and Amortization	2,000,000
= EBITDA	$ 9,200,000

Having made this calculation, a financial analyst would proceed with the knowledge that Acme's normal business operations threw off approximately $9.2 million in cash during 2018.

---

they are allowed to carry forward to future year tax returns the interest expense they were not allowed to deduct in the year the expense was incurred. In other words, the Internal Revenue Service (IRS) allows firms to subtract these expenses from their gross income before computing the tax they owe subject to the new limits on interest expense deductions. We will discuss income taxes later in the chapter.

Net Income

Finally, after we subtract all operating expenses, financing expenses, and taxes from revenues, we arrive at the firm's net income (NI). For Acme, net income in 2018 was $4,117,000. This is the firm's accounting net profit for the year.

Earnings per Share (EPS)

Acme's stockholders are very interested in their individual share of the corporation's earnings. Therefore, under the entry earnings per share (EPS), the income statement shows total net income divided by the number of shares of common stock outstanding. The net income figure comes straight from the income statement.

Net Income (NI)	=	4,117,000
Earnings per Share (EPS) (4.117 million shares)	=	$1.00

The number of shares outstanding comes from the balance sheet. Acme has 4 million shares of common stock outstanding.

To calculate EPS, divide net income by the number of outstanding common stock shares. For Acme, we calculate EPS as follows:

$$EPS = \frac{\text{Net Income}}{\text{Number of shares of common stock outstanding}}$$

$$= \frac{\$4,117,000}{4,117,000}$$

$$= \$1.00$$

Common Stock Dividends and Retained Earnings

A company has two options as to what to do with net income. It can pay stockholder dividends, or it can retain the earnings. Retaining the earnings will likely lead to greater future growth

Take Note
If the amount remaining after paying dividends had been negative, then we would have subtracted our number from retained earnings instead of adding to it. For Acme, there is a positive number to add to retained earnings—$3,717,000.

in sales and new income as new assets are purchased or existing liabilities are paid. In 2018, Acme has chosen to pay $400,000 (9.7 percent of its available earnings) in dividends to common stockholders. The remaining $3,717,000 is an addition to retained earnings of the firm. As shown in Figure 4-1, this amount is added to the earnings retained from past years.

In addition to the income statement, many firms prepare a short statement of retained earnings, as shown in Figure 4-2, that records dividend and retained earnings information. Assuming that Acme's end-of-2017 retained earnings were $7,283,000, Acme's accountants add the 2018 net income less the dividends paid to those stockholders ($4,117,000 − $400,000 = $3,717,000) to the end-of-2018 retained earnings. The result is $11 million ($7,283,000 + $3,717,000) = $11,000,000.

The Balance Sheet

balance sheet The financial statement that shows an economic unit's assets, liabilities, and equity at a given point in time.

If the income statement is like a video, a balance sheet is like a still photograph. The **balance sheet** shows the firm's assets, liabilities, and equity at a given point in time. This snapshot of a company's financial position tells us nothing about the firm's financial position before or after that point in time. Let's examine the end-of-2018 balance sheet for Acme. Figure 4-3 shows the balance sheet for Acme as of the end of the business day, December 31, 2018.

current assets Liquid assets of an economic entity (e.g., cash, accounts receivable, inventory, etc.) usually converted into cash within one year.

On the balance sheet, the firm's assets are listed in order of their liquidity. As we learned in Chapter 1, liquidity is the ease with which you can convert an asset to cash. This means that cash and near-cash assets, **current assets**, are listed first. Assets that are difficult to convert to cash are listed later. On the other side of the balance sheet, the liabilities that are due earliest, **current liabilities**, are listed first. Current liabilities are almost always due within one year. The liabilities due later, such as long-term debt, are listed later on the balance sheet.

current liabilities Liabilities that are coming due soon, usually within one year.

The equity section lists the claims of the owners (Acme's common stockholders). The owners' claims include both the amount the owners contributed when the common stock was first issued and the total earnings retained by the firm at the time of the balance sheet.

The Asset Accounts

Acme has both current and fixed assets. Current assets provide short-term benefits, whereas fixed assets provide long-term benefits to the firm.

Current Assets

Acme has $12 million in cash at the end of 2018. Marketable securities—securities that can quickly and easily be converted to extra cash—are listed next. Acme has $8 million in these securities. Customers owe the company $1 million, the amount of accounts receivable.

The company has $12 million of inventory and $1 million in prepaid expenses. The inventory figure reflects the amount of goods produced but not yet sold to customers. The prepaid expense figure represents future expenses that have been paid in advance. An example of a prepaid expense is the premium paid on an insurance policy. You pay the premium in advance, so the insurance coverage is "owed" to you until the term of coverage expires. Because prepaid expenses, such as insurance premiums, have been paid for but not yet received, they are owed to the company and are considered assets.

The sum of all current assets, including cash, marketable securities, net accounts receivable, inventory, and prepaid expenses, is often referred to as working capital. For Acme, this figure is $34 million.

FIGURE 4-2
Acme Corporation
Statement of Retained
Earnings for the Year
Ended December 31, 2018

Retained Earnings, Dec 31, 2017	$ 7,283,000
+ 2018 Net Income	+ 4,117,000
− 2018 Dividends Paid to Common Stockholders	− 400,000
Retained Earnings, Dec 31, 2018	$ 11,000,000

FIGURE 4-3
Acme Corporation
Balance Sheet for
December 31, 2018

Assets:	
Cash	$ 12,000,000
Accounts Receivable	1,000,000
Inventory	12,000,000
Marketable Securities	8,000,000
Prepaid Expenses	1,000,000
Total Current Assets	34,000,000
Fixed Assets, Gross	28,000,000
Less Accumulated Depreciation	(8,000,000)
Fixed Assets, Net	20,000,000
Total Assets	$ 54,000,000
Liabilities and Equity:	
Accounts Payable	$ 3,830,000
Notes Payable	3,000,000
Accrued Expenses	1,000,000
Total Current Liabilities	7,830,000
Long-Term Debt	15,000,000
Total Liabilities	22,830,000
Common Stock ($1 par)	4,117,000
Capital in Excess of Par	16,053,000
Retained Earnings	11,000,000
Total Common Equity	31,170,000
Total Liabilities and Equity	$ 54,000,000

Fixed Assets

Next to be listed are the fixed assets of the firm. Fixed assets are assets that are expected to provide a benefit to the firm for more than one year. These assets are generally less liquid than the current assets. Acme has $28 million of gross fixed assets, which is listed at the original cost of these assets. The accumulated depreciation figure is the sum of all the depreciation expenses ever taken on the firm's income statements for the assets still carried on the books. Acme's accumulated depreciation figure is $8 million. To find the net fixed assets figure—sometimes called net plant and equipment—subtract the amount of accumulated depreciation from gross fixed assets ($28 million minus $8 million).

The result is $20 million. The $34 million in current assets plus the $20 million in net fixed assets are the total assets of the firm. At the end of 2018, Acme's total assets were $54 million.

The Liabilities and Equity Accounts

The liabilities and equity sections of the balance sheet show how the company's assets were financed. The funds come from those who have liability (debt) claims against the firm or from those who have equity (ownership) claims against the firm.

Liabilities

In the liability section of the balance sheet, current liabilities are listed first. Acme has accounts payable at the end of 2018 of $3.83 million. Accounts payable represent money a business owes to suppliers that have sold the firm materials on account.

Notes payable are $3 million for this company. Notes payable are legal IOUs that represent the debt of the borrower (Acme) and the claim the lender has against that borrower. Acme also has accrued expenses of $1 million. Accrued expenses are business expenses that have not been paid yet. For example, universities often make professors work for a full month before they are paid. The universities accrue wages payable for the month before the payroll checks are finally issued. Acme's accounts payable, notes payable, and accrued expenses add up to $7.83 million in current liabilities.

Net working capital is current assets minus current liabilities. For Acme, this would be $26.17 million ($34 million current assets – $7.83 million current liabilities).

Next, long-term liabilities are listed. Long-term liabilities are liabilities that are not due within one year. Acme has $15 million in long-term bonds payable that mature in 2030. The $15 million figure listed on the balance sheet refers only to the principal on these bonds.

Common Stock and Retained Earnings

The equity section of the balance sheet contains three items: common stock, capital in excess of par, and retained earnings. When Acme Company was founded it issued 3,000,000 shares of common stock, with a par value of $1 per share, at a market price of $5 per share. This made the common stock equity entry $3 million at that time. At the end of 2018, after 1,117,000 additional shares were sold in the primary market also with a $1 per share par value the entry became $4,117,000 (4,117,000 total shares outstanding times $1 per share par value). The end-of-2018 Common Stock entry had gone from $3,000,000 to $4,117,000.

When the company was founded, because the market price of the initial shares sold was $3 per share and the par value was $1 per share, some of that equity capital raised was "in excess of par." To be specific, at the time of that first stock sale 3,000,000 shares were sold to investors at a price that was $2 in excess of the $1 par value. This means that at that time there was an entry of $6,000,000 for the Capital in Excess on the balance sheet ($3 per share market price minus $1 per share par) times 3,000,000 shares sold). During the year 2018 the company issued 1,117,000 additional shares, also with a $1 par value, at a market price of $10 per share. The end-of-2018 Common Stock account increased by $1,117,000 (1,117,000 new shares times $1 per share par). The end-of-2018 Capital in Excess of Par account increased by $10,053,000 (1,117,000 new shares times the difference between the $10 per share market price for the newly issued stock and the $1 per share par value). The end-of-2018 Capital in Excess of Par entry had gone from $6,000,000 to $16,053,000. This increase of $10,053,000 for Capital in Excess of Par is the $9 per share in excess of par figure ($10 market price per share minus $1 par value) times the 1,117,000 new shares sold in the primary market during 2018.

The last entry in the common stock equity section is retained earnings. The retained earnings figure represents the sum of all the net income of a business during its entire history, minus the sum of all the common stock dividends that it has ever paid.[2] Those earnings that were not paid out were, by definition, retained. The retained earnings figure for Acme at the end of 2018 is $11 million.

The Statement of Cash Flows

The third major financial statement required of all publicly traded corporations by the FASB is the *statement of cash flows*. This statement, like the income statement, can be compared to a video: It shows how cash flows into and out of a company over a given period of time.

We construct the statement of cash flows by adjusting the income statement to distinguish between income and cash flow and by comparing balance sheets at the beginning and end of the relevant time period. The statement of cash flows shows cash flows in operating,

Take Note
Do not fall into the trap of thinking that the retained earnings account contains cash. Remember, equity accounts, including this one, represent owners' claims on assets. They are not assets themselves. The earnings not paid out as dividends have already been used to accumulate additional assets or to pay off liabilities.

---

2. There are exceptions. If a company pays a dividend in the form of new common stock instead of cash, then there could be a transfer from retained earnings to the other common stock equity accounts. We will skip this exception for now. The use of stock dividends instead of cash dividends, and the resulting accounting treatment, will be examined in Chapter 16.

Cash Received from (used in) Operations:		
Net Income	$	4,117,000
Depreciation Expense		2,000,000
Decrease (increase) Accounts Receivable		(300,000)
Decrease (increase) Inventory		5,300,000
Decrease (increase) Marketable Securities		1,000,000
Decrease (increase) Prepaid Expenses		0
Increase (decrease) Accounts Payable		(5,170,000)
Increase (decrease) Accrued Expenses		(3,000,000)
Total Cash from Operations	$	3,947,000
Cash Received from (used for) Investments:		
New Fixed Asset Purchases	($	14,000,000)
Total Cash from Investments	($	14,000,000)
Cash Received from (used for) Financing Activities:		
Proceeds from New Long-Term Debt Issue	$	4,283,000
Proceeds from New Common Stock Issue	$	11,170,000
Short-Term Notes Paid Off		(3,000,000)
Dividends		(400,000)
Total Cash from Financing	$	12,053,000
Net Change in Cash Balance	$	2,000,000
Beginning Cash Balance	$	10,000,000
Ending Cash Balance	$	12,000,000

investing, and financing activities, as well as the overall net increase or decrease in cash for the firm. You can see Acme's statement of cash flows for 2018 in Figure 4-4.

Operating Activities

Operating activities on the statement of cash flows shows that Acme had $4,117,000 in net income for 2018. This number represents what was left after Acme paid all the firm's expenses for that year. We adjust that number to determine the operating cash flows for 2018.

Adjustment for Depreciation Expense

Although depreciation expense is a legitimate reduction of income for accounting purposes, it is not a cash outlay. In other words, firms record depreciation expense on financial statements but do not write checks to pay it. We must add the $2 million in depreciation expense because net income was reduced by this amount—even though depreciation is a noncash expense.

Changes in Balance Sheet Accounts

Changes in asset accounts on the balance sheet indicate changes in the company's cash flow. Because firms must pay cash to accumulate new assets, any increase in an asset account between the time one balance sheet is published and the time the next balance sheet is published indicates a cash outflow. Likewise, because firms sell assets to raise cash, any decrease in an asset account indicates a cash inflow. For Acme, balance sheet changes in marketable securities, accounts payable, accounts receivable (net), and inventory are shown in the operations section of Figure 4-4.

Take Note
Be careful not to confuse the statement of cash flows with the income statement. The income statement lists revenues and expenses over a period of time. The statement of cash flows lists where cash came from and what it was used for during a period of time.

Chapter 4 Review of Accounting   69

FIGURE 4-5
Acme Corporation
Balance Sheet Changes
between Dec. 31, 2017
and Dec. 31, 2018

	Dec. 31, 2017	Dec. 31, 2018	Change
Assets:			
Cash	$ 10,000,000	$ 12,000,000	+ 2,000,000
Accounts Receivable	700,000	1,000,000	+ 300,000
Inventory	17,300,000	12,000,000	– 5,300,000
Marketable Securities	9,000,000	8,000,000	– 1,000,000
Prepaid Expenses	1,000,000	1,000,000	0
Total Current Assets	38,000,000	34,000,000	– 4,000,000
Fixed Assets, Gross	14,000,000	28,000,000	+ 14,000,000
Less Accumulated Depreciation	(6,000,000)	(8,000,000)	– 2,000,000
Fixed Assets, Net	8,000,000	20,000,000	+ 12,000,000
Total Assets	$ 46,000,000	$ 54,000,000	+ 8,000,000
Liabilities and Equity:			
Accounts Payable	$ 9,000,000	$ 3,830,000	– 5,170,000
Notes Payable	6,000,000	3,000,000	– 3,000,000
Accrued Expenses	4,000,000	1,000,000	– 3,000,000
Total Current Liabilities	19,000,000	7,830,000	– 11,170,000
Long-Term Debt	10,717,000	15,000,000	+ 4,283,000
Total Liabilities	29,717,000	22,830,000	– 6,887,000
Common Stock ($1 par)	3,000,000	4,117,000	+ 1,117,000
Capital in Excess of Par	6,000,000	16,053,000	10,053,000
Retained Earnings	7,283,000	11,000,000	+ 3,717,000
Total Common Equity	16,283,000	31,170,000	+ 14,887,000
Total Liabilities and Equity	$ 46,000,000	$ 54,000,000	+ 8,000,000

Changes in the liabilities and equity sections of the balance sheet also signal cash flow changes. Because firms must use cash to pay off obligations, any decrease in liability, preferred stock, or common stock equity accounts between the time one balance sheet is published and the time the next balance sheet is published indicates a cash outflow during that time period. To raise additional cash, firms can incur debt or equity obligations; so any increase in liability, preferred stock, or common stock items indicates a cash inflow.

Figure 4-5 shows two balance sheets for Acme side by side. We can compare them and note where the cash inflows and outflows that appear on the statement of cash flows came from.

Operating Activities

In the asset section of the balance sheet, we see that marketable securities decreased by $1 million, signaling that Acme sold some marketable securities to generate a cash inflow of $1 million. Similarly, accounts receivable rose from $700,000 to $1 million, a $300,000 increase. In effect, Acme had a cash outflow of $300,000 in the form of funds recognized as revenue but not collected from its credit customers. In contrast, inventory decreased from $17.3 million to $12 million, which represents a $5.3 million source of cash in the form of inventory items sold that Acme did not have to make or buy.

In the liabilities and equity section of the balance sheet, observe that accounts payable decreased by $3 million. Acme must have paid $3 million in cash to its suppliers to decrease the amount owed by that amount; therefore, this represents a cash outflow. Likewise, the

Take Note
We do not mention the change in accumulated depreciation in the statement of cash flows. The additional accumulated depreciation of $2 million is already included in the depreciation expense figure on the income statement. We don't want to count this twice.

accrued expenses account decreased by $1 million, indicating that Acme used $1 million in cash to pay them.

Investment Activities

The investments section of the statement of cash flows shows investing activities in long-term securities or fixed assets. Increasing investments require a cash outflow, and decreasing investments signal a cash inflow. For instance, observe in Figure 4-5 that Acme's fixed assets increased to $28 million in 2018, up from $14 million in 2017. This $14 million increase reflects a cash outlay used to buy additional assets.

Financing Activities

The financing section of the statement of cash flows shows financing activities related to the sales and retirement of notes, bonds, preferred and common stock, and other corporate securities. The retirement (i.e., buying back) of previously issued securities signals a cash outflow. The issuing of securities is a cash inflow. On the Acme balance sheet, for example, notes payable decreased from $6 million to $3 million. The decrease shows that the firm spent $3 million to pay off outstanding notes.

Further down in the liabilities and equity sections of the balance sheet (Figure 4-5), we see that the common stock account increased by $1.117 million. This increase is the result of 1,117,000 new shares sold in 2018 with a par value of $1 per share. These shares were sold in investors for $10 each which was $9 per share in excess of the $1 par. This is why Common Stock went up by $1,117,000 on the balance sheet in 2018 (1,117,000 shares times $1 per share par) and Capital in Excess of Par went up by $10,053,000 that year (1,117,000 shared by $9 in excess of par) compared to the previous year.

In the equity section of the balance sheet, we see that retained earnings increased from $7,283,000 to $11 million. Although this $3,717,000 increase in retained earnings represents a cash inflow to the firm, it is not recorded on the statement of cash flows. Why? Because the cash inflow it represents was recorded on the statement of cash flows as net income ($4,117,000) less common stock dividends ($400,000). To include the increase in retained earnings again would result in double counting.

Net Cash Flow during the Period

We have now completed the adjustments necessary to convert Acme's net income for 2018 into actual cash flows. Figure 4-4 shows that the cash inflows exceeded the cash outflows, resulting in a net cash inflow of $2 million for Acme in 2018. (Notice in Figure 4-5 that Acme's cash balance of $12 million on December 31, 2018, is $2 million higher than it was on December 31, 2017.)

Depreciation

Depreciation is important to financial managers because it directly affects a firm's tax liabilities—which, in turn, affect cash flows. Here's how: Taxes paid are negative cash flows. Tax savings realized by deducting expenses generate more cash for the firm—the equivalent of a cash inflow.

Accounting depreciation is the allocation of an asset's initial cost over time. Let's look at why it is important to depreciate fixed assets over time. Suppose Acme bought a piece of equipment in 2018 that was expected to last seven years. If Acme paid $5 million cash for the asset and the entire cost were charged as an expense in 2018, the transaction would wipe out all but $2,200,000 of Acme's earnings before taxes for the year ($7,200,000 earnings before taxes – $5,000,000 fixed-asset cost). Nothing would show that Acme had acquired an asset worth $5 million. Then, for the next six years, Acme's income statements would show increases in profits generated by the asset—but there would be no corresponding accounting for the cost of that asset. In effect, it would look like Acme spent a lot of money in 2018, got nothing for it, and increased its profits for no reason over the next six years. This clearly would be misleading.

For more, see 8e Spreadsheet Templates for *Microsoft Excel.*

To get around the problem, accountants apply the *matching principle:* Expenses should be matched to the revenues they help generate. In other words, if you buy an asset and the asset is expected to last for seven years, then you should recognize the cost of the asset over the entire seven-year period. The cost is *amortized,* or spread out, over the seven-year period. In that way, the value of the asset will be properly shown on the financial statements in proportion to its contribution to profits.

The 2017 TCJA left most of the MACRS rules intact but there were some changes to depreciation tax rules. Section 179 property is property that would normally be depreciated but that is allowed to be expensed fully in the year acquired. The limit for Section 179 deductions was $500,000. Beginning in 2018 that limit is raised to $1,000,000 for eligible property. This benefit will begin to phase out when qualifying assets go above $2,500,000.

Accounting depreciation is very different from economic depreciation. The latter attempts to measure the actual change in the value of an asset. Because this involves making value estimates that may turn out to be wrong, accountants use an established set of rules to determine the amount of depreciation to allocate to a certain time period.

Calculating the Amount of Depreciation Expense

Depreciation expense for a given period is determined by calculating the total amount to be depreciated (the *depreciation basis*) and then calculating the percentage of that total to be allocated to a given time period (the *depreciation rules*).

depreciation basis The total value of an asset upon which depreciation expense will be calculated, a part at a time, over the life of the asset.

The total amount to be depreciated over the accounting life of the asset is known as the **depreciation basis**. It is equal to the cost of the asset plus any setup or delivery costs that may be incurred.[3]

Depreciation Methods

The cost of an asset can be allocated over time by using any of several sets of depreciation rules. The two most common depreciation rules used in tax reporting are *straight-line depreciation* and *modified accelerated cost recovery system (MACRS).*

Straight-Line Depreciation The simplest method of depreciation is the straight-line depreciation (SL) method. To use the straight-line depreciation method, you divide the cost of the asset by the number of years of life for the asset, according to classification rules, and charge the result off as depreciation expense each year. For instance, if the managers at Acme bought a $5 million piece of equipment that belonged to the seven-year asset class, then straight-line depreciation for the asset would be computed as follows:

Asset's initial cost: $5,000,000

Divided by length of service: 7 years

Equals depreciation expense each year: $714,286[4]

The Modified Accelerated Cost Recovery System Since the Tax Reform Act of 1986, Congress has allowed firms to use the modified accelerated cost recovery system, or MACRS (pronounced "makers"), to compute depreciation expense for tax purposes. MACRS specifies that some percentage of the cost of assets will be charged each year as depreciation expense during the assets' life. Table 4-1 shows the MACRS percentages for various classes of personal property assets.[5]

---

3. Although in financial statements prepared by public corporations for reporting purposes, salvage value—the value of the asset if sold for salvage—may be subtracted in arriving at the depreciation basis, it is not considered part of the depreciation basis for tax reporting purposes.

4. To be more precise, we would use what is known as the half-year convention in determining the annual depreciation. One-half a year's depreciation would be taken the year the asset was put into service and one-half in the final year. For example, for the preceding asset with a stated seven-year life, depreciation would in fact be spread over eight years. In this case, $357,143 in years 1 and 8, and $714,286 in years 2 through 7.

5. The half-year convention is built into the MACRS depreciation percentages shown in Table 4-1.

TABLE 4-1 MACRS Asset-Class Depreciation

Table 4-1 lists MACRS asset-class depreciation percentage for 3-year to 10-year class assets and examples of assets in each class.

Take Note
In the income statement shown in Figure 4-1, Acme Corporation's taxes are $1,373,000 on before-tax income of $5,490,000. The figure includes Acme's state and local tax obligations as well as the federal amount due.

Asset Class	3-Year Research Equipment and Special Tools	5-Year Computers, Copiers, Cars, and Similar Assets	7-Year Furniture, Fixtures, and Most Manufacturing Equipment	10-Year Equipment for Tobacco, Food, and Petroleum Production
Year	Depreciation Percentages			
1	33.33%	20.00%	14.29%	10.00%
2	44.45%	32.00%	24.49%	18.00%
3	14.81%	19.20%	17.49%	14.40%
4	7.41%	11.52%	12.49%	11.52%
5		11.52%	8.93%	9.22%
6		5.76%	8.92%	7.37%
7			8.93%	6.55%
8			4.46%	6.55%
9				6.56%
10				6.55%
11				3.28%

Source: http://www.irs.gov/publications/p946/ar02.html#d0e11297

So, under the MACRS, Acme's $5 million, seven-year asset would be depreciated 14.29 percent during its first year of life, 24.49 percent during the second year, and so on. Note that a seven-year asset is depreciated over eight years because of the half-year convention built into the table. Note also that MACRS is an accelerated depreciation method—greater percentages of the depreciation basis are subtracted from income in the early years, compared with the percentage applied in the later years. The acceleration is important because the more quickly firms can write off the cost of an asset, the sooner they save taxes from the tax-deductible expenses.

Income Taxes

Federal tax rates are set by Congress. The Internal Revenue Service (IRS) determines the amount of federal income tax a firm owes. The TCJA of 2017 made major changes to the tax rules that apply to corporations effective in tax year 2018. A flat rate of 21% is now applied to all corporate taxable income. Previously, there had been a progressive tax system for corporations with different rates applying to different dollar brackets of taxable income. The rates that had applied to those brackets began at 15% for the first $50,000 and went as high as 39%. For large corporations, the new law is a significant tax cut. Individuals continue to have a progressive tax rate system applied to their taxable income. Those rates begin at 10% for the first $9,525 of taxable income for a single person and go as high as 37% for taxable income above $150,689.50 for a single taxpayer. The top rate for a single person had been 39.6% for a single person. These numbers begin in the tax year 2018. The dollar figures for the brackets will be adjusted in subsequent years for inflation.

What's Next

In this chapter we reviewed basic accounting principles and explained how financial managers use accounting information to create value for the firm. In Chapter 5, we will discuss how to analyze financial statements.

Summary

1. *Explain how financial managers use the three basic accounting financial statements: the income statement, the balance sheet, and the statement of cash flows.*
   Financial managers need to understand the key elements of financial statements to analyze a firm's finances and plan for its future.
   - income statement shows the amount of revenues, expenses, and income a firm has over a specified period of time.
   - balance sheet describes the assets, liabilities, and equity values for a company at a specific point in time.
   - statement of cash flows describes a firm's cash inflows and outflows over a period of time.

2. *Discuss how depreciation affects cash flow and compute depreciation expense.*
   Depreciation is a noncash, tax-deductible expense. Because depreciation is tax deductible, it affects cash flow—the greater a firm's depreciation, the greater its cash flow. Cash flow, in turn, affects the value of the firm. The more cash a firm has, the greater its value.
   To allocate the cost of an asset over time, accountants use different depreciation methods, such as straight-line depreciation or the modified accelerated cost recovery system (MACRS). Whatever method is used, accountants must first find the depreciation basis—the total cost of the asset plus setup and delivery costs. Then they calculate the percentage of that total allocated for the time period at issue, as determined by either the straight-line depreciation method or MACRS.

3. *Explain how the TCJA of 2017 affected the way corporations are taxed.*
   Corporations now pay a flat rate of 21% on taxable income. Interest expenses are no longer fully deductible in the year incurred.

Key Terms

balance sheet The financial statement that shows an economic unit's assets, liabilities, and equity at a given point in time.

capital Funds supplied to a firm.

current assets Liquid assets of an economic entity (e.g., cash, accounts receivable, inventory, etc.) usually converted into cash within one year.

current liabilities Liabilities that are coming due soon, usually within one year.

depreciation basis The total value of an asset upon which depreciation expense will be calculated, a part at a time, over the life of the asset.

income statement A financial statement that presents the revenues, expenses, and income of a business over a specific time period.

mark-to-market Recording an asset or liability according to its recent market price.

10-K reports An audited set of financial statements submitted annually by all public corporations to the Securities and Exchange Commission (SEC).

10-Q reports An unaudited set of financial statements submitted quarterly by all public corporations to the Securities and Exchange Commission (SEC).

Self-Test

ST-1. Brother Mel's Bar-B-Q Restaurant has $80,000 in assets and $20,000 in liabilities. What is the equity of this firm?

ST-2. Cantwell Corporation has sales revenue of $2 million. Cost of goods sold is $1,500,000. What is Cantwell Corporation's gross profit?

ST-3. Adams Computer Store had accumulated depreciation of $75,000 at the end of 2018, and at the end of 2017, this figure was $60,000. Earnings before interest and taxes for 2018 were $850,000. Assuming that no assets were sold in 2018, what was the amount of depreciation expense for 2018?

ST-4. Shattuck Corporation had operating income (EBIT) of $2,500,000 in 2018, depreciation expense of $500,000, and dividends paid of $400,000. What is Shattuck's operating cash flow (EBITDA) for 2018?

ST-5. Bubba's Sporting Goods Company had retained earnings of $3 million at the end of 2017. During 2018, the company had net income of $500,000 and of this paid out $100,000 in dividends. What is the retained earnings figure for the end of 2018?

ST-6. Ron's In-Line Skating Corporation had retained earnings at the end of 2018 of $120,000. At the end of 2017, this figure was $90,000. If the company paid $5,000 in dividends to common stockholders during 2018, what was the amount of earnings available to common stockholders?

ST-7. Hayes Company recently bought a new computer system. The total cost, including setup, was $8,000. If this is five-year asset class equipment, what would be the amount of depreciation taken on this system in year 2 using MACRS rules?

Review Questions

1. Why do total assets equal the sum of total liabilities and equity? Explain.

2. What are the time dimensions of the income statement, the balance sheet, and the statement of cash flows? Hint: Are they videos or still pictures? Explain.

3. Define depreciation expense as it appears on an income statement. How does depreciation affect cash flow?

4. What are retained earnings? Why are they important?

5. Explain how net income and common stock dividends paid, as shown on the current income statement, affect the balance sheet item retained earnings.

6. What is accumulated depreciation?

7. What are the three major sections of the statement of cash flows?

8. How do financial managers compute the amount of taxes owed given the taxable income of a corporation?

9. Identify whether the following items belong on the income statement or the balance sheet.
   a. Interest Expense
   b. Preferred Stock Dividends Paid
   c. Plant and Equipment
   d. Sales
   e. Notes Payable
   f. Common Stock
   g. Accounts Receivable
   h. Accrued Expenses
   i. Cost of Goods Sold
   j. Preferred Stock
   k. Long-Term Debt
   l. Cash
   m. Capital in Excess of Par
   n. Operating Income
   o. Depreciation Expense
   p. Marketable Securities
   q. Accounts Payable
   r. Prepaid Expenses
   s. Inventory
   t. Net Income
   u. Retained Earnings

10. Indicate to which section the following balance sheet items belong (current assets, fixed assets, current liabilities, long-term liabilities, or equity).
    a. Cash
    b. Notes Payable
    c. Common Stock
    d. Accounts Receivable
    e. Accrued Expenses
    f. Preferred Stock
    g. Plant and Equipment
    h. Capital in Excess of Par
    i. Marketable Securities
    j. Accounts Payable
    k. Prepaid Expenses
    l. Inventory
    m. Retained Earnings

Build Your Communication Skills

CS-1. Interview a manager or an owner of an accounting firm. Ask that person what kinds of oral communication skills he or she needs to communicate financial information. Also ask what kinds of writing skills are required. What kinds of communications skills does this accounting firm executive look for when hiring a new person to do accounting or finance work for the firm? Report your findings to the class.

CS-2. Write a report that describes the best sources of financial information about publicly traded corporations. Discuss where you can find the basic financial statements for a corporation, which sources are the easiest to use, and what information sources—the library, the corporation, a brokerage firm, or the Internet—were most useful.

Problems

Financial Statement Connections **4-1.** You are interviewing for an entry-level financial analyst position with Wayne Industries. Bruce Wayne, the senior partner, wants to be sure all the people he hires are very familiar with basic accounting principles. He gives you the following data and asks you to fill in the missing information. Each column is an independent case. Month and day reference are for the current year.

	Case A	Case B
Revenues	200,000	
Expenses		70,000
Net Income		
Retained Earnings, Jan 1	300,000	100,000
Dividends Paid	70,000	30,000
Retained Earnings, Dec 31	270,000	
Current Assets, Dec 31	80,000	
Noncurrent Assets, Dec 31		180,000
Total Assets, Dec 31		410,000
Current Liabilities, Dec 31	40,000	60,000
Noncurrent Liabilities, Dec 31		
Total Liabilities, Dec 31	140,000	
CS and Capital in Excess of Par, Dec 31	520,000	100,000
Total Stockholders' Equity, Dec 31		210,000

Financial Statement Connections **4-2.** Fill in the following missing income statement values. The cases are independent.

For more, see 8e Spreadsheet Templates for *Microsoft Excel*.

	Case A	Case B
Sales		250,000
COGS	200,000	
Gross Profit		150,000
Operating Expenses	60,000	60,000
Operating Income (EBIT)		
Interest Expense	10,000	
Income before Taxes (EBT)		80,000
Tax Expense (40%)	92,000	
Net Income		

Equity **4-3.** Following is a portion of Cyberdie Industries' balance sheet.

Common Stock ($1 par; 400,000 shares authorized; 200,000 shares issued)	$200,000
Capital in Excess of Par	$400,000
Retained Earnings	$100,000

What was the market price per share of the stock when it was originally sold?

After-Tax Earnings **4-4.** This year SanCorp had $10 million in sales, $5.2 million in operating costs, and $200,000 in interest expense. It also paid 25 percent of its pre-tax income to the government as income tax expense. What was SanCorp's net after-tax income for the year?

4-5. A portion of Los Pollos Hermanos' comparative balance sheet follows. What is the amount of depreciation expense you would expect to see on the 2018 income statement? No assets that were on the books at the end of 2017 were sold or otherwise disposed of in 2018.

Depreciation

Los Pollos Hermanos
Balance Sheet as of December 31

	2017	2018
Plant and Equipment	$200,000	$250,000
Less: Accumulated Depreciation	($60,000)	($70,000)
Net Plant and Equipment	$140,000	$180,000

4-6. Use the following table to calculate (a) current assets, (b) net fixed assets, (c) current liabilities, and (d) net working capital.

Balance Sheet

Notes Payable	=	4,000,000
Cash	=	11,000,000
Long-Term Debt	=	16,000,000
Marketable Securities	=	9,000,000
Depreciation	=	8,000,000
Inventory	=	11,000,000
Accounts Receivable	=	3,000,000
Accrued Expenses	=	2,000,000
Fixed Assets	=	30,000,000
Prepaid Expenses	=	1,000,000

4-7. The following financial data correspond to Clayton West Energy's 2018 operations.

Income Statement

Cost of Goods Sold	$200,000
Selling and Administrative Expenses	40,000
Depreciation Expense	85,000
Sales	440,000
Interest Expense	40,000
Applicable Income Tax Rate	25%

Calculate the following income statement items.

a. Gross Profit

b. Operating Income (EBIT)

c. Earnings before Taxes (EBT)

d. Income Taxes

e. Net Income

4-8. Sitwell Enterprises began the year with $1,000,000 in total assets and ended the year with $1,500,000 in total assets. It had no debt at the beginning of the year, but it had $200,000 at the end of the year. What was Sitwell's net worth (that is, total stockholders' equity) at the end of the year?

Net Worth

4-9. Wet Dog Perfume Company (WDPC), a profit-making company, purchased a process line for $131,000 and spent another $12,000 on its installation. The line was commissioned in January 2017, and it falls into the MACRS seven-year class life. Applicable income tax rate for WDPC is 25 percent, and there is no investment tax credit. Calculate the following:

Depreciation

a. 2018 depreciation expense for this process line

b. Amount of tax savings due to this investment

4-10. Refer to the following income statement for Target Telecom (TT):

Total Revenue	$ 4,125,000
Direct Costs	1,237,500
Gross Profit	2,887,500
Operating Expenses:	
Marketing	825,000
Depreciation	42,000
Amortization	15,000
General and Administrative	1,237,500
Total Operating Expenses	2,119,500
Operating Profit	768,000
Interest Expense	10,000
Before-Tax Profit	758,000
Taxes	189,500
After-Tax Profit	$ 568,500

What was TT's Earnings Before Interest, Taxes, Depreciation, and Amortization (EBITDA) for the year?

Taxes

4-11. In 2018, Duff Beer Company purchased $130,000 worth of construction equipment. Duff's taxable income for 2018 without considering the new construction equipment would have been $400,000. The new equipment falls into the MACRS five-year class. Assume the applicable income tax rate is 34 percent.

a. What is the company's 2018 taxable income?

b. How much income tax will Duff pay?

Income Statements

4-12. Last year Momcorp had an operating profit of $600,000 and paid $50,000 in interest expenses. The applicable income tax rate for the year was 34 percent. The company had 100,000 shares of common stock outstanding at the end of last year.

a. What was the amount of Momcorp's earnings per share last year?

b. If the company paid $1.00 per share to its common stockholders, what was the addition to retained earnings last year?

Use the comparative figures of Omni Consumer Products (OCP) to answer problems 4–13 through 4–17 that follow.

For more, see 8e
Spreadsheet Templates
for *Microsoft Excel.*

Omni Consumer Products (OCP)
As of December 31

	2017	2018
Assets:		
Cash	$ 5,534	$ 9,037
Marketable Securities	952	1,801
Accounts Receivable (gross)	14,956	16,110
Less: Allowance for Bad Debts	211	167
Accounts Receivable (net)	14,745	15,943
Inventory	10,733	11,574
Prepaid Expenses	3,234	2,357
Plant and Equipment (gross)	57,340	60,374
Less: Accumulated Depreciation	29,080	32,478
Plant and Equipment (net)	28,260	27,896
Land	1,010	1,007
Long-Term Investments	2,503	4,743

Liabilities:

Accounts Payable	3,253	2,450
Notes Payable	—	—
Accrued Expenses	6,821	7,330
Bonds Payable	2,389	2,112

Stockholders' Equity:

Common Stock	8,549	10,879
Retained Earnings	45,959	51,587

4-13. Compute the following totals for the end of 2017 and 2018.

    Balance Sheet

  a. Current Assets

  b. Total Assets

  c. Current Liabilities

  d. Total Liabilities

  e. Total Stockholders' Equity

4-14. Show whether the basic accounting equation is satisfied in problem 4-13.

    Basic Accounting Equation

4-15. Calculate the cash flows from the changes in the following from the end of 2017 to the end of 2018. Indicate inflow or outflow.

    Balance Sheet

  a. Accumulated Depreciation

  b. Accounts Receivable

  c. Inventories

  d. Prepaid Expenses

  e. Accounts Payable

  f. Accrued Expenses

  g. Plant and Equipment

  h. Marketable Securities

  i. Land

  j. Long-Term Investments

  k. Common Stock

  l. Bonds Payable

4-16. Prepare a statement of cash flows in proper form using the inflows and outflows from question 4-15. Assume net income (earnings after taxes) from the 2018 income statement was $10,628, and $5,000 in common stock dividends were paid. Ignore the income tax effect on the change in depreciation.

    Statement of Cash Flow

4-17. Show whether your net cash flow matches the change in cash between the end-of-2017 and end-of-2018 balance sheets.

    Financial Statement Corrections

4-18. Fill in the missing income statement values for Edelen Enterprises:

    Income Statement Values

Sales	900,000
COGS	_____
Gross Profit	600,000
Operating Expenses	_____
Operating Income (EBIT)	400,000
Interest Expense	_____
Income before Taxes (EBT)	300,000
Tax Expense (25%)	_____
Net Income	_____

| Dividends Paid | → | **4-19.** | Oscorp Technologies' retained earnings at the end of 2017 were $8,000,000; 2018 net income was $1,500,000; and retained earnings for the end of 2018 was $8,700,000. What was the amount paid in dividends to common stockholders in 2018? |

| MACRS Depreciation | → | **4-20.** | Gekko & Company bought a new mash tun in 2017 for $385,000. The mash tun is expected to last for 12 years, but the asset falls into the MACRS 10-year class for depreciation purposes. Calculate the depreciation expense for the new mash tun that should be recorded during each of the next 10 years. |

| MACRS Depreciation | → | **4-21.** | Mortenson has purchased new equipment that initially costs $1,000,000. Setup costs are $100,000 and delivery costs are $50,000. Calculate the year 3 MACRS depreciation of this equipment, which falls into the three-year asset class. |

| MACRS Depreciation | → | **4-22.** | InGen just purchased some new machinery for $7,000,000, and they are going to use the MACRS method for depreciation. The machinery falls into the MACRS asset class of 10 years. What is the amount of depreciation for each year? |

Answers to Self-Test

ST-1. $80,000 assets − $20,000 liabilities = $60,000 equity

ST-2. Cost of goods sold = $1,500,000 Gross profit = $2,000,000 sales revenue − $1,500,000 cost of goods sold = $500,000

ST-3. $75,000 end-of-2018 accumulated depreciation − $60,000 end-of-2017 accumulated depreciation = $15,000 2018 depreciation expense

ST-4. $2,500,000 EBIT + $500,000 = $3,000,000 cash flow from operations (Dividend payments are not operating cash flows; they are financial cash flows)

ST-5. $3,000,000 end-of-2017 retained earnings + $500,000 net income − $100,000 dividends paid = $3,400,000 end-of-2018 retained earnings

ST-6. Beginning retained earnings + net income − dividends paid = ending retained earnings

Therefore:

Net income = ending retained earnings − beginning retained earnings + dividends paid

So, for Ron's In-Line Skating Corporation:

Net income = $120,000 − $90,000 + $5,000 = $35,000

ST-7. $8,000 depreciation basis × .32 (second-year MACRS depreciation percentage for a five-year class asset) = $2,560 year − depreciation expense

Analysis of Financial Statements

"It sounds extraordinary but it's a fact that balance sheets can make fascinating reading."
—Mary Archer

CHAPTER 5

Source: Fariz Alikishibayov/Shutterstock

Learning Objectives

After reading this chapter, you should be able to:

1. Explain how ratio analysis helps to assess the financial health of a company.
2. Compute profitability, liquidity, debt, asset utilization, and market value ratios.
3. Compare financial information over time and among companies.
4. Locate ratio value data for specific companies and industries.

Apple Earnings Break Records for Q1 2015

Earnings for Apple's 2015 Q1 include the last three months of the calendar year 2014, ending on December 27th. Today's earnings announcement from Apple includes a record quarterly revenue of $74.6 billion USD. Apple also announced a record quarterly net profit of $18 billion USD. That's brings on a cool $3.06 USD per diluted share for investors. Apple's gross margin was 39.9 percent this quarter. This compares to a 37.9 percent gross margin this same time one year ago. Apple is doing quite well and investors are quite happy, needless to say.

Apple is providing guidance for next quarter between $52 billion and $55 billion in revenue. The holiday quarter—the one being spoken of today—is generally the biggest and most impressive of the year for Apple.

As expected, Apple's international sales, particularly in China, were up this quarter as well. Apple announced that international sales (those outside of the USA) accounted for 65 percent of the quarter's revenue.

Revenue this quarter is up 30 percent compared to the quarter this time last year at $74.6 billion. EPS growth is up 48 percent over last year, and Apple spent over $8 billion in their capital return program. This brings investor returns to just below $103 billion. Of this $103 billion, said Luca Maestri, Apple's CFO, "$57 billion . . . occurred in just the last 12 months."

Apple generated $33.7 billion in operating cash flow during the quarter—another all-time record.[1]

Financial statements are like puzzles. When you first look at them, many questions arise. What does the picture look like? How do the pieces fit together? What is a company doing? How are they doing it? As the puzzle is assembled, however, the facts begin to surface. This is what the company did. This is how they did it. This is where the money came from. This is where it went. When the puzzle is complete, the company's financial picture lies before you, and with that picture you can make sound judgments about the company's profitability, liquidity, debt management, and market value.

Chapter Overview

In Chapter 4 we reviewed the major financial statements, the primary sources of financial information about a business. In this chapter we will learn how to interpret these financial statements in greater detail. All business owners, investors, and creditors use financial statements and ratio analysis to investigate the financial health of a firm. We will see how financial managers calculate ratios that measure profitability, liquidity, debt, asset activity, and market performance of a firm. We will then explore how financial experts use ratios to compare a firm's performance to managers' goals, the firm's past and present performance, and the firm's performance to similar firms in the industry. We will also discuss sources of financial information.

Assessing Financial Health

Medical doctors assess the health of people. Financial managers assess the health of businesses. When you visit a doctor for an examination, the doctor may check your blood pressure, heart rate, cholesterol, and blood sugar levels. The results of each test should fall within a range of numbers considered "normal" for your age, weight, gender, and height. If they don't, the doctor will probably run additional tests to see what, if anything, is wrong.

Like doctors, financial managers check the health of businesses by running basic tests—such as a financial ratio analysis—to see whether a firm's performance is within the normal range for a company of that type. If it is not, the financial manager runs more tests to see what, if anything, is wrong.

Misleading Numbers

Both medical doctors and financial managers must interpret the information they have and decide what additional information they need to complete an analysis. For instance, suppose a doctor examines a six-foot, 230-pound, 22-year-old male named Dirk. The doctor's chart shows that a healthy male of that age and height should normally weigh between 160 and 180 pounds. Because excess weight is a health risk, the numbers don't look positive.

Before the doctor prescribes a diet and exercise program for Dirk, she asks follow-up questions and runs more tests. She learns that Dirk, a starting fullback for his college football team, has only 6 percent body fat, can bench-press 380 pounds, runs a 40-yard dash in 4.5 seconds, has a blood pressure rate of 110/65, and a resting heart rate of 52 beats per minute. This additional information changes the doctor's initial health assessment. Relying on incomplete information would have led to an inaccurate diagnosis.

Like doctors, financial managers need to analyze many factors to determine the health of a company. Indeed, for some firms the financial statements do not provide the entire picture.

JPMorgan Chase faced multiple legal problems in 2013 and 2014. There were fines levied for a variety of transgressions. One of its securities traders went rogue

---

1. http://www.slashgear.com/apple-earnings-break-records-for-q1-2015-27366390/. February 5, 2015.

in 2012 and lost about $6 billion of the bank's money. In 2013 the bank paid around $1 billion in fines to various regulators for failing to provide proper oversight for this employee, who came to be called the London Whale. There were fines in the ballpark of $2 billion dollars to various regulators for serving as Bernie Madoff's bank while he conducted his pyramid scheme that cheated investors out of approximately $17 billion. JPMorgan Chase was held accountable for not providing proper oversight of Madoff's activities.

As these and other events unfolded, there was great uncertainty about what JPMorgan Chase's responsibility would be and what fines it might ultimately be forced to pay. Accountants don't incorporate such things into financial statements until the legal issues have been resolved. Everyone may know that it is very likely that large fines are going to be assessed, but since the amount is not yet known, such items don't appear in the financial statements. The (potential) liabilities do not appear on the balance sheet. Financial analysis that focuses only on the financial statements prepared according to accounting rules may give an overly optimistic impression of a company's financial health. Just as Dirk's doctor looked beyond the obvious, financial managers using ratio analysis must always seek complete information when conducting a financial analysis. In the sections that follow, we discuss ratios based on financial statements and market information.

Financial Ratios

Financial managers use ratio analysis to interpret the raw numbers on financial statements. A **financial ratio** is a number that expresses the value of one financial variable relative to another. Put more simply, a financial ratio is the result you get when you divide one financial number by another. Calculating an individual ratio is simple, but each ratio must be analyzed carefully to effectively measure a firm's performance.

financial ratio A number that expresses the value of one financial variable relative to the value of another.

Ratios are comparative measures. Because the ratios show relative value, they allow financial analysts to compare information that could not be compared in its raw form.[2] Ratios may be used to compare:

- one ratio to a related ratio
- the firm's performance to management's goals
- the firm's past and present performances
- the firm's performance to similar firms

Financial managers, other business managers, creditors, and stockholders all use financial ratio analysis. Specifically, creditors may use ratios to see whether a business will have the cash flow to repay its debt and interest. Stockholders may use ratios to see what the long-term value of their stock will be.

The Basic Financial Ratios

Financial ratios are generally divided into five categories: profitability, liquidity, debt, asset activity, and market value. The ratios in each group give us insights into different aspects of a firm's financial health.

- *Profitability ratios* measure how much company revenue is eaten up by expenses, how much a company earns relative to sales generated, and the amount earned relative to the value of the firm's assets and equity.

- *Liquidity ratios* indicate how quickly and easily a company can obtain cash for its needs.

- *Debt ratios* measure how much a company owes to others.

---

2. Financial managers who analyze the financial condition of the firms they work for act as financial analysts. The term *financial analyst,* however, also includes financial experts who analyze a variety of firms.

- *Asset activity ratios* measure how efficiently a company uses its assets.

- *Market value ratios* measure how the market value of a company's stock compares with its accounting values.

Calculating the Ratios

We will use the financial statements for the Acme Corporation presented in Chapter 4 as the basis for our ratio analysis. Figure 5-1 shows Acme Corporation's income statement for 2018, and Figure 5-2 shows its December 31, 2018, balance sheet.

Now let's analyze Acme Corporation's financial health by calculating its profitability, liquidity, debt, asset utilization, and market value ratios.

Profitability Ratios

Profitability ratios measure how the firm's returns compare with its sales, asset investments, and equity. Stockholders have a special interest in the profitability ratios because profit ultimately leads to cash flow, a primary source of value for a firm. Managers, acting on behalf of stockholders, also pay close attention to profitability ratios to ensure that the managers preserve the firm's value.

We will discuss five profitability ratios: gross profit margin, operating profit margin, net profit margin, return on assets, and return on equity. Some of the profitability ratios use figures from two different financial statements.

Gross Profit Margin

The *gross profit margin* measures how much profit remains out of each sales dollar after the cost of the goods sold is subtracted. The ratio formula follows:

$$Gross\ Profit\ Margin = \frac{Gross\ Profit}{Sales}$$

$$= \frac{\$10,000,000}{\$15,000,000} = .67,\ or\ 67\%$$

This ratio shows how well a firm generates revenue compared with its costs of goods sold. The higher the ratio, the better the cost controls compared with the sales revenues.

FIGURE 5-1
Acme Corporation Income Statement for the Year Ended December 31, 2018

Acme Corporation Income Statement for the Year Ended December 31, 2018	
Net Sales	$ 15,000,000
Cost of Goods Sold	5,000,000
Gross Profit	10,000,000
Depreciation Expense	2,000,000
S&A Expenses	800,000
Operating Income (EBIT)	7,200,000
Interest Expense	1,710,000
Income before Taxes	5,490,000
Income Taxes (25%) Combined federal and state	1,373,000
Net Income	$ 4,117,000
'Earnings per Share (4,117,000 shares)	$ 1.00
Common Stock Dividends Paid	$ 400,000
Change in Retained Earnings	$ 3,717,000

FIGURE 5-2
Acme Corporation
Balance Sheet for
December 31, 2018

Acme Corporation Balance Sheet
December 31, 2018

Assets:

Cash	$ 12,000,000
Marketable Securities	8,000,000
Accounts Receivable	1,000,000
Inventory	12,000,000
Prepaid Expenses	1,000,000
Total Current Assets	30,000,000
Fixed Assets, Gross	28,000,000
Less Accumulated Depreciation	(8,000,000)
Fixed Assets, Net	20,000,000
Total Assets	$ 54,000,000

Liabilities and Equity:

Accounts Payable	$ 3,830,000
Notes Payable	3,000,000
Accrued Expenses	1,000,000
Total Current Liabilities	7,830,000
Long-Term Debt	15,000,000
Total Liabilities	22,830,000
Common Stock ($1 par)	4,117,000
Capital in Excess of Par	16,053,000
Retained Earnings	11,000,000
Total Common Equity	31,170,000
Total Liabilities and Equity	$ 54,000,000

To find the gross profit margin ratio for Acme, look at Figure 5-1, Acme's income statement. We see that Acme's gross profit for the year was $10 million and its sales revenue was $15 million. Dividing $10 million by $15 million yields Acme Corporation's gross profit margin of .67 or 67 percent. That ratio shows that Acme's cost of products and services sold was 33 percent of sales revenue, leaving the company with 67 percent of sales revenue to use for other purposes.

Operating Profit Margin

The *operating profit margin* measures how much profit remains out of each sales dollar after all the operating expenses are subtracted. This ratio is calculated by dividing earnings before interest and taxes (EBIT or operating income) by sales revenue.

$$\textit{Operating Profit Margin} = \frac{\text{EBIT}}{\text{Sales}}$$

$$= \frac{\$7,200,000}{\$15,000,000} = .48, \text{ or } 48\%$$

Acme's EBIT, as shown on its income statement (see Figure 5-1), is $7,200,000. Dividing $7.2 million by its sales revenue of $15 million gives an operating profit margin of 48 percent (7,200,000 ÷ 15,000,000 = .48 or 48%). Acme's operating profit margin indicates that 48 percent of its sales revenues remain after subtracting all operating expenses.

Net Profit Margin

The *net profit margin* ratio measures how much profit out of each sales dollar is left after all expenses are subtracted—that is, after all operating expenses, interest, and income tax expense are subtracted. It is computed by dividing net income by sales revenue. Acme's net income for the year 2018 was $4.117 million. Dividing $4.117 million by $15 million in sales yields a 27.45 percent net profit margin. Here's the computation:

$$\textit{Net} \text{ Profit Margin} = \frac{\text{Net Income}}{\text{Sales}}$$

$$= \frac{\$4,117,000}{\$15,000,000} = .2745, \text{ or } 27.45\%$$

Net income and the net profit margin ratio are often referred to as "bottom line" measures. The net profit margin includes adjustments for non-operating expenses, such as interest and taxes, and operating expenses. We see that in 2018 Acme Corporation had just over 27 percent of each sales dollar remaining after all expenses were paid.

Return on Assets

The *return on assets* (ROA) ratio indicates how much income each dollar of assets produces on average. It shows whether the business is employing its assets effectively. The ROA ratio is calculated by dividing net income by the total assets of the firm. For Acme Corporation, we calculate this ratio by dividing $4.117 million in net income (see Figure 5-1, Acme income statement) by $54 million of total assets (see Figure 5-2, Acme balance sheet), for a return on assets (ROA) of 7.62 percent. Here's the calculation:

$$\text{Return on Assets} = \frac{\text{Net Income}}{\text{Total Assets}}$$

$$= \frac{\$4,117,000}{\$54,000,000} = .0762, \text{ or } 7.62\%$$

In 2018, each dollar of Acme Corporation's assets produced, on average, income of just over $.07. Although this return on assets figure may seem low, it is not unusual for certain types of companies, such as commercial banks, to have low ROA ratios. This is because such firms are asset intensive and therefore the denominator of the ROA ratio is large relative to the numerator.

Return on Equity

The *return on equity* (ROE) ratio measures the average return on the firm's capital contributions from its owners. For a corporation that means the contributions of common stockholders. It indicates how many dollars of income were produced for each dollar invested by the common stockholders.

ROE is calculated by dividing net income by common stockholders' equity. To calculate ROE for Acme Corporation, divide $4.117 million in net income by $31.170 million in total common stockholders' equity (see Figure 5-2, Acme balance statement). Acme's ROE is 13.21 percent, shown as follows:

$$\text{Return on Equity} = \frac{\text{Net Income}}{\text{Common Stockholders' Equity}}$$

$$= \frac{\$4,117,000}{\$31,170,000} = .1321, \text{ or } 13.21\%$$

The ROE figure shows that in 2018 Acme Corporation returned, on average, 13.21 percent for every dollar that common stockholders invested in the firm.

Mixing Numbers from Income Statements and Balance Sheets

When financial managers calculate the gross profit margin, operating profit margin, and net profit margin ratios, they use only income statement variables. In contrast, analysts use both income statement and balance sheet variables to find the return on assets and return on equity ratios. A mixed ratio is a ratio that uses both income statement and balance sheet variables as inputs.

Because income statement variables show values over a period of time and balance sheet variables show values for one moment in time, using mixed ratios poses the question of how to deal with the different time dimensions. For example, should the analyst select balance sheet variable values from the beginning, the end, or the midpoint of the year? If there is a large change in the balance sheet account during the year, the choice could make a big difference. Consider the following situation:

Total Assets Jan 1, 2018	$ 1,000,000
Total Assets Dec 31, 2018	$ 2,000,000
Net Income in 2018	$ 100,000

Return on assets based on January 1 balance sheet:

$$\$100,000/\$1,000,000 = .10, \text{ or } 10\%$$

Return on assets based on December 31 balance sheet:

$$\$100,000/\$2,000,000 = .05, \text{ or } 5\%$$

Which figure is correct? There is no black-and-white answer to this problem. Some analysts add the beginning-of-the-year balance sheet figure to the end-of-the-year figure and divide by two to get an average figure.

Logic and common sense suggest that analysts should pick figures that best match the returns to the assets or to the equity. Say that Acme purchased a large amount of assets early in the year. The middle- or end-of-year balance sheet figures would probably match the returns to the assets more effectively than beginning-of-the-year figures because assets can only affect profit if they have been used. For simplicity, we used end-of-year balance sheet figures to calculate Acme's mixed profitability ratios.

Liquidity Ratios

Liquidity ratios measure the ability of a firm to meet its short-term obligations. These ratios are important because failure to pay such obligations can lead to bankruptcy. Bankers and other lenders use liquidity ratios to see whether to extend short-term credit to a firm. Generally, the higher the liquidity ratio, the more able a firm is to pay its short-term obligations. Stockholders, however, use liquidity ratios to see how the firm has invested in assets. Too much investment in current—as compared with long-term—assets indicates inefficiency. The interpretation of liquidity ratio values depends on who is doing the analysis. A banker would likely never see a liquidity ratio value she would view as too high. Very high values might make a stockholder, on the other hand, wonder why more resources were not devoted to higher returning fixed assets instead of more liquid but lower returning current assets.

The two main liquidity ratios are the current ratio and the quick ratio.

The Current Ratio

The *current ratio* compares all the current assets of the firm (cash and other assets that can be quickly and easily converted to cash) with all the company's current liabilities (liabilities that must be paid with cash soon). At the end of 2018, Acme Corporation's current

Take Note
Do not confuse the ROE ratio with the return earned by the individual common stockholders on their common stock investment. The changes in the market price of the stock and dividends received determine the total return on an individual's common stock investment.

assets were $34 million and its current liabilities were $7.83 million. Dividing Acme's current assets by its current liabilities, as follows, we see that:

$$\text{Current Ratio} = \frac{\text{Current Assets}}{\text{Current Liabilities}}$$
$$= \frac{\$34,000,000}{\$7,830,000} = 4.34$$

Acme's current ratio value, then, is 4.34. The ratio result shows that Acme has $4.34 of current assets for every dollar of current liabilities, indicating that Acme could pay all its short-term debts by liquidating about a fourth of its current assets.

The Quick Ratio

The *quick ratio* is similar to the current ratio but is a more rigorous measure of liquidity because it excludes inventory from current assets. To calculate the quick ratio, then, divide current assets less inventory by current liabilities.

$$\text{Quick Ratio} = \frac{\text{Current Assets Less Inventory}}{\text{Current Liabilities}}$$
$$= \frac{(\$34,000,000 - \$12,000,000)}{\$7,830,000} = 2.81$$

This more conservative measure of a firm's liquidity may be useful for some businesses. To illustrate, suppose a computer retail store had a large inventory of personal computers with out-of-date Intel i3® microprocessors. The computer store would have a tough time selling its inventory for much money.

At the end of 2018, the balance sheet figures show that Acme Corporation's current assets less inventory are worth $22 million ($34,000,000 – $12,000,000). Its current liabilities are $7.83 million. Dividing $22 million by $7.83 million, we see that its quick ratio is 2.81. A quick ratio of 2.81 means that Acme could pay off 281 percent of its current liabilities by liquidating its current assets, excluding inventory.

If Acme Corporation's inventory is hard to liquidate, the quick ratio is more important. If the company being analyzed had very liquid inventory, such as a government securities dealer, the quick ratio would not be a useful analysis tool compared with the current ratio.

Debt Ratios

Financial analysts use debt ratios to assess the relative size of a firm's debt load and the firm's ability to pay off the debt. The three primary debt ratios are the debt to total assets, debt to equity, and times interest earned ratios.

Current and potential lenders of long-term funds, such as banks and bondholders, are interested in debt ratios. When a business's debt ratios increase significantly, bondholder and lender risk increases because more creditors compete for that firm's resources if the company runs into financial trouble. Stockholders are also concerned with the amount of debt a business has because bondholders are paid before stockholders.

The optimal debt ratio depends on many factors, including the type of business and the amount of risk lenders and stockholders will tolerate. Generally, a profitable firm in a stable business can handle more debt—and a higher debt ratio—than a firm in a volatile business that sometimes records losses on its income statement.

Debt to Total Assets

The *debt to total assets* ratio measures the percentage of the firm's assets that is financed with debt. Acme Corporation's total debt at the end of 2018 was $22.83 million. Its total assets were $54 million. The calculations for the debt to total assets ratio follow:

$$\text{Debt to Total Assets} = \frac{\text{Total Debt}}{\text{Total Assets}}$$

$$= \frac{\$22,830,000}{\$54,000,000} = .42, \text{ or } 42\%$$

Acme's debt to total assets ratio value is 42 percent, indicating that the other 58 percent of financing came from equity investors (the common stockholders).

Times Interest Earned

The *times interest earned* ratio is often used to assess a company's ability to service the interest on its debt with operating income from the current period. The times interest earned ratio is equal to earnings before interest and taxes (EBIT) divided by interest expense. Acme Corporation has EBIT of $7.2 million and interest expense of $1.71 million for 2018. Acme's times interest earned ratio is as follows:

$$\text{Times Interest Earned} = \frac{\text{EBIT}}{\text{Interest Expense}}$$

$$= \frac{\$7,200,000}{\$1,710,000} = 4.2$$

Acme's times interest earned ratio value of 4.2 means that the company earned $4.20 of operating income (EBIT) for each $1 of interest expense incurred during that year.

A high times interest earned ratio suggests that the company will have ample operating income to cover its interest expense. A low ratio signals that the company may have insufficient operating income to pay interest as it becomes due. If so, the business might need to liquidate assets, or raise new debt or equity funds to pay the interest due. Recall, however, that operating income is not the same as cash flow. Operating income figures do not show the amount of cash available to pay interest. Because interest payments are made with cash, the times interest earned ratio is only a rough measure of a firm's ability to pay interest with current funds.

Asset Activity Ratios

Financial analysts use asset activity ratios to measure how efficiently a firm uses its assets. They analyze specific assets and classes of assets. The three asset activity ratios we'll examine here are the average collection period (for accounts receivable), the inventory turnover, and the total asset turnover ratios.

Average Collection Period

The *average collection period* ratio measures how many days, on average, the company's credit customers take to pay their accounts. Managers, especially credit managers, use this ratio to decide to whom the firm should extend credit. Slow payers are not welcome customers. To calculate the average collection period, divide accounts receivable by the company's average credit sales per day. (This in turn, is the company's annual credit sales divided by the number of days in a year, 365.)

$$\text{Average Collection Period} = \frac{\text{Accounts Receivable}}{\text{Average Daily Credit Sales}}$$

$$= \frac{\$1,000,000}{(\$15,000,000/365)}$$

$$= \frac{\$1,000,000}{\$41,096} = 24.3 \text{ days}$$

Acme Corporation had $1 million in accounts receivable and average daily credit sales of $41,096 (i.e., $15 million total credit sales divided by 365 days in one year). Dividing

$1 million by $41,096 gives a value of 24.3. The ratio shows that in 2018 Acme Corporation's credit customers took an average of 24.3 days to pay their account balances.

Notice that, in calculating the ratio, we used Acme Corporation's total sales figure for 2018 in the denominator, assuming that all of Acme's sales for the year were made on credit. We made no attempt to break down Acme's sales into cash sales and credit sales. Financial analysts usually calculate this ratio using the total sales figure when they do not have the credit-sales-only figure.

Inventory Turnover

The *inventory turnover* ratio tells us how efficiently the firm converts inventory to sales. If the company has inventory that sells well, the ratio value will be high. If the inventory does not sell well due to lack of demand or if there is excess inventory, the ratio value will be low.

The inventory turnover formula follows:

$$\text{Inventory Turnover} = \frac{\text{Sales}}{\text{Inventory}}$$

$$= \frac{\$15,000,000}{\$12,000,000} = 1.25$$

Acme Corporation had sales of $15 million and inventory of $12 million in 2018. Dividing $15 million by $12 million, we see that the inventory turnover value is 1.25. This number means that in 2018 Acme "turned" its inventory into sales 1.25 times during the year.[3]

Total Asset Turnover

The *total asset turnover* ratio measures how efficiently a firm utilizes its assets. Stockholders, bondholders, and managers know that the more efficiently the firm operates, the better the returns.

If a company has many assets that do not help generate sales (such as fancy offices and corporate jets for senior management), then the total asset turnover ratio will be relatively low. A company with a high asset turnover ratio suggests that its assets help promote sales revenue.

To calculate the asset turnover ratio for Acme, divide sales by total assets as follows:

$$\text{Total Asset Turnover} = \frac{\text{Sales}}{\text{Total Assets}}$$

$$= \frac{\$15,000,000}{\$54,000,000} = .278$$

The 2018 total asset turnover ratio for Acme Corporation is its sales of $15 million divided by its total assets of $54 million. The result is .28, indicating that Acme's sales were 28 percent of its assets. Put another way, the dollar amount of sales was 28 percent of the dollar amount of its assets.

Market Value Ratios

The ratios examined so far rely on financial statement figures. But market value ratios mainly rely on financial marketplace data, such as the market price of a company's common stock. Market value ratios measure the market's perception of the future earning power of a company, as reflected in the stock share price. The two market value ratios we discuss are the price to earnings ratio and the market to book value ratio.

---

3. Many financial analysts define the inventory turnover ratio using cost of goods sold instead of sales in the numerator. They use cost of goods sold because sales is defined in terms of sales price and inventory is defined in terms of cost. We will use sales in the numerator of the inventory turnover ratio to be consistent with the other turnover ratios.

Price to Earnings Ratio

The *price to earnings (P/E) ratio* is defined as:

$$P/E\ Ratio = \frac{Market\ Price\ per\ Share}{Earnings\ per\ Share}$$

To calculate earnings per share (EPS), we divide net income by the number of shares of common stock outstanding.

Investors and managers use the P/E ratio to gauge the future prospects of a company. The ratio measures how much investors are willing to pay for claim to one dollar of the earnings per share of the firm. The more investors are willing to pay over the value of EPS for the stock, the more confidence they are displaying about the firm's future growth—that is, the higher the P/E ratio, the higher are investors' growth expectations. Consider the following marketplace data for Acme:

Current Market Price of Acme Corporation's Stock:	$20.00
2018 EPS	$1.00

$$P/E\ Ratio = \frac{Market\ Price\ per\ Share}{Earnings\ per\ Share}$$

$$= \frac{\$20}{\$1.00} = 20$$

We see that the $20 per share market price of Acme Corporation's common stock is 20 times the level of its 2018 earnings per share ($1.00 EPS). The result of 20 indicates that stock traders predict that Acme has some growth in its future. It would take 20 years, at Acme's 2018 earnings rate, for the company to accumulate net profits of $20 per share, the amount an investor would pay today to buy this stock.

Market to Book Value

The *market to book value (M/B) ratio* is the market price per share of a company's common stock divided by the accounting book value per share (BPS) ratio. The book value per share ratio is the amount of common stock equity on the firm's balance sheet divided by the number of common shares outstanding.

The book value per share is a proxy for the amount remaining per share after selling the firm's assets for their balance sheet values and paying the debt owed to all creditors and preferred stockholders. We calculate Acme's BPS ratio, based on the following information:

Total Common Stock Equity at Year-End 2018:	$ 31,170,000
Number of Common Shares Outstanding:	÷ 4,117,000
Book Value per Share	= $7.57

Now that we know the book value per share of Acme's stock is $7.57, we can find the market to book value ratio as follows:

$$Market\ to\ Book\ Value\ Ratio = \frac{Market\ Price\ per\ Share}{Book\ Value\ per\ Share}$$

$$= \frac{\$20}{\$7.57} = 2.6$$

We see that Acme's M/B ratio is 2.6. That value indicates that the market price of Acme common stock ($20) is 2.6 times its book value per share ($7.57).

When the market price per share of stock is greater than the book value per share, analysts often conclude that the market believes the company's future earnings are worth more than the firm's liquidation value. The value of the firm's future earnings minus the liquidation value is the going concern value of the firm. The higher the M/B ratio, when it is greater than 1, the greater the going concern value of the company seems to be. In our case, Acme seems to have positive going concern value.

Companies that have a market to book value of less than 1 are sometimes considered to be "worth more dead than alive." Such an M/B ratio suggests that if the company liquidated and paid off all creditors, it would have more left over for the common stockholders than what the common stock could be sold for in the marketplace.

The M/B ratio is useful, but it is only a rough approximation of how liquidation and going concern values compare. This is because the M/B ratio uses an accounting-based book value. The actual liquidation value of a firm is likely to be different than the book value. For instance, the assets of the firm may be worth more or less than the value at which they are currently carried on the company's balance sheet. In addition, the current market price of the company's bonds and preferred stock may also differ from the accounting value of these claims.

Economic Value Added and Market Value Added

economic value added (EVA) The amount of profit remaining after accounting for the return expected by the firm's investors.

Two new financial indicators that have become popular are **economic value added (EVA)** and market value added (MVA). These indicators were developed by Stern Stewart & Company, a consulting firm in New York City. EVA is a measure of the amount of profit remaining after accounting for the return expected by the firm's investors, whereas MVA compares the firm's current value with the amount the current owners paid for it. According to Stern Stewart, the use of the EVA and MVA indicators can help add value to a company because they help managers focus on rewards to stockholders instead of traditional accounting measures.[4] In the following paragraphs we discuss EVA and MVA individually.

Economic Value Added (EVA)

As we mentioned previously, EVA is a measure of the amount of profit remaining after accounting for the return expected by the firm's investors. As such, EVA is said to be an "estimate of true economic profit, or the amount by which earnings exceed or fall short of the required minimum rate of return investors could get investing in other securities of comparable risk."[5] The formula to calculate EVA is as follows:

$$EVA = EBIT(1 - TR) - (IC \times Ka)$$

where EBIT = earnings before interest and taxes
(i.e., operating income)

TR = the effective or average income tax rate

IC = invested capital (explained later)

Ka = investors' required rate of return on their investment (explained later)

Invested capital (IC) is the total amount of capital invested in the company. It is the sum of the market values of the firm's equity and debt capital. Ka is the weighted average of the rates of return expected by the suppliers of the firm's capital, sometimes called the weighted average cost of capital, or WACC.

To illustrate how EVA is calculated, assume Acme's common stock is currently selling for $20 a share, and the weighted average return expected by investors (Ka) is 12 percent. Also assume that the book value of debt on Acme's balance sheet is the same as the market values.[6] Also recall from Figures 5-1 and 5-2 that Acme's EBIT for 2018 is $7,200,000; its effective income tax rate is 25 percent; and there are 4 million shares of common stock outstanding.

---

4. http://www.sternstewart.com.

5. Ibid.

6. This assumption is frequently made in financial analysis to ease the difficulties of locating current market prices for debt securities. Because prices of debt securities do not tend to fluctuate widely, the assumption does not generally introduce an excessive amount of error into the EVA calculation.

The last term we need before calculating Acme's EVA is invested capital (IC). Remember it is the sum of the market values of the firm's equity and debt capital. Acme's IC is found as follows:

$$\text{Market Value of Common Equity} = 4{,}117{,}000 \text{ shares} \times \$20$$
$$= \$82{,}340{,}000$$

$$\text{Market Value of Debt Capital} = \text{Book Value}$$
$$= \text{Notes Payable} + \text{Long-Term Debt}^7$$
$$= \$3{,}000{,}000 + \$15{,}000{,}000$$
$$= \$18{,}000{,}000$$

$$\text{Total Invested Capital (IC)} = \$82{,}340{,}000 + \$18{,}000{,}000$$
$$= \$100{,}340{,}000$$

Now we have all the amounts necessary to solve the EVA equation for Acme in 2018:

$$\text{EVA} = \text{EBIT}(1 - \text{TR}) - (\text{IC} \times \text{Ka})$$
$$\text{EVA} = \$7{,}200{,}000(1 - .25) - (\$100{,}340{,}000 \times .12)$$
$$\text{EVA} = \$5{,}400{,}000 - \$12{,}040{,}800$$
$$\text{EVA} = (\$6{,}640{,}800)$$

Acme's EVA for 2018 is negative, indicating the company did not earn a sufficient amount during the year to provide the return expected by all those who contributed capital to the firm. Even though Acme had $7,200,000 of operating income and $4,117,000 of net income in 2018, it was not enough to provide the 12 percent return expected by Acme's creditors and stockholders.

Does the negative EVA result for 2018 indicate that Acme is in trouble? Not necessarily. Remember the negative result is only for one year, whereas it is the trend over the long term that counts. The negative result for this year could be due to any number of factors, all of which might be approved of by the creditors and stockholders. As long as Acme's average EVA over time is positive, occasional negative years are not cause for alarm.

Market Value Added (MVA)

Market value added (MVA) is the market value of invested capital (IC), minus the book value of IC.[8] MVA is similar to the market to book ratio (M/B). MVA focuses on total market value and total invested capital, whereas M/B focuses on the per share stock price and per share book value. The two measures are highly correlated.

For Acme in 2018:

$$\text{MVA} = \text{market value of debt plus equity} - \text{book value debt plus equity}$$
$$\text{MVA} = (\$18{,}000{,}000 + \$82{,}340{,}000) - (\$18{,}000{,}000 + \$31{,}170{,}000)^9$$
$$\text{MVA} = \$100{,}340{,}000 - \$49{,}170{,}000$$
$$\text{MVA} = \$51{,}170{,}000$$

---

7. Take note that total debt capital is not the same as total liabilities. Liabilities that are spontaneously generated, such as accounts payable and accrued expenses, are not generally included in the definition of debt capital. True debt capital is created when a specified amount of money is lent to the firm at a specified interest rate.

8. Notice that if you make the simplifying assumption (as we have been doing) that the market value of debt capital equals the book value of debt capital, then the formula for MVA becomes the market value of equity minus the book value of equity.

9. Here again we assume the market value of debt equals the book value of debt.

Companies that consistently have high EVAs would normally have a positive MVA. If a company consistently has negative EVAs, it should have a negative MVA too.

In this section we examined the key profitability, liquidity, debt, asset activity, and market value ratios. The value of each ratio tells part of the story about the financial health of the firm. Next we explore relationships among ratios.

Relationships among Ratios: The Du Pont System

As we discussed earlier, ratios may be used to compare one ratio to another related ratio. Financial analysts compare related ratios to see what specific activities add to or detract from a firm's performance.

The Du Pont system of ratio analysis is named for the company whose managers developed the general system. It first examines the relationships between net income relative to sales and sales relative to total assets. The product of the net profit margin and the total asset turnover is the return on assets (or ROA). This equation, known as the Du Pont equation, follows:

Du Pont Equation

Return on Assets = Net Profit Margin × Total Asset Turnover

$$\frac{\text{Net Income}}{\text{Total Assets}} = \frac{\text{Net Income}}{\text{Sales}} \times \frac{\text{Sales}}{\text{Total Assets}} \tag{5-1}$$

Sales, on the right side of the equation, appears in the denominator of the net profit margin and in the numerator of the total asset turnover. These two equal sales figures would cancel each other out if the equation were simplified, leaving net income over total assets on the right. This, of course, equals net income over total assets, which is on the left side of the equal sign, indicating that the equation is valid.

This version of the Du Pont equation helps us analyze factors that contribute to a firm's return on assets. For example, we already know from our basic ratio analysis that Acme Corporation's return on assets for 2018 was 7.6 percent. Now suppose you wanted to know how much of that 7.6 percent was the result of Acme's net profit margin for 2018, and how much was the result of the activity of Acme's assets in 2018. Equation 5-1, the Du Pont equation, provides the following answer:

Return on Assets = Net Profit Margin × Total Asset Turnover

$$\frac{\text{Net Income}}{\text{Total Assets}} = \frac{\text{Net Income}}{\text{Sales}} \times \frac{\text{Sales}}{\text{Total Assets}}$$

$$.076 = \frac{\$4,117,000}{\$15,000,000} \times \frac{\$15,000,000}{\$54,000,000}$$

$$.076 = .274 \times .278$$

or

$$7.6\% = 27.4\% \times .278$$

Acme Corporation, we see, has a fairly healthy net profit margin, 27.4 percent, but its total asset turnover is only .278 times its sales. The .3 total asset turnover has the effect of cutting the 27.4 percent net profit margin, such that ROA is only 7.6 percent.

We might see a low total asset turnover and high net profit margin in a jewelry store, where few items are sold each day but high profit is made on each item sold. A grocery store, however, would have a low net profit margin and a high total asset turnover because many items are sold each day but little profit is made on each dollar of sales.

Another version of the Du Pont equation, called the Modified Du Pont equation, measures how the return on equity (ROE) is affected by net profit margin, asset activity, and debt financing. As shown in Equation 5-2, in the modified Du Pont equation, ROE is the product of net profit margin, total asset turnover, and the equity multiplier (the ratio of total assets to common equity).

Modified Du Pont Equation

Return on Equity = Net Profit Margin × Total Asset Turnover × Equity Multiplier

$$\frac{\text{Net Income}}{\text{Common Stockholders' Equity}} = \frac{\text{Net Income}}{\text{Sales}} \times \frac{\text{Sales}}{\text{Total Assets}} \times \frac{\text{Total Assets}}{\text{Common Stockholders' Equity}} \qquad (5\text{-}2)$$

Notice that sales and total assets appear in both a numerator and a denominator in the right side of the equation and would cancel out if the equation were simplified, leaving net income over equity on both the right and the left of the equal sign, indicating that the equation is valid.

Solving the Modified Du Pont Equation for Acme Corporation in 2018 produces the following:

Return on Equity = Net Profit Margin × Total Asset Turnover × Equity Multiplier

$$\frac{\text{Net Income}}{\text{Common Stockholders' Equity}} = \frac{\text{Net Income}}{\text{Sales}} \times \frac{\text{Sales}}{\text{Total Assets}} \times \frac{\text{Total Assets}}{\text{Common Stockholders' Equity}}$$

$$\frac{\$4,117,000}{\$31,170,000} = \frac{\$4,117,000}{\$15,000,000} \times \frac{\$15,000,000}{\$54,000,000} \times \frac{\$54,000,000}{\$31,170,000}$$

$$.132 = .274 \times .278 \times 1.732$$

or

$$13.2\% = 27.4\% \times .278 \times 1.732$$

Examining the preceding equation, we see that Acme's net profit margin of 27.4 percent is greater than its 13.2 percent ROE. However, Acme's low productivity of assets ($.28 in sales for every dollar of assets employed) reduces the effect of the profit margin—27.4% × .278 = 7.6%. If no other factors were present, Acme's ROE would be 7.6 percent.

Now the equity multiplier comes into play. The equity multiplier indicates the amount of financial leverage a firm has. A firm that uses only equity to finance its assets should have an equity multiplier that equals 1.0. To arrive at this conclusion, recall the basic accounting formula—total assets = liabilities + equity. If a firm had no debt on its balance sheet, its liabilities would equal zero, so equity would equal total assets. If equity equaled total assets, then the equity multiplier would be 1. Multiplying 1 times any other number has no effect, so in such a situation ROE would depend solely on net profit margin and total asset turnover.

If a firm does have debt on its balance sheet (as Acme does), it will have assets greater than equity and the equity multiplier will be greater than 1. This produces a multiplier effect that drives ROE higher (assuming net income is positive) than can otherwise be accounted for by net profit margin and asset turnover.[10]

Acme's equity multiplier of 1.732 indicates that Acme has assets that are 1.732 times its equity. This has the effect (called the leverage effect) of boosting Acme's return on equity from 7.6 percent to 13.2 percent. The leverage effect, caused by debt of $22.83 million shown on Acme's balance sheet, significantly alters Acme's ROE.

For more, see 8e Spreadsheet Templates for *Microsoft Excel*.

In this section we reviewed basic ratios, and analyzed relationships of one ratio to another to assess the firm's financial condition. Next we will investigate how ratio analysis can be used to compare trends in a firm's performance and to compare the firm's performance to other firms in the same industry.

---

10. We discuss leverage in more detail in Chapter 13.

Trend Analysis and Industry Comparisons

Ratios are used to compare a firm's past and present performance and its industry performance. In this section we will examine trend analysis and industry comparison. Comparing a ratio for one year with the same ratio for other years is known as trend analysis. Comparing a ratio for one company with the same ratio for other companies in the same industry is industry comparison.

Trend Analysis

Trend analysis helps financial managers and analysts see whether a company's current financial situation is improving or deteriorating. To prepare a trend analysis, compute the ratio values for several time periods (usually years) and compare them. Table 5-1 shows a five-year trend for Acme Corporation's ROA.

As Table 5-1 shows, Acme Corporation's ROA rose substantially between 2015 and 2018, with the largest growth occurring between 2015 and 2016. Overall, the trend analysis indicates that Acme's 2018 ROA of 6.4 percent is positive, compared to earlier years.

Usually, analysts plot ratio value trends on a graph to provide a picture of the results. Figure 5-3, on the next page, is a graph of Acme's 2014–2018 ROA ratios.

The five-year generally upward trend in ROA, depicted in Figure 5-3, indicates that Acme Corporation increased the amount of profit it generated from its assets.

Trend analysis is an invaluable part of ratio analysis. It helps management spot a deteriorating condition and take corrective action, or identify the company's strengths. By assessing the firm's strengths and weaknesses, and the pace of change in a strength or weakness, management can plan effectively for the future.

Industry Comparisons

Another way to judge whether a firm's ratio is too high or too low is to compare it with the ratios of other firms in the industry (this is sometimes called cross-sectional analysis, or benchmarking). This type of comparison pinpoints deviations from the norm that may indicate problems.

Table 5-2 shows a comparison between Acme Corporation's ROA ratio and the average ROA in Acme Corporation's industry for 2018. It shows that, compared with other firms in Acme's industry, Acme achieved an above-average ROA in 2018. Only Company B managed to do better than Acme.

Benchmarking allows analysts to put the value of a firm's ratio in the context of its industry. For example, Acme's ROA of 7.6% is higher than average for its industry, thus Acme would be looked upon favorably. In another industry, however, the average ROA might be 10 percent, causing Acme's 7.6% to appear too low. Whether a ratio value is good or bad depends on the characteristics of the industry. By putting the ratio in context, analysts compare apples to apples and not apples to oranges.

Note—do not fall into the trap of thinking that a company does not have problems just because its ratios are equal to the industry averages. Maybe the whole industry is in a slump! When a ratio equals the industry average it simply means the company is average in the area that ratio measures.

TABLE 5-1 Acme Corporation ROA, 2014–2018

	2014	2015	2016	2017	2018
ROA	−1.8%	−2.2%	2.6%	4.1%	7.6%

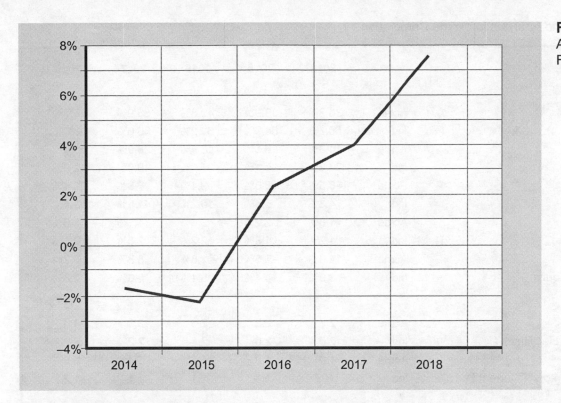

FIGURE 5-3
Acme Corporation
Five-Year Trend in ROA

Summary Analysis: Trend and Industry Comparisons Together

A complete ratio analysis of a company combines both trend analysis and industry comparisons. Table 5-3 shows all the ratios presented in this chapter for Acme Corporation for 2014 through 2018, along with the industry averages for those ratios. (The industry averages are labeled IND in the table.)

First, let's review Acme's profitability ratios compared with the industry average for 2014 to 2018. In 2014 and 2015, Acme Corporation had negative net income. This gave a negative value to the net profit margin, return on assets, and return on equity for each of these years (because net income is the numerator for each ratio). There was steady improvement, however, in the profit ratios from 2014 to 2018.

Acme Corporation had lower gross profit, operating profit, and net profit margins than the industry norm for that five-year time period except for the 2018 operating and net profit margins. For 2014 and 2015, Acme also had a lower return on assets ratio than the

TABLE 5-2 Acme Corporation Cross-Sectional Analysis of ROA 2018

Company	ROA
Acme Corporation	7.6%
Company A	1.0%
Company B	7.1%
Company C	0.9%
Industry Average	3.9%
(ACME + A + B + C) ÷ 4 = 3.9	

TABLE 5-3 Five-Year Ratio Analysis for Acme Corporation

Ratios		2014	2015	2016	2017	2018
Profitability Ratios						
Gross Profit Margin	Acme	36.2%	38.9%	42.8%	58.9%	66.7%
(Gross Profit ÷ Sales)	Ind	55.7%	58.9%	62.2%	66.0%	68.0%
Operating Profit Margin	Acme	14.3%	16.5%	18.6%	28.9%	48.0%
(EBIT ÷ Sales)	Ind	34.2%	35.1%	37.5%	40.0%	42.0%
Net Profit Margin	Acme	–8.5%	–5.8%	3.4%	7.8%	27.4%
(Net Income ÷ Sales)	Ind	4.3%	6.4%	10.2%	11.5%	13.4%
Return on Assets (ROA)	Acme	–1.8%	–2.2%	2.6%	4.1%	7.6%
(Net Income ÷ Total Assets)	Ind	1.2%	1.8%	2.2%	2.5%	2.1%
Return on Equity (ROE)	Acme	–14.6%	–7.5%	2.8%	8.3%	13.2%
(Net Income ÷ Common Equity)	Ind	3.9%	4.4%	5.1%	5.6%	7.8%
Liquidity Ratios						
Current Ratio	Acme	2.2	2.2	2.3	2.6	4.3
(Current Assets ÷ Current Liabilities)	Ind	2.0	2.0	2.1	2.2	2.2
Quick Ratio	Acme	1.0	1.2	1.3	1.4	2.8
(Current Assets Less Inventory ÷ Current Liabilities)	Ind	1.1	1.0	1.1	1.1	1.2
Debt Management Ratios						
Debt to Total Assets	Acme	81.0%	81.0%	82.0%	55.1%	42.3%
(Total Debt ÷ Total Assets)	Ind	62.0%	59.0%	57.0%	58.0%	60.0%
Times Interest Earned	Acme	1.1	1.2	1.2	1.4	4.2
(EBIT ÷ Interest Expense)	Ind	3.7	3.8	4.0	4.2	4.3
Asset Activity Ratios						
Average Collection Period (days)	Acme	33.8	31.5	30.1	28.4	24.3
(Accounts Receivable ÷ Average Daily Credit Sales)	Ind	40.2	39.8	38.4	37.3	40.0
Inventory Turnover (on sales)	Acme	0.4	0.5	0.8	0.5	1.25
(Sales ÷ Inventory)	Ind	0.6	0.7	0.7	0.7	0.7
Total Asset Turnover	Acme	0.3	0.2	0.2	0.2	0.28
(Sales ÷ Total Assets)	Ind	0.2	0.2	0.1	0.2	0.2
Market Value Ratios						
PE Ratio	Acme	—	—	80.0	36.0	20.0
(Market Price per Share ÷ EPS)	Ind	15.0	17.0	19.0	15.0	16.0
Market to Book Ratio	Acme	1.3	1.6	1.8	2.0	2.6
(Market Price per Share ÷ Book Value per Share)	Ind	2.1	2.2	1.9	2.0	2.0

industry average. As the summary analysis shows, the 2014–2018 ROAs are the result of higher asset turnover ratios.

The return on equity figures paint a telling story over this five-year period. From 2014 to 2016, Acme Corporation had a much lower return on equity than the average firm in its industry. In 2014 and 2015, these figures were negative, whereas the industry norms were positive. In 2017 and 2018, however, Acme Corporation had a much higher return on equity than the average firm in its industry.

Next, we examine the liquidity ratios. The previous ratio, 2.2 in 2014, has been rising each year through 2018, when it was 4.3. Having at least two times the amount of current assets as current liabilities is a good target for most companies. Because the industry norm for the current ratio was below the value Acme Corporation had each of these years, Acme had a comparatively high liquidity position.

The quick ratio stayed near the industry norm throughout this period until it spiked to 2.8 in 2018. This means that when inventory is subtracted from total current assets, Acme Corporation's liquidity looked steady. Again, however, 2018's value (2.8 for Acme versus 1.2 for the industry norm) suggests that the company's liquidity is solid.

Acme had a high debt load until 2017. The debt to total asset ratio was consistently above 80 percent, whereas the industry norm for this ratio was 62 percent or less from 2014 to 2017. A high debt load magnifies the changes in the return on equity ratio values.

The times interest earned ratio shows that Acme Corporation barely covered its interest expense with its operating income until 2018. The value of this ratio was slightly more than 1, except for 2018, when it jumped to 4.2.

Now let's look at the asset activity ratios. The average collection period has been significantly lower for Acme than for the average firm in its industry. It appears that Acme is doing a better than average job of collecting its accounts receivable.

The inventory turnover ratio was erratic over this five-year period. The fluctuations suggest that Acme did not match its inventory to its demand for products. The numbers suggest that Acme's managers should have studied its inventory control policies to look for ways to match demand and inventory more closely. There was a big increase in 2018. More about this in Chapter 19.

The total asset turnover ratio was consistently just above the industry norm. This helped the return on assets ratio during the years when net income was positive, as described earlier.

Finally, we turn to the market value ratios. Acme had no meaningful P/E ratios for 2014 and 2015 because net income and, therefore, EPS, were negative. The P/E ratio of 80 in 2017 shows investors had high expectations about Acme's future growth, but these expectations moderated in the next two years as the company matured. The market to book value ratio shows an upward trend over the five-year period showing that investors increasingly valued Acme's future earnings potential above the company's asset liquidation value.

We have just finished a complete ratio analysis of Acme Corporation, including examinations of the company's profitability, liquidity, debt management, asset activity, and market value ratios. To conduct the analysis, we combined trend and industry analysis so we could see how Acme performed over time and how it performed relative to its industry. Managers inside the company can use the results of the analysis to support proposed changes in operations or organization; and creditors and investors outside the company can use the results to support decisions about lending money to the company or buying its stock.

Locating Information about Financial Ratios

Ratio analysis involves a fair amount of research. Before analysts can calculate all the ratios, they must locate the underlying, raw financial data. Analysts can gather information about publicly traded corporations at most libraries and on the Internet.

Two websites where ratios and raw financial data about public companies can be found are www.finance.yahoo.com and www.morningstar.com.

Obtain a quote for the stock of the company you are interested in at either of these websites. Then drill down to "key statistics" at the Yahoo site and "key ratios" at the Morningstar site. Both have company financial statements under "financials." There is a wealth of additional financial information about specific companies at these websites. If your library subscribes to Mergent Online you will also find a wide range of financial information about specific companies there.

What's Next

In this chapter we learned how to calculate and apply financial ratios to analyze the financial condition of the firm. In Chapter 6 we will see how to use analyses to forecast and plan for the company's future.

Summary

1. *Explain how ratio analysis helps to assess the financial health of a company.*
   Just as doctors assess a patient's health, financial analysts assess the financial health of a firm. One of the most powerful assessment tools is financial ratio analysis. Financial ratios are comparative measures that allow analysts to interpret raw accounting data and identify strengths and weaknesses of the firm.

2. *Compute profitability, liquidity, debt, asset activity, and market value ratios.*
   Profitability, liquidity, debt, asset activity, and market value ratios show different aspects of a firm's financial performance. Profitability, liquidity, debt, and asset activity ratios use information from a firm's income statement or balance sheet to compute the ratios. Market value ratios use market and financial statement information.

   Profitability ratios measure how the firm's returns compare with its sales, asset investments, and equity. Liquidity ratios measure the ability of a firm to meet its short-term obligations. Debt ratios measure the firm's debt financing and its ability to pay off its debt. Asset activity ratios measure how efficiently a firm uses its assets. Finally, market value ratios measure the market's perception about the future earning power of a business.

   The Du Pont system analyzes the sources of ROA and ROE. Two versions of the Du Pont equation were covered in this chapter. The first analyzes the contributions of net profit margin and total asset turnover to ROA. The second version analyzes how the influences of net profit margin, total asset turnover, and leverage affect ROE.

3. *Compare financial information over time and among companies.*
   Trend analysis compares past and present financial ratios to see how a firm has performed over time. Industry analysis compares a firm's ratios with the ratios of companies in the same industry. Summary analysis, one of the most useful financial analysis tools, combines trend and industry analysis to measure how a company performed over time in the context of the industry.

4. *Locate ratio value data for specific companies and industries.*
   A number of organizations publish financial data about companies and industries. Many publications contain ratios that are already calculated.

Key Terms

economic value added (EVA) The amount of profit remaining after accounting for the return expected by the firm's investors.

financial ratio A number that expresses the value of one financial variable relative to the value of another.

Equations Introduced in This Chapter

Profitability Ratios:

$$\text{Gross Profit Margin} = \frac{\text{Gross Profit}}{\text{Sales}}$$

$$\text{Operating Profit Margin} = \frac{\text{EBIT}}{\text{Sales}}$$

$$\text{Net Profit Margin} = \frac{\text{Net Income}}{\text{Sales}}$$

$$\text{Return on Assets} = \frac{\text{Net Income}}{\text{Total Assets}}$$

$$\text{Return on Equity} = \frac{\text{Net Income}}{\text{Common Stockholders' Equity}}$$

Liquidity Ratios:

$$\text{Current Ratio} = \frac{\text{Current Assets}}{\text{Current Liabilities}}$$

$$\text{Quick Ratio} = \frac{\text{Current Assets Less Inventory}}{\text{Current Liabilities}}$$

Debt Ratios:

$$\text{Debt to Total Assets} = \frac{\text{Total Debt}}{\text{Total Assets}}$$

$$\text{Times Interest Earned} = \frac{\text{EBIT}}{\text{Interest Expense}}$$

Asset Activity Ratios:

$$\text{Average Collection Period} = \frac{\text{Accounts Receivable}}{\text{Average Daily Credit Sales}}$$

$$\text{Inventory Turnover} = \frac{\text{Sales}}{\text{Inventory}}$$

$$\text{Total Asset Turnover} = \frac{\text{Sales}}{\text{Total Assets}}$$

Market Value Ratios:

$$\text{P/E Ratio} = \frac{\text{Market Price per Share}}{\text{Earnings per Share}}$$

$$\text{Market to Book Value Ratio} = \frac{\text{Market Price per Share}}{\text{Book Value per Share}}$$

Economic Value Added (EVA) and Market Value Added (MVA):

$$\text{EVA} = \text{EBIT}(1 - \text{TR}) - (\text{IC} \times \text{Ka})$$

$$\text{MVA} = \text{market value of debt plus equity} -$$
$$\text{book value debt plus equity}$$

Equation 5-1. The Du Pont Formula:

$$\text{Return on Assets} = \text{Net Profit Margin} \times \text{Total Asset Turnover}$$

$$\frac{\text{Net Income}}{\text{Total Assets}} = \frac{\text{Net Income}}{\text{Sales}} \times \frac{\text{Sales}}{\text{Total Assets}}$$

Equation 5-2. The Modified Du Pont Formula:

$$\text{Return on Equity} = \text{Net Profit Margin} \times \text{Total Asset Turnover} \times \text{Equity Multiplier}$$

$$\frac{\text{Net Income}}{\text{Common Stockholders' Equity}} = \frac{\text{Net Income}}{\text{Sales}} \times \frac{\text{Sales}}{\text{Total Assets}} \times \frac{\text{Total Assets}}{\text{Common Stockholders' Equity}}$$

Self-Test

ST-1 De Marco Corporation has total assets of $5 million and an asset turnover ratio of 4. If net income is $2 million, what is the value of the net profit margin?

ST-2 Francisco Company has current assets of $50,000. Total assets are $200,000; and long-term liabilities and common stock collectively total $180,000. What is the value of the current ratio?

ST-3 If one-half the current assets in ST-2 consist of inventory, what is the value of the quick ratio?

ST-4 Sheth Corporation has a return on assets ratio of 6 percent. If the debt to total assets ratio is .5, what is the firm's return on equity?

ST-5 Mitra Company has a quick ratio value of 1.5. It has total current assets of $100,000 and total current liabilities of $25,000. If sales are $200,000, what is the value of the inventory turnover ratio?

ST-6 Yates Corporation has total assets of $500,000. Its equity is $200,000. What is the company's debt to total asset ratio?

ST-7 Pendell Company has total sales of $4 million. One-fourth of these are credit sales. The amount of accounts receivable is $100,000. What is the average collection period for the company? Use a 365-day year.

Review Questions

1. What is a financial ratio?

2. Why do analysts calculate financial ratios?

3. Which ratios would a banker be most interested in when considering whether to approve an application for a short-term business loan? Explain.

4. In which ratios would a potential long-term bond investor be most interested? Explain.

5. Under what circumstances would market to book value ratios be misleading? Explain.

6. Why would an analyst use the Modified Du Pont system to calculate ROE when ROE may be calculated more simply? Explain.

7. Why are trend analysis and industry comparison important to financial ratio analysis?

Build Your Communication Skills

CS-1. Research a publicly traded company that has a presence in your community. Assess the financial health of this company in the areas of profitability, liquidity, debt, and asset activity. Write a report of your findings. Include in your report a discussion of the strengths and weaknesses of the company, key trends, and how the company's ratios compare with other companies in its industry.

CS-2. You have just been given a job as a loan officer. It is your job to evaluate business loan applications. Your boss would like you to prepare a new set of guidelines to be used by the bank to evaluate loan requests, leading to the approval or denial decision.

Prepare a loan application packet. Include the specific quantitative and qualitative information you would want an applicant for a loan to provide to you. Explain in a brief report, oral or written, how you would use the requested information to decide whether a loan should be approved.

Problems

Profitability Ratios **5-1.** The 2018 income statement for TeleTech is shown here:

Net Sales	$35,000,000
Cost of Goods Sold	15,000,000
Gross Profit	20,000,000
Selling and Admin. Expenses	1,000,000
Depreciation Expense	3,000,000
Operating Income (EBIT)	16,000,000
Interest Expense	2,500,000
Income before Taxes (EBT)	13,500,000
Taxes (25%)	3,375,000
Net Income	10,125,000

Calculate the following:

a. Gross profit margin

b. Operating profit margin

c. Net profit margin

Liquidity Ratios **5-2.** Bob has notes payable of $500, long-term debt of $1,900, inventory of $900, total current assets of $5,000, accounts payable of $850, and accrued expenses of $600. What is Bob's current ratio? What is its quick ratio?

5-3. Weenie Hut Corporation has annual credit sales equal to $5 million, and its accounts receivable account is $500,000. Calculate the company's average collection period.

◀ Asset Activity Ratios

5-4. In 2018, Rock Bottom had sales of $35 million. Its current assets are $15 million, $12 million is in cash, accounts receivable are $600,000, and net fixed assets are $20 million. What is TeleTech's inventory turnover? What is its total asset turnover?

◀ Asset Activity Ratios

5-5. The following data apply to Bikini Bottom Corporation:

◀ Market Value Ratios

Total Common Stock Equity at Year-End 2018	$ 4,500,000
Number of Common Shares Outstanding	650,000
Market Price per Share	$25

Calculate the following:

a. Book value per share

b. Market to book value ratio

For more, see 8e Spreadsheet Templates for *Microsoft Excel*.

Problems 5-6 to 5-11 refer to the consolidated income statement and consolidated balance sheet of Tentacle Acres Company and Subsidiaries that follow.

Tentacle Acres Company and Subsidiaries
Income Statement for 2018 (000 dollars)

Sales	$ 94,001
Cost of Goods Sold	46,623
Gross Profit	47,378
Selling and Administrative Expenses	28,685
Depreciation and R&D Expense (both tax deductible)	5,752
EBIT or Operating Income	12,941
Interest Expense	48
Interest Income	427
Earnings Before Taxes (EBT)	13,320
Income Taxes	4,700
Net Income (NI)	8,620
Earnings per Share	1.72

Tentacle Acres Company and Subsidiaries
Balance Sheet as of End of 2018 (000 dollars)

Assets:	
Cash	$ 5,534
Marketable Securities	952
Accounts Receivable (gross)	14,956
Less: Allowance for Bad Debts	211
Accounts Receivable (net)	14,745
Inventory	10,733
Prepaid Expenses	3,234
Plant and Equipment (gross)	57,340
Less: Accumulated Depreciation	29,080
Plant and Equipment (net)	28,260
Land	1,010
Long-Term Investments	2,503
Total Assets	66,971

Liabilities:	
Accounts Payable	3,253
Notes Payable	—
Accrued Expenses	6,821
Bonds Payable	2,389
Stockholders' Equity:	
Common Stock	8,549
Retained Earnings	45,959
Total Liabilities and Equity	66,971

Profitability Ratios **5-6.** Calculate the following profitability ratios for 2018.

a. Gross profit margin

b. Operating profit margin

c. Net profit margin

d. Return on assets

e. Return on equity

Comment on net profit margin and return on assets ratios if the industry average for these two ratios are 5 percent and 14 percent, respectively.

Liquidity Ratios **5-7.** Calculate the following liquidity ratios for the end of 2018.

a. Current ratio

b. Quick ratio Comment on the company's ability to pay off short-term debts.

Debt Management Ratios **5-8.** Calculate the following debt ratios for the end of 2018.

a. Debt to total assets

b. Times interest earned. Would a banker agree to extend a loan to Pinewood? Explain.

Asset Activity Ratios **5-9.** Calculate the following asset activity ratios for the end of 2018.

a. Average collection period

b. Inventory turnover

c. Total asset turnover. Comment on Pinewood's asset utilization.

Modified Du Pont Equation **5-10.** Construct and solve Tentacle Acres' Modified Du Pont equation for 2018. Use the end of 2018 asset figures. Comment on the company's sources of ROE.

EVA/MVA **5-11.** a. Calculate the economic value added (EVA) for Tentacle Acres, assuming that the firm's income tax rate is 35 percent, the weighted average rate of return expected by the suppliers of the firm's capital is 10 percent, and the market price of the firm's stock is $15. There are 5 million shares outstanding.

b. Comment on your results. What does the EVA value that you calculated indicate?

c. Calculate the market value added (MVA) for Pinewood.

d. Comment on your results. What does the MVA value that you calculated indicate?

EVA/MVA **5-12.** Refer to the following financial statements for the Glove World Company.

Glove World Company
Income Statement
For the Year Ended Dec. 31, 2018

Net Sales	$11,000
Operating Expenses	3,000
Operating Income (EBIT)	8,000

Balance Sheet
Dec. 31, 2018

Assets:

Total Assets	$ 21,000

Liabilities and Equity:

Long-Term Debt	$ 6,000
Total Common Equity	$ 15,000
Total Liabilities and Equity	$ 21,000

a. Calculate the EVA for Glove World, assuming that the firm's income tax rate is 35 percent, the weighted average rate of return expected by the suppliers of the firm's capital is 12 percent, and the market price of the firm's stock is $9. There are 3,000 shares outstanding.

b. Comment on your results. What does the EVA value that you calculated indicate?

c. Calculate the MVA for the Glove World Company.

d. Comment on your results. What does the MVA value that you calculated indicate?

5-13. Refer to the following financial statements for the New Kelp City Corporation.

EVA/MVA

New Kelp City Corporation
Income Statement
For the Year Ended Dec. 31, 2018

Net Sales	$ 10,000
Cost of Goods Sold	3,000
Gross Profit	7,000
Depreciation	200
S&A Expenses	300
Operating Income (EBIT)	6,500
Interest Expense	584
Income before Taxes	5,916
Income Taxes (35%)	2,071
Net Income	$ 3,845
Earnings per Share (3,000 shares)	$ 1.28

> For more, see 8e Spreadsheet Templates for *Microsoft Excel*.

Balance Sheet
Dec. 31, 2018

Assets:

Cash	$ 350
Marketable Securities	300
Accounts Receivable	400
Inventory	680
Prepaid Expenses	200
Total Current Assets	1,930
Fixed Assets, Gross	63,000
Less Accumulated Depreciation	(42,000)
Fixed Assets, Net	21,000
Total Assets	$ 22,930

Liabilities and Equity:

Accounts Payable	$ 740
Notes Payable	630
Accrued Expenses	350
Total Current Liabilities	1,720
Long-Term Debt	6,000
Total Liabilities	7,720
Common Stock	3,000
Capital in Excess of Par	6,610
Retained Earnings	5,600
Total Common Equity	15,210
Total Liabilities and Equity	$ 22,930

The total invested capital of the firm is $33,630.

a. Calculate the EVA for New Kelp City Corporation, assuming that the firm's income tax rate is 35 percent, the weighted average rate of return expected by the suppliers of the firm's capital is 12 percent, and the market price of the firm's stock is $9.

b. Comment on your results. What does the EVA value that you calculated indicate?

c. Calculate the MVA for the New Kelp City Corporation.

d. Comment on your results. What does the MVA value that you calculated indicate?

Du Pont Equation **5-14.** The following financial data relate to Ukulele Bottom Company's business in 2018.

Sales	$ 1,000,000
Net Income	$80,000
Total Assets	$500,000
Debt to Total Assets Ratio	0.5 or 50%

a. Construct and solve the Du Pont and Modified Du Pont equations for Ukulele Bottom.

b. What would be the value of the ROE ratio if the debt to total asset ratio were 70 percent?

c. What would be the value of the ROE ratio if the debt to total asset ratio were 90 percent?

d. What would be the value of the ROE ratio if the debt to total asset ratio were 10 percent?

Financial Relationships **5-15.** From the values of the different ratios that follow, calculate the missing balance sheet items and complete the balance sheet.

Sales	$100,000
Average Collection Period	55 days
Inventory Turnover	15
Debt to Assets Ratio	.4 or 40%
Current Ratio	3
Total Asset Turnover	1.6
Fixed Asset Turnover	2.9

Assets		Liabilities + Equity	
Cash	$ 6,000	Accounts Payable	$ 6,000
Accounts Receivable	_____	Notes Payable	_____
Inventory	_____	Accrued Expenses	600
Prepaid Expenses	_____	Total Current Liabilities	_____
Total Current Assets	_____	Bonds Payable	_____
Fixed Assets	_____	Common Stock	16,000
		Retained Earnings	_____
Total Assets	_____	Total Liabilities + Equity	_____

5-16. Given the partial financial statement information from Palm Bay Corporation, a fried fish supplier, calculate the return on equity ratio.

Financial Relationships

Total Assets	$10,000
Total Liabilities	6,000
Total Sales	5,000
Net Profit Margin	10%

5-17. What is the current ratio of Barnacle Bay Corporation, given the following information from its end of 2018 balance sheet?

Liquidity Ratios

Current Assets	$ 5,000
Long-Term Liabilities	18,000
Total Liabilities	20,000
Total Equity	30,000

5-18. Atlantis, Inc., manufactures windmills. What is Atlantis' total asset turnover if its return on assets is 12 percent and its net profit margin is 4 percent?

Du Pont Equation

Use the following information to answer questions 5-19 to 5-25.

In 2018, Patrick Star opened a small sporting goods retail store called Patrick Star's Sports Stuff (PSSS). It immediately became very popular, and growth was only limited by the amount of capital Patrick could generate through profits and loans. Patrick's financial manager advised him to incorporate. His manager said that by selling stock, Patrick would have the necessary capital to expand his business at an accelerated pace. Answer the following questions relating to Patrick's Sports Stuff.

5-19. The management team at PSSS is looking toward the future. They want to maintain a gross profit margin of 50 percent. If the estimate for net sales in 2019 is $5 million, how much gross profit will be necessary in 2019 to maintain this ratio?

Profitability Ratios

5-20. Using the data in 5-19, if the management team estimated $200,000 in selling and administration expenses and $50,000 in depreciation expenses for 2019, with net sales of $5 million, what operating profit margin can they expect?

Profitability Ratios

5-21. What must net income be in 2019 if PSSS also wants to maintain a net profit margin of 20 percent on net sales of $5 million?

Profitability Ratios

5-22. What will PSSS's return on assets be if its total assets at the end of 2019 are estimated to be $20 million? Net sales are $5 million, and the net profit margin is 20 percent in that year.

Modified Du Pont Equation

5-23. PSSS management knows the astute owners of PSSS stock will sell their stock if the return on stockholders' equity investment (return on equity ratio) drops below 10 percent. Total stockholders' equity for the end of 2019 is estimated to be $15 million. How much net income will PSSS need in 2019 to fulfill the stockholders' expectation of the return on equity ratio of 10 percent?

Profitability Ratios

5-24. Of the $20 million in total assets estimated for the end of 2019, only $2 million will be classified as noncurrent assets. If current liabilities are $4 million, what will PSSS's current ratio be?

Liquidity Ratios

5-25. Inventory on the balance sheet for the end of 2019 is expected to be $3 million. With total assets of $20 million, noncurrent assets of $2 million, and current liabilities of $4 million, what will be the value of PSSS's quick ratio?

Liquidity Ratios

5-26. Given $20 million in total assets, $14 million in total stockholders' equity, and a debt to total asset ratio of 30 percent for Plankton Corporation, what will be the debt to equity ratio?

Debt Ratios

5-27. If total assets are $20 million, noncurrent assets are $2 million, inventory is $3 million, and sales are $5 million for Mr. Krabs Corporation, what is the inventory turnover ratio?

Asset Activity Ratios

5-28. If the net profit margin of Sandy Checks Hotel is maintained at 20 percent and total asset turnover ratio is .25, calculate return on assets.

Du Pont Equation

Du Pont Equation

5-29. The following data are from Gary's Escargot, Inc., 2018 financial statements.

Sales	$2,000,000
Net Income	200,000
Total Assets	1,000,000
Debt to Total Asset Ratio	60%

a. Construct and solve the Du Pont and Modified Du Pont equations for Gary's.

b. What would be the impact on ROE if the debt to total asset ratio were 80 percent?

c. What would be the impact on ROE if the debt to total asset ratio were 20 percent?

Various Ratios

5-30. The following financial information is from two successful retail operations in Bikini Bottom. Squilliam Fancyson owns Squilliam's Fancy Stuff, a lavish jewelry store that caters to the "personal jet-set" crowd. The other store, Squilliam's Cheap Stuff, is a big hit with the typical tourist. It specializes in inexpensive souvenirs such as postcards, mugs, and T-shirts.

Squilliam's Fancy Stuff		Squilliam's Cheap Stuff	
Sales	$ 500,000	Sales	$ 500,000
Net Income	100,000	Net Income	10,000
Assets	5,000,000	Assets	500,000

a. Calculate the net profit margin for each store.

b. Calculate the total asset turnover for each store.

c. Combine the preceding equations to calculate the return on assets for each store.

d. Why would you expect Squilliam's Fancy Stuff's net profit margin to be higher than Squilliam's Cheap Stuff, considering both stores had annual sales of $500,000 and the same figure for return on assets?

Various Ratios

5-31. Reef Cinema Corporation has a current market price for its stock of $40 per share. The latest annual report showed net income of $2,250,000 and total common stock equity of $15 million. The report also listed 1,750,000 shares of common stock outstanding. No common stock dividends are paid.

a. Calculate Reef Cinema's earnings per share (EPS).

b. Calculate Reef Cinema's price to earnings (P/E) ratio.

c. Calculate Reef Cinema's book value per share.

d. What is Reef Cinema's market to book ratio?

e. Based on this information, does the market believe that the future earning power of Reef Cinema Corporation justifies a higher value than could be obtained by liquidating the firm? Why or why not?

Industry Comparisons

5-32. Larry Lobster, the new financial analyst of Golden Products, Inc., has been given the task of reviewing the performance of the company over three recent years against the following industry information (figures in $000):

Year	Net Income	Current Assets	Current Liabilities	Total Assets	Total Liabilities	Sales
2016	$400	$500	$530	$3,800	$2,600	$4,000
2017	425	520	510	3,900	2,500	4,500
2018	440	550	510	4,000	2,400	4,700

The industry averages are

NI/Sales	Current Ratio	Total Assets Turnover
9.42%	1.13	2.00

Should Larry be critical of the company's performance?

Industry Comparisons

5-33. Poppy Puff, another financial analyst of Golden Products, Inc., is working with the same yearly figures shown in 5-32, but is trying to compare the performance trend using another set of industry averages:

The industry averages are

Fixed Asset Turnover	Return on Assets	Debt to Assets Ratio	Return on Equity
1.33	11.00%	0.60	26%

Should Poppy Puff be appreciative of the company's performance?

Probability Ratios

5-34. Squidward Tentacles, the financial analyst reporting to the chief financial officer of Alufab Aluminum Company, is comparing the performance of the company's four separate divisions based on profit margin and return on assets. The relevant figures follow (figures in $000):

	Mining	Smelting	Rolling	Extrusion
Net Income	$ 500	$ 2,600	$ 7,000	$ 2,500
Sales	15,000	30,000	60,000	25,000
Total Assets	12,000	25,000	39,000	18,000

a. Compare profit margin ratios of the four divisions.

b. Compare return on assets ratios of the four divisions.

c. Compute profit margin of the entire company.

d. Compute return on assets of the entire company.

Challenge Problem

5-35. From the values of the different ratios given, calculate the missing balance sheet and income statement items of National Sponge Company.

Average Collection Period	48.67 days
Inventory Turnover	9x
Debt to Asset Ratio	.4 or 40%
Current Ratio	1.6250
Total Asset Turnover	1.5
Fixed Asset Turnover	2.647
Return on Equity	0.242 or 24.2%
Return on Assets	0.145 or 14.5%
Operating Profit Margin	13.33%
Gross Profit Margin	48.89%

For more, see 8e Spreadsheet Templates for *Microsoft Excel*.

National Sponge Company Income Statement for 2018 (000 dollars)

Sales	$45,000
Cost of Goods Sold	_____
Gross Profit	_____
Selling and Administrative Expenses	_____
Depreciation Expense	3,000
Operating Income (EBIT)	_____
Interest Expense	_____
Earnings before Taxes (EBT)	_____
Income Taxes (T = 25%)	1,450
Net Income (NI)	_____

National Sponge Company Balance Sheet as of End 2018

Assets:	$
Cash	_____
Accounts Receivable (gross)	_____
Inventory	_____
Plant and Equipment (net)	_____
Land	1,000

Liabilities:	
Accounts Payable	2,000
Notes Payable	_____
Accrued Expenses	3,000
Bonds Payable	_____
Stockholders' Equity:	
Common Stock	4,000
Retained Earnings	_____

Comprehensive Problem

➡ **5-36.** Bikini Bottom Construction Company (BBCC) manufactures various types of high-quality punching and deep-drawing press tools for kitchen appliance manufacturers. Pearl, the finance manager of BBCC, has submitted a justification to support the application for a short-term loan from the Queensville Interstate Bank (QIB) to finance increased sales. The consolidated income statement and balance sheet of BBCC, submitted with the justification to QIB, follow.

For more, see 8e Spreadsheet Templates for *Microsoft Excel.*

BBCC Income Statement for 2017 and 2018 (000 dollars)

	2017	2018
Sales	$40,909	$45,000
Cost of Goods Sold	20,909	23,000
Gross Profit	20,000	22,000
Selling and Administrative Expenses	11,818	13,000
Depreciation Expense	2,000	3,000
Operating Income (EBIT)	6,182	6,000
Interest Expense	400	412
Earnings before Taxes (EBT)	5,782	5,588
Income Taxes (@ 25%)	1,446	1,397
Net Income (NI)	4,336	4,191
Dividends Paid (@ 20%)	694	671

BBCC Balance Sheet as of End of 2017 and 2018 (000 dollars)

	2017	2018
Assets:		
Cash	$ 2,000	$ 1,800
Accounts Receivable (net)	6,000	7,600
Inventory	5,000	5,220
Plant and Equipment (gross)	26,000	31,000
Less: Accumulated Depreciation	10,000	13,000
Plant and Equipment (net)	16,000	18,000
Land	1,000	1,000
Liabilities:		
Accounts Payable	2,000	2,600
Notes Payable	3,000	3,300
Accrued Expenses	3,000	3,100
Bonds Payable	4,000	4,000
Stockholders' Equity:		
Common Stock	4,000	4,000
Retained Earnings	14,000	16,620

You are the loan officer at QIB responsible for determining whether BBCC's business is strong enough to be able to repay the loan. To do so, accomplish the following:

a. Calculate the following ratios for 2017 and 2018, compare with the industry averages shown in parentheses, and indicate if the company is doing better or worse than the industry and whether the performance is improving or deteriorating in 2018 as compared to 2017.

    i. Gross profit margin (50 percent)

    ii. Operating profit margin (15 percent)

    iii. Net profit margin (8 percent)

    iv. Return on assets (10 percent)

    v. Return on equity (20 percent)

    vi. Current ratio (1.5)

    vii. Quick ratio (1.0)

    viii. Debt to total asset ratio (0.5)

    ix. Times interest earned (25)

    x. Average collection period (45 days)

    xi. Inventory turnover (8)

    xii. Total asset turnover (1.6)

b. Calculate the EVA and MVA for BBCC, assuming that the firm's income tax rate is 40 percent, the weighted average rate of return expected by the suppliers of the firm's capital is 10 percent, and the market price of the firm's stock is $20. There are 1.2 million shares outstanding.

c. Discuss the financial strengths and weaknesses of BBCC.

d. Determine the sources and uses of funds and prepare a statement of cash flows for 2018.

e. Compare and comment on the financial condition as evident from the ratio analysis and the cash flow statement.

f. Which ratios should you analyze more critically before recommending granting of the loan and what is your recommendation?

5-37. Refer to the following financial statements of Bongo Comics Group.   **Ratio Analysis**

Bongo Comic Group
Income Statements
(In 000's, except EPS)

	2016	2017	2018
Net Sales	$ 2,100	$ 3,051	$3,814
Cost of Goods Sold	681	995	1,040
Gross Profit	1,419	2,056	2,774
Selling and Admin. Expenses	610	705	964
Operating Profit	809	1,351	1,810
Interest Expense	11	75	94
Income before Tax	798	1,276	1,716
Income Tax (T = 35%)	279	447	601
Net Income	$ 519	$ 829	$ 1,115
Dividends Paid	$ 0	$ 0	$ 0
Increase in Retained Earnings	519	829	1,115
Common Shares Outstanding	2,500	2,500	2,500
EPS	$ 0.21	$ 0.33	$ 0.45

For more, see 8e Spreadsheet Templates for *Microsoft Excel*.

Bongo Comics Group
Balance Sheets
(In 000's) as of Dec. 31, Years Ended:

	2016	2017	2018
Assets:			
Cash and Equivalents	$ 224	$ 103	$ 167
Accounts Receivable	381	409	564
Inventories	307	302	960
Other Current Assets	69	59	29
Total Current Assets	981	873	1,720
Prop. Plant, and Equip., Gross	1,901	3,023	3,742
Less Accum. Depr.	(81)	(82)	(346)
Prop. Plant, and Equip., Net	1,820	2,941	3,396
Other Assets	58	101	200
Total Assets	$ 2,859	$ 3,915	$ 5,316
Liabilities and Equity:			
Accounts Payable	$ 210	$ 405	$ 551
Short-Term Debt	35	39	72
Total Current Liabilities	245	444	623
Long-Term Debt	17	45	152
Total Liabilities	262	489	775
Common Stock	2,062	2,062	2,062
Retained Earnings	535	1,364	2,479
Total Equity	2,597	3,426	4,541
Total Liabilities and Equity	$ 2,859	$ 3,915	$ 5,316

a. How long, on average, was Bongo Comics Group taking to collect on its receivable accounts in 2018? (Assume all of the company's sales were on credit.)

b. Was Bongo Comics Group more or less profitable in 2018 than in 2016? Justify your answer by examining the net profit margin and return on assets ratios.

c. Was Bongo Comics Group more or less liquid at the end of 2018 than it was at the end of 2016? Justify your answer using the current and quick ratios.

Answers to Self-Test

ST-1. Sales ÷ $5,000,000 = 4, therefore sales = $20,000,000

$2,000,000 net income ÷ $20,000,000 sales
= .1 = 10% net profit margin

ST-2. Current liabilities = $200,000 total assets − $180,000 LTD & CS = $20,000

$50,000 current assets ÷ $20,000 current liabilities
= 2.5 current ratio

ST-3. Current assets − inventory = $50,000 − (.5 × $50,000)
= $25,000

$25,000 ÷ $20,000 current liabilities = 1.25 quick ratio

ST-4. Debt ÷ assets = .5, therefore equity ÷ assets = .5, therefore assets ÷ equity = 1 ÷ .5 = 2

ROE = ROA × (A/E)

= .06 × 2

= .12, or 12%

ST-5. ($100,000 current assets − inventory) ÷ $25,000 = 1.5 quick ratio, therefore inventory = $62,500

$200,000 sales ÷ $62,500 inventory = 3.2 inventory turnover ratio

ST-6. Debt = $500,000 assets − $200,000 equity = $300,000

$300,000 debt ÷ $500,000 assets = .6 = 60% debt to total asset ratio

ST-7. Credit sales = $4,000,000 ÷ 4 = $1,000,000

Average collection period = accounts receivable ÷ average daily credit sales = $100,000

Accounts receivable ÷ ($1,000,000 annual credit sales ÷ 365 days per year) = 36.5 days

Forecasting for Financial Planning

"If you are going to forecast, forecast often."
—Edgar R. Fiedler

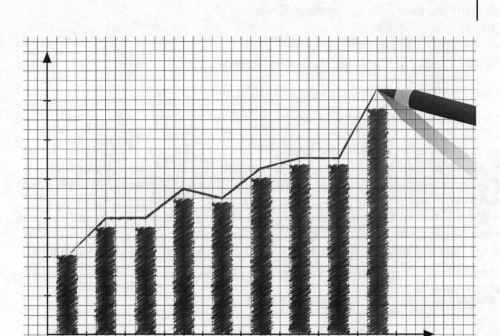

Source: USBFCO/Shutterstock

Learning Objectives

After reading this chapter, you should be able to:

1. Explain why forecasting is vital to business success.
2. Describe the financial statement forecasting process.
3. Prepare *pro forma* (projected) financial statements.
4. Explain the importance of analyzing forecasts.

What's Up with Amazon?

Amazon went public in May of 1997. The initial public offering (IPO) price was $18 per share. Warren Buffett has said he regrets not buying the stock then. Who doesn't? Amazon drastically changes entire industries with it cntcrs thcm. It started by selling books online. Physical bookstores disappeared in large numbers. People used to go to shopping malls to buy stuff. Now connecting to Amazon online, placing an order, and waiting for the delivery truck is much more common.

The company expanded into Web services, offering cloud services to other companies. It allows other merchants to sell their goods through the Amazon website. The Founder, President Chief Executive Officer (CEO), and Chairman of the Board Jeff Bezos was the wealthiest person in the world in early 2018 with an estimated net worth of over $100 billion.

If you own an electronics retail company, a grocery store, or a department store, you look at what happened to bookstores and probably shudder. If you had invested $1,000 in Amazon stock at the IPO price in 1997, by early 2018 your investment would be worth about $900,000.

What business will it enter, and disrupt, next? Financial analysts are busy forecasting sales, earnings, and other financial data for Amazon, for the companies it competes against, and for the companies it might compete against in the future.

Chapter Overview

Business owners who want to run a successful business must be able to answer many questions about the future, including the following:

- How much profit will your business make?

- How much demand will there be for your product or service?

- How much will it cost to produce your product or offer your service?

- How much money will you need to borrow, when, and how will you pay it back?

Business people must estimate the future all the time. The task of estimating future business events is daunting and darn near impossible, but in business it is necessary. Without some idea of what is going to happen in the future, it is impossible to plan and to succeed in business.

We will look first at the forecasting task, discuss why it is important, and explain what forecasting approaches business people use. Then, step by step, we will build a set of projected financial statements. We will conclude with a discussion of how to analyze forecasts to plan for the financial success of the company.

Why Forecasting Is Important

Every day you make decisions based on forecasts. When you go shopping, for example, you decide how much money to spend based on your forecast of how much money you need for other reasons. When you plan trips, you decide how much money to take along based on your forecast of the trip's expenses. You choose what to wear in the morning based on the weather forecaster's prediction of good or bad weather.

The situation is similar in business—particularly in finance. Financial decisions are based on forecasts of situations a business expects to confront in the future. Businesses develop new products, set production quotas, and select financing sources based on forecasts about the future economic environment and the firm's condition. If economists predict interest rates will increase, for example, a firm may borrow now to lock in today's rates.

Forecasting in business is especially important because failing to anticipate future trends can be devastating. The following business examples show why:

- In 2012 Disney released the movie John Carter. This very expensive movie failed to come close to covering the huge investment the company made in it. As of 2015 it is still considered one of the biggest box office bombs in recent history.

- Kodak dominated photography markets for over a century. In 2012 it filed a Chapter 11 bankruptcy petition. It had failed to navigate the transition from film to digital media. Why did this iconic photography company fail while upstart Instagram was selling itself to Facebook for $1 billion in 2012? And, in 2015, speculation was rampant that Pinterest would sell its stock to the public for billions of dollars via an initial public offering (IPO).

Firms often spend a large amount of time, effort, and money to obtain accurate forecasts. Let's take a look at some of the ways forecasters approach the forecasting task.

Forecasting Approaches

Forecasting simply means making projections about what we think will happen in the future. To make these projections, forecasters use different approaches depending on the situation. Financial managers concentrate on three general approaches: *experience*, *probability*, and *correlation*.

Experience

Sometimes we think things will happen a certain way in the future because they happened that way in the past. For instance, if it has always taken you 15 minutes to drive to the grocery store, then you will probably assume that it will take you about 15 minutes the next time you drive to the store. Similarly, financial managers often assume sales, expenses, or earnings will grow at certain rates in the future because that is how the rates grew in the past.

Probability

Sometimes we think things will happen a certain way in the future because the laws of probability indicate that they will be so. For example, let's say insurance company statisticians calculate that male drivers under 25 years of age during a one-year period will have a .25 probability of having an accident. That company insures 10,000 male drivers under 25, so the company's financial manager—based on probability figures—will forecast that 2,500 of the firm's under-25 male policyholders (.25 × 10,000 = 2,500) will have an accident during the coming year. Financial managers use probabilities to forecast the number of customers who won't pay their bills, the number of rejects in a production process, and so on.

Correlation

Sometimes we think things will happen a certain way in the future because there is a high correlation between the behavior of one item and the behavior of another item that we know more about. For example, if you knew that most people buy new cars right after they graduate from college, you could forecast new-car sales to recent graduates fairly accurately. You would base your plans on the amount of correlation between the number of people graduating and new-car sales. In a similar manner, financial managers forecast more sales for snow tires in the winter and more sales of lawn mowers in the summer.

Why Forecasts Are Sometimes Wrong

In general, forecasting the future is based on what has happened in the past (either past experience, past probability, or past correlation). However, just because something has occurred in the past does not *ensure* that it will happen the same way in the future, which is why forecasts are sometimes spectacularly wrong. No one can forecast the future with absolute precision. For example, the 9/11 attacks on the World Trade Center and on the Pentagon in 2001 were completely unforeseen.

The approaches to forecasting range from being quite simple to complex and sophisticated, depending on what is being forecast and how much the business needs to rely on an accurate forecast. In the sections that follow, we will examine some of the approaches that business people use to predict future sales and the way that finance people predict their firms' future.

Forecasting Sales

Producing a sales forecast is not purely a financial task. Estimates of future sales depend on the demand for the firm's products and the strength of the competition. Sales and marketing personnel usually provide assessments of demand and of the competition. Production personnel usually provide estimates of manufacturing capacity and other production constraints. Top management will make strategic decisions affecting the firm as a whole. Sales forecasting, then, is a group effort. Financial managers coordinate, collect, and analyze the sales forecasting information. Figure 6-1 shows a diagram of the process.

FIGURE 6-1
Sales Record, Esoteric
Enterprises

This chart shows how a company's sales forecast is developed from many different sources. Marketing data, company goals, production capabilities, and accounting data are analyzed, weighed, and combined to produce the final sales estimate.

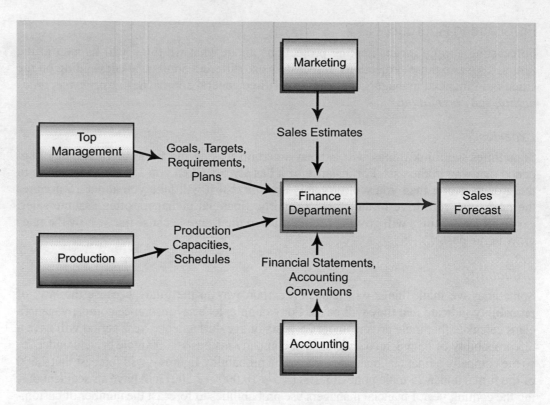

Sometimes financial analysts make a quick estimate of a company's future sales by extending the trend of past sales. Figure 6-2 illustrates this technique, with the sales record of Esoteric Enterprises, Inc., for 2016 to 2019.

The graph in Figure 6-2 shows that Esoteric's sales have been somewhat constant during the five-year period. A forecaster, by extending the past trend, would estimate that Esoteric's sales in 2019 are likely to be about $220,000. The technique of extending a past trend works well when the past trend is discernible and no outside factors, such as new competition, act to change the trend.

Forecasting Financial Statements

After the sales forecast is completed, financial managers determine whether the firm can support the sales forecast financially. They do this by extending the firm's financial statements into future time periods. These forecasted financial statements are commonly referred to as *pro forma* **financial statements.**[1] *Pro forma* financial statements show what the firm will look like if the sales forecasts are indeed realized and management's plans are carried out. By analyzing the projected financial statements, managers can tell if funds needed to make purchases will be available, if the firm will be able to make loan payments on schedule, if external financing will be required, what return on investment the stockholders can expect, and so on.

pro forma financial statements
Projected financial statements.

Budgets

Financial managers use a variety of budgets to help produce *pro forma* financial statements. Budgets contain estimates of future receipts and expenditures for various activities. Financial managers produce *pro forma* statements that assume the budget figures will, in fact, occur.

Two budgets are particularly important to forecasters. These are the cash budget and the capital budget. The **cash budget** shows the projected flow of cash in and out of the firm for specified time periods. The capital budget shows planned expenditures for major

cash budget A document that shows expected cash inflows and outflows during specific future time periods.

---

1. *Pro forma* is a Latin term meaning "as a matter of form." *Pro forma* financial statements show what the business will look like (its form) if expected events take place.

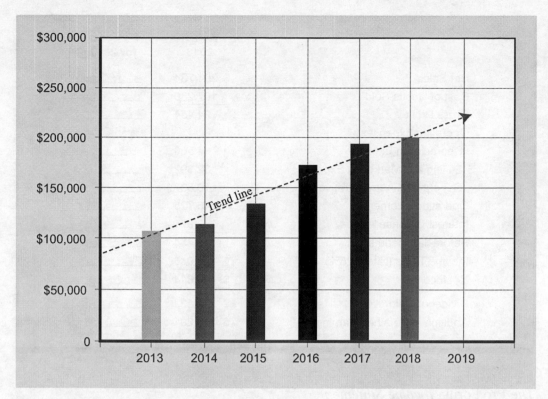

FIGURE 6-2
Sales Record, Esoteric
Enterprises

This chart shows the sales record for Esoteric Enterprises, Inc., during 2013 to 2018. Sales growth has been fairly constant during the five-year period. By extending the sales trend, an analyst might estimate Esoteric's sales in 2019 to be about $220,000.

asset acquisitions. In the sections that follow, we will see how forecasters incorporate data from these budgets into *pro forma* financial statements.

Producing *Pro Forma* Financial Statements

Now that we have reviewed the sales forecast and the budgets from which data are drawn to produce *pro forma* financial statements, we can discuss how to produce *pro forma* financial statements. In the following sections, we explore the step-by-step process of creating both a *pro forma* income statement and a *pro forma* balance sheet for Esoteric Enterprises, Inc.

Esoteric Enterprises makes one product: a rechargeable lithium battery used in industrial facilities throughout the United States to power emergency lights. The company's income statement and balance sheet for 2018 are shown in the first column of Figures 6-3a and 6-3b. We will create a *pro forma* income statement and balance sheet for 2019 by filling in the blanks in the second column of Figures 6-3a and 6-3b.

For convenience, assume that we are preparing this forecast on January 1, 2019. (Being dedicated, we have come in on New Year's Day to do this.)

Choosing the Forecasting Basis

Before we make *pro forma* forecasts of each income statement and balance sheet line item, let's consider our procedure. Unfortunately, no universal procedure applies to all line items on *pro forma* financial statements because forecasters choose values for a variety of reasons. There are three main reasons (1) management specifies a target goal, (2) the value is taken from either the cash or capital budgets, or (3) the value is an extension of a past trend. If management does not specify a target value and if no value from a budget is available, then forecasters must evaluate how the item has behaved in the past and estimate a future value based on experience, probability, or correlation, as discussed earlier in the chapter.

As we consider each financial statement item on Esoteric's *pro forma* statements, we will determine its value by seeing whether management has a target goal or whether a budget sets the value for the item. If not, we will extend the trend based on experience, probability, and correlation.

Let's begin with Esoteric Industries' *pro forma* income statement for 2019.

> **Take Note**
> Developing a cash budget and a capital budget is a complex matter. We discuss cash budgets in Chapter 18, and capital budgets in Chapters 10 and 11.

FIGURE 6-3A

Esoteric Enterprises
Income Statements

The first column in this figure shows Esoteric Enterprises' income statement for 2018. The *pro forma* forecast for 2019 will be inserted in the second column.

	Actual 2018	Forecast for 2019
Net Sales	$ 201,734	_____
Cost of Goods Sold	107,280	_____
Gross Profit	94,454	_____
Operating Expenses:		
Depreciation Expense	4,500	_____
Selling and Marketing Expenses	32,392	_____
General and Administrative Expenses	10,837	_____
Operating Income	46,725	_____
Interest Expense	2,971	_____
Before-Tax Income	43,754	_____
Income Taxes (rate = 25%)	10,940	_____
Net Income	$ 32,814	_____
Dividends Paid	$ 29,533	_____
Addition to Retained Earnings	$ 3,281	_____

The Pro Forma *Income Statement*

To prepare the *pro forma* income statement, we project the values of the following items: sales, costs and expenses associated with sales, general and administrative expenses, depreciation, interest, taxes, dividends paid, and addition to retained earnings. We will examine how to project each value next.

The Sales Projection

At the top of our *pro forma* income statement for 2019 (shown in Figure 6-3a), we need a figure for sales. Assume that our analysis of marketing, production, finance, and management information results in a sales forecast of $221,907. Enter this figure in the "Forecast for 2019" column of Figure 6-3a, as shown:

	Forecast for 2019
Net Sales	$221,907

Cost of Goods Sold (COGS) and Selling and Marketing Expenses

After sales, the next two items are cost of goods sold (COGS) and selling and marketing expenses. We do not have a management target or budget figure for these expenses, so we will forecast them based on past experience. For Esoteric Enterprises, experience suggests that over time both these items have remained a constant percentage of sales. That is, over the years, COGS has been about 53 percent of sales, and selling and marketing expenses have been about 16 percent of sales. So we conclude that in 2019 these items will be 53 percent and 16 percent of sales, respectively, shown as follows:

	Forecast for 2019
Cost of Goods Sold	$221,907 x .53 = $ 117,611
Selling and Marketing Expenses	$221,907 x .16 = $ 35,505

General and Administrative Expenses

General and administrative expenses are closely related to the size of Esoteric's manufacturing plant. For our 2019 forecast we assume that Esoteric's property, plant, and

FIGURE 6-3B
Esoteric Enterprises
Balance Sheets

	Actual Dec 31, 2018	Forecast Dec 31, 2019
Assets		
Current Assets:		
Cash and Marketable Securities	$ 65,313	_____
Accounts Receivable	13,035	_____
Inventory	21,453	_____
Total Current Assets	99,801	_____
Property, Plant, and Equipment, Gross	133,369	_____
Less Accumulated Depreciation	(40,386)	_____
Property, Plant, and Equipment, Net	92,983	_____
Total Assets	$ 192,784	_____
Liabilities and Equity		
Current Liabilities:		
Accounts Payable	$ 4,733	_____
Notes Payable	302	_____
Total Current Liabilities	5,035	_____
Long-Term Debt	37,142	_____
Total Liabilities	42,177	_____
Common Stock (35 mil. shares, $1.00 par value)	35,000	_____
Capital in Excess of Par	32,100	_____
Retained Earnings	83,507	_____
Total Stockholders' Equity	150,607	_____
Total Liabilities and Equity	$ 192,784	_____

The first column in this figure shows Esoteric Enterprises' balance sheet as of December 31, 2018. The *pro forma* forecast for December 31, 2019, will be inserted in the second column.

equipment will not change. This means that our projected value for general and administrative expenses is $10,837, the same value as in the previous year:

	Forecast for 2019
General and Administrative Expenses	$10,837

Depreciation Expense

For our depreciation expenses forecast, let us say that Esoteric Enterprises' capital budget does not include the purchase of any additional property, plant, or equipment, and that no equipment is near the end of its projected useful life. The projected depreciation expense, then, will be $4,500, the same value as it was for 2018.

	Forecast for 2019
Depreciation Expense	$4,500

Interest Expense

The amount of interest to be paid in 2019 depends on the amount of debt outstanding in that year. That hasn't been determined yet because it is part of the balance sheet forecast. At this point we have no information indicating new debt will be obtained or old debt paid off, so we will project that interest expense in 2019 will be $2,971, the same as its 2018 value.

	Forecast for 2019
Interest Expense	$2,971

Take Note
For simplicity, we use the straight-line depreciation method instead of MACRS to determine depreciation expense for 2019. As a result, we obtain a constant depreciation expense value as long as no equipment is replaced.

Chapter 6 Forecasting for Financial Planning 119

Income Taxes

Esoteric's effective 2018 tax rate, shown in Figure 6-3a, is 25 percent.[2] We assume no changes in the tax law for 2019, so to obtain income tax expense for 2019, multiply the 2019 before-tax income by 25 percent, as follows:

	Forecast for 2019
Income Tax Expense	$50,483 x .25 = $12,621

Dividends Paid and Additions to Retained Earnings

Esoteric's management plans to continue the current dividend policy of paying 90 percent of net income in dividends and retaining 10 percent in 2019. We forecast net income in 2019 as $30,290 (see Figure 6-4), so dividends paid and the addition to retained earnings will be as follows:

	Forecast for 2019
Dividends Paid	$30,290 x .90 = $27,261
Addition to Retained Earnings	$30,290 x .10 = $ 3,029

This completes our *pro forma* income statement. The results are summarized in Figure 6-4. Now let's turn to the *pro forma* balance sheet.

The Pro Forma *Balance Sheet*

Now we will create the *pro forma* balance sheet for 2019 (December 31) by examining each individual line item account. If no target value is specified by management and if no value from a budget is available, then we will evaluate the item's past performance and estimate its future value based on experience, probability, or correlation.

Cash and Marketable Securities

The forecast value for cash and marketable securities is normally drawn from the company's *cash budget*, as discussed earlier. Let's assume that financial managers at Esoteric

FIGURE 6-4
Esoteric Enterprises
Pro Forma Income
Statement for 2019

This figure shows Esoteric Enterprises' anticipated 2019 values for each income statement line item. Each forecast value was calculated separately, according to the forecasting assumptions given.

	Forecast for 2019
Net Sales	$ 221,907
Cost of Goods Sold	117,611
Gross Profit	104,296
Operating Expenses:	
Depreciation Expense	4,500
Selling and Marketing Expenses	35,505
General and Administrative Expenses	10,837
Operating Income	53,454
Interest Expense	2,971
Before-Tax Income	50,483
Income Taxes (rate = 25%)	12,621
Net Income	$ 37,862
Dividends Paid	$ 34,076
Addition to Retained Earnings	$ 3,786

---

2. We assume that Esoteric pays 21 percent of its income to the federal government and 4 percent to the state.

have prepared a cash budget that predicts the amount of cash on hand at the end of 2019 will be $71,853.

Accounts Receivable and Inventory

Experience has shown that the accounts receivable and inventory accounts tend to remain the same percentage of sales, similar to the cost of goods sold and selling and marketing expenses on the income statement. In the past, accounts receivable has been 6 percent of sales and inventory has been 11 percent of sales. Therefore, we will assume that these items will be 6 percent and 11 percent of 2019 sales, respectively, at the end of 2019:

	Forecast for 2019
Accounts Receivable	$221,907 x .06 = $13,314
Inventory	$221,907 x .11 = $24,410

Property, Plant, and Equipment

Esoteric's capital budget does not include any provision for purchasing production equipment, buildings, or land. In our income statement forecast, we assumed that in 2019 Esoteric Enterprises will not need any additional equipment, no equipment will be disposed of, and no equipment will reach the end of its useful life. Property, plant, and equipment gross at the end of 2019, then, will be the same as its end of 2018 value of $133,369. Property, plant, and equipment net will be the 2018 gross value less the additional depreciation expense ($4,500) accumulated during 2019. Here are the calculations:

	Forecast for 2019 12/31/19
Property, Plant, and Equipment (gross) (Same as 12/31/18)	$ 133,369
Less:	
Accumulated Depreciation [end of 2018 accumulated depreciation ($40,386) plus 2019 depreciation expense ($4,500)]	$40,386 + $4,500 = $ 44,886
Property, Plant, and Equipment (net)	$ 88,483

Accounts Payable

Experience has shown that, like accounts receivable and inventory, accounts payable tends to remain the same percentage of sales. In the past accounts payable has been about 2 percent of sales. Therefore, we will assume that accounts payable at the end of 2019 will be 2 percent of 2019 sales. Here is the calculation:

	Forecast for 2019 12/31/19
Accounts Payable	$221,907 x .02 = $4,438

Notes Payable

We assume based on experience and management policy that any notes outstanding at the end of a year will be paid off by the end of the following year, resulting in a zero balance in the notes payable account. Accordingly, Esoteric's notes payable value for the end of 2019 will be $0, shown as follows:

	Forecast for 2019 12/31/19
Notes Payable	$0

Long-Term Debt

We will assume that no principal payments on Esoteric's long-term debt are due in 2019, and no new debt financing arrangements have yet been made. Therefore, the long-term debt value at the end of 2019 will be the same as the end of 2018 value, $37,142.

	Forecast for 2019 12/31/19
Long-Term Debt (Same as 2018 value)	$37,142

Common Stock and Capital in Excess of Par

Esoteric's management has no plans to issue or to buy back stock in 2019. The common stock and capital in excess of par values, then, will remain the same at the end of 2019 as they were at the end of 2018, $35,000 and $32,100, respectively. The forecast follows:

	Forecast for 2019 12/31/19
Common Stock (same as 2018 value)	$35,000
Capital in Excess of Par (same as 2018 value)	$32,100

Retained Earnings

As discussed in Chapter 4, the retained earnings account represents the sum of all net income not paid out in the form of dividends to stockholders.

At the end of 2019, the retained earnings value will be the total of the end of 2018 figure ($83,507) plus the 2019 addition to retained earnings ($3,786), as shown on the income statement forecast.

	Forecast for 2019 12/31/19
Retained Earnings	$83,507 + $3,786 = $87,293

This completes our *pro forma* balance sheet. Figure 6-5 summarizes the results.

Additional Funds Needed

When the *pro forma* balance sheet is completed, total assets and total liabilities and equity will rarely match. Our forecast in Figure 6-5—in which total assets are forecast to be $198,060, but total liabilities and equity are forecast to be only $195,973—is typical. The discrepancy between forecasted assets and forecasted liabilities and equity ($2,087 in our example) results when either too little or too much financing is projected for the amount of asset growth expected. The discrepancy is called additional funds needed (AFN) when forecasted assets needed exceed forecasted liabilities and equity. It is called excess financing when forecasted liabilities and equity exceed forecasted assets. Our forecast indicates that $2,087 of additional funds are needed to support Esoteric's needed asset growth.

The determination of additional funds needed is one of the most important reasons for producing *pro forma* financial statements. Armed with the knowledge of how much additional external funding is needed, financial managers can make the necessary financing arrangements in the financial markets before a crisis occurs. Esoteric only needs a small amount, $2,087, so the company would probably obtain the funds from a line of credit with its bank. When large amounts are required, other funding sources include a new bond or stock issue.

A Note on Interest Expense

According to Esoteric's *pro forma* financial statements, the company needs $2,087 of new external financing in 2019. If it borrows the money (as we implied it would),

FIGURE 6-5
Esoteric Enterprises
Pro Forma Balance Sheets
for Dec. 31, 2019

	Forecast Dec. 31, 2019
Assets	
Current Assets:	
Cash and Marketable Securities	$ 71,853
Accounts Receivable	13,314
Inventory	24,410
Total Current Assets	109,577
Property, Plant, and Equipment, Gross	133,369
Less Accumulated Depreciation	(44,886)
Property, Plant, and Equipment, Net	88,483
Total Assets	$ 198,060
Liabilities and Equity	
Current Liabilities:	
Accounts Payable	$ 4,438
Notes Payable	0
Total Current Liabilities	4,438
Long-Term Debt	37,142
Total Liabilities	41,580
Common Stock (35 mil. shares, $1.00 par value)	35,000
Capital in Excess of Par	32,100
Retained Earnings	87,293
Total Stockholders' Equity	154,393
Total Liabilities and Equity	$ 195,973

This figure shows Esoteric Enterprises' projected end of 2019 values for each balance sheet line item. Each forecasted value was calculated separately by assessing management goals, budget figures, or past trends.

then Esoteric will incur new interest charges that were not included in the original *pro forma* income statement. To be accurate, forecasters should revise the *pro forma* income statement to include the new interest. However, if they make this revision, it will reduce 2019's net income—which, in turn, will reduce 2019's retained earnings on the balance sheet forecast. This will change the total liabilities and equity figure for 2019, throwing the balance sheet out of balance again and changing the amount of additional funds needed!

In forecasting circles, this is known as the *balancing problem*. If the forecast is done on an electronic spreadsheet, it is not difficult to recast the financial statements several times over until the additional amount of interest expense becomes negligible. In this chapter, however, to avoid repeating the forecast over and over, we will simply stay with our original interest expense figure.

Now both our *pro forma* financial statements for Esoteric Enterprises are complete. Figures 6-6a and 6-6b contain the complete 2019 forecast, including source notes explaining the reasons for each forecasted item's value.

Analyzing Forecasts for Financial Planning

The most important forecasting task begins after the *pro forma* financial statements are complete. At that time, financial managers must analyze the forecast to determine:

1. What current trends suggest will happen to the firm in the future

2. What effect management's current plans and budgets will have on the firm

3. What actions to take to avoid problems revealed in the *pro forma* statements

FIGURE 6-6A
Esoteric Enterprises Income Statements

The first column in this figure shows Esoteric Enterprises' income statement for 2018. The second column shows the *pro forma* forecast for 2019. The last column contains notes on where each line item value was obtained.

	Actual Dec. 31, 2018	Forecast Dec. 31, 2019	Source Notes
Net Sales	$ 201,734	$ 221,907	Sales forecast
Cost of Goods Sold	107,280	117,611	53% of sales
Gross Profit	94,454	104,296	
Operating Expenses:			
Depreciation	4,500	4,500	Keep same
Selling and Marketing Expenses	32,392	35,505	16% of sales
General and Administrative Expenses	10,837	10,837	Keep same
Operating Income	46,725	53,454	
Interest Expense	2,971	2,971	Keep same
Before-Tax Income	43,754	50,483	
Income Taxes (rate = 25%)	10,939	12,621	Same tax rate, 25%
Net Income	$ 32,815	$ 37,862	
Dividends Paid	$ 29,534	$ 34,076	Same payout policy, 90%
Addition to Retained Earnings	$ 3,281	$ 3,786	Net income— dividends paid

FIGURE 6-6B
Esoteric Enterprises' Balance Sheets

The first column in this figure shows Esoteric Enterprises' balance sheet as of December 31, 2018. The second column shows the *pro forma* forecast for December 31, 2019. The last column contains notes on where each line item value was obtained.

	Actual Dec. 31, 2018	Forecast Dec. 31, 2019	Source Notes
Assets			
Current Assets:			
Cash and Marketable Securities	$ 65,313	$ 71,853	Cash budget
Accounts Receivable	13,035	13,314	6% of sales
Inventory	21,453	24,410	11% of sales
Total Current Assets	99,801	109,577	
Property, Plant, and Equipment, Gross	133,369	133,369	Keep same
Less Accumulated Depreciation	(40,386)	(44,886)	2018 plus 2019 depreciation expense
Property, Plant, and Equipment, Net	92,983	88,483	
Total Assets	$ 192,784	$ 198,060	
Liabilities and Equity			
Current Liabilities:			
Accounts Payable	$ 4,733	$ 4,438	2% of sales
Notes Payable	302	0	Pay off
Total Current Liabilities	5,035	4,438	
Long-Term Debt	37,142	37,142	Keep same
Total Liabilities	42,177	41,580	
Common Stock (35 mil. shares, $1.00 par value)	35,000	35,000	Keep same
Capital in Excess of Par	32,100	32,100	Keep same
Retained Earnings	83,507	87,293	End of year 2018 + total addition to retained earnings
Stockholders' Equity	150,607	154,293	
Total Liabilities and Equity	$ 192,784	$ 195,973	2019 AFN = 2,087

When analyzing the *pro forma* statements, financial managers often see signs of emerging positive or negative conditions. If forecasters discover positive indicators, they will recommend that management continue its current plans. If forecasters see negative indicators, they will recommend corrective action.

To illustrate, let's see how Esoteric Enterprises' financial managers would analyze the company's *pro forma* financial statements and plan for the future.

Scanning the first column in Figure 6-6a, we calculate Esoteric Enterprises' 2018 net profit margin (net income divided by sales) as follows:

$$\text{Current Net Profit Margin} = \$32,815 / \$201,734 = .163 \text{ or } 16.3\%$$

Using the figures from the *pro forma* forecast (see Figure 6-6a, column 2), Esoteric's forecasted net profit margin in 2019 is as follows:

$$\text{Forecasted Net Profit Margin} = \$37,862 / \$221,907 = .171 \text{ or } 17.1\%$$

The expected increase in the net profit margin from 16.3 percent to 17.1 percent is a desirable trend, so Esoteric's financial managers will probably recommend that the business maintain its current course of action.

However, if the analysis had shown a projected decline in the net profit margin to, say, 11 percent, the financial managers would try to determine the cause of this decline (perhaps administrative expenses are too high or asset productivity is too low). After the financial managers found the cause, they would recommend appropriate corrective action. Once the company adjusted its plans to correct the problem, the financial managers would prepare a new set of *pro forma* financial statements that reflected the changes.

We presented a brief example to illustrate the process of analyzing *pro forma* financial statements. A complete analysis would involve calculating profitability ratios, asset productivity ratios, liquidity ratios, and debt management ratios, as described in Chapter 5.

What's Next

In this chapter we described forecasting and prepared *pro forma* statements. In Chapter 7, we turn to the risk/return relationship, one of the key concepts of finance.

Summary

1. *Explain why forecasting is vital to business success.*
   Business planning is based on forecasts of the company's future financial performance. Without forecasting, a business cannot succeed. Incorrect forecasts can be costly—so costly, in some cases, that the mistakes lead to failure.

2. *Describe the financial statement forecasting process.*
   Forecasting means making assumptions about what will happen in the future. The three main approaches to making these assumptions are
   * Experience. We assume things will happen a certain way in the future because they have happened that way in the past.

* Probability. We assume things will happen a certain way in the future because the laws of probability indicate that they will be so.
* Correlation. We assume things will happen a certain way in the future because of a high correlation between the thing we are interested in and another thing we know more about.

Financial managers use the sales forecast, a variety of budgets, and past trend information to produce financial statements for periods in the future. These projected financial statements are *pro forma* financial statements. *Pro forma* financial statements show what assets, liabilities, and equity a firm is expected to have in the future.

3. *Prepare* pro forma *(projected) financial statements.*
   Pro forma financial statements are based on a company's current financial statements. The forecasted value of each current financial statement line item is determined by a target specified by management, a value extracted from a budget, or an extension of a past trend. In *pro forma* financial statement preparation, no general rule can be applied universally to all line items. Instead, each item must be examined individually. If no target value is specified by management and if no value from a budget is available, then forecasters must evaluate the past performance of the account and estimate a future value based on experience, probability, or correlation.

   On the *pro forma* balance sheet, the forecasted values for total assets and total liabilities and equity rarely match. When forecasted assets exceed forecasted liabilities and equity, the difference is called additional funds needed (AFN). When forecasted liabilities and equity exceed forecasted assets, the difference is called excess financing. Additional funds needed is the additional external financing required to support projected asset growth. Excess financing means that too much funding has been set aside for expected asset growth.

4. *Explain the importance of analyzing forecasts.*
   Once the *pro forma* financial statements are complete, financial managers must analyze them to determine if the company should continue with its current plans (as in the case of *pro forma* statements that show a growth in revenues), or if plans need to be modified to avoid problems in the future. Financial managers analyze the *pro forma* statements by using the ratio analysis techniques described in Chapter 5.

Key Terms

cash budget A document that shows expected cash inflows and outflows during specific future time periods.

pro forma **financial statements** Projected financial statements.

Self-Test

ST-1. For the last five years, cost of goods sold (COGS) for Initech Corporation has averaged 60 percent of sales. This trend is expected to continue for the foreseeable future. If sales for 2019 are expected to be $2.5 million, what would be the forecast 2019 value for COGS?

ST-2. In 2018 the Initech Corporation had $180,000 in retained earnings. During 2019, the company expects net income to be $750,000. What will the value of retained earnings be on the company's *pro forma* balance sheet for Dec. 31, 2019, if the company continues its policy of paying 50 percent of net income in dividends?

ST-3. The Globex Company's *pro forma* balance sheet for Dec. 31, 2019, indicates that total assets will be $8,420,000, but total liabilities and equity will be only $7,685,000. What should CFO Hank Scorpio do to resolve Globex's discrepancy between its assets and liabilities?

ST-4. Refer to the *pro forma* financial statements for Esoteric Enterprises, Figures 6-6a and 6-6b. Calculate Esoteric's return on equity (ROE) ratio for 2018 and 2019. Comment on the results.

Review Questions

1. Why do businesses spend time, effort, and money to produce forecasts?

2. What is the primary assumption behind the experience approach to forecasting?

3. Describe the sales forecasting process.

4. Explain how the cash budget and the capital budget relate to *pro forma* financial statement preparation.

5. Explain how management goals are integrated into *pro forma* financial statements.

6. Explain the significance of the term additional funds needed.

7. What do financial managers look for when they analyze *pro forma* financial statements?

8. What action(s) should be taken if analysis of *pro forma* financial statements reveals positive trends? Negative trends?

Build Your Communication Skills

CS-1. Refer to the current and *pro forma* financial statements for Esoteric Enterprises in Figures 6-6a and 6-6b. Analyze the financial statements using the techniques in Chapter 5 and prepare a report of Esoteric's strengths and weaknesses.

CS-2. Form small groups of four to six. Based on each group member's assessment of Esoteric's strengths and weaknesses, discuss whether Esoteric should change its business plans and how. Once the group has prepared a strategy, select a spokesperson to report the group's conclusions to the class.

Problems

6-1. Miniver Corporation grows flowers and sells them to major U.S. retail flower shops. Mrs. Miniver has asked you to prepare a forecast of expected future sales. The chart below shows the Miniver Corporation's sales record for the last six years. Make an estimate of 2019 sales by extending the trend. Justify your estimate to Mrs. Miniver.

◀ **Sales Forecast**

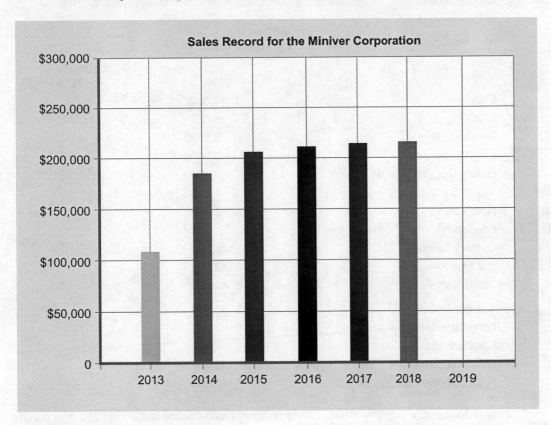

6-2. Complete the following *pro forma* financial statements. Use the forecasting assumptions in the far right-hand column.

◀ **Additional Funds Needed**

	This Year	Next Year	Forecasting Assumption
Sales	100	_____	Sales will grow 20%
Variable Costs	50	_____	Constant % of sales
Fixed Costs	40	_____	Remains same
Net Income	10	_____	
Dividends	5	_____	Keep 50% payout ratio
Current Assets	60	_____	Constant % of sales
Fixed Assets	100	_____	Remains same
Total Assets	160	_____	
Current Liabilities	20	_____	Constant % of sales
Long-Term Debt	20	_____	Remains same
Common Stock	20	_____	Remains same
Retained Earnings	100	_____	
Total Liabilities and Equity	160	_____	
		AFN = _____	

6-3. Vinny's Pizza has just come out with a new pizza that Joe is sure will cause sales to double between 2018 and 2019. Using the following worksheet, complete Vinny's *pro forma* financial forecast and answer the related questions.

You may assume that COGS, current assets, and current liabilities will maintain the same percentage of sales as in 2018. Furthermore, you may assume that no new fixed assets will be needed in 2019, and the current dividend policy will be continued in 2019.

Vinny's Pizza, Inc.
Financial Status and Forecast

	2018	Estimate for 2019
Sales	$ 10,000	
COGS	4,000	
Gross Profit	6,000	
Fixed Expenses	3,000	
Before-Tax Profit	3,000	
Tax @ 33.33%	1,000	
Net Profit	$ 2,000	
Dividends	$ 0	
Current Assets	$ 25,000	
Net Fixed Assets	15,000	
Total Assets	$ 40,000	
Current Liabilities	$ 17,000	
Long-Term Debt	3,000	
Common Stock	7,000	
Retained Earnings	13,000	
Total Liabilities and Equity	$ 40,000	

Will Joe be able to get by without any additional funds needed in 2019? If not, how much will he need?

6-4. Jose Tine owns Sugar Cane Alley, a small candy shop in Aspen, Colorado. He would like to expand his business and open a second store in Vail. Mr. Tine does not have the capital to undertake this project and would like to borrow the money from the local bank. He knows the banker will need projected income statement data for his current store when considering his loan application. Net sales for 2018 were $90,000. Considering previous growth rates in his business and the anticipated increase in tourism, projected net sales for 2019 are $110,000. Answer the questions based on the following assumptions. Cost of goods sold and selling and marketing expenses will remain the same percentage of sales as in 2018. General and administration expenses will remain the same value as 2018 at $5,000. Mr. Tine uses the straight-line method of depreciation, so last year's depreciation expense figure of $2,000 can also be applied to 2019.

a. 2018 cost of goods sold was $48,000. What is the forecasted value of cost of goods sold for 2019?

b. What is the forecasted gross profit for 2019?

c. Selling and marketing expenses for 2018 were $13,000. What is the forecasted value for 2019?

d. Calculate the forecasted operating income for 2019.

e. Assume the interest expense for 2019 will be $800 and the tax rate is 30 percent. Calculate earnings before taxes (EBT) and net income expected for 2019 to the nearest dollar.

f. If $10,000 is distributed in dividends in 2019, what will be 2019's addition to retained earnings?

6-5. After completing the *pro forma* income statement in problem 6-4, Mr. Tine now realizes he should also complete a *pro forma* balance sheet. Net sales in 2018 were $90,000 and his forecasted sales for 2019 are $110,000. All of Sugar Cane Alley's current assets will remain the same percentage of sales as they were in 2018. Mr. Tine does not plan to buy or sell any equipment, so his gross property and equipment amount will remain the same as 2018. In the liabilities and equity section, only accounts payable will remain the same percentage of sales as in 2018. Except for retained earnings, the other accounts are expected to remain the same value as 2018. The following balances were taken from Sugar Cane Alley's end-of-2018 balance sheet:

Cash	$10,000
Accounts Receivable	2,220
Inventory	8,000
Property and Equipment (gross)	25,000
Accumulated Depreciation	4,000
Property and Equipment (net)	21,000
Accounts Payable	1,380
Long-Term Notes Payable	8,000
Retained Earnings	5,000
Common Stock	26,840

a. Calculate the forecasted end-of-2019 values for each of the current asset accounts.

b. Depreciation expense for 2019 is estimated to be $2,000. Calculate the estimated total assets for the end of 2019.

c. Forecast the accounts payable for the end of 2019.

d. What will total liabilities be at the end of 2019?

e. Assuming the forecasted net income for 2019 is $19,351 and cash dividends paid equal $10,000, what total will be forecasted for the end-of-2019 total liabilities and equity?

f. Based on these calculations of the *pro forma* balance sheet, are additional funds needed?

g. Net income for 2018 was $14,840. What was Sugar Cane Alley's net profit margin for 2018? The forecasted net income for 2019 is $19,351. What is Sugar Cane Alley's forecasted 2019 net profit margin?

6-6.

Bluth, Inc.
Balance Sheet, Dec. 31, 2018

Assets		Liabilities + Equity	
Cash	$10,000	Accounts Payable	$10,500
Acct. Rec.	25,000	Notes Payable	10,000
Inventory	20,000	Accrued Expenses	11,000
Prepaid Exp.	2,000	Long-Term Debt	15,000
Total Current Assets	57,000	Common Equity	38,500
Fixed Assets	32,000	Total Liabilities and Equity	85,000
Accum. Dep.	4,000		
Total Assets	85,000		

Bluth's net sales for 2018 were $150 million. Sales growth is expected to be 25 percent in 2019, and all current asset and current liability accounts will have the same percentage of sales as in 2018. Net fixed assets will remain the same dollar amount. There is a 100 percent dividend payout ratio. Prepare a *pro forma* balance sheet for 2019.

➡ 6-7. Fill in the missing values of the *pro forma* income statement for 2019. Sales will increase by 25 percent and the dividend payouts will increase from 40 percent to 55 percent. Variable costs will be 5 percentage points less than the original percentage of sales.

	2018	2019
Sales	1,000	_____
Variable Costs	500	_____
Fixed Costs	160	_____
Net Income	340	_____
Dividends	136	_____

➡ 6.8. The balance sheet of Free Enterprises, Inc., at the end of 2018 follows.

**Free Enterprises, Inc.
Balance Sheet, Dec. 31, 2018
(Thousands of Dollars)**

Assets		Liabilities + Equity	
Cash	$ 4,000	Accounts Payable	$ 4,400
Accounts Receivable	10,000	Notes Payable	4,000
Inventory	13,000	Accrued Expenses	5,000
Prepaid Expenses	400	Total Current Liabilities	13,400
Total Current Assets	27,400	Bonds Payable	6,000
Fixed Assets	11,000	Common Equity	19,000
Total Assets	$ 38,400	Total Liabilities and Equity	$ 38,400

Net sales for 2018 were $85,000,000. The average annual sales growth rate is expected to be 10 percent every year for the next three years. Over the past several years the earnings before taxes (EBT) were 11 percent of net sales and are expected to remain the same over the next three years. The company's tax rate is 25 percent, and it plans to maintain the dividend payout ratio (dividends paid/net income) at 60 percent.

Prepare a *pro forma* balance sheet for Free Enterprises, Inc., for December 31, 2019. Assume the accounts that are not a function of sales (fixed assets, notes payable, and bonds payable) remain the same as they were in 2018. Current assets and current liabilities will remain the same percentage of sales as in 2018. Assume the only change to common equity is for the addition to retained earnings.

➡ 6-9. Consider the current and *pro forma* financial statements that follow.

	2018	2019
Sales	200	220
Variable Costs	100	110
Fixed Costs	80	80
Net Income	20	30
Dividends	10	22
Current Assets	120	132
Fixed Assets	200	200
Total Assets	320	332
Current Liabilities	40	44
Long-Term Debt	40	40
Common Stock	40	40
Retained Earnings	200	208
Total Liabilities and Equity	320	332
		AFN = 0

Compute the following ratios for 2018 and 2019:

	2018	2019
Current Ratio	___	___
Debt to Assets Ratio	___	___
Sales to Assets Ratio	___	___
Net Profit Margin	___	___
Return on Assets	___	___
Return on Equity	___	___

Comment on any trends revealed by your ratio analysis.

6-10. 1. Develop a *pro forma* income statement and balance sheet for the White & Pinkman Corporation. The company's 2018 financial statements are shown below. Base your forecast on the financial statements and the following assumptions:

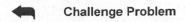 **Challenge Problem**

- Sales growth is predicted to be 20 percent in 2019.

- Cost of goods sold, selling and administrative expense, all current assets, accounts payable, and accrued expenses will remain the same percentage of sales as in 2018.

For more, see 8e Spreadsheet Templates for *Microsoft Excel*.

- Depreciation expense, interest expense, gross plant and equipment, notes payable, long-term debt, and equity accounts other than retained earnings in 2019 will be the same as in 2018.

- The company's tax rate in 2019 will be 40 percent.

- The same dollar amount of dividends will be paid to common stockholders in 2019 as in 2018.

- Bad debt allowance in 2019 will be the same percentage of accounts receivable as it was in 2018.

White & Pinkman Corporation
Income Statement for 2018

Sales	$ 10,000,000
Cost of Goods Sold	4,000,000
Gross Profit	6,000,000
Selling and Administrative Expenses	800,000
Depreciation Expense	2,000,000
Earnings before Interest and Taxes (EBIT)	3,200,000
Interest Expense	1,350,000
Earnings before Taxes (EBT)	1,850,000
Taxes (40%)	740,000
Net Income (NI)	1,110,000
Earnings per Share (EPS) (1 million shares)	$ 1.11
Common Stock Dividends Paid	400,000
Addition to Retained Earnings	710,000

White & Pinkman Corporation
Balance Sheet Dec. 31, 2018

Assets:

Current Assets:

Cash	$ 9,000,000
Marketable Securities	8,000,000
Accounts Receivable (Net)	1,000,000
Inventory	20,000,000
Prepaid Expenses	1,000,000
Total Current Assets	$ 39,000,000
Fixed Assets:	11,000,000
Plant and Equipment (Gross)	20,000,000
Less Accumulated Depreciation	(9,000,0000)
Plant and Equipment (Net)	11,000,000
Total Assets	$ 50,000,000

Liabilities and Equity:

Current Liabilities:

Accounts Payable	$ 12,000,000
Notes Payable	5,000,000
Accrued Expenses	3,000,000
Total Current Liabilities	$ 20,000,000
Bonds Payable (5%, due 2035)	20,000,000
Total Liabilities	$ 40,000,000
Common Stock (1 mil. shares, $1 par)	1,000,000
Capital in Excess of Par	4,000,000
Retained Earnings	5,000,000
Total Equity	10,000,000
Total Liabilities and Equity	$ 50,000,000

2. a. Calculate White & Pinkman's additional funds needed, or excess financing. If additional funds are needed, add them to long-term debt to bring the balance sheet into balance. If excess financing is available, increase common stock dividends paid (and, therefore, decrease 2019 retained earnings) until the balance sheet is in balance.

   b. Calculate White & Pinkman's current ratio for the end of 2018 and 2019.

   c. Calculate White & Pinkman's total asset turnover and inventory turnover ratios for 2019.

   d. Calculate White & Pinkman's total debt to total assets ratio for 2018 and 2019. Assume there has been no additional long-term debt issued in 2019.

   e. Calculate White & Pinkman's net profit margin, return on assets, and return on equity ratios for 2018 and 2019.

3. Comment on White & Pinkman's liquidity, asset productivity, debt management, and profitability based on the results of your ratio analysis in 2b through 2e.

4. What recommendations would you provide to management based on your forecast and analysis?

ST-1. If COGS is expected to remain 60 percent of sales, then in 2019 COGS will be 60 percent of 2010's sales:

$$60 \times \$2,500,000 = \$1,500,000$$

ST-2. If Initech earns $750,000 in 2019 and pays 50 percent of it to stockholders as dividends, then the other 50 percent, or $375,000, will be retained and added to the existing retained earnings account. Therefore, retained earnings on Ishtar's December 31, 2019, *pro forma* balance sheet will be

$$\$180,000 + \$375,000 = \$555,000$$

ST-3. Globex's total liabilities and equity are forecast to be $735,000 less than total assets. This means Globex must arrange for $735,000 in additional financing to support expected asset growth. Possible sources of this financing include bank loans, a bond issue, a stock issue, or perhaps lowering the 2019 dividend (if any).

ST-4.

$$ROE = \frac{Net\ Income}{Common\ Equity}$$

For Esoteric in 2018 (from the 2018 financial statements):

$$ROE = \frac{\$26,252}{\$150,607} = .174,\ or\ 17.4\%$$

For Esoteric in 2019 (from the 2019 *pro forma* financial statements):

$$ROE = \frac{\$30,290}{\$153.636} = .197,\ or\ 19.7\%$$

Note that this is a favorable forecast. The gain of over two percentage points in an already respectable ROE value should be particularly pleasing to the stockholders. Esoteric's financial managers should recommend that the company continue with its current plans, assuming that the increase in ROE does not signal an excessive increase in risk.

> **Take Note**
> Remember that risk and return go hand in hand. The financial managers at Esoteric Enterprises must evaluate the risk associated with the ROE figures before concluding that current plans will lead to desirable results.

Risk and Return

"Take calculated risks. This is quite different from being rash."
—General George S. Patton

Source: ProMediaC/Shutterstock

Learning Objectives

After reading this chapter, you should be able to:

1. Define risk, risk aversion, and the risk-return relationship.
2. Measure risk using the standard deviation and coefficient of variation.
3. Identify the types of risk that business firms encounter.
4. Explain methods of risk reduction.
5. Describe how firms compensate for assuming risk.
6. Explain how the capital asset pricing model (CAPM) relates risk and return.

Are You the "Go-for-It" Type?

The Financial Crisis had people buzzing about "systematic risk." This term means different things in different contexts. Traditionally, systematic risk has referred to the non-diversifiable risk that comes from the impact the overall market has on individual investments. This risk is also known as "market risk" according to the Capital Asset Pricing Model (CAPM) described in this chapter.

With the Financial Crisis, however, people have been using the term systematic risk in a somewhat different way. Many companies, especially financial firms, are connected to each other in significant ways. With a financial instrument known as a swap, for example, one company may have a contract with another company that calls for large payments to be made by one to the other according to specified terms. If the company that is obligated to pay does not, then the company that was supposed to receive the funds might fail. If that company that was supposed to receive the funds fails, then other companies that it owed money to according to other swaps might also fail. This chain reaction of default, failure, default, failure could affect a large number of firms. The larger the firm, the more such relationships it is likely to have and the greater the chain reaction failures that may occur. This is the systematic risk the government is concerned about now.

Systematic risk is why the prestigious Wall Street firm Lehman Brothers declared bankruptcy. The same is true about mortgage giants Fannie Mae and Freddie Mac. Systematic risk led to Wall Street icon Merrill Lynch selling itself at a fire sale price to Bank of America. In May of 2012 JPMorgan Chase lost $6 billion on trades that had been designed to reduce risk the bank had been facing. Using what are called synthetic credit securities the intent had been to create a "hedge" that would reduce the risk this huge bank was facing. In this case an attempt to reduce a risk created a risk instead. The fear of systematic risk is why the federal government pumped billions of dollars into the insurance giant AIG. In 2012 the risk that the economic and financial difficulties in Greece would spread throughout Europe and the rest of the world became a major concern.

This kind of systematic risk clearly has the potential to do great harm. This is part of the overall examination of risk conducted in this chapter.

Chapter Overview

Business firms face risk in nearly everything they do. Assessing risk is one of the most important tasks financial managers perform. The events of recent years have made this painfully obvious. In this chapter we will discuss *risk, risk aversion*, and the *risk-return relationship*. We will measure risk using *standard deviation* and the *coefficient of variation*. We will identify types of risk and examine ways to reduce risk exposure or compensate for risk. Finally, we will see how the capital asset pricing model (CAPM) explains the risk-return relationship.

Risk

The world is a risky place. For instance, if you get out of bed in the morning and go to class, you run the risk of getting hit by a bus. If you stay in bed to minimize the chance of getting run over by a bus, you run the risk of getting coronary artery disease because of a lack of exercise. In everything we do—or don't do—there is a chance that something will happen that we didn't expect. Risk is the potential for unexpected events to occur.

Risk Aversion

Most people try to avoid risks if possible. Risk aversion doesn't mean that some people don't enjoy risky activities, such as skydiving, rock climbing, or automobile racing. In a financial setting, however, evidence shows that most people avoid risk when possible, unless there is a higher expected rate of return to compensate for the risk. Faced with financial alternatives that are equal except for their degree of risk, most people will choose the less risky alternative.

Risk aversion is the tendency to avoid additional risk. Risk-averse people will avoid risk if they can, unless they receive additional compensation for assuming that risk. In finance, the added compensation is a higher expected rate of return.

The Risk-Return Relationship

risk-return relationship
The positive relationship between the risk of an investment and an investor's required rate of return.

The relationship between risk and required rate of return is known as the **risk-return relationship**. It is a positive relationship because the more risk assumed, the higher the required rate of return most people will demand. It takes compensation to convince people to suffer.

Suppose, for instance, that you were offered a job in the Sahara Desert, working long hours for a boss everyone describes as a tyrant. You would surely be averse to the idea of taking such a job. But think about it: Is there any way you would take this job? What if you were told that your salary would be $1 million per year? This compensation might cause you to sign up immediately. Even though there is a high probability you would hate the job, you'd take that risk because of the high compensation.[1]

Not everyone is risk averse, and among those who are, not all are equally risk averse. Some people would demand $2 million before taking the job in the Sahara Desert, whereas others would do it for a more modest salary.

People sometimes engage in very risky financial activities, such as buying lottery tickets or gambling in casinos. This suggests that they like risk and will pay to experience it. Most people, however, view these activities as entertainment rather than financial investing. The entertainment value may be the excitement of being in a casino with all sorts of people, or being able to fantasize about spending the multimillion-dollar lotto jackpot. But in the financial markets, where people invest for the future, they almost always seek to avoid risk unless they are adequately compensated.

Risk aversion explains the positive risk-return relationship. It explains why risky junk bonds carry a higher market interest rate than essentially risk-free U.S. Treasury bonds. Hardly anyone would invest $5,000 in a risky junk bond if the interest rate on the bond were lower than that of a U.S. Treasury bond having the same maturity.

Measuring Risk

We can never avoid risk entirely. That's why businesses must make sure that the anticipated return is sufficient to justify the degree of risk assumed. To do that, however, firms must first determine how much risk is present in a given financial situation. In other words, they must be able to answer the question, "How risky is it?"

Measuring risk quantitatively is a rather tall order. We all know when something feels risky, but we don't often quantify it. In business, risk measurement focuses on the degree of **uncertainty** present in a situation—the chance, or probability, of an unexpected outcome. The greater the probability of an unexpected outcome, the greater the degree of risk.

uncertainty The chance, or probability, that outcomes other than what is expected will occur.

Using Standard Deviation to Measure Risk

In statistics, *distributions* are used to describe the many values variables may have. A company's sales in future years, for example, is a variable with many possible values. So the sales forecast may be described by a distribution of the possible sales values with different probabilities attached to each value. If this distribution is symmetric, its mean—the average of a set of values—would be the expected sales value. Similarly, possible returns on any investment can be described by a *probability distribution*—usually a graph, table, or formula that specifies the probability associated with each possible return the investment may generate. The mean of the distribution is the most likely, or expected, rate of return.

The graph in Figure 7-1 shows the distributions of forecast sales for two companies, Company Calm and Company Bold. Note how the distribution for Company Calm's possible sales values is clustered closely to the mean and how the distribution of Company Bold's possible sales values is spread far above and far below the mean.[2]

The narrowness or wideness of a distribution reflects the degree of uncertainty about the expected value of the variable in question (sales, in our example). The distributions in Figure 7-1 show, for instance, that although the most probable value of sales for both companies is $1,000, sales for Company Calm could vary between $600 and $1,400, whereas sales for Company Bold could vary between $200 and $1,800. Company Bold's relatively wide variations show that there is more uncertainty about its sales forecast than about Company Calm's sales forecast.

---

1. This is not to suggest that people can be coaxed into doing anything they are averse to doing merely by offering them a sufficient amount of compensation. If people are asked to do something that offends their values, there may be no amount of compensation that can entice them.

2. These two distributions are discrete. If sales could take on any value within a given range, the distribution would be continuous and would be depicted by a curved line.

FIGURE 7-1

Sales Forecast Distributions for Companies Calm and Bold

Possible future sales distribution for two companies. Calm has a relatively "tight" distribution, and Bold has a relatively "wide" distribution. Note that sales for Company Bold has many more possible values than the sales for Company Calm.

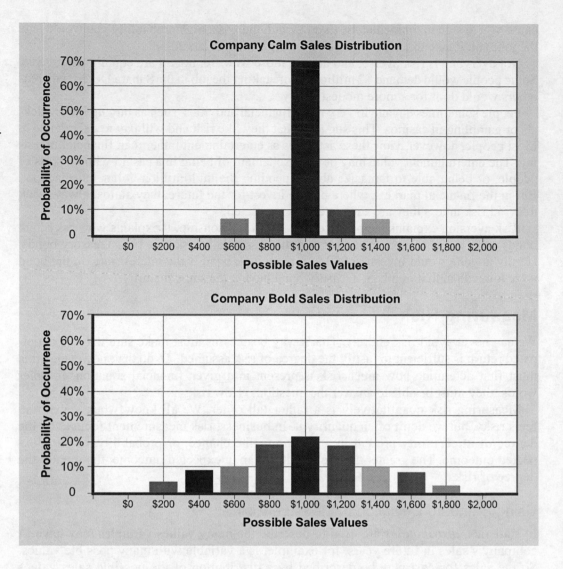

standard deviation A statistic that indicates how widely dispersed actual or possible values are distributed around a mean.

One way to measure risk is to compute the **standard deviation** of a variable's distribution of possible values. The standard deviation is a numerical indicator of how widely dispersed the possible values are around a mean. The more widely dispersed a distribution is, the larger the standard deviation, and the greater the probability that the value of a variable will be significantly above or below the expected value. The standard deviation, then, indicates the likelihood that an outcome different from what is expected will occur.

Let's calculate the standard deviations of the sales forecast distributions for Companies Calm and Bold to illustrate how the standard deviation can measure the degree of uncertainty, or risk, that is present.

Calculating the Standard Deviation

To calculate the standard deviation of the distribution of Company Calm's possible sales, we must first find the expected value, or mean, of the distribution using the following formula:

Formula for Expected Value, or Mean (μ)

$$\mu = \sum (V \times P) \tag{7-1}$$

where: μ = the expected value, or mean

$\sum$ = the sum of

V = the possible value for some variable

P = the probability of the value V occurring

Applying Equation 7-1, we can calculate the expected value, or mean, of Company Calm's forecasted sales. The following values for V and P are taken from Figure 7-1:

Calculating the Mean (μ) of Company Calm's
Possible Future Sales Distribution

Possible Sales Value (V)	Probability of Occurrence (P)	V x P
$ 600	.05	30
$ 800	.10	80
$ 1,000	.70	700
$ 1,200	.10	120
$ 1,400	.05	70
	$\Sigma = 1.00$	$\Sigma = 1,000 = \mu$

Each possible sales value is multiplied by its respective probability. The probability values, taken from Figure 7-1, may be based on trends, industry ratios, experience, or other information sources. We add together the products of each value times its probability to find the mean of the possible sales distribution.

We now know that the mean of Company Calm's sales forecast distribution is $1,000. We are ready to calculate the standard deviation of the distribution using the following formula:

The Standard Deviation (σ) Formula

$$\sigma = \sqrt{\sum P(V - \mu)^2} \qquad (7\text{-}2)$$

where: σ = the standard deviation

$\sum$ = the sum of

P = the probability of the value V occurring

V = the possible value for a variable

To calculate the standard deviation of Company Calm's sales distribution, we subtract the mean from each possible sales value, square that difference, and then multiply by the probability of that sales outcome. These differences squared, times their respective probabilities, are then added together, and the square root of this number is taken. The result is the standard deviation of the distribution of possible sales values.

Calculating the Standard Deviation(s) of Company Calm's
Possible Future Sales Distribution

Possible Sales Value (V)	Probability of Occurrence (P)	$V - \mu$	$(V - \mu)^2$	$P(V - \mu)^2$
$ 600	.05	−400	160,000	8,000
$ 800	.10	−200	40,000	4,000
$ 1,000	.70	0	0	0
$ 1,200	.10	200	40,000	4,000
$ 1,400	.05	400	160,000	8,000
				$\Sigma = 24,000$

$$\sqrt{24,000} = 155 = \sigma$$

This standard deviation result, 155, serves as the measure of the degree of risk present in Company Calm's sales forecast distribution.

Let's calculate the standard deviation of Company Bold's sales forecast distribution.

Mean (μ) and Standard Deviation (σ) of Company Bold's Possible Future Sales Distribution

Possible Sales Value (V)	Probability of Occurrence (P)	Mean Calculation V × P	V − μ	(V − μ)²	P(V − μ)²
$ 200	.04	8	−800	640,000	25,600
$ 400	.07	28	−600	360,000	25,200
$ 600	.10	60	−400	160,000	16,000
$ 800	.18	144	−200	40,000	7,200
$ 1,000	.22	220	0	0	0
$ 1,200	.18	216	200	40,000	7,200
$ 1,400	.10	140	400	160,000	16,000
$ 1,600	.07	112	600	360,000	25,200
$ 1,800	.04	72	800	640,000	25,600

$$\Sigma = 1,000 = \mu \qquad\qquad \Sigma = 148,000$$

$$\sqrt{148,000} = 385 = \sigma$$

As you can see, Company Bold's standard deviation of 385 is over twice that of Company Calm. This reflects the greater degree of risk in Company Bold's sales forecast.

Interpreting the Standard Deviation

Estimates of a company's possible sales, or a proposed project's future possible cash flows, can generally be thought of in terms of a normal probability distribution. The normal distribution is a special type of distribution. It allows us to make statements about how likely it is that the variable in question will be within a certain range of the distribution.

Figure 7-2 shows a normal distribution of possible returns on an asset. The vertical axis measures probability density for this continuous distribution so that the area under the curve always sums to one. Statistics tells us that when a distribution is normal, there is about a 67 percent chance that the observed value will be within one standard deviation of the mean. In the case of Company Calm, that means that, if sales were normally distributed, there would be a 67 percent probability that the actual sales will be $1,000 plus or minus $155 (between $845 and $1,155). For Company Bold it means, if sales were normally distributed, there would be a 67 percent probability that sales will be $1,000 plus or minus $385 (between $615 and $1,385).

Another characteristic of the normal distribution is that approximately 95 percent of the time, values observed will be within two standard deviations of the mean. For Company Calm this means that there would be a 95 percent probability that sales will be $1,000 plus or minus $155 × 2, or $310 (between $690 and $1,310). For Company Bold it means that sales will be $1,000 plus or minus $385 × 2, or $770 (between $230 and $1,770). These relationships are shown graphically in Figure 7-3.

The greater the standard deviation value, the greater the uncertainty about what the actual value of the variable in question will be. The greater the value of the standard deviation, the greater the possible deviations from the mean.

Using the Coefficient of Variation to Measure Risk

Whenever we want to compare the risk of investments that have different means, we use the *coefficient of variation*. We were safe in using the standard deviation to compare the riskiness of Company Calm's possible future sales distribution with that of Company Bold because the mean of the two distributions was the same ($1,000). Imagine, however, that Company Calm's sales were 10 times that of Company Bold. If that were the case and all other factors remained the same, then the standard deviation of Company Calm's possible future sales distribution would increase by a factor of 10, to $1,550. Company Calm's sales would appear to be much more risky than Company Bold's, whose standard deviation was only $385.

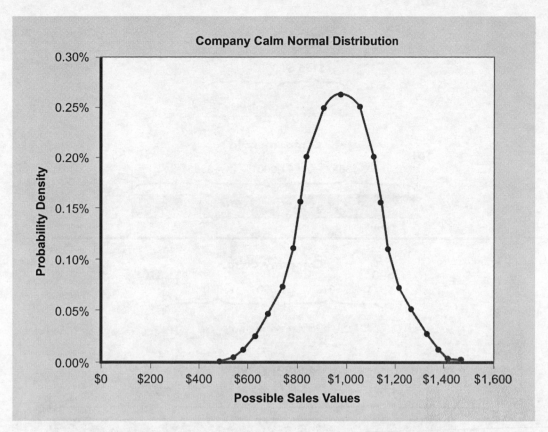

FIGURE 7-2

Normal Distribution

This normal probability distribution of possible returns has a mean, the expected value of $1,000.

To compare the degree of risk among distributions of different sizes, we should use a statistic that measures *relative* riskiness. The **coefficient of variation** (CV) measures relative risk by relating the standard deviation to the mean. The formula follows:

Coefficient of Variation (CV)

$$CV = \frac{\text{Standard Deviation}}{\text{Mean}}$$

(7-3)

coefficient of variation
The standard deviation divided by the mean. A measure of the degree of risk used to compare alternatives with possible returns of different magnitudes.

The coefficient of variation represents the standard deviation's percentage of the mean. It provides a standardized measure of the degree of risk that can be used to compare alternatives.

To illustrate the use of the coefficient of variation, let's compare the relative risk depicted in Company Calm's and Company Bold's possible sales distributions. When we plug the figures into Equation 7-3, we see:

$$\text{Company Calm CV}_{\text{sales}} = \frac{\text{Standard Deviation}}{\text{Mean}} = \frac{155}{1,000} = .155, \text{ or } 15.5\%$$

$$\text{Company Bold CV}_{\text{sales}} = \frac{\text{Standard Deviation}}{\text{Mean}} = \frac{385}{1,000} = .385, \text{ or } 38.5\%$$

Company Bold's coefficient of variation of possible sales (38.5 percent) is more than twice that of Company Calm (15.5 percent). Furthermore, even if Company Calm were 10 times the size of Company Bold—with a mean of its possible future sales of $10,000 and with a standard deviation of $1,550—it would not change the coefficient of variation. This would remain 1,550/10,000 = .155, or 15.5 percent. We use the coefficient of variation instead of the standard deviation to compare distributions that have means with different values because the CV adjusts for the difference, whereas the standard deviation does not.

FIGURE 7-3

The Degree of Risk Present in Company Calm's and Company Bold's Possible Future Sales Values as Measured by Standard Deviation

The standard deviation shows there is much more risk present in Company Bold's sales probability distribution than in Company Calm's. If the distributions are normal, then there is a 67% probability that Company Calm's sales will be between $845 and $1,155, and a 95% probability sales will be between $690 and $1,310. For Company Bold there is a 67% probability that sales will be between $615 and $1,385, and a 95% probability that sales will be between $230 and $1,770.

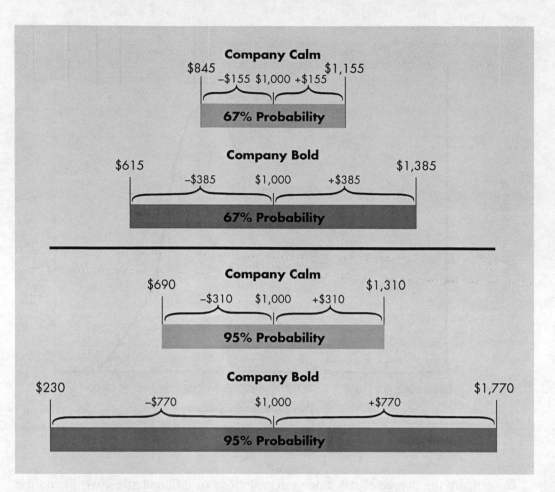

The Types of Risks Firms Encounter

Risk refers to uncertainty—the chance that what you expect to happen *won't* happen. The forms of risk that businesses most often encounter are *business risk, financial risk,* and *portfolio risk.*

Business Risk

Business risk refers to the uncertainty a company has with regard to its operating income (also known as earnings before interest and taxes, or EBIT). The more uncertainty about a company's expected operating income, the more business risk the company has. For example, if we assume that grocery prices remain constant, the only grocery store in a small town probably has little business risk—the store owners can reliably predict how much their customers will buy each month. In contrast, a gold mining firm in Wyoming has a lot of business risk. Because the owners have no idea when, where, or how much gold they will strike, they can't predict how much they will earn in any period with any degree of certainty.

Measuring Business Risk

The degree of uncertainty about operating income (and, therefore, the degree of business risk in the firm) depends on the volatility of operating income. If operating income is relatively constant, as in the grocery store example, then there is relatively little uncertainty associated with it. If operating income can take on many different values, as is the case with the gold mining firm, then there is a lot of uncertainty about it.

We can measure the variability of a company's operating income by calculating the standard deviation of the operating income forecast. A small standard deviation indicates little variability and, therefore, little uncertainty. A large standard deviation indicates a lot of variability and great uncertainty.

Some companies are large and others small. So to make comparisons among different firms, we must measure the risk by calculating the coefficient of variation of possible operating income values. The higher the coefficient of variation of possible operating income values, the greater the business risk of the firm.

Table 7-1 shows the expected value (μ), standard deviation (σ), and coefficient of variation (CV) of operating income for Company Calm and Company Bold, assuming that the expenses of both companies vary directly with sales (i.e., neither company has any fixed expenses).

The Influence of Sales Volatility

Sales volatility affects business risk—the more volatile a company's sales, the more business risk the firm has. Indeed, when no fixed costs are present—as in the case of Company Calm and Company Bold—sales volatility is equivalent to operating income volatility. Table 7-1 shows that the coefficients of variation of Company Calm's and Company Bold's operating income are 15.5 percent and 38.5 percent, respectively. Note that these coefficient numbers are exactly the same numbers as the two companies' coefficients of variation of expected sales.

The Influence of Fixed Operating Costs

In Table 7-1 we assumed that all of Company Calm's and Company Bold's expenses varied proportionately with sales. We did this to illustrate how sales volatility affects operating income volatility. In the real world, of course, most companies have some fixed expenses as well, such as rent, insurance premiums, and the like. It turns out that fixed expenses magnify the effect of sales volatility on operating income volatility. In effect, fixed expenses magnify business risk. The tendency of fixed expenses to magnify business risk is called operating leverage. To see how this works, refer to Table 7-2, in which we assume that all of Company Calm's and Company Bold's expenses are fixed.

As Table 7-2 shows, the effect of replacing each company's variable expenses with fixed expenses increased the volatility of operating income considerably. The coefficient of variation of Company Calm's operating income jumped from 15.49 percent when

> **Take Note**
> One group of businesses that is exposed to an extreme amount of financial risk because they operate almost entirely on borrowed money: banks and other financial institutions. Banks get almost all the money they use for loans from deposits—and deposits are liabilities on the bank's balance sheet. Banks must be careful to keep their revenues stable. Otherwise, fluctuations in revenues would cause losses that would drive the banks out of business. Now you know why the government regulates financial institutions so closely!

TABLE 7-1 Expected Value (μ), Standard Deviation (σ), and Coefficient of Variation (CV) of Possible Operating Income Values for Company Calm and Bold, Assuming All Expenses Are Variable

Company Calm

Probability of Occurrence

	5%	10%	70%	10%	5%
Sales	$ 600	$ 800	$ 1,000	$ 1,200	$ 1,400
Variable Expenses	$ 516	$ 688	$ 860	$ 1,032	$ 1,204
Operating Income (EBIT)	$ 84	$ 112	$ 140	$ 168	$ 196

μ of possible operating income values per equation 7-1: $140

σ of possible operating income values per equation 7-2: $21.69

CV of possible operating income values per equation 7-3: 15.5%

Company Bold

Probability of Occurrence

	4%	7%	10%	18%	22%	18%	10%	7%	4%
Sales	$ 200	$ 400	$ 600	$ 800	$ 1,000	$ 1,200	$ 1,400	$1,600	$ 1,800
Variable Expenses	$ 172	$ 344	$ 516	$ 688	$ 860	$ 1,032	$ 1,204	$1,376	$ 1,548
Operating Income (EBIT)	$ 28	$ 56	$ 84	$ 112	$ 140	$ 168	$ 196	$ 224	$ 252

μ of possible operating income values per equation 7-1: $140

σ of possible operating income values per equation 7-2: $53.86

CV of possible operating income values per equation 7-3: 38.5%

TABLE 7-2 Expected Value (μ), Standard Deviation (σ), and Coefficient of Variation (CV) of Possible Operating Income Values for Company Calm and Bold, Assuming All Expenses Are Fixed

Company Calm

Probability of Occurrence

	5%	10%	70%	10%	5%
Sales	$ 600	$ 800	$ 1,000	$ 1,200	$ 1,400
Fixed Expenses	$ 860	$ 860	$ 860	$ 860	$ 860
Operating Income (EBIT)	($260)	($ 60)	$ 140	$ 340	$ 540

μ of possible operating income values per equation 7-1: $140

σ of possible operating income values per equation 7-2: $154.92

CV of possible operating income values per equation 7-3: 110.7%

Company Bold

Probability of Occurrence

	4%	7%	10%	18%	22%	18%	10%	7%	4%
Sales	$ 200	$ 400	$ 600	$ 800	$ 1,000	$ 1,200	$ 1,400	$1,600	$ 1,800
Fixed Expenses	$ 860	$ 860	$ 860	$ 860	$ 860	$ 860	$ 860	$ 860	$ 860
Operating Income (EBIT)	($660)	($460)	($ 260)	($ 60)	$ 140	$ 340	$ 540	$ 740	$ 940

μ of possible operating income values per equation 7-1: $140

σ of possible operating income values per equation 7-2: $384.71

CV of possible operating income values per equation 7-3: 274.8%

all expenses were variable to over 110 percent when all expenses were fixed. When all expenses are fixed, a 15.49 percent variation in sales is magnified to a 110.66 percent variation in operating income. A similar situation exists for Company Bold.

The greater the fixed expenses, the greater the change in operating income for a given change in sales. Capital-intensive companies, such as electric generating firms, have high fixed expenses. Service companies, such as consulting firms, often have relatively low fixed expenses.

Financial Risk

When companies borrow money, they incur interest charges that appear as fixed expenses on their income statements. (For business loans, the entire amount borrowed normally remains outstanding until the end of the term of the loan. Interest on the unpaid balance, then, is a fixed amount that is paid each year until the loan matures.) Fixed interest charges act on a firm's net income in the same way that fixed operating expenses act on operating income—they increase volatility. The additional volatility of a firm's net income caused by the fixed interest expense is called **financial risk**. The phenomenon whereby a given change in operating income causes net income to change by a larger percentage is called **financial leverage**.

financial risk The additional volatility of a firm's net income caused by the presence of fixed financial costs.

financial leverage The phenomenon whereby a change in operating income causes net income to change by a larger percentage because of the presence of fixed financial costs.

Measuring Financial Risk

Financial risk is the additional volatility of net income caused by the presence of interest expense. We measure financial risk by noting the difference between the volatility of net income when there is no interest expense and when there is interest expense. To measure financial risk, we subtract the coefficient of variation of net income without interest expense from the coefficient of variation of net income with interest expense.

TABLE 7-3 Expected Value (μ), Standard Deviation (σ), and Coefficient of Variation (CV) of Possible Net Income Values for Company Calm and Bold

Company Calm

Probability of Occurrence

	5%	10%	70%	10%	5%
Sales	$ 600	$ 800	$ 1,000	$ 1,200	$ 1,400
Variable Expenses	$ 516	$ 688	$ 860	$ 1,032	$ 1,204
Operating Income (EBIT)	$ 84	$ 112	$ 140	$ 168	$ 196
Interest Expense	$ 40	$ 40	$ 40	$ 40	$ 40
Net Income	$ 44	$ 72	$ 100	$ 128	$ 156

μ of possible net income values per equation 7-1: $100

σ of possible net income values per equation 7-2: $21.69

CV of possible net income values per equation 7-3: 21.7%

Summary:

CV of possible net income values when interest expense is present: 21.7%

CV of possible net income values when interest expense is not present (from Table 7-1): 15.5%

Difference (financial risk) 6.2%

Company Bold

Probability of Occurrence

	4%	7%	10%	18%	22%	18%	10%	7%	4%
Sales	$ 200	$ 400	$ 600	$ 800	$ 1,000	$ 1,200	$ 1,400	$1,600	$ 1,800
Variable Expenses	$ 172	$ 344	$ 516	$ 688	$ 860	$ 1,032	$ 1,204	$1,376	$ 1,548
Operating Income (EBIT)	$ 28	$ 56	$ 84	$ 112	$ 140	$ 168	$ 196	$ 224	$ 252
Interest Expense	$ 40	$ 40	$ 40	$ 40	$ 40	$ 40	$ 40	$ 40	$ 40
Net Income	($ 12)	$ 16	$ 44	$ 72	$ 100	$ 128	$ 156	$ 184	$ 212

μ of possible net income values per equation 7-1: $100

σ of possible net income values per equation 7-2: $53.86

CV of possible net income values per equation 7-3: 53.9%

Summary:

CV of possible net income values when interest expense is present: 53.9%

CV of possible net income values when interest expense is not present (from Table 7-1): 38.5%

Difference (financial risk) 15.4%

The coefficient of variation of net income is the same as the coefficient of variation of operating income when no interest expense is present. Table 7-3 shows the calculation for Company Calm and Company Bold assuming (1) all variable operating expenses and (2) $40 in interest expense.

Financial risk, which comes from borrowing money, compounds the effect of business risk and intensifies the volatility of net income. Fixed operating expenses increase the volatility of operating income and magnify business risk. In the same way, fixed financial expenses (such as interest on debt or a noncancellable lease expense) increase the volatility of net income and magnify financial risk.

Firms that have only equity financing have no financial risk because they have no debt on which to make fixed interest payments. Conversely, firms that operate primarily on borrowed money are exposed to a high degree of financial risk.

Take Note
For simplicity, Table 7-3 assumes that neither firm pays any income taxes. Income tax is not a fixed expense, so its presence would not change the volatility of net income.

Portfolio Risk

A portfolio is any collection of assets managed as a group. Most large firms employ their assets in a number of different investments. Together, these make up the firm's portfolio of assets. Individual investors also have portfolios containing many different stocks or other investments. Firms (and individuals for that matter) are interested in portfolio returns and the uncertainty associated with them. Investors want to know how much they can expect to get back from their portfolio compared with how much they invest (the portfolio's expected return) and what the chances are that they won't get that return (the portfolio's risk).

We can easily find the expected return of a portfolio, but calculating the standard deviation of the portfolio's possible returns is a little more difficult. For example, suppose Company Cool has a portfolio that is equally divided between two assets, Asset A and Asset B. The expected returns and standard deviations of possible returns of Asset A and Asset B are as follows:

	Asset A	Asset B
Expected Return E(R)	10%	12%
Standard Deviation (σ)	2%	4%

Finding the expected return of Company Cool's portfolio is easy. We simply calculate the weighted average expected return, $E(R_p)$, of the two-asset portfolio using the following formula:

Expected Rate of Return of a Portfolio, $E(R_p)$
Comprised of Two Assets, A and B

$$E(R_p) = (w_a \times E(R_a)) + (w_b \times E(R_b))$$

(7-4)

where: $E(R_p)$ = the expected rate of return of the portfolio composed of Asset A and Asset B

w_a = the weight of Asset A in the portfolio

$E(R_a)$ = the expected rate of return of Asset A

w_b = the weight of Asset B in the portfolio

$E(R_b)$ = the expected rate of return of Asset B

According to Equation 7-4, the expected rate of return of a portfolio containing 50 percent Asset A and 50 percent Asset B is

$$E(R_p) = (.50 \times .10) + (.50 \times .12)$$

$$= .05 + .06$$

$$= .11, \text{ or } 11\%$$

Now let's turn to the standard deviation of possible returns of Company Cool's portfolio. Determining the standard deviation of a portfolio's possible returns requires special procedures. Why? Because gains from one asset in the portfolio may offset losses from another, lessening the overall degree of risk in the portfolio. Figure 7-4 shows how this works.

Figure 7-4 shows that even though the returns of each asset vary, the timing of the variations is such that when one asset's returns increase, the other's decrease. Therefore, the net change in the Company Cool portfolio returns is very small—nearly zero. The weighted average of the standard deviations of returns of the two individual assets, then, does not result in the standard deviation of the portfolio containing both assets. The reduction in the fluctuations of the returns of Company Cool (the combination of assets A and B) is called the diversification effect.

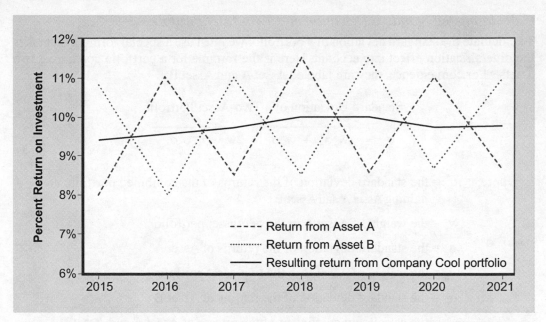

FIGURE 7-4
The Variation in Returns
Over Time for Asset
A, Asset B, and the
Combined Company Cool
Portfolio

Figure 7-4 shows how the
returns of Asset A and Asset B
might vary over time. Notice
that the fluctuations of each
curve are such that gains in
one almost completely offset
losses in the other. The risk
of the Company Cool portfolio
is small due to the offsetting
effects.

Correlation

How successfully diversification reduces risk depends on the degree of correlation between the two variables in question. **Correlation** indicates the degree to which one variable is linearly related to another. Correlation is measured by the correlation coefficient, represented by the letter r. The **correlation coefficient** can take on values between +1.0 (perfect positive correlation) to –1.0 (perfect negative correlation). If two variables are perfectly positively correlated, it means they move together—that is, they change values proportionately in the same direction at the same time. If two variables are perfectly negatively correlated, it means that every positive change in one value is matched by a proportionate corresponding negative change in the other. In the case of Assets A and B in Figure 7-4, the assets are negatively correlated.

The closer r is to +1.0, the more the two variables will tend to move with each other at the same time. The closer r is to –1.0, the more the two variables will tend to move opposite each other at the same time. An r value of zero indicates that the variables' values aren't related at all. This is known as *statistical independence*.

In Figure 7-4, Asset A and Asset B had perfect negative correlation (r = –1.0). So the risk associated with each asset was nearly eliminated by combining the two assets into one portfolio. The risk would have been completely eliminated had the standard deviations of the two assets been equal.

correlation The degree to which one variable is linearly related to another.

correlation coefficient The measurement of degree of correlation, represented by the letter r. Its values range from + 1.0 (perfect positive correlation) to –1.0 (perfect negative correlation).

Calculating the Correlation Coefficient

Determining the precise value of r between two variables can be extremely difficult. The process requires estimating the possible values that each variable could take and their respective probabilities, simultaneously.

We can make a rough estimate of the degree of correlation between two variables by examining the nature of the assets involved. If one asset is, for instance, a firm's existing portfolio, and the other asset is a replacement piece of equipment, then the correlation between the returns of the two assets is probably close to +1.0. Why? Because there is no influence that would cause the returns of one asset to vary any differently than those of the other. A Coca-Cola® Bottling company expanding its capacity would be an example of a correlation of about +1.0.

What if a company planned to introduce a completely new product in a new market? In that case we might suspect that the correlation between the returns of the existing portfolio and the new product would be something significantly less than +1.0. Why? Because the cash flows of each asset would be due to different, and probably unrelated, factors. An example would be Disney buying Marvel Comics, Lucasfilm, Pixar, ESPN, and 20th Century Fox.

Take Note
Any time the correlation coefficient of the returns of two assets is less than +1.0, then the standard deviation of the portfolio consisting of those assets will be less than the weighted average of the individual assets' standard deviations.

Calculating the Standard Deviation of a Two-Asset Portfolio

To calculate the standard deviation of a portfolio, we must use a special formula that takes the diversification effect into account. Here is the formula for a portfolio containing two assets.[3] For convenience, they are labeled Asset A and Asset B:

Standard Deviation of a Two-Asset Portfolio

$$\sigma_p = \sqrt{w_a^2\sigma_a^2 + w_b^2\sigma_b^2 + 2w_aw_br_{a,b}\sigma_a\sigma_b}$$

(7-5)

where: σ_p = the standard deviation of the returns of the combined portfolio containing Asset A and Asset B

w_a = the weight of Asset A in the two-asset portfolio

σ_a = the standard deviation of the returns of Asset A

w_b = the weight of Asset B in the two-asset portfolio

σ_b = the standard deviation of the returns of Asset B

$r_{a,b}$ = the correlation coefficient of the returns of Asset A and Asset B

The formula may look scary, but don't panic. Once we know the values for each factor, we can solve the formula rather easily with a calculator. Let's use the formula to find the standard deviation of a portfolio composed of equal amounts invested in Asset A and Asset B (i.e., Company Cool).

To calculate the standard deviation of possible returns of the portfolio of Company Cool, we need to know that Company Cool's portfolio is composed of 50 percent Asset A (w_a = .5) and 50 percent Asset B (w_b = .5). The standard deviation of Asset A's expected returns is 2 percent (σ_a = .02), and the standard deviation of Asset B's expected returns is 4 percent (σ_b = .04). To begin, assume the correlation coefficient (r) is –1.0, as shown in Figure 7-4.

Now we're ready to use Equation 7-5 to calculate the standard deviation of Company Cool's returns.

$$\begin{aligned}
\sigma_p &= \sqrt{w_a^2\sigma_a^2 + w_b^2\sigma_b^2 + 2w_aw_br_{a,b}\sigma_a\sigma_b} \\
&= \sqrt{(.50^2)(0.02^2) + (.50^2)(0.04^2) + (2)(.50)(.50)(-1.0)(.02)(.04)} \\
&= \sqrt{(.25)(.0004) + (.25)(.0016) - .0004} \\
&= \sqrt{.0001 + .0004 - .0004} \\
&= \sqrt{.0001} \\
&= .01, \text{ or } 1\%
\end{aligned}$$

The diversification effect results in risk reduction. Why? Because we are combining two assets that have returns that are negatively correlated (r = –1.0). The standard deviation of the combined portfolio is much lower than that of either of the two individual assets (1 percent for Company Cool compared with 2 percent for Asset A and 4 percent for Asset B).

Nondiversifiable Risk

nondiversifiable risk
The portion of a portfolio's total risk that cannot be eliminated by diversifying. Factors shared to a greater or lesser degree by most assets in the market, such as inflation and interest rate risk, cause nondiversifiable risk.

Unless the returns of one-half the assets in a portfolio are perfectly negatively correlated with the other half—which is extremely unlikely—some risk will remain after assets are combined into a portfolio. The degree of risk that remains is **nondiversifiable risk**, the part of a portfolio's total risk that can't be eliminated by diversifying.

3. You can adapt the formula to calculate the standard deviations of the returns of portfolios containing more than two assets, but doing so is complicated and usually unnecessary. Most of the time, you can view a firm's existing portfolio as one asset and a proposed addition to the portfolio as the second asset.

Nondiversifiable risk is one of the characteristics of market risk because it is produced by factors that are shared, to a greater or lesser degree, by most assets in the market. These factors might include inflation and real gross domestic product changes. Figure 7-5 illustrates nondiversifiable risk.

In Figure 7-5 we assumed that the portfolio begins with one asset with possible returns having a probability distribution with a standard deviation of 10 percent. However, if the portfolio is divided equally between two assets, each with possible returns having a probability distribution with a standard deviation of 10 percent, and the correlation of the returns of the two assets is, say +.25, then the standard deviation of the returns of the portfolio drops to about 8 percent. If the portfolio is divided among greater numbers of stocks, the standard deviation of the portfolio will continue to fall—as long as the newly added stocks have returns that are less than perfectly positively correlated with those of the existing portfolio.

Note in Figure 7-5, however, that after about 20 assets have been included in the portfolio, adding more has little effect on the portfolio's standard deviation. Almost all the risk that can be eliminated by diversifying is gone. The remainder, about 5 percent in this example, represents the portfolio's nondiversifiable risk.

It is clear that the Financial Crisis was caused, at least in part, by the fact that business leaders and portfolio managers underestimated the extent to which assets could be correlated. It turns out it IS possible for housing prices to go down substantially all over the country at the same time even though the probability of this occurrence had been perceived to be close to zero before the Financial Crisis. With the chain reaction systematic risk described in the opener to this chapter, many assets moved up and down (mostly down) with each other at the same time. The extent to which these assets moved together had not been seen like this since The Great Depression. If you estimate that the correlation coefficient of returns of two assets is .4 and it turns out to be .9, you will be underestimating the risk you are assuming.

Measuring Nondiversifiable Risk

Nondiversifiable risk is measured by a term called **beta (β)**. The ultimate group of diversified assets, the market, has a beta of 1.0. The betas of portfolios, and individual assets, relate their returns to those of the overall stock market. Portfolios with betas higher than

beta (β) The measure of nondiversifiable risk. The stock market has a beta of 1.0. Betas higher than 1.0 indicate more nondiversifiable risk than the market, and betas lower than 1.0 indicate less. Risk-free portfolios have betas of 0.0.

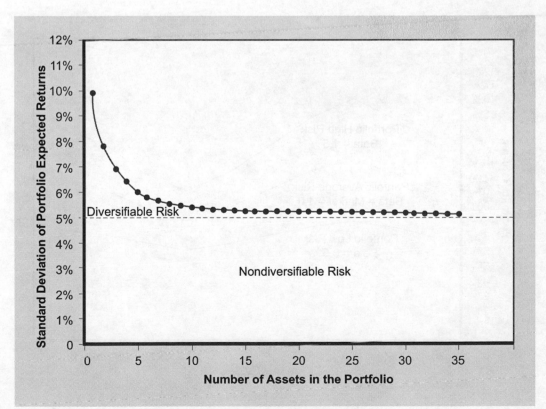

FIGURE 7-5
The Relationship between the Number of Assets in a Portfolio and the Riskiness of the Portfolio

The graph shows that as each new asset is added to a portfolio, the diversification effect causes the standard deviation of the portfolio to decrease. After 20 assets have been added, however, the effect of adding further assets is slight. The remaining degree of risk is nondiversifiable risk.

1.0 are relatively more risky than the market. Portfolios with betas less than 1.0 are relatively less risky than the market. (Risk-free portfolios have a beta of zero.) The more the return of the portfolio in question fluctuates relative to the return of the overall market, the higher the beta, as shown graphically in Figure 7-6.

Figure 7-6 shows that returns of the overall market fluctuated between about 8 percent and 12 percent during the 10 periods that were measured. By definition, the market's beta is 1.0. The returns of the average-risk portfolio fluctuated exactly the same amount, so the beta of the average-risk portfolio is also 1.0. Returns of the low-risk portfolio fluctuated between 6 percent and 8 percent, half as much as the market. So the low-risk portfolio's beta is 0.5, only half that of the market. In contrast, returns of the high-risk portfolio fluctuated between 10 percent and 16 percent, one and a half times as much as the market. As a result, the high-risk portfolio's beta is 1.5, half again as high as the market.

Companies in low-risk, stable industries like public utilities will typically have low beta values because returns of their stock tend to be relatively stable. (When the economy goes into a recession, people generally continue to turn on their lights and use their refrigerators; and when the economy is booming, people do not splurge on additional electricity consumption.) Recreational boat companies, on the other hand, tend to have high beta values. That's because demand for recreational boats is volatile. (When times are tough, people postpone the purchase of recreational boats. During good economic times, when people have extra cash in their pockets, sales of these boats take off.)

Dealing with Risk

Once companies determine the degree of risk present, what do they do about it? Suppose, for example, a firm determined that if a particular project were adopted, the standard deviation of possible returns of the firm's portfolio of assets would double. So what? How should a firm deal with the situation?

There are two broad classes of alternatives for dealing with risk. First, you might take some action to reduce the degree of risk present in the situation. Second (if the degree of risk can't be reduced), you may compensate for the degree of risk you are about to assume. We'll discuss these two classes of alternatives in the following sections.

FIGURE 7-6
Portfolio Fluctuations
and Beta

The relative fluctuation in returns for portfolios of different betas. The higher the beta, the more the portfolio's returns fluctuate relative to the overall market. The market itself has a beta of 1.0.

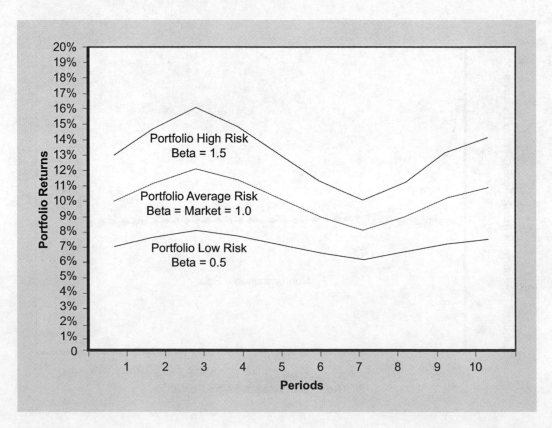

Risk-Reduction Methods

One way companies can avoid risk is simply to avoid risky situations entirely. Most of the time, however, refusing to get involved is an unsatisfactory business decision. Carried to its logical conclusion, this would mean that everyone would invest in risk-free assets only, and no products or services would be produced. Mark Zuckerberg, founder and CEO of Facebook, didn't get rich by avoiding risks. To succeed, businesses must take risks.

If we assume that firms (and individuals) are willing to take some risk to achieve the higher expected returns that accompany that risk, then the task is to reduce the degree of risk as much as possible. The following three methods help to reduce risk: reducing sales volatility and fixed costs, insurance, and diversification.

Reducing Sales Volatility and Fixed Costs

Earlier in the chapter, we discussed how sales volatility and fixed operating costs contribute to a firm's business risk. Firms in volatile industries whose sales fluctuate widely are exposed to a high degree of business risk. That business risk is intensified even further if they have large amounts of fixed operating costs. Reducing the volatility of sales, and the amount of fixed operating costs a firm must pay, then, will reduce risk.

Reducing Sales Volatility

If a firm could smooth out its sales over time, then the fluctuation of its operating income (business risk) would also be reduced. Businesses try to stabilize sales in many ways. For example, retail ski equipment stores sell tennis equipment in the summer, summer vacation resorts offer winter specials, and movie theaters offer reduced prices for early shows to encourage more patronage during slow periods.

Insurance

Insurance is a time-honored way to spread risk among many participants and thus reduce the degree of risk borne by any one participant. Business firms insure themselves against many risks, such as flood, fire, and liability. However, one important risk—the risk that an investment might fail—is uninsurable. To reduce the risk of losing everything in one investment, firms turn to another risk-reduction technique, diversification.

Diversification

Review Figure 7-4 and the discussion following the figure. We showed in that discussion how the standard deviation of returns of Asset A (2 percent) and Asset B (4 percent) could be reduced to 1 percent by combining the two assets into one portfolio. The diversification effect occurred because the returns of the two assets were not perfectly positively correlated. Any time firms invest in ventures whose returns are not perfectly positively correlated with the returns of their existing portfolios, they will experience diversification benefits.

Compensating for the Presence of Risk

In most cases it's not possible to avoid risk completely. Some risk usually remains even after firms use risk-reduction techniques. When firms assume risk to achieve an objective, they also take measures to receive compensation for assuming that risk. In the sections that follow, we discuss these compensation measures.

Adjusting the Required Rate of Return

Most owners and financial managers are generally risk averse. So for a given expected rate of return, less risky investment projects are more desirable than more risky investment projects. The higher the expected rate of return, the more desirable the risky venture will appear. As we noted earlier in the chapter, the risk-return relationship is positive. That is, because of risk aversion, people demand a higher rate of return for taking on a higher-risk project.

> **Take Note**
> Diversification is a hotly debated issue among financial theorists. Specifically, theorists question whether a firm provides value to its stockholders if it diversifies its asset portfolio to stabilize the firm's income. Many claim that individual stockholders can achieve diversification benefits more easily and cheaply than a firm, so firms that diversify actually do a disservice to their stockholders. What do you think?

Take Note
In capital budgeting a rate of return to reflect risk is called a risk-adjusted discount rate. See Chapter 10.

Although we know that the risk-return relationship is positive, an especially difficult question remains: How much return is appropriate for a given degree of risk? Say, for example, that a firm has all assets invested in a chain of convenience stores that provides a stable return on investment of about 6 percent a year. How much more return should the firm require for investing some assets in a baseball team that may not provide steady returns[4]—8 percent? 10 percent? 25 percent? Unfortunately, no one knows for sure, but financial experts have researched the subject extensively.

One well-known model used to calculate the required rate of return of an investment is the **capital asset pricing model** (CAPM). We discuss CAPM next.

capital asset pricing model (CAPM) A financial model that can be used to calculate the appropriate required payment of return for an investment project, given its degree of risk as measured by beta (β).

Relating Return and Risk: The Capital Asset Pricing Model

Financial theorists William F. Sharpe, John Lintner, and Jan Mossin worked on the risk-return relationship and developed the capital asset pricing model, or CAPM. We can use this model to calculate the appropriate required rate of return for an investment project given its degree of risk as measured by beta (β).[5] The formula for CAPM is presented in Equation 7-6.

CAPM Formula

$$k_p = k_{rf} + (k_m - k_{rf}) \times \beta \tag{7-6}$$

where: k_p = the required rate of return appropriate for the investment project

k_{rf} = the risk-free rate of return

k_m = the required rate of return on the overall market

β = the project's beta

risk-free rate of return The rate of return that investors demand in order to take on a project that contains no risk other than an inflation premium.

The three components of the CAPM include the risk-free rate of return (k_{rf}), the market risk premium ($k_m - k_{rf}$), and the project's beta (β). The **risk-free rate of return** (k_{rf}) is the rate of return that investors demand from a project that contains no risk. Risk-averse managers and owners will always demand at least this rate of return from any investment project.

market risk premium The additional return above the risk-free rate demanded by investors for assuming the risk of investing in the market.

The required rate of return on the overall market minus the risk-free rate ($k_m - k_{rf}$) represents the additional return demanded by investors for taking on the risk of investing in the market itself. The term is sometimes called the **market risk premium**. In the CAPM, the term for the market risk premium, ($k_m - k_{rf}$), can be viewed as the additional return over the risk-free rate that investors demand from an "average stock" or an "average-risk" investment project. With the poor performance of the stock market for several years through the 2008–2009 Financial Crisis period and beyond, some have been decreasing their estimates for the market risk premium looking forward. This raises the question of whether we are in a different environment now when stock returns will be lower than they've been in the past. The S&P 500 stock market index is often used as a proxy for the market.

As discussed earlier, a project's beta (β) represents a project's degree of risk relative to the overall stock market. In the CAPM, when the beta term is multiplied by the market risk premium term, ($k_m - k_{rf}$), the result is the additional return over the risk-free rate that investors demand from that individual project. Beta is the relevant risk measure according to the CAPM. High-risk (high-beta) projects have high required rates of return, and low-risk (low-beta) projects have low required rates of return.

Table 7-4 shows three examples of how the CAPM is used to determine the appropriate required rate of return for projects of different degrees of risk.

---

4. Some major league baseball teams lose money and others make a great deal. Television revenues differ greatly from team to team, as do ticket sales and salary expenses.

5. See William Sharpe, "Capital Asset Prices: A Theory of Market Equilibrium," *Journal of Finance* (September 1964); John Lintner, "The Valuation of Risk Assets and the Selection of Risky Investments in Stock Portfolios and Capital Budgets," *Review of Economics and Statistics* (February 1965); and Jan Mossin, "Equilibrium in a Capital Asset Market," *Econometrica* (October 1966).

TABLE 7-4 Using the CAPM to Calculate Required Rates of Return for Investment Projects

Given:

The risk-free rate, k_{rf} = 4%

The required rate of return on the market, k_m = 12%

Project Low Risk's beta = 0.5

Project Average Risk's beta = 1.0

Project High Risk's beta = 1.5

Required rates of return on the project's per the CAPM:

Project Low Risk: $k_p = .04 + (.12 - .04) \times 0.5$

$= .04 + .04$

$= .08,$ or 8%

Project Average Risk: $k_p = .04 + (.12 - .04) \times 1.0$

$= .04 + .08$

$= .12,$ or 12%

Project High Risk: $k_p = .04 + (.12 - .04) \times 1.5$

$= .04 + .12$

$= .16,$ or 16%

Given that the risk-free rate of return is 4 percent and the required rate of return on the market is 12 percent, the CAPM indicates the appropriate required rate of return for a low-risk investment project with a beta of .5 is 8 percent. The appropriate required rate of return for an average-risk project is the same as that for the market, 12 percent, and the appropriate rate for a high-risk project with a beta of 1.5 is 16 percent.

As we can see in Table 7-4, Project High Risk, with its beta of 1.5, has a required rate of return that is twice that of Project Low Risk, with its beta of 0.5. After all, shouldn't we ask for a higher rate of return if the risk is higher? Note also that Project Average Risk, which has the same beta as the market, 1.0, also has the same required rate of return as the market (12 percent). The risk-return relationship for these three projects is shown in Figure 7-7.

Remember that the beta term in the CAPM reflects only the nondiversifiable risk of an asset, not its diversifiable risk. Diversifiable risk is irrelevant because the diversity of each investor's portfolio essentially eliminates (or should eliminate) that risk. (After all, most investors are well diversified. They will not demand extra return for adding a security to their portfolios that contains diversifiable risk.) The return that well-diversified investors demand when they buy a security, as measured by the CAPM and beta, relates to the degree of nondiversifiable risk in the security.

What's Next

In this chapter we examined the risk-return relationship, types of risk, risk measurements, risk-reduction techniques, and the CAPM. In the next chapter, we will discuss the time value of money.

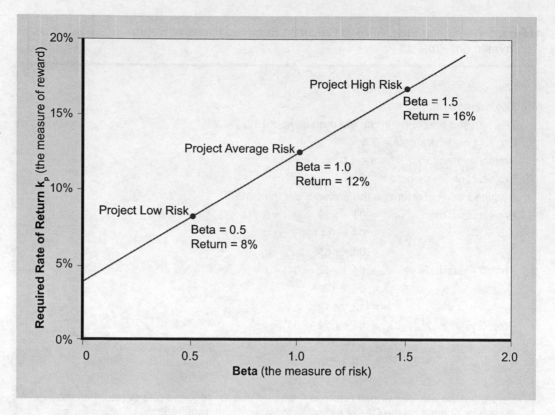

FIGURE 7-7

CAPM and the Risk-Return Relationship

This graph illustrates the increasing return required for increasing risk as indicated by the CAPM beta. This graphical depiction of the risk-return relationship according to the CAPM is called the security market line.

Summary

1. *Define risk, risk aversion, and the risk-return relationship.*
In everything you do, or don't do, there is a chance that something will happen that you didn't count on. Risk is the potential for unexpected events to occur.

 Given two financial alternatives that are equal except for their degree of risk, most people will choose the less risky alternative because they are risk averse. Risk aversion is a common trait among almost all investors. Most investors avoid risk if they can, unless they are compensated for accepting risk. In an investment context, the additional compensation is a higher expected rate of return.

 The risk-return relationship refers to the positive relationship between risk and the required rate of return. Due to risk aversion, the higher the risk, the more return investors expect.

2. *Measure risk using the standard deviation and coefficient of variation.*
Risk is the chance, or probability, that outcomes other than what is expected will occur. This probability is reflected in the narrowness or width of the distribution of the possible values of the financial variable. In a distribution of variable values, the standard deviation is a number that indicates how widely dispersed the possible values are around the expected value. The more widely dispersed a distribution is, the larger the standard deviation, and the greater the probability that an actual value will be different than the expected value. The standard deviation, then, can be used to measure the likelihood that some outcome substantially different than what is expected will occur.

 When the degrees of risk in distributions of different sizes are compared, the coefficient of variation is a statistic used to measure relative riskiness. The coefficient of variation measures the standard deviation's percentage of the expected value. It relates the standard deviation to its mean to give a risk measure that is independent of the magnitude of the possible returns.

3. *Identify the types of risk that business firms encounter.*
Business risk is the risk that a company's operating income will differ from what is expected. The more volatile a company's operating income, the more business risk the firm contains. Business risk is a result of sales volatility, which translates into operating income volatility. Business risk is increased by the presence of fixed costs, which magnify the effect on operating income of changes in sales.

 Financial risk occurs when companies borrow money and incur interest charges that show up as fixed expenses on their income statements. Fixed interest charges act on a firm's net income the same way fixed operating expenses act on operating income—they increase volatility. The additional volatility of a firm's net income caused by the presence of fixed interest expense is called financial risk.

 Portfolio risk is the chance that investors won't get the return they expect from a portfolio. Portfolio risk can be measured by the standard deviation of possible returns of a portfolio. It is affected by the correlation of returns of the assets making up the portfolio. The less correlated these returns are, the more gains on some assets offset losses on others, resulting in a reduction of the portfolio's risk. This phenomenon is known as the diversification effect. Nondiversifiable risk is risk that remains in a portfolio after all diversification benefits have been achieved. Nondiversifiable risk is measured by a term called beta (β). The market has a beta of 1.0. Portfolios with betas greater than 1.0 contain more nondiversifiable risk than the market, and portfolios with betas less than 1.0 contain less nondiversifiable risk than the market.

4. *Explain methods of risk reduction.*
Firms can reduce the degree of risk by taking steps to reduce the volatility of sales or their fixed costs. Firms also obtain insurance policies to protect against many risks, and they diversify their asset portfolios to reduce the risk of income loss.

5. *Describe how firms compensate for assuming risk.*
Firms almost always demand a higher rate of return to compensate for assuming risk. The more risky a project, the higher the return firms demand.

6. *Explain how the capital asset pricing model (CAPM) relates risk and return.*
When investors adjust their required rates of return to compensate for risk, the question arises as to how much return is appropriate for a given degree of risk. The capital asset pricing model (CAPM) is a model that measures the required rate of return for an investment or project, given its degree of nondiversifiable risk as measured by beta (β).

Key Terms

beta (β) The measure of nondiversifiable risk. The stock market has a beta of 1.0. Betas higher than 1.0 indicate more nondiversifiable risk than the market, and betas lower than 1.0 indicate less. Risk-free portfolios have betas of 0.0.

capital asset pricing model (CAPM) A financial model that can be used to calculate the appropriate required payment of return for an investment project, given its degree of risk as measured by beta (β).

coefficient of variation The standard deviation divided by the mean. A measure of the degree of risk used to compare alternatives with possible returns of different magnitudes.

correlation The degree to which one variable is linearly related to another.

correlation coefficient The measurement of degree of correlation, represented by the letter r. Its values range from + 1.0 (perfect positive correlation) to –1.0 (perfect negative correlation).

financial leverage The phenomenon whereby a change in operating income causes net income to change by a larger percentage because of the presence of fixed financial costs.

financial risk The additional volatility of a firm's net income caused by the presence of fixed financial costs.

market risk premium The additional return above the risk-free rate demanded by investors for assuming the risk of investing in the market.

nondiversifiable risk The portion of a portfolio's total risk that cannot be eliminated by diversifying. Factors shared to a greater or lesser degree by most assets in the market, such as inflation and interest rate risk, cause nondiversifiable risk.

risk-free rate of return The rate of return that investors demand in order to take on a project that contains no risk other than an inflation premium.

risk-return relationship The positive relationship between the risk of an investment and an investor's required rate of return.

standard deviation A statistic that indicates how widely dispersed actual or possible values arc distributed around a mean.

uncertainty The chance, or probability, that outcomes other than what is expected will occur.

Equations Introduced in This Chapter

Equation 7-1. The Expected Value, or Mean (μ), of a Probability Distribution:

$$\mu = \sum (V \times P)$$

where: μ = thc expected value, or mean

$\sum$ = the sum of

V = the possible value for some variable

P = the probability of the value V occurring

Equation 7-2. The Standard Deviation:

$$\sigma = \sqrt{\sum P(V - \mu)^2}$$

where: σ = the standard deviation

$\sum$ = the sum of

P = the probability of the value V occurring

V = the possible value for a variable

μ = the expected value

Equation 7-3. The Coefficient of Variation of a Probability Distribution:

$$CV = \frac{\text{Standard Deviation}}{\text{Mean}}$$

Equation 7-4. The Expected Rate of Return, $E(R_p)$, of a portfolio comprised of Two Assets, A and B:

$$E(R_p) = (w_a \times E(R_a)) + (w_b \times E(R_b))$$

where: $E(R_p)$ = the expected rate of return of the portfolio composed of Asset A and Asset B

w_a = the weight of Asset A in the portfolio

$E(R_a)$ = the expected rate of return of Asset A

w_b = the weight of Asset B in the portfolio

$E(R_b)$ = the expected rate of return of Asset B

Equation 7-5. The Standard Deviation of a Two-Asset Portfolio:

$$\sigma_p = \sqrt{w_a^2\sigma_a^2 + w_b^2\sigma_b^2 + 2w_a w_b r_{a,b}\sigma_a\sigma_b}$$

where: σ_p = the standard deviation of the returns of the combined portfolio containing Asset A and Asset B

w_a = the weight of Asset A in the two-asset portfolio

σ_a = the standard deviation of the returns of Asset A

w_b = the weight of Asset B in the two-asset portfolio

σ_b = the standard deviation of the returns of Asset B

$r_{a,b}$ = the correlation coefficient of the returns of Asset A and Asset B

Equation 7-6. The Capital Asset Pricing Model (CAPM):

$$k_p = k_{rf} + (k_m - k_{rf}) \times \beta$$

where: k_p = the required rate of return appropriate for the investment project

k_{rf} = the risk-free rate of return

k_m = the required rate of return on the overall market

β = the project's beta

Self-Test

ST-1. For Tyrion Corporation, the mean of the distribution of next year's possible sales is $5 million. The standard deviation of this distribution is $400,000. Calculate the coefficient of variation (CV) for this distribution of possible sales.

ST-2. Investors in Tyrion Industries common stock have a .2 probability of earning a return of 4 percent, a .6 probability of earning a return of 10 percent, and a .2 probability of earning a return of 20 percent. What is the mean of this probability distribution (the expected rate of return)?

ST-3. What is the standard deviation for the Tyrion Industries common stock return probability distribution described in ST-2?

ST-4. The standard deviation of the possible returns of Boris Company common stock is .08, whereas the standard deviation of possible returns of Natasha Company common stock is .12. Calculate the standard deviation of a portfolio comprised of 40 percent Boris Company stock and 60 percent Natasha Company stock. The correlation coefficient of the returns of Boris Company stock relative to the returns of Natasha Company stock is –.2.

ST-5. The mean of the normal probability distribution of possible returns of Gidney and Cloyd Corporation common stock is 18 percent. The standard deviation is 3 percent. What is the range of possible values that you would be 95 percent sure would capture the return that will actually be earned on this stock?

ST-6. Cercei Corporation common stock has a beta of 1.2. The market risk premium is 6 percent and the risk-free rate is 4 percent. What is the required rate of return on this stock according to the CAPM?

ST-7. Using the information provided in ST-6, what is the required rate of return on the common stock of Zack's Salt Corporation? This stock has a beta of .4.

ST-8. A portfolio of three stocks has an expected value of 14 percent. Stock A has an expected return of 6 percent and a weight of .25 in the portfolio. Stock B has an expected return of 10 percent and a weight of .5 in the portfolio. Stock C is the third stock in this portfolio. What is the expected rate of return of Stock C?

Review Questions

1. What is risk aversion? If common stockholders are risk averse, how do you explain the fact that they often invest in very risky companies?

2. Explain the risk-return relationship.

3. Why is the coefficient of variation often a better risk measure when comparing different projects than the standard deviation?

4. What is the difference between business risk and financial risk?

5. Why does the riskiness of portfolios have to be looked at differently than the riskiness of individual assets?

6. What happens to the riskiness of a portfolio if assets with very low correlations (even negative correlations) are combined?

7. What does it mean when we say that the correlation coefficient for two variables is +1? What does it mean if this value is zero? What does it mean if it is +1?

8. What is nondiversifiable risk? How is it measured?

9. Compare diversifiable and nondiversifiable risk. Which do you think is more important to financial managers in business firms?

10. How do risk-averse investors compensate for risk when they take on investment projects?

11. Given that risk-averse investors demand more return for taking on more risk when they invest, how much more return is appropriate for, say, a share of common stock, than for a Treasury bill?

12. Discuss risk from the perspective of the capital asset pricing model (CAPM).

Build Your Communication Skills

CS-1. Go to the library, use business magazines, computer databases, the Internet, or other sources that have financial information about businesses. (See Chapter 5 for a list of specific resources.) Find three companies and compare their approaches to risk. Do the firms take a conservative or an aggressive approach? Write a one- to two-page report, citing specific evidence of the risk-taking approach of each of the three companies you researched.

CS-2. Research three to five specific mutual funds. Then form small groups of four to six. Discuss whether the mutual funds each group member researched will help investors diversify the risk of their portfolio. Are some mutual funds better than others for an investor seeking good diversification? Prepare a list of mutual funds the group would select to diversify its risk and explain your choices. Present your recommendations to the class.

Problems

7-1. Manager Paul Smith believes an investment project will have the following yearly cash flows with the associated probabilities throughout its life of five years. Calculate the standard deviation and coefficient of variation of the cash flows.

 Standard Deviation and Coefficient of Variation

Cash Flows($)	Probability of Occurrence
$10,000	.05
13,000	.10
16,000	.20
19,000	.30
22,000	.20
25,000	.10
28,000	.05

For more, see 8e Spreadsheet Templates for *Microsoft Excel*.

Measuring Risk **7-2.** Milk-U, an agricultural consulting firm, has developed the following income statement forecast:

Milk-U Income Forecast (in 000's)

	Probability of Occurrence				
	2%	8%	80%	8%	2%
Sales	$500	$700	$1,200	$1,700	$1,900
Variable Expenses	250	350	600	850	950
Fixed Operating Expenses	250	250	250	250	250
Operating Income	0	100	350	600	700

> For more, see 8e Spreadsheet Templates for *Microsoft Excel.*

a. Calculate the expected value of Milk-U's operating income.

b. Calculate the standard deviation of Milk-U's operating income.

c. Calculate the coefficient of variation of Milk-U's operating income.

d. Recalculate the expected value, standard deviation, and coefficient of variation of Milk-U's operating income if the company's sales forecast changed as follows:

	Probability of Occurrence				
	10%	15%	50%	15%	10%
Sales	$500	$700	$1,200	$1,700	$1,900

e. Comment on how Milk-U's degree of business risk changed as a result of the new sales forecast in part *d*.

Standard Deviation and Mean **7-3.** The following data apply to Henshaw Corp. Calculate the mean and the standard deviation, using the following table.

Possible Sales	Probability of Occurrence
$ 1,000	.10
$ 5,000	.20
$ 10,000	.45
$ 15,000	.15
$ 20,000	.10
	$\Sigma = 1.00$

Measuring Risk **7-4.** As a new loan officer in the Springfield Bank, you are comparing the financial riskiness of two firms. Selected information from *pro forma* statements for each firm follows.

Equity Eddie's Company Net Income Forecast (in 000's)

	Probability of Occurrence				
	5%	10%	70%	10%	5%
Operating Income	$100	$200	$400	$600	$700
Interest Expense	0	0	0	0	0
Before-Tax Income	100	200	400	600	700
Taxes (28%)	28	56	112	168	196
Net Income	72	144	288	432	504

> For more, see 8e Spreadsheet Templates for *Microsoft Excel.*

Barry Borrower's Company Net Income Forecast (in 000's)

	Probability of Occurrence				
	5%	**10%**	**70%**	**10%**	**5%**
Operating Income	$110.0	$220.0	$440.0	$660.0	$770.0
Interest Expense	40	40	40	40	40
Before-Tax Income	70	180	400	620	730
Taxes (28%)	19.6	50.4	112	173.6	204.4
Net Income	50.4	129.6	288	446.4	525.6

a. Calculate the expected values of Equity Eddie's and Barry Borrower's net incomes.

b. Calculate the standard deviations of Equity Eddie's and Barry Borrower's net incomes.

c. Calculate the coefficients of variation of Equity Eddie's and Barry Borrower's net incomes.

d. Compare Equity Eddie's and Barry Borrower's degrees of financial risk.

7-5. George Taylor, owner of a toy manufacturing company, is considering the addition of a new product line. Marketing research shows that gorilla action figures will be the next fad for the six- to ten-year-old age group. This new product line of gorilla-like action figures and their high-tech vehicles will be called Go-Rilla. George estimates that the most likely yearly incremental cash flow will be $26,000. There is some uncertainty about this value because George's company has never before made a product similar to the Go-Rilla. He has estimated the potential cash flows for the new product line along with their associated probabilities of occurrence. His estimates follow.

Standard Deviation and Coefficient of Variation

For more, see 8e Spreadsheet Templates for *Microsoft Excel.*

Go-Rilla Project

Cash Flows	Probability of Occurrence
$ 20,000	1%
$ 22,000	12%
$ 24,000	23%
$ 26,000	28%
$ 28,000	23%
$ 30,000	12%
$ 32,000	1%

a. Calculate the standard deviation of the estimated cash flows.

b. Calculate the coefficient of variation.

c. If George's other product lines have an average coefficient of variation of 12 percent, what can you say about the risk of the Go-Rilla Project relative to the average risk of the other product lines?

7-6. Assume that a company has an existing portfolio A with an expected return of 9 percent and a standard deviation of 3 percent. The company is considering adding an asset B to its portfolio. Asset B's expected return is 12 percent with a standard deviation of 4 percent. Also assume that the amount invested in A is $700,000 and the amount to be invested in B is $200,000. If the degree of correlation between returns from portfolio A and project B is zero, calculate:

Portfolio Risk

For more, see 8e Spreadsheet Templates for *Microsoft Excel.*

a. The standard deviation of the new combined portfolio and compare it with that of the existing portfolio.

b. The coefficient of variation of the new combined portfolio and compare it with that of the existing portfolio.

Coefficient of Variation **7-7.** Zazzle Company has a standard deviation of 288 and a mean of 1,200. What is its coefficient of variation (CV)?

Expected Rate of Return **7-8.** What is the expected rate of return on a portfolio that has $4,000 invested in Stock A and $6,000 invested in Stock B? The expected rates of return on these two stocks are 13 percent and 9 percent, respectively.

Standard Deviation **7-9.** A two-stock portfolio has 30 percent in Stock A, with an expected return of 21 percent and a standard deviation of 5 percent, and the remainder in Stock B, with an 18 percent expected return and a standard deviation of 2 percent. The correlation coefficient is 0.6. Determine the standard deviation for this portfolio.

Measuring Risk **7-10.** A firm has an existing portfolio of projects with an expected return of 11 percent a year. The standard deviation of these returns is 4 percent. The existing portfolio's value is $820,000. As financial manager, you are considering the addition of a new project, PROJ1. PROJ1's expected return is 13 percent with a standard deviation of 5 percent. The initial cash outlay for PROJ1 is expected to be $194,000.

  a. Calculate the coefficient of variation for the existing portfolio.

  b. Calculate the coefficient of variation for PROJ1.

  c. If PROJ1 is added to the existing portfolio, calculate the weight (proportion) of the existing portfolio in the combined portfolio.

  d. Calculate the weight (proportion) of PROJ1 in the combined portfolio.

  e. Assume the correlation coefficient of the cash flows of the existing portfolio and PROJ1 is zero. Calculate the standard deviation of the combined portfolio. Is the standard deviation of the combined portfolio higher or lower than the standard deviation of the existing portfolio?

  f. Calculate the coefficient of variation of the combined portfolio.

  g. If PROJ1 is added to the existing portfolio, will the firm's risk increase or decrease?

> For more, see 8e Spreadsheet Templates for *Microsoft Excel.*

CAPM **7-11.** Assume the risk-free rate is 5 percent, the expected rate of return on the market is 15 percent, and the beta of your firm is 1.2. Given these conditions, what is the required rate of return on your company's stock per the capital asset pricing model?

CAPM **7-12.** Calculate the expected rates of return for the low-, average-, and high-risk stocks:

  a. Risk-free rate = 4.5 percent

  b. Market risk premium = 12.5 percent

  c. Low-risk beta = .5

  d. Average-risk beta = 1.0

  e. High-risk beta = 1.6

Challenge Problem **7-13.** Your firm has a beta of 1.5 and you are considering an investment project with a beta of 0.8. Answer the following questions, assuming that short-term Treasury bills are currently yielding 5 percent and the expected return on the market is 15 percent.

  a. What is the appropriate required rate of return for your company per the capital asset pricing model?

  b. What is the appropriate required rate of return for the investment project per the capital asset pricing model?

  c. If your firm invests 20 percent of its assets in the new investment project, what will be the beta of your firm after the project is adopted? (Hint: Compute the weighted average beta of the firm with the new asset, using Equation 7-4.)

The following problems (7-14 to 7-18) relate to the expected business of Power Software Company (PSC) (000's of dollars):

For more, see 8e Spreadsheet Templates for *Microsoft Excel*.

Power Software Company Forecasts

Probability of Occurrence

	2%	8%	20%	40%	20%	8%	2%
Sales	$800	$1,000	$1,400	$2,000	$2,600	$3,000	$3,200

7-14. Calculate the expected value, standard deviation, and coefficient of variation of Measuring Risk sales revenue of PSC. **◀ Measuring Risk**

7-15. Assume that PSC has no fixed expense but has a variable expense that is 60 Business Risk percent of sales as follows: **◀ Business Risk**

Power Software Company Forecasts

Probability of Occurrence

	2%	8%	20%	40%	20%	8%	2%
Sales	$800	$1,000	$1,400	$2,000	$2,600	$3,000	$3,200
Variable Expenses	480	600	840	1,200	1,560	1,800	1,920

Calculate PSC's business risk (coefficient of variation of operating income).

7-16. Now assume that PSC has a fixed operating expense of $400,000, in addition to Business **◀ Business Risk** Risk the variable expense of 60 percent of sales, shown as follows:

Power Software Company Forecasts

Probability of Occurrence

	2%	8%	20%	40%	20%	8%	2%
Sales	$800	$1,000	$1,400	$2,000	$2,600	$3,000	$3,200
Variable Expenses	480	600	840	1,200	1,560	1,800	1,920
Fixed Expenses	400	400	400	400	400	400	400

Recalculate PSC's business risk (coefficient of variation of operating income). How does this figure compare with the business risk calculated with variable cost only?

7-17. Assume that PSC has a fixed interest expense of $60,000 on borrowed funds. Also assume **◀ Various Statistics and Financial Risk** that the applicable tax rate is 30 percent. What are the expected value, standard deviation, and coefficient of variation of PSC's net income? What is PSC's financial risk?

7-18. To reduce the various risks, PSC is planning to take suitable steps to reduce volatility of **◀ Business and Financial Risk** operating and net income. It has projected that fixed expenses and interest expenses can be reduced. The revised figures follow:

Power Software Company Forecasts

Probability of Occurrence

	1%	6%	13%	60%	13%	6%	1%
Sales	$800	$1,000	$1,400	$2,000	$2,600	$3,000	$3,200
Variable Expenses	480	600	840	1,200	1,560	1,800	1,920
Fixed Expenses	250	250	250	250	250	250	250
Interest Expense	40	40	40	40	40	40	40

Recalculate PSC's business and financial risks and compare these figures with those calculated in problems 7-16 and 7-17. The tax rate is 30 percent.

Answers to Self-Test

ST-1. $CV = \sigma \div \mu = \$400,000 \div \$5,000,000 =$
$.08 = 8\%$

ST-2. $\mu = (.2 \times .04) + (.6 \times .10) + (.2 \times .20) = .108 = 10.8\%$

ST-3. $\sigma = ([.2 \times (.04 - .108)^2] + [.6 \times (.10 - .108)^2] + [.2 \times (.20 - .108)^2])^{.5}$

$= [(.2 \times .004624) + (.6 \times .000064) + (.2 \times .008464)]^{.5}$

$= .002656^{.5} = .0515 = 5.15\%$

ST-4. $\sigma_p = [(.4^2 \times .08^2) + (.6^2 + .12^2) + (2 \times .4 \times .6 \times (-.2) \times .08 \times .12)]^{.5}$

$= [(.16 \times .0064) + (.36 \times .0144) + (-.0009216)]^{.5}$

$= .0052864^{.5} = .0727 = 7.27\%$

ST-5. $.18 + (2 \times .03) = .24 = 24\%$

$.18 - (2 \times .03) = .12 = 12\%$

Therefore, we are 95% confident that the actual return will be between 12% and 24%.

ST-6. $k_s = .04 + (.06 \times 1.2) = .112 = 11.2\%$

ST-7. $k_s = .04 + (.06 \times .4) = .064 = 6.4\%$

ST-8. WT of Stock C must be .25 for the total of the weights to equal 1:

$.14 = (.06 \times .25) + (.10 \times .5) + [E(R_C) \times .25]$

$.14 = .065 + [E(R_C) \times .25]$

$.075 = E(R_C) \times .25$

$E(R_C) = .30 = 30\%$

The Time Value of Money

"The importance of money flows from it being a link between the present and the future."
—John Maynard Keynes

CHAPTER 8

Source: Number1411/Shutterstock

Learning Objectives

After reading this chapter, you should be able to:

1. Explain the time value of money and its importance in the business world.
2. Calculate the future value and present value of a single amount.
3. Find the future and present values of an annuity.
4. Solve time value of money problems with uneven cash flows.
5. Solve for the interest rate, number or amount of payments, or the number of periods in a future or present value problem.

Get a Free $1,000 Bond with Every Car Bought This Week!

There is a car dealer who appears on television regularly. He does his own commercials. He is quite loud and is also very aggressive. According to him you will pay way too much if you buy your car from anyone else in town. You might have a car dealer like this in your hometown.

The author of this book used to watch and listen to the television commercials for a particular car dealer. One promotion struck him as being particularly interesting. The automobile manufacturers had been offering cash rebates to buyers of particular cars but this promotion had recently ended. This local car dealer seemed to be picking up where the manufacturers had left off. He was offering "a free $1,000 bond with every new car purchased" during a particular week. This sounded pretty good.

The fine print of this deal was not revealed until the buyer was signing the final sales papers. Even then you had to look close since the print was small. It turns out the "$1,000 bond" offered to each car buyer was what is known as a "zero coupon bond." This means that there are no periodic interest payments. The buyer of the bond pays a price less than the face value of $1,000 and then at maturity the issuer pays $1,000 to the holder of the bond. The investor's return is entirely equal to the difference between the lower price paid for the bond and the $1,000 received at maturity. How much less than $1,000 did the dealer have to pay to get this bond he was giving away?

The amount paid by the dealer is what the bond would be worth (less after paying commissions) if the car buyer wanted to sell this bond now. It turns out that this bond had a maturity of 30 years. This is how long the car buyer would have to wait to receive the $1,000. The value of the bond at the time the car was purchased was about $57. This is what the car dealer paid for each of these bonds and is the amount the car buyer would get from selling the bond. It's a pretty shrewd marketing gimmick when a car dealer can buy something for $57 and get the customers to believe they are receiving something worth $1,000.

In this chapter you will become armed against such deceptions. It's all in the time value of money.

Source: This is inspired by an actual marketing promotion. Some of the details have been changed, and all identities have been hidden, so the author does not get sued.

Chapter Overview

A dollar in hand today is worth more than a promise of a dollar tomorrow. This is one of the basic principles of financial decision making. Time value analysis is a crucial part of financial decisions. It helps answer questions about how much money an investment will make over time and how much a firm must invest now to earn an expected payoff later.

In this chapter we will investigate why money has time value, as well as learn how to calculate the future value of cash invested today and the present value of cash to be received in the future. We will also discuss the present and future values of an annuity—a series of equal cash payments at regular time intervals. Finally, we will examine special time value of money problems, such as how to find the rate of return on an investment and how to deal with a series of uneven cash payments.

Why Money Has Time Value

The time value of money means that money you hold in your hand today is worth more than the same amount of money you expect to receive in the future. Similarly, a given amount of money you must pay out today is a greater burden than the same amount paid in the future.

In Chapter 2 we learned that interest rates are usually positive in part because people prefer to consume now rather than later. Positive interest rates indicate, then, that money has time value. When one person lets another borrow money, the first person requires compensation in exchange for reducing current consumption. The person who borrows the money is willing to pay to increase current consumption. The cost paid by the borrower to the lender for reducing consumption, known as an *opportunity cost*, is the real rate of interest.

pure time value of money The value demanded by an investor to compensate for the postponement of consumption.

The real rate of interest reflects compensation for the **pure time value of money**. The real rate of interest does not include interest charged for expected inflation or the other risk factors discussed in Chapter 2. Recall from the interest rate discussion in Chapter 2 that many factors—including the pure time value of money, inflation risk, default risk, illiquidity risk, and maturity risk—determine market interest rates.

The required rate of return on an investment reflects the pure time value of money, an adjustment for expected inflation, and any other risk premiums present.

Measuring the Time Value of Money

future value The value money or another asset will have in the future.

Financial managers adjust for the time value of money by calculating the **future value** and the present value. Future value and present value are mirror images of each other. Future value is the value of a starting amount at a future point in time, given the rate of growth per period and the number of periods until that future time. How much will $1,000 invested today at a 10 percent interest rate grow to in 15 years? **Present value** is the value of a future amount today, assuming a specific required interest rate for a number of periods until that future amount is realized. How much should we pay today to obtain a promised payment of $1,000 in 15 years if investing money today would yield a 10 percent rate of return per year?

present value Today's value of a promised or expected future value.

The Future Value of a Single Amount

To calculate the future value of a single amount, we must first understand how money grows over time. Once money is invested, it earns an interest rate that compensates for the time value of money and, as we learned in Chapter 2, for default risk, inflation, and other factors. Often, the interest earned on investments is compound interest—interest earned on interest and on the original principal. In contrast, *simple interest* is interest earned only on the original principal.

To illustrate compound interest, assume the financial manager of NileCorp decided to invest $100 of the firm's excess cash in an account that earns an annual interest rate of 5 percent. In one year, NileCorp will earn $5 in interest, calculated as follows:

$$
\begin{aligned}
\text{Balance at the end of year 1} &= \text{Principal} + \text{Interest} \\
&= \$100 + (100 \times .05) \\
&= \$100 \times (1 + .05) \\
&= \$100 \times 1.05 \\
&= \$105
\end{aligned}
$$

The total amount in the account at the end of year 1, then, is $105.

But look what happens in years 2 and 3. In year 2, NileCorp will earn 5 percent of 105. The $105 is the original principal of $100 plus the first year's interest—so the interest earned in year 2 is $5.25, rather than $5.00. The end of year 2 balance is $110.25—$100 in original principal and $10.25 in interest. In year 3, NileCorp will earn 5 percent of $110.25, or $5.51, for an ending balance of $115.76, shown as follows:

	Beginning Balance	×	(1 + Interest Rate)		= Ending Balance	Interest
Year 1	$100.00	×	1.05	=	$105.00	$5.00
Year 2	$105.00	×	1.05	=	$110.25	$5.25
Year 3	$110.25	×	1.05	=	$115.76	$5.51

In our example, NileCorp earned $5 in interest in year 1, $5.25 in interest in year 2 ($110.25 – $105.00), and $5.51 in year 3 ($115.76 – $110.25) because of the compounding effect. If the NileCorp deposit earned interest only on the original principal, rather than on the principal and interest, the balance in the account at the end of year 3 would be $115 ($100 + ($5 × 3) = $115). In our case the compounding effect accounts for an extra $.76 ($115.76 – $115.00 = .76).

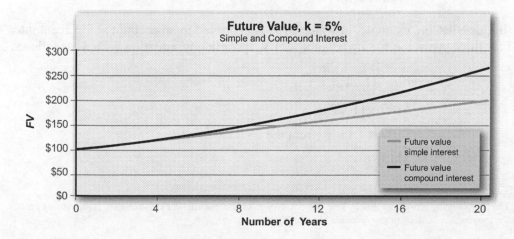

The simplest way to find the balance at the end of year 3 is to multiply the original principal by 1 plus the interest rate per period (expressed as a decimal), $1 + k$, raised to the power of the number of compounding periods, n. Here's the formula for finding the future value—or ending balance—given the original principal, interest rate per period, and number of compounding periods:

Future Value for a Single Amount
Algebraic Method

$$FV = PV \times (1 + k)^n \quad (8\text{-}1a)$$

where: FV = Future Value, the ending amount

PV = Present Value, the starting amount, or original principal

k = Rate of interest per period (expressed as a decimal)

n = Number of periods[1]

In our NileCorp example, PV is the original deposit of $100, k is 5 percent, and n is 3. To solve for the ending balance, or FV, we apply Equation 8-1a as follows:

$$
\begin{aligned}
FV &= PV \times (1 + k)^n \\
&= \$100 \times (1.05)^3 \\
&= \$100 \times 1.1576 \\
&= \$115.76
\end{aligned}
$$

We may also solve for future value using a financial table. Financial tables are a compilation of values, known as interest factors, that represent a term, $(1 + k)^n$ in this case, in time value of money formulas. Table I in the Appendix at the end of the book is developed by calculating $(1 + k)^n$ for many combinations of k and n.

Table I in the Appendix at the end of the book is the **future value factor (FVF)** table. The formula for future value using the FVF table follows:

future value factor (FVF) The factor, which when multiplied by a single amount present value, gives the future value. It equals $(1 + k)^n$ for given values of k and n.

Future Value for a Single Amount
Table Method

$$FV = PV \times \left(FVF_{k, n} \right) \quad (8\text{-}1b)$$

where: FV = Future Value, the ending amount

PV = Present Value, the starting amount

$FVF_{k,n}$ = Future Value Factor given interest rate, k, and number of periods, n, from Table I

In our NileCorp example, in which $100 is deposited in an account at 5 percent interest for three years, the ending balance, or FV, according to Equation 8-1b, is as follows:

$$
\begin{aligned}
FV &= PV \times \left(FVF_{k, n} \right) \\
&= \$100 \times \left(FVF_{5\%, 3} \right) \\
&= \$100 \times 1.1576 \text{ (from the FVF table)} \\
&= \$115.76
\end{aligned}
$$

---

1. The compounding periods are usually years but not always. As you will see later in the chapter, compounding periods can be months, weeks, days, or any specified period of time.

To solve for FV using a financial calculator, we enter the numbers for PV, n, and k (k is depicted as I/Y on the TI BAII PLUS calculator; on other calculators it may be symbolized by i or I), and ask the calculator to compute FV. The keystrokes follow.

Take Note
Because future value interest factors are rounded to four decimal places in Table I, you may get a slightly different solution compared to a problem solved by the algebraic method.

TI BAII PLUS Financial Calculator Solution

Step 1: First press **2nd** **CLR TVM**. This clears all the time value of money keys of all previously calculated or entered values.

Step 2: Press **2nd** **P/Y** 1 **ENTER** , **2nd** **QUIT** . This sets the calculator to the mode where one payment per year is expected, which is the assumption for the problems in this chapter.

Older TI BAII PLUS financial calculators were set at the factory to a default value of 12 for P/Y. Change this default value to 1 as shown here if you have one of these older calculators. For the past several years TI has made the default value 1 for P/Y. If after pressing you see the value 1 in the display window you may press CE/C twice on your calculator to back out of this. No changes to the P/Y value are needed if your calculator is already set to the default value of 1. You may similarly skip this adjustment throughout this chapter where the financial calculator solutions are shown if your calculator already has its P/Y value set to 1. If your calculator is an older one that requires you to change the default value of P/Y from 12 to 1, you do not need to make that change again. The default value of P/Y will stay set to 1 unless you specifically change it.

Step 3: Input values for principal (PV), interest rate (k or I/Y on the calculator), and number of periods (n).

100 **+/−** **PV** 5 **I/Y** 3 **N** **CPT** **FV**   **Answer: 115.76**

In the NileCorp example, we input −100 for the present value (PV), 3 for number of periods (N), and 5 for the interest rate per year (I/Y). Then we ask the calculator to compute the future value, FV. The result is $115.76. Our TI BAII PLUS is set to display two decimal places. You may choose a greater or lesser number if you wish. This future value problem can also be solved using the FV function in the spreadsheet below.

E10		✕ ✓ *fx*	=FV(D10,C10,0,-B10)		

	A	B	C	D	FV(rate, nper, pmt, [pv], [type])	F	G
1							
2			The Future Value of a Single Amount				
3							
4	This Excel spreadsheet computes the future value of $100 earning 5% annual interest						
5	for three years. This is a future value of a single amount problem with annual compounding.						
6	Note how the FV Function inputs the $100 present value amount as a negative value						
7	since you are paying out that amount now at the time of the deposit.						
8							
9		PV	n	k	FV	Function	
10		$100.00	3	5%	$115.76	<— =FV(D10,C10,0,-B10)	
11							
12							
13					Excel FV()		
14					Function		
15							

We have learned four ways to calculate the future value of a single amount: the algebraic method, the financial table method, the financial calculator method, and the spreadsheet method. In the next section, we see how future values are related to changes in the interest rate, k, and the number of time periods, n. We also input −100 for the PV value in the spreadsheet.

The Sensitivity of Future Values to Changes in Interest Rates or the Number of Compounding Periods

Future value has a positive relationship with the interest rate, k, and with the number of periods, n. That is, as the interest rate increases, future value increases. Similarly, as the number of periods increases, so does future value. In contrast, future value decreases with decreases in k and n values.

It is important to understand the sensitivity of future value to k and n because increases are exponential, as shown by the $(1 + k)^n$ term in the future value formula. Consider this: A business that invests $10,000 in a savings account at 5 percent for 20 years will have a future value of $26,532.98. If the interest rate is 8 percent for the same 20 years, the future value of the investment is $46,609.57. We see that the future value of the investment increases as k increases. Figure 8-1a shows this graphically.

Now let's say that the business deposits $10,000 for 10 years at a 5 percent annual interest rate. The future value of that sum is $16,288.95. Another business deposits $10,000 for 20 years at the same 5 percent annual interest rate. The future value of that $10,000 investment is $26,532.98. Just as with the interest rate, the higher the number of periods, the higher the future value. Figure 8-1b shows this graphically.

The Present Value of a Single Amount

Present value is today's dollar value of a specific future amount. With a bond, for instance, the issuer promises the investor future cash payments at specified points in time. With an investment in new plant or equipment, certain cash receipts are expected. When we calculate the present value of a future promised or expected cash payment, we discount it (mark it down in value) because it is worth less if it is to be received later rather than now. Similarly, future cash outflows are less burdensome than present cash outflows of the same amount. Future cash outflows are similarly discounted (made less negative). In present value analysis, then, the interest rate used in this discounting process is known as the discount rate. The discount rate is the required rate of return on an investment. It reflects

FIGURE 8-1A

Future Value at Different Interest Rates

Figure 8-1a shows the future value of $10,000 after 20 years at interest rates of 5 percent and 8 percent.

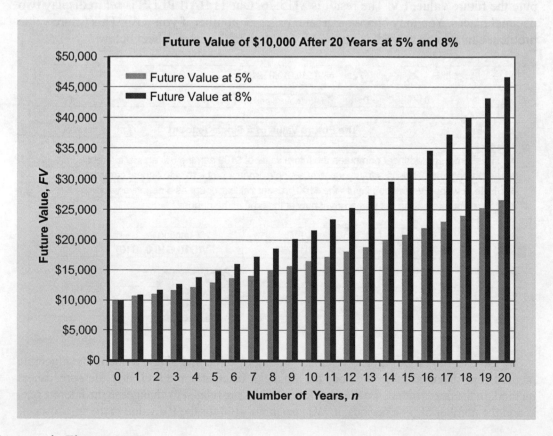

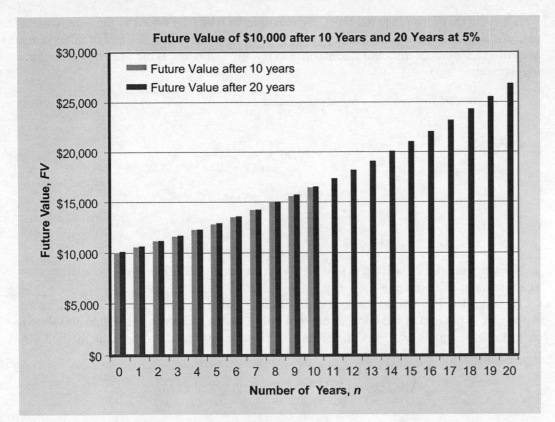

FIGURE 8-1B
Future Value at Different
Times

Figure 8-1b shows the
future value of $10,000 after
10 years and 20 years at an
interest rate of 5 percent.

the lost opportunity to spend or invest now (the opportunity cost) and the various risks assumed because we must wait for the funds. Discounting is the inverse of compounding. Compound interest causes the value of a beginning amount to increase at an increasing rate.

Discounting causes the present value of a future amount to decrease at a decreasing rate. To demonstrate, imagine the NileCorp financial manager needed to know how much to invest now to generate $115.76 in three years, given an interest rate of 5 percent. Given what we know so far, the calculation would look like this:

$$FV = PV \times (1 + k)^n$$

$$\$115.76 = PV \times 1.05^3$$

$$\$115.76 = PV \times 1.157625$$

$$PV = \$100.00$$

To simplify solving present value problems, we modify the future value for a single amount equation by multiplying both sides by $1/(1 + k)^n$ to isolate PV on one side of the equal sign. The present value formula for a single amount follows:

The Present Value of a Single Amount Formula
Algebraic Method

$$PV = FV \times \frac{1}{(1 + k)^n}$$

(8-2a)

where: PV = Present Value, the starting amount

FV = Future Value, the ending amount

k = Discount rate of interest per period (expressed as a decimal)

n = Number of periods

Applying this formula to the NileCorp example, in which its financial manager wanted to know how much the firm should pay today to receive $115.76 at the end of three years, assuming a 5 percent discount rate starting today, the following is the present value of the investment:

$$PV = FV \times \frac{1}{(1 + k)^n}$$

$$= \$115.76 \times \frac{1}{(1 + .05)^3}$$

$$= \$115.76 \times .86384$$

$$= \$100.00$$

NileCorp should be willing to pay $100 today to receive $115.76 three years from now at a 5 percent discount rate.

To solve for PV, we may also use the Present Value Factor Table in Table II in the Appendix at the end of the book. A **present value factor (PVF)**, is calculated and shown in Table II. It equals $1/(1 + k)^n$ for given combinations of k and n. The table method formula, Equation 8-2b, follows:

present value factor (PVF) Today's value of promised or expected future value. It equals

$$\frac{1}{(1 + k)^n}$$

for given values of k and n.

The Present Value of a Single Amount Formula
Table Method

$$PV = FV \times (PVF_{k, n}) \qquad (8\text{-}2b)$$

where: PV = Present Value

FV = Future Value

$PVF_{k,n}$ = Present Value Factor given discount rate, k per period, and number of periods, n, from Table II

In our example, NileCorp's financial manager wanted to solve for the amount that must be invested today at a 5 percent annual interest rate to accumulate $115.76 within three years. Applying the present value table formula, we find the following solution:

$$PV = FV \times \left(PVF_{k, n}\right)$$

$$= \$115.76 \times \left(PVF_{5\%, 3}\right)$$

$$= \$115.76 \times .8638 \text{ (from the PVF table)}$$

$$= \$99.99 \text{ (slightly lower than \$100 due to the rounding to four places in the table)}$$

The present value of $115.76, discounted back three years at a 5 percent annual discount rate, is $100.

To solve for present value using a financial calculator, enter the numbers for future value, FV, the number of periods, n, and the interest rate, k—symbolized as I/Y on the calculator—then hit the CPT (compute) and PV (present value) keys. The sequence follows:

Step 1: Press `2nd` `CLR TVM` to clear previous values.

Step 2: Press `2nd` `P/Y` 1 `ENTER` `2nd` `QUIT` to ensure the calculator is in the mode for annual interest payments.

Step 3: Input the values for future value, the interest rate, and number of periods, and compute PV.

115.76 `FV` 5 `I/Y` 3 `N` `CPT` `PV`   **Answer: –100.00**

The financial calculator result is displayed as a negative number to show that the present value sum is a cash outflow—that is, that sum will have to be invested to earn $115.76 in three years at a 5 percent annual interest rate. This present value problem can also be solved using the PV function in the spreadsheet that follows.

E10	▾	:	X	✓	*fx*	=PV(D10,C10,0,B10)		
	A	B	C	D	PV(rate, nper, pmt, [fv], [type]) F		G	
1								
2			**The Present Value of a Single Amount**					
3								
4	This Excel spreadsheet shows you how to compute the present value of $115.76							
5	discounted back 3 years with a 5% annual discount rate. Note that the computed							
6	PV has a negative value indicating that you should be willing to pay that amount							
7	now for the right to receive $115.76 in three years with a 5% discount rate.							
8								
9		FV	n	k	PV	Function		
10		$115.76	3	5%	–$100.00	<– =PV(D10,C10,0,B10)		
11								
12						Excel PV()		
13						Function		
14								
15								

We have examined how to find present value using the algebraic, table, financial calculator, and spreadsheet methods. Next, we see how present value analysis is affected by the discount rate, k, and the number of compounding periods, n.

The Sensitivity of Present Values to Changes in the Interest Rate or the Number of Compounding Periods

In contrast with future value, present value is inversely related to k and n values. In other words, present value moves in the opposite direction of k and n. If k increases, present value decreases; if k decreases, present value increases. If n increases, present value decreases; if n decreases, present value increases.

Consider this: A business that expects a 5 percent annual return on its investment (k = 5%) should be willing to pay $3,768.89 today (the present value) for $10,000 to be received 20 years from now. If the expected annual return is 8 percent for the same 20 years, the present value of the investment is only $2,145.48. We see that the present value of the investment decreases as the value of k increases. The way the present value of the $10,000 varies with changes in the required rate of return is shown graphically in Figure 8-2a.

Now let's say that a business expects to receive $10,000 ten years from now. If its required rate of return for the investment is 5 percent annually, then it should be willing to pay $6,139 for the investment today (the present value is $6,139). If another business

FIGURE 8-2A
Present Value at Different Interest Rates

Figure 8-2a shows the present value of $10,000 to be received in 20 years at interest rates of 5 percent and 8 percent.

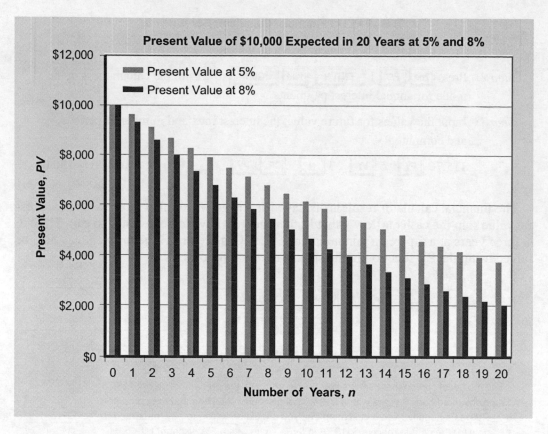

Present Value of $10,000 Expected in 20 Years at 5% and 8%

- Present Value at 5%
- Present Value at 8%

Present Value, *PV* vs Number of Years, *n*

FIGURE 8-2B
Present Value at Different Times

Figure 8-2b shows the present value of $10,000 to be received in 10 years and 20 years at an interest rate of 5 percent.

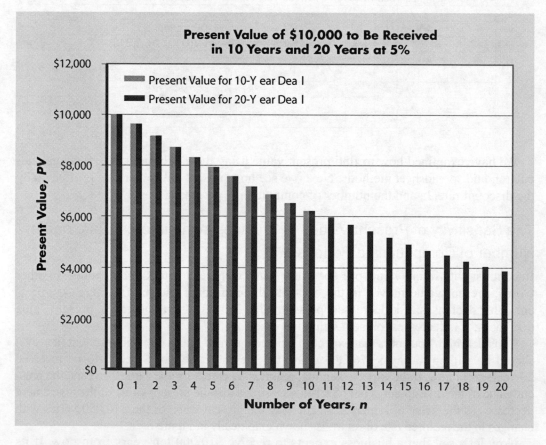

Present Value of $10,000 to Be Received in 10 Years and 20 Years at 5%

- Present Value for 10-Year Deal
- Present Value for 20-Year Deal

Present Value, *PV* vs Number of Years, *n*

expects to receive $10,000 twenty years from now and it has the same 5 percent annual required rate of return, then it should be willing to pay $3,769 for the investment (the present value is $3,769). Just as with the interest rate, the greater the number of periods, the lower the present value. Figure 8-2b shows how it works.

In this section we have learned how to find the future value and the present value of a single amount. Next, we will examine how to find the future value and present value of several amounts.

Working with Annuities

Financial managers often need to assess a series of cash flows rather than just one. One common type of cash flow series is the **annuity**—a series of equal cash flows, spaced evenly over time.

Professional athletes often sign contracts that provide annuities for them after they retire, in addition to the signing bonus and regular salary they may receive during their playing years. Consumers can purchase annuities from insurance companies as a means of providing retirement income. The investor pays the insurance company a lump sum now in order to receive future payments of equal size at regularly spaced time intervals (usually monthly). Another example of an annuity is the interest on a bond. The interest payments are usually equal dollar amounts paid either annually or semiannually during the life of the bond.

Annuities are a significant part of many financial problems. You should learn to recognize annuities and determine their value, future or present. In this section we will explain how to calculate the future value and present value of annuities in which cash flows occur at the end of the specified time periods. Annuities in which the cash flows occur at the end of each of the specified time periods are known as *ordinary annuities*. Annuities in which the cash flows occur at the beginning of each of the specified time periods are known as *annuities due*.

annuity A series of equal cash payments made at regular time intervals.

Future Value of an Ordinary Annuity

Financial managers often plan for the future. When they do, **they often need to know how much money to save on a regular basis to accumulate a given amount of cash at a** specified future time. The future value of an annuity is the amount that a given number of annuity payments, n, will grow to at a future date, for a given periodic interest rate, k.

For instance, suppose the NileCorp Company plans to invest $500 in a money market account at the end of each year for the next four years, beginning one year from today. The business expects to earn a 5 percent annual rate of return on its investment. How much money will NileCorp have in the account at the end of four years? The problem is illustrated in the timeline in Figure 8-3. The t values in the timeline represent the end of each time period. Thus, t_1 is the end of the first year, t_2 is the end of the second year, and so on. The symbol t_0 is now, the present point in time.

Because the $500 payments are each single amounts, we can solve this problem one step at a time. Looking at Figure 8-4, we see that the first step is to calculate the future value of the cash flows that occur at t_1, t_2, t_3, and t_4 using the future value formula for a single amount. The next step is to add the four values together. The sum of those values is this ordinary annuity's future value.

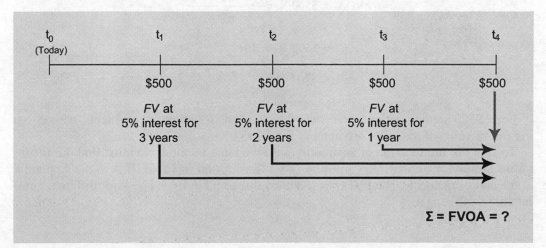

FIGURE 8-3
NileCorp FVOA Timeline

FIGURE 8-4
Future Value of the
NileCorp Ordinary Annuity

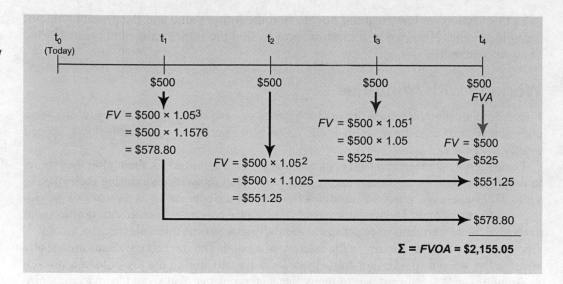

As shown in Figure 8-4, the sum of the future values of the four end-of-year single amounts is the ordinary annuity's future value, $2,155.05. However, the step-by-step process illustrated in Figure 8-4 is time-consuming even in this simple example. Calculating the future value of a 20- or 30-year ordinary annuity, such as would be the case with many bonds, would take an enormous amount of time. Instead, we can calculate the future value of an ordinary annuity easily by using the following formula:

Future Value of an Ordinary Annuity
Algebraic Method

$$FVOA = PMT \times \frac{(1 + k)^n - 1}{k}$$

(8-3a)

where: FVOA = Future Value of an Ordinary Annuity

PMT = Amount of each annuity payment

k = Interest rate per period expressed as a decimal

n = Number of periods

Using Equation 8-3a in our NileCorp example, we solve for the future value of the annuity at 5 percent interest (k = 5%) with four $500 end-of-year payments (n = 4 and PMT = $500), as follows:

$$FVOA = \$500 \times \left[\frac{(1 + .05)^4 - 1}{.05} \right]$$

$$= \$500 \times 4.3101$$

$$= \$2,155.05$$

future value factor for an ordinary annuity (FVFOA) The factor, which when multiplied by an expected annuity payment, gives the sum of the future values of an ordinary annuity stream. It equals

$$\left[\frac{(1 + k)^n - 1}{k} \right]$$ for given

values of k and n.

For a $500 annuity with a 5 percent interest rate and four annuity payments, we see that the future value of the NileCorp annuity is $2,155.05.

To find the future value of an annuity with the table method, we must find the **future value factor for an ordinary annuity (FVFOA)**, found in Table III-A in the Appendix at the end of the book. The $FVFOA_{k, n}$ is the value of $[(1 + k)^n - 1] \div k$ for different combinations of k and n.

Future Value of an Ordinary Annuity Formula
Table Method

$$FVOA = PMT \times FVFOA_{k,n} \qquad (8\text{-}3b)$$

where: FVOA = Future Value of an Ordinary Annuity

      PMT = Amount of each annuity payment

      $FVFOA_{k,n}$ = Future Value Factor for an Ordinary Annuity from Table III-A

             k = Interest rate per period

             n = Number of periods

In our NileCorp example, then, we need to find the FVFOA for a discount rate of 5 percent with four end-of-year annuity payments. Table III-A in the Appendix shows that the $FVFOA_{k=5\%, n=4}$ is 4.3101. Using the table method, we find the following future value of the NileCorp annuity:

$$FVOA = \$500 \times FVFOA_{5\%, 4}$$

$$= \$500 \times 4.3101 \text{ (from the FVFOA table)}$$

$$= \$2,155.05$$

To find the future value of an ordinary annuity using a financial calculator, key in the values for the annuity payment (PMT), n, and k (remember that the notation for the interest rate on the TI BAII PLUS calculator is I/Y, not k). Then compute the future value of the ordinary annuity (FV on the calculator). For a series of four $500 end-of-year (ordinary annuity) payments where n = 4 and k = 5 percent, the computation is as follows:

TI BAII PLUS Financial Calculator Solution

Step 1: Press `2nd` `CLR TVM` to clear previous values.

Step 2: Press `2nd` `P/Y` 1 `ENTER`, `2nd` `BGN` `2nd` `SET` `2nd` `SET`. Repeat `2nd` `SET` until END shows in the display `2nd` `QUIT` to set the annual interest rate mode and to set the annuity payment to end of period mode.

Step 3: Input the values and compute.

0 `PV`   5 `I/Y`   4 `N`   500 `+/-` `PMT`   `CPT` `FV`   **Answer: 2,155.06**

The spreadsheet that follows solves this same future value problem using the FV function.

E9		✕ ✓ *fx*	=FV(D9,C9,-B9)		

	A	B	C	D	FV(rate, nper, pmt, [pv], [type])	G	H
1							
2			The Future Value of an Ordinary Annuity				
3							
4	This Excel spreadsheet computes the future value of a 4 year, $500 annual ordinary annuity						
5	earning a 5% annual interest rate. Note that the FV function inputs the $500 annuity payment as a						
6	negative value since you are paying that amount out in order to receive $2,155.06 at the future point in time.						
7							
8		PMT	n	k	FV	Function	
9		$500.00	4	5%	$2,155.06	<-- =FV(D9,C9,-B9)	
10							
11							
12					Excel FV()		
13					Function		
14							

In the financial calculator and spreadsheet inputs, note that the payment is keyed in as a negative number to indicate that the payments are cash outflows—the payments flow out from the company into an investment. The [pv] input for the FV function is omitted since it doesn't apply to this problem and the [type] input is omitted since the default is to compute the ordinary annuity value. Later in this chapter the value of an annuity due (beginning-of-period) will be computed and the necessary [type] value will be input at that time.

The Present Value of an Ordinary Annuity

Because annuity payments are often promised (as with interest on a bond investment) or expected (as with cash inflows from an investment in new plant or equipment), it is important to know how much these investments are worth to us today. For example, assume that the financial manager of Buy4Later, Inc. learns of an annuity that promises to make four annual payments of $500, beginning one year from today. How much should the company be willing to pay to obtain that annuity? The answer is the present value of the ordinary annuity.

Because an annuity is nothing more than a series of equal single amounts, we could calculate the present value of an annuity with the present value formula for a single amount and sum the totals, but that would be a cumbersome process. Imagine calculating the present value of a 50-year annuity! We would have to find the present value for each of the 50 annuity payments and total them.

Fortunately, we can calculate the present value of an annuity in one step with the following formula:

The Present Value of an Ordinary Annuity Formula
Algebraic Method

$$PVOA = PMT \times \left[\frac{1 - \frac{1}{(1 + k)^n}}{k} \right] \times (1 + k)$$

(8-4a)

where: PVOA = Present Value of an Ordinary Annuity

PMT = Amount of each annuity payment

k = Discount rate per period expressed as a decimal

n = Number of periods

Figure 8-5 and Figure 8-6 show a diagram of this problem. Using our example of a four-year ordinary annuity with payments of $500 at the end of each year and a 5 percent discount rate, we solve for the present value of the ordinary annuity as follows:

$$PVOA = 500 \times \left[\frac{1 - \frac{1}{(1 + .05)^4}}{.05} \right]$$

$$= 500 \times 3.5459505$$

$$= \$1,772.98$$

The present value of the four-year ordinary annuity with equal end-of-year payments of $500 at a 5 percent discount rate is $1,772.98.

We can also use the financial table for the **present value factor for an ordinary annuity (PVFOA)** to solve present value of ordinary annuity problems. The PVFOA table is found in Table IV-A in the Appendix at the end of the book. The formula for the table method follows:

present value factor for an ordinary annuity (PVFOA) The factor which, when multiplied by an expected ordinary annuity payment, gives the sum of the present values of the ordinary annuity stream. It equals

$$\left[\frac{(1 + k)^n - 1}{k} \right]$$ for given

values of k and n.

The Present Value of an Ordinary Annuity Formula
Table Method

$$PVOA = PMT \times PVFOA_{k, n} \qquad (8\text{-}4b)$$

where: PVOA = Present Value of an Ordinary Annuity

PMT = Amount of each annuity payment

$PVFOA_{k, n}$ = Present Value Factor for an Ordinary Annuity from Table IV-A

k = Discount rate per period

n = Number of periods

Applying Equation 8-4b, we find that the present value of the four-year annuity with $500 equal payments and a 5 percent discount rate is as follows:[2]

$$PVOA = \$500 \times PVFOA_{5\%, 4}$$
$$= \$500 \times 3.5460$$
$$= \$1,773.00[2]$$

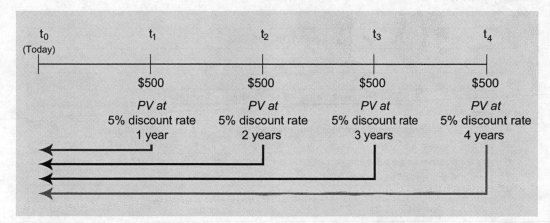

FIGURE 8-5
NileCorp PVOA Timeline

FIGURE 8-6
Present Value of the
NileCorp Ordinary Annuity

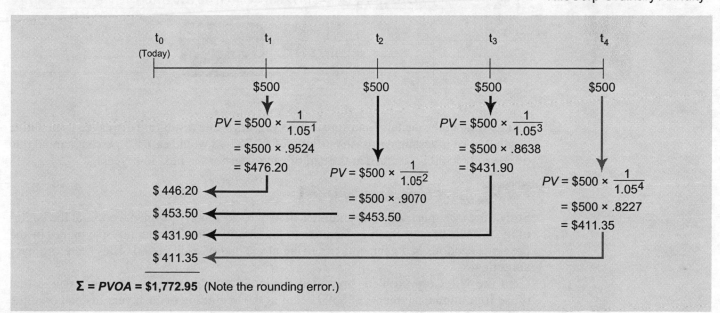

---

2. The $.02 difference between the algebraic result and the table formula solution is due to rounding to 4 decimal places in the table.

We may also solve for the present value of an ordinary annuity with a financial calculator or spreadsheet. For the financial calculator, simply key in the values for the payment, PMT, number of payment periods, n, and the interest rate, k—symbolized by I/Y on the TI BAII PLUS calculator—and ask the calculator to compute PVA (PV on the calculator). For the series of four $500 payments where n = 4 and k = 5 percent, the computation follows:

TI BAII PLUS Financial Calculator Solution

Step 1: Press 2nd CLR TVM to clear previous values.

Step 2: Press 2nd P/Y 1 ENTER , 2nd BGN 2nd SET 2nd SET . Repeat 2nd SET until END shows in the display 2nd QUIT to set the annual interest rate mode and to set the annuity payment to end of period mode.

Step 3: Input the values and compute.

5 I/Y   4 N   500 PMT CPT PV   **Answer: –1,772.98**

The PV function in the spreadsheet below also solves this present value of an ordinary annuity problem.

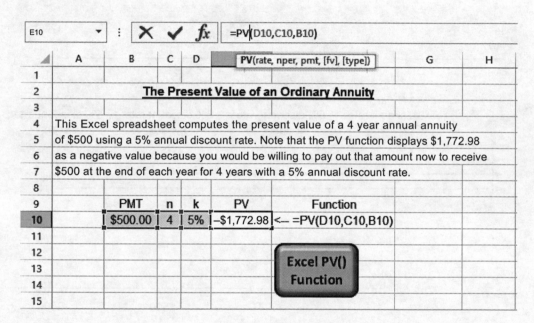

The financial calculator and spreadsheet present value results are displayed as negative numbers. An investment (a cash outflow) of $1,772.98 would earn a 5 percent annual rate of return if $500 is received at the end of each year for the next four years.

Future Value of an Annuity Due

Sometimes we must deal with annuities in which the annuity payments occur at the beginning of each period. Such an annuity is an annuity due. The annuity payments in the previous sections had payments occurring at the end of each period. They were ordinary annuities.

In the NileCorp problem presented earlier in this chapter, let us now assume that those four annual payments of $500 occur at the beginning of each year instead of at the end of each year. Before doing any computations we know that the future value of must be greater than the $2,155.05 value obtained for the future value of an ordinary annuity problem. This is because each $500 annual payment is earning interest sooner, when it is received at the beginning of each year instead of at the end.

We can again solve this future value of an annuity due (FVAD) problem a step at a time. Looking at the numbers in Figure 8-8 we can compute the future value of the cash flows that occur at t_0, t_1, t_2, and t_3 using the future value of a single amount formula. The next step is to add these four future values together. The sum of those values is the future value of the annuity due four years in the future.

We may also use the Future Value Factor for an Annuity Due (FVFAD) in Table III-B in the Appendix at the end of the book. The factors in Table III-B are obtained by applying Equation 8-3a for a range of possible values of k and n and then multiplying that number by $(1 + k)$. The difference between Table III-A and Table III-B, therefore, is that the factors in Table III-B reflect the corresponding factor in Table III-A multiplied by $(1 + k)$ to convert the ordinary annuity factor to its corresponding annuity due factor.

Future Value of an Annuity Due
Algebraic Method

$$FVAD = PMT \times \left[\frac{(1+k)^n - 1}{k} \right] \times (1 + k)$$

(8-5a)

where: FVAD = Future Value of an Annuity Due

PMT = Amount of each annuity payment

k = Interest rate per period expressed as a decimal

n = Number of periods

To solve for FVAD, we can use the algebraic approach described in Equation 8-5a. We solve this problem that specifies four $500 annual annuity due payments (n = 4 and PMT = $500) with a 5% interest rate (k = .05 expressed as a decimal), as follows:

$$FVAD = \$500 \times \left[\frac{(1 + .05)^4 - 1}{.05} \right] \times (1 + .05)$$

$$= \$500 \times 4.310125 \times 1.05$$

$$= \$2,262.82$$

For a $500 annuity due with a 5 percent interest rate and four annual annuity payments, we get a future value of$2,262.82. Figure 8-7 and Figure 8-8 show a diagram of this problem.

Using the table method we find the **future value factor for an annuity due (FVFAD)** found in Table III-B in the Appendix at the end of the book. The $FVFAD_{k,n}$ is the value of $[[(1 + k)^n - 1] \div k] \times (1 + k)$ for different combinations of k and n.

Future Value of an Annuity Due Formula
Table Method

$$FVAD = PMT \times FVFAD_{k,n}$$

(8-5b)

where: FVAD = Future Value of an Annuity

PMT = Amount of each annuity payment

$FVFAD_{k,n}$ = Future Value Factor for an Annuity Due from Table III-B

k = Interest rate per period

n = Number of periods

future value factor for an annuity due (FVFAD) The factor, which when multiplied by an expected annuity payment, gives the sum of the future values of an annuity due stream. It equals

$$\left[\frac{(1 + k)^n - 1}{k} \right] \times (1 + k)$$

for given values of k and n.

Table III-B gives us an FVFAD value of 4.5256 for an interest rate of 5% per period with four annuity due payments. Using $500 for the annuity due value we compute:

$$FVAD = \$500 \times FVFAD_{5\%,4}$$

$$= \$500 \times 4.5256 \text{ (from the FVFAD table in Appendix III-B)}$$

$$= \$2,262.80 \text{ (note the } \$0.02 \text{ rounding discrepancy when only four decimal places are used as found in the table)}$$

FIGURE 8-7
NileCorp FVAD Timeline

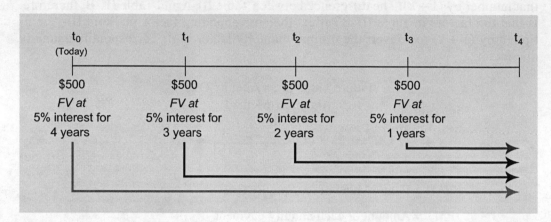

FIGURE 8-8
Future Value of the NileCorp Annuity Due

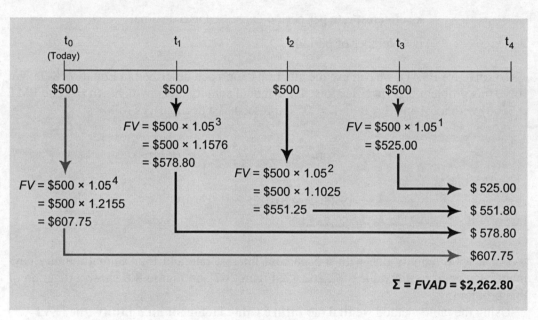

The FVAD is $2,262.80 using the table method. Note we are limited to four decimal places for FVFAD when using the table. Next we can solve this problem using the financial calculator.

Future Value of a Four-Year, $500 Annuity Due, k = 5%

TI BAII PLUS Financial Calculator Solution

Step 1: Press [2nd] [CLR TVM] to clear previous values.

Step 2: Press [2nd] [P/Y] 1 [ENTER], [2nd] [BGN] [2nd] [SET] [2nd] [SET]. Repeat [2nd] [SET] command until the display shows BGN, [2nd] [QUIT] to set to the annual interest rate mode and to set the annuity payment to beginning of period mode.

Step 3: Input the values for the annuity due and compute.

5 [I/Y] 4 [N] 500 [+/-] [PMT] [CPT] [FV] **Answer: 2,262.82**

The answer is $2,262.82 according to the financial calculator for this future value of an annuity due problem.

The spreadsheet can solve this problem by using the FV function. We must be sure to make the [type] value equal to 1 since this is an annuity due problem. When we were solving for the future value of an ordinary annuity the [type] value was 0 which is the default value used by the spreadsheet when this input is omitted. This means that the FV function assumes the annuity problem is an ordinary annuity, and this input may be left out for such problems. When we have an annuity due problem, as here, the value of 1 must be specified for the [type] input value in the FV function.

E10	▼	:	✕ ✓ *fx*	=FV(D10,C10,-B10,0,1)			
◢	A	B	C	D	FV(rate, nper, pmt, [pv], [type])	G	H
1							
2			The Future Value of an Annuity Due				
3							
4	This Excel spreadsheet computes the future value of a 4 year annual annuity due of $500						
5	using a 5% annual discount rate. Note that the FV function inputs the $500 annuity						
6	payment as negative because you would pay out that amount at the beginning of each						
7	year to have $2,262.82 in 5 years.						
8							
9		PMT	n	k	FV	Function	
10		$500.00	4	0.05	$2,262.82	<-- =FV(D10,C10,–B10,0,–1)	
11							
12							
13				Excel FV()			
14				Function			
15							

In this section we learned how to compute the future value and present value of ordinary annuities. We now turn to annuities due.

Present Value of an Annuity Due

Sometimes we run into a series of beginning-of-period annuity payments for which we would like to compute the present value. We can compute the future value of an annuity due in one-step using Equation 8-6a.

Present Value of an Annuity Due
Algebraic Method

$$PVAD = PMT \times \left[\frac{1 - \dfrac{1}{(1+k)^n}}{k} \right] \times (1+k) \qquad \text{8-6a}$$

where: PVAD = Present Value of an Annuity Due

PMT = Amount of each annuity payment

k = Interest rate per period expressed as a decimal

n = Number of periods

Figure 8-9 shows such a timeline and Figure 8-10 shows the timeline with numbers. Using Equation 8-7a in our NileCorp example, we solve for the present value of the annuity due at 5 percent interest (k = .05 expressed as a decimal) with four $500 beginning-of-year payments (n = 4 and PMT = $500), as follows:

$$PVAD = \$500 \times \left[\frac{1 - \dfrac{1}{(1+.05)^4}}{.05}\right] \times (1+.05)$$

$$= \$500 \times 3.545951 \times 1.05$$

$$= \$1,861.62$$

present value factor for an annuity due (PVFAD) The factor, which when multiplied by an expected annuity payment, gives the sum of the present values of an annuity due stream.It equals

$$\left[\frac{1 - \dfrac{1}{(1+k)^n}}{k}\right] \times (1+k)$$

for given values of k and n.

Figure 8-9 and Figure 8-10 show a diagram of this problem. We can also use the financial table for the **present value factor for an annuity due (PVFAD)** to solve present value of annuity problems. The PVFAD table is found in Table IV-B in the Appendix at the end of the book. The formula for the table method follows:

The Present Value of an Annuity Due Formula
Table Method

$$PVAD = PMT \times PVFAD_{k,n} \qquad (8\text{-}6b)$$

where: PVAD = Present Value of an Annuity

PMT = Amount of each annuity payment

$PVFAD_{k,n}$ = Present Value Factor for an Annuity Due from Table IV-B

k = Discount rate per period

n = Number of periods

Applying Equation 8-6b, we find that the present value of the four-year annuity with $500 equal payments and a 5 percent discount rate per period is as follows:

$$PVAD = \$500 \times PVFAD_{5\%, 4}$$

$$= \$500 \times 3.7233$$

$$= \$1,861.65^3$$

FIGURE 8-9
NileCorp PVAD Timeline

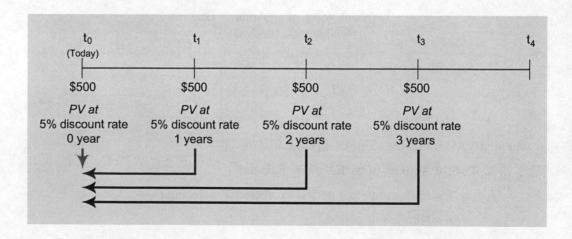

---

3. The $.03 difference between the algebraic result and the table formula solution is due to differences in rounding.

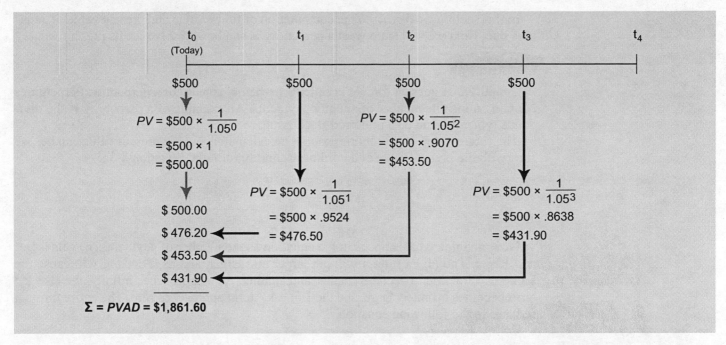

$\Sigma = PVAD = \$1,861.60$

The financial calculator solution for this annuity due problem is shown next.

FIGURE 8-10
Present Value of the
NileCorp Annuity Due

Present Value of a Four-Year, $500 Annuity Due, k = 5%

TI BAII PLUS Financial Calculator Solution

Step 1: Press `2nd` `CLR TVM` to clear previous values.

Step 2: Press `2nd` `P/Y` 1 `ENTER`, `2nd` `BGN` `2nd` `SET` `2nd` `SET`. Repeat `2nd` `SET` command until the display shows BGN, `2nd` `QUIT` to set to the annual interest rate mode and to set the annuity payment to beginning of period mode.

Step 3: Input the values for the annuity due and compute.

5 `I/Y`   4 `N`   500 `PMT`   `CPT` `PV`   **Answer: −1,861.62**

Here is the spreadsheet solution. Note how the [type] value in the PV function is again set to "1" to indicate that this is an annuity due problem.

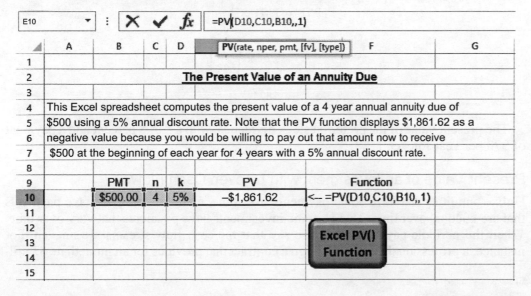

In this section we discussed the computation of future value and present value of annuities due. Next we will learn what a perpetuity is and how to solve for its present value.

Perpetuities

An annuity that goes on forever is called a perpetual annuity or a perpetuity. Perpetuities contain an infinite number of annuity payments. An example of a perpetuity is the dividends typically paid on a preferred stock issue.

The future value of perpetuities cannot be calculated, but the present value can be. We start with the present value of an ordinary annuity formula, Equation 8-3a.

$$PVOA = PMT \times \left[\frac{1 - \dfrac{1}{(1 + k)^n}}{k} \right]$$

Now imagine what happens in the equation as the number of payments (n) gets larger and larger. The $(1 + k)^n$ term will get larger and larger, and as it does, it will cause the $1/(1 + k)^n$ fraction to become smaller and smaller. As n approaches infinity, the $(1 + k)^n$ term becomes infinitely large, and the $1/(1 + k)^n$ term approaches zero. The entire formula reduces to the following equation:

Present Value of Perpetuity

$$PVP = PMT \times \left[\frac{1 - 0}{k} \right]$$

or

$$PVP = PMT \times \left(\frac{1}{k} \right)$$

(8-7)

where: PVP = Present Value of a Perpetuity

k = Discount rate expressed as a decimal

Neither the table method nor the financial calculator can solve for the present value of a perpetuity. Suppose you had the opportunity to buy a share of preferred stock that pays $70 per year forever. If your required rate of return is 8 percent, what is the present value of the promised dividends to you? In other words, given your required rate of return, how much should you be willing to pay for the preferred stock? The answer, found by applying Equation 8-5, follows:

$$PVP = PMT \times \left(\frac{1}{k} \right)$$

$$= \$70 \times \left(\frac{1}{.08} \right)$$

$$= \$875$$

The present value of the preferred stock dividends, with a k of 8 percent and a payment of $70 per year forever, is $875.

Present Value of an Investment with Uneven Cash Flows

Unlike annuities that have equal payments over time, many investments have payments that are unequal over time. That is, some investments have payments that vary over time. When the periodic payments vary, we say that the cash flow streams are uneven. For instance, a professional athlete may sign a contract that provides for an immediate $7 million signing bonus, followed by a salary of $2 million in year 1, $4 million in year 2, then $6 million in years 3 and 4. What is the present value of the promised payments that total $25 million? Assume a discount rate of 8 percent. The present value calculations are shown in Table 8-1.

As we see from Table 8-1, we calculate the present value of an uneven series of cash flows by finding the present value of a single amount for each series and summing the totals.

We can also use a financial calculator to find the present value of this uneven series of cash flows. The worksheet mode of the TI BAII PLUS calculator is especially helpful in solving problems with uneven cash flows. The C display shows each cash payment following CF_0, the initial cash flow. The F display key indicates the frequency of that payment. The keystrokes follow.

TI BAII PLUS Financial Calculator PV Solution
Uneven Series of Cash Flows

Keystrokes	Display
CF	CF_0 = old contents
2nd CLR Work	CF_0 = 0.00
7000000 ENTER	7,000,000.00
↓ 2000000 ENTER	C01 = 2,000,000.00
↓	F01 = 1.00
↓ 4000000 ENTER	C02 = 4,000,000.00
↓	F02 = 1.00
↓ 6000000 ENTER	C03 = 6,000,000.00
↓ 2 ENTER	F03 = 2.00
NPV	I = 0.00
8 ENTER	I = 8.00
↓ CPT	NPV = 21,454,379.70

TABLE 8-1 The Present Value of an Uneven Stream of Cash Flows

Time	Cash Flow	PV of Cash Flow
t_0	$7,000,000	$7,000,000 \times \dfrac{1}{1.08^0} = \$7,000,000$
t_1	$2,000,000	$2,000,000 \times \dfrac{1}{1.08^1} = \$1,851,852$
t_2	$4,000,000	$4,000,000 \times \dfrac{1}{1.08^2} = \$3,429,355$
t_3	$6,000,000	$6,000,000 \times \dfrac{1}{1.08^3} = \$4,762,993$
t_4	$6,000,000	$6,000,000 \times \dfrac{1}{1.08^4} = \$4,410,179$
		Sum of the PVs = $21,454,380

We see from the calculator keystrokes that we are solving for the present value of a single amount for each payment in the series except for the last two payments, which are the same. The value of F03, the frequency of the third cash flow after the initial cash flow, was 2 instead of 1 because the $6 million payment occurred twice in the series (in years 3 and 4).

We have seen how to calculate the future value and present value of annuities, the present value of a perpetuity, and the present value of an investment with uneven cash flows. Now we turn to time value of money problems in which we solve for k, n, or the annuity payment.

Special Time Value of Money Problems

Financial managers often face time value of money problems even when they know both the present value and the future value of an investment. In those cases, financial managers may be asked to find out what return an investment made—that is, what the interest rate is on the investment. Still other times financial managers must find either the number of payment periods or the amount of an annuity payment. In the next section, we will learn how to solve for k and n. We will also learn how to find the annuity payment (PMT).

Finding the Interest Rate

Financial managers frequently have to solve for the interest rate, k, when firms make a long-term investment. The method of solving for k depends on whether the investment is a single amount or an annuity.

Finding k for a Single-Amount Investment

Financial managers may need to determine how much periodic return an investment generated over time. For example, imagine that you are head of the finance department of GrabLand, Inc. Say that GrabLand purchased a house on prime land 20 years ago for $40,000. Recently, GrabLand sold the property for $106,131. What average annual rate of return did the firm earn on its 20-year investment?

First, the future value—or ending amount—of the property is $106,131. The present value—the starting amount—is $40,000. The number of periods, n, is 20. Armed with those facts, you could solve this problem using the table version of the future value of a single amount formula, Equation 8-1b, as follows:

$$FV = PV \times \left(FVF_{k,n}\right)$$
$$\$106{,}131 = \$40{,}000 \times \left(FVF_{k=?,n=20}\right)$$
$$\$106{,}131 \div \$40{,}000 = FVF_{k=?,n=20}$$
$$2.6533 = FVF_{k=?,n=20}$$

Now find the FVF value in Table I, shown in part below. The whole table is in the Appendix at the end of the book. You know n = 20, so find the n = 20 row on the left-hand side of the table. You also know that the FVF value is 2.6533, so move across the n = 20 row until you find (or come close to) the value 2.6533. You find the 2.6533 value in the k = 5% column. You discover, then, that GrabLand's property investment had an interest rate of 5 percent.

Future Value Factors, Compounded at k Percent per Period for n Periods, Part of Table I

Number of Periods, n	Interest Rate, k									
	1%	2%	3%	4%	5%	6%	7%	8%	9%	10%
18	1.1961	1.4282	1.7024	2.0258	2.4066	2.8543	3.3799	3.9960	4.7171	5.5599
19	1.2081	1.4568	1.7535	2.1068	2.5270	3.0256	3.6165	4.3157	5.1417	6.1159
20	1.2202	1.4859	1.8061	2.1911	2.6533	3.2071	3.8697	4.6610	5.6044	6.7275
25	1.2824	1.6406	2.0938	2.6658	3.3864	4.2919	5.4274	6.8485	8.6231	10.8347

Solving for k using the FVF table works well when the interest rate is a whole number, but it does not work well when the interest rate is not a whole number. To solve for the interest rate, k, we rewrite the algebraic version of the future value of a single amount formula, Equation 8-1a, to solve for k:

$$\text{The Rate of Return, k}$$

$$k = \left(\frac{FV}{PV}\right)^{\frac{1}{n}} - 1 \qquad (8\text{-}8)$$

where:　k = Rate of return per period expressed as a decimal

　　　　FV = Future Value

　　　　PV = Present Value

　　　　n = Number of periods

Let's use Equation 8-8 to find the average annual rate of return on GrabLand's house investment. Recall that the company bought it 20 years ago for $40,000 and sold it recently for $106,131. We solve for k applying Equation 8-6 as follows:

$$k = \left(\frac{FV}{PV}\right)^{\frac{1}{n}} - 1$$

$$= \left(\frac{\$106,131}{\$40,000}\right)^{\frac{1}{20}} - 1$$

$$= 2.653275^{.05} - 1$$

$$= 1.05 - 1$$

$$= .05, \text{ or } 5\%$$

Equation 8-6 will find any rate of return or interest rate given a starting value, PV, an ending value, FV, and a number of compounding periods, n.

To solve for k with a financial calculator, key in all the other variables and ask the calculator to compute k (depicted as I/Y on your calculator). For GrabLand's house-buying example, the calculator solution follows:

TI BAII PLUS Financial Calculator Solution

Step 1: Press [2nd] [CLR TVM] to clear previous values.

Step 2: Press [2nd] [P/Y] 1 [ENTER] , [2nd] [QUIT] .

Step 3: Input the values and compute.

　　40000 [+/−] [PV]　106131 [FV]　20 [N]　[CPT] [I/Y]　　　**Answer: 5.00**

The spreadsheet RATE function can also find this value.

E10		X ✓ *fx*	=RATE(D10,0,-B10,C10)			

	A	B	C	D		G
					RATE(nper, pmt, pv, [fv], [type], [guess])	
1						
2			**Finding k for a Single-Amount Investment**			
3						
4	This Excel spreadsheet computes the interest rate per period you would					
5	earn on a single amount $40,000 investment that grows to $106,131 over 20 years.					
6	Note that the RATE function inputs the $40,000 present value as negative because					
7	you would pay out that amount now to receive $106,131 in 20 years.					
8						
9		PV	FV	n	k	Function
10		$40,000	$106,131	20	5%	<-- =RATE(D10,0,-B10,C10)
11						
12						
13						Excel RATE ()
14						Function
15						

Remember when using the financial calculator or spreadsheet to solve for the rate of return, you must enter cash outflows as a negative number. In our example, the $40,000 PV is entered as a negative number because GrabLand spent that amount to invest in the house.

Finding k for an Annuity Investment

Financial managers may need to find the interest rate for an annuity investment when they know the starting amount (PVOA), n, and the annuity payment (PMT), but they do not know the interest rate, k. For example, suppose GrabLand wanted a 15-year, $100,000 amortized loan from a bank. An amortized loan is a loan that is paid off in equal amounts that include principal as well as interest.[4] According to the bank, Grab-Land's payments will be $12,405.89 per year for 15 years. What interest rate is the bank charging on this loan?

To solve for k when the known values are PVOA (the $100,000 loan proceeds), n (15), and PMT (the loan payments $12,405.89), we start with the present value of an ordinary annuity formula, Equation 8-4a, as follows:

$$PVOA = PMT \times (PVFOA_{k,n})$$

$$\$100,000 = \$12,405.89 \times (PVFOA_{k = ?, n = 15})$$

$$8.0607 = PVFOA_{k = ?, n = 15}$$

Now refer to the PVFOA values in Table IV-A, shown in part on the next page. The whole table is in the Appendix at the end of the book. You know n = 15, so find the n = 15 row on the left-hand side of the table. You have also determined that the PVFOA value is 8.0607 ($100,000/$12,405 = 8.0607), so move across the n = 15 row until you find (or come close to) the value of 8.0607. In our example, the location on the table where n = 15 and the PVIFA is 8.0607 is in the k = 9% column, so the interest rate on GrabLand's loan is 9 percent.

---

4. Amortize comes from the Latin word *mortalis*, which means "death." You will kill off the entire loan after making the scheduled payments.

Present Value Factors for an Ordinary Annuity, Discounted at k Percent per Period for n Periods, Part of Table IV-A

Number of Periods, n	Interest Rate, k									
	1%	2%	3%	4%	5%	6%	7%	8%	9%	10%
13	12.1337	11.3484	10.6350	9.9856	9.3936	8.8527	8.3577	7.9038	7.4869	7.1034
14	13.0037	12.1062	11.2961	10.5631	9.8986	9.2950	8.7455	8.2442	7.7862	7.3667
15	13.8651	12.8493	11.9379	11.1184	10.3797	9.7122	9.1079	8.5595	8.0607	7.6061
16	14.7179	13.5777	12.5611	11.6523	10.8378	10.1059	9.4466	8.8514	8.3126	7.8237

To solve this problem with a financial calculator, key in all the variables but k, and ask the calculator to compute k (depicted as I/Y on the TI calculator) as follows:

TI BAII PLUS Financial Calculator Solution

Step 1: Press [2nd] [CLR TVM] to clear previous values.

Step 2: Press [2nd] [P/Y] 1 [ENTER] , [2nd] [BGN] [2nd] [SET] [2nd] [SET]. Repeat [2nd] [SET] until END shows in the display. Press [2nd] [QUIT] after you see END in the display.

Step 3: Input the values and compute.

100000 [PV] 15 [N] 12405.89 [+/-] [PMT] [CPT] [I/Y]   **Answer: 9.00**

Again here the spreadsheet RATE function can compute this value.

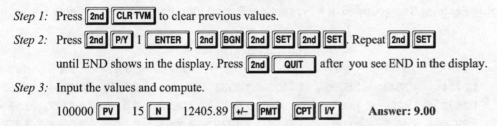

Note how in the financial calculator solution we took the perspective of the borrower, making the $12,405.89 PMT negative and the $100,000 loan amount PV positive. In the spreadsheet we took the bank's perspective, showing the loan amount as negative and the payments as positive. You can see that both approaches gave the same 9% answer for the interest rate.

Finding the Number of Periods

Suppose you found an investment that offered you a return of 6 percent per year. How long would it take you to double your money? In this problem you are looking for n, the number of compounding periods it will take for a starting amount, PV, to double in size (FV = 2 × PV).

To find n in our example, start with the formula for the future value of a single amount and solve for n as follows:

$$FV = PV \times \left(FVF_{k,n}\right)$$

$$2 \times PV = PV \times \left(FVF_{k=6\%,\, n=?}\right)$$

$$2.0 = FVF_{k=6\%,\, n=?}$$

Now refer to the FVF values, shown below in part of Table I. You know k = 6%, so scan across the top row to find the k = 6% column. Knowing that the FVF value is 2.0, move down the k = 6% column until you find (or come close to) the value 2.0. Note that it occurs in the row in which n = 12. Therefore, n in this problem, and the number of periods it would take for the value of an investment to double at 6 percent interest per period, is 12.

Future Value Factors, Compounded at k Percent per Period for n Periods, Part of Table I

Number of Periods, n	Interest Rate, k									
	1%	2%	3%	4%	5%	6%	7%	8%	9%	10%
11	1.1157	1.2434	1.3842	1.5395	1.7103	1.8983	2.1049	2.3316	2.5804	2.8531
12	1.1268	1.2682	1.4258	1.6010	1.7959	2.0122	2.2522	2.5182	2.8127	3.1384
13	1.1381	1.2936	1.4685	1.6651	1.8856	2.1329	2.4098	2.7196	3.0658	3.4523
14	1.1495	1.3195	1.5126	1.7317	1.9799	2.2609	2.5785	2.9372	3.3417	3.7975

This problem can also be solved on a financial calculator quite quickly. Just key in all the known variables (PV, FV, and I/Y) and ask the calculator to compute n.

TI BAII PLUS Financial Calculator Solution

Step 1: Press [2nd] [CLR TVM] to clear previous values.

Step 2: Press [2nd] [P/Y] 1 [ENTER] , [2nd] [QUIT] .

Step 3: Input the values and compute.

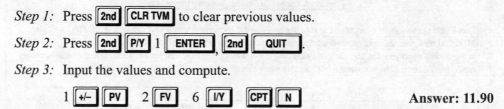

1 [+/−] [PV]   2 [FV]   6 [I/Y]   [CPT] [N]   **Answer: 11.90**

The spreadsheet NPER function solves for the number of periods for this problem.

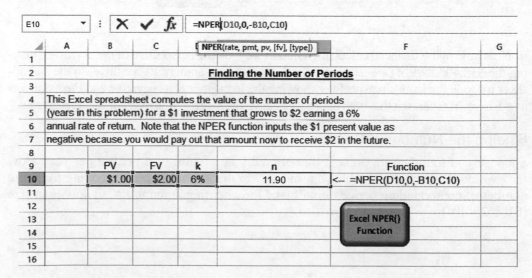

In our example n = 12 when $1 is paid out and $2 received with a rate of interest of 6 percent. That is, it takes approximately 12 years to double your money at a 6 percent annual rate of interest.

Solving for the Payment

Lenders and financial managers frequently have to determine how much each payment—or installment—will need to be to repay an amortized loan. For example, suppose you are a business owner and you want to buy an office building for your company that costs $200,000. You have $50,000 for a down payment and the bank will lend you the $150,000 balance at a 6 percent annual interest rate. How much will the annual payments be if you obtain a 10-year amortized loan?

As we saw earlier, an amortized loan is repaid in equal payments over time. Amortized loans are ordinary annuity problems, not annuities due. The period of time may vary. Let's assume in our example that your payments will occur annually, so that at the end of the 10-year period you will have paid off all interest and principal on the loan (FV = 0).

Because the payments are regular and equal in amount at the end of each year, this is an ordinary annuity problem. The present value of the ordinary annuity (PVOA) is the $150,000 loan amount, the annual interest rate (k) is 6 percent, and n is 10 years. The payment amount (PMT) is the only unknown value.

Because all the variables but PMT are known, the problem can be solved by solving for PMT in the present value of an ordinary annuity formula, equation 8-4a, as follows:

$$PVOA = PMT \times \left[\frac{1 - \frac{1}{(1 + k)^n}}{k} \right]$$

$$\$150,000 = PMT \times \left[\frac{1 - \frac{1}{(1.06)^{10}}}{.06} \right]$$

$$\$150,000 = PMT \times 7.36009$$

$$\frac{\$150,000}{7.36009} = PMT$$

$$\$20,380.19 = PMT$$

We see, then, that the payment for an ordinary annuity with a 6 percent interest rate, an n of 10, and a present value of $150,000 is $20,380.19.

We can also solve for PMT using the table formula, Equation 8-4b, as follows:

$$PVOA = PMT \times \left(PVFOA_{k, n} \right)$$

$$\$150,000 = PMT \times \left(PVFOA_{6\%, \, 10 \, years} \right)$$

$$\$150,000 = PMT \times 7.3601 \text{ (look up PVFOA, Table IV-A)}$$

$$\frac{\$150,000}{7.3601} = PMT$$

$$\$20,380.16 = PMT \text{ (note the \$0.03 rounding error)}$$

The table formula shows that the payment for a loan with the present value of $150,000 at an annual interest rate of 6 percent and an n of 10 is $20,380.16.

With the financial calculator, simply key in all the variables but PMT and have the calculator compute PMT as follows:

TI BAII PLUS Financial Calculator Solution

Step 1: Press [2nd] [CLR TVM] to clear previous values.

Step 2: Press [2nd] [P/Y] 1 [ENTER] , [2nd] [BGN] [2nd] [SET]. Repeat [2nd] [SET] command until the display shows END, [2nd] [QUIT] to set to the annual interest rate mode and to set the annuity payment to end of period mode.

Step 3: Input the values for the ordinary annuity and compute.

150,000 [PV]   6 [I/Y]   10 [N]   [CPT] [PMT]   Answer: −20,380.19

The financial calculator and the spreadsheet that follows will display the payment, $20,380.19, as a negative number because it is a cash outflow for the borrower who received the $150,000 loan amount.

F10	▼	:	X ✓ *fx*	=PMT(E10,D10,B10)			
	A	B	C	D	E PMT(rate, nper, pv, [fv], [type])	F	G	H
1							
2			**Amortized Loan - Solving for the Annual Payment**				
3							
4	This Excel spreadsheet computes the annual payment on an amortized loan. The amount						
5	borrowed is $150,000 with annual payments for 10 years and a 6% annual interest rate. Note						
6	that the Excel PMT function displays the PMT value as a negative value since you are paying						
7	out that amount at the end of each year.						
8							
9		PV	FV	n	k	PMT	Function
10		$150,000.00	$0.00	10	6%	−$20,380.19	<-- =PMT(E10,D10,B10)
11							
12							
13							Excel PMT() Function
14							
15							

Loan Amortization

As each payment is made on an amortized loan, the interest due for that period is paid, along with a repayment of some of the principal that must also be "killed off." After the last payment is made, all the interest and principal on the loan have been paid. This step-by-step payment of the interest and principal owed is often shown in an *amortization table*. The amortization table for the ten-year 6 percent annual interest rate loan of $150,000 that was discussed in the previous section is shown in Table 8-2. The annual payment, calculated in the previous section, is $20,380.19.

We see from Table 8-2 how the balance on the $150,000 loan is killed off a little each year until the balance at the end of year 10 is zero. The payments reflect an increasing amount going toward principal and a decreasing amount going toward interest over time.

Compounding More Than Once per Year

So far in this chapter, we have assumed that interest is compounded *annually*. However, there is nothing magical about annual compounding. Many investments pay interest that is compounded semiannually, quarterly, or even daily. Most banks, savings and loan associations, and credit unions, for example, compound interest on their deposits more frequently than annually.

Suppose you deposited $100 in a savings account that paid 12 percent annual interest, compounded annually. After one year you would have $112 in your account ($112 = $100 × 1.121).

Now, however, let's assume the bank used *semiannual compounding*. With semiannual compounding you would receive half a year's interest (6 percent) after six months. In the second half of the year, you would earn interest both on the interest earned in the first six months *and* on the original principal. The total interest earned during the year on a $100 investment at 12 percent annual interest would be:

$ 6.00	(interest for the first six months)
+ $ .36	(interest on the $6 interest during the second 6 months)[5]
+ $ 6.00	(interest on the principal during the second six months)
= $ 12.36	total interest in year 1

At the end of the year, you will have a balance of $112.36 if the interest is compounded semiannually, compared with $112.00 with annual compounding—a difference of $.36.

Here's how to find answers to problems in which the compounding period is less than a year: Apply the relevant present value or future value equation, but adjust k and n so they reflect the actual compounding periods.

To demonstrate, let's look at our example of a $100 deposit in a savings account at 12 percent for one year with semiannual compounded interest. Because we want to find out what the future value of a single amount will be, we use that formula to solve for the future value of the account after one year. Next, we divide the annual interest rate, 12 percent, by two because interest will be compounded twice each year. Then, we multiply the

TABLE 8-2 Amortization Table for a $150,000 Loan, 6 percent Annual Interest Rate, 10-Year Term

		Loan Amortization Schedule		
Amount Borrowed:	$150,000			
Interest Rate:	6.0%			
Term:	10 years			
Required Payments:	$20,380.19 *(found using Equation 8-4a)*			

	Col. 1	Col. 2	Col. 3 Col. 1 x .06	Col. 4 Col. 2 - Col. 3	Col. 5 Col. 1 - Col. 4
Year	Beginning Balance	Total Payment	Payment of Interest	Payment of Principal	Ending Balance
1	$ 150,000.00	$ 20,380.19	$ 9,000.00	$ 11,380.19	$ 138,619.81
2	$ 138,619.81	$ 20,380.19	$ 8,317.19	$ 12,063.01	$ 126,556.80
3	$ 126,556.80	$ 20,380.19	$ 7,593.41	$ 12,786.79	$ 113,770.02
4	$ 113,770.02	$ 20,380.19	$ 6,826.20	$ 13,553.99	$ 100,216.02
5	$ 100,216.02	$ 20,380.19	$ 6,012.96	$ 14,367.23	$ 85,848.79
6	$ 85,848.79	$ 20,380.19	$ 5,150.93	$ 15,229.27	$ 70,619.52
7	$ 70,619.52	$ 20,380.19	$ 4,237.17	$ 16,143.02	$ 54,476.50
8	$ 54,476.50	$ 20,380.19	$ 3,268.59	$ 17,111.60	$ 37,364.90
9	$ 37,364.90	$ 20,380.19	$ 2,241.89	$ 18,138.30	$ 19,226.60
10	$ 19,226.60	$ 20,380.19	$ 1,153.60	$ 19,226.60	$ 0.00

---

5. The $.36 was calculated by multiplying $6 by half of 12%: $6.00 × .06 = $.36.

number of years n (one in our case) by two because with semiannual interest there are two compounding periods in a year. The calculation follows:

$$FV = PV \times (1 + k/2)^{n \times 2}$$
$$= \$100 \times (1 + .12/2)^{1 \times 2}$$
$$= \$100 \times (1 + .06)^2$$
$$= \$100 \times 1.1236$$
$$= \$112.36$$

The future value of $100 after one year, earning 12 percent annual interest compounded semiannually, is $112.36.

To use the table method for finding the future value of a single amount, find the $FVF_{k,n}$ in Table I in the Appendix at the end of the book. Then, divide the k by two and multiply the n by two as follows:

$$FV = PV \times \left(FVF_{k/2, n \times 2}\right)$$
$$= \$100 \times \left(FVF_{12\%/2, 1 \times 2 \text{ periods}}\right)$$
$$= \$100 \times \left(FVF_{6\%, 2 \text{ periods}}\right)$$
$$= \$100 \times 1.1236$$
$$= \$112.36$$

To solve the problem using a financial calculator, divide the k (represented as I/Y on the TI BAII PLUS calculator) by two and multiply the n by two. Next, key in the variables as follows:

TI BAII PLUS Financial Calculator Solution

Step 1: Press [2nd] [CLR TVM] to clear previous values.

Step 2: Press [2nd] [P/Y] 1 [ENTER] , [2nd] [QUIT] .

Step 3: Input the values and compute.

100 [+/−] [PV] 6 [I/Y] 2 [N] [CPT] [FV]   **Answer: 112.36**

The future value of $100 invested for two periods at 6 percent per period is $112.36.[6] This future value is computed with a spreadsheet here.

---

6. Note that the interest rate and number of periods are expressed in semi-annual terms when using the TI BAII PLUS calculator and the FV function in the Excel spreadsheet. We used the semiannual interest rate of 6 percent, not the annual interest rate of 12 percent. Similarly, n was expressed as the number of semiannual periods, two in one year.

E11			$\times$ $\checkmark$ f_x	=FV(D11/2,C11*2,0,-B11)	

	A	B	C	D	F
				FV(rate, nper, pmt, [pv], [type])	
1					
2			The Future Value of a Single Amount With Semi-Annual Compounding		
3					
4	This Excel spreadsheet computes the future value of $100 invested for 1 year at a 12% annual				
5	interest rate (6% per semiannual period) for 1 year (2 semiannual periods). Note that the FV				
6	function interest rate is divided by 2 and the number of years multiplied by 2 for this semiannual				
7	compounding problem and that it inputs the $100 present value as a negative number since				
8	that amount is being paid out.				
9					
10		PV	n Years	Annual k	FV	Function
11		$100.00	1	12%	$112.36	<-- =FV(D11/2,C11*2,0,-B11)
12						
13						
14						Excel FV()
15						Function
16						

Other compounding rates, such as quarterly or monthly rates, can be found by modifying the applicable formula to adjust for the compounding periods. With a quarterly compounding period, then, annual k should be divided by four and annual n multiplied by four. For monthly compounding, annual k should be divided by twelve and annual n multiplied by twelve. Similar adjustments could be made for other compounding periods.

Annuity Compounding Periods

Many annuity problems also involve compounding or discounting periods of less than a year. For instance, suppose you want to buy a car that costs $20,000. You have $5,000 for a down payment and plan to finance the remaining $15,000 at 6 percent annual interest for four years. What would your monthly loan payments be?

First, change the stated annual rate of interest, 6 percent, to a monthly rate by dividing by 12 (6%/12 = 1/2% or .005). Second, multiply the four-year period by 12 to obtain the number of months involved (4 × 12 = 48 months). Now solve for the annuity payment size using the annuity formula.

In our case, we apply the present value of an ordinary annuity formula, equation 8-4a, as follows:

$$PVOA = PMT \times \left[\frac{1 - \frac{1}{(1 + k)^n}}{k} \right]$$

$$\$15,000 = PMT \times \left[\frac{1 - \frac{1}{(1.005)^{48}}}{.005} \right]$$

$$\$15,000 = PMT \times 42.5803$$

$$\frac{\$15,000}{42.5803} = PMT$$

$$\$352.28 = PMT$$

The monthly payment on a $15,000 car loan with a 6 percent annual interest rate (.5 percent per month) for four years (48 months) is $352.28.

Solving this problem with the PVFOA table in Table IV-A in the Appendix at the end of the book would be difficult because the .5 percent interest rate is not listed in the PVFOA table. If the PVFOA were listed, we would apply the table formula, make the adjustments to reflect the monthly interest rate and the number of periods, and solve for the present value of the annuity.

On a financial calculator, we would first adjust the k and n to reflect the same time period—monthly, in our case—and then input the adjusted variables to solve the problem as follows:

TI BAII PLUS Financial Calculator Solution

Step 1: Press [2nd] [CLR TVM] to clear previous values.

Step 2: Press [2nd] [P/Y] 1 [ENTER], [2nd] [BGN] [2nd] [SET] [2nd] [SET]. Repeat [2nd] [SET] command until the display shows END, [2nd] [QUIT] to set to the annual interest rate mode and to set the annuity payment to end of period mode.

Step 3: Input the values for the ordinary annuity and compute.

15,000 [PV] .5 [I/Y] 48 [N] [CPT] [PMT]   **Answer: −352.28**

The following spreadsheet also solves for the monthly payment of this amortized loan.

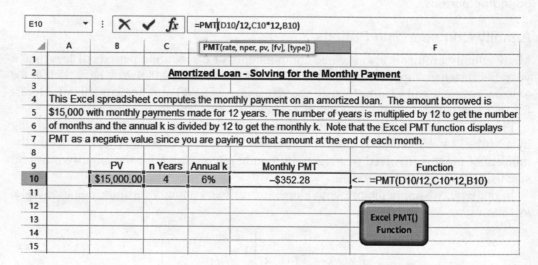

The interest rate we entered was not the 6 percent rate per year but rather the .5 percent rate per month. We entered not the number of years, four, but rather the number of months, 48. Because we were consistent in entering the k and n values in monthly terms, the calculator and spreadsheet gave us the correct monthly payment of −352.28 (an outflow of $352.28 per month). The values of RATE and NPER were similarly adjusted in the spreadsheet.

Continuous Compounding

The effect of increasing the number of compounding periods per year is to increase the future value of the investment. The more frequently interest is compounded, the greater the future value. The smallest compounding period is used when we do continuous compounding—compounding that occurs every tiny unit of time (the smallest unit of time imaginable).

Recall our $100 deposit in an account at 12 percent for one year with annual compounding. At the end of year 1, our balance was $112. With semiannual compounding, the amount increased to $112.36.

When continuous compounding is involved, we cannot divide k by infinity and multiply n by infinity. Instead, we use the term e, which you may remember from your math class. We define e as follows:

$$e = \lim_{h \to \infty} \left[1 + \frac{1}{h} \right]^h \approx 2.71828$$

The value of e is the natural antilog of 1 and is approximately equal to 2.71828. This number is one of those like pi (approximately equal to 3.14159), which we can never express exactly but can approximate. Both e and pi are irrational numbers. Using e, the formula for finding the future value of a given amount of money, PV, invested at annual rate, k, for n years, with continuous compounding, is as follows:

Future Value with Continuous Compounding

$$FV = PV \times e^{(k \times n)} \tag{8-9}$$

where k (expressed as a decimal) and n are expressed in annual terms.

Applying Equation 8-9 to our example of a $100 deposit at 12 percent annual interest with continuous compounding, at the end of one year we would have the following balance:

$$FV = \$100 \times 2.71828^{(.12 \times 1)}$$

$$= \$112.75$$

The future value of $100, earning 12 percent annual interest compounded continuously, is $112.75.

As this section demonstrates, the compounding frequency can impact the value of an investment. Investors, then, should look carefully at the frequency of compounding. Is it annual, semiannual, quarterly, daily, or continuous? Other things being equal, the more frequently interest is compounded, the more interest the investment will earn.

What's Next

In this chapter we investigated the importance of the time value of money in financial decisions and learned how to calculate present and future values for a single amount, for ordinary annuities, and for annuities due. We also learned how to solve special time value of money problems, such as finding the interest rate or the number of periods.

The skills acquired in this chapter will be applied in later chapters, as we evaluate proposed projects, bonds, and preferred and common stock. They will also be used when we estimate the rate of return expected by suppliers of capital. In the next chapter, we will turn to the cost of capital.

Summary

1. *Explain the time value of money and its importance in the business world.*
   Money grows over time when it earns interest. Money expected or promised in the future is worth less than the same amount of money in hand today. This is because we lose the opportunity to earn interest when we have to wait to receive money. Similarly, money we owe is less burdensome if it is to be paid in the future rather than now. These concepts are at the heart of investment and valuation decisions of a firm.

2. *Calculate the future value and present value of a single amount.*
   To calculate the future value and the present value of a single dollar amount, we may use the algebraic, table, or calculator methods. Future value and present value are mirror images of each other. They are compounding and discounting, respectively. With future value, increases in k and n result in an exponential increase in future value. Increases in k and n result in an exponential decrease in present value.

3. *Find the future and present values of an annuity.*
   Annuities are a series of equal cash flows. An annuity that has payments that occur at the end of each period is an ordinary annuity. An annuity that has payments that occur at the beginning of each period is an annuity due. A perpetuity is a perpetual annuity. To find the future and

present values of an ordinary annuity, we may use the algebraic, table, or financial calculator method. To find the future and present values of an annuity due, multiply the applicable formula by $(1 + k)$ to reflect the earlier payment.

4. *Solve time value of money problems with uneven cash flows.*
   To solve time value of money problems with uneven cash flows, we find the value of each payment (each single amount) in the cash flow series and total each single amount. Sometimes the series has several cash flows of the same amount. If so, calculate the present value of those cash flows as an annuity and add the total to the sum of the present values of the single amounts to find the total present value of the uneven cash flow series.

5. *Solve for the interest rate, number or amount of payments, or the number of periods in a future or present value problem.*
   To solve special time value of money problems, we use the present value and future value equations and solve for the missing variable, such as the loan payment, k, or n. We may also solve for the present and future values of single amounts or annuities in which the interest rate, payments, and number of time periods are expressed in terms other than a year. The more often interest is compounded, the larger the future value.

Key Terms

annuity A series of equal cash payments made at regular time intervals.

future value The value money or another asset will have in the future.

future value factor (FVF) The factor, which when multiplied by a single amount present value, gives the future value. It equals $(1 + k)^n$ for given values of k and n.

future value factor for an annuity due (FVFAD) The factor, which when multiplied by an expected annuity payment, gives the sum of the future values of an annuity due stream.

It equals $\left[\dfrac{(1 + k)^n - 1}{k} \right] \times (1 + k)$ for given values of k and n.

future value factor for an ordinary annuity (FVFOA) The factor, which when multiplied by an expected annuity payment, gives the sum of the future values of an ordinary annuity stream.

It equals $\left[\dfrac{(1 + k)^n - 1}{k} \right]$ for given values of k and n.

present value factor (PVF) The factor, which when multiplied by a single amount future value, gives the present value.

It equals $\dfrac{1}{(1 + k)^n}$ for given values of k and n.

present value factor for an annuity due (PVFAD) The factor, which when multiplied by an expected annuity payment, gives the sum of the present values of an annuity due stream. It equals

$$\left[\dfrac{1 - \dfrac{1}{(1 + k)^n}}{k} \right] \times (1 + k)$$ given values of k and n.

present value factor for an ordinary annuity (PVFOA) The factor which, when multiplied by an expected ordinary annuity payment, gives you the sum of the present values of the ordinary annuity stream.

It equals $$\left[\dfrac{1 - \dfrac{1}{(1 + k)^n}}{k} \right]$$ for given values of k and n.

present value Today's value of a promised or expected future value.

pure time value of money The value demanded by an investor to compensate for the postponement of consumption.

Equations Introduced in This Chapter

Equation 8-1a. Future Value of a Single Amount—Algebraic Method:

$$FV = PV \times (1 + k)^n$$

where: FV = Future Value, the ending amount

            PV = Present Value, the starting amount, or original principal

            k = Rate of interest per period expressed as a decimal

            n = Number of time periods

Equation 8-1b. Future Value of a Single Amount—Table Method:

$$FV = PV \times \left(FVF_{k, n} \right)$$

where: FV = Future Value, the ending amount

            PV = Present Value, the starting amount

        $FVF_{k,n}$ = Future Value Factor given interest rate per period, k, and number of periods, n, from Table I

Equation 8-2a. Present Value of a Single Amount—Algebraic Method:

$$PV = FV \times \frac{1}{(1 + k)^n}$$

where: PV = Present Value, the starting amount

            FV = Future Value, the ending amount

            k = Discount rate of interest per period expressed as a decimal

            n = Number of time periods

Equation 8-2b. Present Value of a Single Amount—Table Method:

$$PV = FV \times \left(PVF_{k, n} \right)$$

where: PV = Present Value

            FV = Future Value

$PVF_{k, n}$ = Present Value Factor given discount rate per period, k, and number of periods, n, from Table II

Equation 8-3a. Future Value of an Ordinary Annuity—Algebraic Method:

$$FVOA = PMT \times \left[\frac{(1 + k)^n - 1}{k} \right]$$

where: $FVOA$ = Future Value of an Ordinary Annuity

        PMT = Amount of each annuity payment

            k = Interest rate per period expressed as a decimal

            n = Number of periods

Equation 8-3b. Future Value of an Ordinary Annuity—Table Method:

$$FVOA = PMT \times FVFOA_{k,\,n}$$

where: FVOA = Future Value of an Annuity

PMT = Amount of each annuity payment

$FVFOA_{k,\,n}$ = Future Value Factor for an Ordinary Annuity from Table III-A

k = Interest rate per period expressed as a decimal

n = Number of periods

Equation 8-4a. Present Value of an Ordinary Annuity—Algebraic Method:

$$PVOA = PMT \times \left[\dfrac{1 - \dfrac{1}{(1+k)^n}}{k}\right] \times (1+k)$$

where: PVOA = Present Value of an Ordinary Annuity

PMT = Amount of each annuity payment

k = Discount rate per period expressed as a decimal

n = Number of periods

Equation 8-4b. Present Value of an Ordinary Annuity—Table Method:

$$PVOA = PMT \times PVFOA_{k,\,n}$$

where: PVOA = Present Value of an Ordinary Annuity

PMT = Amount of each annuity payment

$PVFOA_{k,\,n}$ = Present Value Factor for an Ordinary Annuity from Table IV-A

k = Discount rate per period

n = Number of periods

Equation 8-5a. The Future Value of an Annuity Due Formula—Algebraic Method

$$FVAD = PMT \times \left[\dfrac{(1+k)^n - 1}{k}\right] \times (1+k)$$

where: FVAD = Future Value of an Annuity Due

PMT = Amount of each annuity payment

k = Interest rate per period expressed as a decimal

n = Number of periods

Equation 8-5b. The Future Value of an Annuity Due Formula—Table Method

$$FVAD = PMT \times FVFAD_{k,n}$$

where: FVAD = Future Value of an Annuity Due

PMT = Amount of each annuity payment

$FVFAD_{k,\,n}$ = Future Value Factor for an Annuity Due from Table III-B

k = Interest rate per period

n = Number of periods

Equation 8-6a. The Present Value of an Annuity Due—Algebraic Method

$$PVAD = PMT \times \left[\dfrac{1 - \dfrac{1}{(1+k)^n}}{k} \right] \times (1+k)$$

where: PVAD = Present Value of an Annuity Due

PMT = Amount of each annuity payment

k = Discount rate per period expressed as a decimal

n = Number of periods

Equation 8-6b. The Present Value of an Annuity Due Formula—Table Method

$$PVAD = PMT \times PVFAD_{k,n}$$

where: PVAD = Present Value of an Annuity Due

PMT = Amount of each annuity payment

$PVFAD_{k,n}$ = Present Value Factor for an Annuity Due from Table IV-B

k = Discount rate per period

n = Number of periods

Equation 8-7. Present Value of a Perpetuity:

$$PVP = PMT \times \left(\dfrac{1}{k} \right)$$

where: PVP = Present Value of a Perpetuity

k = Discount rate expressed as a decimal

Equation 8-8. Rate of Return:

$$k = \left(\dfrac{FV}{PV} \right)^{\frac{1}{n}} - 1$$

where: k = Rate of return per period expressed as a decimal

FV = Future Value

PV = Present Value

n = Number of compounding periods

Equation 8-9. Future Value with Continuous Compounding:

$$FV = PV \times e^{(k \times n)}$$

where: FV = Future Value

PV = Present Value

e = Natural antilog of 1

k = Stated annual interest rate expressed as a decimal

n = Number of years

Self-Test

ST-1. Jed is investing $5,000 into an eight-year certificate of deposit (CD) that pays 6 percent annual interest with annual compounding. How much will he have when the CD matures?

ST-2. Tim has found a 2013 Toyota 4-Runner on sale for $19,999. The dealership says that it will finance the entire amount with a one-year loan, and the monthly payments will be $1,776.98. What is the annualized interest rate on the loan (the monthly rate times 12)?

ST-3. Heidi's grandmother died and provided in her will that Heidi will receive $100,000 from a trust when Heidi turns 21 years of age, 10 years from now. If the appropriate discount rate is 8 percent, what is the present value of this $100,000 to Heidi?

ST-4. Zack wants to buy a new Ford Mustang automobile. He will need to borrow $20,000 to go with his down payment in order to afford this car. If car loans are available at a 6 percent annual interest rate, what will Zack's monthly payment be on a four-year loan?

ST-5. Bridget invested $5,000 in a growth mutual fund, and in 10 years her investment had grown to $15,529.24. What annual rate of return did Bridget earn over this 10-year period?

ST-6. If Tom invests $1,000 a year beginning today into a portfolio that earns a 10 percent return per year, how much will he have at the end of 10 years? (Hint: Recognize that this is an annuity due problem.)

Review Questions

1. What is the time value of money?

2. Why does money have time value?

3. What is compound interest? Compare compound interest to discounting.

4. How is present value affected by a change in the discount rate?

5. What is an annuity?

6. Suppose you are planning to make regular contributions in equal payments to an investment fund for your retirement. Which formula would you use to figure out how much your investments will be worth at retirement time, given an assumed rate of return on your investments?

7. How does continuous compounding benefit an investor?

8. If you are doing PVA and FVA problems, what difference does it make if the annuities are ordinary annuities or annuities due?

9. Which formula would you use to solve for the payment required for a car loan if you know the interest rate, length of the loan, and the borrowed amount? Explain.

Build Your Communication Skills

CS-1. Obtain information from four different financial institutions about the terms of their basic savings accounts. Compare the interest rates paid and the frequency of the compounding. For each account, how much money would you have in 10 years if you deposited $100 today? Write a one- to two-page report of your findings.

CS-2. Interview a mortgage lender in your community. Write a brief report about the mortgage terms. Include in your discussion comments about what interest rates are charged on different types of loans, why rates differ, and what fees are charged in addition to the interest and principal that mortgagees must pay to this lender. Describe the advantages and disadvantages of some of the loans offered.

Problems

All these problems may be solved using algebra, tables, financial calculator, or Excel. The algebra, table, and financial calculator approaches are presented in the body of this chapter. Those who wish to solve these problems using Excel may learn the skills to do so for each type of problem presented here by going to www.textbookmedia.com and going to the area of the website for this textbook.

Future Value **8-1.** What is the future value of $1,000 invested today if you earn 2 percent annual interest for five years?

Future Value **8-2.** Calculate the future value of $20,000 ten years from now if the annual interest rate is

    a. 0 percent

    b. 2 percent

    c. 5 percent

    d. 10 percent

Future Value **8-3.** How much will you have in 10 years if you deposit $5,000 today and earn 3 percent annual interest?

8-4. Calculate the future value of $20,000 invested today fifteen years from now based on the following annual interest rates: ⬅   **Future Value**

     a. 3 percent

     b. 6 percent

     c. 9 percent

     d. 12 percent

8-5. Calculate the future values of the following amounts at 4 percent for twenty years: ⬅   **Future Value**

     a. $50,000

     b. $75,000

     c. $100,000

     d. $125,000

8-6. Calculate the future value of $40,000 at 5 percent for the following years: ⬅   **Future Value**

     a. 5 years

     b. 10 years

     c. 15 years

     d. 20 years

8-7. What is the present value of $90,000 to be received ten years from now using a 7 percent annual discount rate?   ⬅   **Present Value**

8-8. Calculate the present value of $15,000 to be received twenty years from now at an annual discount rate of: ⬅   **Present Value**

     a. 0 percent

     b. 5 percent

     c. 10 percent

     d. 20 percent

8-9. Jimbo Jones is going to receive a graduation present of $10,000 from his grandparents in four years. If the annual discount rate is 3 percent, what is this gift worth today?

8-10. Calculate the present values of $25,000 to be received in ten years using the following annual discount rates: ⬅   **Present Value**

     a. 3 percent

     b. 6 percent

     c. 9 percent

     d. 12 percent

8-11. Calculate the present values of the following using a 4 percent annual discount rate at the end of 15 years: ⬅   **Present Value**

     a. $20,000

     b. $60,000

     c. $90,000

     d. $130,000

8-12. Calculate the present value of $100,000 at a 5 percent annual discount rate to be received in: ⬅   **Present Value**

     a. 5 years

     b. 10 years

     c. 15 years

     d. 20 years

8-13. What is the present value of a $2,000 ten-year annual ordinary annuity at a 4 percent annual discount rate?   ⬅   **Present Value of an Ordinary Annuity**

Present Value of an Ordinary Annuity → **8-14.** Calculate the present value of a $25,000 thirty-year annual ordinary annuity at an annual discount rate of:

    a. 0 percent

    b. 5 percent

    c. 10 percent

    d. 15 percent

Present Value of an Ordinary Annuity → **8-15.** What is the present value of a ten-year ordinary annuity of $40,000, using a 2 percent annual discount rate?

Present Value of an Ordinary Annuity → **8-16.** Find the present value of a four-year ordinary annuity of $10,000, using the following annual discount rates:

    a. 2 percent

    b. 4 percent

    c. 6 percent

    d. 10 percent

Future Value of an Ordinary Annuity → **8-17.** What is the future value of a five-year annual ordinary annuity of $900, using a 4 percent annual interest rate?

Future Value of an Ordinary Annuity → **8-18.** Calculate the future value of a twelve-year, $15,000 annual ordinary annuity, using an annual interest rate of:

    a. 0 percent

    b. 5 percent

    c. 10 percent

    d. 15 percent

Future Value of an Ordinary Annuity → **8-19.** What is the future value of a forty-year ordinary annuity of $5,000, using an annual interest rate of 4 percent?

Future Value of an Ordinary Annuity → **8-20.** What is the future value of an eight-year ordinary annuity of $12,000, using a 7 percent annual interest rate?

Future Value of an Ordinary Annuity → **8-21.** Find the future value of the following five-year ordinary annuities, using a 3 percent annual interest rate.

    a. $1,000

    b. $10,000

    c. $75,000

    d. $125,000

Future Value of an Annuity Due → **8-22.** Starting today, you invest $10,000 a year into your individual retirement account (IRA). If your IRA earns 8 percent a year, how much will be available at the end of 40 years?

Future Value of an Annuity Due → **8-23.** Dolph Starbeam will deposit $5,000 at the beginning of each year for twenty years into an account that has an annual interest rate of 4 percent. How much will Dolph have to withdraw in twenty years?

Future Value of an Annuity Due → **8-24.** An account manager has found that the future value of $10,000, deposited at the end of each year, for five years at an annual interest rate of 2 percent will amount to $52,040.40. What is the future value of this scenario if the account manager deposits the money at the beginning of each year?

Present Value of an Annuity Due → **8-25.** If your required annual rate of return is 6 percent, how much will an investment that pays $50 a year at the beginning of each of the next 40 years be worth to you today?

8-26. Allison Taylor has won the lottery and is going to receive $100,000 per year for 25 years; she received her first check today. The current annual discount rate is 5 percent. Find the present value of her winnings.

◄ Present Value of an Annuity Due

8-27. Leon Kompowsky pays a debt service of $1,300 a month and will continue to make this payment for 15 years. What is the present value of these payments discounted at 6 percent if he mails his first payment in today? Be sure to do monthly discounting.

8-28. You invested $50,000, and 10 years later the value of your investment has grown to $185,361.07. What is your compounded annual rate of return over this period?

◄ Solving for k

8-29. You invested $1,000 five years ago, and the value of your investment has fallen to $903.92. What is your compounded annual rate of return over this period?

◄ Solving for k

8-30. What is the rate of return on an investment that grows from $50,000 to $89,542.38 in 10 years?

◄ Solving for k

8-31. What is the present value of a $50 annual perpetual annuity using a discount rate of 2 percent?

◄ Present Value of a Perpetuity

8-32. A payment of $70 per year forever is made with an annual discount rate of 6 percent. What is the present value of these payments?

◄ Present Value of a Perpetuity

8-33. You are valuing a preferred stock that makes a dividend payment of $65 per year, and the current discount rate is 6.5 percent. What is the value of this share of preferred stock?

◄ Present Value of a Perpetuity (Preferred Stock)

8-34. Herman Hermann is financing a new boat with an amortizing loan of $24,000, which is to be repaid in 10 annual installments of $3,576.71 each. What interest rate is Herman paying on the loan?

◄ Solving for a Loan Interest Rate

8-35. On June 1, 2012, Selma Bouvier purchased a home for $220,000. She put $20,000 down on the house and obtained a 30-year fixed-rate mortgage for the remaining $200,000. Under the terms of the mortgage, Selma must make payments of $898.09 a month for the next 30 years starting June 30. What is the effective annual interest rate on Selma's mortgage?

◄ Solving for the Monthly Interest Rate on a Mortgage

8-36. What is the amount you have to invest today at 4 percent annual interest to be able to receive $10,000 after

  a. 5 years?

  b. 10 years?

  c. 20 years?

◄ Present Value

8-37. How much money would Alexis Whitney need to deposit in her savings account at Great Western Bank today in order to have $26,850.58 in her account after five years? Assume she makes no other deposits or withdrawals and the bank guarantees a 6 percent annual interest rate, compounded annually.

◄ Future Value

8-38. If you invest $15,000 today, how much will you receive after

  a. 7 years at a 2 percent annual interest rate?

  b. 10 years at a 4 percent annual interest rate?

◄ Future Value

8-39. The Apple stock you purchased twelve years ago for $23 a share is now worth $535.86. What is the compounded annual rate of return you have earned on this investment?

◄ Solving for k

8-40. Jessica Lovejoy deposited $1,000 in a savings account. The annual interest rate is 10 percent, compounded semiannually. How many years will it take for her money to grow to $4,321.94?

◄ Solving for k

8-41. Beginning a year from now, Clancy Wiggum will receive $80,000 a year from his pension fund. There will be fifteen of these annual payments. What is the present value of these payments if a 3 percent annual interest rate is applied as the discount rate?

◄ Present Value of an Ordinary Annuity

Future Value of an Annuity Due ➡ **8-42.** If you invest $6,000 per year into your Individual Retirement Account (IRA), earning 8 percent annually, how much will you have at the end of twenty years? You make your first payment of $6,000 today.

Future Value of an Ordinary Annuity ➡ **8-43.** What would you accumulate if you were to invest $500 every quarter for ten years into an account that returned 8 percent annually? Your first deposit would be made one quarter from today. Interest is compounded quarterly.

Future Value of an Ordinary Annuity ➡ **8-44.** If you invest $2,000 per year for the next fifteen years at a 6 percent annual interest rate, beginning one year from today compounded annually, how much are you going to have at the end of the fifteenth year?

Future Value of an Ordinary Annuity (Challenge Problem) ➡ **8-45.** It is the beginning of the quarter and you intend to invest $750 into your retirement fund at the end of every quarter for the next thirty years. You are promised an annual interest rate of 8 percent, compounded quarterly.

    a. How much will you have after thirty years upon your retirement?

    b. How long will your money last if you start withdrawing $9,000 at the end of every quarter after you retire?

Solving for a Loan Payment ➡ **8-46.** A $50,000 loan obtained today is to be repaid in equal annual installments over the next seven years starting at the end of this year. If the annual interest rate is 2 percent, compounded annually, how much is to be paid each year?

Future Value ➡ **8-47.** Janey Powell invested $1,000 in a certificate of deposit (CD) that pays 4% annual interest, compounded continuously, for twenty years. How much money will she have when this CD matures?

Present Value of a Perpetuity ➡ **8-48.** Aristotle Amadopolis is moving to Central America. Before he packs up his wife and son he purchases an annuity that guarantees payments of $10,000 a year in perpetuity. How much did he pay if the annual interest rate is 4 percent?

Future Value ➡ **8-49.** Ned and Maud Flanders deposited $1,000 into a savings account the day their son, Todd, was born. Their intention was to use this money to help pay for Todd's wedding expenses when and if he decided to get married. The account pays 5 percent annual interest with continuous compounding. Upon his return from a graduation trip to Hawaii, Todd surprises his parents with the sudden announcement of his planned marriage to Francine. The couple set the wedding date to coincide with Todd's twenty-third birthday. How much money will be in Todd's account on his wedding day?

Time to Triple Your Money ➡ **8-50.** You deposit $2,000 in an account that pays 8 percent annual interest, compounded annually. How long will it take to triple your money?

Time to Pay Off a Credit Card Balance ➡ **8-51.** Upon reading your most recent credit card statement, you are shocked to learn that the balance owed on your purchases is $4,000. Resolving to get out of debt once and for all, you decide not to charge any more purchases and to make regular monthly payments until the balance is zero. Assuming that the bank's credit card annual interest rate is 19.5 percent and the most you can afford to pay each month is $350, how long will it take you to pay off your debt?

Solving for k ➡ **8-52.** Waylon Smithers borrows $17,729.75 for a new car. He is required to repay the amortized loan with four annual payments of $5,000 each. What is the annual interest rate on his loan?

Future Value of an Annuity (Challenge Problem) ➡ **8-53.** Ernst and Gunter are planning for their eventual retirement from the magic business. They plan to make quarterly deposits of $2,000 into an IRA starting three months from today. The guaranteed annual interest rate is 4 percent, compounded quarterly. They plan to retire in 15 years.

    a. How much money will be in their retirement account when they retire?

    b. Using the preceding interest rate and the total account balance from part a, for how many years will Ernst and Gunter be able to withdraw $6,000 at the end of each quarter?

8-54. Moe Szyslak comes to you for financial advice. He is considering adding video games to his tavern to attract more customers. The company that sells the video games has given Moe a choice of four different payment options. Which of the following four options would you recommend that Moe choose? Why?

Challenge Problem

Option 1. Pay $5,900 cash immediately.

Option 2. Pay $6,750 cash in one lump sum two years from now.

Option 3. Pay $800 at the end of each quarter for two years.

Option 4. Pay $1,000 immediately plus $5,250 in one lump sum two years from now.

Moe tells you he can earn 6 percent annual interest, compounded quarterly, on his money. You have no reason to question his assumption.

8-55. Titania wants to borrow $225,000 from a mortgage banker to purchase a $300,000 house. The mortgage loan is to be repaid in monthly installments over a thirty-year period. The annual interest rate is 6 percent. How much will Titania's monthly mortgage payments be?

Solving for a Mortgage Loan Payment

8-56. Carl Carlson's family has found the house of their dreams. They have $50,000 to use as a down payment and they want to borrow $400,000 from the bank. The current mortgage annual interest rate is 6 percent. If they make equal monthly payments for twenty years, how much will their monthly mortgage payment be?

Solving for a Mortgage Loan Payment

8-57. Otto Mann has his heart set on a new Miata sports car. He will need to borrow $28,000 to get the car he wants. The bank will loan Otto the $28,000 at an annual interest rate of 3 percent.

Solving for Auto Loan Payments

a. How much would Otto's monthly car payments be for a four-year loan?

b. How much would Otto's monthly car payments be if he obtains a six-year loan at the same interest rate?

8-58. Assume the following set of cash flows:

Challenge Problem (Value of Missing Cash Flow)

End of Year 1	End of Year 2	End of Year 3	End of Year 4
$100	$150	?	$100

At an annual discount rate of 10 percent, the total present value of all the cash flows above, including the missing cash flow, is $452.22. Given these conditions, what is the value of the missing cash flow?

For more, see 8e Spreadsheet Templates for *Microsoft Excel.*

8-59. You are considering financing the purchase of an automobile that costs $22,000. You intend to finance the entire purchase price with a four-year amortized loan with a 6 percent annual interest rate.

Loan Amortization Table

a. Calculate the amount of the monthly payments for this loan.

b. Construct an amortization table for this loan using the format shown in Table 8-2. Use monthly payments.

For more, see 8e Spreadsheet Templates for *Microsoft Excel.*

c. If you elected to pay off the balance of the loan at the end of the thirty-sixth month how much would you have to pay?

Answers to Self-Test

ST-1. FV = $5,000 × 1.068 = $7,969.24 = Jed's balance when the eight-year CD matures.

ST-2. $19,999 = $1,776.98 × $\left(\text{PVFOA}_{k=?, n=12}\right)$

$11.2551 = \text{PVFOA}_{k=?, n=12}$

k = 1% monthly (from the PVIFA Table at the end of the n = 12 row,

k = 1%)

Annual Rate = 1% × 12 = 12%

ST-3. PV = $100,000 × (1/1.08^{10}) = $46,319.35

= the present value of Heidi's $100,000

ST-4. $20,000 = PMT × [1 − (1/1.005^{48})] / .005

$20,000 = PMT × 42.5803

PMT = $469.70 = Zack's car loan payment

ST-5. $5,000 × FVF_{k=?, n=10} = $15,529.24

$FVF_{k=?, n=10} = 3.1058$, therefore k = 12% = Bridget's annual rate of return on the mutual fund.

ST-6. FV = PMT × $\left(\text{FVFOA}_{k\%, n}\right)$ × $\left(1 + k\right)$

= $1,000 × $\left(\text{FVFOA}_{10\%, 10}\right)$ × $\left(1 + .10\right)$

= $1,000 × 15.9374 × 1.10

= $17,531.14

Capital Budgeting and Business Valuation

PART 3

Source: Lipskiy/Shutterstock

Chapter 9
The Cost of Capital

Chapter 10
Capital Budgeting Decision Methods

Chapter 11
Estimating Incremental Cash Flows

Chapter 12
Business Valuation

Capital budgeting and business valuation concern two subjects near and dear to financial people's hearts: What should we do with the firm's money and how much is the company worth? The two subjects are closely related because the decision about what to do with the firm's money often affects the value of the firm. Chapter 9, "The Cost of Capital," begins this section with a discussion of how to estimate the minimum rate of return that the firm must seek when it makes investments. Chapter 10, "Capital Budgeting Decision Methods," explains how to decide if an investment meets the firm's requirements and how to rank order competing investments. Chapter 11, "Estimating Incremental Cash Flows," goes on to describe how to estimate the cash inflows and outflows associated with investments. Finally, Chapter 12, "Business Valuation," explains how to use the techniques in Chapters 9 through 11 (and those in Chapter 8) to estimate the market value of the firm.

The Cost of Capital

"There's no such thing as a free lunch."
—Milton Friedman

CHAPTER 9

Source: rvlsoft/Shutterstock

Learning Objectives

After reading this chapter, you should be able to:

1. Describe the sources of capital and how firms raise capital.
2. Estimate the cost of capital for each financing source.
3. Estimate the weighted average cost of capital.
4. Use the marginal cost of capital (MCC) schedule to make capital budgeting decisions.
5. Explain the importance of the marginal cost of capital (MCC) schedule in financial decision making.

You Can Almost Always Get Capital If Your Idea Is Good Enough

This chapter on the cost of capital and those that follow on capital budgeting are all interconnected. What return do the suppliers of capital to a firm expect? To answer this we must assess the risk these would-be suppliers of capital are facing. What expected return would be sufficient to compensate for this risk?

The suppliers of equity capital have a greater required rate of return on their investment than do the suppliers of debt capital because the former are taking a greater risk. Equity investors are paid after lenders.

If capital is invested in good value-adding projects the suppliers of that capital can be paid the rate of return they required to part with that capital. If funds are not already in hand they can be raised. Raising funds will not be difficult if the would-be suppliers of those funds expect to get a return on their investment that is sufficient to justify the risk of their investment.

If a company has a history of not delivering to its capital suppliers the returns they needed, considering the risk taken by these investors, then this company will probably have difficulty in the future raising funds at a reasonable cost.

Companies with good projects waiting to be financed will find it easier to raise the funds needed for those projects. The cost of this capital will be reasonable since would-be investors will want to be part of this successful venture.

Chapter Overview

In capital budgeting decisions, financial managers must analyze many factors to determine whether a project will add value to a firm, including estimated incremental cash flows, the timing of those cash flows, risk, and the project's required rate of return.

capital Funds supplied to a firm.

One of the key components of the capital budgeting decision is the cost of capital. **Capital** is the term for funds that firms use. Businesses raise capital from creditors and owners. All capital raised has a cost because the suppliers of capital demand compensation for the funds provided.

In this chapter we examine the costs of different types of capital. We see how to estimate the cost of capital from a particular source, as well as the overall cost of capital for a firm. We also see how estimating a firm's cost of capital affects a firm's financing and investment decisions.

The Cost of Capital

To properly evaluate potential investments, firms must know how much their capital costs. Without a measure of the cost of capital, for example, a firm might invest in a new project with an expected return of 10 percent, even though the capital used for the investment costs 15 percent. If a firm's capital costs 15 percent, then the firm must seek investments that return at least that much. It is vital, then, that managers know how much their firm's capital costs before committing to investments.

Suppliers and users of capital use cost estimates before making short- or long-term financial decisions. Investors must determine their required rate of return, k, to value either a bond or stock before they invest. That required rate of return, k, for each type of security issued is the cost of capital for that source. Overall, the cost of capital is the compensation investors demand of firms that use their funds, adjusted for taxes and transaction costs in certain cases, as we will explain later in this chapter.

In Chapter 10, we will see that firms determine their required rate of return before deciding whether to accept a capital budgeting project. The discount rate or hurdle rate, k, is the firm's cost of capital for that project. Investors supply capital, so they require a return, and firms use capital, so they must pay suppliers of capital for the use of those funds.

Sources of Capital

A firm's capital is supplied by its creditors and owners. Firms raise capital by borrowing it (issuing bonds to investors or promissory notes to banks), or by issuing preferred or common stock. The overall cost of a firm's capital depends on the return demanded by each of these suppliers of capital.

To determine a firm's overall cost of capital, the first step is to determine the cost of capital from each category of supplier. The cost of capital from a particular source, such as bondholders or common stockholders, is known as the **component cost of capital**.

component cost of capital The cost of raising funds from a particular source, such as bondholders or common stockholders.

In the following sections, we estimate the cost of debt capital, k_d; the cost of capital raised through a preferred stock issue, k_p; and the cost of equity capital supplied by common stockholders, k_s for internal equity and k_n for new external equity.

The Cost of Debt

When a firm borrows money at a stated rate of interest, determining the cost of debt, k_d, is relatively straightforward. As shown in Figure 9-1, the lender's cost of capital is the required rate of return on either a company's new bonds or on a new promissory note

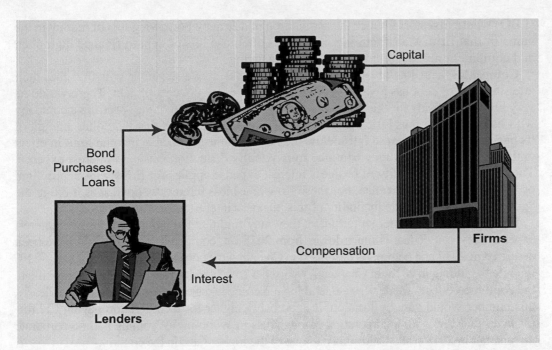

FIGURE 9-1
The Flow of Debt Capital
from Investors to Firms

Figure 9-1 shows how debt
investors supply capital to and
receive interest from the firm.

when a bank loan is obtained. The firm's **cost of debt** when it borrows money by issuing bonds is the interest rate demanded by the bond investors. When borrowing money from an individual or financial institution, the interest rate on the loan is the firm's cost of debt.

When the Financial Crisis hit, companies with all but the highest credit ratings found that they had to pay much higher interest rates to borrow money. Their cost of debt increased significantly.

cost of debt (k_d) The lender's required rate of return on a company's new bonds or other instrument of indebtedness.

The After-Tax Cost of Debt (AT k_d)

The **after-tax cost of debt, AT k_d,** is the tax adjusted cost to the company of obtaining debt funds. The computation of the after-tax cost of debt has gotten a little more complicated since the Tax Cuts and Jobs Act of 2017 (TCJA) went into effect in 2018. Businesses, including corporations, cannot deduct business interest expenses on their taxes without limit as they could pre-2018.

Effective in 2018 only business interest expenses up to 30% of "adjusted taxable income" are deductible. Adjusted taxable income adds back depreciation, amortization, and depletion expenses to taxable income through 2021. From 2022 on those items cannot be added back, thus placing a stricter limit on the amount of business interest expense that can be deducted on the company's tax return. There is no limit on business interest expense deductions for companies with $25 million or less of annual sales revenue. For those companies that do run into the limit, they are allowed to carry forward to future year tax returns the business interest expense they were not allowed to deduct in the year the expense was incurred. A company with a large amount of business interest expense, however, might find itself in a position where it would take many decades or more, before the disallowed business interest expenses from earlier years are finally deducted using this carry forward provision. The carry forward only has value to the firm in those future years if the company is below the 30% limit in those years. The firm could apply the carry forward to bring its deductions in that future year up from the business expenses in that year to the 30% limit. A company with business interest expense above the 30% limit could deduct the amount of that year's business interest expense up to that limit, but not the amount above the limit. Since we are talking about the cost of new debt, by definition the business interest expense on that debt would be above the limit for such firms and therefore not deductible in that year.

The TCJA of 2017 will have a severe negative impact on businesses with lots of debt on their balance sheets. Many companies with junk bond level credit ratings have lots of debt. So too do many businesses that have recently gone through a leverage buyout

after-tax cost of debt (AT k_d) The after-tax cost to a company of obtaining debt funds.

(LBO) where investors finance the acquisition of a firm by borrowing lots of money in the name of that firm. Manufacturing companies often use lots of debt to finance high plant and equipment needs with mortgage bond financing.

Companies with lots of business interest expense above the limit will find that their after-tax cost of debt has a value very close to the before-tax cost of debt. There would be very little tax subsidy for this borrowed money. At the other end of the spectrum a company with little debt and thus little business interest expense may find that the dollar amount of its business interest expense falls below the 30% of adjusted taxable income limit in effect until 2022 will find that they continue to have fully deductible business interest expense. The same full deductibility of business interest expense applies for firms with $25 million or less of annual sales revenue. For these firms, business interest works just as it did in the "good old days" of full deductibility of this business interest expense prior to 2018.

For those businesses not so fortunate, they may find that the amount of business interest expense they can deduct is much lower from 2018 on, compared to what could have been deducted in 2017 and before. As described in Chapter 4 the corporate income tax rate is a 21% flat rate beginning in 2018. In Chapter 4, we used a 25% blended rate for taxes to approximate the combined effect of federal, state, and local income taxes owed by a corporation. Clearly, this number would vary by location. It is probably higher for a corporation paying California taxes and lower for a corporation paying taxes in Wyoming. Wyoming had no corporate income tax in 2018 while California had one of the higher rates in the country.

When computing the cost of capital we are talking about new capital. If the company were raising new funds from debt, preferred stock, or common equity sources what would be the cost it incurs? Taxes can affect only the cost of debt capital. For many years textbooks like this one computed the after tax cost by taking the before tax cost of debt and multiplying that figure by one minus the marginal tax rate of the firm. This was the correct approach prior to 2018.

Formula for the After-Tax Cost of Debt

$$AT\,k_d = k_d\,(1 - ISTR) \tag{9-1}$$

where: k_d = The before tax cost of debt

          ISTR = The firm's interest subsidy tax rate

For example, pre-2018, if the before tax cost of debt were 10% and the firm's marginal tax rate were 35% we would have:

$$BT\,k_d \times (1 - T) = AT\,k_d$$

Where $BT\,k_d$ = the before-tax cost of debt

         T = the firm's marginal tax rate

         $AT\,k_d$ = the after-tax cost of debt

e.g., $10\% \times (1 - .35) = 6.5\%$ the after tax cost of debt.

In our post-TCJA world, clearly a different process is called for. The firm's marginal tax rate is no longer the relevant number to use for the after-tax adjustment. For example, for a firm with annual sales above $25 million, and with business interest expense greater or equal to 30% of adjusted taxable income in a given year, there would be no tax subsidy for the amount of its business interest expense above the 30% threshold. Since we are talking about new borrowings in a given year, the cost of this new debt would receive no tax subsidy in that year with the possibility of tax benefits in subsequent years from carry forwards. Now your after-tax cost of debt is equal to your before tax cost (ignoring any future benefit that might exist from carry forwards). We'd have:

$$BT\,k_d \times (1 - ISTR) = AT\,k_d$$

Where $BT\ k_d$ = the before-tax cost of debt

                 ISTR = the firm's interest subsidy tax rate

                 $AT\ k_d$ = the after-tax cost of debt

e.g., $10\% \times (1 - 0) = 10\%$ the after tax cost of debt.

For a firm with annual sales of \$25 million or less, or with total business interest expense less than 30% of adjusted taxable income, all the business interest expense would be tax deductible. If we take the new federal flat corporate tax rate of 21% and add 4 percentage points for state and local taxes, we would have:

$$BT\ k_d \times (1 - ISTR) = AT\ k_d$$

Where $BT\ k_d$ = the before-tax cost of debt

                 ISTR = the firm's interest subsidy tax rate

                 $AT\ k_d$ = the after-tax cost of debt

e.g., $10\% \times (1 - .25) = 7.5\%$ the after tax cost of debt.

Such a company would see its interest subsidy on its business debt to be the same as it was for all firms pre-TCJA.

Clearly, firms could fall between the 0% ISTR and the 25% ISTR. The firm with the 0% ISTR might receive some tax benefit in future years from the business interest expense not deductible in the current year. If this were the case, we would need to consider the present value of future tax savings from the indefinite carry forward provision. Business interest expense not deductible in the current year might not be deductible in future years either if the company finds itself year after year with business interest expense above the 30% threshold.

In this chapter, the costs of debt, preferred stock, internal common equity, and external common equity are computed for fictional company Ellis Industries. Taxes affect only the cost of debt for a company raising the capital. The before-tax cost of debt is converted to the after-tax cost of debt by multiplying the before-tax cost by one minus the interest subsidy tax rate of 15%. Remember, for a company with no limit on its business interest tax deductions because it has business interest expense below 30% of adjustable taxable income or annual sales of \$25 million or less the marginal rate would be closer to the 25% blended rate we have been using. Such a company would get the same tax subsidy for its debt as did all companies before 2018. A company with lots of business interest expense and annual sales above \$25 million might have an interest subsidy tax rate below 15%, perhaps even 0%, for the adjustment of the before-tax cost of debt to arrive at the after-tax cost of debt. Such a company would receive a lower subsidy for its debt financings compared to the pre-2018 days, possibly much lower. The 15% rate we will use in this chapter is a compromise between the two extremes. The lower the interest subsidy tax rate used, the closer the after-tax cost of debt will be to the before-tax cost. Real world companies will have to determine how much of their business interest expense is being subsidized by the federal, state, and local income tax authorities to determine how much, if at all, their after-tax cost of debt is less than their before-tax cost.

The Cost of Preferred and Common Stock

When corporations raise capital by issuing preferred or common stock, these investors expect a return on their investments. If that return is not realized, investors will sell their stock, driving the stock price down. Although the claim of preferred and common stockholders may not be contractual, as it is for bondholders, there is a cost nonetheless. To calculate the cost of using preferred and common stockholders' money, then, the firm must estimate the rate of return that these investors demand. Figure 9-2 shows how firms raise capital from, and compensate, equity investors.

FIGURE 9-2
The Flow of Capital from Equity Investors to Firms

Figure 9-2 shows how equity investors supply capital to the firm and receive dividends from it.

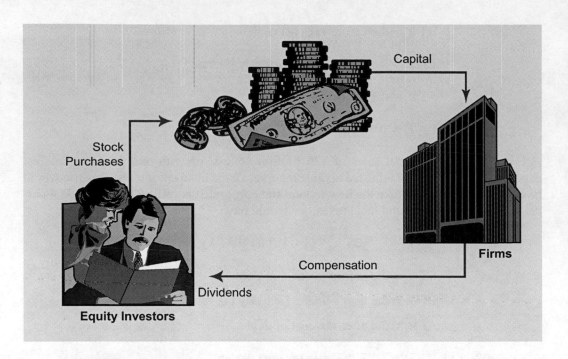

Equity Investors

Stock Purchases

Capital

Firms

Compensation

Dividends

The Cost of Preferred Stock (k_p)

cost of preferred stock (k_p) Investors' required rate of return on a company's new preferred stock.

flotation cost Fees that companies pay (to investment bankers and to others) when new securities are issued.

The **cost of preferred stock (k_p)** is the rate of return investors require on a company's new preferred stock, plus the cost of issuing the stock. Therefore, to calculate k_p, a firm's managers must estimate the rate of return that preferred stockholders would demand and add in the cost of the stock issue. Because preferred stock investors normally buy preferred stock to obtain the stream of constant preferred stock dividends associated with the preferred stock issue, their return on investment can normally be measured by dividing the amount of the firm's expected preferred stock dividend by the price of the shares. The cost of issuing the new securities, known as **flotation cost**, includes investment bankers' fees and commissions, and attorneys' fees. These costs must be deducted from the preferred stock price paid by investors to obtain the net price received by the firm. Equation 9-2 shows how to estimate the cost of preferred stock:

Formula for the Cost of Preferred Stock

$$k_p = \frac{D_p}{(P_p - F)}$$

(9-2)

where: k_p = The cost of the preferred stock issue; the expected return

D_p = The amount of the expected preferred stock dividend

P_p = The current price of the preferred stock

F = The flotation cost per share

Take Note
There is no tax adjustment in the cost of preferred stock calculation. Unlike interest payments on debt, firms may never deduct preferred stock dividends on their tax returns. The dividends are paid out of after-tax profits.

The cost of using the company's preferred stock is k_p. The value of k_p, the expected return from the preferred stock issue, is the minimum return the firm's managers must earn when they use the money supplied by preferred stockholders. If they cannot earn this return, the preferred stockholders will sell their shares, causing the preferred stock's price to fall. This means the firm must issue more shares of the stock than before the stock price fell to raise the same amount of funds.

Suppose Ellis Industries has issued preferred stock that has been paying annual dividends of $2.50 and is expected to continue to do so indefinitely. The current price of Ellis's preferred stock is $22 a share, and the flotation cost is $2 per share. According to Equation 9-2, the cost of Ellis's preferred stock is as follows:

$$k_p = \frac{\$2.50}{(\$22 - \$2)}$$

$$= .125, \text{ or } 12.5\%$$

We see that Ellis Industries' cost of new preferred stock, assuming that stock pays dividends of $2.50 per year and has a market price of $22, is 12.5 percent.

The cost of preferred stock, k_p, is higher than the before-tax cost of debt, k_d, because a company's bondholders and bankers have a prior claim on the earnings of the firm and on its assets in the event of a liquidation. Preferred stockholders, as a result, take a greater risk than bondholders or bankers and demand a correspondingly greater rate of return.

Preferred stock prices tumbled during the Financial Crisis. This led to an increase in the cost of preferred stock capital when companies tried to issue such securities to investors who were looking primarily at safer investments such as U.S. Treasury securities.

The Cost of Internal Common Equity (k_s)

The **cost of internal common equity (k_s)** is the required rate of return on funds supplied by existing common stockholders. The cost of equity depends on the rate of return the common stockholders demand for holding the company's common stock. Calculating k_s is more difficult than calculating k_p because common stockholders do not receive a constant stream of dividends. Instead, investors own the firm, including the corporate earnings left over after other claimants on the firm have been paid. Neither creditors nor preferred stockholders have a claim on these residual earnings. Corporations may either retain the residual earnings or return them in the form of common stock dividends. Retained earnings have a cost, however. The cost of retained earnings, another name for the cost of internal equity, is the rate of return that the company must earn to justify retaining the earnings instead of paying them as dividends. These are internally generated (within the firm) equity funds.

As noted, common stock dividend payments change from year to year or may not be paid at all. Ultimately, however, dividends are the only payments a corporation makes to its common stockholders. The corporation may pay regular dividends, or it may pay a liquidation dividend sometime in the future. For companies that pay regular dividends that grow at a constant rate, the constant dividend growth model may be used to estimate the cost of equity. For companies that do not pay regular dividends, or when the market approach to risk is more appropriate, the capital asset pricing model (CAPM) may be used to estimate the cost of equity.

cost of internal common equity (k_s) The required rate of return on funds supplied by existing common stockholders through earnings retained.

Using the Dividend Growth Model to Estimate k_s

The dividend growth model (sometimes called the Gordon Model after its developer, financial economist Myron Gordon) uses the time value of money concepts in Chapter 8 to calculate the present value of a continuing stream of future dividends:

$$P_0 = \frac{D_1}{k_s - g}$$

where: P_0 = The current price of the common stock

D_1 = The dollar amount of the common stock dividend expected one period from now

k_s = Required rate of return per period on this common stock investment

g = Expected constant growth rate per period of the company's common stock dividends[1]

---

1. This is the constant growth version of the dividend growth model. It assumes that the company's dividends grow at the same rate indefinitely.

Rearranging the terms in the dividend growth model to solve for k_s, we rewrite the formula as follows:

Formula for the Cost of Common Stock Equity (k_s)
(Dividend Growth Model Approach)

$$k_s = \frac{D_1}{P_0} + g$$

(9-3)

By making use of Equation 9-3, we can solve for k_s, assuming we know the values of the terms P_0, D_1, and g. The term D_1/P_0 in Equation 9-3 represents the stock's dividend yield, and the g term represents dividend growth rate from year to year.

To apply Equation 9-3, suppose that Ellis Industries' common stock is selling for $40 a share. Next year's common stock dividend is expected to be $4.20, and the dividend is expected to grow at a rate of 5 percent per year indefinitely. Given these conditions, Equation 9-3 tells us that the expected rate of return on Ellis's common stock is as follows:

$$k_s = \frac{\$4.20}{\$40} + .05$$

$$= .105 + .05$$

$$= .155, \text{ or } 15.5\%$$

At a stock share price of $40, a dividend of $4.20, and an expected dividend growth rate of 5 percent, the expected return from Ellis's common stock is 15.5 percent. The expected return of 15.5 percent is the minimum return the firm's managers must earn when they use money supplied by common stockholders. If they cannot achieve this return, common stockholders will sell their shares, causing the stock's price to fall. This will make it necessary to sell more shares to raise the desired amount of funds. The cost of using money supplied by the company's common stockholders, then, is 15.5 percent. Because dividends paid are not tax deductible to the corporation, there is no tax adjustment to the k_s calculation.

When common stock prices plunged during the Financial Crisis it took more shares than before the plunge to raise the same amount of equity capital. This increased the cost of common stock equity capital. With the economy in a bad recession, few companies were looking to expand their operations. The higher cost of common equity capital they faced made them even less interested in raising such capital.

The CAPM Approach to Estimating k_s

A firm may pay dividends that grow at a changing rate; it may pay no dividends at all; or the managers of the firm may believe that market risk is the relevant risk. In such cases, the firm may choose to use the capital asset pricing model (CAPM) to calculate the rate of return that investors require for holding common stock. The CAPM solves for the rate of return that investors demand for holding a company's common stock according to the degree of nondiversifiable risk[2] present in the stock. The CAPM formula, Equation 9-4, follows:

CAPM Formula for the Cost of Common Stock Equity (k_s)

$$k_s = k_{rf} + (k_m - k_{rf}) \times \beta$$

(9-4)

---

2. According to the CAPM, common stockholders hold well-diversified portfolios, so the only relevant risk measure is nondiversifiable (market) risk.

where: k_s = The required rate of return from the company's common stock equity

k_{rf} = The risk-free rate of return

k_m = The expected rate of return on the overall stock market

β = The beta of the company's common stock, a measure of the amount of nondiversifiable risk

Suppose Ellis Industries has a beta of 1.39, the risk-free rate as measured by the rate on short-term U.S. Treasury bills is 3 percent, and the expected rate of return on the overall stock market is 12 percent. Given those market conditions, according to Equation 9-4, the required rate of return for Ellis's common stock is as follows:

$$k_s = .03 + (.12 - .03) \times 1.39$$
$$= .03 + (.09 \times 1.39)$$
$$= .03 + .1251$$
$$= .1551, \text{ or about } 15.5\%$$

According to the CAPM, we see that the cost of using money supplied by Ellis's common stockholders is about 15.5 percent, given a company beta of 1.39, a risk-free rate of 3 percent, and an expected market rate of return of 12 percent.

Deciding How to Estimate k_s

Should you use the dividend growth model, Equation 9-3, or the CAPM, Equation 9-4, to estimate a firm's cost of common equity? The choice depends on the firm's dividend policy, available data, and management's view of risk. As a financial manager, if you were confident that your firm's dividends would grow at a fairly constant rate in the future, you could apply the dividend growth model to calculate k_s. If your firm's growth rate were erratic or difficult to determine, you might use the CAPM instead, assuming that you agreed with the CAPM's underlying hypothesis that common stockholders hold well-diversified portfolios and that nondiversifiable risk is what is priced in the market. When possible, practitioners apply both models and use their business judgment to reconcile differences between the two outcomes.

The Cost of Equity from New Common Stock (k_n)

The cost incurred by a company when new common stock is sold is the **cost of equity from new common stock (k_n)**. In the preceding section, we discussed the cost of using funds supplied by the firm's existing stockholders. Capital from existing stockholders is internal equity capital. That is, the firm already has these funds. In contrast, capital from issuing new stock is external equity capital. The firm is trying to raise new funds from outside sources.

New stock is sometimes issued to finance a capital budgeting project. The cost of this capital includes not only stockholders' expected returns on their investment but also the flotation costs incurred to issue new securities. Flotation costs make the cost of using funds supplied by new stockholders slightly higher than using retained earnings supplied by the existing stockholders.

To estimate the cost of using funds supplied by new stockholders, we use a variation of the dividend growth model that includes flotation costs:

Formula for the Cost of New Common Stock Equity (k_n)

$$k_n = \frac{D_1}{P_0 - F} + g$$

(9-5)

cost of equity from new common stock (k_n) The cost of external equity, including the costs incurred to issue new common stock.

where: k_n = The cost of new common stock equity

P_0 = The price of one share of the common stock

D_1 = The amount of the common stock dividend expected to be paid in one year

F = The flotation cost per share

g = The expected constant growth rate of the company's common stock dividends

Equation 9-5 shows mathematically how the cost of new common stock, k_n, is greater than the cost of existing common stock equity, k_s. By subtracting flotation costs, F, from the common stock price in the denominator, the k_n term becomes larger.

Let's look at the cost of new common stock for Ellis Industries. Suppose again that Ellis Industries' anticipated dividend next year is $4.20 a share, its growth rate is 5 percent a year, and its existing common stock is selling for $40 a share. New shares of stock can be sold to the public for the same price, but to do so Ellis must pay its investment bankers 5 percent of the stock's selling price, or $2 per share. Given these conditions, we use Equation 9-5 to calculate the cost of Ellis Industries' new common equity as follows:

$$k_n = \frac{\$4.20}{\$40 - \$2} + .05$$

$$= .1105 + .05$$

$$= .1605, \text{ or } 16.05\%$$

Because of the $2 flotation costs, Ellis Industries keeps only $38 of the $40 per share paid by investors. As a result, the cost of new common stock is higher than the cost of existing equity—16.05 percent compared to 15.5 percent.

If the cost of new common equity is higher than the cost of internal common equity, the cost of preferred stock, and the cost of debt, why use it? Sometimes corporations have no choice.

Also, if the amount of debt a firm has incurred continues to increase, and internal equity funds have run out, it may be necessary to issue new common stock to bring the weight of debt and equity on the balance sheet into line.[3]

We have examined the sources of capital and the cost of each capital source. Next, we investigate how to measure the firm's overall cost of capital.

The Weighted Average Cost of Capital (WACC)

To estimate a firm's overall cost of capital, the firm must first estimate the cost for each component source of capital. The component sources include the after-tax cost of debt, AT k_d; the cost of preferred stock, k_p; the cost of common stock equity, k_s; and the cost of new common stock equity, k_n. In the following section, we first discuss all component sources except k_n, which we discuss separately.

To illustrate the first step in estimating a firm's overall cost of capital, let's review Ellis Industries' component costs of capital. From our previous calculations, we know the following costs of capital:

$$\text{AT } k_d = 8.5\%$$

$$k_p = 12.5\%$$

$$k_s = 15.5\%$$

The next step in finding a firm's overall cost of capital is assessing the firm's *capital structure.* In practice, the assets of most firms are financed with a mixture of debt, preferred stock, and common equity. The mixture of capital used to finance a firm's assets is

3. This issue will be discussed in detail in Chapter 13.

called the **capital structure** of the firm. To analyze the capital structure of a business, we must find the percentage of each type of capital source.

To illustrate how to assess a firm's capital structure, assume that Ellis Industries finances its assets through a mixture of capital sources, as shown on its balance sheet:[4]

capital structure The mixture of sources of capital that a firm uses (for example, debt, preferred stock, and common stock).

Total Assets	$ 1,000,000
Long- and Short-Term Debt	$ 400,000
Preferred Stock	100,000
Common Equity	500,000
Total Liabilities and Equity	$ 1,000,000

In percentage terms, then, the mixture of capital used to finance Ellis's $1 million worth of assets is as follows:

Debt: 400,000/1,000,000 = .40, or 40%

Preferred Stock: 100,000/1,000,000 = .10, or 10%

Common Equity: 500,000/1,000,000 = .50, or 50%

Our calculations show that Ellis Industries' capital structure consists of 40 percent debt, 10 percent preferred stock, and 50 percent common equity. If Ellis Industries thinks that this mixture is optimal and wants to maintain it, then it will finance new capital budgeting projects with a mixture of 40 percent debt, 10 percent preferred stock, and 50 percent common equity. This mixture might not be used for each and every project. But in the long run, the firm is likely to seek this capital structure if it is believed to be optimal.

The final step in estimating a firm's overall cost of capital is to find the weighted average of the costs of each individual financing source. The **weighted average cost of capital (k_a or WACC)** is the mean of all component costs of capital, weighted according to the percentage of each component in the firm's optimal capital structure. We find the WACC by multiplying the individual source's cost of capital times its percentage of the firm's capital structure, then adding these results. For Ellis Industries, the weighted average of the financing sources follows:

weighted average cost of capital (k_a) or (WACC) The average of all the component costs of capital, weighted according to the percentage of each component in the firm's optimal capital structure.

$$(.40 \times \text{AT } k_d) + (.10 \times k_p) + (.50 \times k_s)$$

$$= (.40 \times .085) + (.10 \times .125) + (.50 \times .155)$$

$$= .034 + .0125 + .0775$$

$$= .124, \text{ or } 12.4\%$$

Ellis Industries' weighted average cost of capital is 11.4 percent. The general formula for any firm's WACC is shown in Equation 9-6:

Formula for the Weighted Average Cost of Capital (WACC)

$$k_a = (WT_d \times \text{AT } k_d) + (WT_p \times k_p) + (WT_s \times k_s) \qquad (9\text{-}6)$$

where: k_a = The weighted average cost of capital (WACC)

WT_d = The weight, or proportion, of debt used to finance the firm's assets

$\text{AT } k_d$ = The after-tax cost of debt

WT_p = The weight, or proportion, of preferred stock being used to finance the firm's assets

k_p = The cost of preferred stock

WT_s = The weight, or proportion, of common equity being used to finance the firm's assets

k_s = The cost of common equity

4. Ideally, the percentage of each component in the capital structure would be measured on the basis of market values instead of accounting values. For the sake of simplicity, we use accounting values here, as do many real-world companies.

A firm must earn a return equal to the WACC to pay suppliers of capital the return they expect given the amount of risk they are taking. In the case of Ellis Industries, for instance, its average-risk capital budgeting projects must earn a return of 12.4 percent to pay its capital suppliers the return they expect.

In the long run, companies generally try to maintain an optimal mixture of capital from different sources. In the short run, however, one project may be financed entirely from one source. Even if a particular project is financed entirely from one source, the WACC should still be used as the required rate of return for an average-risk project. Say, for instance, such a project is entirely financed with debt, a relatively cheap source of capital. The cost of debt should not be used as that project's cost of capital. Why? Because the firm's risk would increase with the increase in debt, and the costs of all sources of capital would increase.

The Marginal Cost of Capital (MCC)

A firm's weighted average cost of capital will change if one component cost of capital changes. Often, a change in WACC occurs when a firm raises a large amount of capital. For example, lenders may increase the interest rate they charge, k_d, if they think the firm's debt load will be too heavy after new funds are borrowed. Or a firm's cost of equity may increase when new stock is issued after new retained earnings run out. This is because of the flotation costs incurred when new stock is issued.

marginal cost of capital (MCC) The weighted average cost of capital for the next dollar of funds raised.

Firms, then, must consider how increasing component costs of capital affect the WACC. The weighted average cost of the next dollar of capital to be raised is the **marginal cost of capital (MCC)**. To find the MCC, financial managers must (1) assess at what point a firm's cost of debt or equity will change the firm's WACC, (2) estimate how much the change will be, and (3) calculate the cost of capital up to and after the points of change.

The Firm's MCC Schedule

The marginal cost of the *first* dollar of capital a firm raises is the same as the firm's basic WACC. However, as the firm raises more capital, a point is reached at which the marginal cost of capital changes. Why? Because one of the component sources of capital changes. This point is the *break point* in the firm's MCC schedule. Capital above the break point can only be raised at a higher cost.

Finding the Break Points in the MCC Schedule

To find break points in the MCC schedule, financial managers determine what limits, if any, there are on the firm's ability to raise funds from a given source at a given cost. Break points in the MCC schedule consist of one or more *debt break points* and an *equity break point*.

Debt Break Points

Suppose that Ellis Industries' financial managers, after consulting with bankers, determined that the firm can borrow up to $300,000 at an interest rate of 10 percent, but any money borrowed above that amount will cost 12 percent. To calculate Ellis Industries' after-tax cost of debt, assume the firm's interest subsidy tax rate is 15 percent. We apply Equation 9-1 as follows:

$$AT\,k_d = k_d\,(1 - ISTR)$$
$$= .10 \times (1 - .15)$$
$$= .085, \text{ or } 8.5\%$$

We see that at an interest rate of 10 percent and a tax rate of 40 percent, Ellis's after-tax cost of debt is 8.5 percent. However, if Ellis Industries borrows more than $300,000, then its interest rate increases to 12 percent. At an interest subsidy tax rate of 15 percent and an interest rate of 12 percent, the firm's after-tax k_d for amounts borrowed over $300,000 is

$$\text{AT } k_d \text{ (for over \$300,000 borrowed)} = .12\,(1 - .15)$$

$$= .102, \text{ or } 10.2\%$$

Because Ellis's AT k_d increases when it borrows more than $300,000, its MCC will also increase when it borrows more than $300,000. (We'll see how much it increases in the next section.) The financial managers at Ellis Industries want to know how much total capital they can raise before the debt portion reaches $300,000, causing an increase in the AT k_d and the MCC.

Ellis Industries' marginal cost of capital break point is not $300,000 because the firm's capital structure is 40 percent debt, 10 percent preferred stock, and 50 percent common stock. At $300,000, then, only 40 percent of that capital is debt. Instead, the financial managers of Ellis Industries must figure out at what point the firm will use $300,000 of debt capital.

To find a firm's marginal cost of capital break point, we use Equation 9-7:

Formula for the Marginal Cost of Capital (MCC) Break Point

$$BP = \frac{\text{Limit}}{\text{Proportion of Total}} \qquad (9\text{-}7)$$

where: BP = The capital budget size at which the MCC changes (break point)

Limit = The point at which the cost of the source of capital changes

Proportion of Total = The percentage of this source of capital in the firm's capital structure

In our Ellis Industries example, we know that the firm has a $300,000 debt limit before its after-tax cost of debt will increase and that debt is 40 percent of the firm's capital structure. Applying Equation 9-7 to our Ellis example, we see that its debt break point is the following:

$$BP_d = \frac{\$300,000}{.40}$$

$$= \$750,000$$

We find that Ellis Industries' break point is $750,000. By applying Equation 9-7, Ellis's financial managers know that they may raise up to $750,000 in capital before their borrowing costs will rise from 8.5 percent to 10.2 percent. Any capital raised over $750,000 will reflect the higher cost of borrowing, as shown in Figure 9-3.

Notice we used subscript $_d$ with BP in Equation 9-7. That was to identify the break point as a *debt break point*. There could be other debt break points for Ellis Industries. If, for instance, the company's lenders set additional limits on the company's borrowing, the debt break points would be denoted as BP_{d1}, BP_{d2}, and so on. For our example, let's assume that Ellis's bankers will lend the firm an unlimited amount of money over $300,000 at 10.2 percent, so there are no further debt break points.

The Equity Break Point

The equity break point is the point at which the MCC changes because the cost of equity changes. Equity costs may change because firms exhaust the supply of funds from the firm's existing common stockholders—that is, they exhaust additions to retained earnings. After firms exhaust their supply of internal equity, which has a capital cost of k_s, they will have to raise additional equity funds by issuing new stock, which has a higher cost, k_n. This additional equity is external equity capital. The MCC increases accordingly.

FIGURE 9-3

Ellis Industries
Debt Break Point

Figure 9-3 shows how Ellis Industries can raise up to $750,000 of total capital before the $300,000 of lower-cost debt is exhausted.

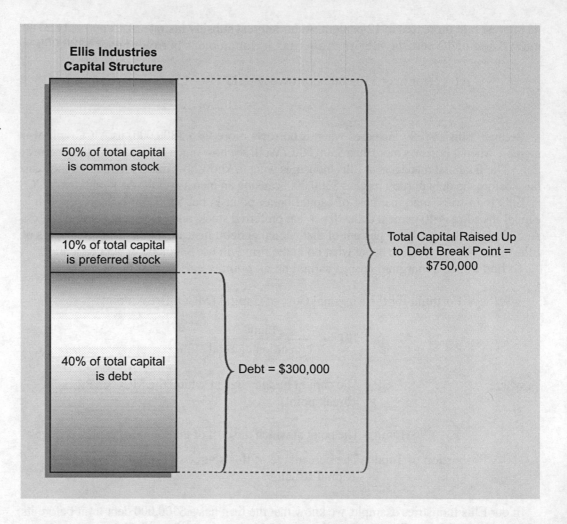

Ellis Industries Capital Structure

50% of total capital is common stock

10% of total capital is preferred stock

40% of total capital is debt

Debt = $300,000

Total Capital Raised Up to Debt Break Point = $750,000

Let's illustrate how the MCC increases because of changes in the cost of equity. We'll assume that Ellis Industries expects to realize $600,000 in income this year after it pays preferred stockholders their dividends. The $600,000 in earnings belong to the common stockholders. The firm may either pay dividends or retain the earnings. Let's assume Ellis retains the $600,000. The finite supply of capital from the existing common stockholders is the $600,000 addition to retained earnings. To find the equity break point, then, Ellis's managers must know at what point the firm will exhaust the common equity capital of $600,000, assuming existing common stock equity is 50 percent of the firm's capital budget. Figure 9-4 graphically depicts the Ellis equity break point analysis.

To find the equity break point, we apply Equation 9-7, the MCC break point formula. We know that the existing common stock capital limit is $600,000 and that common equity finances 50 percent of the total capital budget. Using Equation 9-7, we solve for the equity break point, BP_e, as follows:

$$BP_e = \frac{\$600,000}{.50}$$

$$= \$1,200,000$$

Our calculations show that the Ellis equity break point is $1,200,000. If the capital budget exceeds $1,200,000, the portion financed with common equity will exceed $600,000. At that point, Ellis will need to issue new common stock to raise the additional capital. The new common stock's cost, k_n, will be greater than the cost of internal common equity, k_s, so the MCC will rise when the capital budget exceeds $1,200,000, as shown in Figure 9-4.

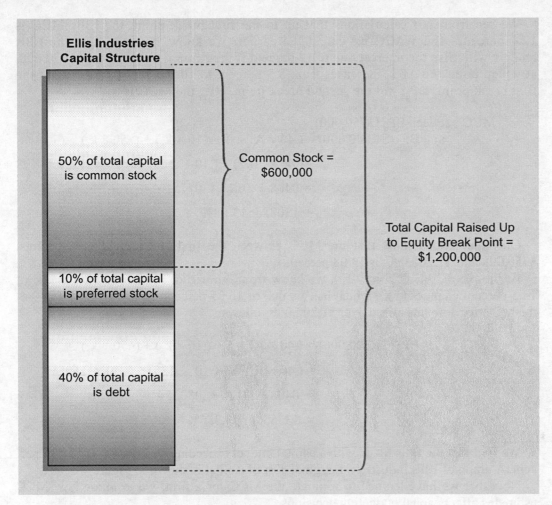

FIGURE 9-4
Ellis Industries
Equity Breakpoint

Figure 9-4 shows how Ellis Industries can raise up to $1,200,000 of total capital before the $600,000 of lower-cost internal equity is exhausted.

Calculating the Amount the MCC Changes

To calculate MCC changes, we must first identify the break points. In our Ellis Industries example, we identified two break points at which the firm's MCC will change:

$$\text{Debt Break Point, } BP_d = \$750,000$$

$$\text{Equity Break Point, } BP_e = \$1,200,000$$

The next step in the MCC analysis is to estimate how much the change in the MCC will be for varying amounts of funds raised.

The MCC Up to the First Break Point

Because the MCC is simply the weighted average cost of the next dollar of capital to be raised, we can use the WACC formula, Equation 9-6, to calculate the MCC as well.

We assume that Ellis Industries wants to maintain its current capital structure of 40 percent debt, 10 percent preferred stock, and 50 percent common equity. We assume further that its after-tax cost of debt, $AT\,k_d$, is 8.5 percent; its cost of preferred stock, k_p, is 12.5 percent; and its cost of internal common equity, k_s, is 15.5 percent. With these values, we use Equation 9-6 to find the Ellis MCC for capital raised up to the first break point, BP_d, as follows:

$$\text{MCC up to } BP_d \,(\$750,000) = (.40 \times AT\,k_d) + (.10 \times k_p) + (.50 \times k_s)$$

$$= (.40 \times .085) + (.10 \times .125) + (.50 \times .155)$$

$$= .034 + .0125 + .0775$$

$$= .124, \text{ or } 12.4\%$$

We see from our calculations that up to the first break point, the Ellis MCC is 12.4 percent—the WACC we calculated earlier. We know, however, that the Ellis lenders will raise the interest rate to 12 percent if the firm raises more than $750,000, at which point the AT k_d increases from 8.5 percent to 10.2 percent. So between the first break point, BP_d, and the second break point, BP_e, the MCC is

$$\text{MCC between } BP_d\ (\$750,000)$$
$$\text{and } BP_e\ (\$1,200,000) = (.40 \times AT\ k_d) + (.10 \times k_p) + (.50 \times k_s)$$
$$= (.40 \times .102) + (.10 \times .125) + (.50 \times .155)$$
$$= .0408 + .0125 + .0775$$
$$= .1308, \text{ or } 13.08\%$$

Our calculations show that the MCC between the first and second break points, $750,000 and $1,200,000, is 13.08 percent.

At the second break point, BP_e, we know from our earlier Ellis discussion that k_s of 15.5 percent changes to k_n, which has a value of 16.05 percent. Applying Equation 9-6, the MCC for amounts raised over $1,200,000 follows:

$$\text{MCC over } BP_e\ (\$1,200,000) = (.40 \times AT\ k_d) + (.10 \times k_p) + (.50 \times k_s)$$
$$= (.40 \times .102) + (.10 \times .125) + (.50 \times .1605)$$
$$= .0408 + .0125 + .08025$$
$$= .13355, \text{ or } 13.355\%$$

We find that the Ellis MCC with a capital budget exceeding $1,200,000 is 13.335 percent. A graph of Ellis Industries' marginal cost of capital is shown in Figure 9-5.

Now that we have learned to estimate the MCC for a firm, we examine how MCC estimates affect capital budgeting decisions.

FIGURE 9-5

Ellis Industries Marginal Cost of Capital Schedule

Figure 9-5 shows the marginal cost of capital (MCC) schedule that reflects the cost of debt and cost of equity break points.

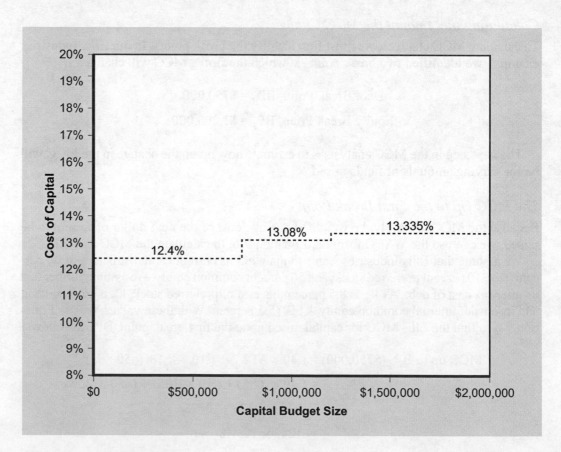

The MCC Schedule and Capital Budgeting Decisions

Firms use the MCC schedule to identify which new capital budgeting projects should be selected for further consideration and which should be rejected. For example, assume that Ellis Industries has identified the following projects for possible adoption:

Project	Initial Investment Required	Project's Expected Rate of Return
A	$500,000	18.00%
B	$300,000	14.00%
C	$200,000	13.5%
D	$300,000	12.5%
E	$700,000	9.00%

The projects are ranked from highest to lowest expected rate of return. The list of proposed capital budgeting projects ranked by expected rate of return is the firm's investment opportunity schedule (IOS). To determine which proposed projects should be accepted, the Ellis financial managers determine which projects have expected rates of return that exceed their respective costs of capital. To compare the projects' expected rates of return to the firm's cost of capital, the financial managers plot the IOS on the same graph as the MCC. Figure 9-6 shows this technique.

The projects with the highest expected rates of return are plotted first. The Ellis financial managers should start with Project A, which has an expected rate of return of 18 percent. That project requires a capital investment of $500,000. Next, they should add Project B, a project with an expected rate of return of 14 percent and an investment of $300,000. The total capital budget with Projects A and B is $800,000. Then Project C, with an expected rate of return of 13.5 percent, should be accepted because it would be financed with capital costing 13.08%. This means that the optimal capital budget is $100,000 consisting of the combined initial investment values for Projects A, B, and C.

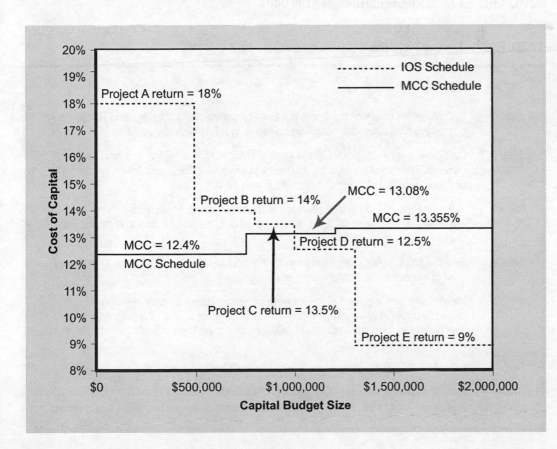

FIGURE 9-6

Ellis Industries MCC and IOS Schedules

Figure 9-6 shows the MCC and IOS schedules. Those projects on the IOS schedule above the MCC schedule are accepted.

Note that if Project D were the only project under consideration it would be accepted. Its expected rate of return is 12.5% and the funds to finance it, if it were the only project under consideration would be 12.4%. Figure 9-6 shows why it is important to consider all the projects under consideration at the same time so that the optimal decision, the one that increases the value of the firm the most, is made. When the projects are considered at the same time we see that Project D is financed partly with capital costing 13.08% and partly with capital costing 13.335% while offering an expected rate of return of only 12.5%. It, therefore, should be rejected. Project E is also rejected since it would be financed entirely with capital costing 13.355% while having an expected rate of return of 9%. Combining the IOS and MCC schedules is an effective tool to see whether a firm should accept or reject a project.

The Optimal Capital Budget

optimal capital budget
The list of all accepted projects and the total amount of their initial cash outlays.

When we integrate the IOS and the MCC schedules, as shown in Figure 9-6, we see that Ellis Industries' optimal capital budget is $1 million, consisting of Projects A, B, and C. The **optimal capital budget** is the list of all accepted projects and the total amount of initial cash outlays for these projects. All projects on the IOS schedule that are above the MCC schedule are accepted; the rest are rejected.

Table 9-1 summarizes the seven steps to calculate the optimal capital budget.

The Importance of MCC to Capital Budgeting Decisions

Analyzing the combined IOS and MCC schedules allows financial managers to examine many projects at once, rather than each project in isolation. This way they choose the best projects.

To demonstrate how important the MCC schedule is to capital budgeting decisions, look at Figure 9-6 again. Notice that Projects D and E are rejected because they are below the MCC line. Because Project D's expected rate of return is only 12.5 percent, it's a poor investment. However, this statement is only true because Projects A, B, and C were already considered before Project D. Together, Projects A, B, and C require $1 million of capital investment. Given that $1 million has already been spent for Projects A, B, and C, the $300,000 required for Project D can only be raised at costs of 13.08 percent (the first $200,000) and 13.335 percent (the last $100,000).

TABLE 9-1 Determining the Optimal Capital Budget

STEPS	ACTIONS
Step 1	Calculate the costs of the firm's sources of capital, AT k_d, k_p, k_s, and Record any borrowing limits and the resulting changes in AT k_d with those limits.
Step 2	Calculate the break points in the capital budget size at which the MCC will change. There will always be an equity break point, BP_e, and there may be one or more debt break points, BP_{d1}, BP_{d2}, and so on.
Step 3	Calculate the MCC up to, between, and above all the break points. The MCC increases at each break point. Record the MCC values before and after each break point.
Step 4	Plot the MCC values on a graph with the capital budget size on the X axis and cost of capital/rate of return on the Y axis.
Step 5	Identify the firm's potential investment projects. Record each investment project's initial investment requirement and expected rate of return. Make an investment opportunity schedule (IOS) by lining up the projects from highest return to lowest.
Step 6	Plot the IOS on the same graph with the MCC.
Step 7	Note the point where the IOS and MCC schedules cross. Projects on the IOS line above the MCC line should be accepted, and those below the MCC line rejected.

This example illustrates the importance of using a firm's MCC, not the firm's initial WACC, to evaluate investments. If all investment projects are treated in isolation and evaluated using the firm's initial WACC, then some of them may be overvalued. The discrepancy will become apparent when the firm tries to raise the entire amount of capital to support the complete capital budget and finds that the cost of the last dollar raised exceeds the expected rate of return of the last project adopted.

Crowdfunding

Crowdfunding is a relatively recent phenomenon whereby companies raise capital from a large number of different people who have a connection with the company. These suppliers of capital could be customers of the company. The word "company" is used loosely here. The suppliers of the capital could be fans of a musical group. Those fans could offer capital to the musicians to finance the group's tour.

The concept seems to have begun as a way to connect artists with their fans. A visual artist, filmmaker, or musician might seek funding from individuals who are fans. These suppliers of funds are typically not "investors" in the way we would normally think of it. The "return" might be in the form of preferential treatment in the purchase of tickets for an art opening or concert. There would be no promissory note or ownership share conveyed by the entity seeking the funds. There are some more traditional crowdfunding ventures, with the suppliers of capital taking either a debt or equity interest in the entity seeking the funds. Crowdfunding for purely charitable purposes is also seen. This might involve a worthy cause that goes "viral" that attracts the interest of many people who wish to support the person in need by supplying funds through the crowdfunding model.

Crowdfunding is usually done through a website on the Internet. Reviews of some of the more popular such websites can be seen at www.crowdfunding-websitereviews.com/. Kickstarter is one of the more popular crowdfunding websites. As this phenomenon continues to grow, more traditional start-up companies are turning to these crowdfunding websites for capital. As is typical for this type of website, the entity seeking funding establishes an amount of funding it seeks. If it fails to raise that amount, it gets nothing. Traditional for-profit start-up companies are seeking investors in the more traditional sense as described in this chapter. These investors are seeking a return on their investments, a return that is appropriate given the risk being taken.

Crowdfunding is beginning to take the place of venture capital (VC) firms. Such VC firms have been around for a long time and have been an important source of funding for start-up companies. VC firms are traditionally owned by a small number of wealthy and sophisticated investors who are seeking to profit by getting in on the group floor as equity investors in a promising new company. Such VC firms often require significant management control over the companies in which they invest. One of the appeals for start-up companies of crowdfunding is that the founders can often maintain more control over their firms. These entrepreneurs can pursue their dreams without the kind of outside interference that often comes when VC capital is accepted. The other side of this coin is that VC investors typically bring management expertise to the emerging company, expertise that might be lacking by the company founders.

In April 2012 President Obama signed the Jumpstart Our Business Startups (JOBS) Act. Eligible companies, designated as emerging growth companies (EGCs), are now allowed to raise up to $1 million over a twelve-month period from small investors without going through the normal Securities and Exchange Commission (SEC) registration process. To be eligible for classification as an EGC a company must have less than $1 billion in gross revenues for its past fiscal year.

Go to http://www.gibsondunn.com/publications/Pages/JOBSActChangesPublic-PrivateCapitalMarketsLandscape.aspx for additional information on the JOBS Act.

What's Next

In this chapter we learned how to calculate a firm's individual component costs of capital and how to calculate its WACC and its MCC. In Chapter 10, we discuss the decision techniques that firms use to select projects.

Summary

1. *Describe the sources of capital and how firms raise capital.*
   Firms raise debt capital from lenders or bondholders. They also raise funds from preferred stockholders, from current stockholders, and from investors who buy newly issued shares of common stock. All suppliers of capital expect a rate of return proportionate to the risk they take. To ensure a supply of capital to meet their capital budgeting needs, firms must pay that return to capital suppliers. To compensate creditors, firms must pay the interest and principal on loans. For bondholders, firms must pay the market required interest rate. For preferred stockholders, the dividend payments serve as compensation. To compensate common stock investors, firms pay dividends or reinvest the stockholders' earnings.

2. *Estimate the cost of capital for each financing source.*
   To find a firm's overall cost of capital, a firm must first estimate how much each source of capital costs. The after-tax cost of debt, AT k_d, is the market's required rate of return on the firm's debt, adjusted for the tax savings realized if interest payments are deducted from taxable income. The before-tax cost of debt, k_d, is multiplied by one minus the interest subsidy tax rate $(1 - ISTR)$ to arrive at the firm's after-tax cost of debt. The cost of preferred stock, k_p, is the investor's required rate of return on that security. The cost of common stock equity, k_s, is the opportunity cost of new retained earnings, the required rate of return on the firm's common stock. The cost of new common stock, k_n (external equity), is the required rate of return on the firm's common stock, adjusted for the flotation costs incurred when new common stock is sold in the market.

3. *Estimate the weighted average cost of capital.*
   The weighted average cost of capital, k_a or WACC, is the overall average cost of funds considering each of the component capital costs and the weight of each of those components in the firm's capital structure. To estimate WACC, we multiply the individual source's cost of capital times its percentage of the firm's capital structure and then add the results.

4. *Use the marginal cost of capital (MCC) schedule to make capital budgeting decisions.*
   A firm's WACC changes as the cost of debt or equity increases as more capital is raised. Financial managers calculate the break points in the capital budget size at which the MCC will change. There will always be an equity break point, BP_e, and there may be one or more debt break points, BP_{d1}, BP_{d2}, and so on. Financial managers then calculate the MCC up to, between, and above all the break points and plot the MCC values on a graph showing how the cost of capital changes as capital budget size changes. Financial managers create an IOS by ranking all potential capital budgeting projects from the highest internal rate of return to the lowest and then plotting the IOS on the same graph with the MCC. To increase the value of the firm, projects on the IOS line above the MCC line should be accepted and those below the MCC line rejected.

5. *Explain the importance of the marginal cost of capital (MCC) schedule in financial decision making.*
   The MCC schedule forces financial managers to match a project's rate of return with the cost of funds for that specific project. This marginal analysis prevents financial managers from estimating a project's value incorrectly because of faulty cost of capital estimates that fail to consider how a larger capital budget increases capital costs.

Key Terms

after-tax cost of debt (AT k_d) The after-tax cost to a company of obtaining debt funds.

capital Funds supplied to a firm.

capital structure The mixture of sources of capital that a firm uses (for example, debt, preferred stock, and common stock).

component cost of capital The cost of raising funds from a particular source, such as bondholders or common stockholders.

cost of debt (k_d) The lender's required rate of return on a company's new bonds or other instrument of indebtedness.

cost of equity from new common stock (k_n) The cost of external equity, including the costs incurred to issue new common stock.

cost of internal common equity (k_s) The required rate of return on funds supplied by existing common stockholders through earnings retained.

cost of preferred stock (k_p) Investors' required rate of return on a company's new preferred stock.

flotation costs Fees that companies pay (to investment bankers and to others) when new securities are issued.

marginal cost of capital (MCC) The weighted average cost of capital for the next dollar of funds raised.

optimal capital budget The list of all accepted projects and the total amount of their initial cash outlays.

weighted average cost of capital (k_a) or (WACC) The average of all the component costs of capital, weighted according to the percentage of each component in the firm's optimal capital structure.

Equations Introduced in This Chapter

Equation 9-1. Formula for the After-Tax Cost of Debt (AT k_d):

$$AT\ k_d = k_d\ (1 - ISTR)$$

where: k_d = The before-tax cost of debt

ISTR = The firm's interest subsidy tax rate

Equation 9-2. Formula for the Cost of Preferred Stock (k_p):

$$k_p = \frac{D_p}{(P_p - F)}$$

where: k_p = The cost of the preferred stock issue; the expected return

D_p = The amount of the expected preferred stock dividend

P_p = The current price of the preferred stock

F = The flotation cost per share

Equation 9-3. Formula for the Cost of Common Stock Equity (k_s)
(Dividend Growth Model Approach):

$$k_s = \frac{D_1}{P_0} + g$$

where: P_0 = The current price of the common stock

D_1 = The amount of the common stock dividend expected one period from now

g = The expected constant growth rate of the company's common stock dividends

Equation 9-4. CAPM Formula for the Cost of Common Equity (k_s):

$$k_s = k_{rf} + (k_m - k_{rf}) \times \beta$$

where: k_s = The required rate of return from the company's common stock equity

k_{rf} = The risk-free rate of return

k_m = The expected rate of return on the overall stock market

β = The beta of the company's common stock, a measure of the amount of nondiversifiable risk

Equation 9-5. Formula for the Cost of New Common Equity (k_n):

$$k_n = \frac{D_1}{P_0 - F} + g$$

where: k_n = The cost of new common stock equity

P_0 = The price of one share of the common stock

D_1 = The amount of the common stock dividend expected to be paid in one year

F = The flotation cost per share

g = The expected constant growth rate of the company's common stock dividends

Equation 9-6. Formula for the Weighted Average Cost of Capital (WACC):

$$k_a = (WT_d \times AT\,k_d) + (WT_p \times k_p) + (WT_s \times k_s)$$

where: k_a = The weighted average cost of capital (WACC)

WT_d = The weight, or proportion, of debt used to finance the firm's assets

$AT\,k_d$ = The after-tax cost of debt

WT_p = The weight, or proportion, of preferred stock being used to finance the firm's assets

k_p = The cost of preferred stock

WT_s = The weight, or proportion, of common equity being used to finance the firm's assets

k_s = The cost of common equity

Equation 9-7. Formula for the Marginal Cost of Capital (MCC) Break Point:

$$BP = \frac{Limit}{Proportion\ of\ Total}$$

where: BP = The capital budget size at which the MCC changes (break point)

Limit = The point at which the cost of the source of capital changes

Proportion
of Total = The percentage of this source of capital in the firm's capital structure

Self-Test

ST-1. Jules' Security Company can issue new bonds with a market interest rate of 14 percent. Jules' interest subsidy tax rate is 25 percent. Compute the after-tax cost of debt, $AT\,k_d$, for this company.

ST-2. Mr. White's company, The Problem Solvers, wants to issue new preferred stock. The preferred dividend is $3.00 per share, the stock can be sold for $30, and the flotation costs are $1. What is the cost of preferred stock, k_p?

ST-3. Vincent's Dance Studio, Inc., has a beta of 1.9. The risk-free rate of interest is 4 percent. The market portfolio has an expected rate of return of 10 percent. What is the cost of internal equity, k_s, for this company using the CAPM approach?

ST-4. Marsalis's Entertainment Corporation has an after-tax cost of debt of 8 percent, a cost of preferred stock of 12 percent, and a cost of equity of 16 percent. What is the WACC, k_a, for this company? The capital structure of Marsalis's company contains 20 percent debt, 10 percent preferred stock, and 70 percent equity.

ST-5. Quinten's Movie Company has been told by its investment banking firm that it could issue up to $8 million in bonds at an after-tax cost of debt of 10 percent. But after that, additional bonds would have a 12 percent after-tax cost. Quinten's company uses 40 percent debt and 60 percent equity for major projects. How much money could this company raise, maintaining its preferred capital structure, before the after-tax cost of debt would jump to 12 percent?

Review Questions

1. Which is lower for a given company: the cost of debt or the cost of equity? Explain. Ignore taxes in your answer.

2. When a company issues new securities, how do flotation costs affect the cost of raising that capital?

3. What does the "weight" refer to in the weighted average cost of capital?

4. How do tax considerations affect the cost of debt and the cost of equity?

5. If dividends paid to common stockholders are not legal obligations of a corporation, is the cost of equity zero? Explain your answer.

6. What is the investment opportunity schedule (IOS)? How does it help financial managers make business decisions?

7. What is a marginal cost of capital (MCC) schedule? Is the schedule always a horizontal line? Explain.

8. For a given IOS and MCC, how do financial managers decide which proposed capital budgeting projects to accept and which to reject?

Build Your Communication Skills

CS-1. Prepare a brief paper in which you explain to the CEO of a fictional company why the cost of equity is greater than either the cost of debt or the cost of preferred stock. Be sure to explain why equity funds have a cost even though those costs are not reflected on the income statement. Finally, discuss why it is important for a firm to know its cost of capital.

CS-2. Write a short report that analyzes the role of the MCC schedule in making capital budgeting decisions. In your report, explain how the IOS affects this decision-making process. Be sure to explain your rationale for choosing some proposed projects while rejecting others.

Problems

9-1. **a.** What would be the after-tax cost of debt for a company with the following yields to maturity for its new bonds, if the applicable interest subsidy tax rate 20 percent?

     1. YTM = 7%

     2. YTM = 11%

     3. YTM = 13%

     b. How would the cost of debt change if the applicable interest subsidy tax rate were 25 percent?

Cost of Debt

9-2. Calculate the after-tax cost of debt for loans with the following effective annual interest rates and interest subsidy tax rates.

     a. Interest rate, 10%; interest subsidy tax rate, 0%.

     b. Interest rate, 10%; interest subsidy tax rate, 22%.

     c. Interest rate, 10%; interest subsidy tax rate, 25%.

Cost of Debt

9-3. What would be the cost of debt for the following companies given their yields to maturity (YTM) for new bonds and the applicable interest subsidy tax rates?

Cost of Debt

Company	YTM	Interest Subsidy Tax Rate
A	8%	10%
B	11%	15%
C	14%	25%

9-4. Ellen Ripley is the chief financial officer of Weyland Industries. She has asked Trudy Jones, one of the financial analysts, to calculate the after-tax cost of debt based on different bond yield to maturity rates. Magnolia Steel's interest subsidy tax rate is 15 percent. Calculate the after-tax cost-of-debt figures that will be shown in Ms. Jones's report at each tax rate for the following YTM rates.

     a. Yield to maturity, 8%.

     b. Yield to maturity, 14%.

     c. Yield to maturity, 16%.

9-5. A firm is issuing new bonds that pay 8 percent annual interest. The market required annual rate of return on these bonds is 13 percent. The firm has an interest subsidy rate of 25 percent.

     a. What is the before-tax cost of debt?

     b. What is the after-tax cost of debt?

Cost of Debt

9-6. A company's creditors charge 9.5 percent annual interest on loans to the company. The company's interest subsidy tax rate is 25 percent. What is the company's after-tax cost of debt?

Cost of Debt

Cost of Preferred Stock	➡ **9-7.**	A company can sell preferred stock for $26 per share, and each share of stock is expected to pay a dividend of $2. If the flotation cost per share of stock is $0.75, what would be the estimate of the cost of capital from this source?
Cost of Debt and Preferred Stock	➡ **9-8.**	Frank Underwood, the treasurer of a manufacturing company, thinks that debt (YTM = 11%, tax rate = 40%) will be a cheaper option for acquiring funds compared to issuing new preferred stock. The company can sell preferred stock at $61 per share and pay a yearly preferred dividend of $8 per share. The cost of issuing preferred stock is $1 per share. Is Frank correct?
Cost of Preferred Stock	➡ **9-9.**	One-Eyed Jacks Corporation needs money to fund a new production line of playing cards. Rio Longworth, manager of the finance department, suggests they sell preferred stock for $50 per share. They expect to pay $6 per share annual dividends. What is the estimate of the cost of preferred stock if the flotation cost is $2.25 per share?
Cost of Preferred Stock	➡ **9-10.**	El Norte Industries will issue $100 par, 12 percent preferred stock. The market price for the stock is expected to be $89 per share. El Norte must pay flotation costs of 5 percent of the market price. What is El Norte's cost of preferred stock?
Cost of Preferred Stock	➡ **9-11.**	A company's investment bankers say that a proposed new issue of 7.5 percent cumulative preferred stock with a par value of $10 a share can be sold to the public for $27 a share. The transaction costs will be $1 a share. What is the company's cost of preferred stock financing?
Cost of Equity	➡ **9-12.**	Twister Corporation is expected to pay a dividend of $7 per share one year from now on its common stock, which has a current market price of $143. Twister's dividends are expected to grow at 13 percent.
		a. Calculate the cost of the company's retained earnings.
		b. If the flotation cost per share of new common stock is $4, calculate the cost of issuing new common stock.
Cost of Retained Earnings	➡ **9-13.**	Amy Jolly is the treasurer of her company. She expects the company will grow at 4 percent in the future, and debt securities (YTM = 14%, tax rate = 30%) will always be a cheaper option to finance the growth. The current market price per share of its common stock is $39, and the expected dividend in one year is $1.50 per share. Calculate the cost of the company's retained earnings and check if Amy's assumption is correct.
Cost of Equity CAPM Approach	➡ **9-14.**	Free Willy, Inc., (Nasdaq: FWIC) has a beta of 1.4. If the rate on U.S. Treasury bills is 4.5 percent and the expected rate of return on the stock market is 12 percent, what is Free Willy's cost of common equity financing?
Challenge Problem	➡ **9-15.**	Pedro Muzquiz and Tita de la Garza are the CEOs of a large bakery chain, Chocolates, Inc. The common stock sells on the NASDAQ with a current market price of $65 per share. A $7 dividend is planned for one year from now. Business has been good and they expect the dividend growth rate of 10 percent to continue.
		a. Calculate the cost of the corporation's retained earnings.
		b. At the beginning of the year, 1 million shares were authorized, with 500,000 issued and outstanding. They plan to issue another 200,000 shares. Calculate the cost of capital of the new common stock if the flotation cost per share is $3. Do you expect the cost of new common equity (external) to be higher than the cost of the internal equity? Why?
Cost of Equity CAPM Approach	➡ **9-16.**	Margo Channing, the financial analyst for Eve's Broadway Production Company, has been asked by management to estimate a cost of equity for use in the analysis of a project under consideration. In the past, dividends declared and paid have been very sporadic. Because of this, Ms. Channing elects to use the CAPM approach to estimate the cost of equity. The rate on the short-term U.S. Treasury bills is 3 percent, and the expected rate of return on the overall stock market is 11 percent. Eve's Broadway Production Company has a beta of 1.6. What will Ms. Channing report as the cost of equity?

9-17. African Queen River Tours, Inc. has capitalized on the renewed interest in riverboat travel. Charlie Allnut, the lone financial analyst, estimates the firm's earnings, dividends, and stock price will continue to grow at the historical 5 percent rate. AQRT's common stock is currently selling for $30 per share. The dividend just paid was $2. They pay dividends every year. The rate of return expected on the overall stock market is 12 percent.

Cost of Common Equity

   a. What is AQRT's cost of equity?

   b. If they issue new common stock today and pay flotation costs of $2 per share, what is the cost of new common equity?

   c. If AQRT has a risk-free rate of 3 percent and a beta of 1.4, what will be AQRT's cost of equity using the CAPM approach?

9-18. Alvin C. York, the founder of York Corporation, thinks that the optimal capital structure of his company is 30 percent debt, 15 percent preferred stock, and the rest common equity. If the company has a 25 percent interest subsidy tax rate, compute its weighted average cost of capital given that:

Weighted Average Cost of Capital

   • YTM of its debt is 10 percent.

   • New preferred stock will have a market value of $31, a dividend of $2 per share, and flotation costs of $1 per share.

   • Price of common stock is currently $100 per share, and new common stock can be issued at the same price with flotation costs of $4 per share. The expected dividend in one year is $4 per share, and the growth rate is 6 percent.

   Assume the addition to retained earnings for the current period is zero.

9-19. A company has an optimal capital structure as follows:

Weighted Average Cost of Capital

Total Assets	$600,000
Debt	$300,000
Preferred Stock	$100,000
Common Equity	$200,000

   What would be the minimum expected return from a new capital investment project to satisfy the suppliers of the capital? Assume the applicable interest subsidy tax rate is 25 percent, YTM of its debt is 11 percent, flotation cost per share of preferred stock is $0.75, and flotation cost per share of common stock is $4. The preferred and common stocks are selling in the market for $26 and $143 a share, respectively, and they are expected to pay a dividend of $2 and $7, respectively, in one year. The company's dividends are expected to grow at 13 percent per year. The firm would like to maintain the foregoing optimal capital structure to finance the new project.

9-20. Great Expectations, a wedding and maternity clothing manufacturer, has a cost of equity of 16 percent and a cost of preferred stock of 14 percent. Its before-tax cost of debt is 12 percent, and its marginal tax rate is 40 percent. Assume that the most recent balance sheet shown here reflects the optimal capital structure. Calculate Great Expectations' after-tax WACC.

Weighted Average Cost of Capital

Great Expectations Balance Sheet
Dec. 31, 2015

Assets		Liabilities and Equity	
Cash	$ 50,000		
Accounts Receivable	90,000	Long-Term Debt	$ 600,000
Inventories	300,000	Preferred Stock	250,000
Plant and Equipment, net	810,000	Common Stock	400,000
Total Assets	$ 1,250,000	Total Liabilities and Equity	$ 1,250,000

Weighted Average Cost of Capital

9-21. Puppet Masters is considering a new capital investment project. The company has an optimal capital structure and plans to maintain it. The yield to maturity on Puppet Masters' debt is 10 percent, and its interest subsidy tax rate is 20 percent. The market price of the new issue of preferred stock is $25 per share, with an expected per share dividend of $2 at the end of this year. Flotation costs are set at $1 per share. The new issue of common stock has a current market price of $140 per share, with an expected dividend in one year of $5. Flotation costs for issuing new common stock are $4 per share. Puppet Masters' dividends are growing at 10 percent per year, and this growth is expected to continue for the foreseeable future. Selected figures from last year's balance sheet follow:

Total Assets	$1,000,000
Long-Term Debt	300,000
Preferred Stock	100,000
Common Stock	600,000

Calculate the minimum expected return from the new capital investment project needed to satisfy the suppliers of the capital.

Weighted Average Cost of Capital

9-22. Jay Lo Enterprises finances its assets with 60 percent debt, 10 percent preferred stock, and 30 percent common stock. Jay Lo's after-tax cost of debt is 5 percent, its cost of preferred stock is 8 percent, and its cost of common equity financing is 12 percent. Given these conditions, what is Jay Lo's WACC?

Weighted Average Cost of Capital

9-23. The law firm of Dewey, Cheatem, and Howe (DCH) has the following balance sheet:

Assets		Liabilities and Equity	
Cash	$ 110,000	Accounts Payable	$ 70,000
Receivables	240,000	Long-Term Debt	160,000
Office Equipment	80,000	Preferred Stock	100,000
Total Assets	$ 430,000	Common Equity	100,000
		Total Liabilities and Equity	$ 430,000

DCH's creditors charge 9.5 percent annual interest on loans to the company. It can sell preferred stock with a $10 per share dividend to the public for $50 a share (net to the company after commissions). The company's interest subsidy tax rate is 15 percent, its beta is 1.1, the risk-free rate is 4 percent, and the expected rate of return on the stock market is 12 percent. Given these conditions, what is DCH's WACC?

Marginal Cost of Capital Schedule

9-24. Fans By Fay Company has a capital structure of 60 percent debt and 40 percent common equity. The company expects to realize $200,000 in net income this year and will pay no dividends. The effective annual interest rate on its new borrowings increases by 3 percent for amounts over $500,000.

a. At what capital budget size will Fans By Fay's cost of equity increase? In other words, what is its equity break point?

b. At what capital budget size will its cost of debt increase (debt break point)?

Marginal Cost of Capital Schedule

9-25. Babe's Dog Obedience School, Inc., wants to maintain its current capital structure of 50 percent common equity, 10 percent preferred stock, and 40 percent debt. Its cost of common equity is 13 percent, and the cost of preferred stock is 12 percent. The bank's effective annual interest rate is 11 percent for amounts borrowed that are less than or equal to $1 million and 13 percent for amounts between $1 million and $2 million. If more than $2 million is borrowed, the effective annual interest rate charged is 15 percent. Babe's tax rate is 40 percent. The firm expects to realize $2,750,000 in net income this year after preferred dividends have been paid.

a. Calculate the MCC if $900,000 is needed for an upcoming project.

b. Calculate the MCC if $3,000,000 is needed for the project instead.

c. If a different project is adopted and $5,005,000 is needed for it, what is the MCC?

9-26. Stone Wood Products has a capital structure of 35 percent debt and 65 percent common equity. The managers consider this mix to be optimal and want to maintain it in the future. Net income for the coming year is expected to be $1.2 million dollars. Duke Mantee, the loan officer at the local bank, has set up the following schedule for Stone Wood Products' borrowings. There are 40,000 shares of common stock outstanding. The firm's interest subsidy tax rate is 40 percent.

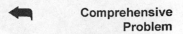

Comprehensive Problem

For more, see 8e Spreadsheet Templates for *Microsoft Excel*.

Loan Amount	Interest Rate
$0 to $750,000	10%
> $750,000	12%

The market price per share of Stone Wood Products' common stock is $50 per share. They have declared a $5 dividend to be paid in one year. The company's expected growth rate is 9 percent. The flotation costs for new common stock issued are set at 8 percent of the market price.

The managers are considering several investment opportunities for the upcoming year. They have asked the senior financial analyst, Gabrielle Maple, to recommend which of the following projects the firm should undertake. Because you are the newest member of her team and need the experience, she has passed this management request on to you.

Investment Opportunities

Project	Initial Investment (in millions)	Rate of Return
A	$0.5	16%
B	$1.6	12%
C	$0.6	15%
D	$1.5	18%

a. Calculate all of Stone Wood Products' component costs of capital (after-tax cost of debt, cost of equity, and cost of new equity).

b. Calculate all of the MCC break points.

c. Calculate all of the MCC figures.

d. Make an IOS by listing the projects from the highest to the lowest internal rates of return.

e. Plot the MCC values and the IOS values on the same graph.

f. Which projects will you recommend management adopt for the next year?

Answers to Self-Test

ST-1. $.14 \times (1 - .25) = .105 = 10.5\%$ AT k_d

ST-2. Using Equation 9-7, $k_p = D_p /(P_p - F) = \$3/(\$30 - \$1) = .1034$, or 10.34%

ST-3. $.04 + (.10 - .04) \times 1.9 = .154 = 15.4\%$ k_s

ST-4. $(.08 \times .2) + (.12 \times .10) + (.16 \times .70) = .14 = 14\%$ k_a

ST-5. The break point in the MCC schedule caused by the increase in the cost of debt, BP_d, after $8,000,000 is borrowed, equals $8,000,000 ÷ .40 = $20,000,000.

Capital Budgeting Decision Methods

"Everything is worth what its purchaser will pay for it."
—Publilius Syrus

Source: Alfa Photo/Shutterstock

Learning Objectives

After reading this chapter, you should be able to:

1. Explain the capital budgeting process.

2. Calculate the payback period, net present value, internal rate of return, and modified internal rate of return for a proposed capital budgeting project.

3. Describe capital rationing and how firms decide which projects to select.

4. Measure the risk of a capital budgeting project.

5. Explain risk-adjusted discount rates.

Apple Investments

In early 2018, Apple Computer announced its plan to construct another campus facility. Taking advantage of benefits the company expects to receive from the Tax Cuts and Jobs Act of 2017 (TCJA) the company announced plans to contribute $350 billion to the U.S. economy over the next five years. This huge figure includes generous estimates of spillover effects in the economy triggered by Apple's own investments. The direct pledge from Apple for 2018 was to spend $55 billion of its own money while creating 20,000 new jobs. The company also announced that it plans to bring back to the U.S. 94% of its $252 billion in cash that it had been holding overseas. If it had brought this cash back to the U.S. before TCJA passed the company would have had to pay taxes of approximately 35% of the amount it repatriated. Evidently, the new corporate tax rate of 21% is more to the company's liking.

When a company decides to shell out this kind of money, it needs a framework for deciding how much to spend on what projects. That is what this chapter addresses. Individual projects need to be evaluated with consideration of the benefits and costs of the proposal, including the costs of the funds intended for each project. Clearly, as seen with Apple's plans, the stakes can be very large.

Sources: https://www.nytimes.com/2018/01/17/technology/apple-tax-bill-repatriate-cash.html
https://www.bostonglobe.com/business/2018/01/17/apple-says-will-build-second-corporate-campus/A1C5Vc9Yob1gfhYOrjlQ3L/story.html
https://techcrunch.com/2018/01/17/apple-pledges-350-billion-investment-in-us-economy-over-next-five-years/

Chapter Overview

We now look at the decision methods that analysts use to determine whether to approve a given investment project and how they account for a project's risk. Investment projects such as Apple's new investment firm project can fuel a firm's success, so effective project selection often determines a firm's value. The decision methods for choosing acceptable investment projects, then, are some of the most important tools financial managers use.

We begin by looking at the capital budgeting process and four capital budgeting decision methods: *payback, net present value, internal rate of return,* and *modified internal rate of return*. Then we discuss how to select projects when firms limit their budget for capital projects, a practice called capital rationing. Finally, we look at how firms measure and compensate for the risk of capital budgeting projects.

The Capital Budgeting Process

All businesses budget for capital projects—an airline that considers purchasing new planes, a production studio that decides to buy new film cameras, or a pharmaceutical company that invests in research and development for a new drug. **Capital budgeting** is the process of evaluating proposed large, long-term investment projects. The projects may be the purchase of fixed assets, investments in research and development, advertising, or intellectual property. For instance, Apple Computer's development of the iPhone was a capital budgeting project.

capital budgeting The process of evaluating proposed projects.

Long-term projects may tie up cash resources, time, and additional assets. They can also affect a firm's performance for years to come. As a result, careful capital budgeting is vital to ensure that the proposed investment will add value to the firm.

Before we discuss the specific decision methods for selecting investment projects, we briefly examine capital budgeting basics: capital budgeting decision practices, types of capital budgeting projects, the cash flows associated with such projects, and the stages of the capital budgeting process.

Decision Practices

Financial managers apply two decision practices when selecting capital budgeting projects: *accept/reject* and *ranking*. The accept/reject decision focuses on the question of whether the proposed project would add value to the firm or earn a rate of return that is acceptable to the company. The ranking decision lists competing projects in order of desirability to choose the best one.

The accept/reject decision determines whether a project is acceptable in light of the firm's financial objectives. That is, if a project meets the firm's basic risk and return requirements, it will be accepted. If not, it will be rejected.

Ranking compares projects to a standard measure and orders the projects based on how well they meet the measure. If, for instance, the standard is how quickly the project pays off the initial investment, then the project that pays off the investment most rapidly would be ranked first. The project that paid off most slowly would be ranked last.

Types of Projects

Firms invest in two categories of projects: independent projects and mutually exclusive projects. **Independent projects** do not compete with each other. A firm may accept none, one, some, or all from among a group of independent projects. Say, for example, that a firm is able to raise funds for all worthwhile projects it identifies. The firm is considering two new projects—a new telephone system and a warehouse. The telephone system and the warehouse would be independent projects. Accepting one does not preclude accepting the other.

In contrast, **mutually exclusive projects** compete against each other. The best project from among a group of acceptable mutually exclusive projects is selected. For example, if a company needed only one copier, one proposal to buy a Xerox™ copier and a second proposal to buy a Toshiba™ copier would be two projects that are mutually exclusive.

independent projects A group of projects such that any or all could be accepted.

mutually exclusive projects A group of projects that compete against each other; only one of the mutually exclusive projects may be chosen.

Capital Budgeting Cash Flows

Although decision makers examine accounting information such as sales and expenses, capital budgeting decision makers base their decisions on relevant cash flows associated with a project. The relevant cash flows are **incremental cash flows**—cash flows that will occur if an investment is undertaken but that won't occur if it isn't.

For example, imagine that you are an animator who helps create children's films. Your firm is considering whether to buy a computer to help you design your characters more quickly. The computer would enable you to create two characters in the time it now takes you to draw one, thereby increasing your productivity.

The incremental cash flows associated with the animation project are (1) the initial investment in the computer and (2) the *additional* cash the firm will receive because you will double your animation output for the life of the computer. These cash flows will occur if the new computer is purchased and will not occur if it is not purchased. These are the cash flows, then, that affect the capital budgeting decision.

Estimating these incremental cash flows, the subject of Chapter 11, is a major component of capital budgeting decisions, as we see in the next section.

incremental cash flows Cash flows that will occur only if an investment is undertaken.

Stages in the Capital Budgeting Process

The capital budgeting process has four major stages:

1. Finding projects
2. Estimating the incremental cash flows associated with projects
3. Evaluating and selecting projects
4. Implementing and monitoring projects

This chapter focuses on stage 3—how to evaluate and choose investment projects. We assume that the firm has found projects in which to invest and has estimated the projects' cash flows effectively.

> **Take Note**
> Capital budgeting techniques are usually used only for projects with large cash outlays. Small investment decisions are usually made by the "seat of the pants." For instance, if your office supply of pencils is running low, you order more. You know that the cost of buying pencils is justified without undergoing capital budgeting analysis.

Capital Budgeting Decision Methods

The four formal capital budgeting decision methods we will examine are payback, net present value, internal rate of return, and modified internal rate of return. Let's begin with the payback method.

The Payback Method

One of the simplest capital budgeting decision methods is the payback method. To use it, analysts find a project's **payback period**—the number of time periods it will take before the cash inflows of a proposed project equal the amount of the initial project investment (a cash outflow).

payback period The expected amount of time a capital budgeting project will take to generate cash flows that cover the project's initial cash outlay.

How to Calculate the Payback Period

To calculate the payback period, simply add up a project's projected positive cash flows, one period at a time, until the sum equals the amount of the project's initial investment. That number of time periods it takes for the positive cash flows to equal the amount of the initial investment is the payback period.

To illustrate, imagine that you work for a firm called the AddVenture Corporation. AddVenture is considering two investment proposals, Projects X and Y. The initial investment for both projects is $5,000. The finance department estimates that the projects will generate the following cash flows:

Cash Flows

	For Initial Investment	End of Year 1	End of Year 2	End of Year 3	End of Year 4
Project X	−$5,000	$2,000	$3,000	$ 500	$ 0
Project Y	−$5,000	$2,000	$2,000	$1,000	$ 2,000

By analyzing the cash flows, we see that Project X has a payback period of two years because the project's initial investment of $5,000 (a cash flow of −$5,000) will be recouped (by offsetting positive cash flows) at the end of year 2. In comparison, Project Y has a payback of three years.

Payback Method Decision Rule

To apply the payback decision method, firms must first decide what payback time period is acceptable for long-term projects. In our case, if the firm sets two years as its required payback period, it will accept Project X but reject Project Y. If, however, the firm allows a three-year payback period, then both projects will be accepted if they are independent.

Problems with the Payback Method

The payback method is used in practice because of its simplicity, but it has a big disadvantage in that it does not consider cash flows that occur after the payback period. For example, suppose Project Y's cash flows in year 4 were $10 million instead of $2,000. It wouldn't make any difference. Project Y would still be rejected under the payback method if the company's policy were to demand a payback of no more than two years. Failing to look beyond the payback period can lead to poor business decisions, as shown.

Another deficiency of the payback method is that it does not consider the time value of money. For instance, compare the cash flows of Projects A and B:

Cash Flows

	For Initial Investment	End of Year 1	End of Year 2
Project A	−$5,000	$3,000	$2,000
Project B	−$5,000	$2,000	$3,000

Assuming the required payback period is two years, we see that both projects are equally preferable—they both pay back the initial investment in two years. However, time value of money analysis indicates that if both projects are equally risky, then Project A is better than Project B because the firm will get more money sooner. Nevertheless, timing of cash flows makes no difference in the payback computation.

Because the payback method does not factor in the time value of money, or the cash flows after the payback period, its usefulness is limited. Although it does provide a rough measure of a project's liquidity and can help to supplement other techniques, financial managers should not rely on it as a primary decision method.

The Net Present Value (NPV) Method

The project selection method that is most consistent with the goal of owner wealth maximization is the net present value method. The **net present value (NPV)** of a capital budgeting project is *the dollar amount of the change in the value of the firm as a result of undertaking the project*. The change in firm value may be positive, negative, or zero, depending on the NPV value.

net present value (NPV) The estimated change in the value of the firm that would occur if a project is accepted.

If a project has an NPV of zero, it means that the firm's overall value will not change if the new project is adopted. Why? Because the new project is expected to generate exactly the firm's required rate of return—no more and no less. A positive NPV means that the firm's value will increase if the project is adopted because the new project's estimated return exceeds the firm's required rate of return. Conversely, a negative NPV means the firm's value will decrease if the new project is adopted because the new project's estimated return is less than what the firm requires.

Calculating NPV

To calculate the net present value of a proposed project, we add the present value of a project's projected cash flows and then subtract the amount of the initial investment.[1] The result is a dollar figure that represents the change in the firm's value if the project is undertaken.

Formula for Net Present Value (NPV), Algebraic Method

$$NPV = \left(\frac{CF_1}{(1+k)^1}\right) + \left(\frac{CF_2}{(1+k)^2}\right) + \ldots + \left(\frac{CF_n}{(1+k)^n}\right) - \text{Initial Investment}$$

(10-1a)

where: CF = Cash flow at the indicated times

k = Discount rate, or required rate of return per period for the project

n = Life of the project measured in the number of periods

To use financial tables to solve present value problems, write the NPV formula as follows:

Formula for Net Present Value (NPV), Table Method

$$NPV = CF_1(PVIF_{k,1}) + CF_2(PVIF_{k,2}) + \ldots + CF_n(PVIF_{k,n}) - \text{Initial Investment}$$ (10-1b)

where: $PVIF$ = Present Value Interest Factor

k = Discount rate, or required rate of return per period for the project

n = Life of the project measured in the number of periods

To use the TI BAII Plus financial calculator to solve for NPV, switch the calculator to the spreadsheet mode, enter the cash flow values in sequence, then the discount rate, depicted as I on the TI BAII Plus calculator, then compute the NPV.

For simplicity, we use only the algebraic equation and the financial calculator to calculate NPV. If you prefer using financial tables, simply replace Equation 10-1a with Equation 10-1b.[2]

To show how to calculate NPV, let's solve for the NPVs of our two earlier projects, Projects X and Y. First, note the following cash flows of Projects X and Y:

Cash Flows

	For Initial Investment	End of Year 1	End of Year 2	End of Year 3	End of Year 4
Project X	−$5,000	$2,000	$3,000	$ 500	$ 0
Project Y	−$5,000	$2,000	$2,000	$1,000	$ 2,000

---

1. We use many of the time value of money techniques learned in Chapter 8 to calculate NPV.

2. If the future cash flows are in the form of an annuity, Equations 10-1a and 10-1b can be modified to take advantage of the present value of ordinary annuity formulas discussed in Chapter 8, Equations 8-4a and 8-4b.

Assume the required rate of return for Projects X and Y is 10 percent. Now we have all the data we need to solve for the NPV of Projects X and Y.

Applying Equation 10-1a and assuming a discount rate of 10 percent, the NPV of Project X follows:

$$\text{NPV} = \left(\frac{\$2,000}{(1 + .10)^1} \right) + \left(\frac{\$3,000}{(1 + .10)^2} \right) + \left(\frac{\$500_n}{(1 + .10)^3} \right) - \$5,000$$

$$= \frac{\$2,000}{1.1} + \frac{\$3,000}{1.21} + \frac{\$500}{1.331} - \$5,000$$

$$= \$1,818.1818 + \$2,479.3388 + \$375.6574 - \$5,000$$

$$= -\$326.82$$

We may also find Project X's NPV with the financial calculator at a 10 percent discount rate as follows:

TI BAII PLUS Financial Calculator Solutions
Project X NPV

Keystrokes	Display		Keystrokes	Display
CF	CF_0 = old contents		↓	F02 = 1.00
2nd CLR Work	CF_0 = 0.00		↓ 500 ENTER	C03 = 500.00
5000 +/− ENTER	CF_0 = −5,000.00		↓	F03 = 1.00
↓ 2000 ENTER	C01 = 2,000.00		NPV	I = 0.00
↓	F01 = 1.00		10 ENTER	I = 10.00
↓ 3000 ENTER	C02 = 3,000.00		↓ CPT	NPV = −326.82

(continued to right)

E11	▾ : ✗ ✔ *fx*	=NPV(D11,C12:C14)+C11		

	A	B	C	NPV(rate, value1, [value2], [value3], ...)	F
1					
2		**The Net Present Value Approach**			
3	This Excel spreadsheet computes the net present value (NPV) of a proposed project.				
4	Note that the initial investment is listed as a negative cash flow and positive				
5	cash flows for years 1 through 3 are discounted and then the cash flow				
6	-$5,000 is added to the sum of the discounted positive cash flows. The				
7	discount rate of 10% is the first argument in the NPV function and the cash				
8	flows to be discounted are specified in cells C12 through C14.				
9					
10		End of Year	Cash Flows	k	NPV	Function
11		0	-$5,000	10%	-$326.82	<-- =NPV(D11,C12:C14)+C11
12		1	$2,000			
13		2	$3,000		Excel NPV()	
14		3	$500		Function	
15						
16						

The preceding calculations show that at a 10 percent discount rate, an initial cash outlay of $5,000, and cash inflows of $2,000, $3,000, and $500 at the end of years 1, 2, and 3, the NPV for Project X is –326.82.

To find the NPV of Project Y, we apply Equation 10-1a as follows:

$$NPV = \frac{\$2,000}{(1 + .10)^1} + \frac{\$2,000}{(1 + .10)^2} + \frac{\$1,000}{(1 + .10)^3} + \frac{\$2,000}{(1 + .10)^4} - \$5,000$$

$$= \frac{\$2,000}{1.1} + \frac{\$2,000}{1.21} + \frac{\$1,000}{1.331} + \frac{\$2,000}{1.4641} - \$5,000$$

$$= \$1,818.1818 + \$1,652.8926 + \$751.3148 + \$1,366.0269 - \$5,000$$

$$= \$588.42$$

Using the financial calculator, we solve for Project Y's NPV at a 10 percent discount rate as follows:

TI BAII PLUS Financial Calculator Solutions
Project Y NPV

Keystrokes	Display	Keystrokes	Display
CF	CF_0 = old contents	↓	F02 = 1.00
2nd CLR Work	CF_0 = 0.00	↓ 2000 ENTER	C03 = 2,000.00
5000 +/– ENTER	CF_0 = –5,000.00	↓	F03 = 1.00
↓ 2000 ENTER	C01 = 2,000.00	NPV	I = 0.00
↓ 2 ENTER	F01 = 2.00	10 ENTER	I = 10.00
↓ 1000 ENTER	C02 = 1,000.00	↓ CPT	NPV = 588.42

(continued to right)

E11	▼ :	X ✓ *fx*	=NPV(D11,C12:C15)+C11

	A	B	C	NPV(rate, value1, [value2], [value3], ...)		F
1						
2		**The Net Present Value Approach**				
3		This Excel spreadsheet computes the net present value (NPV) of a proposed project.				
4		Note that the initial investment is listed as a negative cash flow and positive				
5		cash flows for years 1 through 3 are discounted and then the cash flow				
6		-$5,000 is added to the sum of the discounted positive cash flows. The				
7		discount rate of 10% is the first argument in the NPV function and the cash				
8		flows to be discounted are specified in cells C12 through C15.				
9						
10		End of Year	Cash Flows	k	NPV	Function
11		0	-$5,000	10%	–$588.42	<-- =NPV(D11,C12:C15)+C11
12		1	$2,000			
13		2	$2,000		Excel NPV()	
14		3	$1,000		Function	
15		4	$2,000			
16						

Our calculations show that with a required rate of return of 10 percent, an initial cash outlay of $5,000, and positive cash flows in years 1 through 4 of $2,000, $2,000, $1,000, and $2,000, respectively, the NPV for Project Y is $588.42. If we compare Project X's NPV of –326.82 to Project Y's NPV of $588.42, we see that Project Y would add value to the business and Project X would decrease the firm's value.

NPV Decision Rules

NPV is used in two ways: (1) to determine if independent projects should be accepted or rejected (the accept/reject decision), and (2) to compare acceptable mutually exclusive projects (the ranking decision). The rules for these two decisions are

- NPV Accept/Reject Decision—A firm should accept all independent projects having NPVs greater than or equal to zero. Projects with positive NPVs will add to the value of the firm if adopted. Projects with NPVs of zero will not alter the firm's value but (just) meet the firm's requirements. Projects with NPVs less than zero should be rejected because they will reduce the firm's value if adopted. Applying this decision rule, Project X would be rejected and Project Y would be accepted.

- NPV Ranking Decision—The project from the mutually exclusive list with the highest positive NPV should be ranked first, the next highest should be ranked second, and so on. Under this decision rule, if the two projects in our previous example were mutually exclusive, Project Y would be ranked first and Project X second. (Not only is Project X second in rank here, but it is unacceptable because it has a negative NPV.)

The NPV Profile

The k value is the cost of funds used for the project. It is the discount rate used in the NPV calculation because the cost of funds for a given project is that project's required rate of return. The relationship between the NPV of a project and k is inverse—the higher the k, the lower the NPV, and the lower the k, the higher the NPV.[3]

Because a project's NPV varies inversely with k, financial managers need to know how much the value of NPV will change in response to a change in k. If k is incorrectly specified, what appears to be a positive NPV could in fact be a negative NPV and vice versa—a negative NPV could turn out to be positive. Mutually exclusive project rankings could also change if an incorrect k value is used in the NPV computations.[4]

To see how sensitive a project's NPV value is to changes in k, analysts often create an NPV profile. The NPV profile is a graph that shows how a project's NPV changes when different discount rate values are used in the NPV computation.

Building an NPV profile is straightforward. First, the NPV of the project is calculated at a number of different discount rates. Then the results are plotted on the graph, with k values on one axis and the resulting NPV values on the other. If more than one project is included on the graph, the process is repeated for each project until all are depicted. To illustrate, we will build an NPV profile of Projects X and Y. We will plot Project X and then Project Y on the graph.

To begin, we first calculate the NPV of Project X with a number of different discount rates. The different k values may be chosen arbitrarily. For our purposes, let's use 0 percent, 5 percent, 10 percent, 15 percent, and 20 percent. The results of Project X's NPV calculations follow:

---

3. We are assuming here that the project is a typical one, meaning that it has an initial negative cash flow, the initial investment, followed by all positive cash flows. It is possible that if a project has negative cash flows in the future, the relationship between NPV and k might not be inverse.

4. The estimation of the cost of funds used for capital budgeting projects was covered in Chapter 9.

Discount Rate	Project X NPV
0%	$ 500.00
5%	$ 57.77
10%	−$ 326.82
15%	−$ 663.68
20%	−$ 960.65

Now Project X's NPV values may be plotted on the NPV profile graph. Figure 10-1 shows the results.

When the data points are connected in Figure 10-1, we see how the NPV of Project X varies with the discount rate changes. The graph shows that with a k of about 5.7 percent, the value of the project's NPV is zero. At that discount rate, then, Project X would provide the firm's required rate of return, no more and no less.

Next, we add project Y to the NPV profile graph. We calculate the NPV of Project Y at a number of different discount rates, 0 percent, 5 percent, 10 percent, 15 percent, and 20 percent. The results follow:

Discount Rate	Project Y NPV
0%	$2,000.00
5%	$1,228.06
10%	$ 588.42
15%	$ 52.44
20%	−$ 401.23

Figure 10-2 shows these NPV values plotted on the NPV profile graph.

Notice in Figure 10-2 that Project Y's NPV profile falls off more steeply than Project X's. This indicates that Project Y is more sensitive to changes in the discount rate than Project X. Project X's NPV becomes negative and, thus, the project is unacceptable when the discount rate rises above about 6 percent. Project Y's NPV becomes negative and, thus, the project is unacceptable when the discount rate rises above about 16 percent.

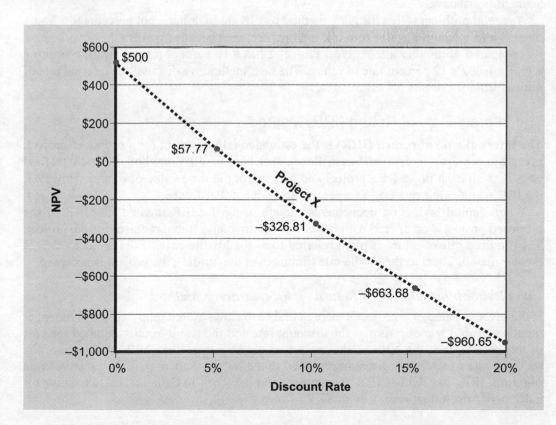

FIGURE 10-1
NPV Profile of Project X

The NPV profile shows how the NPV of project X varies inversely with the discount rate, k. Project X's NPV is highest ($500) when the discount rate is zero. Its NPV is lowest (−$960.65) when the discount rate is 20 percent.

FIGURE 10-2
NPV Profile of Projects X
and Y

The NPV file shows how the
NPVs of two capital budgeting
projects, Projects X and
Y, vary inversely with the
discount rate, k.

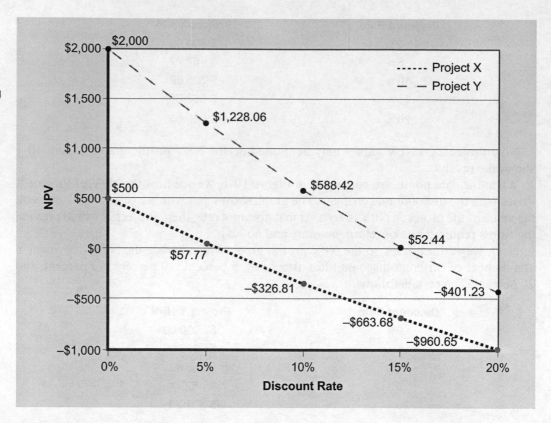

Problems with the NPV Method

Although the NPV method ensures that a firm will choose projects that add value to a firm, it suffers from two practical problems. First, it is difficult to explain NPV to people who are not formally trained in finance. Few nonfinance people understand phrases such as "the present value of future cash flows" or "the change in a firm's value given its required rate of return." As a result, many financial managers have difficulty using NPV analysis persuasively.

A second problem is that the NPV method results are in dollars, not percentages. Many owners and managers prefer to work with percentages because percentages can be easily compared with other alternatives; Project 1 has a 10 percent rate of return compared with Project 2's 12 percent rate of return. The next method we discuss, the internal rate of return, provides results in percentages.

The Internal Rate of Return (IRR) Method

internal rate of return (IRR)
The estimated rate of return for a proposed project, given the size of the project's incremental cash flows and their timing.

The **internal rate of return (IRR)** is the estimated rate of return for a proposed project, given the project's incremental cash flows. Just like the NPV method, the IRR method considers all cash flows for a project and adjusts for the time value of money. However, the IRR results are expressed as a percentage, not a dollar figure.

When capital budgeting decisions are made using the IRR method, the IRR of the proposed project is compared with the rate of return management requires for the project. The required rate of return is often referred to as the **hurdle rate**. If the project's IRR is greater than or equal to the hurdle rate (jumps over the hurdle), the project is accepted.

hurdle rate The minimum rate of return that management demands from a proposed project before that project will be accepted.

Calculating Internal Rate of Return: Trial-and-Error Method

If the present value of a project's incremental cash flows were computed using management's required rate of return as the discount rate and the result exactly equaled the cost of the project, then the NPV of the project would be zero. When NPV equals zero, the required rate of return, or discount rate used in the NPV calculation, is the projected rate of return, IRR. To calculate IRR, then, we reorder the terms in Equation 10-1a to solve for a discount rate, k, that results in an NPV of zero.

The formula for finding IRR, Equation 10-2, follows:

Formula for IRR

$$NPV = 0 = \left(\frac{CF_1}{(1 + k)^1}\right) + \left(\frac{CF_2}{(1 + k)^2}\right) + \ldots + \left(\frac{CF_n}{(1 + k)^n}\right) - \text{Initial Investment}$$

$$(10\text{-}2)$$

To find the IRR of a project using Equation 10-2, fill in the cash flows, the n values, and the initial investment figure. Then choose different values for k (all the other values are known) until the result equals zero. The IRR is the k value that causes the left-hand side of the equation, the NPV, to equal zero.

To illustrate the process, let's calculate the IRR for Project X. Recall that the cash flows associated with Project X were as follows:

Cash Flows

	For Initial Investment	Year 1	Year 2	Year 3	Year 4
Project X	−$5,000	$2,000	$3,000	$500	$0

First, we insert Project X's cash flows and the times they occur into Equation 10-2.

$$NPV = 0 = \left(\frac{\$2,000}{(1 + k)^1}\right) + \left(\frac{\$3,000}{(1 + k)^2}\right) + \left(\frac{\$500}{(1 + k)^3}\right) - \$5,000$$

Next, we try various discount rates until we find the value of k that results in an NPV of zero. Let's begin with a discount rate of 5 percent.

$$0 = \left(\frac{\$2,000}{(1 + .05)^1}\right) + \left(\frac{\$3,000}{(1 + .05)^2}\right) + \left(\frac{\$500}{(1 + .05)^3}\right) - \$5,000$$

$$= \left(\frac{\$2,000}{1.05}\right) + \left(\frac{\$3,000}{1.1025}\right) + \left(\frac{\$500}{1.157625}\right) - \$5,000$$

$$= \$1,904.76 + \$2,721.09 + \$431.92 - \$5,000$$

$$= \$57.77$$

This is close, but not quite zero. Let's try a second time, using a discount rate of 6 percent.

$$0 = \left(\frac{\$2,000}{(1 + .06)^1}\right) + \left(\frac{\$3,000}{(1 + .06)^2}\right) + \left(\frac{\$500}{(1 + .06)^3}\right) - \$5,000$$

$$= \left(\frac{\$2,000}{1.06}\right) + \left(\frac{\$3,000}{1.1236}\right) + \left(\frac{\$500}{1.191016}\right) - \$5,000$$

$$= \$1,886.79 + \$2,669.99 + \$419.81 - \$5,000$$

$$= -\$23.41$$

This is close enough for our purposes. We conclude the IRR for Project X is slightly less than 6 percent.

Although calculating IRR by trial and error is time-consuming, the guesses do not have to be made entirely in the dark. Remember that the discount rate and NPV are inversely related. When an IRR guess is too high, the resulting NPV value will be too low. When an IRR guess is too low, the NPV will be too high.

Calculating Internal Rate of Return: Financial Calculator

Finding solutions to IRR problems with a financial calculator is simple. After clearing previous values, enter the initial cash outlay and other cash flows and compute the IRR value.

The TI BAII PLUS financial calculator keystrokes for finding the IRR for Project X are shown next.

TI BAII PLUS Financial Calculator Solution IRR

Keystrokes	Display
CF	CF_0 = old contents
2nd CLR Work	CF_0 = 0.00
5000 +/- ENTER	–5,000.00
↓ 2000 ENTER	C01 = 2,000.00
↓	F01 = 1.00
↓ 3000 ENTER	C02 = 3,000.00
↓	F02 = 1.00
↓ 500 ENTER	C03 = 500.00
↓	F03 = 1.00
IRR	IRR = 0.00
CPT	IRR = 5.71

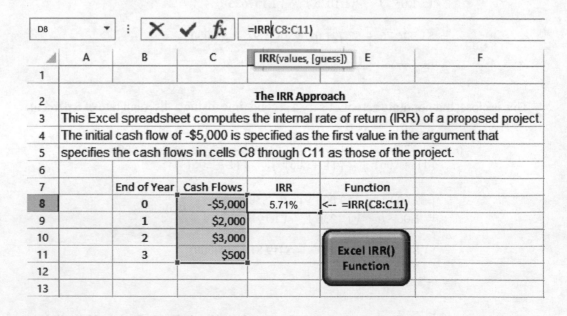

We see that with an initial cash outflow of $5,000 and Project X's estimated cash inflows in years 1 through 3, the IRR is 5.71 percent.

IRR and the NPV Profile

Notice in Figure 10-2 that the point where Project X's NPV profile crosses the zero line is, in fact, the IRR (5.71 percent). This is no accident. When the required rate of return, or discount rate, equals the expected rate of return, IRR, then NPV equals zero. Project Y's NPV profile crosses the zero line just below 16 percent. If you use your financial calculator, you will find that the Project Y IRR is 15.54 percent. If an NPV profile graph is available, you can always find a project's IRR by locating the point where a project's NPV profile crosses the zero line.

IRR Decision Rule

When evaluating proposed projects with the IRR method, those that have IRRs equal to or greater than the required rate of return (hurdle rate) set by management are accepted, and those projects with IRRs that are less than the required rate of return are rejected. Acceptable, mutually exclusive projects are ranked from highest to lowest IRR.

Take Note
If you are using a financial calculator other than the TI BAII PLUS, the calculator procedure will be similar but the keystrokes will differ. Be sure to check your calculator's instruction manual.

Benefits of the IRR Method

The IRR method for selecting capital budgeting projects is popular among financial practitioners for three primary reasons:

1. IRR focuses on all cash flows associated with the project.

2. IRR adjusts for the time value of money.

3. IRR describes projects in terms of the rate of return they earn, which makes it easy to compare them with other investments and the firm's hurdle rate.

Problems with the IRR Method

The IRR method has several problems, however. First, because the IRR is a percentage number, it does not show how much the value of the firm will change if the project is selected. If a project is quite small, for instance, it may have a high IRR but a small effect on the value of the firm. (Consider a project that requires a $10 investment and returns $100 a year later. The project's IRR is 900 percent, but the effect on the value of the firm if the project is adopted is negligible.)

If the primary goal for the firm is to maximize its value, then knowing the rate of return of a project is not the primary concern. What is most important is the amount by which the firm's value will change if the project is adopted, which is measured by NPV.

To drive this point home, ask yourself whether you would rather earn a 100 percent rate of return on $5 (which would be $5) or a 50 percent rate of return on $1,000 (which would be $500). As you can see, it is not the rate of return that is important but the dollar value. Why? Dollars, not percentages, comprise a firm's cash flows. NPV tells financial analysts how much value in dollars will be created. IRR does not.

A second problem with the IRR method is that, in rare cases, a project may have more than one IRR, or no IRR. This is shown in detail in Appendix 10A.

The IRR can be a useful tool in evaluating capital budgeting projects. As with any tool, however, knowing its limitations will enhance decision making.

Conflicting Rankings between the NPV and IRR Methods

As long as proposed capital budgeting projects are independent, both the NPV and IRR methods will produce the same accept/reject indication. That is, a project that has a positive NPV will also have an IRR that is greater than the discount rate. As a result, the project will be acceptable based on both the NPV and IRR values. However, when mutually exclusive projects are considered and ranked, a conflict occasionally arises. For instance, one project may have a higher NPV than another project, but a lower IRR.

To illustrate how conflicts between NPV and IRR can occur, imagine that the AddVenture Company owns a piece of land that can be used in different ways. On the one hand, this land has minerals beneath it that could be mined, so AddVenture could invest in mining equipment and reap the benefits of retrieving and selling the minerals. On the other hand, the land has perfect soil conditions for growing grapes that could be used to make wine, so the company could use it to support a vineyard.

Clearly, these two uses are mutually exclusive. The mine cannot be dug if there is a vineyard, and the vineyard cannot be planted if the mine is dug. The acceptance of one of the projects means that the other must be rejected.

Now let's suppose that AddVenture's finance department has estimated the cash flows associated with each use of the land. The estimates are presented next:

Time	Cash Flows for the Mining Project	Cash Flows for the Vineyard Project
t_0	($ 736,369)	($ 736,369)
t_1	$ 500,000	$ 0
t_2	$ 300,000	$ 0
t_3	$ 100,000	$ 0
t_4	$ 20,000	$ 50,000
t_5	$ 5,000	$ 200,000
t_6	$ 5,000	$ 500,000
t_7	$ 5,000	$ 500,000
t_8	$ 5,000	$ 500,000

Note that although the initial outlays for the two projects are the same, the incremental cash flows associated with the projects differ in amount and timing. The Mining Project generates its greatest positive cash flows early in the life of the project, whereas the Vineyard Project generates its greatest positive cash flows later. The differences in the projects' cash flow timing have considerable effects on the NPV and IRR for each venture.

Assume AddVenture's required rate of return for long-term projects is 10 percent. The NPV and IRR results for each project given its cash flows are summarized as follows:

	NPV	IRR
Mining Project	$ 65,727.39	16.05%
Vineyard Project	$ 194,035.65	14.00%

These figures were obtained with our TI BAII PLUS calculator, in the same manner as shown earlier in the chapter.

The NPV and IRR results show that the Vineyard Project has a higher NPV than the Mining Project ($194,035.65 versus $65,727.39), but the Mining Project has a higher IRR than the Vineyard Project (16.05 percent versus 14.00 percent). AddVenture is faced with a conflict between NPV and IRR results. Because the projects are mutually exclusive, the firm can only accept one.

In cases of conflict among mutually exclusive projects, the one with the highest NPV should be chosen because NPV indicates the dollar amount of value that will be added to the firm if the project is undertaken. In our example, then, AddVenture should choose the Vineyard Project (the one with the higher NPV) if its primary financial goal is to maximize firm value.

The Modified Internal Rate of Return (MIRR) Method

One problem with the IRR method that was not mentioned earlier is that the only way you can actually receive the IRR indicated by a project is if you reinvest the intervening cash flows in the project at the IRR. If the intervening cash flows are reinvested at any rate lower than the IRR, you will not end up with the IRR indicated at the end of the project.

For example, assume you have a project in which you invest $100 now and expect to receive four payments of $50 at the end of each of the next four years:

t_0	t_1	t	t_3	t_4
−100	+50	+50	+50	+50

The IRR of this investment, calculated using either the trial-and-error or financial calculator methods, is 34.9 percent. On the surface, this sounds like a fabulous investment. But, as they say, don't count your chickens before they hatch. If you can't reinvest each $50 payment at the IRR of 34.9 percent, forget it; you won't end up with an overall return of 34.9 percent. To see why, consider what would happen if, for example, you simply put each $50 payment in your pocket. At the end of the fourth year, you would have $200 in your pocket. Now, using Equation 8-8, calculate the average annual rate of return necessary to produce $200 in four years with a beginning investment of $100:

Actual return on the investment per Equation 8-8

$$k = \left(\frac{200}{100}\right)^{\left(\frac{1}{4}\right)} - 1$$

$$= .189, \text{ or } 18.9\% \text{ (not } 34.9\%)$$

Despite the fact that the IRR of the investment was 34.9 percent, you only ended up with an 18.9 percent annual return. The only way you could have obtained an annual return of 34.9 percent was to have reinvested each of the $50 cash flows at 34.9 percent. This is called the *IRR reinvestment assumption.*

To get around the IRR reinvestment assumption, a variation on the IRR procedure has been developed, called the **modified internal rate of return (MIRR)** method. The MIRR method calls for assuming that the intervening cash flows from a project are reinvested at a rate of return equal to the cost of capital. To find the MIRR, first calculate how much you would end up with at the end of a project, assuming the intervening cash flows were invested at the cost of capital. The result is called the project's *terminal value.* Next, calculate the annual rate of return it would take to produce that end amount from the beginning investment. That rate is the MIRR.

Here is the MIRR calculation for the project in our example, in which $100 is invested at time zero, followed by inflows of $50 at the end of each of the next four years. Let us assume for this example that the cost of capital is 10 percent.

modified internal rate of return (MIRR) The estimated rate of return for a proposed project for which the projected cash flows are assumed to be reinvested at the cost of capital rate.

Step 1: Calculate the project's terminal value:

Time	Cash	FV of Cash Flow at t_4 if reinvested @ 10% Cost of Capital Flow (per Equation 8-1a)	
t_1	$50	FV = $50 × (1 + .10)³ =	$ 66.55
t_2	$50	FV = $50 × (1 + .10)² =	$ 60.50
t_3	$50	FV = $50 × (1 + .10)¹ =	$ 55.00
t_4	$50	FV = $50 × (1 + .10)⁰ =	$ 50.00
		Project's Terminal Value:	$ 232.05

Step 2: Calculate the annual rate of return that will produce the terminal value from the initial investment:

Project's Terminal Value: $232.05

PV of Initial Investment: $100

per Equation 8-8:

$$MIRR = \left(\frac{232.05}{100}\right)^{\left(\frac{1}{4}\right)} - 1$$

$$= .234, \text{ or } 23.4\%$$

| | E8 | | ▼ | : | × ✓ f_x | =MIRR(C8:C12,,D8) |

	A	B	C			F
1					MIRR(values, finance_rate, reinvest_rate)	
2					**The MIRR Approach**	
3	This Excel spreadsheet computes the modified internal rate of return (MIRR) of a proposed project.
4	Note the initial investment is listed as a negative cash flow in cell C8 and positive cash flows are
5	shown in cells C9 through C12. The k value is the reinvestment rate for the positive cash flows.
6						
7		End of Year	Cash Flows	k	MIRR	Function
8		0	-$100	10%	23.4%	<-- =MIRR(C8:C12,,D8)
9		1	$50			
10		2	$50			
11		3	$50			Excel MIRR() Function
12		4	$50			
13						

Earning this 23.4% MIRR value is a more realistic expectation than the 34.9 percent return from the project indicated by the IRR method. Remember, any time you consider investing in a project, you will not actually receive the IRR unless you can reinvest the project's intervening cash flows at the IRR. Calculate the MIRR to produce a more conservative measure of return, since the positive cash flows are assumed to be reinvested at the lower cost of capital rate instead of the higher IRR rate that one must earn on reinvested cash flows if the IRR is the rate to be earned. The MIRR value is always less than the IRR value for projects that have an IRR value greater than the cost of capital. This is so since the IRR is greater than or equal to the cost of capital for acceptable projects. If the IRR value is less than the cost of capital then we do not care what the MIRR value is since the project is unacceptable.

In this section, we looked at four capital budgeting decision methods: the payback method, the net present value method, the internal rate of return method, and the modified internal rate of return method. We also investigated how to resolve conflicts between NPV and IRR decision methods. Next, we turn to a discussion of capital rationing.

Capital Rationing

Our discussion so far has shown that all independent projects with NPVs greater than or equal to zero should be accepted. All such projects that are adopted will add value to the firm. To act consistently with the goal of shareholder wealth maximization, then, it seems that if a firm locates $200 billion worth of independent positive NPV projects, it should accept all the projects. In practice, however, many firms place dollar limits on the total amount of capital budgeting projects they will undertake. They may wish to limit spending on new projects to keep a ceiling on business size. This practice of setting dollar limits on capital budgeting projects is known as **capital rationing**.

If capital rationing is imposed, then financial managers should seek the combination of projects that maximizes the value of the firm within the capital budget limit. For example, suppose a firm called BeLimited does not want its capital budget to exceed $200,000. Seven project proposals, Proposals A to G, are available, as shown in Table 10-1.

Note that all the projects in Table 10-1 have positive net present values, so they are all acceptable. However, BeLimited cannot adopt them all because that would require the expenditure of more than $200,000, its self-imposed capital budget limit.

Under capital rationing, BeLimited's managers try different combinations of projects seeking the combination that gives the highest NPV without exceeding the $200,000 limit. For example, the combination of Projects B, C, E, F, and G costs $200,000 and yields a total NPV of $23,700. A better combination is that of Projects A, B, C, D, and F, which costs $200,000 and has a total NPV of $30,600. In fact, this combination has the highest total NPV, given the $200,000 capital budget limit (try a few other combinations to see for yourself), so that combination is the one BeLimited should choose.

In this section, we explored capital rationing. In the following section, we will examine how risk affects capital budgeting decisions.

capital rationing The process whereby management sets a limit on the amount of cash available for new capital budgeting projects.

Risk and Capital Budgeting

Suppose you are a financial manager for AddVenture Corporation. You are considering two capital budgeting projects, Project X (discussed throughout the chapter) and Project X2. Both projects have identical future cash flow values and timing, and both have the same NPV, if discounted at the same rate, k, and the same IRR. The two projects appear equally desirable.

Now suppose you discover that Project X's incremental cash flows are absolutely certain, but Project X2's incremental cash flows, which have the same expected value, are highly uncertain. These cash flows could be higher or lower than forecast. In other words, Project X is a sure thing and Project X2 appears to be quite risky. As a risk-averse person, you would prefer Project X over Project X2.

Financial managers are not indifferent to risk. Indeed, the riskier a project, the less desirable it is to the firm. To incorporate risk into the NPV and IRR evaluation techniques, we use the standard deviation and coefficient of variation (CV) measures discussed in Chapter 7. We begin by examining how to measure the risk of a capital budgeting project. Then we explain how to include the risk measurement in the NPV and IRR evaluation.

TABLE 10-1 BeLimited Project Proposals

Project	Initial Cash Outlay	Net Present Value
A	$20,000	$8,000
B	$50,000	$7,200
C	$40,000	$6,500
D	$60,000	$5,100
E	$50,000	$4,200
F	$30,000	$3,800
G	$30,000	$2,000

Measuring Risk in Capital Budgeting

Financial managers may measure three types of risk in the capital budgeting process. The first type is *project-specific risk,* or the risk of a specific new project. The second type is *firm risk,* which is the impact of adding a new project to the existing projects of the firm. The third is *market (or beta) risk,* which is the effect of a new project on the stockholders' nondiversifiable risk.

In this chapter, we focus on measuring firm risk. To measure firm risk, we compare the coefficient of variation (CV) of the firm's portfolio before and after a project is adopted. The before-and-after difference between the two CVs serves as the project's risk measure from a firm perspective. If the CAPM approach (discussed in Chapter 7) is preferred, a financial manager could estimate the risk of a project by calculating the project's beta instead of the change in firm risk.

Computing Changes in the Coefficient of Variation

Let's reconsider our earlier example, Project X. Recall that the IRR of Project X was 5.71 percent. Now suppose that after careful analysis, we determine this IRR is actually the most likely value from a range of possible values, each with some probability of occurrence. We find the expected value and standard deviation of Project X's IRR distribution using Equations 7-1 and 7-2, respectively. We find that the expected value of the IRR distribution is 5.71 percent and the standard deviation is 2.89 percent.

To see how adding Project X to the firm's existing portfolio changes the portfolio's coefficient of variation (CV), we follow a five-step procedure.

Step 1: **Find the CV of the Existing Portfolio.** Suppose the expected rate of return and standard deviation of possible returns of AddVenture's existing portfolio are 6 percent and 2 percent, respectively. Given this information, calculate the CV of the firm's existing portfolio using Equation 7-3:

$$CV = \frac{\text{Standard Deviation}}{\text{Mean, or Expected Value}}$$

$$= \frac{.02}{.06}$$

$$= .3333, \text{ or } 33.33\%$$

Step 2: **Find the Expected Rate of Return of the New Portfolio (the Existing Portfolio Plus the Proposed Project).** Assume that the investment in Project X represents 10 percent of the value of the portfolio. In other words, the new portfolio after adding Project X will consist of 10 percent Project X and 90 percent of the rest of the firm's assets. With these figures, solve for the expected rate of return of the new portfolio using Equation 7-4. In the calculations, Asset A represents Project X and Asset B represents the firm's existing portfolio.

$$E(R_p) = (w_a \times E(R_a)) + (w_b \times E(R_b))$$

$$= (.10 \times .0571) + (.90 \times .06)$$

$$= .00571 + .05400$$

$$= .05971, \text{ or } 5.971\%$$

$$\sigma_p = \sqrt{w_a^2\sigma_a^2 + w_b^2\sigma_b^2 + 2w_aw_br_{a,b}\sigma_a\sigma_b}$$

$$= \sqrt{(.10^2)(0.0289^2) + (.90^2)(0.02^2) + (2)(.10)(.90)(0.0)(.0289)(.02)}$$

$$= \sqrt{(.01)(.000835) + (.81)(.0004) + 0}$$

$$= \sqrt{.00000835 + .000324}$$

$$= \sqrt{.000332352}$$

$$= .0182, \text{ or } 1.82\%$$

Step 3: Find the Standard Deviation of the New Portfolio (the Existing Portfolio Plus the Proposed Project). Calculate the standard deviation of the new portfolio using Equation 7-5. Assume the degree of correlation (r) between project X (Asset A) and the firm's existing portfolio (Asset B) is zero. Put another way, there is no relationship between the returns from Project X and the returns from the firm's existing portfolio.

Step 4: Find the CV of the New Portfolio (the Existing Portfolio Plus the Proposed Project). To solve for the CV of the new portfolio with Project X included, we use Equation 7-3, as follows:

$$CV = \frac{\text{Standard Deviation}}{\text{Mean, or Expected value}}$$

$$= \frac{.0182}{.05971}$$

$$= .3048, \text{ or } 30.48\%$$

Step 5: Compare the CV of the Portfolio with and without the Proposed Project. To evaluate the effect of Project X on the risk of the AddVenture portfolio, we compare the CV of the old portfolio (without Project X) to the CV of the new portfolio (with Project X). The coefficients follow:

CV of the Portfolio without Project X	CV of the Portfolio with Project X	Change in CV
33.33%	30.48%	−2.85

The CV of the firm's portfolio dropped from 33.33 percent to 30.48 percent with the addition of Project X. This 2.85 percentage point decrease in CV is the measure of risk in Project X from the firm's perspective.

Adjusting for Risk

Most business owners and financial managers are risk averse, so they want the capital budgeting process to reflect risk concerns. Next, we discuss how to adjust for risk in the capital budgeting process—risk-adjusted discount rates. The discount rate is the cost of capital discussed in Chapter 9. A project's risk-adjusted discount rate is the cost of capital for that specific project.

Risk-Adjusted Discount Rates (RADRs)

One way to factor risk into the capital budgeting process is to adjust the rate of return demanded for high- and low-risk projects. Risk-adjusted discount rates (RADRs), then, are discount rates that differ according to their effect on a firm's risk. The higher the risk, the higher the RADR, and the lower the risk, the lower the RADR. A project with a normal risk level would have an RADR equal to the actual discount rate.

To find the RADR for a capital budgeting project, we first prepare a risk adjustment table like the one in Table 10-2. We assume in Table 10-2 that the coefficient of variation, CV, is the risk measure to be adjusted for. The CV is based on the probability distribution of the IRR values.

Table 10-2 shows how the discount rates for capital budgeting projects might be adjusted for varying degrees of risk. The discount rate of a project that decreased the CV of the firm's portfolio of assets by 2.5 percentage points, for example, would be classified as a low-risk project. That project would be evaluated using a discount rate two percentage points lower than that used on average projects.

This has the effect of making Project X a more desirable project. That is, financial managers would calculate the project's NPV using an average discount rate that is two percentage points lower, which would increase the project's NPV. If the firm uses the IRR method, financial managers would compare the project's IRR to a hurdle rate two percentage points lower than average, which would make it more likely that the firm would adopt the project.

RADRs are an important part of the capital budgeting process because they incorporate the risk–return relationship. All other things being equal, the more a project increases risk, the less likely it is that a firm will accept the project; the more a project decreases risk, the more likely it is that a firm will accept the project.

What's Next

In this chapter, we explored the capital budgeting process and decision methods. We examined four capital budgeting techniques—the payback method, net present value method, internal rate of return method, and modified internal rate of return method. We also discussed capital rationing and how to measure and adjust for risk when making capital budgeting decisions.

In the next chapter, we'll investigate how to estimate incremental cash flows in capital budgeting.

TABLE 10-2 Risk-Adjustment Table

If Adoption of the Proposed Capital Budgeting Project Would Change the CV of the Firm's Portfolio IRR by the Following Amount:	Then Assign the Project to the Following Risk Category:	And Adjust the Discount Rate for the Project as Follows:
More than a 1 percent increase	High risk	+2%
Between a 1 percent decrease and a 1 percent increase	Average risk	0
More than a 1 percent decrease	Low risk	–2%

Summary

1. *Explain the capital budgeting process.*
   Capital budgeting is the process of evaluating proposed investment projects. Capital budgeting projects may be independent—the projects do not compete with each other— or mutually exclusive—accepting one project precludes the acceptance of the other(s) in that group.

   Financial managers apply two decision practices when selecting capital budgeting projects: accept/reject decisions

and ranking decisions. The accept/reject decision is the determination of which independent projects are acceptable in light of the firm's financial objectives. Ranking is a process of comparing projects to a standard measure and ordering the mutually exclusive projects based on how well they meet the measure. The capital budgeting process is concerned only with incremental cash flows; that is, those cash flows that will occur if an investment is undertaken but won't occur if it isn't.

2. *Calculate the payback period, net present value, internal rate of return, and modified internal rate of return for a proposed capital budgeting project.*

The payback period is defined as the number of time periods it will take before the cash inflows from a proposed capital budgeting project will equal the amount of the initial investment. To find a project's payback period, add all the project's positive cash flows, one period at a time, until the sum equals the amount of the initial cash outlay for the project. The number of time periods it takes to recoup the initial cash outlay is the payback period. A project is acceptable if it pays back the initial investment within a time frame set by firm management.

The net present value (NPV) of a proposed capital budgeting project is the dollar amount of the change in the value of the firm that will occur if the project is undertaken. To calculate NPV, total the present values of all the projected incremental cash flows associated with a project and subtract the amount of the initial cash outlay. A project with an NPV greater than or equal to zero is acceptable. An NPV profile—a graph that shows a project's NPV at many different discount rates (required rates of return)—shows how sensitive a project's NPV is to changes in the discount rate.

The internal rate of return (IRR) is the projected percentage rate of return that a proposed project will earn, given its incremental cash flows and required initial cash outlay. To calculate IRR, find the discount rate that makes the project's NPV equal to zero. That rate of return is the IRR. A project is acceptable if its IRR is greater than or equal to the firm's required rate of return (the hurdle rate).

The IRR method assumes that intervening cash flows in a project are reinvested at a rate of return equal to the IRR. This can result in overly optimistic expectations when the IRR is high and the intervening cash flows can't be reinvested at that rate. To produce more realistic results, the Modified Internal Rate of Return (MIRR) method was developed. The MIRR method calls for assuming that the intervening cash flows from a project are reinvested at a rate of return equal to the cost of capital. To find the MIRR, first calculate how much you would end up with at the end of a project, assuming the intervening cash flows were invested at the cost of capital. The result is called the project's terminal value. Next, calculate the annual rate of return it would take to produce that end amount from the beginning investment. That rate is the MIRR.

3. *Describe capital rationing and how firms decide which projects to select.*

The practice of placing dollar limits on the total size of the capital budget is called capital rationing. Under capital rationing, the firm will select the combination of projects that yields the highest NPV without exceeding the capital budget limit.

4. *Measure the risk of a capital budgeting project.*

To measure the risk of a capital budgeting project, we determine how the project would affect the risk of the firm's existing asset portfolio. We compare the coefficient of variation of possible returns of the firm's asset portfolio with the proposed project and without it. The difference between the two coefficients of variation is the measure of the risk of the capital budgeting project.

5. *Explain risk-adjusted discount rates.*

To compensate for the degree of risk in capital budgeting, firms may adjust the discount rate for each project according to risk. The more risk is increased, the higher the discount rate. The more risk is decreased, the lower the discount rate. Rates adjusted for the risk of projects are called risk-adjusted discount rates (RADRs).

Key Terms

capital budgeting The process of evaluating proposed projects.

capital rationing The process whereby management sets a limit on the amount of cash available for new capital budgeting projects.

hurdle rate The minimum rate of return that management demands from a proposed project before that project will be accepted.

incremental cash flows Cash flows that will occur only if an investment is undertaken.

independent projects A group of projects such that any or all could be accepted.

internal rate of return (IRR) The estimated rate of return for a proposed project, given the size of the project's incremental cash flows and their timing.

modified internal rate of return (MIRR) The estimated rate of return for a proposed project for which the projected cash flows are assumed to be reinvested at the cost of capital rate.

mutually exclusive projects A group of projects that compete against each other; only one of the mutually exclusive projects may be chosen.

net present value (NPV) The estimated change in the value of the firm that would occur if a project is accepted.

payback period The expected amount of time a capital budgeting project will take to generate cash flows that cover the project's initial cash outlay.

Equation 10-1a. NPV Formula, Algebraic Method:

$$NPV = \left(\frac{CF_1}{(1+k)^1}\right) + \left(\frac{CF_2}{(1+k)^2}\right) + \ldots + \left(\frac{CF_n}{(1+k)^n}\right) - \text{Initial Investment}$$

where:　　CF = Cash flow at the indicated times

k = Discount rate, or required rate of return per period for the project

n = Life of the project measured in the number of periods

Equation 10-1b. NPV Formula, Table Method:

$$NPV = CF_1(PVF_{k,1}) + CF_2(PVF_{k,2}) + \ldots + CF_n(PVF_{k,n}) - \text{Initial Investment}$$

where:　PVF = Present Value Factor

k = Discount rate, or required rate of return per period for the project

n = Life of the project measured in the number of periods

Equation 10-2.　Formula for IRR Using Equation 10-1a:

$$NPV = 0 = \left(\frac{CF_1}{(1+k)^1}\right) + \left(\frac{CF_2}{(1+k)^2}\right) + \ldots + \left(\frac{CF_n}{(1+k)^n}\right) - \text{Initial Investment}$$

where:　　k = the IRR value

Fill in cash flows (CFs) and periods (n). Then choose values for k by trial and error until the NPV equals zero. The value of k that causes the NPV to equal zero is the IRR.

Self-Test

ST-1. What is the NPV of the following project?

Initial investment	$50,000
Net cash flow at the end of year 1	$20,000
Net cash flow at the end of year 2	$40,000
Discount rate	11%

ST-2. What is the IRR of the project in ST-1?

ST-3. You've been assigned to evaluate a project for your firm that requires an initial investment of $200,000, is expected to last for 10 years, and is expected to produce after-tax net cash flows of $44,503 at the end of each year. If your firm's annual required rate of return is 14 percent, should the project be accepted?

ST-4. What is the IRR of the project in ST-3?

ST-5. What is the MIRR of the project in ST-3?

ST-6. Assume you have decided to reinvest your portfolio in zero-coupon bonds. You like zero-coupon bonds because they pay off a known amount, $1,000 at maturity, and involve no other cash flows other than the purchase price. Assume your required rate of return is 12 percent. If you buy some 10-year zero-coupon bonds for $400 each today, will the bonds meet your return requirements? (Hint: Compute the IRR of the investment given the cash flows involved.)

ST-7. Joe, the cut-rate bond dealer, has offered to sell you some zero-coupon bonds for $300. (Remember, zero-coupon bonds pay off $1,000 at maturity and involve no other cash flows other than the purchase price.) If the bonds mature in 10 years and your required rate of return for cut-rate bonds is 20 percent, what is the NPV of Joe's deal?

Review Questions

1. How do we calculate the payback period for a proposed capital budgeting project? What are the main criticisms of the payback method?

2. How does the net present value relate to the value of the firm?

3. What are the advantages and disadvantages of the internal rate of return method?

4. Provide three examples of mutually exclusive projects.

5. What is the decision rule for accepting or rejecting proposed projects when using net present value?

6. What is the decision rule for accepting or rejecting proposed projects when using internal rate of return?

7. What is capital rationing? Should a firm practice capital rationing? Why?

8. Explain how to resolve a ranking conflict between the net present value and the internal rate of return. Why should the conflict be resolved as you explained?

9. Explain how to measure the firm risk of a capital budgeting project.

10. Why is the coefficient of variation a better risk measure to use than the standard deviation when evaluating the risk of capital budgeting projects?

11. Explain why we measure a project's risk as the change in the CV.

12. Explain how using a risk-adjusted discount rate improves capital budgeting decision making compared with using a single discount rate for all projects.

Build Your Communication Skills

CS-1. Arrange to have a person who has no training in finance visit the class on the next day after the net present value (NPV) evaluation method has been covered. Before the visitor arrives, choose two teams who will brief the visitor on the results of their evaluation of a capital budgeting project. The visitor will play the role of the CEO of the firm. The CEO must choose one capital budgeting project for the firm to undertake. The CEO will choose the project based on the recommendations of Team A and Team B.

Now have each team describe the following projects:

	Team A	Team B
	Solar Energy Satellite (a plan to beam energy down from orbit)	**Fresh Water Extraction Project** (a plan to extract drinking water from the sea)
Initial Investment	$ 40 million	$ 40 million
NPV	$ 10 million	$ 8 million
IRR	12%	18%

After the projects have been described, have the CEO ask each team for its recommendation about which project to adopt. The CEO may also listen to input from the class at large.

When the debate is complete, have the CEO select one of the projects (based on the class's recommendations). Then critique the class's recommendations.

CS-2. Divide the class into groups of two members each. Have each pair prepare a written description (closed book) of how to measure the risk of a capital budgeting project. When the explanations are complete, select a volunteer from each group to present their findings to the class.

Problems

10-1. You are investing in a new business known informally as Zombiebook. The initial investment is $5 million. Future cash flows are projected to be $2 million at the end of years one, two, three, and four. A different business in which you are considering investing is called Angry Rabbits. It too would cost $5 million. Future cash flows for Angry Rabbits are projected to be $1 million at the end of years one, two, and three, followed by a positive cash flow of $20 million at the end of year 4. Compute the payback period for Zombiebook and for Angry Rabbits. On the basis of the two payback computations, which of the two companies would you choose? Does this choice cause you any concern?

 Payback

NPV and IRR **10-2.** An heiress has a rich grandfather who set up a trust that will pay her $5 million per year for 20 years beginning on her 25th birthday. Assume her 25th birthday is 4 years from now. Further assume that you are a wealthy investor and this heiress is anxious to get her hands on some serious cash. You are offered the opportunity to purchase the rights to receive the promised cash flows from the trust.

    a. If you were to pay $80 million today for the right to receive these cash flows promised to the heiress, what is the net present value (NPV) of this investment, assuming a 10% discount rate is appropriate?

    b. What is the internal rate of return (IRR) of this $80 million investment?

Payback **10-3.** Three separate projects each have an initial cash outlay of $10,000. The cash flow for Peter's Project is $4,000 per year for three years. The cash flow for Paul's Project is $2,000 in years 1 and 3, and $8,000 in year 2. Mary's Project has a cash flow of $10,000 in year 1, followed by $1,000 each year for years 2 and 3.

    a. Use the payback method to calculate how many years it will take for each project to recoup the initial investment.

    b. Which project would you consider most liquid?

Net Present Value **10-4.** You have just paid $20 million in the secondary market for the winning Powerball lottery ticket. The prize is $2 million at the end of each year for the next 25 years. If your required rate of return is 8 percent, what is the net present value (NPV) of the deal?

Internal Rate of Return **10-5.** What is the internal rate of return (IRR) of the Powerball deal in question 4?

Modified Internal Rate of Return **10-6.** What is the modified internal rate of return (MIRR) of the Powerball deal in question 4?

Payback Period **10-7.** RejuveNation needs to estimate how long the payback period would be for their new facility project. They have received two proposals and need to decide which one is best. Project Weights will have an initial investment of $200,000 and generate positive cash flows of $100,000 at the end of year 1, $75,000 at the end of year 2, $50,000 at the end of year 3, and $100,000 at the end of year 4. Project Waters will have an initial investment of $300,000 and will generate positive cash flows of $200,000 at the end of year 1 and $150,000 at the end of years 2, 3, and 4. What is the payback period for Project Waters? What is the payback period for Project Weights? Which project should RejuveNation choose?

NPV **10-8.** Calculate the NPV of each project in problem 10-7 using RejuveNation's cash flows and an 8 percent discount rate.

NPV and IRR **10-9.** The Bedford Falls Bridge Building Company is considering the purchase of a new crane. George Bailey, the new manager, has had some past management experience while he was the chief financial officer of the local savings and loan. The cost of the crane is $17,291.42, and the expected incremental cash flows are $5,000 at the end of year 1, $8,000 at the end of year 2, and $10,000 at the end of year 3.

    a. Calculate the net present value if the required rate of return is 9 percent.

    b. Calculate the internal rate of return.

    c. Should Mr. Bailey purchase this crane?

NPV **10-10.** Lin McAdam and Lola Manners, managers of the Winchester Company, do not practice capital rationing. They have three independent projects they are evaluating for inclusion in this year's capital budget. One is for a new machine to make rifle stocks. The second is for a new forklift to use in the warehouse. The third project involves the purchase of automated packaging equipment. The Winchester Company's required rate of return is 13 percent. The initial investment (a negative cash flow) and the expected positive net cash flows for years 1 through 4 for each project follow:

Expected Net Cash Flow

Year	Rifle Stock Machine	Forklift	Packaging Equipment
0	$(9,000)	$(12,000)	$(18,200)
1	2,000	5,000	0
2	5,000	4,000	5,000
3	1,000	6,000	10,000
4	4,000	2,000	12,000

a. Calculate the net present value for each project.

b. Which project(s) should be undertaken? Why?

10-11. The Trask Family Lettuce Farm is located in the fertile Salinas Valley of California. Adam Trask, the head of the family, makes all the financial decisions that affect the farm. Because of an extended drought, the family needs more water per acre than what the existing irrigation system can supply. The quantity and quality of lettuce produced are expected to increase when more water is supplied. Cal and Aron, Adam's sons, have devised two different solutions to their problem. Cal suggests improvements to the existing system. Aron is in favor of a completely new system. The negative cash flow associated with the initial investment and expected positive net cash flows for years 1 through 7 for each project follow. Adam has no other alternatives and will choose one of the two projects. The Trask Family Lettuce Farm has a required rate of return of 8 percent for these projects.

NPV and IRR

Expected Net Cash Flow

Year	Cal's Project	Aron's Project
0	$(100,000)	$(300,000)
1	22,611	63,655
2	22,611	63,655
3	22,611	63,655
4	22,611	63,655
5	22,611	63,655
6	22,611	63,655
7	22,611	63,655

a. Calculate the net present value for each project.

b. Calculate the internal rate of return for each project.

c. Which project should Adam choose? Why?

d. Is there a conflict between the decisions indicated by the NPVs and the IRRs?

10-12. Buzz Lightyear has been offered an investment in which he expects to receive payments of $4,000 at the end of each of the next 10 years in return for an initial investment of $10,000 now.

IRR and MIRR

a. What is the IRR of the proposed investment?

b. What is the MIRR of the proposed investment? Assume a cost capital of 10%.

c. Why is the MIRR thought of as a more realistic indication of a project's potential than the IRR?

10-13. Dave Hirsh publishes his own manuscripts and is unsure which of two new printers he should purchase. He is a novelist living in Parkman, Illinois. Having slept through most of his Finance 300 course in college, he is unfamiliar with cash flow analysis. He enlists the help of the finance professor at the local university, Dr. Gwen French, to assist him. Together they estimate the following expected initial investment (a negative cash flow) and net positive cash flows for years 1 through 3 for each machine. Dave only needs one printer and estimates it will be worthless after three years of heavy use. Dave's required rate of return for this project is 8 percent.

	Expected Net Cash Flow	
Year	Printer 1	Printer 2
0	$(2,000)	$(2,500)
1	900	1,500
2	1,100	1,300
3	1,300	800

a. Calculate the payback period for each printer.

b. Calculate the net present value for each printer.

c. Calculate the internal rate of return for each printer.

d. Which printer do you think Dr. French will recommend? Why?

e. Suppose Dave's required rate of return were 16 percent. Does the decision about which printer to purchase change?

NPV, IRR, and MIRR

10-14. Matrix.com has designed a virtual-reality program that is indistinguishable from real life to those experiencing it. The program will cost $20 million to develop (paid up front), but the payoff is substantial: $1 million at the end of year 1, $2 million at the end of year 2, $5 million at the end of year 3, and $6 million at the end of each year thereafter, through year 10. Matrix.com's weighted average cost of capital is 15 percent. Given these conditions, what are the NPV, IRR, and MIRR of the proposed program?

Independent and Mutually Exclusive Projects

10-15. Project A has an initial investment of $11,000, and it generates positive cash flows of $4,000 each year for the next six years. Project B has an initial investment of $17,000, and it generates positive cash flows of $4,500 each year for the next six years. Assume the discount rate, or required rate of return, is 13 percent.

a. Calculate the net present value of each project. If Project A and Project B are mutually exclusive, which one would you select?

b. Assume Projects A and B are independent. Based on NPV, which one(s) would you select?

c. Calculate the internal rate of return for each project.

d. Using IRR for your decision, which project would you select if Project A and Project B were mutually exclusive? Would your answer change if these two projects were independent instead of mutually exclusive?

e. Project C was added to the potential capital budget list at the last minute as a mutually exclusive alternative to Project B. It has an initial cash outlay of $17,000, and it generates its only positive cash flow of $37,500 in the sixth year. Years 1 through 5 have $0 cash flow. Calculate Project C's NPV. Which alternative, Project B or C, would you choose?

f. Now calculate the IRR of Project C and compare it with Project B's IRR. Based solely on the IRRs, which project would you select?

g. Because Projects B and C are mutually exclusive, would you recommend that Project B or Project C be added to the capital budget for this year? Explain your choice.

10-16. Joanne Crale is an independent petroleum geologist. She is taking advantage of every opportunity to lease the mineral rights of land she thinks lies over oil reserves. She thinks there are many reservoirs with oil reserves left behind by major corporations when they plugged and abandoned fields in the 1960s. Ms. Crale knows that with today's technology, production can be sustained at much lower reservoir pressures than was possible in the 1960s. She would like to lease the mineral rights from George Hansen and Ed McNeil, the landowners. Her net cost for this current oil venture is $5 million. This includes costs for the initial leasing and three planned development wells. The expected positive net cash flows for the project are $1.85 million each year for four years. On depletion, she anticipates a negative cash flow of $250,000 in year 5 because of reclamation and disposal costs. Because of the risks involved in petroleum exploration, Ms. Crale's required rate of return is 10 percent.

NPV, and IRR

a. Calculate the net present value for Ms. Crale's project.

b. Calculate the internal rate of return for this project.

c. Would you recommend the project?

10-17. Silkwood Power Company is considering two projects with the following predicted cash flows:

NPV Profile
Analysis

	Hydroelectric Upgrade	Geothermal Upgrade
Initial Investment CFs	($100,000)	($100,000)
End of year 1 CFs	20,000	80,000
End of year 2 CFs	30,000	40,000
End of year 3 CFs	40,000	30,000
End of year 4 CFs	90,000	10,000

These two projects are mutually exclusive.

a. Construct a chart showing the NPV profiles of both projects.

b. Which project(s) would be accepted if the company's cost of capital were 6 percent?

c. Which project(s) would be accepted if the company's cost of capital were 15 percent?

d. At what cost of capital would Silkwood value each project equally?

e. At what cost of capital would the hydroelectric project become unacceptable?

f. At what cost of capital would the geothermal project become unacceptable?

10-18. The product development managers at World Series Innovations are about to recommend their final capital budget for next year. They have a self-imposed budget limit of $100,000. Five independent projects are being considered. Vernon Simpson, the chief scientist and CEO, has minimal financial analysis experience and relies on his managers to recommend the projects that will increase the value of the firm by the greatest amount. Given the following summary of the five projects, which ones should the managers recommend?

Challenge Problem

Projects	Initial Cash Outlay	Net Present Value
Chalk Line Machine	($10,000)	$4,000
Gel Padded Glove	($25,000)	$3,600
Insect Repellent	($35,000)	$3,250
Titanium Bat	($40,000)	$2,500
Recycled Base Covers	($20,000)	$2,100

Various Capital Budgeting Issues

 10-19. A project you are considering has an initial investment of $5,669.62. It has positive net cash flows of $2,200 each year for three years. Your required rate of return is 10 percent.

a. Calculate the net present value of this project.

b. Would you undertake this project if you had the cash available?

c. What would the discount rate have to be before this project's NPV would be positive? Construct an NPV profile with discount rates of 0 percent, 5 percent, and 10 percent to answer this question.

d. What other method might you use to determine at what discount rate the net present value would become greater than 0?

Expected IRR

 10-20. The internal rate of return (IRR) of a capital investment, Project B, is expected to have the following values with the associated probabilities for an economic life of five years. Calculate the expected value, standard deviation, and coefficient of variation of the IRR distribution.

IRR	Probability of Occurrence
0%	0.05
1%	0.10
3%	0.20
6%	0.30
9%	0.20
11%	0.10
12%	0.05

Capital Budgeting Risk

 10-21. Four capital investment alternatives have the following expected IRRs and standard deviations.

Project	Expected IRR	Standard Deviation
A	14%	2%
B	16%	6%
C	11%	5%
D	14%	4%

If the firm's existing portfolio of assets has an expected IRR of 13 percent with a standard deviation of 3 percent, identify the lowest- and the highest-risk projects in the preceding list. You may assume the correlation coefficient of returns from each project relative to the existing portfolio is .50 and the investment in each project would constitute 20 percent of the firm's total portfolio.

Capital Budgeting Risk and RADRs

 10-22. Assume that a company has an existing Portfolio A, with an expected IRR of 10 percent and standard deviation of 2 percent. The company is considering adding a Project B, with expected IRR of 11 percent and standard deviation of 3 percent, to its portfolio. Also assume that the amount invested in Portfolio A is $700,000 and the amount to be invested in Project B is $200,000.

a. If the degree of correlation between returns from Portfolio A and Project B is .90 (r = +.9), calculate:

1. the coefficient of variation of Portfolio A

2. the expected IRR of the new combined portfolio

3. the standard deviation of the new combined portfolio

4. the coefficient of variation of the new combined portfolio

b. What is the change in the coefficient of variation as a result of adopting Project B?

c. Assume the firm classifies projects as high risk if they raise the coefficient of variation of the portfolio 2 percentage points or more, as low risk if they lower the coefficient of variation of the portfolio 2 percentage points or more, and as average risk if they change the coefficient of variation of the portfolio by less than 2 percent in either direction. In what risk classification would Project B be?

d. The required rate of return for average-risk projects for the company in this problem is 13 percent. The company policy is to adjust the required rate of return downward by 3 percent for low-risk projects and to raise it 3 percent for high-risk projects (average-risk projects are evaluated at the average required rate of return). The expected cash flows from Project B are as follows:

CF of Initial Investment	($200,000)
end of year 1	55,000
end of year 2	55,000
end of year 3	55,000
end of year 4	100,000

Calculate the NPV of Project B when its cash flows are discounted at:

1. the average required rate of return
2. the high-risk discount rate
3. the low-risk discount rate

10-23. Dorothy Gale is thinking of purchasing a Kansas amusement park, Glinda's Gulch. She already owns at least one park in each of the surrounding states and wants to expand her operations into Kansas. She estimates the IRR from the project may be one of a number of values, each with a certain probability of occurrence. Her estimated IRR values and the probability of their occurrence follow.

← Risk in Capital Budgeting

Glinda's Gulch

Possible IRR Value	Probability
2%	.125
5%	.20
9%	.35
13%	.20
16%	.125

Now Dorothy wants to estimate the risk of the project. Assume she has asked you to do the following for her:

a. Calculate the mean, or expected, IRR of the project.

b. Calculate the standard deviation of the possible IRRs.

c. Assume the expected IRR of Dorothy's existing portfolio of parks is 8 percent, with a standard deviation of 2 percent. Calculate the coefficient of variation of Dorothy's existing portfolio.

d. Calculate the expected IRR of Dorothy's portfolio if the Glinda's Gulch project is adopted. For this calculation, assume that Dorothy's new portfolio will consist of 80 percent existing parks and 20 percent new Glinda's Gulch.

e. Again assuming that Dorothy's new portfolio will consist of 80 percent existing parks and 20 percent new Glinda's Gulch, calculate the standard deviation of Dorothy's portfolio if the Glinda's Gulch project is added. Because Glinda's Gulch is identical to Dorothy's other parks, she estimates the returns from Glinda's Gulch and her existing portfolio are perfectly positively correlated (r = +1.0).

f. Calculate the coefficient of variation of Dorothy's new portfolio with Glinda's Gulch.

g. Compare the coefficient of variation of Dorothy's existing portfolio with and without the Glinda's Gulch project. How does the addition of Glinda's Gulch affect the riskiness of the portfolio?

Risk in Capital Budgeting

10-24. Four capital investment alternatives have the following expected IRRs and standard deviations.

Project	Expected IRR	Standard Deviation
A	18%	9%
B	15%	5%
C	11%	3%
D	8%	1%

The firm's existing portfolio of projects has an expected IRR of 12 percent and a standard deviation of 4 percent.

a. Calculate the coefficient of variation of the existing portfolio.

b. Calculate the coefficient of variation of the portfolio if the firm invests 10 percent of its assets in Project A. You may assume that there is no correlation between the returns from Project A and the returns from the existing portfolio (r = 0). (Note: In order to calculate the coefficient of variation, you must first calculate the expected IRR and standard deviation of the portfolio with Project A included.)

c. Using the same procedure as in b and given the same assumptions, calculate the coefficient of variation of the portfolio if it includes, in turn, Projects B, C, and D.

d. Which project has the highest risk? Which has the lowest risk?

Firm Risk

10-25. A firm has an existing portfolio of projects with a mean, or expected, IRR of 15 percent. The standard deviation of this estimate is 5 percent. The existing portfolio is worth $820,000. The addition of a new project, PROJ1, is being considered. PROJ1's expected IRR is 18 percent with a standard deviation of 9 percent. The initial investment for PROJ1 is expected to be $194,000. The returns from PROJ1 and the existing portfolio are perfectly positively correlated (r = +1.0).

a. Calculate the coefficient of variation for the existing portfolio.

b. If PROJ1 is added to the existing portfolio, calculate the weight (proportion) of the existing portfolio in the combined portfolio.

c. Calculate the weight (proportion) of PROJ1 in the combined portfolio.

d. Calculate the standard deviation of the combined portfolio. Is the standard deviation of the combined portfolio higher or lower than the standard deviation of the existing portfolio?

e. Calculate the coefficient of variation of the combined portfolio.

f. If PROJ1 is added to the existing portfolio, will the firm's risk increase or decrease?

Risk in Capital Budgeting

10-26. VOTD Pharmaceuticals is considering the mass production of a new sleeping pill. Neely O'Hara, VOTD's financial analyst, has gathered all the available information from the finance, production, advertising, and marketing departments and has estimated that the yearly net incremental cash flows will be $298,500. She estimates the initial investment for this project will be $2 million. The pills are expected to be marketable for 10 years, and Neely does not expect that any of the investment costs will be recouped at the end of the 10-year period. VOTD's required rate of return for average-risk projects is 8 percent. Two percent is added to the required rate of return for high-risk projects.

a. Calculate the net present value of the project if VOTD management considers it to be average risk.

b. A lot of uncertainty is associated with the potential competition of new drugs that VOTD's competitors might introduce. Because of this uncertainty, VOTD management has changed the classification of this project to high risk. Calculate the net present value at the risk-adjusted discount rate.

c. Assuming the risk classification does not change again, should this project be adopted?

d. What will the yearly net incremental cash flow have to be to have a positive NPV when using the high-risk discount rate?

10-27. Aluminum Building Products Company (ABPC) is considering investing in either of the two mutually exclusive projects described as follows:

Project 1. Buying a new set of roll-forming tools for its existing roll forming line to introduce a new cladding product. After its introduction, the product will need to be promoted. This means that cash inflows from additional production will start sometime after and will gradually pick up in subsequent periods.

Project 2. Modifying its existing roll-forming line to increase productivity of its available range of cladding products. Cash inflows from additional production will start immediately and will reduce over time as the products move through their life cycle.

Sarah Brown, project manager of ABPC, has requested that you do the necessary financial analysis and give your opinion about which project ABPC should select. The projects have the following net cash flow estimates:

Year	Project 1	Project 2
0	($200,000)	($200,000)
1	0	90,000
2	0	70,000
3	20,000	50,000
4	30,000	30,000
5	40,000	10,000
6	60,000	10,000
7	90,000	10,000
8	100,000	10,000

Both these projects have the same economic life of eight years and average risk characteristics. ABPC's weighted average cost of capital, or hurdle rate, is 7.2 percent.

a. Which project would you recommend Ms. Brown accept to maximize value of the firm? (Hint: Calculate and compare NPVs of both projects.)

b. What are the IRRs of each project? Which project should be chosen using IRR as the selection criterion?

c. Draw the NPV profiles of both projects. What is the approximate discount rate at which both projects would have the same NPV? What is that NPV?

d. Does the selection remain unaffected for i) WACC > 5.4 percent; ii) WACC > 8.81 percent; and iii) WACC > 14.39 percent?

e. Further market survey research indicates that both projects have lower-than- average risk and, hence, the risk-adjusted discount rate should be 5 percent. What happens to the ranking of the projects using NPV and IRR as the selection criteria? Explain the conflict in ranking, if any.

f. Answer questions a, d, and e, assuming the projects are independent of each other.

Answers to Self-Test

ST-1. The NPV of the project can be found using Equation 10-1a as follows:

$$NPV = \left(\frac{\$20,000}{(1 + .11)^1}\right) + \left(\frac{\$40,000}{(1 + .11)^2}\right) - \$50,000$$

$$= \left(\frac{\$20,000}{1.11}\right) + \left(\frac{\$40,000}{1.2321}\right) - \$50,000$$

$$= \$18,018 + \$32,465 - \$50,000$$

$$= \$483$$

ST-2. To find the IRR, we solve for the k value that results in an NPV of zero in the NPV formula (Equation 10-1a) by trial and error.

Try using k = 11%:

$$0 = \left(\frac{\$20,000}{(1 + .11)^1}\right) + \left(\frac{\$40,000}{(1 + .11)^2}\right) - \$50,000$$

$$= \left(\frac{\$20,000}{1.11}\right) + \left(\frac{\$40,000}{1.2321}\right) - \$50,000$$

$$= \$18,018 + \$32,465 - \$50,000$$

$$= \$483$$

The result does not equal zero. Try again using a slightly higher discount rate.

Second, try using k = 11.65%:

$$0 = \left(\frac{\$20,000}{(1 + .1165)^1}\right) + \left(\frac{\$40,000}{(1 + .1165)^2}\right) - \$50,000$$

$$= \left(\frac{\$20,000}{1.1165}\right) + \left(\frac{\$40,000}{1.24657225}\right) - \$50,000$$

$$= \$17,913 + \$32,088 - \$50,000$$

$$= \$1$$

Close enough. The IRR of the project is almost exactly 11.65 percent.

ST-3. The NPV of the project must be calculated to see if it is greater or less than zero. Because the project in this problem is an annuity, its NPV can be found most easily using a modified version of Equation 10-1b as follows:

$$NPV = PMT(PVFOA_{k, n}) - \text{Initial Investment}$$

We include this problem (and some others that follow) to show you that Equations 10-1a and 10-1b can be modified to take advantage of the present value of an annuity formulas covered in Chapter 8, Equations 8-4a and 8-4b.

The problem could also be solved using the basic forms of Equations 10-1a and 10-1b, but those would take longer.

In this problem, the initial investment is $200,000, the annuity payment is $44,503, the discount rate, k, is 14 percent, and the number of periods, n, is 10.

$$NPV = \$44,503(PVFOA_{14\%, 10}) - \$200,000$$
$$= \$44,503(5.2161) - \$200,000$$
$$= \$232,132 - \$200,000$$
$$= \$32,132$$

Because the NPV is positive, the project should be accepted.

ST-4. The IRR is found by setting the NPV formula to zero and solving for the IRR rate, k. In this case, there are no multiple cash flows, so the equation can be solved algebraically. For convenience, we use Equation 10-1b modified for an annuity:

$$0 = \$44,503\left(PVFOA_{k\%, 10}\right) - \$200,000$$

$$\$200,000 = \$44,503\left(PVFOA_{k\%, 10}\right)$$

$$\frac{\$200,000}{\$44,503} = PVFOA_{k\%, 10}$$

$$4.49408 = PVFOA_{k\%, 10}$$

Finding the PVFOA in Table IV-A in the Appendix, we see that 4.4941 (there are only four decimal places in the table) occurs in the year 10 row in the 18 percent column. Therefore, the IRR of the project is 18 percent.

ST-5. To calculate the MIRR, first calculate the project's terminal value. Next, calculate the annual rate of return it would take to produce that end amount from the beginning investment. That rate is the MIRR.

For the project in ST-3:

Step 1: Calculate the project's terminal value. Note—The terminal value could be calculated by adding up the future values of each individual cash flow, as was done on the MIRR explanation on pages 244–246. In this case, however, that would be a lengthy procedure because there are 10 cash flows. Recognizing that the cash flows are an annuity, we can make use of the future value of an annuity formula, Equation 8-3a, to calculate the terminal value:

$$FVOA = \$44,503 \left[\frac{(1+.14)^{10} - 1}{.14} \right]$$

$$FVOA = \$44.503 \left[19.3372951 \right]$$

$$TV = \text{Project's Terminal Value} = \$860,568$$

Step 2: Calculate the annual rate of return that will produce the terminal value from the initial investment.

Project's Terminal Value: $860,568

PV of Initial Investment: $200,000

per Equation 8-8:

$$MIRR = \left(\frac{860,568}{200,000} \right)^{\left(\frac{1}{10} \right)} - 1$$

$$MIRR = .1571, \text{ or } 15.71\%$$

ST-6. There are only two cash flows in this problem, a $400 investment at time 0 and the $1,000 payoff at the end of year 10. To find the IRR, we set the NPV formula to zero, fill in the two cash flows and periods, and solve for the IRR rate, k, that makes the right-hand side of the equation equal zero. Equation 10-1b is more convenient to use in this case:

$$0 = \$1,000 \left(PVF_{k\%, 10} \right) - \$400$$

$$\$400 = \$1,000 \left(PVF_{k\%, 10} \right)$$

$$\frac{\$400}{\$1,000} = PVF_{k\%, 10}$$

$$.4000 = PVF_{k\%, 10}$$

If we find the PVF in Table II inside the book cover, we see that .4000 occurs in the year 10 row between the 9 percent and 10 percent columns. Therefore, the IRR of the project is between 9 percent and 10 percent. (The exact value of the IRR is 9.596 percent.) Because your required rate of return in this problem was 12 percent, the bonds would not meet your requirements.

ST-7. Solve for the NPV using Equation 10-1a or b. Equation 10-1a would be the more convenient version for this problem. The cash flows are a $300 investment at time 0 and a $1,000 future value (FV) in 10 years. The discount rate is 20 percent.

$$NPV = \left(\frac{\$1,000}{(1 + .20)^{10}} \right) - \$300$$

$$= \left(\frac{\$1,000}{6.191736} \right) - \$300$$

$$= \$161.51 - \$300$$

$$= -\$138.49$$

Appendix 10A

Wrinkles in Capital Budgeting

In this appendix, we discuss three situations that change the capital budgeting decision process. First, we examine nonsimple projects, projects that have a negative initial cash flow, in addition to one or more negative future cash flows. Next, we explore projects that have multiple IRRs. Finally, we discuss how to compare mutually exclusive projects with unequal project lives.

Nonsimple Projects

Most capital budgeting projects start with a negative cash flow—the initial investment—at t_0, followed by positive future cash flows. Such projects are called **simple projects**. **Nonsimple projects** are projects that have one or more negative future cash flows after the initial investment.

To illustrate a nonsimple project, consider Project N, the expected cash flows for a nuclear power plant project. The initial investment of $500 million is a negative cash flow at t_0, followed by positive cash flows of $25 million per year for 30 years as electric power is generated and sold. At the end of the useful life of the project, the storage of nuclear fuel and the shutdown safety procedures require cash outlays of $100 million at the end of year 31. The timeline depicted in Figure 10A-1 shows the cash flow pattern.

With a 20 percent discount rate, an initial investment of $500 million, a 30-year annuity of $25 million, and a shutdown cash outlay of $100 million in year 31, the NPV of Project N follows (in millions), per Equation 10-1a:

$$NPV_n = \$25 \left[\frac{1 - \dfrac{1}{\left(1 + .20\right)^{30}}}{.20} \right] - \left(\frac{\$100}{\left(1 + .20\right)^{31}} \right) - \$500$$

$$= \left(\$25 \times 4.9789364\right) - \left(\frac{\$100}{284.8515766} \right) - \$500$$

$$= \$124.47341 - \$.35106 - \$500$$

$$= -\$375.8776$$

We find that at a discount rate of 20 percent, Project N has a negative net present value of minus $375.88, so the firm considering Project N should reject it.

> **Take Note**
> The $25 million annual payment for 30 years constitutes an annuity, so we were able to adapt Equation 10-1a by using the present value of annuity formula, Equation 8-4a.

Multiple IRRs

Some projects may have more than one internal rate of return. That is, a project may have several different discount rates that result in a net present value of zero.

Here is an example. Suppose Project Q requires an initial cash outlay of $160,000 and is expected to generate a positive cash flow of $1 million in year 1. In year 2, the project will require an additional cash outlay in the amount of $1 million. The cash flows for Project Q are shown on the timeline in Figure 10A-2.

FIGURE 10A-1
Cash Flow Timeline for Project N (in millions)

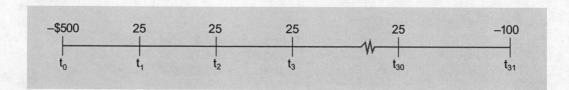

−$500	25	25	25	25	−100
t_0	t_1	t_2	t_3	t_{30}	t_{31}

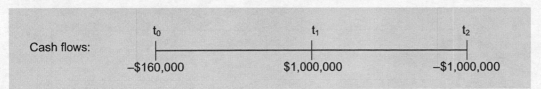

We find the IRR of Project Q by using the trial-and-error procedure, Equation 10-2. When k = 25 percent, the NPV is zero.

$$0 = \left(\frac{\$1,000,000}{(1 + .25)^1}\right) - \left(\frac{\$1,000,000}{(1 + .25)^2}\right) - \$160,000$$

$$= \left(\frac{\$1,000,000}{1.25}\right) - \left(\frac{\$1,000,000}{1.5625}\right) - \$160,000$$

$$= \$800,000 - \$640,000 - \$160,000$$

$$= \$0$$

Because 25 percent causes the NPV of Project Q to be zero, the IRR of the project must be 25 percent. But wait! If we had tried k = 400%, the IRR calculation would look like this:

$$0 = \left(\frac{\$1,000,000}{(1 + 4.00)^1}\right) - \left(\frac{\$1,000,000}{(1 + 4.00)^2}\right) - \$160,000$$

$$= \left(\frac{\$1,000,000}{5.00}\right) - \left(\frac{\$1,000,000}{25.00}\right) - \$160,000$$

$$= \$200,000 - \$40,000 - \$160,000$$

$$= \$0$$

Because 400 percent results in an NPV of zero, 400 percent must also be the IRR of the Project Q. Figure 10A-3 shows the net present value profile for Project Q. By examining this graph, we see how 25 percent and 400 percent both make the net present value equal to zero.

As the graph shows, Project Q's net present value profile crosses the horizontal axis (has a zero value) in two different places, at discount rates of 25 percent and 400 percent.

Project Q had two IRRs because the project's cash flows changed from negative to positive (from t_0 to t_1) and then from positive to negative at (from t_1 to t_2). It turns out that a nonsimple project may have (but does not have to have) as many IRRs as there are sign changes. In this case, two sign changes resulted in two internal rates of return.

Whenever we have two or more IRRs for a project, the IRR method is not a useful decision-making tool. Remember the IRR accept/reject decision rule: Firms should accept projects with IRRs higher than the discount rate and reject projects with IRRs lower than the discount rate. With more than one discount rate, decision makers will not know which IRR to use for the accept/reject decision. In projects that have multiple IRRs, then, switch to the NPV method.

Mutually Exclusive Projects with Unequal Project Lives

When mutually exclusive projects have different expected useful lives, selecting among the projects requires more than comparing the projects' NPVs. To illustrate, suppose you are a business manager considering a new business telephone system. One is the Cheap Talk System, which requires an initial cash outlay of $10,000 and is expected to last three years. The other is the Rolles Voice System, which requires an initial cash outlay of $50,000 and is expected to last 12 years. The Cheap Talk System is expected to generate positive

FIGURE 10A-3

Net Present Value Profile for Project Q

The net present value profile for project Q crosses the zero line twice, showing that two IRRs exist.

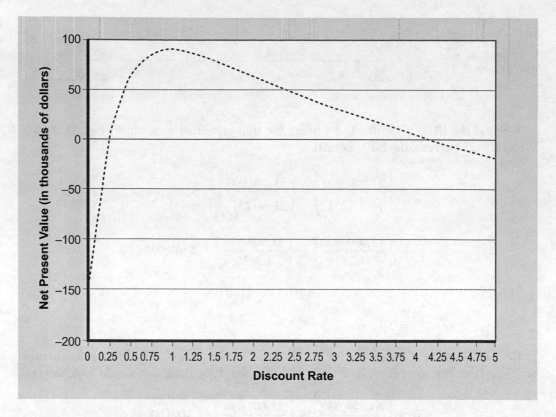

cash flows of $5,800 per year for each of its three years of life. The Rolles Voice System is expected to generate positive cash flows of $8,000 per year for each of its 12 years of life. The cash flows associated with each project are summarized in Figure 10A-4.

To decide which project to choose, we first compute and compare their NPVs. Assume the firm's required rate of return is 10 percent. We solve for the NPVs as follows:

1. NPV of Cheap Talk.

$$\text{NPV}_{CT} = \$5,800 \left[\frac{1 - \dfrac{1}{(1 + .10)^3}}{.10} \right] - \$10,000$$

$$= (\$5,800 \times 2.48685) - \$10,000$$

$$= \$14.424 - \$10,000$$

$$= \$4,424$$

FIGURE 10A-4

Cash Flows for the Cheap Talk and Rolles Voice Communications System (in thousands)

This figure shows the cash flows for two projects with unequal lives, Project Cheap Talk and Project Rolles Voice.

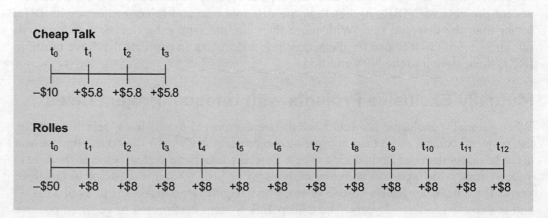

2. NPV of Rolles Voice.

$$NPV_{Rolles} = \$8,000 \left[\frac{1 - \dfrac{1}{(1 + .10)^{12}}}{.10} \right] - \$50,000$$

$$= \left(\$8,000 \times 6.81369\right) - \$50,000$$

$$= \$54,510 - \$50,000$$

$$= \$4,510$$

We find that Project Cheap Talk has an NPV of \$4,424, compared with Project Rolles's NPV of \$4,510. We might conclude based on this information that the Rolles Voice System should be selected over the Cheap Talk system because it has the higher NPV. However, before making that decision, we must assess how Project Cheap Talk's NPV would change if its useful life were 12 years, not three years.

Comparing Projects with Unequal Lives

Two possible methods that allow financial managers to compare projects with unequal lives are the replacement chain approach and the equivalent annual annuity (EAA) approach.

The Replacement Chain Approach

The replacement chain approach assumes each of the mutually exclusive projects can be replicated, until a common time period has passed in which the projects can be compared. The NPVs for the series of replicated projects are then compared to the project with the longer life. An example illustrates this process. Project Cheap Talk could be repeated four times in the same time span as the 12-year Rolles Voice project. If a business replicated project Cheap Talk four times, the cash flows would look as depicted in Figure 10A-5.

The NPV of this series of cash flows, assuming the discount rate is 10 percent, is (in thousands) \$12,121. Each cash flow, be it positive or negative, is discounted back the appropriate number of years to get the NPV of the four consecutive investments in the Cheap Talk system.

The NPV of \$12,121 for Cheap Talk system is the sum of the NPVs of the four repeated Cheap Talk projects, such that the project series would have a life of 12 years, the same life as the Rolles Voice System Project. We are now comparing apples to apples. Cheap Talk's replacement chain NPV is \$12,121, whereas the NPV of Project Rolles Voice is \$4,510 over the same 12-year period. If a firm invested in project Cheap Talk four successive times, it would create more value than investing in one project Rolles Voice.

The Equivalent Annual Annuity (EAA)

The equivalent annual annuity (EAA) approach converts the NPVs of the mutually exclusive projects into their equivalent annuity values. The equivalent annual annuity is the amount of the annuity payment that would give the same present value as the actual future

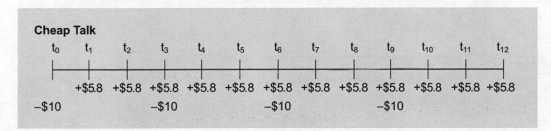

FIGURE 10A-5
Cash Flows for the Cheap Talk System Repeated 4 times (in thousands)

cash flows for that project. The EAA approach assumes that you could repeat the mutually exclusive projects indefinitely as each project came to the end of its life.

The equivalent annuity value (EAA) is calculated by dividing the NPV of a project by the present value interest factor for an annuity (PVFOA) that applies to the project's life span.

Formula for an Equivalent Annual Annuity (EAA)

$$EAA = \frac{NPV}{PVFOA_{k,n}}$$

(10A-1)

where: k = Discount rate used to calculate the NPV

n = Life span of the project

The NPVs of Cheap Talk ($4,424) and Rolles Voice ($4,510) were calculated earlier, assuming a required rate of return of 10 percent. With the project's NPV and the discount rate, we calculate each project's EAA, per Equation 10A-1, as follows:

1. EAA of Project Cheap Talk:

$$EAA_{CT} = \frac{\$4,424}{2.48685}$$

$$= \$1,778.96$$

2. EAA of Project Rolles

$$EAA_{Rolles} = \frac{\$4,510}{6.81369}$$

$$= \$661.90$$

Take Note
Note that the unequal lives problem is only an issue when the projects under consideration are mutually exclusive. If the projects were independent, we would adopt both.

The EAA approach decision rule calls for choosing whichever mutually exclusive project has the highest EAA. Our calculations show that Project Cheap Talk has an EAA of $1,778.96 and Project Rolles Voice System has an EAA of $661.90. Because Project Cheap Talk's EAA is higher than Project Rolles's, Project Cheap Talk should be chosen.

Both the replacement chain and the EAA approach assume that mutually exclusive projects can be replicated. If the projects can be replicated, then either the replacement chain or the equivalent annual annuity methods should be used because they lead to the same correct decision. Note in our case that the EAA method results in the same project selection (Project Cheap Talk) as the replacement chain method. If the projects cannot be replicated, then the normal NPVs should be used as the basis for the capital budgeting decision.

Equations Introduced in This Appendix

Equation 10A-1. The Formula for an Equivalent Annual Annuity:

$$EAA = \frac{NPV}{PVFOA_{k,n}}$$

where: k = Discount rate used to calculate the NPV

n = Life span of the project

Estimating Incremental Cash Flows

"We (NFL team executives) paid our starting quarterback a $20 million signing bonus plus a salary of $15 million per year in salary. His performance on the field this year is horrible and it is clear that our backup quarterback to whom we paid a $5 million signing bonus and $3 million dollars per year in salary is a better player. We have to stick with our starter, however, because of all the money we have tied up in him.
—An example of the sunk cost fallacy

Learning Objectives

After reading this chapter, you should be able to:

1. Explain the difference between incremental cash flows and sunk costs.

2. Identify types of incremental cash flows in a capital budgeting project.

3. Explain why cash flows associated with project financing are not included in incremental cash flow estimates.

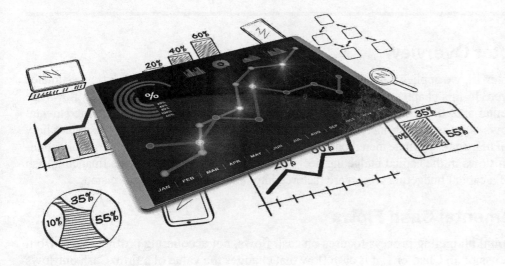

Source: pedrosek/Shutterstock

Saving Money?

The story you are about to read is true. The company name has been withheld to protect those guilty of poor financial decision making.

Company X is a large multinational corporation with many facilities throughout the United States and the rest of the world. Employees at a variety of U.S. sites frequently are required to travel to the home office in Headquarters City. On a typical day there may be a dozen or more employees traveling to Headquarters City from any given satellite city site.

Company X has many corporate jets at airports throughout the United States near the larger satellite cities. Senior executives routinely fly on these corporate jets when traveling to Headquarters City. Middle-level managers fly on commercial aircraft, usually located at a much greater distance from the workplace. The reason for this is that the department of the traveling employee is "billed" $800 if the corporate jet is used. This $800 expense goes into the financial report of that department, which goes to corporate headquarters. Managers can frequently find commercial airfares under $300 for employees traveling to Headquarters City.

Because each department would rather be charged $300 a trip instead of $800 when reporting its financial performance, only a few of the most senior executives fly the corporate jets. This means that each corporate jet typically has a dozen empty seats for its daily flights to Headquarters City. It is clearly in the interest of each department manager to keep his or her expenses down. Is it in the interests of the stockholders to have mostly empty planes fly each day to Headquarters City? The cost of adding an additional passenger, or 12 additional passengers, to a corporate jet is almost zero. A very small amount of additional fuel would be consumed. The stockholders would save $300 for each additional person who took an otherwise-empty seat on a corporate jet instead of flying on a commercial airline.

Consider the interests of the department managers and those of the stockholders of Company X as you read Chapter 11.

Chapter Overview

In Chapter 10, we applied capital budgeting decision methods, taking the cash flow estimates as a given. In this chapter, we see how financial managers determine which cash flows are incremental and, therefore, relevant to a capital budgeting decision. We define incremental cash flows and distinguish incremental cash flows from sunk costs. We also examine how financial managers estimate incremental initial investment cash flows and incremental operating cash flows in the capital budgeting decision. Finally, we explore how the financing cash flows of a capital budgeting project are factored into the capital budgeting decision.

Incremental Cash Flows

The capital budgeting process focuses on cash flows, not accounting profits. Recall from our discussion in Chapter 1, it is cash flow that changes the value of a firm. Cash outflows reduce the value of the firm, whereas cash inflows increase the value of the firm.

In capital budgeting, incremental cash flows are the positive and negative cash flows directly associated with a project. They occur if a firm accepts a project, but they do not occur if the project is rejected.

For instance, suppose that the chief financial officer of Photon Manufacturing, Mr. Sulu, is analyzing the cash flows associated with a proposed project. He finds that the CEO hired a consultant to assess the proposed project's environmental effects. The consultant will be paid $50,000 for the work. Although the $50,000 fee is related to the project, it is not an incremental cash flow because the money must be paid whether the project is accepted or rejected. Therefore, the fee should not be included as a relevant cash flow of the expansion project decision. Cash flows that have already occurred, or will occur whether a project is accepted or rejected, are sunk costs.

Financial managers carefully screen out irrelevant cash flows, such as sunk costs, from the capital budgeting decision process. If they include irrelevant cash flows in their capital budgeting decision, then their calculations of a project's payback period, net present value (NPV), internal rate of return (IRR), and modified internal rate of return (MIRR) will be distorted and inaccurate. The calculations may be so distorted that they lead to an incorrect decision about a capital budgeting project.

Types of Incremental Cash Flows

To accurately assess the value of a capital budgeting project, financial managers must identify and estimate many types of incremental cash flows. The three main types of incremental cash flows are *initial investment cash flows, operating cash flows,* and *shutdown cash flows.* We examine these three types of incremental cash flows in the sections that follow.

Initial Investment Cash Flows

Generally, financial managers begin their incremental cash flow estimates by assessing the costs of the initial investment. The negative cash flow associated with the initial investment occurs only if the project is accepted. Initial investment cash flows include the purchase price of the asset or materials to produce the asset, the installation and delivery costs, and the additional investment in net working capital.

Purchase Price, Installation, and Delivery

Financial managers usually obtain quotes on the purchase price and installation and delivery costs from suppliers. These figures, then, can usually be estimated with a high degree of accuracy.

Changes in Net Working Capital

Aside from the setup costs and purchase price of a proposed capital budgeting project, a company may have to invest in changes in net working capital. As explained in Chapter 4, net working capital is defined as current assets (working capital) minus current liabilities. If a proposed capital budgeting project will require a positive change in net working capital (the most likely scenario), the cash outlay needed to finance this must be included in the cash flow estimates.

Recall that working capital consists of cash, accounts receivable, and inventory, along with other current assets if any. Companies invest in these assets in much the same way they invest in plant and equipment. Accepting a new project often triggers an increased need for cash, accounts receivable, and inventory investments. Working capital investments tie up cash the same way as investment in a new piece of equipment.

A company's current liabilities—such as accounts payable, accrued wages, and accrued taxes—may also be affected if a firm accepts a capital budgeting project. For example, if a plant is expanded, the company may place larger orders with suppliers to accommodate the increased production. The increase in orders is likely to lead to an increase in accounts payable.

Increases in current liabilities create cash inflows. It is unlikely that current liabilities will increase sufficiently to finance all the needed current asset buildup. This is the reason that an investment in net working capital is almost always required.

Table 11-1 shows an example of the incremental changes in net working capital that might occur with a proposed capital budgeting project for the McGuffin Company.

As Table 11-1 indicates, the McGuffin Company project has an estimated increase of $27,000 in needed current assets and a $10,000 increase in new current liabilities, resulting in a $17,000 change in needed net working capital. That is, the firm will have to spend $17,000 to increase its net working capital by this amount—a negative cash flow.

Once financial managers estimate the initial investment incremental cash flows, they analyze the operating cash flows of a capital budgeting project. We turn to those cash flows next.

TABLE 11-1 Change in McGuffin Company Net Working Capital if New Project Is Accepted

Current Asset Changes	Current Liability Changes
$5,000 Increase in Cash	$8,000 Increase in Accounts Payable
$7,000 Increase in Receivables	$2,000 Increase in Accruals
$15,000 Increase in Inventory	
Total Current Asset Changes: $27,000	Total Current Liability Changes: $10,000
Increase in Needed Net Working Capital (NWC): $27,000 − $10,000 = $17,000	
Incremental Cash Flow Due to the Increase in NWC = −$17,000	

Operating Cash Flows

Operating cash flows are those cash flows that the project generates after it is in operation. For example, cash flows that follow a change in sales or expenses are operating cash flows. Those operating cash flows incremental to the project under consideration are the ones relevant to our capital budgeting analysis. Incremental operating cash flows also include tax changes, including those due to changes in depreciation expense, opportunity costs, and externalities.

Taxes

The change in taxes that will occur if a project is accepted is part of the incremental cash flow analysis. Tax effects are considered because a tax increase is equivalent to a negative cash flow, and a tax decrease is equivalent to a positive cash flow. In a capital budgeting decision, then, financial managers must examine whether and how much tax the firm will pay on additional income that the proposed project generates during a given period. They must also see whether and how much taxes will decrease if the project increases the firm's periodic operating expenses (such as payments for labor and materials), thereby creating additional tax deductions.

Depreciation and Taxes

Financial managers estimate changes in depreciation expense as part of the incremental cash flow analysis because increases in depreciation expense may increase a firm's cash flow. How? Depreciation expense is deductible for tax purposes. The greater the depreciation expense deduction, the less tax a firm must pay, and the less cash it must give to the IRS. Financial managers estimate the amount of depreciation expense a capital budgeting project will have, therefore, to see how much the firm's taxable income, and taxes owed, will decrease.

Incremental depreciation expense is the change in depreciation expense that results from accepting a proposed capital budgeting project. Incremental depreciation expense affects the change in taxes attributable to a capital budgeting project.

To illustrate how incremental depreciation expense changes taxes due, recall how we converted after-tax net profits into operating cash inflows in Chapter 4. We added all noncash charges (including depreciation) that were deducted as expenses on the firm's income statement to net profits after taxes. Once the tax effects of a project's depreciation expense are calculated, we add this incremental depreciation expense back to the project's net profits after taxes.

The following example, illustrated in Table 11-2, demonstrates how to estimate the incremental depreciation expense of a capital budgeting project. Suppose your firm is considering a project that is expected to earn $100,000 in cash sales in year 1. Suppose that, in addition to the sales increase, the project is expected to increase cash operating expenses by $50,000 and new depreciation expense will be $10,000. Assume your firm's marginal tax rate is 25 percent. First, compute the net operating cash flows from the project for this year, as shown in Table 11-2.

Compare line 3 and line 7 in Table 11-2. Note that once we used the new project incremental depreciation expense of $10,000 to make the tax change calculations, we

TABLE 11-2 Net Operating Cash Flows for New Project

1. New Project Sales (cash inflow)	$ 100,000
2. New Project Cash Operating Expenses (cash outflow)	− 50,000
3. New Project Depreciation Expense (noncash expense)	− 10,000
4. Net New Project Taxable Income	40,000
5. Taxes on New Project Income (25%) (cash outflow)	− 10,000
6. Net New Project After-Tax Income	30,000
7. Plus Depreciation Expense (added back)	+ 10,000
8. Net Incremental Cash Flow	$ 40,000

added the $10,000 depreciation expense back to the new project's after-tax net income to calculate the incremental operating cash flow for this year from the new project. The incremental depreciation expense affected cash flow only because of its effect on taxes.

Opportunity Costs

Sometimes accepting a capital budgeting project precludes other opportunities for the firm. For instance, if an industrial mixer already owned by a toy company is used to make a new product called Slime #4, then that mixer will not be available to make the Slime #2 currently produced in that mixer. The forgone benefits of the alternative not chosen are opportunity costs.

Opportunity costs are incremental cash flows that financial managers consider in a capital budgeting decision. In our example, the opportunity cost comes from the lost use of the industrial mixer for other products our firm makes. If our cash flows decrease by $30,000 due to the decrease in sales of Slime #2 that we can no longer make, then this $30,000 is the opportunity cost of choosing to produce the new product, Slime #4.

Externalities

In estimating incremental operating cash flows, financial managers consider the effect a capital budgeting project might have on cash flows related to other parts of the business. Externalities are the positive or negative effects on existing projects if a new capital budgeting project is accepted.

For instance, suppose that a tennis ball manufacturer decides to start making tennis racquets but does not want to hire any additional managers. The current managers may become overworked because the expansion project requires manager time and oversight. This is a negative externality. Existing projects suffer due to manager inattention, but it is difficult to measure the size of those incremental costs.

On the other hand, the new racquet project may give the company more visibility than it had before and increase sales of its existing tennis ball business, thereby leading to an increase in cash flows. Because these cash flows from the increased tennis ball sales are incremental to the tennis racquet project under consideration, they should be considered in the capital budgeting analysis. This is a positive externality. Here again, however, the positive externalities are likely to be difficult to measure.

If the impact of externalities can be measured, they should be incorporated in the capital budgeting analysis. If the cost of externalities cannot be measured precisely—as is likely the case—most firms use a subjective analysis of externalities before making a project's final accept or reject decision. For example, if the NPV of a project is only slightly greater than zero, company officials may reject the project if they believe significant unmeasured negative externalities are present.

Shutdown Cash Flows

Financial managers estimate the shutdown cash flows that are expected to occur at the end of the useful life of a proposed capital budgeting project. Shutdown cash flows may include those from the project's salvage value, taxes tied to the sale of the used asset, and the reduction of net working capital.

If a project is expected to have a positive salvage value at the end of its useful life, there will be a positive incremental cash flow at that time. However, this salvage value incremental cash flow must be adjusted for tax effects.

Four possible tax scenarios may occur when the used asset is sold, depending on the asset's sale price. First, the asset may be sold for more than its purchase price. In this instance, the difference between the purchase and the sale price is taxed at the capital gains tax rate. (The capital gain is the portion of the sale price that exceeds the purchase price.) In addition, the purchase price minus depreciation book value is taxed at the ordinary income rate.

TABLE 11-3 Tax Effects of the Sale of an Asset at the End of Its Useful Life

Type of Sale	Tax Effect
The asset is sold for more than its purchase gains rate.	This difference is taxed at the capital gains rate. In addition, the purchase price minus the depreciation book value is ordinary income and is taxed at the ordinary rate.
The asset is sold for less than its purchase price but for more than its depreciation book value.	The sales price minus the depreciation book value is ordinary income and is taxed at the ordinary income tax rate.
The asset is sold for its depreciation book value.	There is no tax effect.
The asset is sold for less than its depreciation book value.	The depreciation book value minus the sales price is an ordinary loss and reduces the firm's tax liability by that amount times the ordinary income tax rate.

Second, the asset may be sold for less than the purchase price but for more than its depreciation book value. The amount that the sales price exceeds the depreciation book value is ordinary income, so it is taxed at the ordinary income tax rate.

Third, the asset may be sold for its depreciation book value. In that case, the asset sale has no tax effects.

Fourth, the asset may be sold for less than its depreciation book value. The amount by which the depreciation book value exceeds the sales price is an ordinary loss. The firm's tax liability is reduced by the amount of the loss times the ordinary income tax rate.

The situation is summarized in Table 11-3.

Financing Cash Flows

Suppose a company planned to borrow or sell new common stock to raise part or all of the funds needed for a proposed capital budgeting project. The company would receive a cash inflow on receipt of the loan or the sale of new common stock. Conversely, the company must make the interest and principal payments on the loan, or may make dividend payments to stockholders. Financing cash flows are the cash outflows that occur as creditors are paid interest and principal, and stockholders are paid dividends.

If a capital budgeting project is rejected, financing cash flows will not occur, so they are relevant cash flows in the capital budgeting decision. However, as we saw in Chapter 10, financing costs are factored into the discount rate (required rate of return) in the NPV calculation. Those costs are also included in the hurdle rate of the IRR decision rule. Therefore, to avoid double counting, we do not include financing costs in our operating incremental cash flow estimates when we make capital budgeting decisions. If we did include financing costs as part of the incremental operating cash flows, then the NPV or IRR analysis would be distorted. That distortion could lead in turn to a poor capital budgeting decision.

Figure 11-1 summarizes the cash flow estimation process and its role in capital budgeting.

Incremental Cash Flows of an Expansion Project

To practice capital budgeting cash flow estimation, let's examine a proposed expansion project. An expansion project is one in which the company adds a project and does not replace an existing one. Imagine a company called Photon Manufacturing, which makes torpedoes. It is considering a project to install $2.5 million worth of new machine tools in its main plant. The new tools are expected to last for five years. Photon operations management

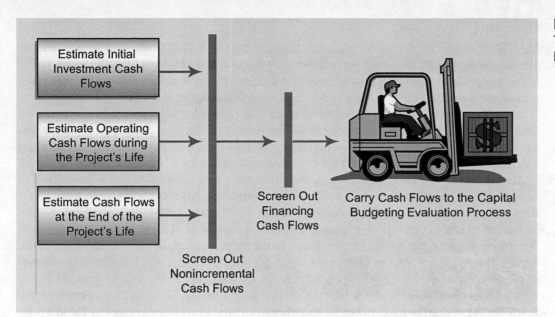

FIGURE 11-1
The Cash Flow Estimation
Process

and marketing experts estimate that during those five years the tools will result in a sales increase of $800,000 per year.

The Photon Manufacturing CEO has asked Mr. Sulu, the company CFO, to identify all incremental cash flows associated with the project and to calculate the project's NPV and IRR. Based on the incremental cash flow analysis and Sulu's recommendation, the company will make an accept or reject decision about the project.

Sulu's first step is to identify the relevant (incremental) cash flows associated with the project. He begins with the initial investment in the project, then looks at the operating cash flows, and finally the shutdown cash flows.

Initial Investment Cash Flows

The cash flows that will occur as soon as the project is implemented (at t_0) make up the project's initial investment. The initial investment includes the cash outflows for the purchase price, installation, delivery, and increase in net working capital.

Sulu knows that its tool supplier gave Photon a bid of $2.5 million to cover the cost of the new tools, including setup and delivery. Photon inventory and accounting specialists estimate that if the tools are purchased, inventory will need to increase by $40,000, accounts receivable by $90,000, and cash by $10,000. This is a $140,000 increase in current assets (working capital).

Also, Photon experts estimate that if the tools are purchased, accounts payable will increase by $20,000 as larger orders are placed with suppliers, and accruals (wages and taxes) will increase by $10,000—a $30,000 increase in current liabilities. Subtracting the increases in current liabilities from the increases in current assets ($140,000 – $30,000) results in a $110,000 increase in net working capital associated with the expansion project.

Sulu concludes after extensive research that he has found all the initial investment incremental cash flows. Those cash flows are summarized in Table 11-4.

TABLE 11-4 Photon Manufacturing Expansion Project Initial Investment Incremental Cash Flows at t_0

	Cost of Tools and Setup	$ 2,500,000
+	Investment in Additional NWC	110,000
=	Total Initial Cash Outlay	$ 2,610,000

Operating Cash Flows

Now Sulu examines the operating cash flows, those cash flows expected to occur from operations during the five-year period after the project is implemented (at t_1 through t_5). The Photon expansion project operating cash flows reflect changes in sales, operating expenses, and depreciation tax effects. We assume these cash flows occur at the end of each year.

Sulu learns from the vice president of sales that cash sales are expected to increase by $800,000 per year because the new tools will increase manufacturing capacity. If purchased, the tools will be used to perform maintenance on other equipment at Photon, so operating expenses (other than depreciation) are expected to decrease by $100,000 per year.

Depreciation is a noncash expense, but remember that Sulu must use depreciation to compute the change in income tax that Photon must pay. After taxes are computed, Sulu then will add back the change in depreciation in the operating cash flow analysis.

To calculate depreciation expense, Sulu looks at MACRS depreciation rules and finds that the new manufacturing tools are in the three-year asset class. According to the MACRS rules, 33.3 percent of the new tools' $2.5 million cost will be charged to depreciation expense in the tools' first year of service, 44.5 percent in the second year, 14.8 percent in the third year, and 7.4 percent in the fourth year.[1] Now Sulu summarizes the incremental operating cash flows for the Photon capital budgeting project in Table 11-5.

Sulu is not quite through yet. He must include in his analysis additional shutdown cash flows that occur at t_5, the end of the project's life.

Shutdown Cash Flows

Photon company experts estimate that the actual economic life of the tools will be five years, after which time the tools should have a salvage value of $800,000. Under MACRS depreciation rules, assets are depreciated to zero at the end of their class life, so at t_5 the book value of the new tools is zero. Therefore, if the tools are sold at the end of year 5 for their salvage value of $800,000, Photon Manufacturing will realize a taxable gain on the sale of the tools of $800,000 ($800,000 − $0 = $800,000). The income tax on the gain at Photon's marginal tax rate of 25 percent will be $800,000 × .25 = $200,000.

TABLE 11-5 Photon Manufacturing Expansion Project Incremental Operating Cash Flows, Years 1–5

		t_1	t_2	t_3	t_4	t_5
+	Change in Sales	+ 800,000	800,000	800,000	800,000	800,000
+	Reduction in Nondepreciation Operating Expenses	+ 100,000	100,000	100,000	100,000	100,000
−	Change in Depreciation Exp.	− 832,500	1,112,500	370,000	185,000	0
=	Change in Operating Income	= 67,500	(212,500)	530,000	715,000	900,000
−	Incremental tax from New Income (See Note)	− 16,875	(53,125)	132,500	178,750	225,000
=	Change in Earnings After Taxes	= 50,625	(159,375)	397,500	536,250	675,000
+	Add Back Change in Dep. Expense	+ 832,500	1,112,500	370,000	185,000	0
=	Net Incremental Operating Cash Flow	= 883,125	953,125	767,500	721,250	675,000

Note: The change in taxes at t_2 is negative, which means the change in earnings after taxes on the line above for that year is increased by the amount of the taxes saved. The negative incremental operating income in year 2 of ($212,500) causes a decrease in the taxes Photon owes during year two of $53,125, due to the value of the offset of this amount against taxable income elsewhere in the company.

---

1. Depreciation expenses for the tools are spread over four years instead of three because the MACRS depreciation rules apply a half-year convention—all assets are assumed to be purchased and sold halfway through the first and last years, respectively. If an asset with a three-year life is assumed to be purchased halfway through year 1, then the three years will be complete halfway through year 4.

The net amount of cash that Photon will receive from the sale of the tools is the salvage value minus the tax paid:

$800,000	Salvage Value
− 200,000	Taxes Paid
$600,000	Net Proceeds

The net proceeds from the tool sale at the end of year 5, then, are $600,000.

Finally, if the new tools are sold at t_5, Sulu concludes (based on sales department information) that Photon's sales will return to the level they were before the new tools were installed. Consequently, there will be no further need for the additional investment in net working capital that was made at t_0. When the $110,000 investment in net working capital is recaptured,[2] that amount is recovered in the form of a positive cash flow.

The additional incremental cash flows from the sale of the tools and the change in net working capital are summarized in Table 11-6.

Cash Flow Summary and Valuation

Tables 11-4, 11-5, and 11-6 contain all the incremental cash flows associated with Photon Manufacturing's proposed expansion project. Sulu's next step is to summarize the total incremental net cash flows occurring at each point in time in one table. Table 11-7 shows the results.

Table 11-7 contains the bottom-line net incremental cash flows associated with Photon's proposed expansion project. The initial cash flow at t_0 is –$2,610,000. The operating cash flows from t_1 to t_5 total $4,490,000. The sum of all the incremental positive and negative cash flows for the project is $1,380,000.

Now Sulu is ready to compute the NPV, IRR, and MIRR of the expansion project based on the procedures described in Chapter 10.

Assuming that Photon's discount rate is 10 percent, Sulu computes the NPV of the project using Equation 10-1 as follows:

For more, see 8e Spreadsheet Templates for *Microsoft Excel*.

Initial Investment at t_0: $2,610,000

Net Incremental Cash Flows:

t_1	t_2	t_3	t_4	t_5
$883,125	$953,125	$767,500	$721,250	$1,385,000

$$NPV = \left(\frac{\$883,125}{(1 + .10)^1}\right) + \left(\frac{\$953,125}{(1 + .10)^2}\right) + \left(\frac{\$767,500}{(1 + .10)^3}\right) + \left(\frac{\$721,250}{(1 + .10)^4}\right) + \left(\frac{\$1,385,000}{(1 + .10)^5}\right) - \$2,610,000$$

$$= \frac{\$883,125}{1.1} + \frac{\$953,125}{1.21} + \frac{\$767,500}{1.331} + \frac{\$721,250}{1.4641} + \frac{\$1,385,000}{1.61051} - \$2,610,000$$

$$= \$802,841 + \$787,707 + \$576,634 + \$492,623 + \$859,976 - \$2,610,000$$

$$= \$909,781$$

TABLE 11-6 Photon Manufacturing Expansion Project Shutdown Cash Flows at t_5

	Salvage Value	800,000
−	Taxes on Salvage Value	− 200,000
=	Net Cash Inflow from Sale of Tools	= 600,000
+	Cash from Reduction in NWC	+ 110,000
=	Total Additional Cash Flows at t_5	= 710,000

---

2. Current assets, in the amount by which they exceed current liabilities, are sold and not replaced because they are no longer needed.

TABLE 11-7 Photon Manufacturing Expansion Project Summary of Incremental Cash Flows

	t_0	t_1	t_2	t_3	t_4	t_5
For Purchase and Setup	(2,500,000)					
For Additional NWC	(110,000)					
From Operating Cash Flows		883,125	953,125	767,500	721,250	675,000
From Salvage Value Less Taxes						600,000
From Reducing NWC						110,000
Net Incremental Cash Flows	(2,610,000)	883,125	953,125	767,500	721,250	1,385,000

Assuming a discount rate of 10 percent, the NPV of the project is $909,781.

Next, Sulu uses Equation 10-2 and the trial-and-error method described in Chapter 10 to find the IRR of the project:

D8		✕ ✓ fx	=IRR(C8:C13)		

	A	B	C	D	E	F
1						
2			**The IRR Approach**			
3	This Excel template shows how to calculate the IRR of the Sulu investment project.					
4	The initial cash flow of -$2,610,000 is specified as the first agument for the IRR function					
5	followed by the positive values for the end of years 1 - 5.					
6						
7		End of Year	Cash Flows	IRR		
8		0	-$2,610,000	22.26% <- Formula		
9		1	$883,125			
10		2	$953,125			
11		3	$767,500			
12		4	$721,250			
13		5	$1,385,000			
14						

$$\text{NPV} = 0 = \frac{\text{CF}_1}{(1 + k)^1} + \frac{\text{CF}_2}{(1 + k)^2} + \frac{\text{CF}_3}{(1 + k)^3} + \frac{\text{CF}_4}{(1 + k)^4} + \frac{\text{CF}_5}{(1 + k)^5} - \text{Initial Investment}$$

$$0 = \frac{\$883,125}{(1 + k)^1} + \frac{\$953,125}{(1 + k)^2} + \frac{\$767,500}{(1 + k)^3} + \frac{\$721,250}{(1 + k)^4} + \frac{\$1,385,000}{(1 + k)^5} - \$2,610,000$$

If you insert the 22.26% rate found with the IRR function, expressed as a decimal, we can see that the NPV ≈ $0

$$0 \approx \frac{\$883,125}{(1 + .2226)^1} + \frac{\$953,125}{(1 + .2226)^2} + \frac{\$767,500}{(1 + .2226)^3} + \frac{\$721,250}{(1 + .2226)^4} + \frac{\$1,385,000}{(1 + .2226)^5} - \$2,610,000$$

Therefore IRR = .2226, or 22.26%. You get an NPV value equal to $0.00 if you use a discount rate of 22.2564192. Therefore, that is the IRR value computed to seven decimal places.

Finally, Sulu uses the method described in Chapter 10 to find the MIRR of the project:

Time	Cash Flow	FV of Cash Flow at t_5 if Reinvested @ 10% Cost of Capital (per Equation 8-1a)
t_1	$ 883,125	x $(1 + .10)^4$ = $ 1,292,983
t_2	$ 953,125	x $(1 + .10)^3$ = $ 1,286,609
t_3	$ 767,500	x $(1 + .10)^2$ = $ 928,675
t_4	$ 721,250	x $(1 + .10)^1$ = $ 793,375
t_5	$ 1,385,000	x $(1 + .10)^0$ = $ 1,385,000
		Terminal Value: $ 5,686,642
		Initial Investment: $ 2,610,000

MIRR per Equation 8-8:

$$k = \left(\frac{\$5,686,642}{\$2,610,000} \right)^{\frac{1}{5}} - 1$$

$$k = .1685, \text{ therefor MIRR} = .1685 \text{ or } 16.85\%$$

Because the project's NPV of $909,781 is positive, the IRR of 22.26 percent exceeds the required rate of return of 10 percent, and the MIRR of 16.85 percent exceeds the required rate of return, Sulu will recommend that Photon proceed with the expansion project.

In this discussion, we examined how a firm determines the incremental costs of an expansion project, and the project's NPV, IRR, and MIRR. We turn next to replacement projects and their incremental costs.

Asset Replacement Decisions

Often a company considers replacing existing equipment with new equipment. A replacement decision is a capital budgeting decision to purchase a new asset and replace and retire an old asset, or to keep the old asset. Financial managers identify the *differences* between the company's cash flows with the old asset versus the company's cash flows if the new asset is purchased and the old asset retired. As illustrated in Figure 11-2, these differences are the incremental cash flows of the proposed new project.

Real Options

Externalities and opportunity costs are not the only elements of the capital budgeting decision that are difficult to reduce to an incremental cash flow estimate. Many projects have options embedded in them that add to the value of the project and, therefore, of the firm. For example, a project may provide management with the option to revise a capital budgeting project at a later date. This characteristic is called a real option. It is a real option because it is related to a real asset such as a piece of equipment or a new plant. You may already be familiar with financial options (calls and puts) that give the holder the opportunity to buy or sell financial assets such as stocks or bonds at a later date. Real options are similar except that their value is related to the value of real assets rather than to the value of financial assets. Note that the word *option* indicates that the future alternative does not have to be taken. It will be taken only if it is seen as adding value.

The flexibility that is provided by a real option to revise a project at a later date has value. This option may be to expand a project, to abandon it, to create another project that is an offshoot of the current project, or something else. For example, a restaurant with room to expand is more valuable than one that is confined to its original fixed space, other things being equal. A project that can be shut down before its scheduled useful life if it turns out to be a failure is more valuable, other things being equal, than a similar failed project that must continue operating while it is losing money. An investment in a research

For more, see 8e Spreadsheet Templates for *Microsoft Excel.*

FIGURE 11-2
Comparing Cash Flows: Replacing an Asset vs. Keeping It

Figure 11-2 illustrates how firms compare the difference between the cash flows of replacing an old asset with a new one or keeping the old asset.

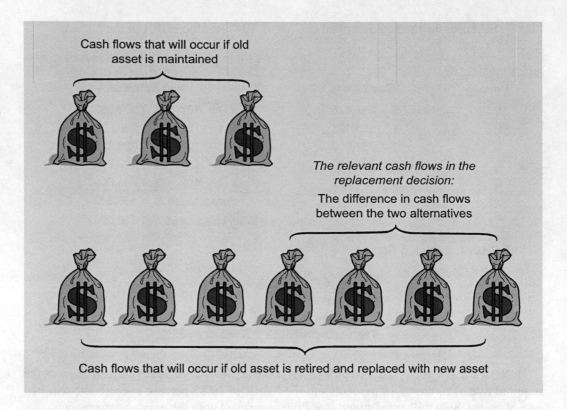

Cash flows that will occur if old asset is maintained

The relevant cash flows in the replacement decision:

The difference in cash flows between the two alternatives

Cash flows that will occur if old asset is retired and replaced with new asset

laboratory that is working on a new drug that might open the door to other drugs that treat other conditions would be more valuable than a research lab that was working on just one drug without any spinoff potential.

Traditional NPV and IRR analysis often overlooks the value that may come from real options because this value cannot be reduced to a simple incremental cash flow estimate. Faced with this difficulty, managers usually omit from capital budgeting analysis real options that are part of a project. This causes the NPV and IRR figures to be understated. As a result, the value real options add to the firm and the increase in the project rates of return they provide are not recognized.

The NPV process can be modified to reflect the value that real options add to the firm. This involves computing the traditional NPV and then adding today's value of any real options that may be present. The following paragraphs illustrate the mechanics of the process.

Real options can be incorporated into the capital budgeting process by using *decision trees*. Decision trees show the different paths a project could take, including the various options that may be available. Each place at which the decision tree branches is called a node. There are two kinds of nodes, decision nodes and outcome nodes.

- A decision node is one that shows the alternatives available for management at that point in time.

- An outcome node is one that shows the various things that can happen once a decision path is chosen.

Let's go through an NPV analysis using a decision tree and real options to illustrate how the process works. Suppose that Jason and Jennifer are business partners who think their hometown of Fort Fun would support a new Mexican restaurant, which they have decided to call Super Marg. Figure 11-3 shows the decision tree for Super Marg Mexican Restaurant. In Figure 11-3, A, C, and D are decision nodes, whereas B and E are outcome nodes.

Jason and Jennifer's first expenditure is the $250,000 investment required to build the restaurant. This initial cash outflow is shown at the left side of Figure 11-3. This is decision node A. Once the new restaurant is built, customers will determine how successful it is. According to Jason and Jennifer's estimates, the probability is 3 that it will be a smash hit, 6

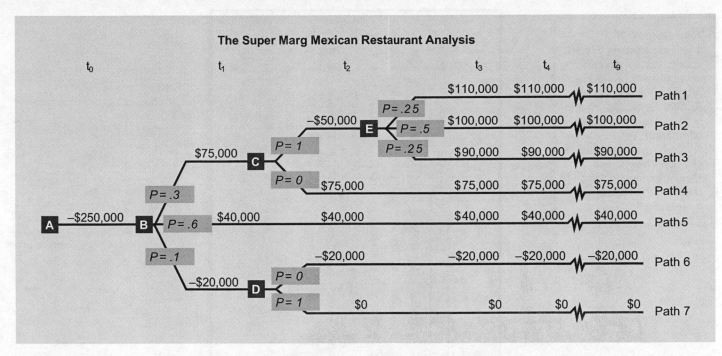

FIGURE 11-3 A Real Options Decision Tree

that it will be moderately successful, and .1 that it will be a bomb. Outcome node B shows these three possibilities. Note that all the probabilities associated with a node must sum to 1.0. If the restaurant is a smash hit, operating cash flows of $75,000 in year 1 are expected. If it is a smash hit, Jason and Jennifer will expand the business after one year of operation, making an additional investment of $50,000 at t_2. Decision node C indicates where the management decision to expand the business would be made. Paths 1, 2, and 3 show the possible outcomes if the business is expanded. Path 4 indicates the path that would not be taken if the expansion option is pursued. Jason and Jennifer can do better than this if the restaurant is a smash hit.

After expansion, the probability is .25 that subsequent operating cash flows will be $110,000, .50 that they will be $100,000, and .25 that they will be $90,000. Each of these cash flow streams would continue for seven years, until t_9. Outcome node E in Figure 11-3 shows these three possibilities. If the restaurant is moderately successful, operating cash flows of $40,000 per year for nine years are expected. Path 5 shows this cash flow stream.

If the restaurant is a bomb, an operating cash flow of –$20,000 at (subscript) is expected. This outcome would cause Jason and Jennifer to abandon the business after one year. Decision node D shows this abandonment option. Note that the probability is 1.0 that Jason and Jennifer will abandon the project if cash flows in t_1 are –$20,000. Path 6 shows the negative cash flows from t_2 to t_9 that are avoided if the project is abandoned. Path 7 shows the $0 cash flows that are preferred to the $20,000 cash flows that would have occurred.

Once all the decisions, outcomes, and probabilities are plotted on the decision tree, the net present value and joint probability of each path can be computed. Note in Figure 11-3 that there are seven possible paths the operation can take. The probabilities associated with each possible path are multiplied together to give a joint probability for that path. The sum of the joint probabilities is 1.0. When the net present value for each path is multiplied by its joint probability and these results added, the expected net present value for the entire deal is obtained.

Table 11-8 shows the NPV calculations for the Super Marg Restaurant project, assuming that Jason and Jennifer's required rate of return is 10 percent. The NPV of each of the seven paths is calculated using Equation 10-1a. In the far right-hand column of Table 11-8, the NPVs of each path are multiplied by the joint probability of that path occurring to give a composite score for each path called the *product*. The sum of the products, $15,161, is the expected NPV of the project. Because the expected NPV is greater than zero, the project would be accepted. Note that Path 5 has a higher probability than any of the other six paths, and it has a negative NPV. The overall expected NPV is positive, however, due to the very good outcomes from Paths 1–3.

TABLE 11-8 Real Options NPV Analysis for the Super Marg Mexican Restaurant

Real Options NPV Analysis				Cash Flows							Joint Probability of Occurrence	NPV	Product
	t_0	t_1	t_2	t_3	t_4	t_5	t_6	t_7	t_8	t_9			
Path 1	($250,000)	$75,000	($50,000)	$110,000	$110,000	$110,000	$110,000	$110,000	$110,000	$110,000	0.075	$219,443	$16,458
Path 2	($250,000)	$75,000	($50,000)	$100,000	$100,000	$100,000	$100,000	$100,000	$100,000	$100,000	0.15	$179,208	$26,881
Path 3	($250,000)	$75,000	($50,000)	$90,000	$90,000	$90,000	$90,000	$90,000	$90,000	$90,000	0.075	$138,973	$10,423
Path 4	($250,000)	$75,000	$75,000	$75,000	$75,000	$75,000	$75,000	$75,000	$75,000	$75,000	$0	$181,927	$0
Path 5	($250,000)	$40,000	$40,000	$40,000	$40,000	$40,000	$40,000	$40,000	$40,000	$40,000	0.60	($19,639)	($11,783)
Path 6	($250,000)	($20,000)	($20,000)	($20,000)	($20,000)	($20,000)	($20,000)	($20,000)	($20,000)	($20,000)	0	($365,180)	$0
Path 7	($250,000)	($20,000)	$0	$0	$0	$0	$0	$0	$0	$0	0.1	($268,182)	($26,818)

Sum = 1.0   Exp NPV = $15,161

Required rate of return (k) = 10%

What's Next

In this chapter, we learned how financial managers estimate incremental cash flows as part of the capital budgeting process. We described the difference between sunk costs and incremental cash flows. We also discussed various types of incremental cash flows. In Chapter 12, we examine business valuation.

Summary

1. *Explain the difference between incremental cash flows and sunk costs.*

   Incremental cash flows are the cash flows that will occur if a capital budgeting project is accepted. They will not occur if the investment is rejected. Sunk costs are costs that will occur whether a project is accepted or rejected. Financial managers must screen out sunk costs from the capital budgeting analysis to prevent distortion in cash flow estimates. Any distortion in these estimates will, in turn, lead to inaccurate NPV or IRR values and could result in poor capital budgeting decisions.

2. *Identify types of incremental cash flows in a capital budgeting project.*

   Financial managers must examine three main types of cash flows to estimate the incremental cash flows of a proposed capital budgeting project. First, they must assess the cost of the initial investment: the purchase price, the installation and delivery costs, and any change in net working capital. Then the financial manager must analyze incremental operating cash flows. These may include tax changes due to changes in sales and depreciation expense, opportunity costs, and externalities. Finally, a financial manager must examine the project shutdown cash flows, such as those cash flows from the project's salvage value, the reduction of net working capital, and the tax-related cash flows from the sale of the used asset.

3. *Explain why cash flows associated with project financing are not included in incremental cash flow estimates.*

   Incremental operating cash flows are treated separately from incremental financing cash flows. The latter are captured in the discount rate used in the NPV calculation and in the hurdle rate used when applying the IRR decision rule. Financial managers do not include financing costs as incremental operating cash flows to avoid distorting the NPV or IRR calculations in the capital budgeting process. Double counting would result if financing costs were reflected in both the operating cash flows and the discount rate.

Self-Test

ST-1. Fat Tire Corporation had $20,000 in depreciation expense last year. Assume a joint federal and state marginal tax rate of 25 percent. How much are the firm's taxes reduced (and cash flow increased) by the depreciation deduction on federal and state income tax returns?

ST-2. Left Hand Corporation had net income of $2 million and depreciation expense of $400,000. What was the firm's operating cash flow for the year?

ST-3. Powder Hound Ski Company is considering the purchase of a new helicopter for $1.5 million. The company paid an aviation consultant $20,000 to advise them on the need for a new helicopter. The decision about buying the helicopter hasn't been made yet. If it is purchased, what is the total initial cash outlay that will be used in the NPV calculation?

ST-4. Rich Folks Ski Area is considering the replacement of one of its older ski lifts. By replacing the lift, Rich Folks expects sales revenues to increase by $500,000 per year. Maintenance expenses are expected to increase by $75,000 per year if the new lift is purchased. Depreciation expense would be $100,000 per year. (The company uses the straight-line method.) The old lift has been fully depreciated. The firm's marginal tax rate is 25 percent. What would the firm's incremental annual operating cash flows be if the new lift is purchased?

ST-5. Snorkel Ski Company is considering the replacement of its aerial tram. Sales are expected to increase by $900,000 per year, and depreciation expense is also expected to rise by $300,000 per year. The marginal tax rate is 25 percent. The purchase will be financed with a $900,000 bond issue carrying a 10 percent annual interest rate. What are the annual incremental operating cash flows if this project is accepted?

Review Questions

1. Why do we focus on cash flows instead of profits when evaluating proposed capital budgeting projects?

2. What is a sunk cost? Is it relevant when evaluating a proposed capital budgeting project? Explain.

3. How do we estimate expected incremental cash flows for a proposed capital budgeting project?

4. What role does depreciation play in estimating incremental cash flows?

5. How and why does working capital affect the incremental cash flow estimation for a proposed large capital budgeting project? Explain.

6. How do opportunity costs affect the capital budgeting decision-making process?

7. How are financing costs generally incorporated into the capital budgeting analysis process?

Build Your Communication Skills

CS-1. Pick a company and obtain a copy of its recent income statement, balance sheet, and statement of cash flows. Compare its profit and cash flow for the period covered by the income statement. Use the statement of cash flows to describe where the firm's cash came from and where it went during that period. Examine the balance sheet to assess the cash position of the firm at that point in time. Submit a written report that analyzes the firm's cash position.

CS-2. Stock market analysts often compare a firm's reported quarterly earnings and its expected quarterly earnings. Quarterly earnings that come in below expectations often mean a drop in the stock price, whereas better than expected earnings usually mean a stock price increase. Is this consistent with the view that cash flows and not accounting profits are the source of firm value? Divide into small groups and discuss these issues with the group members for 15 minutes. Select a spokesperson to present the group's key points to the class.

Problems

Expansion Project, Initial Investment Cash Flows

 11-1. Tru-Green Landscaping is shopping for a new lawn mower. The purchase price of the model the company has selected is $6,000. However, Tru-Green plans to add some special attachments that will cost $5,000, and painting the company's name on the side of the mower will cost $300. Building a garage and maintenance facility for the mower and several other items of new equipment will cost $12,000. What is the total cash outflow at t_0 for the mower?

Salvage Value Cash Flows

 11-2. An asset falling under the MACRS five-year class was purchased three years ago for $200,000 (its original depreciation basis). Calculate the cash flows if the asset is sold now at

a. $60,000

b. $80,000

Assume the applicable tax rate is 25 percent.

Operating Cash Flows

 11-3. Marshall Mathers is evaluating the purchase of new trenching equipment for Scorpio Enterprises. For now, he is only figuring the incremental operating cash flow from the proposed project for the first year. Mathers estimates that the firm's sales of earth-moving services will increase by $10,000 in year 1. Using the new equipment will add an additional $3,000 to their operating expenses. Interest expense will increase by $100 because the machine will be partly financed by a loan from the bank. The additional depreciation expense for the new machine will be $2,000. Scorpio Enterprises' marginal tax rate is 25 percent.

a. Calculate the change in operating income (EBIT) for year 1.

b. Calculate the cash outflow for taxes associated with this new income.

c. What is the net new after-tax income (change in earnings after taxes)?

d. Calculate the net incremental operating cash flow from this project for year 1.

e. Are there any expenses listed that you did not use when estimating the net incremental cash flow? Explain.

Expansion Project, Operating Cash Flows

 11-4. Calvin Broadus owns a golf course and bought a lawn mower for $20,000. With this new machine, the company was able to increase its business, raising its annual revenue from $250,000 to $350,000 each year. Operating costs went up as well, however, from $70,000 to $100,000 annually. The mower falls in the MACRS five-year class for depreciation expense, and the company's combined federal and state income tax rate is 21 percent. What is the net incremental operating cash flow in year 1 for the new lawn mower investment?

11-5. Never Brown Landscaping has a lawn mower that it bought three years ago for $10,000. The mower has an actual operating life of six years, at the end of which the mower can be sold for $2,000. For depreciation purposes, the mower is in the MACRS five-year class. Never Brown's combined federal and state income tax rate is 25 percent. What are the terminal cash flows associated with the mower investment?

Expansion Project, Terminal Cash Flows

11-6. Andre Young, a financial analyst at Rhodes Manufacturing Corporation, is trying to analyze the feasibility of purchasing a new piece of equipment that falls under the MACRS five-year class. The initial investment, including the cost of equipment and its start-up, would be $375,000. Over the next six years, the following earnings before depreciation and taxes (EBDT) will be generated from using this equipment:

Estimating Cash Flows

End of Year	EBDT ($)
1	120,000
2	90,000
3	70,000
4	70,000
5	70,000
6	70,000

For more, see 8e Spreadsheet Templates for *Microsoft Excel.*

Rhodes's discount rate is 13 percent and the company is in the 40 percent tax bracket. There is no salvage value at the end of year 6. Should Mr. Young recommend acceptance of the project?

11-7. Assume the same cash flows, initial investment, MACRS class, discount rate, and income tax rate as given in problem 11-6. Now assume that the resale value of the equipment at the end of six years will be $50,000. Calculate the NPV and recommend whether the project should be accepted.

Estimating Cash Flows

For more, see 8e Spreadsheet Templates for *Microsoft Excel.*

11-8. George Kaplan is considering adding a new crop-dusting plane to his fleet at North Corn Corner, Inc. The new plane will cost $85,000. He anticipates spending an additional $20,000 immediately after the purchase to modify it for crop-dusting. Kaplan plans to use the plane for five years and then sell it. He estimates that the salvage value will be $20,000. With the addition of the new plane, Kaplan estimates revenue in the first year will increase by 10 percent over last year. Revenue last year was $125,000. Other first-year expenses are also expected to increase. Operating expenses will increase by $20,000, and depreciation expense will increase by $10,500. Kaplan's marginal tax rate is 40 percent.

Initial Investment, Operating Cash Flows, and Salvage Value

a. For capital budgeting purposes, what is the net cost of the plane? Or, stated another way, what is the initial net cash flow?

b. Calculate the net incremental operating cash flow for year 1.

c. In which year would the salvage value affect the net cash flow calculations?

11-9. Ghost Squadron Historical Aircraft, Inc. (GSHAI) is considering adding a rare World War II B-24 bomber to its collection of vintage aircraft. The plane was forced down in Burma in 1942, and it has remained there ever since. Flying a crew to Burma and collecting the wreckage will cost $100,000. Transporting all the parts to the company's restoration facility in Texas will cost another $35,000. Restoring the plane to flyable condition will cost an additional $600,000 at t_0.

Evaluating an Expansion Project

GSHAI's operating costs will increase by $40,000 a year at the end of years 1 through 7 (on top of the restoration costs). At the end of years 3 through 7, revenues from exhibiting the plane at airshows will be $70,000. At the end of year 7, the plane will be retired. At that time, the plane will be sold to a museum for $500,000.

For more, see 8e Spreadsheet Templates for *Microsoft Excel.*

The plane falls into the MACRS depreciation class for seven-year assets. GSHAI's combined federal and state income tax rate is 35 percent, and the company's weighted average cost of capital is 12 percent. Calculate the NPV and IRR of the proposed investment in the plane.

**Changes in Net
Working Capital**

11-10. The management of the local cotton mill is evaluating the replacement of low-wage workers by automated machines. If this project is adopted, production and sales are expected to increase significantly: Norma Rae, the mill's financial analyst, expects cash will have to increase by $8,000 and the accounts receivable will increase by $10,000 in response to the increase in sales volume. Because of the higher level of production, inventory will have to increase by $12,000, with an associated $6,000 increase in accounts payable. Accrued taxes and wages, even with the decrease in the number of laborers, are estimated to increase by $2,500.

a. Calculate the change in net working capital if the automation project is adopted.

b. Is this change in NWC a cash inflow or outflow?

c. Given the limited information about the duration of the project, in what year should this change affect the net incremental cash flow calculations?

**Cash Flows and
Capital Budgeting**

For more, see 8e
Spreadsheet Templates
for *Microsoft Excel.*

11-11. Kendrick Duckworth has entrusted financial analyst Flower Belle Lee with the evaluation of a project that involves buying a new asset at a cost of $90,000. The asset falls under the MACRS three-year class and will generate the following revenue stream:

End of Year	1	2	3	4
Revenues ($)	50,000	30,000	20,000	20,000

The asset has a resale value of $10,000 at the end of the fourth year. Duckworth's discount rate is 11 percent. The company has an income tax rate of 30 percent. Should Flower recommend purchase of the asset?

**Replacement
Decision and
Cash Flows**

For more, see 8e
Spreadsheet Templates
for *Microsoft Excel.*

11-12. Moonstone, Inc., a competitor of Duckworth in problem 11-11, is considering purchasing similar equipment with the same revenue, initial investment, MACRS class, and resale value. Moonstone's discount rate is 10 percent and its income tax rate is 40 percent. However, Moonstone is considering the new asset to replace an existing asset with a book value of $20,000 and a resale value of $10,000. What would be the NPV of the replacement project?

**Changes in Net
Working Capital**

For more, see 8e
Spreadsheet Templates
for *Microsoft Excel.*

11-13. You have just joined Moonstone, Inc. as its new financial analyst. You have learned that accepting the project described in problem 11-12 will require an increase of $10,000 in current assets and will increase current liabilities by $5,000. The investment in net working capital will be recovered at the end of year 4. What would be the new NPV of the project?

Challenge Problem

For more, see 8e
Spreadsheet Templates
for *Microsoft Excel.*

11-14. You have been hired by Egon Spengler, Peter Venkman, and Ray Stantz to help them with NPV analysis for a replacement project. These three New York City parapsychologists need to replace their existing supernatural beings detector with the new, upgraded model. They have calculated all the necessary figures but are unsure about how to account for the sale of their old machine. The original depreciation basis of the old machine is $20,000, and the accumulated depreciation is $12,000 at the date of the sale. They can sell the old machine for $18,000 cash. Assume the tax rate for their company is 30 percent.

a. What is the book value of the old machine?

b. What is the taxable gain (loss) on the sale of the old equipment?

c. Calculate the tax on the gain (loss).

d. What is the net cash flow from the sale of the old equipment? Is this a cash inflow or an outflow?

e. Assume the new equipment costs $40,000 and they do not expect a change in net working capital. Calculate the incremental cash flow for t_0.

f. Assume they could only sell the old equipment for $6,000 cash. Recalculate parts *b* through *e*.

11-15. Mitch and Lydia Brenner own a small factory located in Bodega Bay, California. They manufacture rubber snakes used to scare birds away from houses, gardens, and playgrounds. The recent and unexplained increase in the bird population in northern California has significantly increased the demand for the Brenners' products. To take advantage of this marketing opportunity, they plan to add a new molding machine that will double the output of their existing facility. The cost of the new machine is $20,000. The machine setup fee is $2,000. With this purchase, current assets must increase by $5,000 and current liabilities will increase by $3,000. The economic life of the new machine is four years, and it falls under the MACRS three-year depreciation schedule. The machine is expected to be obsolete at the end of the fourth year and have no salvage value.

Cash Flows and
Capital Budgeting

The Brenners anticipate recouping 100 percent of the additional investment in net working capital at the end of year 4. Sales are expected to increase by $20,000 each year in years 1 and 2. By year 3, the Brenners expect sales to be mostly from repeat customers purchasing replacements instead of sales to new customers. Therefore, the increase in sales for years 3 and 4 is estimated to only be $10,000 in each year. The increase in operating expenses is estimated to be 20 percent of the annual change in sales. Assume the marginal tax rate is 40 percent.

For more, see 8e Spreadsheet Templates for *Microsoft Excel.*

a. Calculate the initial net incremental cash flow.

b. Calculate the net incremental operating cash flows for years 1 through 4. Round all calculations to the nearest whole dollar. Use Table 4-1 to calculate the depreciation expense.

c. Assume the Brenners' discount rate is 14 percent. Calculate the net present value of this project. Would you recommend the Brenners add this new machine to their factory?

11-16. The RHPS Corporation specializes in the custom design, cutting, and polishing of stone raw materials to make ornate building facings. These stone facings are commonly used in the restoration of older mansions and estates. Janet Weiss and Brad Majors, managers of the firm, are evaluating the addition of a new stone-cutting machine to their plant. The machine's cost to RHPS is $150,000. Installation and calibration costs will be $7,500. They do not anticipate an increase in sales, but the reduction in the operating expenses is estimated to be $50,000 annually. The machine falls under the MACRS three-year depreciation schedule. The machine is expected to be obsolete after five years. At the end of five years, Weiss and Majors expect the cash received (less applicable capital gains taxes) from the sale of the obsolete machine to offset the shutdown and dismantling costs. The RHPS cost of capital is 10 percent, and the marginal tax rate is 35 percent.

Cash Flows and
Capital Budgeting

For more, see 8e Spreadsheet Templates for *Microsoft Excel.*

a. Calculate the net present value for the addition of this new machine. Round all calculations to the nearest whole dollar.

b. Would you recommend that Weiss and Majors go forward with this project?

11-17. The Chemical Company of Baytown purchased new processing equipment for $40,000 on December 31, 2016. The equipment had an expected life of four years and was classified in the MACRS three-year class. Due to changes in environmental regulations, the operating cost of this equipment has increased. The company is considering replacing this equipment with a more-efficient process line at the end of 2018. The salvage value of the old equipment is estimated to be $4,000. The marginal tax rate is 40 percent.

Comprehensive
Problem

a. Calculate the cash flow from the sale of this equipment. Assume the sale occurred at the end of 2018. Use Table 4-1 to calculate the depreciation.

For more, see 8e Spreadsheet Templates for *Microsoft Excel.*

b. The new process line has a higher capacity than the old one and is expected to boost sales. As a result, the cash requirement will increase by $1,000, accounts receivable by $5,000, and inventory by $10,000. It will also increase accounts payable by $6,000 and accrued expenses by $3,000. Calculate the incremental cash flow due to the change in the net working capital.

c. The new equipment will cost $180,000, including installation and start-up costs. Calculate the net cash outflow at the end of 2018 if the new process line is installed and is ready to operate by the end of the year.

d. Beginning in January 2019, this new equipment is expected to generate additional sales of $60,000 each year for the next four years. It will have an economic life of four years and will fall under the MACRS three-year classification. Being more efficient, the new equipment will reduce yearly operating expenses by $6,000. Calculate the net incremental operating cash flows for 2022 through 2025. Assume the marginal tax rate will remain at 40 percent. Round calculations to the nearest whole dollar.

e. At the end of its economic life, the new process line is expected to be sold for $20,000. The cost of capital for the company is 6 percent. Calculate the net present value and the internal rate of return (only if you have a financial calculator) for this project. Round calculations to the nearest whole dollar. Recommend whether the replacement project should be adopted or rejected. (Hint: Preparation of a summary of incremental cash flows similar to Table 11-5 may be helpful.)

f. Draw an NPV profile for the project.

Real Options Approach

➡

For more, see 8e Spreadsheet Templates for *Microsoft Excel*.

11-18. Joe and Tim are business partners who are considering opening a brewpub in Breckenridge, Colorado. It is to be called J&T's Double Diamond Brewhouse. Joe and Tim's first expenditure is the $300,000 investment required to build the brewpub. Once it is built, customers will determine how successful it is. According to Joe and Tim's estimates, the probabilities are .25 that it will be a smash hit, .50 that it will be moderately successful, and .25 that it will be a bomb.

If the brewpub is a smash hit, operating cash flows of $200,000 at the end of years 1 and 2 are expected. In that case, Joe and Tim will expand the business at the end of year 2 at a cost of $100,000. After expansion, the probabilities are .50 that subsequent operating cash flows at the end of year 3 will be $400,000, .30 that they will be $200,000, and .20 that they will be $90,000. Each of these cash flow streams would continue in years 4 and 5.

If the brewpub is moderately successful, operating cash flows of $100,000 per year at the end of years 1 through 5 are expected.

If the brewpub is a bomb, operating cash flows of –$40,000 per year at the end of years 1 through 5 are expected. This outcome would cause Joe and Tim to abandon the business at the end of year 1. The probability is 1.0 that Joe and Tim will abandon the project if cash flows at the end of year 1 are –$40,000.

a. Plot the decisions, outcomes, and probabilities associated with the new project on a decision tree similar to Figure 11-3.

b. Calculate the NPV and joint probability of each path in the decision tree. Assume that Joe and Tim's required rate of return is 14 percent.

c. Calculate the expected NPV of the entire deal. Again, assume that Joe and Tim's required rate of return is 10 percent.

Answers to Self-Test

ST-1. $20,000 × .25 = $20,000 × .25 = $5,000 tax savings

ST-2. $2,000,000 + $400,000 = $2,400,000 operating cash flow

ST-3. $1,500,000 total initial cash outlay (The $20,000 for the consultant is a sunk cost.)

ST-4. ($500,000 – $75,000 – $100,000) × (1 – .25)

= $325,000 × .75 = $243,750 incremental net income

$243,750 + $100,000 depreciation expense

= $343,750 incremental cash flow

ST-5. ($900,000 – $300,000) × (1 – .25)

= $600,000 × .75 = $450,000 incremental net income

$450,000 + $300,000 depreciation expense

= $750,000 incremental operating cash flow

(The finance costs are not part of operating cash flows. They will be reflected in the required rate of return.)

Business Valuation

"Managers and investors alike must understand that accounting numbers are the beginning, not the end, of business valuation."
—Warren Buffet

CHAPTER 12

Source: gguy/Shutterstock

Learning Objectives

After reading this chapter, you should be able to:

1. Explain the importance of business valuation.
2. Discuss the concept of business valuation.
3. Compute the market value and the yield to maturity of a bond.
4. Calculate the market value and expected yield of preferred stock.
5. Compute the market value per share of common stock.
6. Compute the market value of total common equity.
7. Compute the yield on common stock.
8. Compute the value of a complete business.

Valuing the M&M Mushroom Company

Melissa and Mark were young and in love. They also shared a passion for mushrooms. In fact, they were so passionate about mushrooms they liked to grow them in their basement. They were quite good at it, and often had more mushrooms than they knew what to do with. Then they had the idea of selling their mushrooms to friends and neighbors. This endeavor was successful beyond their wildest dreams and soon they had quite a business going. They expanded out of their basement into dedicated production facilities, incorporated under the name "M&M Mushrooms," and became quite famous in the local area for having the best tasting mushrooms around.

The M&M Mushroom Company grew steadily for ten years, enlarging its sales territory to five states and employing 150 people in three plants. That's when the trouble began. Melissa wanted to keep expending the business, but Mark missed the small, informal operation they used to have years ago. Also, Mark had recently begun taking flying lessons and had developed a close relationship with his flight instructor. Mark and Melissa began spending more and more time apart, and began having more and more disagreements, until it was apparent that everyone would be better off if they went their separate ways.

The divorce was amicable, as Melissa and Mark had no children and the only major assets they owned were their common stock shares in the M&M Mushroom Corporation (Melissa and Mark each owned 50% of the shares outstanding, 500 shares each). Since Melissa wanted to continue managing the business and Mark wanted out, he agreed to sell her his 500 shares. However, they could not agree on a price. Melissa was of the opinion that the shares were worth in the neighborhood of $1,000 each, making the total value of Mark's 500 shares $500,000. Mark disagreed. Pointing to their steady growth during the past ten years, and current wide area of operations, he maintained the shares were worth at least $2,000 each for a total of $1,000,000.

Melissa and Mark could not settle their differences on their own and soon found themselves facing each other in court. The primary issue before the court was to establish the "fair market value" of the shares in question. Each side engaged an expert to provide an opinion on the value of the shares.

Now suppose you were approached by Melissa or Mark's attorney and asked if you would write a report containing an estimate of the fair market value per share of M&M Mushroom company's stock. How would you go about this task? The stock is privately held, and not traded on any stock exchange, so it would appear that you face a formidable task.

The valuation task is formidable, but it is not impossible. Indeed, professional appraisers do it regularly, not only to support opposing sides in court cases, but also to establish a value when the business is to be used for collateral for a loan, an asking price when the sale of the business is contemplated, or a value for tax purposes when the business is a part of an estate settlement.

The techniques appraisers use to estimate market value vary from case to case, but at their heart, they generally involve the calculation of the present value of an assumed set of future cash flows. You are already familiar with this technique from your studies of the time value of money in Chapter 8. In this chapter, we show you how to adapt those techniques specifically to the task of valuing stocks, bonds, and complete businesses.

Chapter Overview

In this chapter, we will discuss how to value businesses in a dynamic marketplace. First, we will investigate the importance of business valuation and introduce a general model that analysts and investors use to value assets. Then we will show how to adapt the model to bonds, preferred stock, and common stock. For common stock, we'll explore additional valuation techniques.

The Importance of Business Valuation

As Chapter 1 explained, the primary financial goal of financial managers is to maximize the market value of their firm. It follows, then, that financial managers need to assess the market value of their firms to gauge progress.

Accurate business valuation is also a concern when a corporation contemplates selling securities to raise long-term funds. Issuers want to raise the most money possible from selling securities. Issuers lose money if they undervalue their businesses. Likewise, would-be purchasers are concerned about businesses' value because they don't want to pay more than what the businesses are worth.

A General Valuation Model

The value of a business depends on its future earning power. To value a business then, we consider three factors that affect future earnings:

- Size of cash flows
- Timing of cash flows
- Risk associated with the cash flows

These three factors also determine the value of individual assets belonging to a business, or interests in a business, such as those possessed by bondholders and stockholders.

In Chapter 7, we examined how risk factors affect an investor's required rate of return. In Chapter 8 we learned that time value of money calculations can determine an investment's value, given the size and timing of the cash flows. In Chapters 9, 10, and 11 we learned how to evaluate future cash flows.

Financial managers determine the value of a business, a business asset, or an interest in a business by finding the present value of the future cash flows that the owner of the business, asset, or interest could expect to receive. For example, we can calculate a bond's value by taking the sum of the present values of each of the future cash flows from the bond's interest and principal payments. We can calculate a stock's value by taking the sum of the present values of future dividend cash flow payments.

Analysts and investors use a general valuation model to calculate the present value of future cash flows of a business, business asset, or business interest. This model, the **discounted cash flow (DCF) model**, is a basic valuation model for an asset that is expected to generate cash payments in the form of cash earnings, interest and principal payments, or dividends. The DCF equation is shown in Equation 12-1:

discounted cash flow (DCF) model A model that estimates the value of an asset by calculating the sum of the present values of all future cash flows.

The Discounted Cash Flow Valuation Model

$$V_0 = \frac{CF_1}{(1 + k)^1} + \frac{CF_2}{(1 + k)^2} + \frac{CF_3}{(1 + k)^3} + \dots + \frac{CF_n}{(1 + k)^n}$$

(12-1)

where: V_0 = Present value of the anticipated cash flows from the asset, its current value

$CF_{1, 2, 3, \text{ and } n}$ = Cash flows expected to be received one, two, three, and so on up to n periods in the future

k = Discount rate, the required rate of return per period

The DCF model values an asset by calculating the sum of the present values of all expected future cash flows.

The discount rate in Equation 12-1 is the investor's required rate of return per time period, which is a function of the risk of the investment. Recall from Chapter 7 that the riskier the security, the higher the required rate of return.

The discounted cash flow model is easy to use if we know the cash flows and discount rate. For example, suppose you were considering purchasing a security that entitled you to receive payments of $100 in one year, another $100 in two years, and $1,000 in three years. If your required rate of return for securities of this type were 20 percent, then we would calculate the value of the security as follows:

$$V_0 = \frac{\$100}{(1 + .20)^1} + \frac{\$100}{(1 + .20)^2} + \frac{\$1,000}{(1 + .20)^3}$$

$$= \$83.3333 + \$69.4444 + \$578.7037$$

$$= \$731.48$$

The total of the security's three future cash flows at a 20 percent required rate of return yields a present value of $731.48.

In the sections that follow, we'll adapt the discounted cash flow valuation model to apply to businesses and business components.

Applying the General Valuation Model to Businesses

According to the general valuation model, Equation 12-1, the value of a business's assets is the present value of the anticipated cash flows from the asset. The value of a complete business, therefore, is the present value of the cash flows expected to be generated by the business. In order to use the general valuation model to estimate the value of a complete business, we must forecast the cash flows expected to be generated by the business and discount them to the present using the required rate of return appropriate for the business. This sounds relatively simple, but in fact, it is an extremely complex task requiring the cash flow estimation techniques that you learned in Chapter 11 and the cost of capital estimation techniques that you learned in Chapter 9.

Instead of tackling the value of a complete business all at once, we will begin with the present values of the components of the business, as illustrated in Figure 12-1.

As Figure 12-1 shows, the value of all of a business's assets (that is, the complete business) equals the sum of the present values of its current liabilities, long-term debt, preferred stock, and common stock. In the remainder of this chapter, we will apply this approach, first examining the valuation of current liabilities and long-term debt (corporate bonds), then preferred stock, and finally common stock. Following those individual discussions, we will show how the same techniques can be used to estimate the total value of a business.

Valuing Current Liabilities and Long-Term Debt

Current liabilities are short-term obligations of a company that are fixed by agreement. Accounts payable, for example, represents amounts that the company has purchased from its suppliers and has agreed to pay for in a specified amount of time. Because the time to maturity of these obligations is not lengthy, the market value of current liabilities is most often taken to be equal to their book value. Therefore, when analysts value the current-liability component of a complete business, they normally just read the value of the current liabilities from the firm's balance sheet.

Long-Term Debt

A company's long-term obligations may be long-term loans from a commercial bank or a private investor, corporate bonds, or notes issued to the public. In each case, the value

FIGURE 12-1

Total Market Value of a Business

This figure illustrates how the total market value of a business is the sum of the present values of the components of the business.

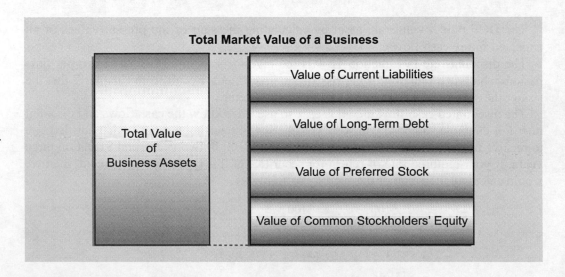

Total Market Value of a Business

Total Value of Business Assets

Value of Current Liabilities

Value of Long-Term Debt

Value of Preferred Stock

Value of Common Stockholders' Equity

of the debt is the present value of the future cash flows that would accrue to the owner of the debt, as we have explained previously. In this chapter, we will discuss the valuation of long-term debt when it is in the form of bonds.

Bond Valuation

Remember from Chapter 2 that a bond's cash flows are determined by the bond's coupon interest payments, face value, and maturity.

Because coupon interest payments occur at regular intervals throughout the life of the bond, those payments are an annuity. Instead of using several terms representing the individual cash flows from the future coupon interest payments (CF_1, CF_2, and so on), we adapt Equation 12-1 by using one term to show the annuity. The remaining term represents the future cash flow of the bond's face value, or principal, that is paid at maturity. Equation 12-2 shows the adapted valuation model:

The Bond Valuation Formula (Algebraic Method)

$$V_B = INT \times \left[\frac{1 - \frac{1}{(1 + k_d)^n}}{k_d} \right] + \frac{M}{(1 + k_d)^n}$$

(12-2)

where: V_B = Current market value of the bond

INT = Dollar amount of each periodic interest payment

n = Number of times the interest payment is received (which is also the number of periods until maturity)

M = Principal payment received at maturity

k_d = Required rate of return per period on the bond debt instrument

The table version of the bond valuation model is shown in Equation 12-3, as follows:

$$V_B = (INT \times PVFOA_{k, n}) + (M \times PVF_{k, n})$$

(12-3)

where: $PVFOA_{k, n}$ = Present Value Factor for an Ordinary Annuity from Table IV-A

$PVF_{k, n}$ = Present Value Factor for a single amount from Table II

To use a calculator to solve for the value of a bond, enter the dollar value of the interest payment as [PMT], the face value payment at maturity as [FV], the number of payments as n, and the required rate of return, k_d depicted as [I/Y] on the TI BAII Plus calculator. Then compute the present value of the bond's cash flows.

Now let's apply the bond valuation model. Suppose Microsoft Corporation issues a 7 percent coupon interest rate bond with a maturity of 20 years. The face value of the bond, payable at maturity, is $1,000.

First, we calculate the dollar amount of the coupon interest payments. At a 7 percent coupon interest rate, each payment is .07 × $1,000 = $70.

Next, we need to choose a required rate of return, k_d. Remember that k_d is the required rate of return that is appropriate for the bond based on its risk, maturity, marketability, and tax treatment. Let's assume that 8 percent is the rate of return the market determines to be appropriate.

Now we have all the factors we need to solve for the value of Microsoft Corporation's bond. We know that k_d is 8 percent, n is 20, the coupon interest payment is $70 per year, and the face value payment at maturity is $1,000. Using Equation 12-2, we calculate the bond's value as follows:

$$V_B = \$70 \times \left[\frac{1 - \frac{1}{(1 + .08)^{20}}}{.08} \right] + \frac{\$1,000}{(1 + .08)^{20}}$$

$$= (\$70 \times 9.8181474) + \left(\frac{\$1,000}{4.660957} \right)$$

$$= \$687.270318 + \$214.548214$$

$$= \$901.82$$

Notice that the value of Microsoft Corporation's bond is the sum of the present values of the 20 annual $70 coupon interest payments plus the present value of the one-time $1,000 face value to be paid 20 years from now, given a required rate of return of 8 percent.

To find the Microsoft bond's value using present value tables, recall that the bond has a face value of $1,000, a coupon interest payment of $70, a required rate of return of 8 percent, and an n value of 20. We apply Equation 12-3 as shown:

$$V_B = (\$70 \times PVFOA_{8\%, \ 20 \ yrs}) + (\$1,000 \times PVF_{8\%, \ 20 \ yrs})$$
$$= (\$70 \times 9.8181) + (\$1,000 \times .2145)$$
$$= \$687.267 + \$214.500$$
$$= \$901.77$$

We see that the sum of the present value of the coupon interest annuity, $687.267, plus the present value of the principal, $214.500, results in a bond value of $901.77. There is a five-cent rounding error in this example when the tables are used.

Here's how to find the bond's value using the TI BAII PLUS financial calculator. Enter the $70 coupon interest payment as PMT, the one-time principal payment of $1,000 as FV, the 20 years until maturity as n (N on the TI BAII PLUS), and the 8 percent required rate of return—depicted as I/Y on the TI BAII Plus. As demonstrated in Chapter 8 calculator solutions, clear the time value of money TVM registers before entering the new data. Skip steps 2 and 3 if you know your calculator is set to one payment per year and is also set for end-of-period payment mode.

TI BAII PLUS Financial Calculator Solution

Step 1: Press [2nd] [CLR TVM] to clear previous values.

Step 2: Press [2nd] [P/Y] 1 [ENTER], [2nd] [BGN] [2nd] [SET] [2nd] [SET] repeat [2nd] [SET] until END shows in the display [2nd] [QUIT] to set the annual interest rate mode and to set the annuity payment to end of period mode.

Step 3: Input the values and compute.

1000 [FV]   8 [I/Y]   20 [N]   70 [PMT]   [CPT] [PV]   **Answer: –901.82**

The $901.82 is negative because it is a cash outflow—the amount an investor would pay to buy the bond today.

We have shown how to value bonds with annual coupon interest payments in this section. Next, we show how to value bonds with semiannual coupon interest payments.

Semiannual Coupon Interest Payments

In the hypothetical bond valuation examples for Microsoft Corporation, we assumed the coupon interest was paid annually. However, most bonds issued in the United States pay interest semiannually (twice per year). With semiannual interest payments, we must adjust the bond valuation model accordingly. If the Microsoft bond paid interest twice per year, the adjustments would look like this:

	Annual Basis	Semiannual Basis
Coupon Interest Payments	$70	÷ 2 = $35 per six-month period
Maturity	20 yrs	× 2 = 40 six-month periods
Required Rate of Return	8%	÷ 2 = 4% semiannual rate

These values can now be used in Equation 12-2, Equation 12-3, or a financial calculator, in the normal manner. For example, if Microsoft's 7 percent coupon, 20-year bond paid interest semiannually, its present value per Equation 12-2 would be

$$V_B = \$35 \times \left[\frac{1 - \frac{1}{(1 + .04)^{40}}}{.04} \right] + \frac{\$1,000}{(1 + .04)^{40}}$$

$$= \left(\$35 \times 19.792774 \right) + \left(\frac{\$1,000}{4.801021} \right)$$

$$= \$692.74709 + \$208.2890$$

$$= \$901.04$$

The value of our Microsoft bond with semiannual interest and a 4 percent per semiannual period discount rate is $901.04. This compares to a value of $901.82 for the same bond if it pays annual interest and has an 8 percent annual discount rate. Note that a required rate of return of 4 percent per semiannual period is not the same as 8 percent per year. The difference in the frequency of discounting gives a slightly different answer. The spreadsheet can also be used to compute the price of this bond for both annual and semi-annual interest payments.

G12		✕ ✓ *fx*	=-PV(F12/E12,C12*E12,B12*D12/E12,B12)

	A	B	C	D			H
1					PV(rate, nper, pmt, [fv], [type])		
2					**The Price of a Coupon Bond**		
3							
4	This Excel spreadsheet computes the price of a bond having a $1,000 face value, 7% annual						
5	coupon rate, and 20 year maturity. It shows how to compute the price for both annual						
6	coupon payment and semi-annual coupon payment frequency. Note the negative sign						
7	before the PV in the PV function. This converts what would be a negative number in cells						
8	G11 and G12 to positive values.						
9							
10		Face Value	Years	Coupon Rate	Frequency	k	Price	Function
11		$1,000.00	20	7%	1	8%	$901.82	<-- =-PV(F11/E11,C11*E11,B11*D11/E11,B11)
12		$1,000.00	20	7%	2	8%	$901.04	<-- =-PV(F12/E12,C12*E12,B12*D12/E12,B12)
13								
14								
15						Excel PV()		
16						Function		
17								
18								

The Yield to Maturity of a Bond

Most investors want to know how much return they will earn on a bond to gauge whether the bond meets their expectations. That way, investors can tell whether they should add the bond to their investment portfolio. As a result, investors often calculate a bond's yield to maturity before they buy a bond. **Yield to maturity (YTM)** represents the average rate of return on a bond if all promised interest and principal payments are made on time and if the interest payments are reinvested at the YTM rate given the price paid for the bond.

yield to maturity (YTM) The investor's return on a bond, assuming that all promised interest and principal payments are made on time and the interest payments are reinvested at the YTM rate.

For more, see 8e Spreadsheet Templates for *Microsoft Excel.*

Calculating a Bond's Yield to Maturity

To calculate a bond's YTM, we apply the bond valuation model. However, we apply it differently than we did when solving for a bond's present value (price) because we solve for k_d, the equivalent of YTM.

To compute a bond's YTM, we must know the values of all variables except k_d. We take the market price of the bond, P_B, as the value of a bond, V_B.

Finding a bond's YTM can be simply done with the help of a financial calculator. Simply plug in the values on the calculator and solve for k_d, as shown:

TI BAII PLUS Financial Calculator Solution

Step 1: Press 2nd CLR TVM to clear previous values.

Step 2: Press 2nd P/Y 1 ENTER , 2nd BGN 2nd SET 2nd SET repeat 2nd SET until END shows in the display 2nd QUIT to set the annual interest rate mode and to set the annuity payment to end of period mode.

Step 3: Input the values and compute.

1,114.70 +/– PV   1000 FV   20 N   70 PMT   CPT I/Y

Answer: 6.00

Using the financial calculator, we find that the YTM of the Microsoft $1,000 face value 20-year bond with a coupon rate of 7 percent and a market price of $1,114.70 is 6 percent. A spreadsheet can also be used to obtain the YTM for this bond using its RATE function.

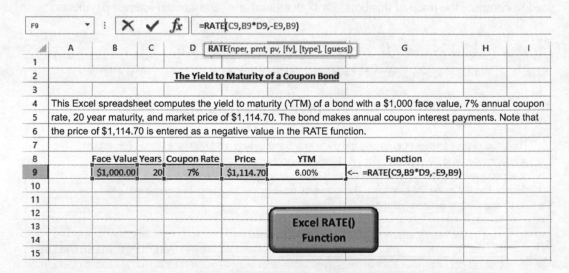

The Relationship between Bond YTM and Price

A bond's market price depends on its yield to maturity. When a bond has a YTM greater than its coupon rate, it sells at a *discount* from its face value. When the YTM is equal to the coupon rate, the market price equals the face value. When the YTM is less than the coupon rate, the bond sells at a *premium* over face value.

Figure 12-2 shows the relationship between YTM and the price of a bond.

The inverse relationship between bond price and YTM is important to bond traders. Why? Because if market YTM interest rates rise, bond prices fall. Conversely, if market YTM interest rates fall, bond prices rise. The suggestion that the Fed might raise interest rates is enough to send the bond market reeling as bond traders unload their holdings.

In this section, we examined bond valuation for bonds that pay annual and semiannual interest. We also investigated how to find a bond's yield to maturity and the relationship between a bond's YTM and its price. We turn next to preferred stock valuation.

For more, use 8e Spreadsheet TutorPak™

Preferred Stock Valuation

To value preferred stock, we adapt the discounted cash flow valuation formula, Equation 12-1, to reflect the characteristics of preferred stock. First, recall that the value of any security is the present value of its future cash payments. Second, review the characteristics of preferred stock. Preferred stock has no maturity date, so it has no maturity value. Its future cash payments are dividend payments that are paid to preferred stockholders at regular time intervals for as long as they (or their heirs) own the stock. Cash payments from preferred stock dividends are scheduled to continue forever. To value preferred stock, then, we must adapt the discounted cash flow model to reflect that preferred stock dividends are a perpetuity.

Finding the Present Value of Preferred Stock Dividends

To calculate the value of preferred stock, we need to find the present value of its future cash flows—which are a perpetuity. In Chapter 8, we learned how to find the present value of a perpetuity. We use the formula for the present value of a perpetuity, Equation 8-5, but adapt the terms to reflect the nature of preferred stock.[1]

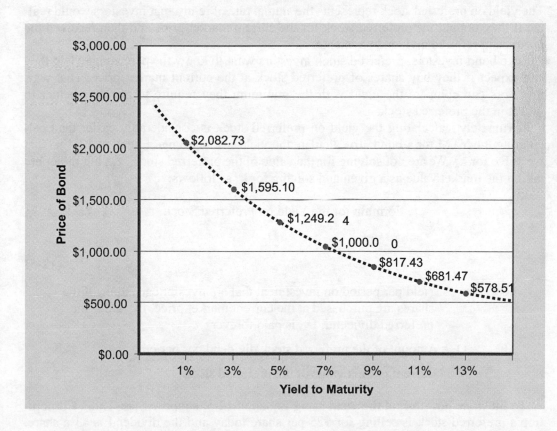

FIGURE 12-2
Bond YTM versus Bond Price

Figure 12-2 shows the inverse relationship between the price and the YTM for a $1,000 face value, 20-year, 7% coupon interest rate bond that pays annual interest.

---

1. Equation 8-5 is PV = PMT/k. In Equation 12-4, V_p substitutes for PV, D_p replaces PMT, and k_p replaces k.

The preferred stock valuation calculations require that we find the present value (V_p) of preferred stock dividends (D_p), discounted at required rate of return, k_p. The formula for preferred stock valuation follows:

The Formula for the Present Value of Preferred Stock

$$V_P = \frac{D_p}{k_p}$$

(12-4)

where: V_P = Current market value of the preferred stock

D_p = Amount of the preferred stock dividend per period

k_p = Required rate of return per period for this issue of preferred stock

Let's apply Equation 12-4 to an example. Suppose investors expect an issue of preferred stock to pay an annual dividend of $2 per share. Investors in the market have evaluated the issuing company and market conditions and have concluded that 10 percent is a fair rate of return on this investment. The present value for one share of this preferred stock, assuming a 10 percent required rate of return follows:

$$V_P = \left(\frac{\$2}{.10} \right)$$
$$= \$20$$

We find that for investors whose required rate of return (k_p) is 10 percent, the value of each share of this issue of preferred stock is $20.

The Yield on Preferred Stock

The yield on preferred stock represents the annual rate of return that investors would realize if they bought the preferred stock for the current market price and then received the promised preferred dividend payments.

Like bond investors, preferred stock investors want to know the percentage yield they can expect if they buy shares of preferred stock at the current market price. That way, investors can compare the yield with the minimum they require to decide whether to invest in the preferred stock.

Fortunately, calculating the yield on preferred stock is considerably easier than calculating the YTM for a bond. To calculate the yield, we rearrange Equation 12-4 so that we solve for k_p. We are not solving for the value of the preferred stock, V_P, but rather are taking the market value as a given and solving for k_p as follows:

Formula for the Yield on Preferred Stock

$$k_P = \frac{D_P}{V_P}$$

(12-5)

where: k_p = Yield per period on investment that an investor can expect if the shares are purchased at the current market price, P_P, and if the preferred dividend, D_p, is paid forever

D_p = Amount of the preferred stock dividend per period

V_P = Current market value of the preferred stock

To illustrate how to find the yield using Equation 12-5, suppose Sure-Thing Corporation's preferred stock is selling for $25 per share today and the dividend is $3 a share. Now assume you are a potential buyer of Sure-Thing's preferred stock, so you want to find the expected annual percent yield on your investment. You know that the current market value of the stock, V_p, is \$25, and the stock dividend, D_p, is \$3. Applying Equation 12-5, you calculate the yield as follows:

$$k_P = \frac{\$3}{\$25}$$
$$= .12, \text{ or } 12\%$$

You find that the yield for Sure-Thing's preferred stock is 12 percent. If your minimum required rate of return is less than or equal to 12 percent, you would invest in the Sure-Thing preferred stock. If your required rate of return is greater than 12 percent, you would look for another preferred stock that had a yield of more than 12 percent.

Common Stock Valuation

The valuation of common stock is somewhat different from the valuation of bonds and preferred stock. Common stock valuation is complicated by the fact that common stock dividends are difficult to predict compared with the interest and principal payments on a bond or dividends on preferred stock. Indeed, corporations may pay common stock dividends irregularly or not pay dividends at all. Moreover, because owners of more than 50 percent of a corporation's stock have control over the affairs of the business and can force their will, the value of a controlling interest of common stock is relatively more valuable than the value of one share. This means that different procedures must be used to value controlling interests (or total common stockholders' equity) than are used to value one share. Often, ownership of less than 50 percent of a corporation's common stock can result in control if the percentage owned is significant and if the remaining shares are widely disbursed among investors not working in concert with each other.

In the sections that follow, we examine the most popular methods of valuing individual shares of common stock. We will then illustrate how these methods are applied to the valuation of total common stockholders' equity.

Valuing Individual Shares of Common Stock

As with bonds and preferred stock, we value individual shares of common stock by estimating the present value of the expected future cash flows from the common stock. Those future cash flows are the expected future dividends and the expected price of the stock when the stock is sold. The discounted cash flow valuation model, Equation 12-1, adapted for common stock is shown in Equation 12-6:

The DCF Valuation Model Applied to Common Stock

$$P_0 = \frac{D_1}{\left(1 + k_s\right)^1} + \frac{D_2}{\left(1 + k_s\right)^2} + \frac{D_3}{\left(1 + k_s\right)^3} + \ldots + \frac{P_n}{\left(1 + k_s\right)^n}$$

(12-6)

where: P_0 = Present value of the expected dividends, the current price of the common stock

D_1, D_2, D_3, etc. = Common stock dividends expected to be received at the end of periods 1, 2, 3, and so on until the stock is sold

P_n = Anticipated selling price of the stock in n periods

k_s = Required rate of return per period on this common stock investment

In practice, however, using Equation 12-6 to value shares of common stock is problematic because an estimate of the future selling price of a share of stock is often speculative. This severely limits the usefulness of the model.

Instead, some analysts use models that are a variation of Equation 12-6 that do not rely on an estimate of a stock's future selling price. We turn to those models next.

The Constant Growth Dividend Model

Common stock dividends can grow at different rates. The two growth patterns we examine here are constant growth and nonconstant, or supernormal, growth.

The constant growth dividend model assumes common stock dividends will be paid regularly and grow at a constant rate. The constant growth dividend model (also known as the Gordon growth model because financial economist Myron Gordon helped develop and popularize it) is shown in Equation 12-7:

The Constant Growth Version of the Dividend Valuation Model

$$P_0 = \frac{D_1}{k_s - g}$$

(12-7)

where: P_0 = Current price of the common stock

D_1 = Dollar amount of the common stock dividend expected one period from now

k_s = Required rate of return per period on this common stock investment

g = Expected constant growth rate per period of the company's common stock dividends

Equation 12-7 is easy to use if the stock dividends grow at a constant rate. For example, assume your required rate of return (k_s) for Wendy's common stock is 10 percent. Suppose your research leads you to believe that Wendy's Corporation will pay a $0.25 dividend in one year (D_1), and for every year after the dividend will grow at a constant rate (g) of 8 percent a year. Using Equation 12-7, we calculate the present value of Wendy's common stock dividends as follows:

$$
\begin{aligned}
P_0 &= \frac{\$0.25}{.10 - .08} \\
&= \frac{\$0.25}{.02} \\
&= \$12.50
\end{aligned}
$$

We find that with a common stock dividend in one year of $0.25, a constant growth rate of 8 percent, and a required rate of return of 10 percent, the value of the common stock is $12.50.

In a no-growth situation, g, in the denominator of Equation 12-7 becomes zero. To value stocks that have no growth is particularly easy because the value is simply the expected dividend (D1) divided by k_s.

The Nonconstant, or Supernormal, Growth Model

In addition to the constant growth dividend cash flow pattern that we discussed in the previous section, some companies have very high growth rates, known as supernormal growth of the cash flows. Valuing the common stock of such companies presents a special problem because high growth rates cannot be sustained indefinitely. A young high-technology firm may be able to grow at a 40 percent rate per year for a few years, but that growth must slow down because it is not sustainable given the population and productivity growth rates. In fact, if the firm's growth rate did not slow down, its sales would surpass the gross domestic product of the entire nation over time. Why? The company has a 40 percent growth rate that will compound annually, whereas the gross domestic product may grow at a 4 percent compounded average annual growth rate.

The constant growth dividend model for common stock, Equation 12-7, then, must be adjusted for those cases in which a company's dividend grows at a supernormal rate that will not be sustained over time. We do this by dividing the projected dividend cash flow stream of the common stock into two parts: the initial supernormal growth period and the next period, in which normal and sustainable growth is expected. We then calculate the present value of the dividends during the fast-growth time period first. Then we solve for the present value of the dividends during the constant growth period that are a perpetuity. The sum of these two present values determines the current value of the stock.

To illustrate, suppose Supergrowth Corporation is expected to pay an annual dividend of $2 per share one year from now and that this dividend will grow at a 30 percent annual rate during each of the following four years (taking us to the end of year 5). After this supernormal growth period, the dividend will grow at a sustainable 5 percent rate each year beyond year 5. The cash flows are shown in Figure 12-3.

The valuation of a share of Supergrowth Corporation's common stock is described in the following three steps.

Step 1: Add the present values of the dividends during the supernormal growth period. Assume that the required rate of return, k_s, is 14 percent.

$$
\begin{array}{rl}
\$2.00 \times 1/1.14^1 = & \$\ 1.75 \\
\$2.60 \times 1/1.14^2 = & \$\ 2.00 \\
\$3.38 \times 1/1.14^3 = & \$\ 2.28 \\
\$4.39 \times 1/1.14^4 = & \$\ 2.60 \\
\$5.71 \times 1/1.14^5 = & \underline{\$\ 2.97} \\
\Sigma = & \$11.60
\end{array}
$$

Step 2: Calculate the sum of the present values of the dividends during the normal growth period, from t_6 through infinity in this case. To do this, pretend for a moment that t_6 is t_1. The present value of the dividend growing at the constant rate of 5 percent to perpetuity could be computed using Equation 12-7.

$$
P_0 = \frac{D_1}{k_s - g}
$$

Substituting our values, we would have:

$$
P_0 = \frac{\$6.00}{.14 - .05}
$$
$$
= \$66.67
$$

Because the $6.00 dividend actually occurs at t_6 instead of t_1, the $66.67 figure is not a t_0 value, but rather a t_5 value. Therefore, it needs to be discounted back five years at our required rate of return of 14 percent. This gives us $66.67 \times (1/1.14^5) = \$34.63$. The result of $34.63 is the present value of the dividends from the end of year 6 through infinity.

FIGURE 12-3 Timeline of Supergrowth Common Stock Dividend with Initial Supernormal Growth

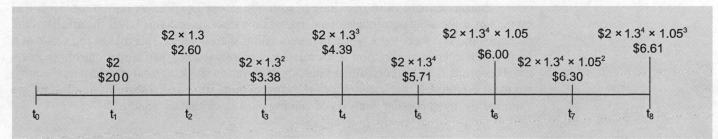

Step 3: Finally, we add the present values of the dividends from the supernormal growth period and the normal growth period. In our example we add $11.60 + $34.63 = $46.23. The sum of $46.23 is the appropriate market price of Supergrowth Corporation's common stock, given the projected dividends and the 14 percent required rate of return on those dividends.

The P/E Model

Many investment analysts use the price to earnings, or P/E, ratio to value shares of common stock. As we discussed in Chapter 6, the P/E ratio is the price per share of a common stock divided by the company's earnings per share:

$$\text{P/E ratio} = \frac{\text{Price per Share}}{\text{Earnings per Share}}$$

The P/E ratio indicates how much investors are willing to pay for each dollar of a stock's current earnings. So, a P/E ratio of 20 means that investors arc willing to pay $20 for $1 of a stock's earnings. A high P/E ratio indicates that investors believe the stock's earnings will increase, or that the risk of the stock is low, or both.

Financial analysts often use a P/E model to estimate common stock value for businesses that are not public. First, analysts compare the P/E ratios of similar companies within an industry to determine an appropriate P/E ratio for companies in that industry. Second, analysts calculate an appropriate stock price for firms in the industry by multiplying each firm's earnings per share (EPS) by the industry average P/E ratio. The P/E model formula, Equation 12-8, follows:

The P/E Model

$$\text{Appropriate Stock Price} = \text{Industry P/E Ratio} \times \text{EPS} \tag{12-8}$$

To illustrate how to apply the P/E model, let's value the common stock of the Zumwalt Corporation. Suppose that Zumwalt Corporation has current earnings per share of $2 and, given the risk and growth prospects of the firm, the analyst has determined that the company's common stock should sell for 15 times current earnings. Applying the P/E model, we calculate the following price for Zumwalt Corporation's common stock:

$$\text{Appropriate Stock Price} = \text{Industry P/E Ratio} \times \text{EPS}$$

$$= 15 \times \$2$$

$$= \$30$$

Our P/E model calculations show that $30 per share is the appropriate price for common stock that has a $2 earnings per share and an industry P/E ratio of 15. The industry P/E ratio would be adjusted up or down according to the individual firm's growth prospects and risk relative to the industry norm.

Valuing Total Common Stockholders' Equity

As we said earlier, different procedures must be used to value total common stockholders' equity than are used to value one share of common stock. The primary reason for this is that owners of some large percentage of a corporation's stock have control over the affairs of the business and can force their will on the remaining shareholders. This makes the value of a controlling interest of common stock relatively more valuable than a noncontrolling interest. Therefore, to value controlling interests of common stock, or total stockholders' equity, we must use models that account for this "control premium." In the sections that follow, we examine the most popular methods of valuing total stockholders' equity.

Book Value

One of the simplest ways to value total common stockholders' equity is to subtract the value of the firm's liabilities and preferred stock, if any, as recorded on the balance sheet from the value of its assets. The result is the **book value,** or **net worth**.

book value, net worth
The total amount of common stockholders' equity on a company's balance sheet.

$$\text{Book Value of Common Equity} \qquad\qquad (12\text{-}9)$$

Book Value of Common Equity = Total Assets – Total Liabilities – Preferred Stock

The book value approach has severe limitations. The asset values recorded on a firm's balance sheet usually reflect what the current owners originally paid for the assets, not the current market value of the assets. Due to these and other limitations, the book value is rarely used to estimate the market value of common equity.

Liquidation Value

The liquidation value and book value valuation methods are similar, except that the liquidation method uses the market values of the assets and liabilities, not book values, as in Equation 12-9. The market values of the assets are the amounts the assets would earn on the open market if they were sold (or liquidated). The market values of the liabilities are the amounts of money it would take to pay off the liabilities.

The *liquidation value* is the amount each common stockholder would receive if the firm closed, sold all assets and paid off all liabilities and preferred stock, and distributed the net proceeds to the common stockholders.

Although more reliable than book value, liquidation value is a worst-case valuation assessment. A company's common stock should be worth at least the amount generated at liquidation. Because liquidation value does not consider the earnings and cash flows the firm will generate in the future, it may provide misleading results for companies that have significant future earning potential.

The Free Cash Flow DCF Model

The Free Cash Flow DCF Model is very similar to the nonconstant, or supernormal, dividend growth model discussed earlier, but instead of discounting dividend cash flows, the free cash flow model discounts the total cash flows that would flow to the suppliers of the firm's capital. Once the present value of those cash flows is determined, liabilities and preferred stock (if any) are subtracted to arrive at the present value of common stockholders' equity.

Free Cash Flows

Free cash flows represent the total cash flows from business operations that flow to the suppliers of a firm's capital each year. In forecasts, free cash flows are calculated as follows:

   Cash Revenues
– Cash Expenses
= Earnings Before Interest, Taxes, Depreciation, and Amortization (EBITDA)
– Depreciation and Amortization
= Earnings Before Interest and Taxes (EBIT)
– Federal and State Income Taxes
= Net Operating Profit After-Tax (NOPAT)
+ Add Back Depreciation and Amortization
– Capital Expenditures
– New Net Working Capital
= Free Cash Flow

Free cash flow represents those amounts in each operating period that are "free" to be distributed to the suppliers of the firm's capital—that is, the debt holders, the preferred stockholders, and the common stockholders. In the previous calculation, you can see that free cash flow is that amount remaining after cash expenses, income taxes, capital expenditures, and new net working capital are subtracted from cash revenues.

A Real World Example

In July 2001, the Abiomed Corporation of Danvers, Massachusetts, received a lot of publicity when the company's AbioCor self-contained artificial heart was implanted in a terminally ill patient, marking the first time that such a device was used on a human being. Let us put ourselves in the shoes of someone valuing this company on April 1, 2006, and that you work for a firm that is interested in acquiring Abiomed. In support of the acquisition analysis, you have been asked to prepare an estimate of the market value of the firm's common equity. The methodology you have chosen is the discounted free cash flow model.

Following a lengthy analysis of the artificial heart market, the medical equipment industry, and Abiomed's financial statements, you produce the discounted free cash flow forecast and valuation shown in Figure 12-4. In the following paragraphs, we explain the procedure. The forecasting variables that form the basis for the valuation are listed at the top of Figure 12-4 (these are the product of your lengthy analysis). For convenience, we have numbered each line in the figure at the left-hand side.

The "Actual 2006" column in Figure 12-4 contains Abiomed's operating results for the fiscal year ended March 31, 2006, as recorded on the firm's SEC Form 10-K.[2] The remaining columns contain the forecast for the next 10 years.

Product revenues (line 12) are expected to accelerate from 20 to 50 percent annual growth over four years, with the growth rate decreasing 10 percentage points a year after that until the ninth year of the forecast, when revenue growth settles out at an expected long-term growth rate of 5 percent a year (the growth factor is on line 1). Funded research and development revenue (line 13), on the other hand, is expected to decrease 50 percent a year until it is almost negligible after 10 years (the growth factor is on line 2). These factors produce total revenues (line 14) exceeding $52 million in 2007 and $376 million in 2016.

Direct costs of revenues on line 15 are a function of the expected gross profit margin on line 3. In Abiomed's forecast, 2006's gross margin of 77 percent is extended for each year through 2016. This produces gross profits (see line 16) ranging from just over $40 million in 2007 to over $289 million in 2016. Given the forecasted gross profit figures, direct costs on line 15 are "plugged" by subtracting gross profit from total revenues.

Research and development expenses (line 17) are expected to grow by 10 percent in 2007 and then to decrease by 10 percent a year through 2016. Selling, general, and administrative expenses (line 18) are forecast as a percentage of revenue, starting at 70 percent of revenue in 2007 (the same percentage as in 2006) and declining to 54 percent in 2016. Subtracting these operating expenses from gross profit leaves earnings before interest, taxes, depreciation, and amortization (EBITDA on line 19) of negative $15.176 million in 2007, positive $2.067 million in 2010, and positive $78.966 million in 2016.

Although they are noncash expenses, depreciation and amortization are included in discounted free cash flow forecasts in order to calculate income tax expense. In the case of Abiomed, depreciation and amortization expense (line 20) is forecast to be 6 percent of revenue each year. Subtracting depreciation and amortization expense from EBITDA produces earnings before interest and taxes (EBIT), also known as operating income (see line 21).

As shown in Figure 12-4, line 22, Abiomed has $94.159 million in tax-loss carryforwards at the beginning of FY 2006. Operating income was a negative $16.985 million in 2006, so $94.159 million + $16.985 million = $111.144 million in tax-loss carryforwards are available at the beginning of 2007. This situation continues until 2016, when the carryforwards are finally used up, and Abiomed reports $10.738 million in net taxable earnings. After 2016, operating income is fully taxable.

---

2. The "Edgar" database at *www.sec.gov.*

The forecast assumes a combined federal and state income tax rate of 40 percent (see line 9). Applying this rate to Abiomed's net taxable earnings (line 23) in 2016, and $0 to the earlier years, produces the income tax expenses shown on line 24. Subtracting taxes from EBIT produces the company's net operating profit after tax (NOPAT on line 25), which is negative $18.314 million in 2007 rising to positive $52.109 million in 2016.

Once NOPAT has been determined, three further adjustments are necessary to calculate free cash flow. First, on line 26, depreciation and amortization are added back to NOPAT, because these noncash items were subtracted earlier only for the purpose of calculating income tax expense. Next, on line 27, expected capital expenditures are subtracted. Capital expenditures are amounts expected to be spent to procure new plant and equipment. For this forecast, we assume that your research indicates that Abiomed will need to spend about the same amount on plant and equipment in 2007 than it did in 2006 (see line 7), and that this spending may be decreased 10 percent a year in each year after 2007. The resulting capital expenditure budget, shown in Figure 12-4, line 27, gradually decreases from $2.92 million in 2007 to just over $1.13 million in 2016.

Finally, on line 28, new net working capital investment is subtracted. Net working capital is the difference between current assets and current liabilities that must be financed from long-term capital sources (debt and equity). When businesses grow, they typically need more working capital in the form of cash, inventory, and receivables, and not all of it can be financed spontaneously from current liabilities. For this reason, the company's long-term debt and equity holders must invest additional amounts each year to "take up the slack." In the case of Abiomed, we will assume that your research indicates that the typical ratio of net working capital to sales in the medical equipment industry is 10 percent (see line 8). In other words, for every $10 of new sales a company realizes, $1 of new net working capital will be needed. In Figure 12-4, line 28, this is calculated by multiplying the difference in product revenue each year by .10. In 2007, for example, ($51,986 − $43,322) × .10, and rounded to even thousands = $866,000 of new net working capital is needed. The remaining years are calculated similarly.

After all the calculations have been completed, the resulting figures on line 29 represent amounts that are free to be distributed to the suppliers of Abiomed's capital, either in the form of interest to the debt holders or dividends to the stockholders. These free cash flows range from negative $18.962 million in 2007 to positive $71.750 million in 2016.

In the previous paragraphs, we explicitly forecast the free cash flows for 2007 through 2016. But what about the years after that? After all, Abiomed is not expected to suddenly cease operating at the end of 2016 but to continue operating indefinitely into the future as a going concern.

To forecast the free cash flows in the years beyond 2016, we rely on a variation of the constant growth dividend valuation model, Equation 12-7. After 2016, Abiomed's free cash flows are expected to grow at a constant rate of 5 percent a year indefinitely. We adapt Equation 12-7 to value these constantly growing free cash flows as follows:

Constant Growth Free Cash Flow Valuation Model

$$V_{fcft} = \frac{FCF_t(1+g)}{k-g}$$

(12-10)

where: V_{fcft} = the value of future free cash flows at time t

FCF_t = free cash flow at time t

k = the discount rate per period

g = the long-term constant growth rate per period of free cash flows

FIGURE 12-4
Discounted Free Cash Flow Forecast and Valuation for Abiomed (in $ thousands)

Line	Forecasting Variables:	Actual 2006	2007	2008
1	Product revenue growth factor	14%	20%	30%
2	Research revenue growth factor		−10%	−10%
3	Expected gross profit margin	77%	77%	77%
4	R&D expense growth factor		10%	−10%
5	S, G, & A expense % of revenue	71%	71%	70%
6	Depr. & Amort. % of revenue	6%	6%	6%
7	Capital expenditure growth factor		0%	−10%
8	Net working capital to sales ratio		10%	10%
9	Income tax rate	40%		
10	Assumed long-term sustainable growth rate	5% per year		
11	Discount rate	20%		

Line	Forecast and Valuation:	Actual 2006	2007	2008
12	Product revenue	$ 43,322	$ 51,986	$ 67,582
13	Funded research and development revenue	348	313	282
14	Total revenue	43,670	52,299	67,864
15	Direct costs	10,251	12,029	15,609
16	Gross profit	33,419	40,270	52,255
17	Research and development expenses	16,739	18,413	16,572
18	Selling, general and administrative expenses	30,923	37,033	47,574
19	Earnings before interest, taxes, depr. & amort. (EBITDA)	(14,243)	(15,176)	(11,891)
20	Depreciation and amortization	2,742	3,138	4,072
21	Earnings before interest and taxes (EBIT)	(16,985)	(18,314)	(15,963)
22	Available tax-loss carryforwards	(94,159)	(111,144)	(129,458)
23	Net taxable earnings	(16,985)	(18,314)	(15,963)
24	Federal and state income taxes	0	0	0
25	Net operating profit after-tax (NOPAT)	(16,985)	(18,314)	(15,963)
26	Add back depreciation and amortization	2,742	3,138	4,072
27	Subtract capital expenditures	(2,920)	(2,920)	(2,628)
28	Subtract new net working capital	0	(866)	(1,560)
29	Free cash flow	($17,163)	($18,962)	($16,079)
30	Terminal value, 2016			
31	Present value of free cash flows @ 20%		(15,802)	(11,166)
32	Total present value of company operations	$100,140		
33	Plus current assets	46,443*		
34	Less current liabilities	(8,739)*		
35	Less long-term debt	(310)*		
36	Less preferred stock	0*		
37	Net market value of common equity	$137,534	*from Abiomed's March 31, 2006 Balance Sheet	

2009	2010	2011	2012	2013	2014	2015	2016
40%	50%	40%	30%	20%	10%	5%	5%
−10%	−10%	−10%	−10%	−10%	−10%	−10%	−10%
77%	77%	77%	77%	77%	77%	77%	77%
−10%	−10%	−10%	−10%	−10%	−10%	−10%	−10%
68%	66%	64%	62%	60%	58%	56%	54%
6%	6%	6%	6%	6%	6%	6%	6%
−10%	−10%	−10%	−10%	−10%	−10%	−10%	−10%
10%	10%	10%	10%	10%	10%	10%	10%

Years Ending March 31
Forecast

2009	2010	2011	2012	2013	2014	2015	2016
$94,615	$141,923	$198,692	$258,300	$309,960	$340,956	$358,004	$375,904
254	229	206	185	167	150	135	122
94,869	142,152	198,898	258,485	310,127	341,106	358,139	376,026
21,820	32,695	45,747	59,452	71,329	78,454	82,372	86,486
73,049	109,457	153,151	199,033	238,798	262,652	275,767	289,540
14,915	13,424	12,082	10,874	9,787	8,808	7,927	7,134
64,608	93,966	127,499	160,526	186,394	198,191	200,925	203,440
(6,474)	2,067	13,570	27,633	42,617	55,653	66,915	78,966
5,692	8,529	11,934	15,509	18,608	20,466	21,488	22,562
(12,166)	(6,462)	1,636	12,124	24,009	35,187	45,427	56,404
(45,421)	(157,587)	(164,049)	(162,413)	(150,289)	(126,280)	(91,093)	(45,666)
(12,166)	(6,462)	0	0	0	0	0	10,738
0	0	0	0	0	0	0	4,295
(12,166)	(6,462)	1,636	12,124	24,009	35,187	45,427	52,109
5,692	8,529	11,934	15,509	18,608	20,466	21,488	22,562
(2,365)	(2,129)	(1,916)	(1,724)	(1,552)	(1,397)	(1,257)	(1,131)
(2,703)	(4,731)	(5,677)	(5,961)	(5,166)	(3,100)	(1,705)	(1,790)
($ 11,542)	($ 4,793)	$ 5,977	$ 19,948	$ 35,899	$ 51,156	$ 63,953	$ 71,750
							$502,250
(6,679)	(2,311)	2,402	6,681	10,019	11,897	12,395	92,704

According to Equation 12-10, and assuming a discount rate of 20 percent (see line 11),[3] the value as of the end of 2016 of Abiomed's free cash flows in years 2017 and beyond, in thousands, would be

$$V_{\text{fcf } 2016} = \frac{\$71,750\left(1 + .05\right)}{.20 - .05}$$
$$= \$502,250$$

Take Note
Do not confuse the market value of Abiomed's common equity, as calculated here, with the actual price of the firm's common stock on the open market. The $137.534 million is what the company's stock is worth to an investor with a required rate of return of 20 percent a year, given the assumptions in the model in Figure 12-4. Stock traders in the market may be making any number of different assumptions about Abiomed and may have different required rates of return. As a result, the actual price of Abiomed's stock in the market may be completely different than the *intrinsic* value shown here.[5]

The value of the free cash flows at the end of 2016 and beyond is called the *terminal value* of the company's operations at the end of 2016. The amount is shown in Figure 12-4 on line 30.

On line 31, the present value of the free cash flows is calculated using Equation 8-2a, assuming a discount rate of 20 percent. The present values are then summed up on line 32 to produce the total value of Abiomed's operations on April 1, 2006, which is $100.140 million.

Let us say a few words about this value before proceeding. As we said earlier, the present value of the company's free cash flows ($100.140 million in the case of Abiomed) represents the market value of the firm's core income-producing operations. In the world of finance and investing, this is sometimes called the firm's *enterprise value*. It is NOT the total market value of the entire company, however, or the total market value of the company's assets, because the current, or nonoperating, assets of the company have not yet been accounted for.

We shall have more to say about this issue later in the chapter in the section on valuing complete businesses. For now, just remember that the present value of the company's free cash flows equals the market value of the firm's core income-producing operations (called enterprise value). The relationship is illustrated in Figure 12-5.

In the analysis in Figure 12-4, we have calculated the market value of Abiomed's operating, or income-producing assets, as shown in the lower-left portion of Figure 12-5. From Figure 12-5, it is clear that to obtain the value of Abiomed's common stock (which is our ultimate goal), we must take line 32 and add the value of the firm's current assets and then subtract the values of current liabilities, long-term debt, and preferred stock. In Figure 12-4, this is done on lines 33, 34, 35, and 36. The values for current assets, current liabilities, long-term debt, and preferred stock were taken from Abiomed's March 31, 2006, balance sheet.[4]

Line 37 of Figure 12-4 shows the final result after adding Abiomed's current assets ($46.443 million) and subtracting current liabilities ($8.739 million), long-term debt ($.310 million), and preferred stock ($0) from the present value of the firm's operations ($100.140 million). This final result, $137.534 million, is the total market value of Abiomed's common equity as of April 1, 2006. A lot of things have changed, of course, since 2006. In early 2018 Abiomed had a total market value of about $11.6 billion.

The Yield on Common Stock

We calculate the yield for common stock by rearranging the terms in Equation 12-7 to arrive at the constant growth dividend model, as shown in Equation 12-11:

The Yield, or Total Return, on Common Stock

$$k_s = \frac{D_1}{P_0} + g$$

(12-11)

---

3. The discount rate represents the weighted average required rates of return of Abiomed's debt holders and common stockholders. Calculating this weighted average return was discussed in detail in Chapter 9.

4. To be precise, we should have calculated the market values of Abiomed's current assets, current liabilities, and long-term debt before making the adjustments. In practice, however, the book values from the balance sheet are often used instead because the process of valuing the items is difficult and the market values often do not differ materially from the book values.

5. In fact, Abiomed's stock closed at $12.90 on Friday, March 31, 2006, the day before our valuation date. $12.90 per share equates to a total common equity value of $341.438 million, not including a control premium. This is almost $204 million higher than the $137.534 million estimated by our model. In April 2015, the stock was trading at $69 per share.

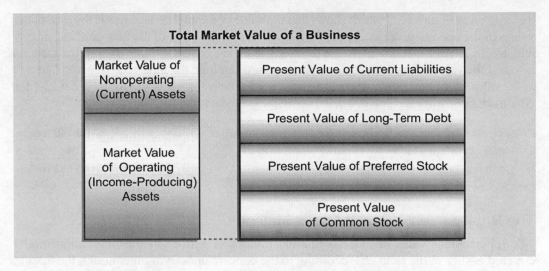

FIGURE 12-5
Total Market Value of a Business

This figure is an extension of Figure 12-1, showing how total assets are made up of operating (income-producing) assets plus nonoperating (current) assets.

where: D_1 = Amount of the common stock dividend anticipated in one period

P_0 = Current market price of the common stock

g = Expected constant growth rate of dividends per period

k_s = Expected rate of return per period on this common stock investment

Equation 12-11 is also called the formula for an investor's total rate of return from common stock. The stock's **dividend yield** is the term D_1/P_0.

To demonstrate how Equation 12-11 works, suppose you found that the price of BP common stock today was $52 per share. Then suppose you believe that BP will pay a common stock dividend next year of $4.80 a share, and the dividend will grow each year at a constant annual rate of 4 percent. If you buy one share of BP common stock at the listed price of $52, your expected annual percent yield on your investment will be

$$k_s = \frac{D_1}{P_0} + g$$
$$= \frac{\$4.80}{\$52} + .04$$
$$= .0923 + .04$$
$$= .1323, \text{ or } 13.23\%$$

dividend yield A stock's annual dividend divided by its current market price.

If your minimum required rate of return for BP common stock, considering its risk, were less than 13.23 percent, you would proceed with the purchase. Otherwise, you would look for another stock that had an expected return appropriate for its level of risk.

Valuing Complete Businesses

Up to this point in the chapter, we have dealt with the values of business components as shown in the right-hand "pillar" in Figure 12-1. Now we turn our attention to valuing the complete business all at once, or the total value of the business's assets as shown in the left-hand "pillar" in Figure 12-1.

The Free Cash Flow DCF Model Applied to a Complete Business

As it turns out, using the Free Cash Flow Model to value a complete business is quite straightforward once you have learned how to use it to value common equity. This is because the Free Cash Flow Model values the complete business as a part of the procedure to value common equity.

Refer again to Figure 12-5, which shows that the value of a complete business is the sum of the values of the operating, or income-producing, assets plus the value of the nonoperating, or current, assets. All that is necessary to use the Free Cash Flow Model to value a complete business is to add the value of the company's current assets, taken from the most recent balance sheet,[6] to the value of the company's operations, calculated exactly the same way as in Figure 12-4 for Abiomed. Following this procedure, the complete business value for Abiomed would be

Present value of company operations (or enterprise value)	$100.140 million
+ Value of current assets	46.443 million
= Complete business value of Abiomed	$146.583 million

(see Figure 12-4, lines 32 and 33)

The Replacement Value of Assets Method

The replacement value of assets valuation method is similar to the liquidation model covered earlier in the chapter. According to the concept underlying the model, the market value of a complete business cannot exceed the amount it would take to buy all of the firm's assets on the open market. For example, you would not be willing to pay the owners of Abiomed $146.583 million for the company if you could buy all the assets necessary to duplicate the company for $100 million.

Although it is simple in concept, the replacement value of assets method is not often applied to complete business valuations for two reasons:

1. It is frequently very difficult to locate similar assets for sale on the open market.

2. Some of a business's assets are difficult to define and quantify (how do you quantify a business's reputation, for example, or the strength of its brands?).

Although it is difficult to use the replacement value of assets method to value a complete business, the model can be quite useful for estimating the value of individual assets in a business. For example, the value of a company's nonproprietary software can be estimated by listing the various programs in use and then noting the prices of those programs in retail stores, catalogs, and on the Internet. The sum of the lowest prices at which the programs could be obtained is the replacement value of the company's software. In another example, it is possible to estimate the value of a company's machinery and equipment by calculating what it would cost to replace all the machinery and equipment. This is normally done by noting the prices for machinery and equipment of similar age and in similar condition on the open market. Alternatively, analysts sometimes note the prices of new machinery and equipment and adjust those prices to reflect the age and condition of the machinery and equipment belonging to the company.

Individual asset valuations of this type are most often employed when one business buys another and it is necessary to allocate the purchase price among the assets purchased. In such cases, the "fair market value" of the individual assets is estimated (using the replacement value of assets method, the discounted free cash flow method, or some other method), and any amounts remaining are assigned to "goodwill."

What's Next

In this chapter, we investigated valuation methods for bonds, preferred stock, common stock, and complete businesses. The valuation methods applied risk and return, and time value of money techniques learned in Chapters 7 and 8, respectively. In the next chapter, we will explore capital structure issues.

---

6. As we said earlier, to be precise, one should use the market value of the current assets, rather than the book value from the balance sheet. However, because estimating the market value of the current assets is time-consuming and the results are often not materially different from the book value, many analysts simply use the book value in their complete business valuations.

Summary

1. *Explain the importance of business valuation.*
   When corporations contemplate selling their businesses, they do not want to undervalue the businesses because they want to raise the most money possible. Likewise, would-be purchasers of businesses use valuation methods to avoid paying more than the businesses are worth.

2. *Discuss the concept of business valuation.*
   To value any business, business asset, or security, we apply risk and return and time value of money techniques. In sum, the value of a business, asset, or security is the present value of the expected future cash flows. Bond cash flows are the periodic interest payments and the principal at maturity. Stock and business cash flows come from the future earnings that the assets produce for the firm, usually leading to cash dividend payments.

   To value businesses, assets, and securities, investors and financial managers use a general valuation model to calculate the present value of the expected future cash flows. That model incorporates risk and return, and time value of money concepts.

3. *Compute the market value and the yield to maturity of a bond.*
   The market value of a bond is the sum of the present values of the coupon interest payments plus the present value of the face value to be paid at maturity, given a market's required rate of return.

   The yield to maturity of a bond (YTM) is the average annual rate of return that investors realize if they buy a bond for a certain price, receive the promised interest payments and principal on time, and reinvest the interest payments at the YTM rate.

   A bond's market price and its YTM vary inversely. That is, when the YTM rises, the market price falls, and vice versa. When a bond has a YTM greater than its coupon rate, it sells at a discount to its face value. When the YTM is equal to the coupon rate, the market price equals the face value. When the YTM is less than the coupon rate, the bond sells at a premium over face value.

4. *Calculate the market value and expected yield of preferred stock.*
   The market value of preferred stock is the present value of the stream of preferred stock dividends, discounted at the market's required rate of return for that investment. Because the dividend cash flow stream is a perpetuity, we adapt the present value of a perpetuity formula, Equation 8-5, to value preferred stock.

   The yield on preferred stock represents the annual rate of return that investors realize if they buy the stock for the current market price and then receive the promised dividend payments on time.

5. *Compute the market value per share of common stock.*
   The market value of common stock is estimated in a number of ways, including (1) finding the present value of all the future dividends the stock is expected to pay,

discounted at the market's required rate of return for that stock; and (2) finding the price implied, given the level of earnings per share and the appropriate P/E ratio. The dividend growth model and the P/E valuation approaches assume the firm will be a going concern. That is, the models value the future cash flows that a firm's assets are expected to produce. Two versions of the dividend growth model are commonly used, one for situations in which the future growth of the firm's dividends is expected to be constant, and the other for situations in which the future growth of the firm's dividends is expected to be nonconstant, or supernormal. Supernormal growth implies a period of high growth followed by a settling out at the long-term constant growth rate.

6. *Compute the market value of total common equity.*
   The market value of total common equity is estimated in a number of ways, including (1) estimating common equity value based on the book value of the firm's assets as recorded on the balance sheet, less all liabilities and preferred stock (if any); (2) estimating the value of the firm's assets if they were to be liquidated on the open market and all claims on the firm were to be paid off; and (3) employing a discounted free cash flow model that calculates the present value of expected free cash flows to the suppliers of the firm's capital. The discounted free cash flow model is similar to the nonconstant dividend growth model in that it involves making a forecast of free cash flows during a specified period (usually 7 to 10 years). This is followed by the calculation of the value of the cash flows expected to be received after the forecast period (called the terminal value). The present values of the free cash flows and the present value of the terminal value are summed to produce the total present value of the firm's operations. This figure, in turn, is adjusted by adding current assets and subtracting current liabilities, long-term debt, and preferred stock (if any) to produce the total value of common equity.

7. *Compute the yield on common stock.*
   The yield on common stock is the percentage return investors can expect if they purchase the stock at the prevailing market price and receive the expected cash flows. It is calculated by solving for k in the constant growth dividend model.

8. *Compute the value of a complete business.*
   The market value of a complete business can be found by applying the discounted free cash flow model used to estimate the value of common equity. In the complete business application, current assets are added to the present value of the firm's operations to produce the value of the complete business. Sometimes the value of complete businesses can also be found by calculating the amount that would be required to replace the firm's assets, but this method is usually more effective when applied to the valuation of individual business assets.

Key Terms

book value, net worth The total amount of common stock-holders' equity on a company's balance sheet.

discounted cash flow (DCF) model A model that estimates the value of an asset by calculating the sum of the present values of all future cash flows.

dividend yield A stock's annual dividend divided by its current market price.

yield to maturity (YTM) The investor's return on a bond, assuming that all promised interest and principal payments are made on time and the interest payments are reinvested at the YTM rate.

Equations Introduced in This Chapter

Equation 12-1. The Discounted Cash Flow Valuation Model:

$$V_0 = \frac{CF_1}{(1+k)^1} + \frac{CF_2}{(1+k)^2} + \frac{CF_3}{(1+k)^3} + \ldots + \frac{CF_n}{(1+k)^n}$$

where: V_0 = Present value of the anticipated cash flows from the asset, its current value

$CF_{1, 2, 3, \text{ and } n}$ = Cash flows expected to be received one, two, three, and so on up to n periods in the future

k = Discount rate, the required rate of return per period

Equation 12-2. The Bond Valuation Formula (Algebraic Method):

$$V_B = INT \times \left[\frac{1 - \frac{1}{(1+k_d)^n}}{k_d} \right] + \frac{M}{(1+k_d)^n}$$

where: V_B = Current market value of the bond

INT = Dollar amount of each periodic interest payment

n = Number of times the interest payment is received (which is also the number of periods until maturity)

M = Principal payment received at maturity

k_d = Required rate of return per period on the bond debt instrument

Equation 12-3. The Bond Valuation Formula (Table Method):

$$V_B = (INT \times PVFOA_{k, n}) + (M \times PVF_{k, n})$$

where: $PVFOA_{k, n}$ = Present Value Factor for an Ordinary Annuity from Table IV-A

$PVF_{k, n}$ = Present Value Factor for a single amount from Table II

Equation 12-4. The Formula for the Present Value of Preferred Stock:

$$V_P = \frac{D_p}{k_p}$$

where: V_P = Current market value of the preferred stock

D_p = Amount of the preferred stock dividend per period

k_p = Required rate of return for this issue of preferred stock

Equation 12-5. Formula for the Yield on Preferred Stock:

$$k_p = \frac{D_p}{V_P}$$

where: k_p = Yield per period on investment that an investor can expect if the shares are purchased at the current market price, P_p, and if the preferred dividend, D_p, is paid forever

D_p = Amount of the preferred stock dividend per period

V_P = Current market value of the preferred stock

Equation 12-6. The DCF Valuation Model Applied to Common Stock:

$$P_0 = \frac{D_1}{\left(1 + k_s\right)^1} + \frac{D_2}{\left(1 + k_s\right)^2} + \frac{D_3}{\left(1 + k_s\right)^3} + \ldots + \frac{P_n}{\left(1 + k_s\right)^n}$$

where: P_0 = Present value of the expected dividends, the current price of the common stock

D_1, D_2, D_3, etc. = Common stock dividends expected to be received at the end of periods 1, 2, 3, and so on until the stock is sold

P_n = Anticipated selling price of the stock in n periods

k_s = Required rate of return per period on this common stock investment

Equation 12-7. The Constant Growth Version of the Dividend Valuation Model:

$$P_0 = \frac{D_1}{k_s - g}$$

where: P_0 = Current price of the common stock

D_1 = Dollar amount of the common stock dividend expected one period from now

k_s = Required rate of return per period on this common stock investment

g = Expected constant growth rate per period of the company's common stock dividends

Equation 12-8. The P/E Model for Valuing Common Stock:

Appropriate Stock Price = Industry P/E Ratio × EPS

Equation 12-9. The Book Value of Common Stock:

Book Value of Common Stock = Total Assets − Total Liabilities − Preferred Stock

Equation 12-10. The Constant Growth Free Cash Flow Valuation Model

$$V_{fcft} = \frac{FCF_t(1+g)}{k - g}$$

where: V_{fcft} = the value of future free cash flows at time t

FCF_t = free cash flow at time t

k = the discount rate per period

g = the long-term constant growth rate per period of free cash flows

Equation 12-11. The Yield, or Total Return, on Common Stock:

$$k_s = \frac{D_1}{P_0} + g$$

where: D_1 = Amount of the common stock dividend anticipated in one period

P_0 = Current market price of the common stock

g = Expected constant growth rate of dividends per period

k_s = Expected rate of return per period on this common stock investment

Self-Test

ST-1. The General Motors Corporation has issued a 10.95 percent annual coupon rate bond that matures December 31, 2035. The face value is $1,000. If the required rate of return on bonds of similar risk and maturity is 9 percent, and assuming the time now is January 1, 2019, what is the current value of DaimlerChrysler's bond?

ST-2. General Motors' 10.95 percent coupon rate, 2035 bond is currently selling for $1,115. At this price, what is the yield to maturity of the bond? Assume the time is January 1, 2019.

ST-3. McDonald's is offering preferred stock that pays a dividend of $1.93 a share. The dividend is expected to continue indefinitely. If your required rate of return for McDonald's preferred stock is 8 percent, what is the value of the stock?

ST-4. PepsiCo's next annual dividend is expected to be $1.14 a share. Dividends have been growing at a rate of 6 percent a year, and you expect this rate to continue indefinitely. If your required rate of return for this stock is 9 percent, what is the maximum price you should be willing to pay for it?

ST-5. Goodyear Corporation stock is currently selling for $38. The company's next annual dividend is expected to be $1.00 a share. Dividends have been growing at a rate of 5 percent a year, and you expect this rate to continue indefinitely. If you buy Goodyear at the current price, what will be your yield, or total return?

Review Questions

1. Describe the general pattern of cash flows from a bond with a positive coupon rate.

2. How does the market determine the fair value of a bond?

3. What is the relationship between a bond's market price and its promised yield to maturity? Explain.

4. All other things held constant, how would the market price of a bond be affected if coupon interest payments were made semiannually instead of annually?

5. What is the usual pattern of cash flows for a share of preferred stock? How does the market determine the value of a share of preferred stock, given these promised cash flows?

6. Name two patterns of cash flows for a share of common stock. How does the market determine the value of the most common cash flow pattern for common stock?

7. Define the P/E valuation method. Under what circumstances should a stock be valued using this method?

8. Compare and contrast the book value and liquidation value methods for common stock. Is one method more reliable? Explain.

9. Answer the following questions about the discounted free cash flow model illustrated in Figure 12-4:
   a. What are "free cash flows"?
   b. Explain the terminal-value calculation at the end of the forecast period. Why is it necessary?
   c. Explain the term *present value of the firm's operations* (also known as *enterprise value*). What does this number represent?
   d. Explain the adjustments necessary to translate enterprise value to the total present value of common equity.

10. Explain the difference between the discounted free cash flow model as it is applied to the valuation of common equity and as it is applied to the valuation of complete businesses.

11. Why is the replacement value of assets method not generally used to value complete businesses?

Build Your Communication Skills

CS-1. Check the current price of Texas Instruments Corporation stock or a stock of your choice in the financial press. Then research financial information from last year predicting how Texas Instruments stock (or the stock you chose) would fare and analyze what valuation methods the analysts used. Next, compare the current price with the analysts' price predictions. Prepare a brief oral report that you present to the class discussing your assessment of the analysts' stock valuation.

CS-2. Choose a stock in the financial press. Check its current price. Then estimate the value of the stock using the dividend growth model, Equation 12-7. Compare the value of the stock with its current price and prepare a short memo in which you explain why the two figures might differ.

Problems

12-1. Owen Meany is considering the purchase of a $1,000 Amity Island Municipal Bond. The city is raising funds for a much-needed advertising campaign to promote its East Coast resort community. The stated coupon rate is 6 percent, paid annually. The bond will mature in 10 years. The YTM for similar bonds in the market is 8 percent.

Bond Valuation

    a. How much will the annual interest payments be?

    b. What is the market price of the bond today?

    c. Is the interest received on a municipal bond generally tax free?

12-2. Assume Disney Studios is offering a corporate bond with a face value of $1,000 and an annual coupon rate of 12 percent. The maturity period is 15 years. The interest is to be paid annually. The annual YTM for similar bonds in the market is currently 8 percent.

Bond Valuation

    a. What is the amount of interest to be paid annually for each bond?

    b. What is the value of this $1,000 bond today?

    c. What would be the present value of the interest and principal paid to holders of one of their bonds if the interest payments were made semiannually instead of annually?

12-3. After a major earthquake, the San Francisco Opera Company is offering zero coupon bonds to fund the needed structural repairs to its historic building. Buster Norton is considering the purchase of several of these bonds. The bonds have a face value of $2,000 and are scheduled to mature in 10 years. Similar bonds in the market have an annual YTM of 12 percent. If Mr. Norton purchases three of these bonds today, how much money will he receive 10 years from today at maturity?

Bond Valuation

12-4. Two best friends, Thelma and Louise, are making long-range plans for a road trip vacation to Mexico. They will embark on this adventure in five years and want to invest during the five-year period to earn money for the trip. They decide to purchase a $1,000 Grand Canyon Oil Company bond with an annual coupon rate of 10 percent with interest to be paid semiannually. The bond will mature in five years. The YTM of similar bonds is 8 percent. How much should they be willing to pay for the bond if they purchase it today?

Bonds with Semiannual Interest Payments

12-5. Assume that Intel Corporation's $1,000 face value 9 percent coupon rate bond matures in 10 years and sells for $1,100. If you purchase the bond for $1,100 and hold it to maturity, what will be your average annual rate of return on the investment?

Expected Rate of Return on a Corporate Bond

12-6. Clancy Submarines, Inc. is offering $1,000 par value bonds for sale. The bonds will mature 10 years from today. The annual coupon interest rate is 12 percent, with payments to be made annually. James Hobson just purchased one bond at the current market price of $1,125.

Bond YTM and Pricing

For more, see 8e Spreadsheet Templates for *Microsoft Excel.*

    a. Will the YTM of this bond be greater than or less than the coupon interest rate? Answer this part without doing any calculations.

    b. To the nearest whole percent, what is the YTM of Mr. Hobson's bond? You'll need to crunch some numbers for this part.

    c. What would the YTM have to be to make the market price of the bond equal to the face value? No number crunching is needed to answer.

12-7. A corporate bond has a face value of $1,000 and an annual coupon interest rate of 7 percent. Interest is paid annually. Of the original 20 years to maturity, only 10 years of the life of the bond remain. The current market price of the bond is $872. To the nearest whole percent, what is the YTM of the bond today?

Bond YTM

For more, see 8e Spreadsheet Templates for *Microsoft Excel.*

12-8. The new Shattuck Corporation will offer its preferred stock for sale in the very near future. These shares will have a guaranteed annual dividend of $10 per share. As you research the market, you find that similar preferred stock has an expected rate of return of 12 percent. If this preferred stock could be purchased today, what price per share would you expect to pay for it?

Preferred Stock Valuation

Preferred Stock k

12-9. Lucky Jackson knows that one share of Grand Prix Enterprises preferred stock sells for $20 per share on the open market. From its annual reports, he sees that Grand Prix pays an annual dividend of $1.75 per share on this preferred stock. What is the market's required rate of return on Grand Prix's stock?

Preferred Stock Valuation

12-10. Tiny Shipping Corporation is planning to sell preferred stock that will pay an annual dividend of $8 per share. The current expected rate of return from similar preferred stock issues is 13 percent.

    a. What price per share would you expect to have to pay to purchase this stock?

    b. If the stock is actually selling for $50 per share, what is the market's required rate of return for this stock?

Common Stock Valuation per Share

12-11. China S. Construction, Inc., is in the business of building electrical power plants in the eastern United States. Jack Godell and the rest of the board members of the firm have just announced a $4 per share dividend on the corporation's common stock to be paid in one year. Because the quality of some of its recent projects is under attack by investigative television reporters, the expected constant dividend growth rate is only estimated to be 1 percent. The required rate of return for similar stocks in this industry is 16 percent.

    a. What is the present value of the expected dividends from one share of China S. Construction's common stock?

    b. What is the stock's dividend yield (D_1/P_0)?

Yield on Common Stock

12-12. The current listed price per share of a certain common stock is $15. The cash dividend expected from this corporation in one year is $2 per share. All market research indicates that the expected constant growth rate in dividends will be 4 percent per year in future years. What is the rate of return on this investment that an investor can expect if shares are purchased at the current listed price?

Common Stock Valuation per Share

12-13. Golden Manufacturing Company is expected to pay a dividend of $8 per share of common stock in one year. The dollar amount of the dividends is expected to grow at a constant 3 percent per year in future years. The required rate of return from shares of similar common stock in the present environment is 14 percent.

    a. What would you expect the current market price of a share of Golden common stock to be?

    b. Assuming the cash dividend amount and the growth rate are accurate, what is the annual rate of return on your investment in Golden common stock if you purchased shares at the stock's actual listed price of $65 per share?

Bond Valuation

12-14. Micron issues a 9 percent coupon bond with a maturity of 5 years. The face value of the bond, payable at maturity, is $1,000. What is the value of this bond if your required rate of return is 12 percent?

Bond Valuation (Semiannual Interest)

12-15. Sam wants to purchase a bond that has a par value of $1,000, an annual coupon rate of 7 percent, and a maturity of 10 years. The bond's interest is paid semiannually. Sam's annual required rate of return is 11 percent. What should Sam be willing to pay for this particular bond?

Discounted Cash Flows (DCF)

12-16. What is the value of a security that entitles you to receive the following payments if your required rate of return for this type of security is 23 percent?

$80—end of year 1

$150—end of year 2

$1,500—end of year 3

Preferred Stock Valuation

12-17. Tom expects the issue of InVest preferred stock to pay an annual dividend of $3 per share. He also has researched the company and feels that 12 percent is a fair rate of return for this investment. Calculate the value of each share of stock.

12-18. Analysts forecast that Dixie Chicks, Inc. (DCI) will pay a dividend of $2.20 a share at the end of this year, continuing a long-term growth trend of 9 percent a year. If this trend is expected to continue indefinitely and investors' required rate of return for DCI is 18 percent, what is the market value per share of DCI's common stock?

Common Stock Valuation, Constant Growth

12-19. PepsiCo (NYSE: PEP) paid a dividend of $0.58 per share this year. Dividends at the end of each of the next five years are expected to be as follows:

Common Stock Valuation, Constant Growth

Year 1	$0.70
Year 2	$0.83
Year 3	$0.96
Year 4	$1.09
Year 5	$1.22

After year 5, dividends are expected to grow indefinitely at 10 percent a year.

If your required rate of return for PepsiCo common stock is 12 percent, what is the most that you would pay per share for PepsiCo today?

12-20. Regis knows that CRS stock sells for $82 per share, has a growth rate of 7 percent, and a dividend that was just paid of $3.82. What can Regis expect as an annual percent yield if he purchases a share of CRS stock?

Common Stock Yield

12-21. Gwenyth just purchased a bond for $1,250 that has a maturity of 10 years and a coupon interest rate of 8.5 percent, paid annually. What is the YTM of the $1,000 face value bond that she purchased?

Yield to Maturity (YTM)

12-22. Analysts forecast that free cash flows from Dixie Chicks, Inc. (DCI) will be $2.1 million in the coming year, continuing a long-term growth trend of 9 percent a year. If this trend is expected to continue indefinitely and investors' required rate of return for DCI is 18 percent, what will be the total enterprise value of DCI?

Enterprise Value, Constant Growth

12-23. The free cash flow for PepsiCo (NYSE: PEP) this year was $1,026,600,000. Free cash flows at the end of each of the next five years are expected to be as follows:

Enterprise Value, Nonconstant Growth

Year 1	$1,231,920,000
Year 2	$1,453,665,600
Year 3	$1,686,252,096
Year 4	$1,922,327,389
Year 5	$2,153,006,676

After year 5, free cash flows are expected to grow indefinitely at 10 percent a year.

If the weighted average cost of capital (WACC) for PepsiCo is 12 percent, what is the enterprise value of the company today?

12-24. Jack and Frank Baker know their piano renditions of lounge songs have limited appeal on the nightclub circuit, so they work part-time as investment consultants. They are researching relatively unknown corporations, one of which is Susie Diamond Enterprises. To get a quick idea of the value of SDE's common stock, they have taken the following numbers from the most recent financial statements.

Book Value

Total Assets	$675,000
Total Liabilities	$120,000
250,000 Shares of Common Stock Issued	
100,000 Shares of Common Stock Outstanding	

What is the book value (net worth) of Susie Diamond Enterprises?

12-25. The most recent balance sheet of Free Enterprise, Inc., follows.

**Free Enterprise, Inc., Balance Sheet December 31, 2018
(thousands of dollars)**

Assets		Liabilities + Equity	
Cash	$ 4,000	Accounts Payable	$ 4,400
Accounts Receivable	10,000	Notes Payable	4,000
Inventory	13,000	Accrued Expenses	5,000
Prepaid Expenses	400	Total Current Liabilities	13,400
Total Current Assets	27,400	Bonds Payable	6,000
Fixed Assets	11,000	Common Equity	19,000
Total Assets	$ 38,400	Total Liabilities + Equity	$ 38,400

   a. What was Free Enterprise's book value (net worth) at the beginning of 2019?

   b. If the company had 750,000 shares of common stock authorized and 500,000 shares outstanding, what was the book value per share of common stock at the beginning of 2019?

   c. Net income of Free Enterprise, Inc. was $5,610,000 in 2018. Calculate the earnings per share of Free Enterprise's common stock.

   d. The P/E ratio for a typical company in Free Enterprise, Inc.'s industry is estimated to be 6. Using the EPS from part c) above, calculate the price of one share of common stock at the beginning of 2019, assuming that Free Enterprise commands a P/E ratio value equal to that of an average company in its industry.

   e. What would you infer about the company's total assets shown on the balance sheet when comparing this calculated stock price with the company's book value per share?

   f. Calculate the liquidation value of Free Enterprise's common stock assuming the market value of the total assets is $50 million and the market value of total liabilities is $20 million, as estimated by your analyst.

 12-26. Lucky Jackson is trying to choose from among the best of the three investment alternatives recommended to him by his full-service investment broker. The alternatives are

   a. The corporate bond of Star Mining Company has a face value of $1,000 and an annual coupon interest rate of 13 percent. The bond is selling in the market at $1,147.58. Of the original 20 years to maturity, only 16 years of the life of the bond remain.

   b. The preferred stock of Supernova Minerals Company has a par value of $100 per share and it offers an annual dividend of $14 per share. The market price of the stock is $140 per share.

   c. The common stock of White Dwarf Ores Company sells in the market at $300 per share. The company paid a dividend of $39 per share yesterday. The company is expected to grow at 3 percent per annum in the future.

   Which of the three alternatives should Lucky choose? Remember the priority of claims for bondholders, preferred stockholders, and common stockholders from Chapters 1 and 4.

 12-27. Suppose Flash in the Pan Corporation is expected to pay an annual dividend of $3 per share one year from now and that this dividend will grow at the following rates during each of the following four years (to the end of year 5): Year 2, 20 percent; Year 3, 30 percent; Year 4, 20 percent; Year 5, 10 percent. After this supernormal growth period, the dividend will grow at a sustainable 5 percent rate each year beyond year 5.

a. What is the present value of the dividends to be paid during the supernormal growth period? Assume that the required rate of return, k_s, is 15 percent.

b. What is the present value of the dividends to be paid during the normal growth period (from year 6 through infinity)?

c. What is the total present value of one share of Flash in the Pan's common stock?

For more, see 8e Spreadsheet Templates for *Microsoft Excel.*

12-28. Assume that you are the owner of a pet foods company and you are interested in acquiring the stock of Hardi-Pets, an up-and-coming company that markets a new type of dog food that causes pets that eat it to never get sick and to never need shots. Selected financial data for Hardi-Pets is shown.

Discounted Free Cash Flow Model for Total Common Equity (Challenge Problem)

Hardi-Pets, Inc., Selected Financial Data for 2018

Total Revenue	$ 1,000,000
Cost of Goods Sold	500,000
Gross Profit	500,000
Selling, General and Administrative Expenses	200,000
Earnings before Interest, Taxes, Depr. & Amort. (EBITDA)	300,000
Depreciation and Amortization	100,000
Earnings before Interest and Taxes (EBIT)	200,000
Capital Expenditures	$ 15,000
Combined Federal and State Income Tax Rate	40%
Current Assets, Dec. 31, 2018	$ 100,000
Current Liabilities, Dec. 31, 2018	80,000
Long-Term Debt, Dec. 31, 2018	500,000
Preferred Stock Outstanding, Dec. 31, 2018	0

For more, see 8e Spreadsheet Templates for *Microsoft Excel.*

Prepare a valuation analysis of Hardi-Pets total common equity using the discounted free cash flow model. Use a spreadsheet format similar to the example shown in Figure 12-4. The following forecasting variables apply. Assume that the time now is January 1, 2019.

	2019	2020	2021	2022	2023	2024	2025	2026	2027	2028
Revenue Growth Factor	10%	15%	20%	25%	30%	25%	20%	15%	10%	5%
Expected Gross Profit Margin	50%	50%	50%	50%	50%	50%	50%	50%	50%	50%
S, G, & A Exp % of Revenue	20%	20%	20%	20%	20%	20%	20%	20%	20%	20%
Depr. & Amort. % of Revenue	10%	10%	10%	10%	10%	10%	10%	10%	10%	10%
Capital Expend. Growth Factor	10%	10%	10%	10%	−10%	−10%	−10%	−10%	−10%	−10%
Net Working Cap to Sales Ratio	10%	10%	10%	10%	10%	10%	10%	10%	10%	10%

Income tax rate = 40%

Assumed long-term sustainable growth rate = 5% per year after 2028

Discount rate = 20%

For more, see 8e
Spreadsheet Templates
for *Microsoft Excel.*

12-29. The Great Expectations Company just finished its first year of operations in which the company realized $2 million in revenue. Company managers are looking forward to a number of years of rapid growth ahead, and to this end, they are seeking $10 million in long-term debt financing from the Capital 4 U Financing Company. However, before the loan can be approved, an independent appraisal of Great Expectations is required to establish the fair market value of the company.

Assume that you are a financial analyst working for Value Plus, Independent Appraisers. Capital 4 U has engaged your firm to estimate the fair market value of Great Expectations as a complete business. Selected financial data for Great Expectations is shown.

Great Expectations, Inc., Selected Financial Data for 2018

Total Revenue	$ 2,000,000
Cost of Goods Sold	1,200,000
Gross Profit	800,000
Selling, General and Administrative Expenses	1,200,000
Earnings before Interest, Taxes, Depr. & Amort. (EBITDA)	(400,000)
Depreciation and Amortization	200,000
Earnings before Interest and Taxes (EBIT)	(600,000)
Capital Expenditures	$ 1,000,000
Combined Federal and State Income Tax Rate	40%
Current Assets, Dec. 31, 2018	$ 500,000

Prepare a valuation analysis of Great Expectations as a complete business using the discounted free cash flow model. Use a spreadsheet format similar to the example shown in Figure 12-4, modified for a complete business. The following forecasting variables apply. Assume that the time now is January 1, 2019.

	2019	2020	2021	2022	2023	2024	2025	2026	2027	2028
Revenue Growth Factor	20%	30%	40%	50%	60%	50%	40%	30%	20%	10%
Expected Gross Profit Margin	50%	51%	52%	53%	54%	55%	56%	57%	58%	59%
S, G, & A Exp % of Revenue	50%	40%	30%	29%	28%	27%	26%	25%	24%	23%
Depr. & Amort. % of Revenue	10%	10%	10%	10%	10%	10%	10%	10%	10%	10%
Capital Expend. Growth Factor	40%	35%	30%	25%	20%	−10%	−15%	−20%	−25%	−30%
Net Working Cap to Sales Ratio	19%	18%	17%	16%	15%	14%	13%	12%	11%	10%

Income tax rate = 40%

Assumed long-term sustainable growth rate = 5% per year after 2028

Discount rate = 20%

ST-1. The present value of General Motors 10.95 percent 2035 bond can be found using Equation 12-2:

$$V_B = INT \times \left[\frac{1 - \dfrac{1}{(1 + k_d)^n}}{k_d} \right] + \frac{M}{(1 + k_d)^n}$$

Face value is $1,000

The coupon interest payment is 10.95 percent of $1,000, or $109.50.

$n = 16$

$k_d = 9\%$

$$V_B = \$109.50 \times \left[\frac{1 - \dfrac{1}{(1 + .09)^{16}}}{.09} \right] + \frac{\$1,000}{(1 + .09)^{16}}$$

$$= \left(\$109.50 \times 8.312558193 \right) + \left(\frac{\$1,000}{3.970305881} \right)$$

$$= \$910.2251 + \$251.8698$$

$$= \$1,162.09$$

So the present value of the interest and principal and thus the price of the bond is $1,162.09.

ST-2. Using the financial calculator, we enter:

1000 [FV]; 109.50 [PMT]; 16 [N]; 1115 [+/–] [PV]; and then [CPT] [I/Y] to get the YTM value of 9.52%. The same answer could be obtained using the Excel RATE function.

ST-3. Equation 12-5 is used to find the value of preferred stock as follows:

$$V_P = \frac{D_p}{k_p}$$

D_p is $1.93 and k_p is 8 percent.

$$V_P = \frac{\$1.93}{.08}$$

$$= \$24.125$$

ST-4. The maximum price you are willing to pay for PepsiCo is what it is worth to you, or its value. Because the characteristics of the stock fit the constant dividend growth model, use Equation 12-7 to compute the value.

$$P_0 = \frac{D_1}{k_s - g}$$

D_1 is $1.14, k_s is 9 percent, and g is 6 percent.

Given these conditions, the value of Quaker Oats stock is

$$P_0 = \frac{\$1.14}{.09 - .06}$$

$$= \frac{\$1.14}{.03}$$

$$= \$38$$

ST-5. The yield on common stock can be found using Equation 12-11.

$$k_s = \frac{D_1}{P_0} + g$$

D_1 is $1.00, P_0 is $38, and g is 5 percent. Given these conditions, the yield on Goodyear common stock is as follows:

$$k_s = \frac{\$1.00}{\$38} + .05$$

$$= .0263 + .05$$

$$= .0763, \text{ or } 7.63\%$$

Long-Term Financing Decisions

PART 4

Source: MaxxiGo/Shutterstock

Chapter 13
Capital Structure Basics

Chapter 14
Corporate Bonds, Preferred Stock, and Leasing

Chapter 15
Common Stock

Chapter 16
Dividend Policy

Long-term financing decisions concern how the firm finances its assets over the long term (that is, for more than one year). At issue are the proper balance between debt and equity financing, and the procedures associated with raising money from the various long-term financing sources. Chapter 13 begins this section with an introduction to capital structure theory, which examines the aspects of financing with debt and financing with equity and how the blend affects the firm. Chapter 14 covers long-term debt financing and financing from sources that are similar to long-term debt: preferred stock and leasing. Chapter 15 covers financing obtained from the firm's owners in the form of common stock ownership. Chapter 16 ends the section with the study of what to do with the firm's excess funds, examining the factors that lead to either distributing the funds to stockholders in the form of dividends or retaining it for growth.

Capital Structure Basics

"The only person who sticks closer to you in adversity than a friend is a creditor."
—Unknown

CHAPTER 13

Source: Light And Dark Studio/Shutterstock

Learning Objectives

After reading this chapter, you should be able to:

1. Define capital structure.
2. Explain operating, financial, and combined leverage effects and the resulting business and financial risks.
3. Find the breakeven level of sales for a firm.
4. Describe the risks and returns of a leveraged buyout.
5. Explain how changes in capital structure affect a firm's value.

A Popcorn Venture

Jason is a college student who wants to start his own business. Jason's business idea is to sell popcorn from a cart, just as he has seen done in the downtown area of the city in which he lives. The downtown vendor sells about 500 bags of popcorn a day, and Jason thinks he might be able to do as well with a similar popcorn stand near the college in his town.

However, the wagon contains both a popcorn-making machine and a storage room for supplies, so it isn't cheap. Also, if Jason went into this business, he would need an expensive business operator's license from the city. The downtown vendor charges only $1 for a bag of popcorn, so Jason would have to sell a lot of popcorn to recoup the high price of the wagon and the license, $8,000 and $4,000, respectively. His variable costs are $0.04 per bag.

Is this a viable business idea or not? What are the risks and the potential returns of this business? Is this a better path than taking a McJob, as many of Jason's friends have done? In this chapter we'll look at some of these issues.

Source: Jason's popcorn venture is based on actual events. The entrepreneur's name has been changed and approximate numbers have been used, because data about this private company are confidential.

Chapter Overview

In this chapter, we investigate how fixed costs affect the volatility of a firm's operating and net income. We see how fixed operating costs create *operating leverage*, which magnifies the effect of sales changes on operating income. We also examine how fixed financial costs create *financial leverage*, which magnifies the effect of changes in operating income on net income. Then we analyze the risk and return of leveraged buyouts (LBOs). Finally, we see how changes in a firm's capital structure affect the firm's overall value.

Capital Structure

Capital structure is the mixture of funding sources (debt, preferred stock, or common stock) that a firm uses to finance its assets. A central question in finance is what blend of these financing sources is best for the firm. That is, how much of a firm's assets should be financed by borrowing? How much should be financed by preferred stockholders? How much should be financed by the common stockholders? The question is important because each of these financing sources has a different cost, as you learned in Chapter 9, and each of them has a different degree of risk. Therefore, the choice of financing directly affects a firm's weighted average cost of capital and the degree of riskiness in the firm.

leverage Something that creates a magnifying effect, such as when fixed operating or fixed financial costs cause a magnifying effect on the movements of operating income or net income.

When a firm uses debt to finance its assets this creates **leverage**. A firm with a lot of debt in its capital structure is said to be highly levered. A firm with no debt is said to be unlevered. In physics, the term *leverage* describes how a relatively small force input can be magnified to create a larger force output. For example, if a farmer wants to move a large boulder in a field, he can wedge a long board (a lever) between the large boulder and a small rock (a fulcrum), which gives him enough leverage to push down on the end of the long board and easily move the boulder.

The power of leverage can also be harnessed in a financial setting. Its magnifying power can help or hurt a business. A firm that has leverage will earn or lose more than it would without leverage. In the sections that follow, we investigate specific types of leverage and the risks associated with each type.

Operating Leverage

operating leverage The effect of fixed operating costs on operating income; because of fixed costs, any change in sales results in a larger percentage change in operating income.

Operating leverage refers to the phenomenon whereby a small change in sales triggers a relatively large change in operating income (or earnings before interest and taxes, also known as EBIT). Operating leverage occurs because of fixed costs in the operations of the firm. A firm with fixed costs in the production process will see its EBIT rise by a larger percentage than sales when unit sales are increasing. If unit sales drop, however, the firm's EBIT will decrease by a greater percentage than its sales.

Table 13-1 illustrates the operating leverage effect for a firm in which all production costs, a total of $5,000, are fixed. Observe how the presence of the fixed costs causes a 10 percent change in sales to produce a 20 percent change in operating income.

Calculating the Degree of Operating Leverage

degree of operating leverage (DOL) The percentage change in operating income divided by the percentage change in sales.

The degree of operating leverage, or DOL, measures the magnitude of the operating leverage effect. The **degree of operating leverage** is the percentage change in earnings before interest and taxes (%ΔEBIT) divided by the percentage change in sales (% Δ Sales):

TABLE 13-1 The Operating Leverage Effect—Fixed Costs Only

	Period 1	Period 2	Percent Change
Sales	$ 10,000	$ 11,000	10%
Fixed Costs	− 5,000	− 5,000	
Operating Income	$ 5,000	$ 6,000	20%

Degree of Operating Leverage (DOL)

$$DOL = \frac{\%\Delta \ EBIT}{\%\Delta \ Sales}$$

(13-1)

where: $\%\Delta$ EBIT = Percentage change in earnings before interest and taxes

$\%\Delta$ Sales = Percentage change in sales

According to Equation 13-1, the DOL for the firm in Table 13-1 is

$$DOL = \frac{20\%}{10\%}$$
$$= 2.0$$

We see that, for a firm with a 10 percent change in sales and a 20 percent change in EBIT, the DOL is 2.0. A DOL greater than 1 shows that the firm has operating leverage. That is, when sales change by some percentage, EBIT will change by a greater percentage.

The Effect of Fixed Costs on DOL

Table 13-2 shows the projected base-year and second-year income statement for Jason's Popcorn Wagon. The income statement allows us to analyze Jason's operating leverage. (Note that Table 13-2 divides the operating expenses into two categories, fixed and variable.) We see that sales and operating expenses are likely to change in the second and subsequent years. We also see the predicted impact on EBIT, given the sales forecast.

We see from Table 13-2 that Jason's percentage change in sales is 10 percent, and his percentage change in EBIT (or operating income) is 17.1 percent. We use Equation 13-1 to find Jason's DOL, as follows:

$$
DOL = \frac{\%\Delta \ EBIT}{\%\Delta \ Sales}
$$
$$
= \frac{(19,680 - 16,800)/16,800}{(33,000 - 30,000)/30,000}
$$
$$
= \frac{.171}{.10}
$$
$$
= 1.71
$$

Our DOL calculations indicate that if Jason's Popcorn Wagon business sales increase by 10 percent from the base year to the next year, EBIT will increase by 17.1 percent.

TABLE 13-2 Jason's Popcorn Wagon Projected Income Statement (Fixed Costs Are $12,000, Variable Costs Are $0.04 per Unit, and Price per Unit is $1.00)

	Base Year	Year 2	
Sales	$30,000	$33,000	$\%\Delta = \dfrac{33,000 - 30,000}{30.000} = .10$, or 10%
– VC	– 1,200	– 1,320	
– FC	– 12,000	– 12,000	
= EBIT	= $16,800	= $19,680	$\%\Delta = \dfrac{19,680 - 16,800}{16.800} = .171$, or 17.1%

This larger percentage increase in EBIT is caused by the company's fixed operating costs. No matter how much popcorn Jason produces and sells, his wagon and license costs stay the same. The fixed costs cause the EBIT to increase faster than sales. If sales decrease, the fixed costs must still be paid. As a result, the fixed costs cause EBIT to drop by a greater percentage than sales.

The Alternate Method of Calculating DOL

Instead of using Equation 13-1, we may also find the DOL by using only numbers found in the base-year income statement. Subtract total variable costs from sales, divide that number by sales minus total variable costs minus fixed costs, and solve for DOL. The formula for the alternate method of finding DOL, Equation 13-2, follows:

Degree of Operating Leverage (DOL) (alternate)

$$DOL = \frac{Sales - VC}{Sales - VC - FC}$$

(13-2)

where: VC = Total variable costs

FC = Total fixed costs

From Table 13-2, we know that in the base year, Jason's Popcorn Wagon has sales of $30,000, variable costs of $1,200, and fixed costs of $12,000. Using the alternate formula, we find that Jason has the following DOL:

$$
\begin{aligned}
DOL &= \frac{Sales - VC}{Sales - VC - FC} \\
&= \frac{30,000 - 1,200}{30,000 - 1,200 - 12,000} \\
&= \frac{28,800}{16,800} \\
&= 1.71
\end{aligned}
$$

We find a DOL of 1.71, just as we did with Equation 13-1. How did this happen? The alternate formula, Equation 13-2, uses only numbers from the base year income statement, whereas Equation 13-1 requires information from the base year and year 2.[1] Why use two different ways to calculate DOL when they both give the same answer? The answer is that each method reveals different information about operating leverage.

The percentage change version of the DOL formula, Equation 13-1, shows the effect of the leverage—sales change by a certain percentage, triggering a greater percentage change in operating income if the DOL is greater than 1. The percentage change in operating income, then, is the product of the percentage change in sales and this degree of operating leverage.

The alternate DOL formula, Equation 13-2, shows that fixed costs cause the leveraging effect. Whenever fixed costs are greater than 0, DOL is greater than 1, indicating a leverage effect (the percentage change in EBIT is greater than the percentage change in sales). The larger the amount of fixed costs, the greater the leveraging effect.

Taken together, the two formulas demonstrate that leverage has the effect of triggering a greater percentage change in operating income when a percentage change in sales occurs and that fixed costs cause operating leverage. Equation 13-3 shows how changes in sales and DOL combine to determine the change in EBIT.

---

1. Equations 13-1 and 13-2 give the same numeric result when sales price per unit, fixed costs, and variable costs per unit are constant.

Percentage Change in EBIT

$$\%\Delta\ \text{EBIT} = \%\Delta\ \text{Sales} \times \text{DOL} \qquad (13\text{-}3)$$

where: %Δ Sales = Percentage change in sales

DOL = Degree of operating leverage

The Risk of Operating Leverage

As we know from Chapter 7, the risk associated with operating leverage is business risk. Recall that business risk refers to the volatility of operating income. The more uncertainty about what a company's operating income will be, the higher its business risk. Volatility of sales triggers business risk. The presence of fixed costs, shown by the amount of DOL, magnifies business risk. The total degree of business risk that a company faces is a function of both sales volatility and the degree of operating leverage.

Financial Leverage

Fluctuations in sales and the degree of operating leverage determine the fluctuations in operating income (also known as EBIT). Now let's turn our attention to financial leverage. **Financial leverage** is the additional volatility of net income caused by the presence of fixed-cost funds (such as fixed-rate debt) in the firm's capital structure. Interest on fixed-rate debt is a fixed cost because a firm must pay the same amount of interest, no matter what the firm's operating income.

financial leverage
The phenomenon whereby a change in operating income causes net income to change by a larger percentage because of the presence of fixed financial costs.

Calculating the Degree of Financial Leverage (DFL)

The **degree of financial leverage (DFL)** is the percentage change in net income (%ΔNI) divided by the percentage change in EBIT (%ΔEBIT). The formula for DFL follows:

degree of financial leverage (DFL) The percentage change in net income divided by the percentage change in operating income.

Degree of Financial Leverage (DFL)

$$\text{DFL} = \frac{\%\Delta\ \text{NI}}{\%\Delta\ \text{EBIT}}$$

$$(13\text{-}4)$$

where: %Δ NI = Percentage change in net income

%Δ EBIT = Percentage change in earnings before interest and taxes

If net income changes by a greater percentage than EBIT changes, then the DFL will have a value greater than 1, and this indicates a financial leverage effect.[2]

Table 13-3 shows the entire base-year income statement for Jason's Popcorn Wagon and the projections for year 2. Notice that the lower portion of the income statements contains fixed interest expense, so we would expect the presence of financial leverage.

As shown in Table 13-3, the percentage change in EBIT from the base year to year 2 is 17.1 percent, and the percentage change in net income from the base year to year 2 is 18 percent. Jason's degree of financial leverage according to Equation 13-4 follows:

$$\begin{aligned}
\text{DFL} &= \frac{\%\Delta\ \text{NI}}{\%\Delta\ \text{EBIT}} \\[6pt]
&= \frac{.18}{.171} \\[6pt]
&= 1.05
\end{aligned}$$

---

2. Note that the degree of financial leverage calculated using Equation 13-4 will be faced by preferred stockholders and common stockholders together. If you were interested in finding the degree of financial leverage faced by common stockholders only, you would modify Equation 13-4 by subtracting preferred dividends from net income.

TABLE 13-3 Jason's Popcorn Wagon Projected Income Statements

	Base Year	Year 2	
Sales	$30,000	$33,000	$\%\Delta = \dfrac{33,000 - 30,000}{30,000} = .10,$ or 10%
− VC	− 1,200	− 1,320	
− FC	− 12,000	− 12,000	
= EBIT	= $16,800	= $19,800	$\%\Delta = \dfrac{19,680 - 16,800}{16,800} = .171,$ or 17.1%
− Int	− 800	− 800	
= EBT	= 16,000	= 18,880	
− Tax(15%)	− 2,400	− 2,832	
= NI	= 13,600	= 16,048	$\%\Delta = \dfrac{16,048 - 13,600}{13,600} = .18,$ or 18%

Our calculations show that Jason's Popcorn Wagon business has a degree of financial leverage of 1.05.

Another Method of Calculating Financial Leverage

Just as with DOL, there are two ways to compute DFL. Instead of using Equation 13-4, the percentage change in NI divided by the percentage change in EBIT, we could instead calculate the DFL using only numbers found in the base-year income statement. By dividing EBIT by EBIT minus interest expense (Int), we can find DFL. The equation looks like this:

Degree of Financial Leverage (DFL) (alternate)

$$DFL = \frac{EBIT}{EBIT - Int}$$

(13-5)

where: EBIT = Earnings before interest and taxes

Int = Interest expense

The base-year income statement numbers in Table 13-3 show that Jason's EBIT is $16,800 and his interest expense is $800. To find the degree of financial leverage, we apply Equation 13-5 as follows:

$$DFL = \frac{EBIT}{EBIT - Int}$$
$$= \frac{16,800}{16,800 - 800}$$
$$= \frac{16,800}{16,000}$$
$$= 1.05$$

Equation 13-5 yields the same DFL for Jason's business as Equation 13-4.[3] Both formulas are important because they give us different but equally important insights about

---

3. Equations 13-4 and 13-5 give the same DFL value only if the fixed financial costs (interest expense) and the tax rate are constant.

financial leverage. Equation 13-4 shows the effect of financial leverage—net income (NI) will vary by a larger percentage than operating income (EBIT). Equation 13-5 pinpoints the source of financial leverage—fixed interest expense. The degree of financial leverage, DFL, will be greater than 1 if interest expense (I) is greater than 0. In sum, interest expense magnifies the volatility of NI as operating income changes.

How Interest Expense Affects Financial Leverage

To illustrate the financial leverage effect, suppose that to help start his business, Jason borrowed $10,000 from a bank at an annual interest rate of 8 percent. This 8 percent annual interest rate means that Jason will have to pay $800 ($10,000 × .08) in interest each year on the loan. The interest payments must be made, no matter how much operating income Jason's business generates. In addition to Jason's fixed operating costs, he also has fixed financial costs (the interest payments on the loan) of $800.

The fixed financial costs magnify the effect of a change in operating income on net income. For instance, even if Jason's business does well, the bank interest payments do not increase, even though he could afford to pay more. If Jason's business does poorly, however, he cannot force the bank to accept less interest simply because he cannot afford the payments.

The Risk of Financial Leverage

The presence of debt in a company's capital structure and the accompanying interest cost create extra risk for a firm. As we know from Chapter 7, the extra volatility in NI caused by fixed interest expense is financial risk. The financial risk of the firm compounds the effect of business risk and magnifies the volatility of net income. Just as fixed operating expenses increase the volatility of operating income and business risk, so too fixed financial expenses increase the volatility of NI and increase financial risk. This is shown in Equation 13-6.

$$\text{Percentage Change in Net Income}$$

$$\%\Delta\, NI = \%\Delta\, EBIT \times DFL \qquad (13\text{-}6)$$

where: $\%\Delta\, EBIT$ = Percentage change in earnings before interest and taxes

DFL = Degree of financial leverage

Now we explore the combined effect of operating and financial leverage next.

Combined Leverage

The combined effect of operating leverage and financial leverage is known as **combined leverage**. Combined leverage occurs when net income changes by a larger percentage than sales, which occurs if there are any fixed operating or financial costs. The following combined leverage formula solves for the net income change due to sales changes that occur when fixed operating and financial costs are present.

The **degree of combined leverage (DCL)** is the percentage change in net income ($\%\Delta\, NI$) divided by the percentage change in sales ($\%\Delta\, Sales$), as shown in Equation 13-7:

$$\text{Degree of Combined Leverage (DCL)}$$

$$DCL = \frac{\%\Delta\, NI}{\%\Delta\, Sales} \qquad (13\text{-}7)$$

where: $\%\Delta\, NI$ = Percentage change in net income

$\%\Delta\, Sales$ = Percentage change in sales

combined leverage
The phenomenon whereby a change in sales causes net income to change by a larger percentage because of fixed operating and financial costs.

degree of combined leverage (DCL) The percentage change in net income divided by the percentage change in sales.

The alternate DCL formula follows:

Degree of Combined Leverage (DCL) (alternate 1)

$$DCL = \frac{Sales - VC}{Sales - VC - FC - Int} \qquad (13\text{-}8)$$

where: VC = Total variable costs

               FC = Total fixed costs

               Int = Interest expense

We can also calculate the degree of combined leverage (DCL) a third way: multiplying the degree of operating leverage (DOL) by the degree of financial leverage (DFL). The third DCL formula is shown in Equation 13-9.

Degree of Combined Leverage (DCL) (alternate 2)

$$DCL = DOL \times DFL \qquad (13\text{-}9)$$

where: DOL = Degree of operating leverage

               DFL = Degree of financial leverage

Equation 13-10 shows the combined effect of DOL and DFL on net income (NI).

Percentage Change in Net Income (NI)

$$\%\Delta\, NI = \%\Delta\, Sales \times DOL \times DFL \qquad (13\text{-}10)$$

where: %Δ Sales = Percentage change in sales

               DOL = Degree of operating leverage

               DFL = Degree of financial leverage

Equation 13-10 shows how the change in net income is determined by the change in sales and the compounding effects of operating and financial leverage.

Fixed Costs and Combined Leverage

Fixed operating costs create operating leverage, fixed financial costs create financial leverage, and these two types of leverage together form combined leverage. If fixed operating costs (FC) and fixed interest costs (Int) were both zero, there would be no leverage effect. The percentage change in net income (NI) would be the same as the percentage change in sales. If either, or both, fixed operating costs and fixed financial costs exceed zero, a leverage effect will occur (DCL > 1).

Firms that have high operating leverage need to be careful about how much debt they pile onto their balance sheets, and the accompanying interest costs they incur because of combined leverage effects. Remember that for Jason's Popcorn Wagon, the degree of operating leverage (DOL) was 1.71 and the degree of financial leverage was 1.05. The degree of combined leverage for Jason's business according to Equation 13-8 is 1.80 (1.71 × 1.05 = 1.80 rounded to two decimal places). Jason is quite confident that his sales will be high enough so that this high leverage will not be a problem. If the sales outlook were questionable, though, the combined leverage effect could magnify poor sales results.

Leverage is helpful when sales increase (positive percentage changes). Magnifying this positive change benefits the firm. However, leverage is harmful when sales decrease because it magnifies the negative change. Because future sales for most companies are uncertain, most companies view leverage with mixed feelings.

Breakeven Analysis and Leverage

Investments in projects may change a firm's fixed operating and financing costs, thereby affecting firm value. Fixed costs may affect firm value because of *leverage effects* and the resulting risk from those leverage effects.

To understand a firm's potential for risk and return, then, financial managers must understand two types of leverage effects: operating leverage and financial leverage.

Breakeven analysis is a key to understanding *operating leverage*. In breakeven analysis we examine fixed and variable operating costs. **Fixed costs** are those costs that do not vary with the company's level of production. **Variable costs** are those costs that change as the company's production levels change.

In breakeven analysis, the **sales breakeven point** is the level of sales that a firm must reach to cover its operating costs. Put another way, it is the point at which the operating income (earnings before interest and taxes) equals zero.

A company with high fixed operating costs must generate high sales revenue to reach the sales breakeven point. A company with low fixed operating costs requires relatively low sales revenue to reach its sales breakeven point.

We usually observe a high/low trade-off in breakeven analysis. Firms with high fixed operating costs tend to have low variable costs, and vice versa. A company that automates a factory, for instance, commits to significant fixed costs—the expensive equipment. But the company's variable labor costs are likely to be low at a highly automated plant that operates with relatively few employees. In contrast, a company that produces handmade pottery with little overhead and hires hourly workers as needed, is likely to have low fixed costs but high variable costs.[4]

To demonstrate the high/low trade-off, we gather data for a sales breakeven chart for two firms. The first firm has high fixed and low variable costs. The second firm has low fixed and high variable costs.

> **fixed costs** Costs that do not vary with the level of production.
>
> **variable costs** Costs that vary with the level of production.
>
> **sales breakeven point** The level of sales that must be achieved such that operating income equals zero.

Constructing a Sales Breakeven Chart

A breakeven chart shows graphically how fixed costs, variable costs, and sales revenue interact. Analysts construct the chart by plotting sales revenue and costs at various unit sales levels on a graph. To illustrate, let's construct the breakeven chart for Jason's Popcorn Wagon, featured in the opening of the chapter.

The first step in constructing the breakeven chart is to find the breakeven point for the business. Let's look at some of the numbers for Jason's business and calculate the level of sales Jason must achieve to break even. Recall that at the breakeven point, operating income equals zero. If sales are below the breakeven point, Jason suffers an operating loss. If sales are above the breakeven point, Jason enjoys an operating profit. (Interest and taxes, subtracted after finding operating income, will be discussed in the last section of the chapter.)

Jason wants to know that his business venture has the potential for a positive operating profit, so he is keenly interested in finding his breakeven point. To find this point, we need to know how many bags of popcorn he must sell before the sales revenue contributed by each bag sold just covers his fixed and variable operating costs. The relevant sales breakeven figures for Jason's proposed business are shown in Table 13-4.

The numbers in Table 13-4 show that Jason's fixed costs are high compared with his sales price of $1 per bag of popcorn. The fixed costs include the $8,000 annual rental fee for the wagon and the $4,000 annual license fee. Jason must pay these costs no matter how much popcorn he produces and sells.

In contrast to the high fixed operating costs, Jason's variable operating costs per unit are a tiny fraction of his sales price of $1 per unit. The bag, oil, salt, and popcorn that help produce one bag of popcorn cost a total of $0.04. Each bag of popcorn that is sold,

---

4. Labor costs can be either fixed or variable. If workers are guaranteed pay for a certain minimum number of hours per week, as might be called for in a union contract, the labor costs associated with this minimum guaranteed pay would be fixed costs. The costs associated with hourly worker pay with no guaranteed minimum are variable.

TABLE 13-4 Jason's Relevant Figures for Breakeven Analysis

Fixed Costs:	
Wagon (annual rental)	$ 8,000
City License (annual fee)	$ 4,000
Total	$ 12,000
Variable Costs per Unit:	
One Paper Bag	$ 0.020
Oil	$ 0.005
Salt	$ 0.003
Popcorn	$ 0.012
Total	$ 0.040
Sales Price per Unit:	$ 1.00

then, contributes $0.96 to cover the fixed costs, and ultimately the profit of the business ($1.00 – $0.04 = $0.96). The sales price per unit minus the variable cost per unit, $.96 in this case, is the contribution margin.

From the numbers presented in Table 13-4, we can calculate the breakeven level of sales for Jason's business. We find the level of sales needed to reach the operating income breakeven point by applying the following formula:

The Breakeven Point in Unit Sales, $Q_{b.e.}$

$$Q_{b.e.} = \frac{FC}{p - vc}$$

(13-11)

where: $Q_{b.e.}$ = Quantity unit sales breakeven level

FC = Total fixed costs

p = Sales price per unit

vc = Variable cost per unit

For Jason's business, the total fixed costs are $12,000, the price per unit is $1, and the variable cost per unit is $.04. According to Equation 13-11, Jason's popcorn business has the following sales breakeven point:

$$Q_{b.e.} = \frac{\$12,000}{\$1.00 - \$.04}$$
$$= \frac{\$12,000}{\$.96}$$
$$= 12,500$$

We find that Jason's sales breakeven point with $12,000 in fixed costs, $.04 per unit in variable costs, and a $1 per bag sales price, is 12,500 units. At $1 per bag, this is $12,500 in sales to reach the breakeven point.

Now that we know Jason's sales breakeven point, we need revenue and cost information to construct the breakeven chart.

Revenue Data

At any given level of unit sales, Jason's total sales revenue can be found using Equation 13-12:

$$\text{Total Revenue (TR)}$$
$$TR = p \times Q \qquad\qquad (13\text{-}12)$$

where: p = Sales price per unit

Q = Unit sales (Quantity sold)

Table 13-5 shows how to calculate Jason's sales revenues at different sales levels. For instance, we see that if Jason sells 5,000 bags of popcorn at the price of $1 per bag, his total revenue will be $5,000 \times \$1.00 = \$5,000$. If Jason sells 10,000 bags, his total revenue will be $10,000.

Cost Data

By definition, Jason's fixed costs will remain $12,000, regardless of the level of unit production and sales. His variable costs, however, increase by $0.04 for each unit sold. Jason's total costs for any given level of unit production and sales can be found using Equation 13-13 as follows:

$$\text{Total Costs (TC)}$$
$$TC = FC + (vc \times Q) \qquad\qquad (13\text{-}13)$$

where: FC = Fixed costs

vc = Variable costs per unit

Q = Units produced

Table 13-6 demonstrates how we use Equation 13-13 to calculate Jason's total costs for different production and sales levels. For instance, we see that if Jason sells 5,000 bags of popcorn at a variable cost of $0.04 per bag and fixed costs of $12,000, his total cost will be $12,200. At 10,000 bags, his total cost will be $12,400. We assume the number of units produced equals the number of units sold.

Plotting Data on the Breakeven Chart

Jason's breakeven chart is shown in Figure 13-1. The chart is constructed with units produced and sold (Q) on the horizontal axis and cost and revenue dollars on the vertical axis. Total revenues from Table 13-5 are shown on the TR line, and total costs from Table 13-6 are shown on the TC line.

TABLE 13-5 Revenues at Different Unit Sales Levels

Unit Sales (Q)	x	Price (P)	=	Total Revenue (TR)
0	x	$1	=	$ 0
5,000	x	$1	=	$ 5,000
10,000	x	$1	=	$ 10,000
15,000	x	$1	=	$ 15,000
20,000	x	$1	=	$ 20,000
25,000	x	$1	=	$ 25,000
30,000	x	$1	=	$ 30,000

FIGURE 13-1
Breakeven Chart for Jason's Popcorn Wagon

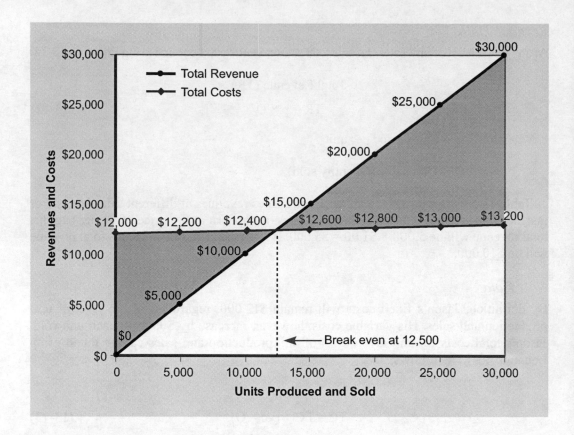

TABLE 13-6 Jason's Total Costs for Different Sales Levels

Fixed Costs (FC)	+	Variable Cost/Unit (vc)	x	Units Produced (Q)	=	Total Cost (TC)
$12,000	+	($.04	x	0)	=	$12,000
$12,000	+	($.04	x	5,000)	=	$12,200
$12,000	+	($.04	x	10,000)	=	$12,400
$12,000	+	($.04	x	15,000)	=	$12,600
$12,000	+	($.04	x	20,000)	=	$12,800
$12,000	+	($.04	x	25,000)	=	$13,000
$12,000	+	($.04	x	30,000)	=	$13,200

We see from the chart that to break even, Jason has to sell $12,500 worth of popcorn at $1 per bag—a quantity of 12,500 bags.

Applying Breakeven Analysis

Although 12,500 bags of popcorn may seem like a lot of sales just to break even, Jason has watched another vendor downtown sell on average 500 bags of popcorn a day. Jason plans to sell for three months during the summer, four weeks a month, five days a week. He estimates that he could sell 30,000 bags of popcorn (500 bags × 3 months × 4 weeks × 5 days) during the summer. At this sales level, Jason expects $30,000 in gross sales revenue at $1 per bag and $16,800 in operating income [$30,000 total revenue −$12,000 fixed costs − ($30,000 × .04 variable costs) = $16,800 operating income]. Not a bad summer job income.

How is it possible to make so much money selling popcorn? Note how once Jason passes the breakeven point in sales, each additional $1 bag of popcorn he sells generates $0.96 of operating profit. The $0.04 in variable costs incurred in the production of that bag of popcorn represents a small part of the $1 in revenue generated. Operating profit rises rapidly as sales climb above the breakeven point of 12,500 units, as shown by Figure 13-1. Were Jason's sales potential not so promising, however, his risk of loss (negative operating income) would be a greater concern. The red area of the graph in Figure 13-1 shows Jason's loss potential.

The breakeven chart allows Jason to see the different sales scenarios to understand his profit and loss potential. Because the total revenue line in Figure 13-1 is much steeper than the total cost line (because the sales price per unit is much greater than the variable cost per unit) the profit potential is great. Because of the high fixed costs, however, the loss potential is great, too. What happens depends on how much popcorn Jason can sell.

To illustrate what happens with a low breakeven business, let's construct a breakeven chart for Carey, another college student, who wants to sell hotplate mini-cookbooks (only five pages long) to college students.[5]

Because Carey plans to operate from her apartment and use her own recipes for the mini-cookbook, her only fixed cost would be a $1,000 printer's design fee. Her variable costs consist of her paper printing costs at $0.60 per unit. Carey plans to sell her cookbook for $1 per unit.

This is a low-risk business. The design fee is modest and there are no other fixed costs. The contribution margin is $0.40 ($1.00 sales price – $0.60 variable cost per unit). We can find Carey's breakeven point using Equation 13-11:

$$Q_{b.e.} = \frac{FC}{p - vc}$$

$$= \frac{\$1,000}{\$1 - \$.60}$$

$$= \frac{\$1,000}{\$.40}$$

$$= 2,500$$

We find that Carey's breakeven point is 2,500 units. Carey figures she can sell to friends in the dorm. Beyond that, however, the sales potential is uncertain. She may or may not reach the breakeven point.

To find Carey's breakeven point, we find her total revenue and total costs at different sales levels and plot them on a breakeven chart (see Figure 13-2).

Note how small the loss potential is for Carey's business, as shown in the red area in Figure 13-2, compared with Jason's loss potential, shown in the red area in Figure 13-1. Carey's loss potential is small because her breakeven level of sales ($0 operating income) is 2,500 units, compared with Jason's 12,500 unit breakeven point. Even if she sold nothing, Carey would lose only the $1,000 in fixed costs that she had to pay (compared with Jason's $12,000). Table 13-7 shows the profit and loss potential for Jason and Carey.

The risk of Jason's business is also evident when we look at sales of 15,000 units for each business. Jason has a profit of only $2,400, whereas Carey would earn a profit of $5,000; at 30,000 units sold, however, Jason earns a profit of $16,800 and Carey earns only $11,000, as shown in Table 13-7. Jason's profits are much more dependent on selling a large number of units than Carey's.

Now compare the profit potential for the two proposed businesses. Jason has the potential to make much more profit (operating income) than Carey. At a sales level of 30,000, Table 13-7 shows Jason makes $16,800, whereas Carey would make only $11,000. Even though Jason's business has more risk—he stands to lose much more if sales don't go well—he has the potential for greater returns.

Whether the high fixed cost and low variable cost per unit business (like Jason's) is better than the low fixed cost and high variable cost per unit business (like Carey's) depends on two factors: how many units you think you can sell and how much tolerance you have for risk. High fixed costs and low variable costs per unit mean high profit potential and

> **Take Note**
> Long-distance telephone and cable companies are examples of firms with high fixed costs and low variable costs per unit. A consulting firm would be an example of a firm with low fixed costs and high variable costs.

---

5. Believe it or not, Carey's business is also inspired by a true story.

FIGURE 13-2
Breakeven Chart for
Carey's Mini-Cookbooks

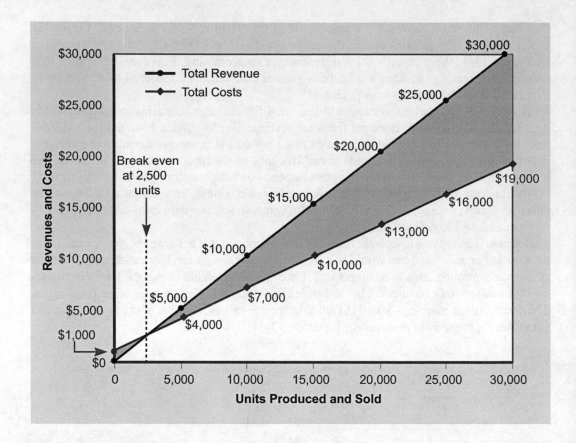

TABLE 13-7 Jason's and Carey's Profit and Loss Potential

Units Produced and Sold	Jason			Carey		
	$Total Costs	$Total Revenue	$Operating Income	$Total Costs	$Total Revenue	$Operating Income
0	12,000	0	−12,000	1,000	0	−1,000
5,000	12,200	5,000	−7,200	4,000	5,000	1,000
10,000	12,400	10,000	−2,400	7,000	10,000	3,000
15,000	12,600	15,000	2,400	10,000	15,000	5,000
20,000	12,800	20,000	7,200	13,000	20,000	7,000
25,000	13,000	25,000	12,000	16,000	25,000	9,000
30,000	13,200	30,000	16,800	19,000	30,000	11,000
35,000	13,400	35,000	21,600	22,000	35,000	13,000
40,000	13,600	40,000	26,400	25,000	40,000	15,000

high loss potential, as in the case of Jason's proposed business. Conversely, low fixed costs and high variable costs per unit mean low profit potential and low loss potential, as in the case of Carey's proposed business. You may vary the fixed costs, price per unit, and variable cost per unit numbers in the Spreadsheet Tutorpak ™ to see the resulting effects on break-even, profit potential, and loss potential.

LBOs

Many publicly owned corporations have been bought out by a small group of investors, including top management of the firm, using a large amount of borrowed money. Such a purchase is called a *leveraged buyout*, or LBO. The leverage referred to is financial leverage. Safeway and PetSmart went through LBOs in 2014 as did Dell in 2013.

In an LBO, investment banking firms work to identify attractive target companies. These investment banking firms solicit investors to acquire the target. To take over the target, the purchasing group raises cash, mostly borrowed, to purchase the common stock shares from the general public. The stock purchase converts the publicly owned corporation to a privately owned one. The investment banking firm would collect fees for its advice and for underwriting the bond issue that helped raise the additional debt capital Because of the limits placed on tax deductions for business interest by the Tax Cuts and Jobs Act or 2017 (TCJA), LBOs will be less attractive from 2018 on than they were pre-2018.

Because of the dramatic increase in financial leverage, some LBOs have worked out well for investors and others have been disasters. For instance, Kohlberg, Kravis, & Roberts made a 50 percent annual rate of return on its $1.34 billion investment after the Beatrice Company LBO. Other companies purchased through LBOs include Toys "R" Us, Neiman Marcus, Borg-Warner, Montgomery Ward, Safeway, Southland, and RJR Nabisco. Bain Capital, Blackstone Group, Carlyle Group, and Kohlberg Kravis Roberts & Co. were reported in May of 2006 to have joined forces with Grupo Televisa SA to launch an LBO of Univision Communications Inc., the Spanish-language television company. This target company is known for its soccer announcer who yells "goooooooooooooooooooal" after a score.

When a company with a normal debt load goes through an LBO, investors holding the company's bonds issued before the LBO are often hurt. The surge in the company's debt results in more financial risk. With higher risk, the market requires a higher rate of return, so the bonds issued before the LBO will see their market interest rates rise—and their market prices fall—after the company announces an LBO.

The risk of an LBO is large because of financial leverage effects. Investors who took over Beatrice through an LBO did very well. Revco, on the other hand, went bankrupt after its LBO. Financial leverage helped the Beatrice LBO investors and hurt those for Revco. Bondholders may suddenly see the value of their bonds drop precipitously after an LBO announcement. In Chapter 14, we discuss how bondholders can protect themselves against this risk.

Now that we have analyzed how fixed operating and financial costs can create leverage effects and risk, we will consider the optimal capital structure for a firm.

Capital Structure Theory

Every time a company borrows, it increases its financial leverage and financial risk. New equity financing decreases financial leverage and risk. Changes in financial leverage, we have seen, bring the potential for good and bad results. How then do financial managers decide on the right balance of debt and equity? Financial managers analyze many factors, including the tax effects of interest payments and how the comparative costs of debt and equity affect firm value.

Tax Deductibility of Interest

Debt in a firm's capital structure can be beneficial. First, debt creates the potential for leveraged increases in net income (NI) when operating income (EBIT) is rising. Second, debt gives the company a tax deduction for the interest that is paid on the debt if that firm qualifies for the business interest tax deduction after the TCJA. If the firm has annual sales of $25 million or less it can deduct all its interest expense on its income tax return as could all firms prior to 2018. For firms with a higher level of sales, interest expense up to 30% of taxable income plus depreciation, amortization, and depletion expenses. In 2022 those additions to taxable income go away so that the amount of deductible interest expense for firms governed by this rule decreases. In contrast to debt, an issue of common stock to raise equity funds results in no tax break. In short, interest paid on business debt is tax deductible, but dividends paid to common stockholders are not. The tax laws, therefore, give some companies an incentive to use debt in their capital structures.

Although the tax deductibility of interest payments on debt is a benefit, debt has costs, too. We know that the financial risk of the firm increases as debt increases. As financial risk increases, including an increasing risk of bankruptcy, a company will incur costs to deal with this risk. For example, suppliers may refuse to extend trade credit to the company, and lawyers' fees may drain funds that could go to either bond holders or common stock investors.

Modigliani and Miller

How does a company balance the costs and benefits of debt? In 1958, Franco Modigliani and Merton Miller wrote a seminal paper that has influenced capital structure discussion ever since. Modigliani and Miller (known in economics and finance circles as M&M) concluded that when interest payments are tax deductible to a firm, a capital structure of all debt is optimal.

In reaching this conclusion, M&M assumed the following:

1. There were no transaction costs.

2. Purchasers of a company's bonds or common stock paid no income tax.

3. Corporations and investors can borrow at the same rate of interest.

4. Investors and management have the same information about the firm.

5. Debt the firm issues is riskless.

6. Operating income is not affected by the use of debt.

In such an environment, M&M showed that the tax benefits to the firm from issuing debt were so beneficial that the benefits allowed the company to increase its value by issuing more and more debt. Given the assumptions, a 100 percent debt capital structure is optimal.

The assumptions, of course, do not exist in the real world. Companies don't seek a 100 percent debt capital structure, suggesting that capital structure is not optimal. In the real world, capital structures vary widely.

Toward an Optimal Capital Structure

Firms seek to balance the costs and benefits of debt to reach an optimal mix that maximizes the value of the firm. Figure 13-3 shows the component costs and weighted cost of capital according to the view of most financial managers. Given the way suppliers of capital react in the real world, many financial managers believe this view is more realistic than the M&M model.

Figure 13-3 illustrates what many believe happens to the cost of debt, equity, and the weighted average cost of capital (WACC) as the capital structure of the firm changes. First, the graph shows that debt is cheaper than equity capital. Second, it shows that the weighted average cost of capital equals the cost of equity when the firm has no debt. Third, it shows that at point Z firms minimize the weighted average cost of capital, so at that point the capital structure maximizes the value of the firm. The cost advantage that debt has over equity dominates the increasing risk up to point Z. At this point, the greater risk begins to dominate and causes the weighted average cost of capital to begin to turn upward.

We learned in Chapter 9 how to estimate the costs of debt and equity and weighted average figures. Here we study how capital structure changes may affect the firm's cost of capital and its value.

The Lower Cost of Debt

Figure 13-3 shows that debt capital has a lower cost than equity capital. Debt is cheaper than equity for two reasons. As mentioned earlier, interest payments made by a firm are tax deductible and dividend payments made to common stockholders are not. Even without the tax break, however, debt funds are cheaper than equity funds. The required rate of return on a bond is lower than the required rate of return on common stock for a given company because its debt is less risky than its equity to investors. Debt is less risky because bondholders have a claim superior to that of common stockholders on the earnings and assets of the firm.

FIGURE 13-3
Cost of Capital and Capital
Structure

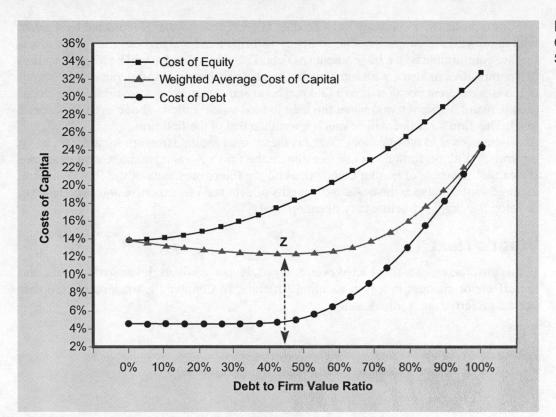

How Capital Costs Change as Debt Is Added

If we examine the WACC line in Figure 13-3, we see that the weighted average cost of capital equals the cost of equity when the firm has no debt. Then, as debt is added, the cost advantage (to the issuing company) of debt over equity makes the weighted average cost of capital decrease, up to a point, as more of the cheaper debt funds and less of the more expensive equity funds are used. The effect of adding debt to capital structure is shown in Figure 13-3 as we move along the horizontal axis from the origin.

The Effect of Risk

What causes the WACC to increase, as shown in Figure 13-3, beyond point Z? As the firm moves to a capital structure with higher debt (moves to the right along the horizontal axis of Figure 13-3), the risk of the firm increases. As financial risk rises with additional debt, the required return of both debt and equity investors increases. Notice that the cost of equity curve starts to climb sooner than the cost of debt curve. This is because common stockholders get paid *after* bondholders.

As both the cost of debt and the cost of equity curves turn upward, the curve depicting the weighted average of the cost of debt and the cost of equity eventually turns upward, too. According to the capital structure view depicted in Figure 13-3, if a firm has less debt than the amount at Z, the WACC is higher than it needs to be. Likewise, if a firm has more debt than the amount at Z, the WACC is higher than it needs to be. Only at the capital structure at point Z do firms minimize the weighted average cost of capital. This is the capital structure, then, that maximizes the value of the firm.

Establishing the Optimal Capital Structure in Practice

In the real world, it is unlikely that financial managers can determine an exact point for Z where the WACC is minimized. Many financial managers try instead to estimate Z and set a capital structure close to it. Unfortunately, no formula can help estimate point Z. The optimal capital structure for a firm depends on the future prospects of that firm.

For example, say a company has a product in great demand that is protected by a patent with many years to expiration. The company will find that bond and common stock investors are comfortable with a large amount of debt. This firm's Z value will be high. But a firm in a competitive industry, with some quality control problems and soft demand for its product, is in a different position. It will find that bond and common stock investors get nervous (and demand higher returns) when the debt to total value[6] ratio is above even a moderate level. This firm's Z value will be much lower than that of the first firm.

So the answer to the question, "What is the optimal capital structure for a firm?" is, "It depends." With no formula to use to estimate the firm's Z value, management examines the capital structure of similar companies and the future prospects of the firm. Financial managers must balance the costs and benefits of debt and use expertise and experience to develop the capital structure they deem optimal.

What's Next

In this chapter, we examined breakeven analysis, leverage effects, leveraged buyouts, and the effects of changes in a firm's capital structure. In Chapter 14, we look at corporate bonds, preferred stock, and leasing.

---

6. Total value here refers to the total market value of the firm's outstanding debt and equity.

Summary

1. *Define capital structure.*
   Capital structure is the mixture of funding sources (debt, preferred stock, or common stock) that a firm uses to finance its assets. A central question in finance is what blend of these financing sources is best for the firm. That is, how much of a firm's assets should be financed by borrowing? How much should be financed by preferred stockholders? How much should be financed by the common stockholders? The question is important because each of these financing sources has a different cost, and each of them has a different degree of risk. Therefore, the choice of financing directly affects a firm's weighted average cost of capital and the degree of riskiness in the firm.

2. *Explain operating, financial, and combined leverage effects and the resulting business and financial risks.*
   Firms with high fixed costs have high operating leverage—that is, a small change in sales triggers a relatively large change in operating income. Firms with low fixed costs have less operating leverage. The effect of low operating leverage is that small changes in sales do not cause large changes in operating income.

   Business risk refers to the volatility of a company's operating income. Business risk is triggered by sales volatility and magnified by fixed operating costs.

   If a company uses fixed-cost funds (such as fixed interest rate bonds) to raise capital, financial leverage results. With financial leverage, fixed interest costs cause

net income to change by a greater percentage than a given percentage change in EBIT.

The presence of financial leverage creates financial risk for a firm—the risk that the firm will not be able to make its interest payments if operating income drops. Financial risk compounds the business risk already present.

The total effect of operating leverage and financial leverage is called combined leverage. The value of the degree of financial leverage is multiplied by the value of the degree of operating leverage to give the degree of combined leverage (DCL). The DCL gives the percentage change in net income for a given percentage change in sales.

3. *Find the breakeven level of sales for a firm.*
   The costs of operating a business can be categorized as fixed or variable. Operating costs that do not vary with the level of production are fixed; operating costs that do vary with the level of production are variable. High fixed costs are usually tied to low variable costs per unit, and low fixed costs are usually tied to high variable costs per unit.

   The breakeven point is the level of sales that results in an operating income of zero. At sales levels above the breakeven point, a firm begins to make a profit. A company with high fixed operating costs must generate high sales revenue to cover its fixed costs (and its variable costs) before reaching the sales breakeven point. Conversely, a firm with low fixed operating costs will break even with a relatively low level of sales revenue.

4. *Describe the risks and returns of a leveraged buyout.* LBOs, or leveraged buyouts, occur when publicly owned corporations are bought out by a small group of investors using mostly borrowed funds. The purchase is leveraged because the investors finance it with a large amount of borrowed money. Consequently, when a firm is purchased in an LBO, it is saddled with a large amount of debt in its capital structure and a large amount of financial leverage and financial risk.

5. *Explain how changes in capital structure affect a firm's value.* Capital structure theory deals with the mixture of debt, preferred stock, and equity a firm utilizes. Because interest on business loans is a tax-deductible expense, and because lenders demand a lower rate of return than stockholders for a given company (because lending money is not as risky as owning shares), debt capital is cheaper than equity capital. However, the more a company borrows, the more it increases its financial leverage and financial risk. The additional risk causes lenders and stockholders to demand a higher rate of return. Financial managers use capital structure theory to help determine the mix of debt and equity at which the weighted average cost of capital is lowest.

Key Terms

combined leverage The phenomenon whereby a change in sales causes net income to change by a larger percentage because of fixed operating and financial costs.

degree of combined leverage (DCL) The percentage change in net income divided by the percentage change in sales.

degree of financial leverage (DFL) The percentage change in net income divided by the percentage change in operating income.

degree of operating leverage (DOL) The percentage change in operating income divided by the percentage change in sales.

financial leverage The phenomenon whereby a change in operating income causes net income to change by a larger percentage because of the presence of fixed financial costs.

fixed costs Costs that do not vary with the level of production.

leverage Something that creates a magnifying effect, such as when fixed operating or fixed financial costs cause a magnifying effect on the movements of operating income or net income.

operating leverage The effect of fixed operating costs on operating income; because of fixed costs, any change in sales results in a larger percentage change in operating income.

sales breakeven point The level of sales that must be achieved such that operating income equals zero.

variable costs Costs that vary with the level of production.

Equations Introduced in This Chapter

Equation 13-1. Degree of Operating Leverage (DOL):

$$DOL = \frac{\%\Delta \; EBIT}{\%\Delta \; Sales}$$

where: $\%\Delta$ EBIT = Percentage change in earnings before interest and taxes

$\%\Delta$ Sales = Percentage change in sales

Equation 13-2. Degree of Operating Leverage (DOL) (alternate):

$$DOL = \frac{Sales - VC}{Sales - VC - FC}$$

where: VC = Total variable costs

FC = Total fixed costs

Equation 13-3. Percentage Change in EBIT:

$\%\Delta$ EBIT = $\%\Delta$ Sales × DOL

where: $\%\Delta$ Sales = Percentage change in sales

DOL = Degree of operating leverage

Equation 13-4. Degree of Financial Leverage (DFL):

$$DFL = \frac{\%\Delta \; NI}{\%\Delta \; EBIT}$$

where: $\%\Delta$ NI = Percentage change in net income

$\%\Delta$ EBIT = Percentage change in earnings before interest and taxes

Equation 13-5. Degree of Financial Leverage (DFL) (alternate):

$$DFL = \frac{EBIT}{EBIT - Int}$$

where: EBIT = Earnings before interest and taxes

Int = Interest expense

Equation 13-6. Percentage Change in Net Income:

$$\%\Delta\,NI = \%\Delta\,EBIT \times DFL$$

where: $\%\Delta\,EBIT$ = Percentage change in earnings before interest and taxes

DFL = Degree of financial leverage

Equation 13-7. Degree of Combined Leverage (DCL):

$$DCL = \frac{\%\Delta\,NI}{\%\Delta\,Sales}$$

where: $\%\Delta\,NI$ = Percentage change in net income

$\%\Delta\,Sales$ = Percentage change in sales

Equation 13-8. Degree of Combined Leverage (DCL) (alternate 1):

$$DCL = \frac{Sales - VC}{Sales - VC - FC - Int}$$

where: VC = Total variable costs

FC = Total fixed costs

Int = Interest expense

Equation 13-9. Degree of Combined Leverage (DCL) (alternate 2):

$$DCL = DOL \times DFL$$

where: DOL = Degree of operating leverage

DFL = Degree of financial leverage

Equation 13-10. Percentage Change in Net Income (NI):

$$\%\Delta\,NI = \%\Delta\,Sales \times DOL \times DFL$$

where: $\%\Delta\,Sales$ = Percentage change in sales

DOL = Degree of operating leverage

DFL = Degree of financial leverage

Equation 13-11. The Breakeven Point in Unit Sales, $Q_{b.e.}$:

$$Q_{b.e.} = \frac{FC}{p - vc}$$

where: $Q_{b.e.}$ = Quantity unit sales breakeven level

FC = Total fixed costs

p = Sales price per unit

vc = Variable cost per unit

Equation 13-12. Total Revenue, TR:

$$TR = p \times Q$$

where: p = Sales price per unit

Q = Unit sales (Quantity sold)

Equation 13-13. Total Costs, TC:

$$TC = FC + (vc \times Q)$$

where: FC = Fixed costs

vc = Variable costs per unit

Q = Units produced

Self-Test

ST-1. Kendrick Lamar's firm has fixed costs of $40,000, variable costs per unit of $4, and a selling price per unit of $9. What is Mr. Lamar's breakeven level of sales (in units)?

ST-2. HAL's computer store has sales of $225,000, fixed costs of $40,000, and variable costs of $100,000. Calculate the degree of operating leverage (DOL) for this firm.

ST-3. HAL's computer store has operating income (EBIT) of $85,000 and interest expense of $10,000. Calculate the firm's degree of financial leverage (DFL).

ST-4. Drake's Down Comforters has an after-tax cost of debt of 6 percent. The cost of equity is 14 percent. The firm believes that its optimal capital structure is 30 percent

debt and 70 percent equity, and it maintains its capital structure according to these weights. What is the weighted average cost of capital?

ST-5. Johnny Ringo's Western Shoppe expects its sales to increase by 20 percent next year. If this year's sales are $500,000 and the degree of operating leverage (DOL) is 1.4, what is the expected level of operating income (EBIT) for next year if this year's EBIT is $100,000?

ST-6. Marion Pardoo's Bookstore has a degree of operating leverage (DOL) of 1.6 and a degree of financial leverage (DFL) of 1.8. What is the company's degree of combined leverage (DCL)?

Review Questions

1. What is the operating leverage effect and what causes it? What are the potential benefits and negative consequences of high operating leverage?

2. Does high operating leverage always mean high business risk? Explain.

3. What is the financial leverage effect and what causes it? What are the potential benefits and negative consequences of high financial leverage?

4. Give two examples of types of companies likely to have high operating leverage. Find examples other than those cited in the chapter.

5. Give two examples of types of companies that would be best able to handle high debt levels.

6. What is an LBO? What are the risks for the equity investors and what are the potential rewards?

7. If an optimal capital structure exists, what are the reasons that too little debt is as undesirable as too much debt?

Build Your Communication Skills

CS-1. Using publicly available sources, identify four companies having very high debt ratios and four having very low debt ratios. Write a one- to two-page report describing the characteristics of the companies with high debt ratios and those with low debt ratios. Can you identify characteristics that seem to be common to the four high-debt firms? What are characteristics common to the four low-debt firms?

CS-2. Interview the owner of a small business in your community. Ask that person to describe the fixed operating costs and the variable costs of the business. Write a report or give an oral presentation to your class on the nature of the business risk of this firm.

Problems

Breakeven Point **13-1.** Lilies, a flower shop, has the following data for the most recent fiscal year:

Fixed Costs	$2,300/month
Variable Costs (per unit):	
Packets	$ 0.75
Décor	$ 3.00
Misc	$ 2.00
Sales Price	$50.00

    a. What is Lilies' breakeven point in sales per month?

    b. The owner of Lilies is planning on moving to a new location that will cut fixed costs by 30 percent. The price can be lowered to $45 per unit. What is the new breakeven point in sales (per month)?

Total Revenue,
Total Costs **13-2.** ViSorb sells its deluxe cell phone model for $125, its advanced model for $90, and its basic model for $55. The company has fixed costs of $10,000 per month, and variable costs are $15 per unit sold.

    a. Calculate the total revenue if 30 units of each model are sold.

    b. What are the total costs if 30 units of each model are sold?

    c. What is the company's total revenue if it sells 10 deluxe models, 15 advanced models, and 35 basic models?

    d. What would its total costs be at the sales level in (c)?

Degree of Operating
Leverage **13-3.** The following is an income statement for Gabotti Enterprises:

	2018	2019
Net Sales	$15,000,000	$25,000,000
Fixed Costs	3,800,000	3,800,000
Variable Costs	1,980,000	3,300,000
Operating Income	$9,220,000	$17,900,000
Interest Expense	1,710,000	1,710,000
EBT	7,510,000	16,190,000
Taxes (30%)	2,253,000	4,857,000
Net Income	$5,257,000	$11,333,000

Calculate Gabotti Enterprises' DOL. Use both methods and compare results.

Degree of Financial
Leverage **13-4.** From the table in problem 13-3, calculate Gabotti Enterprises' DFL using both methods.

Breakeven Analysis **13-5.** Howard Beal Co. manufactures molds for casting aluminum alloy test samples. Fixed costs amount to $20,000 per year. Variable costs for each unit manufactured are $16. Sales price per unit is $28.

    a. What is the contribution margin of the product?

    b. Calculate the breakeven point in unit sales and dollars.

    c. What is the operating profit (loss) if the company manufactures and sells

        1. 1,500 units per year?

        2. 3,000 units per year?

    d. Plot a breakeven chart using the foregoing figures.

Breakeven Analysis **13-6.** UBC Company, a competitor of Howard Beal Co. in problem 13-5, has a comparatively labor-intensive process with old equipment. Fixed costs are $10,000 per year and variable costs are $20 per unit. Sales price is the same, $28 per unit.

a. What is the contribution margin of the product?

b. Calculate the breakeven point in unit sales and dollars.

c. What is the operating profit (loss) if the company manufactures and sells

   1. 1,500 units per year?

   2. 3,000 units per year?

d. Plot a breakeven chart using the foregoing figures.

e. Comment on the profit and loss potential of UBC Company compared with Howard Beal Co.

13-7. Use the same data given in problem 13-5 (fixed cost = $20,000 per year, variable cost = $16 per unit, and sales price = $28 per unit) for Howard Beal Co. The company sold 3,000 units in 2018 and expects to sell 3,300 units in 2019. Fixed costs, variable costs per unit, and sales price per unit are assumed to remain the same in 2018 and 2019.

Operating Leverage

a. Calculate the percentage change in operating income and compare it with the percentage change in sales.

b. Comment on the operating leverage effect.

c. Calculate the degree of operating leverage using

   1. data for 2018 and 2019

   2. data for 2018 only

d. Explain what the results obtained in (c) tell us.

13-8. Use the same data given in problems 13-5 and 13-7 (fixed cost = $20,000 per year, variable cost per unit = $16, sales price per unit = $28, 2018 sales = 3,000 units, and expected 2019 sales = 3,300 units) for Howard Beal Co. Fixed costs, variable costs per unit, and sales price per unit are assumed to remain the same in 2018 and 2019. The company has an interest expense of $2,000 per year. Applicable income tax rate is 30 percent.

Financial Leverage

a. Calculate the percentage change in net income and compare it with the percentage change in operating income (EBIT).

b. Comment on the financial leverage effect.

c. Calculate the degree of financial leverage using

   1. data for 2018 and 2019

   2. data for 2018 only

d. Explain what the results obtained in (c) tell us about financial leverage.

13-9. Tony Manero owns a small company that refinishes and maintains the wood flooring of many dance clubs in Brooklyn. Because of heavy use, his services are required at least quarterly by most of the clubs. Tony's annual fixed costs consist of depreciation expense for his van, polishing equipment, and other tools. These expenses were $9,000 this year. His variable costs include wood-staining products, wax, and other miscellaneous supplies. Tony has been in this business since 1977 and accurately estimates his variable costs at $1.50 per square yard of dance floor. Tony charges a rate of $15 per square yard.

Breakeven Analysis

a. How many square yards of dance floor will he need to work on this year to cover all of his expenses but leave him with zero operating income?

b. What is this number called?

c. Calculate the breakeven point in dollar sales.

d. Tony has little competent competition in the Brooklyn area. What happens to the breakeven point in sales dollars if Tony increases his rate to $18 per square yard?

e. At the $18 per square yard rate, what are Tony's operating income and net income if he completes work on 14,000 square yards this year? Assume his tax rate is 40 percent and he has a $25,000 loan outstanding on which he pays 12 percent interest annually.

**Operating Leverage
and Breakeven
Analysis** **13-10.** Otis Day's company manufactures and sells men's suits. His trademark gray flannel suits are popular on Wall Street and in boardrooms throughout the East. Each suit sells for $800. Fixed costs are $200,000 and variable costs are $250 per suit.

    a. What is the firm's operating income on sales of 600 suits? On sales of 3,000 suits?

    b. What is Mr. Day's degree of operating leverage (DOL) at a sales level of 600 suits? At a sales level of 3,000 suits?

    c. Calculate Mr. Day's breakeven point in sales units and sales dollars.

    d. If the cost of the gray flannel material increases so that Mr. Day's variable costs are now $350 per suit, what will be his new breakeven point in sales units and sales dollars?

    e. Considering the increase in variable costs, by how much will he need to increase the selling price per suit to reach the original operating income for sales of 3,000 suits calculated in part *a*?

Operating Leverage **13-11.** Company A, Company B, and Company C all manufacture and sell identical products. They each sell 12,000 units annually at a price of $10 per unit. Assume Company A has $0 fixed costs and variable costs of $5 per unit. Company B has $10,000 in fixed costs and $4 in variable costs per unit. Company C has $40,000 fixed costs and $1 per unit variable costs.

    a. Calculate the operating income (EBIT) for each of the three companies.

    b. Before making any further calculations, rank the companies from highest to lowest by their relative degrees of operating leverage. Remember what you read about how fixed costs affect operating leverage.

Operating Leverage **13-12.** Faber Corporation, a basketball hoop manufacturing firm in Hickory, Indiana, plans to branch out and begin producing basketballs in addition to basketball hoops. It has a choice of two different production methods for the basketballs. Method 1 will have variable costs of $6 per ball and fixed costs of $700,000 for the high-tech machinery, which requires little human supervision. Method 2 employs many people to hand-sew the basketballs. It has variable costs of $16.50 per ball, but fixed costs are estimated to be only $100,000. Regardless of which method CEO Norman Dale chooses, the basketballs will sell for $30 each. Marketing research indicates sales in the first year will be 50,000 balls. Sales volume is expected to increase to 60,000 in year 2.

    a. Calculate the sales revenue expected in years 1 and 2.

    b. Calculate the percentage change in sales revenue.

    c. Calculate the earnings before interest and taxes for each year for both production methods.

    d. Calculate the percentage change in EBIT for each method.

    e. Calculate the year 1 degree of operating leverage for each method, using your answers from parts *b* and *d*.

    f. Calculate the degree of operating leverage again. This time use only revenue, fixed costs and variable costs from year 1 (your base year) for each production method.

    g. Under which production method would EBIT be more adversely affected if the sales volume did not reach the expected levels?

    h. What would drive this adverse effect on EBIT?

    i. Recalculate the year 1 base year EBIT and the degree of operating leverage for both production methods if year 2 sales are expected to be only 53,000 units.

Financial Leverage **13-13.** Three companies manufacture and sell identical products. They each have earnings before interest and taxes of $100,000. Assume Company A is an all equity company and, therefore, has zero debt. Company B's capital structure is 10 percent debt and 90 percent equity. It makes annual interest payments of $2,000. Company C's capital structure is just the opposite of B. It has 90 percent debt and 10 percent equity. Company C has annual interest expense of $40,000. The tax rate for each of the three companies is 40 percent.

    a. Before making any calculations, rank the companies from highest to lowest by their relative degrees of financial leverage (DFL). Remember what you read about how debt and the interest expense that comes with it affects financial leverage.

b. Calculate the degree of financial leverage for each company. Was your answer to part *a* correct?

c. Calculate the net income for each company.

13-14. Michael Dorsey and Dorothy Michaels each own their own companies. They design and supply custom-made costumes for Broadway plays. The income statement from each company shows they each have earnings before interest and taxes of $50,000 this year. Mr. Dorsey has an outstanding loan for $70,000, on which he pays 13 percent interest annually. When she started her business, Ms. Michaels only needed to borrow $10,000. She is still paying 9 percent annual interest on the loan. Each company expects EBIT for next year to be $60,000. The tax rate for each is 40 percent and is not expected to change for next year.

← Financial Leverage

a. Calculate the net income for each company for this year and next year.

b. Calculate the percentage change in net income for each company.

c. Calculate the percentage change in EBIT for each company.

For more, see 8e Spreadsheet Templates for *Microsoft Excel.*

d. Calculate this year's degree of financial leverage for each company using your answers from parts *b* and *c*.

e. Calculate the degree of financial leverage for each company again. This time use only EBIT and interest expense for this year.

f. If earnings before interest and taxes do not reach the expected levels, in which company would net income be more adversely affected?

g. What would drive this adverse effect on net income?

h. Recalculate the degree of financial leverage and the net income expected for next year for both companies if EBIT only increases to $53,000.

13-15. In 2018, Calaire had net income of $75,000 and sales of $230,000. John Mastore, the financial manager, has forecast the 2019 net income to be $200,000 and sales to be $400,000. What is Calaire's degree of combined leverage if these numbers become fact?

← Degree of Combined Leverage

13-16. Fanny Brice, owner of Funny Girl Comics, has sales revenue of $200,000, earnings before interest and taxes of $95,000, and net income of $30,000 this year. She is expecting sales to increase to $225,000 next year. The degree of operating leverage is 1.35 and the degree of financial leverage is relatively low at 1.09.

← Challenge Problem

a Calculate the percentage change in EBIT Ms. Brice can expect between this year and next year.

For more, see 8e Spreadsheet Templates for *Microsoft Excel.*

b. How much will EBIT be next year in dollars?

c. Calculate the percentage change in net income Ms. Brice can expect between this year and next year.

d. How much net income should Ms. Brice expect next year?

e. Calculate this year's degree of combined leverage (DCL).

f. Ms. Brice is considering a price increase. This would mean the percentage change in sales revenue between this year and next year would be 20 percent. If this is true, what net income (in dollars) can she expect for next year?

13-17. Clint Reno owns Real Cowboy, a western wear store that has current annual sales of $2,800,000. The degree of operating leverage (DOL) is 1.4. EBIT is $600,000. Real Cowboy has $2 million in debt, on which it pays 10 percent annual interest. Calculate the degree of combined leverage for Real Cowboy.

← Degree of Combined Leverage

13-18. Chad Gates owns Strings Attached, a store that sells guitars. The company has $5 million in current annual sales, fixed operating costs of $300,000, and $700,000 in variable operating costs, for a total EBT of $2.5 million. The firm has debt of $16,666,666.67, on which it pays 9 percent annual interest. The degree of combined leverage (DCL) for Strings Attached is 1.72.

← DOL, DFL, and DCL Interactions

a. Calculate the degree of operating leverage (DOL).

b. What is the degree of financial leverage (DFL) for Strings Attached? Calculate your answer using the EBIT and interest expense figures and your knowledge of how DOL and DFL jointly determine DCL.

c. If sales next year increase by 20 percent, what will be the percent change in net income?

13-19. Soccer International, Inc., produces and sells soccer balls. Partial information from the income statements for 2018 and 2019 follows.

Soccer International, Inc., Income Statement for the Year
Ending December 31

	2018	2019
Sales Revenue	$560,000	616,000
Variable Costs	240,000	264,000
Fixed Costs	160,000	160,000
EBIT		
Interest Expense	40,000	40,000
EBT		
Income Taxes (30%)		
Net Income		

For more, see 8e
Spreadsheet Templates
for *Microsoft Excel*.

Soccer International sells each soccer ball for $16.

a. Fill in the missing values in the income statements of 2018 and 2019.

b. Calculate Soccer International's breakeven point in sales units for 2018 and 2019.

c. Calculate the breakeven point in dollar sales for 2018 and for 2019.

d. How many soccer balls need to be sold to have an operating income of $200,000 in 2018?

e. What is the operating profit (loss) if the company sells (i) 18,000 and (ii) 24,000 balls in 2018?

f. Calculate the degree of operating leverage for 2018 and for 2019.

g. If sales revenue is expected to increase by 10 percent in 2019, calculate the percentage increase in EBIT and the dollar amount of EBIT for 2019.

h. Calculate the degree of financial leverage for 2018 and for 2019.

i. Calculate the percentage change in net income and the dollar amount of net income expected in 2019.

j. Calculate the degree of combined leverage for 2018 and for 2019.

k. Assume Soccer International raises its selling price and that sales revenue increases to $650,000 in 2018. How much net income can be expected in 2019?

Percentage Change
in Net Income

13-20. Los Amigos has an operating income of $35,000 in 2018 and a projected operating income of $50,000 in 2019. It estimates its DFL to be 1.71. At this estimated DFL, what will be the change in net income?

Answers to Self-Test

ST-1. Sales breakeven point (in units) = $40,000 ÷ ($9.00 − $4.00) = 8,000 units

ST-2. Degree of operating leverage (DOL) = ($225,000 − $100,000) ÷ ($225,000 − $100,000 − $40,000) = 1.47

ST-3. Degree of financial leverage (DFL) = $85,000 ÷ ($85,000 − $10,000) = 1.13

ST-4. Weighted average cost of capital, k_a = (.3 × 6%) + (.7 × 14%) = 11.6%

ST-5. Next year's change in EBIT equals (this year's EBIT × 20% × 1.4) + this year's EBIT = ($100,000 × 20% × 1.4) + $100,000 = $128,000

ST-6. Degree of combined leverage (DCL) = DOL × DFL = 1.6 × 1.8 = 2.88

Corporate Bonds, Preferred Stock, and Leasing

CHAPTER 14

"The borrower is servant to the lender."
—Proverbs 22:7

Source: designer491

Learning Objectives

After reading this chapter, you should be able to:

1. Describe the contract terms of a bond issue.
2. Distinguish the various types of bonds and describe their major characteristics.
3. Describe the key features of preferred stock.
4. Compare and contrast a genuine lease and a disguised purchase contract.
5. Explain why some leases must be shown on the balance sheet.

Negative Interest Rates?

In 2015 negative interest rates were being observed for many bonds that had been issued by a variety of different entities around the world. This was seen for some government bonds issued by various European countries and by Japan. On the face of this it doesn't seem to make sense. In Chapter 2 the components that determine market interest rates were described. Those were the real rate of interest along with premiums for expected inflation, default risk, illiquidity risk, and maturity risk.

The real world sometimes throws complexities at us, however. What if inflation were negative? This is also known as deflation. If the general level of prices were expected to drop significantly, this negative premium could overwhelm the other premia that are positive. There is also the possibility that some investors are willing to pay someone to store their cash such that a negative interest rate would be accepted by this investor. Suppose you managed a very large institutional portfolio and you were very concerned about the future of the world economy and looking for a safe place to store your money. A small investor could deposit cash into an insured bank account that would provide insurance protection of up to $250,000. This is of little help to the institutional investor looking for a place to invest $1 billion in a safe place. Such an investor might be willing to invest in a government bond with a negative interest rate, knowing that the investment is backed by the full faith and credit of that government.

The investor is effectively paying a fee so the government will hold the money in a safe place, much as a person might pay a storage fee for the safekeeping of gold.

In late 2014 there were some U.S. Treasury bills that had market interest rates slightly into negative territory. The U.S. Treasury at that time would not issue its Treasury bills in the weekly primary market auctions with negative interest rates. The Treasury, however, has no control over what the price might be for its securities when those securities subsequently trade in the secondary market. If the prices of those Treasury bills are bid up in the market to a level above the face value of the bill, negative interest rates occur.

Chapter Overview

In Chapter 2, we examined the basic characteristics and terminology of corporate bonds. In Chapter 12, we learned how to estimate the value of bonds. In this chapter we investigate how corporate bonds and preferred stock play a role in the financing decisions of a corporation. We also explore how leasing decisions affect a firm's finances.

Bond Basics

corporate bond A security that represents a promise by the issuing corporation to make certain payments, according to a certain schedule, to the owner of the bond.

A **corporate bond** is a security that represents a promise by the issuing corporation to make certain payments to the owner of the bond, according to a certain schedule. The corporation that issues a bond is the debtor, and the investor who buys the bond is the creditor.

indenture The contract between the issuing corporation and the bond's purchaser.

The **indenture** is the contract between the issuing corporation and the bond's purchaser. It spells out the various provisions of the bond issue, including the face value, coupon interest rate, interest payment dates, maturity date, and other details. The yield to maturity is not in the indenture because it is market determined and changes with market conditions. The major features of bond indentures are described in the next section.

The investment bankers who underwrite the new bond issue help the firm set the terms of that issue. This usually means obtaining a rating for the bonds from one or more of the major rating companies, such as Moody's and Standard & Poor's. Bond ratings shown in Table 14-1 reflect the likelihood that the issuer will make the promised interest and principal payments on time. Many institutional investors, the main purchasers of bonds, are prohibited, either by law or by client demands, from purchasing unrated bonds.

investment-grade bonds Bonds rated Baa3 or above by Moody's bond rating agency and BBB– or above by Standard & Poor's.

Bonds rated Baa3 or above by Moody's and BBB2 or above by Standard & Poor's are called **investment-grade bonds**. Bonds with lower than investment-grade ratings (Ba1 or below by Moody's and BB+ or below by Standard & Poor's) are called **junk bonds**. We'll have more to say about junk bonds later in the chapter.

junk bonds Bonds with lower than investment-grade ratings.

Features of Bond Indentures

In addition to the basic characteristics of the bond (interest, principal, maturity, and specific payment dates), the bond indenture specifies other features of the bond issue. These features include:

- Any security to be turned over to the bond's owner in the event the issuing corporation defaults
- The plan for paying off the bonds at maturity
- Any provisions for paying off the bonds ahead of time
- Any restrictions the issuing company places on itself to provide an extra measure of safety to the bondholder
- The name of an independent trustee to oversee the bond issue

Thus, every key feature of the bond issue is spelled out in the bond indenture.

TABLE 14-1 Moody's and Standard & Poor's Bond Rating Categories

Moody's	Standard & Poor's	Remarks
Aaa	AAA	Best Quality
Aa1	AA+	
Aa2	AA	High Quality
Aa3	AA2	
A1	A+	
A2	A	Upper Medium Grade
A3	A2	
Baa1	BBB+	
Baa2	BBB	Medium Grade
Baa3	BBB2	
Ba1	BB+	
Ba2	BB	Speculative
Ba3	BB2	
B1	B+	
B2	B	Very Speculative
B3	B2	
Caa	CCC	
Ca	CC	Very, Very Speculative
C	C	
	D	In Default

Security

A person who buys a newly issued bond is, in effect, lending money to the issuing corporation for a specified period of time. Like other creditors, bondholders are concerned about getting their money back. A provision in the loan agreement (the indenture) that provides security[1] to the lender in case of default will increase the bond's value, compared with a loan agreement without a security provision. The value of the bond is higher because the investor has an extra measure of protection. A bond that has a security provision in the indenture is a **secured bond**. A bond that does not pledge any specific asset(s) as security is a **debenture**. Debentures are backed only by the company's ability and willingness to pay.

secured bond A bond backed by specific assets that the investor may claim if there is a default.

debenture A bond that is unsecured.

Plans for Paying Off Bond Issues

Bonds are paid off, or retired, by a variety of means. Some of the more popular methods include *staggered maturities*, *sinking funds*, and *call provisions*.

Staggered Maturities

Some bond issues are packaged as a series of different bonds with different or staggered maturities. Every few years a portion of the bond issue matures and is paid off. Staggering maturities in this fashion allows the issuing company to retire the debt in an orderly fashion without facing a large one-time need for cash, as would be the case if the entire issue were to mature at once. **Serial payments** pay off bonds according to a staggered maturity schedule.

serial payments A mode of payment in which the issuer pays off bonds according to a staggered maturity schedule.

---

1. Chapter 2 used a different definition of security (a financial claim such as a stock or bond). Security has another definition, as used here. This definition is any asset (such as a piece of equipment, real estate, or a claim on future profits) that is promised to the investor in the event of a default.

Sinking Funds

Although *sinking* is not an appealing word, sending your debt to the bottom of the ocean has its appeal. When a sinking fund provision is included in the bond's indenture, the issuing company makes regular contributions[2] to a fund that is used to buy back outstanding bonds. Putting aside a little money at a time in this fashion ensures that the amount needed to pay off the bonds will be available.

Call Provisions

call provision A bond indenture provision that allows the issuer to pay off a bond before the stated maturity date at a specified price.

Many corporate bonds have a provision in their indentures that allows the issuing corporation to pay off the bonds before the stated maturity date, at some stated price. This is known as a **call provision**. The price at which the bonds can be purchased before the scheduled maturity date is the call price.

Call provisions allow issuing corporations to refinance their debt if interest rates fall, just as homeowners refinance their mortgage loans when interest rates fall. For example, a company that issued bonds in 2015 with a 9 percent coupon interest rate would be making annual interest payments of 9 percent of $1,000, or $90 on each bond. Suppose that in 2019 the market rate of the company's bonds were to fall to 7 percent. If the bond indenture contained a call provision,[3] the company could issue 7 percent bonds in 2019 and use the proceeds from the issue to "call in" or pay off the 9 percent bonds. The company's new interest payments would be only 7 percent of $1,000, or $70, thus saving the company $20 on each bond each year.

call premium The premium the issuer pays to call in a bond before maturity. The excess of the call price over the face value.

When bonds are called, convention is that the call price the issuer must pay is generally more than the face value. This excess of the call price over the face value is known as the **call premium**. The call premium may be expressed as a dollar amount or as a percentage of par.

refunding Issuing new bonds to replace old bonds.

Issuing new bonds to replace old bonds is known as a **refunding** operation. Remember, the option to call a bond is held by the issuing corporation. The owners of the bonds have no choice in the matter. If investors don't turn in their bonds when the bonds are called, they receive no further interest payments.

A company approaches a bond refunding the same way it does any capital budgeting decision. The primary incremental cash inflows come from the interest savings realized when old high-interest debt is replaced with new low-interest debt. The primary incremental cash outflows are the call premium, if any, and the flotation costs associated with the new bond issue. All these variables must be adjusted for taxes and then evaluated by the firm. If the net present value of the incremental cash flows associated with the refunding is greater than or equal to zero, the refunding is done. If the NPV is negative, the company allows the old bonds to remain outstanding. This is the same thing you do when deciding whether to refinance a mortgage loan on a home.

Occasionally, a corporation will refund a bond issue even though there are no significant interest savings to be had. If the outstanding bonds have indenture provisions that the issuing company now finds oppressive or too limiting, the old bonds could be called and new bonds issued without the offending features. Let's go through a typical bond refunding decision.

A Sample Bond Refunding Problem

Suppose the Mega-Chip Corporation has $50 million worth of bonds outstanding with an annual coupon interest rate of 10 percent. However, market interest rates have fallen to 8 percent since the bonds were issued five years ago. Accordingly, the Mega-Chip Corporation would like to replace the old 10 percent bonds with a new issue of 8 percent bonds. In so doing, the firm could save 2 percent × $50 million = $1 million a year in interest

---

2. These are called "contributions" in the same sense that the government refers to the money you pay into the Social Security system as contributions. You have no choice; you must pay. If a company fails to make its required contributions to a sinking fund as described in the indenture, the bond issue can be declared to be in default.

3. If a bond issue is callable, there is usually a certain amount of time that must pass before the bonds can be called. This is known as a deferred call provision. The indenture specifies the call date. The issuer can call bonds in from investors on, or after, this call date.

payments. The original maturity of the 10 percent bonds was 20 years. The relevant financial data are summarized in Table 14-2.

The Mega-Chip Corporation will be issuing new bonds having the same maturity as the number of years remaining to maturity on the old bonds (15 years). The call premium on the old bonds is the amount specified in the original bond indenture that the company must pay the bond owners if the bonds are called. The call premium is expressed as a percentage of the bond's face value. Thus, in this case, Mega-Chip will have to pay the old bondholders 5 percent of $50 million, or $2.5 million, in addition to the face value of the bonds, if it calls the bonds in.

The amount of the underwriting costs and the interest savings realized as a result of the refund are numbers that are essentially certain, so a very low discount rate is called for in this capital budgeting problem. The usual custom is to use the after-tax cost of debt for the discount rate. In this case the number is 6 percent.[4]

The calculations for this refunding capital budgeting problem are shown in Table 14-3.

The cash outflows in Table 14-3 are fairly straightforward. The 5 percent call premium on the old bonds and the 3 percent underwriting costs on the new bonds add up to a total outflow of $4 million.

The cash inflows are more complicated. There is an annual interest savings of $1 million per year for 15 years. This amounts to $750,000 after taxes. The present value of these after-tax annual savings is $7,284,187, using the after-tax cost of debt of 6 percent as the discount rate. The interest rate subsidy rate used to compute the after-tax cost of debt is 25%. This reflects the tax law that went into effect in 2018 with the passage of the Tax Cuts and Jobs Act of 2017 (TCJA). We are assuming here that Mega-Chip has annual sales of $25 million or less, or that it has total interest expense below 30% of adjusted taxable income. Such a firm would get a tax deduction for its business interest the same as all companies did before 2018. In our case, with a 25% interest subsidy tax rate (21% federal plus 4% for state and local) the company is saving $0.25 on its taxes for every $1.00 in interest it pays on its debt. This means if its before tax cost of debt is 8% then its after-tax cost of debt would be $8\% \times (1 - .25)$ which is 6%. Companies that did not qualify for the full deduction of business interest, because of the level of their annual sales or adjusted taxable income, would have a lower interest subsidy tax rate and thus their after-tax cost of debt would be higher (closer to the before-tax cost of debt). Refer back to Chapter 9 for a fuller description of how the TCJA changed the rules for

TABLE 14-2 Mega-Chip Bond Refunding Problem

Old Bond Issue:	$50,000,000; 10% annual interest rate; interest paid annually; 20 years original maturity. 15 years remaining to maturity
Call Premium on Old Bond:	5%
Underwriting Costs on Old Bonds When Issued 5 Years Ago:	2% of amount issued
New Bond Issue:	$50,000,000; 8% annual interest rate; interest paid semiannually; 15 years to maturity
Underwriting Costs on New Bonds:	3% of amount issued
Marginal Tax Rate:	25%
Interest Subsidy Tax Rate:	25%
After-Tax Cost of Debt:	AT k_d = 6%

---

4. This number was found using Equation 9-1. Mega-Chip's current before-tax cost of debt is 8 percent and its interest subsidy tax rate is 25 percent. Per Equation 9-1, its after-tax cost of debt is:

$$\text{After-Tax } k_d = \text{Before-Tax } k_d \times (1 - \text{Interest Subsidy Tax Rate})$$
$$= .08 \times (1 - .25)$$
$$= .06, \text{ or } 6\%$$

TABLE 14-3 Mega-Chip Bond Refunding Calculations

Cash Outflows	Calculations	Incremental Cash Flows
Call Premium Paid	$50,000,000 x .05 =	$ 2,500,000
New Bond Underwriting Costs	$50,000,000 x .03 =	$ 1,500,000
Total Outflows		$ 4,000,000

Cash Inflows

Interest Savings

Interest on old bonds:

$50,000,000 x .10 = $5,000,000

Interest on new bonds:

$50,000,000 x .08 = $4,000,000

$1,000,000 difference each year for 15 years

Less taxes on the additional Income at 25%:

$1,000,000 x .25 = ($250,000)

Net Savings = 750,000 per year

Present value of the net savings for 15 years at 6%:

$$\$750,000 \times \left[\frac{1 - \dfrac{1}{1.06^{15}}}{.06} \right] = \$750,000 \times 9.712249 = \qquad \$ 7,284,187$$

Tax Savings on Call Premium Paid
(the call premium is a tax
deductible expense amortized
over the life of the bond issue)

$50,000,000 x .05 x .25 = $625,000

Amortized over 15 years =

$625,000/15 years = $41,666.67 per year

Present value of the savings for 15 years at 6%:

$41,666.67 x 9.712279 = $ 404,678

Tax Savings from Writing Off
Balance of Old Bond
Underwriting Costs

Unamortized Amount = $50,000,000 x .02 x (15/20)[a]
= $750,000 Immediate Deduction

PV of unamortized amount if bond is not called:[a]

($750,000/15) x 9.712279 = $485,614

Net Tax Savings = ($750,000 − 485,614) x .25 = $ 66,097

Tax Savings from New Bond
Underwriting Costs

($50,000,000 x .03)/15 = $100,000 per Year Write-off

Tax Savings = $100,000 x .25 = $25,000

PV of Tax Savings = $25,000 x 9.712279 = $ 242,807

Total Inflows	$ 7,997,769
Net Present Value = $7,997,769 − $4,000,000 =	$ 3,997,769

Note: There are 5 of the original 20 years' worth of underwriting costs on the old bonds that have been written off. This leaves 15 of the 20 years, which is all written off immediately if the bonds are refunded.

[a] This is the PV of the tax savings you would have received anyhow without the refunding. The difference is the incremental cash flow from the refunding associated with the underwriting costs on the old bonds that have not yet been written off.

the deduction of business interest. The tax savings on the call premium paid on the old bonds is $404,678. The tax deductions from the underwriting costs on the old bonds were amortized over the original 20-year scheduled life of the bond. Thus, if the bonds are called now, the entire balance of the underwriting costs not yet claimed as a tax deduction will become immediately deductible.

The difference between the immediate tax savings from this deduction and the present value of the tax savings that would have been realized over the next 15 years is the incremental cash inflow relating to these underwriting costs. That figure is shown to be $66,097 in this case. We see from our calculations, then, that the present value of the tax savings from the amortization of the underwriting costs on the new bonds is $242,807.

Netting out all the incremental cash outflows and inflows gives a net present value figure of $3,997,768. Because this NPV figure is greater than zero, Mega-Chip will accept the project and proceed with the bond refunding.[5]

Restrictive Covenants

A company that seeks to raise debt capital by issuing new bonds often makes certain promises to would-be investors to convince them to buy the bonds being offered or to make it possible to issue the bonds at a lower interest rate. These promises made by the issuer to the investor, to the benefit of the investor, are **restrictive covenants**. They represent something like a courtship. If the suitor does not give certain assurances about the way the other party will be treated, there is little chance the relationship will blossom.

In a bond issuer–bond investor relationship, these assurances may include limitations on future borrowings, restrictions on dividends, and minimum levels of working capital that must be maintained.

restrictive covenants Promises made by the issuer of a bond to the investor, to the benefit of the investor.

Limitations on Future Borrowings

Investors who lend money to a corporation by buying its bonds expect that the corporation will not borrow excessively in the future. A company in too much debt may be unable to pay bond principal and interest payments on time. Bond investors would be worried if, after buying the bonds of a firm with a 20 percent debt to total assets ratio, the company then issued $100 million of additional bonds, increasing that ratio to over 90 percent. The new debt would make the earlier issued bonds instantly more risky and would lower their price in the market.

A restrictive covenant in which the corporation promises not to issue a large amount of future debt would protect the company's current bondholders from falling bond ratings and plunging market prices. A bond issue with this restriction in the indenture will have more value than a bond issue without this guarantee. As a result, the bonds could be issued at a lower coupon interest rate than bonds without the restriction in the indenture.

Restrictions on Dividends

An indenture may also include restrictions on the payment of common stock dividends if a firm's times interest earned ratio drops below a specified level. This restriction protects the bondholders against the risk of the common stockholders withdrawing value (cash for dividends that may be needed to make future interest payments) from the firm during difficult times. The bondholders are supposed to have priority over common stockholders. A bond issue with this sort of protection for investors can be issued at a lower interest rate than a bond issue without it.

Minimum Levels of Working Capital

Current assets can generally be quickly and easily converted to cash to pay bills. Having a good liquidity position protects all creditors, including bondholders. Minimum working capital guarantees in an indenture provide an additional margin of protection for bondholders and, therefore, reduce the interest rate required on such bonds.

The Independent Trustee of the Bond Issue

trustee The party that oversees a bond issue and makes sure all the provisions set forth in the indenture are carried out.

Violations of any of the provisions included in the indenture could constitute a default. Therefore, an independent **trustee** is named in the indenture to oversee the bond issue and

---

5. This assumes that the management of Mega-Chip Corporation does not expect interest rates to fall further in the months to come. If managers are confident in a forecast for even lower interest rates to come, they may wait, expecting an even greater NPV in the near future.

to make sure all the provisions spelled out in the indenture are adhered to. The trustee is usually a commercial bank.

Most people think a default is a failure to make a scheduled interest or principal payment on time. Actually, this is only one possible type of default because the promise to pay interest and principal on their due dates is only part of the promise made by the bond issuer in the indenture. Failure to keep any of the substantive promises mentioned in the indenture constitutes a default.

Types of Bonds

Some of the more innovative new financial instruments have been developed in the bond market. Let's now look more closely at the many kinds of bonds, both traditional and new.

Secured Bonds

A secured bond is backed by specific assets pledged by the issuing corporation. In the event of a default, the investors in these secured bonds would have a claim on these assets.

Mortgage Bonds

mortgage bond A bond secured by real property.

A bond backed by real assets (not financial assets) is known as a **mortgage bond**. When you buy a house and finance the purchase with a mortgage loan, you are pledging your house (a real asset) as collateral for that loan. You are issuing a mortgage bond to the lender. That is what corporations do when they pledge real assets, such as airplanes and railroad cars, as collateral for the bonds issued to purchase those assets.

first mortgage A mortgage bond (a bond secured by real property) that gives the holder first claim on the real property pledged as security if there is a foreclosure.

Different mortgage bonds can be issued that pledge the same real assets as collateral. Different classes of mortgage bonds signal the priority each investor has on the asset. An investor in a **first-mortgage** bond has first claim on the proceeds from the sale of the pledged assets if there is a default. A later lender may be an investor in a **second-mortgage** bond. In the event of default, the holder of the second mortgage receives proceeds from the sale of the pledged assets only after the first-mortgage bond investors have received all payments due to them. Similarly, third-mortgage bonds, fourth-mortgage bonds, and so forth can be issued with correspondingly lower priorities.

second mortgage A mortgage bond (a bond secured by real property) that gives the holder second claim (after the first-mortgage bond-holder) on the real property pledged as security.

Unsecured Bonds (Debentures)

A bond that is not backed by any collateral is called a debenture. A debenture is backed only by the ability and willingness of the issuing corporation to make the promised interest and principal payments as scheduled. If a debenture were to go into default, the bondholders would be unsecured creditors. They would only have a general claim on the issuing company, not a right to the firm's specific assets.

senior debenture An unsecured bond having a superior claim on the earnings and assets of the issuing firm relative to other debentures.

There may be different classes of debentures. Certain issues may have a higher priority for payment than others. If bond issue A has priority for payment over bond issue B, according to their respective indentures, then bond issue A is said to be a **senior debenture** and bond issue B is said to be a **subordinated debenture**. A senior debenture has a prior claim to the earnings and liquidation proceeds from the general assets of the firm (those assets not specifically pledged as security for other bonds) relative to the claim of subordinated debenture investors.

subordinated debenture An unsecured bond having an inferior claim on the earnings and assets of the issuing firm relative to other debentures.

Subordinated debentures have a lower-priority claim on the firm's earnings and assets. Because subordinated debentures are riskier than senior debentures, investors demand and issuers pay higher interest rates on them. This higher interest rate is consistent with the risk–return relationship—the greater the risk of a security, the greater the required rate of return. Holders of first-mortgage bonds assume less risk than holders of second-mortgage bonds. Debenture holders have more risk than secured bondholders, and subordinated debenture holders have more risk than senior debenture holders. Preferred stock investors take more risk than a bond investor, and common stock investors take more risk still for a given company. This risk hierarchy, reflecting the relative priority of claims, is shown in Figure 14-1.

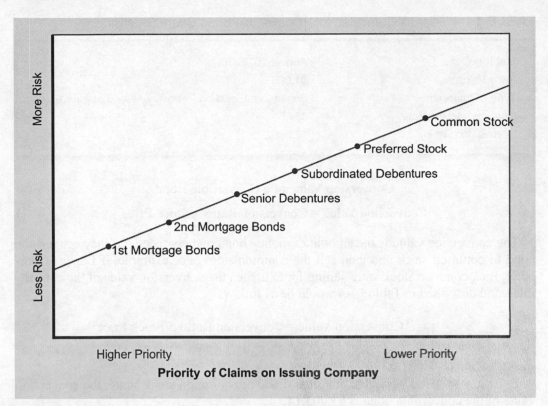

FIGURE 14-1
The Risk Hierarchy

Figure 14-1 shows the different priorities of claims that creditors and investors have on a company in default. First mortgage bondholders are paid first, whereas common stockholders are paid last.

Convertible Bonds

One of the special types of bonds available is called a **convertible bond**. A convertible bond is a bond that may be converted, at the option of the bond's owner, into a certain amount of another security issued by the same company. In the vast majority of the cases, the other security is common stock.[6] This means that the investor who bought the convertible bond may send it back to the issuing company and "convert" it into a certain number of shares of that company's common stock.

convertible bond A bond that may be converted, at the option of the bond's owner, into a certain amount of a different type of security issued by the company.

Features of Convertible Bonds

Convertible bonds have a face value, coupon rate, interest payment frequency, and maturity spelled out in their indenture, as do regular nonconvertible bonds. The indenture also spells out the terms of conversion, if the investor chooses to exercise that option. If the bond's owner elects not to convert the bond, the owner continues to receive interest and principal payments as with any other bond.

The Conversion Ratio

Each convertible bond has a conversion ratio. The **conversion ratio** is the number of shares of common stock that an investor would get if the convertible bond were converted. For example, Banana Computer, Inc., issued a convertible $1,000 bond that matures in 2030, with a conversion ratio of 12.5392 (see details in Table 14-4). That means the bond's owner can trade in the bond for 12.5392 shares of Banana Computer common stock at any time.

conversion ratio The number of shares (usually of common stock) that the holder of a convertible bond would receive if he or she exercised the conversion option.

The Conversion Value

To find the conversion value of a bond, multiply the conversion ratio by the market price per share of the company's common stock, as shown in Equation 14-1:

---

6. Some convertible bonds can be converted into a certain amount of preferred stock or some other security issued by the company.

TABLE 14-4 Banana Computer, Inc., Convertible Bond Characteristics

Maturity Date:	August 15, 2030
Face Value:	$1,000
Type of Interest:	Semiannual, paid on February 14 and August 14
Coupon Interest Rate:	3%
Conversion Ratio:	12.5392

Conversion Value of a Convertible Bond

$$\text{Conversion Value} = \text{Conversion Ratio} \times \text{Stock Price} \qquad (14\text{-}1)$$

The conversion value is the amount of money bond owners receive if they convert the bond to common stock and then sell the common stock. For example, if Banana Computer, Inc., common stock were selling for $80, then the conversion value of the convertible bond described in Table 14-4 would be as follows:

$$\text{Conversion Value} = \text{Conversion Ratio} \times \text{Stock Price}$$

$$= 12.5392 \times \$80 = \$1,003.14$$

Equation 14-1 shows us that at a rate of $80 per common stock share, the conversion value of the convertible bond is $1,003.14.

The Straight Bond Value

If a convertible bond is not converted into stock, then it is worth at least the sum of the present values of its interest and principal payments.[7] The value coming from the interest and principal is called the convertible bond's straight bond value. The discount rate used to compute this straight bond value is the required rate of return for a nonconvertible bond having characteristics (risk, maturity, tax treatment, and liquidity) similar to the convertible bond.

As shown in Table 14-4, Banana Computer's convertible bond has a coupon interest rate of 3 percent and a maturity date of August 15, 2030. The bond was issued in 2010. With a face value of $1,000, the annual interest payments will be $30 ($1,000 × .03). Because interest is paid semiannually, actual interest payments of $15 ($30 ÷ 2) are made twice a year. If the required rate of return on similar nonconvertible bonds is 8 percent annual interest (4 percent semiannually),[8] then according to Equation 12-2, the bond's straight bond value as of August 15, 2018, follows:[9]

$$V_B = \$15 \times \left[\frac{1 - \dfrac{1}{(1.04)^{24}}}{.04} \right] + \frac{\$1,000}{(1.04)^{24}}$$

$$= \left(\$15 \times 15.24696314 \right) + \left(\frac{\$1,000}{2.563304165} \right)$$

$$= \$228.7044471 + \$390.1214743$$

$$= \$618.83$$

---

7. Equation 12-2 in Chapter 12 gives the present value of a bond's interest and principal payments.

8. Actually, if 8 percent were the annual required market rate of return, then the corresponding semiannual required rate of return would be 3.923 percent (1.039232 − 1 = .08 or 8 percent) and not 4 percent. We will round this to 4 percent to simplify the calculation.

9. The number used for n in the equation is 24 because 24 semiannual periods remain until the bond matures.

We find that the present value of the interest and principal payments on a twelve-year, semiannual convertible bond with a face value of $1,000 and a 3 percent annual coupon interest rate is $618.83.

A rational investor may convert a bond if it is advantageous but will not convert it if it is disadvantageous. A convertible bond, then, is always worth the conversion value or the straight bond value, whichever is greater. For this Banana Computer bond the conversion value of $1,003.14 is greater than the straight bond value of $618.83. Because the conversion value is greater, this bond must sell for at least that higher number of $1,003.14.

Variable-Rate Bonds

Although most corporate bonds pay a fixed rate of interest (the coupon interest rate is constant), some pay a variable rate. With a **variable-rate bond**, the initial coupon rate is adjusted according to an established timetable and a market rate index.

The variable bond rates could be tied to any rate, such as a Treasury bond rate or the London Interbank Offer Rate (LIBOR). Bond issuers check this market rate on every adjustment date specified in the indenture and reset the coupon rate accordingly.

The variable rate protects investors from much of the interest rate risk inherent in fixed-rate bonds. Rising inflation hurts investors in fixed-rate bonds because the price of fixed-rate bonds falls as rising inflation increases an investor's required rate of return. In times of rising inflation, the price of a variable-rate bond does not fall as much because the investor knows that a coupon rate adjustment will occur to adjust to new, higher interest rates. However, investors who buy bonds with fixed coupon interest rates will be better off when market interest rates are falling. A variable-rate bond would have its coupon rate drop as market interest rates fell.

An issuing corporation can benefit from issuing variable-rate bonds if market rates are historically high and a drop in rates is expected. Of course, high rates can rise even further, in which case the issuing company could lose money.

> **variable-rate bonds** Bonds that have periodic changes in their coupon rates, usually tied to changes in market interest rates

Putable Bonds

A **putable bond** is a bond that can be cashed in before maturity at the option of the bond's owner. This is like the callable bond described earlier in the chapter except that the positions of the issuer and the bond's owner with respect to the option have been reversed. Investors may exercise the option to redeem their bonds early when it is in their best interest to do so. Investors usually redeem fixed-rate bonds if interest rates have risen. The existing, lower-interest-rate bond can be redeemed and the proceeds used to buy a new higher-interest-rate bond.

> **putable bonds** Bonds that can be redeemed before the scheduled maturity date, at the option of the bondholder.

Junk Bonds

Another type of bond that is popular with aggressive investors seeking high levels of income is the junk bond. Junk bonds, also known as *high-yield bonds*, have a bond rating below investment grade. As shown earlier in this chapter, according to Moody's ratings, a junk bond would have a rating of Ba1 or below; according to Standard & Poor's ratings, it would have a rating of BB+ or below. The name *junk* is perhaps unfairly applied because these bonds are usually not trash; they are simply riskier than bonds having an investment grade. For instance, many bonds used to finance corporate takeovers have below-investment-grade ratings.

Some junk bonds start out with investment-grade ratings but then suffer a downgrade—the issuing company may have fallen on hard financial times or may have gone through a major financial restructuring that increased the risk of the outstanding bonds. Such junk bonds are known as *fallen angels*. Mattel was downgraded to junk bond status by Moody's and Fitch in December of 2017. Other companies whose bonds have become fallen angels over the years include Sony, Panasonic, Kodak, Rite Aid, and CenturyLink.

International Bonds

international bonds Bonds that are sold in countries other than where the issuer is domiciled.

An **international bond** is a bond sold in countries other than where the corporate headquarters of the issuing company is located. The bonds may be denominated in the currency of the issuing company's country or in the currency of the country in which the bonds are sold. Foreign corporations issue bonds in the United States, sometimes denominated in their home currencies and sometimes in U.S. dollars. In turn, U.S. corporations frequently issue bonds outside the United States. These bonds may be denominated in U.S. dollars or in some other currency.

Eurobonds are bonds denominated in the currency of the issuing company's home country and sold in another country. For example, if General Motors issued a dollar-denominated bond in Italy it would be called a Eurobond. Similarly, if Ferrari, an Italian company, issued a euro-denominated bond in the United States, the bond would be called a Eurobond. If the Ferrari bond were denominated in dollars instead of euros, it would be referred to as a *Yankee bond*.

Super Long-Term Bonds

IBM, the Disney Corporation, Coca-Cola, and Nacional Electricidad SA, the largest power company in Chile, have issued bonds with a maturity of 100 years, which is a much longer maturity than is typical among corporate bond issuers. Investors who purchase these bonds must have confidence in the future cash flow of these companies.

In this section we have described types of bonds. Next, we examine preferred stock, its characteristics, and those who purchase it.

Preferred Stock

Preferred stock is so called because owners of preferred stock have a priority claim over common stockholders to the earnings and assets of a corporation. That is, preferred stockholders receive their dividends before common stockholders. Preferred stock is not issued by many corporations except in certain industries, such as public utilities.

The preferred stock dividend is usually permanently fixed, so the potential return on investment for a preferred stockholder is not as high as it is for a common stockholder. Common stockholders are entitled to all residual income of the firm (which could be considerable).

Preferred stock is known as a hybrid security. It is a hybrid because it has both debt and equity characteristics. Preferred stock is like debt primarily because preferred stockholders do not have an ownership claim, nor do they have any claim on the residual income of the firm. It is also like equity because it has an infinite maturity and a lower-priority claim against the firm than bondholders have.

Preferred Stock Dividends

Issuers of preferred stock generally promise to pay a fixed dollar amount of dividends to the investor. This promise, however, does not result in bankruptcy if it is broken. Unlike failure to make a scheduled interest or principal payment to bondholders, failure to pay a scheduled dividend to preferred stockholders is not grounds for bankruptcy of the company that issued the preferred stock.

Occasionally, participating preferred stock is issued. This type of preferred stock offers the chance for investors to share the benefits of rising earnings with the common stockholders. This is quite rare, however.

Preferred stock can be either cumulative or noncumulative with respect to its dividends. With cumulative preferred stock, if a dividend is missed, it must be paid at a later date before dividends may resume to common stockholders. Seldom is any interest paid, however, to compensate preferred stockholders for the fact that when dividends are resumed, they are received later than when promised. Noncumulative preferred stock does not make up missed dividends. If the dividends are skipped, they are lost forever to the investors.

Preferred Stock Investors

Corporations can generally exclude 50 percent of the dividend income received on preferred stock issued by another corporation from their taxable income. This 50% exclusion number dropped from 70% in 2018 with the passage of the Tax Cuts and Jobs Act of 2017. As a result, corporations are the major investors in preferred stock. The tax exclusion is 65 percent with the passage of the TCJA of 2017 if the investor corporation owns more than 20 percent of the stock of the other corporation.

Because of the favorable tax treatment corporations receive on this dividend income, they bid up the price on preferred stock, thus lowering the expected rate of return. The lower expected rate of return is the price they pay for receiving the preferential tax treatment. Individuals cannot exclude any dividend income on their personal tax returns and must pay taxes on all of it, so preferred stock is not often recommended by financial planners as a good investment for individuals.

Convertible Preferred Stock

Occasionally companies issue preferred stock that is convertible into a fixed number of shares of common stock. The convertible preferred stock may be either cumulative or noncumulative, just like "regular" preferred stock. For example, in June, 2009, The Callaway Golf Company raised approximately $134 million from an issue of 1,250,000 shares of 7.50 percent cumulative convertible preferred stock to MEHC Investment, Inc. Each share of the preferred stock is convertible into 14.1844 shares of Callaway common stock.[10]

In some cases, convertible preferred stock may also be exchanged for a certain number of convertible bonds with the identical pre-tax cash flow and common stock conversion terms. This type of stock is called convertible exchangeable preferred stock.

Leasing

Debt is often incurred to acquire an asset. An alternative to borrowing and buying an asset is to lease the asset. A **lease** is an arrangement in which one party that owns an asset contracts with another party to use that asset for a specified period of time, without conveying legal ownership of that asset. The party who owns the asset is known as the **lessor**. The party who uses the asset is the **lessee**. The lessee makes lease payments to the lessor for the right to use the asset for the specified time period.

A lease contract that is long term and noncancelable is very similar to a debt obligation from the perspective of the lessee. Some contracts that look like genuine leases are not, according to federal tax laws. There are different types of lease contracts. These different types have different accounting treatments, which we turn to next.

lease A contract between an asset owner (lessor) and another party who uses that asset (lessee) that allows the use of the asset for a specified period of time, specifies payment terms, and does not convey legal ownership.

lessor The party in a lease contract who owns the asset.

lessee The party in a lease contract who uses the asset.

Genuine Leases versus Fakes

When a business leases an asset, the entire amount of the lease payments made by the lessee to the lessor is tax deductible to the lessee. When bonds are issued, or a bank loan obtained, only the interest portion of the loan payment may be tax deductible depending on the amount of annual sales of the company and the amount of total interest expense it has relative to the interest deduction limit imposed by the TCJA of 2017. This sometimes leads a company to enter into a contract that looks like a lease, to obtain the large tax deductions, but which is not in fact a lease. The IRS is ever vigilant in ferreting out these fake lease contracts and denying the associated deductions.

To illustrate, suppose you needed a new truck for your business. The purchase price of the truck you want is $40,000. If you buy the truck and depreciate it over five years (ignore the half-year convention), you would have tax-deductible depreciation expense of $8,000 per year for five years. What if instead of buying the truck for $40,000, you leased it from the truck dealer for $40,000 in up-front cash, followed by additional lease payments of $1 per year for four years and then an option to buy the truck at the end of five years for

---

10. https://www.sec.gov/Archives/edgar/data/837465/000119312509219017/d424b3.htm

$10? The extra $14 paid, with the exercising of the purchase option, would be a drop in the bucket compared to the tax savings you would realize in year 1 from the $40,000 tax deduction for the "lease payments." Because money has time value, a $40,000 deduction in year 1 is much preferred to deductions of $8,000 per year for five years.

The foregoing lease is a sham, a fake. What we have here is an installment purchase, disguised as a lease. In an audit, the IRS would deny the $40,000 year 1 "lease payment" and reclassify the deduction as a (much lower) depreciation expense. Your business would probably also be hit with interest charges and penalties.

The IRS standards for a genuine lease are as follows:

1. The remaining life of the asset at the end of the lease term must be the greater of 20 percent of the original useful life or one year.

2. The lease payments must provide the lessor with a reasonable rate of return.

3. Renewal options must contain terms consistent with the market value of the asset.

4. Purchase options must be for an amount close to the asset's fair market value at the time the option is exercised.

5. The property must not be limited-use (custom made for only one firm's use) property.

You can see immediately that in our truck example, the purchase option specifies a price ($10) that is much lower than the fair market value of the truck in five years. The IRS would consider this "lease" to be a sham.

Operating and Financial (Capital) Leases

operating lease A lease that has a term substantially shorter than the useful life of the asset and is usually cancelable by the lessee.

financial (capital) lease A lease that is generally long term and non-cancelable, with the lessee using up most of the economic value of the asset by the end of the lease's term.

Once a lease passes the tests for being classified as a genuine lease, it must be further classified for accounting purposes as an operating or financial (capital) lease. An **operating lease** has a term substantially shorter than the useful life of the asset and is usually cancelable by the lessee. A **financial (capital) lease** is long term and noncancelable. The lessee uses up most of the economic value of the asset by the end of the lease's term with a financial lease.

If you went on a business trip and leased a car for the week to make your business calls, this would be an operating lease. This same car will be leased again to many other customers, and in one week you will use up a small fraction of the car's economic value. Your company, which is paying your travel expenses, would deduct these lease payments as business expenses on the income statement.

If your company signed a 10-year, noncancelable lease on a $20 million supercomputer, this is likely to be a financial lease (also known as a capital lease). After 10 years the supercomputer is likely to be obsolete. Your company would have used up most, if not all, its economic value by the end of the 10-year lease period. The lessor surely would demand lease payments high enough to recognize this fact and also to compensate for the time value of money that is paid over a 10-year period. The fact that the payments are spread out over time means that the lessor must be compensated for the cost of the asset and for the delay in the receipt of the lease payments.

Accounting Treatment of Leases

Both operating and financial (capital) lease payments show up on the income statement. Assuming that a lease is genuine, payments made by the lessee to the lessor are shown on the income statement as tax-deductible business expenses for both types of leases. These are costs of doing business for the lessee.

Financial leases have another accounting impact, however, that operating leases do not. A financial lease also shows up on the company's balance sheet because it is functionally equivalent to buying the asset and financing the purchase with borrowed money. If the asset had been purchased and financed with debt, the asset and the liability associated with the debt would both show up on the balance sheet. Because a financial lease is functionally equivalent to a purchase financed with debt, the Financial Accounting Standards Board (FASB) has ruled that the accounting treatment should be similar.

Failure to make a bond payment can lead to bankruptcy, as can failure to make a contractual lease payment on a noncancelable lease. The leased asset is shown in the asset section of the lessee's balance sheet, with a corresponding liability entry in the amount of the present value of all the lease payments owed to the lessor.

A lease is classified as a financial (capital) lease if it meets *any one* of the following four criteria:

1. Ownership of the asset is transferred to the lessee at the end of the lease's term.

2. There is an option for the lessee to buy the asset at a bargain purchase price at the end of the lease period.

3. The lease period is greater than or equal to 75 percent of the estimated useful life of the asset.

4. The present value of the lease payments equals 90 percent or more of the fair market value of the asset at the time the lease is originated, using the lower of the lessee's cost of debt or the lessor's rate of return on the lease as the discount rate.

Only if none of these four criteria applies is the lease considered an operating lease, with no balance sheet entry.

Lease or Buy?

Leasing is growing in popularity. Whether an asset should be leased or bought depends on the relative costs of the two alternatives. Leasing is most nearly comparable to a buy–borrow alternative. Because signing a debt contract is similar to signing a lease contract, comparisons are usually made between the lease option and the buy with borrowed funds option.

The alternative that has the lower present value of after-tax costs is usually chosen. The tax factor considered for the lease alternative would be the tax deductibility of the lease payments that would be made (assuming the lease is genuine and passes IRS muster). The tax factors for the buy with borrowed funds alternative would come primarily from two sources. One is the tax deduction that comes with the payment of interest on the borrowed funds. The other is the tax deduction that comes with the depreciation expense on the purchased asset.

A Lease or Buy Decision Example

Let's go through an example of a lease or buy decision to illustrate the computations involved. For our example, we will use Mr. Sulu in the Photon Manufacturing Company, whose project was described in Chapter 11. Recall that Mr. Sulu was considering a project to install $3 million worth of new machine tools in the company's main torpedo manufacturing plant. According to the analysis in Chapter 11, the NPV of the project was positive, so Mr. Sulu decided to obtain the new machine tools. Now the decision about how to finance the acquisition must be made. For simplicity, let us assume that two alternatives are available: (1) The machine tools can be purchased using the proceeds from a $3 million, five-year, 10 percent interest rate loan from a bank, or (2) the machine tools can be leased for $500,000 a year, payable at the beginning of each of the next five years. At the end of the lease term, the tools would be returned to the lessor for disposal.[11] If the tools are purchased, they can be sold for salvage at the end of five years for $800,000.

The decision to lease or to borrow and purchase the machine tools can be made by comparing the present value of the cash flows associated with each alternative. Table 14-5 contains the analysis for Mr. Sulu's new machine tools. Notice in Table 14-5 that the

---

11. For simplicity in this example, we will assume that the lease is a straightforward operating lease, so no other accounting considerations are required.

TABLE 14-5 Photon Manufacturing Company Lease–Buy Analysis

PART 1, THE BUY OPTION
Assumptions

Cost of New Tools	$ 3,000,000
Expected Life	5 years
Salvage Value	$ 800,000
Amount to Be Borrowed	$ 3,000,000
Interest Rate on Loan	10%

MACRS Depreciation	Yr 1	Yr 2	Yr 3	Yr 4
(3-Year Asset Class)	33.3%	44.5%	14.8%	7.4%

Cost of capital　　8.5% (after-tax cost of debt with an interest subsidy tax rate (ISTR) of 15%)

Corporate tax rate　　25% (21% federal rate plus 4% assumed for state and local)

Interest subsidy tax rate (ISTR)　　15%

Estimated Incremental Cash Flows to Equity

Year	0	1	2	3	4	5
Cost of New Tools	$(3,000,000)					
Amount to Be Borrowed	3,000,000					
Depreciation on New Tools		$ (999,000)	$(1,335,000)	$ (444,000)	$ (222,000)	$ 0
Tax Savings on Depreciation		249,750	333,750	111,000	55,500	0
Interest Payments on Loan		$ (300,000)	(300,000)	(300,000)	(300,000)	(300,000)
Tax Savings on Interest		45,000	45,000	45,000	45,000	45,000
Repayment of Principal on Loan						(3,000,000)
Salvage Value of New Tools						800,000
Tax on Gain						(200,000)
Net Incremental Cash Flows	$ 0	$ (5,250)	$ 78,750	$(144,000)	$(199,500)	$(2,655,000)
PV of Cash Flows	$ 0	$ (4,839)	$ 66,895	$(112,739)	$(143,954)	$(1,765,696)

Total PV of Cash Flows Associated with the Buy Option = $(1,960,333)

Cost of Buying with Borrowed Funds = $ 1,960,333

PART 2, THE LEASE OPTION
Assumptions

Annual Lease Payment	$ (500,000) paid at the beginning of each year
Lease Term	5 years
Value at Termination of Lease	$0

Estimated Incremental Cash Flows to Equity

Year	0	1	2	3	4	5
Lease Payment	$(500,000)	$(500,000)	$(500,000)	$(500,000)	$(500,000)	
Tax Savings on Lease Payment	$ 125,000	$ 125,000	$ 125,000	$ 125,000	$ 125,000	
Net Incremental Cash Flows	$(375,000)	$(375,000)	$(375,000)	$(375,000)	$(375,000)	
PV of Cash Flows	$(375,000)	$(345,622)	$(318,546)	$(293,591)	$(270,590)	

Total PV of Cash Flows Associated with the Lease Option = $(1,603,349)

Cost of Leasing = $ 1,603,349

Net Advantage to Leasing (NAL) = Total Cost of Buying with Borrowed Funds – Cost of Leasing = $ 356,984

analysis is conducted from the point of view of Photon Manufacturing's stockholders, so it is the incremental cash flows to equity that are relevant.

In the top portion of Table 14-5, the analysis of the buy option is presented, in which the asset is purchased with borrowed funds. The analysis begins with the $3,000,000 cash outflow for the purchase of the tools, which is offset by a $3,000,000 cash inflow from the proceeds from the loan, making the net cash flow at t_0 zero dollars. Next, the cash flows at the end of years 1 through 5 are considered. Depreciation expense will be recorded at the end of years 1 through 4, because the tools fall into the MACRS three-year asset class. The depreciation expense is tax-deductible, so at the end of years 1 through 4 the firm will experience tax savings equal to the depreciation expense times the firm's income tax rate of 25 percent. Depreciation is a noncash expense, but the income tax savings represent real cash inflows to the firm at the end of years 1 through 4.

Interest payments on the loan in the amount of $3,000,000 times 10 percent must be made at the end of years 1 through 5. Also at the end of year 5, the $3,000,000 must be repaid. Finally, when the tools are sold for salvage at the end of the fifth year, their book value is zero, so income tax must be paid on the $800,000. The amount to be paid is $800,000 × 25 percent = $200,000.

When all the cash flows are added up, the net incremental cash flows are negative $5,250 in year 1, $78,750 in year 2, negative $144,000 in year 3, negative $199,500 in year 4, and negative $2,655,000 in year 5, as shown in Table 14-5. To calculate the present value of the cash flows, they are discounted at the after-tax cost of borrowing the $3,000,000, which in this case is 10% × (1 − .15) = 8.5%. The results indicate that the total present value of the cash flows associated with buying the machine tools is negative $1,960,333.

In the bottom portion of Table 14-5, the analysis of the lease option is presented. In this case the only relevant cash flows are the lease payments and the associated tax savings that occur because the lease payments are tax-deductible. The tax savings are calculated by multiplying the lease payment ($500,000) by the firm's tax rate (25 percent). Note that the five annual lease payments are made at the beginning of each year. Adding the tax savings and the lease payment produces the net incremental cash flow associated with leasing each year, which is $375,000. Because the cash flows associated with leasing are almost certain, like the firm's debt cash flows, the lease cash flows are discounted at the after-tax cost of debt (8.5 percent) to calculate their present values. Their total present value, as shown in Table 14-5, is negative $1,603,349.

To decide whether to lease or buy the new machine tools, Mr. Sulu compares the present value of the cash flows associated with buying with the present value of the cash flows associated with leasing:

Cost of Buying with Borrowed Funds	$ 1,960,333
Cost of Leasing	$ 1,603,349
Net Advantage to Leasing (NAL)	$ 356,984

Observing that the cost of leasing is $356,984 less than the cost of buying with borrowed funds, Mr. Sulu directs his staff to proceed with the leasing arrangements.

Companies that are likely to see a clear advantage to leasing instead of buying are those that are losing money. Such companies, because they have negative taxable income, pay no taxes. The deductions for interest and depreciation expenses could not be used (subject to carry back and carry forward provisions of losses to earlier or later years). If the asset is leased instead from a profitable lessor, the lessor can take advantage of the interest and depreciation expense tax deductions and the lessee can negotiate a lease payment that is lower than it otherwise would be, so that these tax benefits are shared by the lessor and the lessee.

Many airlines are losing money. The next time you take a plane trip, look for a small sign just inside the passenger entrance of the plane. It may say that the airplane you are about to travel on is owned by a leasing company (the lessor) and leased by the airline (the lessee).

What's Next

In this chapter we learned about the basic characteristics of bonds and the different types of bonds available. We also examined preferred stock and leasing. In Chapter 15 we will discuss common stock, how it is issued, and the nature of the equity claim of the common stockholders.

Summary

1. *Describe the contract terms of a bond issue.*
   The indenture is the contract that spells out the terms of the bond issue. A call provision gives the issuer the option to buy back the bonds before the scheduled maturity date. A conversion provision gives the bondholder the option to exchange the bond for a given number of shares of stock. Restrictive covenants may include limits on future borrowings by the issuer, minimum working capital levels that must be maintained, and restrictions on dividends paid to common stockholders.

2. *Distinguish the various types of bonds and describe their major characteristics.*
   All bonds are debt instruments that give the holder a liability claim on the issuer. A mortgage is a bond secured by real property. A debenture is an unsecured bond. A convertible bond is convertible, at the option of the bondholder, into a certain number of shares of common stock (sometimes preferred stock or another security).

   A variable-rate bond has a coupon interest rate that is not fixed but is tied to a market interest rate indicator. A putable bond can be cashed in by the bondholder before maturity. Bonds that are below investment grade are junk bonds. An international bond, a bond sold in a country other than the country of the corporate headquarters of the issuing company, differs from a Eurobond. A Eurobond is a bond denominated in the currency of the issuing company's home country and sold in another country. A super long-term bond is one that matures in 100 years.

3. *Describe the key features of preferred stock.*
   Preferred stock is a hybrid security that has debt and equity characteristics. Preferred stockholders have a superior claim relative to the common stockholders to a firm's earnings and assets, and their dividend payments are usually fixed. Those traits resemble debt. In addition, preferred stock has an infinite maturity and lower-priority claim to assets and earnings than bondholders. Because of the corporate tax exclusion of some preferred stock dividends from taxable income, corporations are much more likely to invest in stock than individuals.

4. *Compare and contrast a genuine lease and a disguised purchase contract.*
   Because lease payments are entirely tax deductible, many attempt to disguise purchase contracts as genuine leases. A lease is an arrangement in which the owner of an asset contracts to allow another party the use of the asset over time. In order for the lease to be genuine, the lessee (the party to whom the asset is leased) must not have an effective ownership of the asset. The IRS has six standards that a lease must meet to qualify for the lease tax deductions. Failure to comply with IRS rules will result in the less favorable tax treatment of a purchase contract.

5. *Explain why some leases must be shown on the balance sheet.*
   Operating leases are usually short term and cancelable. Financial (capital) leases are long term and noncancelable. Both operating and financial leases appear on the income statement of the lessee because they are tax-deductible business expenses. Because financial leases are functionally equivalent to a purchase financed with debt, FASB rules require that businesses treat them similarly for accounting purposes. Financial leases, therefore, appear on the balance sheet.

Key Terms

call premium The premium the issuer pays to call in a bond before maturity. The excess of the call price over the face value.

call provision A bond indenture provision that allows the issuer to pay off a bond before the stated maturity date at a specified price.

conversion ratio The number of shares (usually of common stock) that the holder of a convertible bond would receive if he or she exercised the conversion option.

convertible bond A bond that may be converted, at the option of the bond's owner, into a certain amount of a different type of security issued by the company.

corporate bond A security that represents a promise by the issuing corporation to make certain payments, according to a certain schedule, to the owner of the bond.

debenture A bond that is unsecured.

financial (capital) lease A lease that is generally long term and non-cancelable, with the lessee using up most of the economic value of the asset by the end of the lease's term.

first mortgage A mortgage bond (a bond secured by real property) that gives the holder first claim on the real property pledged as security if there is a foreclosure.

indenture The contract between the issuing corporation and the bond's purchaser.

international bonds Bonds that are sold in countries other than where the issuer is domiciled.

investment-grade bonds Bonds rated Baa3 or above by Moody's bond rating agency and BBB– or above by Standard & Poor's.

junk bonds Bonds with lower than investment-grade ratings.

lease A contract between an asset owner (lessor) and another party who uses that asset (lessee) that allows the use of the asset for a specified period of time, specifies payment terms, and does not convey legal ownership.

lessee The party in a lease contract who uses the asset.

lessor The party in a lease contract who owns the asset.

mortgage bond A bond secured by real property.

operating lease A lease that has a term substantially shorter than the useful life of the asset and is usually cancelable by the lessee.

putable bonds Bonds that can be redeemed before the scheduled maturity date, at the option of the bondholder.

refunding Issuing new bonds to replace old bonds.

restrictive covenants Promises made by the issuer of a bond to the investor, to the benefit of the investor.

second mortgage A mortgage bond (a bond secured by real property) that gives the holder second claim (after the first-mortgage bond-holder) on the real property pledged as security.

secured bond A bond backed by specific assets that the investor may claim if there is a default.

senior debenture An unsecured bond having a superior claim on the earnings and assets of the issuing firm relative to other debentures.

serial payments A mode of payment in which the issuer pays off bonds according to a staggered maturity schedule.

subordinated debenture An unsecured bond having an inferior claim on the earnings and assets of the issuing firm relative to other debentures.

trustee The party that oversees a bond issue and makes sure all the provisions set forth in the indenture are carried out.

variable-rate bonds Bonds that have periodic changes in their coupon rates, usually tied to changes in market interest rates.

Equations Introduced in This Chapter

Equation 14-1. Conversion Value of a Convertible Bond:

$$\text{Conversion Value} = \text{Conversion Ratio} \times \text{Stock Price}$$

Self-Test

ST-1. Explain the features of a bond indenture.

ST-2. What is a callable bond?

ST-3. What is the straight bond value of a convertible bond?

ST-4. What is cumulative preferred stock?

ST-5. Which financial statement(s) would a financial lease affect? Why?

ST-6. What is the conversion value of a convertible bond having a current stock price of $15 and a conversion ratio of 20?

Review Questions

1. How does a mortgage bond compare with a debenture?

2. How does a sinking fund function in the retirement of an outstanding bond issue?

3. What are some examples of restrictive covenants that might be specified in a bond's indenture?

4. Define the following terms that relate to a convertible bond: conversion ratio, conversion value, and straight bond value.

5. If a convertible bond has a conversion ratio of 20, a face value of $1,000, a coupon rate of 8 percent, and the market price for the company's stock is $15 per share, what is the convertible bond's conversion value?

6. What is a callable bond? What is a putable bond? How do each of these features affect their respective market interest rates?

Build Your Communication Skills

CS-1. Select a corporate bond and research its indenture provisions. What must the issuer do and what must the issuer not do? Write a brief report of one to two pages on your findings.

CS-2. Does a bond issuer owe potential investors full disclosure of plans that might affect the value of the bonds, or is the issuer's duty to investors only what is explicitly stated in the indenture contract? Divide into small groups to debate this issue.

Problems

Straight Bond Value **14-1.** Sean Thornton has invested in a convertible bond issued by Cohan Enterprises. The conversion ratio is 20. The market price of Cohan common stock is $60 per share. The face value is $1,000. The coupon rate is 8 percent and the annual interest is paid until the maturity date 10 years from now. Similar nonconvertible bonds are yielding 12 percent (YTM) in the marketplace. Calculate the straight bond value of this bond.

Straight Bond Value **14-2.** Use the same data given in problem 14-1. Now assume that interest is paid semiannually ($40 every six months). Calculate the straight bond value.

Conversion Value **14-3.** Using the data in problem 14-1, calculate the conversion value of the Cohan Enterprises convertible bond.

Conversion Value **14-4.** Danny Brown purchased 10 convertible bonds from Raingers in 2015 that mature in 2019 with a conversion ratio of 26.5 each. Currently Raingers stock is selling for $32 per share. Danny wants to convert six of his bonds. What is the conversion value of these six bonds?

Straight Bond Value **14-5.** Kendrick Lamar has a balance in his savings account of $10,000. He wants to invest 10 percent of this amount into a convertible bond issued by the Hamptom Corp. The market price of Hamptom Corp. common stock is $85 per share. The convertible bond has a conversion ratio of 30. This bond has a 9 percent annual coupon rate (paid quarterly), a maturity of 15 years, and a face value of $1,000. Nonconvertible bonds with similar attributes are yielding 15 percent. Calculate the straight bond value for this bond.

Conversion Value **14-6.** Using the values in 14-5, find the conversion value of this bond.

Straight Bond Value **14-7.** Characteristics of Tanbs, Inc., convertible bonds.

Conversion Ratio	25.885
Face Value	$1,000
Maturity Date	15 years hence
Coupon Interest Rate	6.75% annual
Interest Paid	semiannually

Calculate Tanbs, Inc.'s straight bond value on its convertible bonds. The current market interest rate on similar nonconvertible bonds is 8 percent.

Sinking Fund **14-8.** Two years ago a company issued $10 million in bonds with a face value of $1,000 and a maturity of 10 years. The company is supposed to put aside $1 million in a sinking fund each year to pay off the bonds. Dolly Frisco, the finance manager of the company, has found out that the bonds are selling at $800 apiece in the open market now when a deposit to the sinking fund is due. How much would Dolly save (before transaction costs) by purchasing 1,000 of these bonds in the open market instead of calling them in at $1,000 each?

Call Provision **14-9.** Five years ago BLK issued bonds with a 7 percent coupon interest rate. The bond's indenture stated that the bonds were callable after three years. So, four years later interest rates fell to 5 percent, the company called the old bonds and refunded at the 5 percent rate. If BLK issued 30,000 10-year bonds, how much did BLK save in interest per year?

Call Provision **14-10.** A company where Chief Keef works as the vice president of finance issued 20,000 bonds 10 years ago. The bonds had a face value of $1,000, annual coupon rate of 10 percent, and a maturity of 20 years. This year the market yield on the company's bond is 8 percent. The bonds are callable after five years at par. If Chief Keef decides in favor of exercising the call option, financing it through a refunding operation, what would be the annual savings in interest payments for the company? (Interest is paid annually.)

14-11. Use the same information given in problem 14-10. Now assume that the call premium is 5 percent and the bonds were called back today. Chief Keef purchased 10 bonds when they were originally issued at $950 per bond. Calculate the realized rate of return for Chief Keef.

Call Premium

14.12. Chief Keef of problem 14-11, after getting his bonds called back by the original issuing company, can now invest in a $1,000 par, 8 percent annual coupon rate, 10-year maturity bond of equivalent risk selling at $950. (Interest is paid annually.)

Total Return on Investment

   a. What is the overall return for Keef over the 20 years, assuming the bond is held until maturity?

   b. Compare the overall return with the return on the bonds in problem 14-8 if they had not been called. Did Keef welcome the recall?

14-13. Captain Nathan Brittles invested in a $1,000 par, 20-year maturity, 9 percent annual coupon rate convertible bond with a conversion ratio of 20 issued by a company six years ago. What is the conversion value of Captain Brittles's investment if the current market price for the company's common stock is $70 per share? (Interest is paid annually.)

Conversion Value

14-14. Use the same information given in problem 14-13. If the current required rate of return on a similar nonconvertible bond is 7 percent, what is the straight bond value for the bond? Should Captain Brittles convert the bond into common stock now?

Straight Bond Value

14-15. Jaime Lannister invested in a $1,000 par, 10-year maturity, 11 percent coupon rate convertible bond with a conversion ratio of 30 issued by a company five years ago. The current market price for the company's common stock is $30 per share. The current required rate of return on similar but nonconvertible bonds is 13 percent. Should Mr. Lannister consider converting the bond into common stock now?

Bond Conversion

14-16. Six years ago Ruby Carter invested $1,000 in a $1,000 par, 20-year maturity, 9 percent annual coupon rate putable bond, which can be redeemed at $900 after five years. If the current required rate of return on similar bonds is 13 percent, should Ruby redeem the bond? What is the realized rate of return after redeeming? (Interest is paid annually.)

Putable Bond

14-17. Five years ago Diana Troy invested $1,000 in a $1,000 par, 10-year maturity, 9 percent annual coupon rate putable bond, which can be redeemed at $900 after five years. If the current required rate of return on similar bonds is 14 percent, should Diana redeem the bond? What is the realized rate of return after redeeming? If Diana reinvests the sum in a $1,000 par, five years to maturity, 13 percent annual coupon rate bond selling at $900 and holds it until maturity, what is her realized rate of return over the next five years? What is her realized rate of return over the entire 10 years?

Putable Bond Reinvesting

14-18. Hot Box Insulators, a public company, initially issued investment-grade, 20-year maturity, 8 percent annual coupon rate bonds 10 years ago at $1,000 par. A group of investors bought all of Hot Box's common stock through a leveraged buyout, which turned the bonds overnight into junk bonds. Similar junk bonds are currently yielding 25 percent in the market. Calculate the current price of the original bonds.

Challenge Problem

14-19. Profit Unlimited Company is in bankruptcy. The company has the following liability and equity claims:

Priority of Claim

First-Mortgage Bonds	$ 5 million
Second-Mortgage Bonds	5 million
Senior Debentures	10 million
Subordinated Debentures	4 million
Common Stock	10 million (par value)

Mortgaged assets have been sold for $7 million and other assets for $13 million. According to priority of claims, determine the distribution of $20 million obtained from the sale proceeds.

14-20. Suppose the Builders-R-Us Real Estate Finance Corporation has $60 million worth of bonds outstanding with an annual coupon interest rate of 8 percent. However, market interest rates have fallen to 6 percent since the bonds were issued 10 years ago. Accordingly, Builders-R-Us would like to replace the old 8 percent bonds with a new issue of 6 percent bonds.

For more, see 8e Spreadsheet Templates for *Microsoft Excel.*

The relevant financial data are summarized here:

Old Bond Issue	$60,000,000, 8% annual interest rate, interest paid semiannually, 20 years original maturity, 10 years remaining to maturity
Call Premium on Old Bond	4%
Underwriting Costs on Old Bonds When Issued 5 Years Ago	2% of amount issued
New Bond Issue	$60,000,000, 6% annual interest rate, interest paid semiannually, 10 years to maturity
Underwriting Costs on New Bonds	3% of amount issued
Marginal Tax Rate	25%
Interest Subsidy Tax Rate	15%
Discount Rate for Present Value Analysis (After-Tax Cost of Debt)	5.1%

The Builders-R-Us Corporation will be issuing new bonds having the same maturity as the number of years remaining to maturity on the old bonds.

a. What are the total cash outflows that Builders-R-Us will incur at time zero if the company implements the proposed bond refunding program?

b. What is the annual before-tax savings in interest payments that Builders-R-Us would realize?

c. What is the annual after-tax savings in interest payments that Builders-R-Us would realize?

d. What is the present value of the annual after-tax interest savings?

e. What are the annual tax savings on the call premium that will be paid in the refunding program?

f. What is the present value of the annual tax savings on the call premium?

g. What are the net tax savings from writing off the balance of the old bond underwriting costs?

h. What are the tax savings from the new bond underwriting costs?

i. What is the present value of the tax savings from the new bond underwriting costs?

j. What is the present value of the total cash inflows that will occur if the bond refunding program is implemented?

k. What is the net present value of the proposed bond refunding program? Would you advise Builders-R-Us to proceed with the program?

14-21. Regina Hitechia, the CIO of Aurora Glass Fibers, Inc., is considering whether to lease or buy some new computers in the company's manufacturing plant. The new computers can be purchased for $800,000 with the proceeds from a 4-year, 10 percent interest rate loan, or leased for $250,000 a year, payable at the beginning of each year for the next four years. The computers fall into MACRS depreciation three-year asset class and have an expected useful life of four years. The salvage value of the computers at the end of the fourth year is $100,000. If the computers are leased, they will be returned to the leasing company at the end of the fourth year. Aurora's marginal tax rate is 40 percent.

For more, see 8e Spreadsheet Templates for *Microsoft Excel.*

a. What is the present value of the cash flows associated with buying the computers?

b. What is the present value of the cash flows associated with leasing the computers?

c. Should Ms. Hitechia purchase or lease the new computers?

ST-1. A bond indenture is the contract that spells out the provisions of a bond issue. It always contains the face value, coupon rate, interest payment dates, and maturity date. It may also include terms of security in the case of default, if any; the plan for paying off the bonds at maturity; provisions for paying off the bonds ahead of time; restrictive covenants to protect bondholders; and the trustee's name.

ST-2. A callable bond is a bond that can be paid off early by the issuer at the issuer's option.

ST-3. The straight bond value of a convertible bond is the value a convertible bond would have without its conversion feature. It is the present value of the interest and principal using the required rate of return on a similar nonconvertible bond as the discount rate.

ST-4. Cumulative preferred stock is preferred stock for which missed dividends must be made up (paid) by the issuing company before common stock dividends may be resumed.

ST-5. A financial (capital) lease would show up on both the income statement and the balance sheet. Lease payments are business expenses that belong on the income statement, and FASB rules call for financial leases to be reflected on the balance sheet also.

ST-6. $15 market price of the stock × 20 conversion ratio = $300 conversion value of the convertible bond.

Common Stock

"Where your treasure is, there will your heart be also."
—Matthew 6:21

CHAPTER 15

Source: Tupungato/Shutterstock

Learning Objectives

After reading this chapter, you should be able to:

1. Describe the characteristics of common stock.
2. Explain the disadvantages and advantages of equity financing.
3. Explain the process of issuing new common stock.
4. Describe the features of rights and warrants.

GoPro Goes Public

GoPro went public on July 26, 2014 with an initial public offering (IPO) price of $24 per share. The price of the stock immediately jumped when it began trading and closed at $31.34 on that IPO date. The lead underwriters were JP Morgan, Citigroup, and Barclays. The value of the company was about $3 billion on its IPO date.

The company sells wearable sports cameras. The stock now sells on the Nasdaq market under the ticker symbol GPRO. On March 8, 2018 the stock was selling for $5.74 per share after the company fell upon bad times. Stocks being sold through an IPO are usually offered at an initial price that is lower than what the market price subsequently is. This is why investors seek to obtain from the underwriters the right to obtain shares at the IPO price. This is difficult to do, however. The underwriters usually allocate shares at the IPO price to their best customers. "Best" in this case means those customers who trade frequently and in large amounts so that they are profitable to the underwriter.

Chapter Overview

In this chapter we explore the characteristics and types of common stock, types of common stock owners, and the pros and cons of issuing stock to raise capital. Then we investigate how firms issue common stock. Finally, we examine rights and warrants, and their risk and return features.

The Characteristics of Common Stock

common stock A security that indicates ownership of a corporation.

residual income Income left over, and available to common stockholders, after all other claimants have been paid.

As we learned in Chapter 2, **common stock** is a security that represents an equity claim on a firm. Having an equity claim means that the one holding the security (the common stockholder) is an owner of the firm, has voting rights, and has a claim on the residual income of the firm. **Residual income** is income left over after other claimants of the firm have been paid. Residual income can be paid out in the form of a cash dividend to common stockholders, or it can be reinvested in the firm. Reinvesting this residual income increases the market value of the common stock due to the new assets acquired or liabilities reduced.

Corporations sometimes have different classes of stockholders. For example, a corporation's charter may provide for a certain class of stockholders to have greater voting rights than other classes. Or one class of stock may receive its dividends based on the performance of only a certain part of the company. Facebook has two different classes of common stock. The stock owned by CEO Mark Zuckerberg has much greater voting power than the shares you could buy on the Nasdaq stock market.

All classes of stock have values that are determined when those stocks are traded from one investor to another at the various stock exchanges and in the over-the-counter market, as was described in Chapter 2. The market takes into account the characteristics of a given class and values each class accordingly. Figure 15-1 shows a certificate of ownership for 288 shares of the common stock of Central Jersey Bancorp.

Common stockholders are paid dividends determined by the ability and willingness of the firm to pay. This dividend decision is made by the board of directors of the corporation. Residual income not paid out to the common stockholders in the form of dividends is reinvested in the firm. It benefits the common stockholders there as well (because they are the owners of the corporation).

All corporations issue stock reflecting the owners' claims. But some corporations are privately owned, whereas others are owned by members of the general public. The rules for private and public corporations differ, as we see next.

FIGURE 15-1
Stock Certificate for 288 Shares of Central Jersey Bankcorp Common Stock

Stock Issued by Private Corporations

Private corporations (also known as closely held corporations) are so called because their common stock is not traded openly in the marketplace. Private corporations do not report financial information to the government through the Securities and Exchange Commission. (Tax returns, of course, are filed with the IRS, but this information is confidential.) Privately held corporations are usually small, and the stockholders are often actively involved in the management of the firm. The corporate form of organization is attractive to many small firms because the owners face only limited liability.

private corporation
A corporation that does not offer its shares to the general public and that can keep its financial statements confidential.

Stock Issued by Publicly Traded Corporations

AT&T. McDonald's. Motorola. These are just some examples of well-known publicly traded corporations. A **publicly traded corporation** is a corporation whose common stock can be bought by any interested party and that must release audited financial statements to the public. It is typically run by a professional management team, which likely owns only a tiny fraction of the outstanding shares of common stock.

The professional management team that handles the operations of the firm reports to a group called the **board of directors**. The board of directors, in turn, is elected by the common stockholders to represent their interests. The board is an especially important body for large public corporations because management typically owns such a small percentage of the firm. The agency problem discussed in Chapter 1 described the conflict of interest that can occur when those who run a firm own very little of it. The common stockholders elect the board members, and the board members oversee the management of the company.

Members of the board of directors have a fiduciary responsibility to the common stockholders who elected them. **Fiduciary responsibility** is the legal duty to act in the best interests of the person who entrusted you with property or power. When stockholders elect board members to represent them, they entrust the board members with the management of their company. Those board members owe it to common stockholders to act in the common stockholders' interest. Stockholders may vote directly on some major issues, such as a proposal to merge or liquidate the company.

publicly traded corporations
Corporations that have common stock that can be bought in the marketplace by any interested party and that must release audited financial statements to the public.

board of directors A group of individuals elected by the common stockholders to oversee the management of the firm.

fiduciary responsibility
The legal requirement that those who are managing assets owned by someone else do so in a prudent manner and in accordance with the interests of the person(s) they represent.

Institutional Investors, Proxy Advisory Firms, and Activist Investors

Much of the stock of publicly traded corporations is owned by institutional investors. Such investors include mutual funds, trust departments, endowments, pension funds, and insurance companies. It is not uncommon for a corporation to have over fifty percent of its stock held by a small number of these institutional investors. This means that these large institutional investors have great voting power, and senior managers of the corporations owned in large measure by these investors must pay attention to what those investors want. Some corporate decisions require approval of the holders of the firm's common stock. In addition to voting on members of the board of directors, shareholders are frequently asked to approve major decisions such as mergers, dissolution of the firm, amendments to the corporate charter, and the sale of a large portion of the firm. Shareholder approval may also be needed to approve stock options offered to executives and the salaries of those executives. Shareholders may petition the board of directors to place a topic on the agenda of the stockholders' meeting. Such petitions could request a change in dividend policy, a change in the composition of the board, or a major restructuring of the firm. Those items that require shareholder approval may be specified by regulators or by the company itself as spelled out in its charter.

When shareholders vote, they do not normally do so themselves in person at the stockholders' meeting. Shareholders usually sign a proxy document. This transfers the right to cast the votes of the shareholder to another party who then casts the votes for that shareholder at the meeting. Small shareholders frequently sign proxies giving management of the company the right to vote their shares. Large institutional shareholders usually hire a proxy advisory firm to advise them on how to vote and to vote those shares at the stockholders' meeting. The two biggest companies in this proxy services business are Institutional Shareholder Services (ISS) and Glass, Lewis & Co LLC.

Many large institutional investors vote together in a block. These investors are likely to vote in a block if the institutional shareholders use the same proxy advisory firm. ISS is the largest. It is not unusual for an ISS representative to walk into a corporation's stockholder meeting holding proxies for well in excess of fifty percent of the voting shares of that company.

Some institutional investors, and some large individual investors, try to push through specific proposals representing their personal agendas at these stockholder meetings. These are called **activist investors**. An activist investor is a person or institutional investor owning a large number of shares, but not a majority, seeking to lobby other investors and the company itself for specific actions by the company. Sometimes a hedge fund will act as an activist investor. A hedge fund is similar to a mutual fund, but only accredited (rich) investors can own shares, and the hedge fund frequently makes investment moves that are much riskier than what a mutual fund would do. Carl Icahn, Dan Loeb, Mick McGuire of Marcato Capital Management, Starboard, and Voce Capital engaged in activist investor activities in 2014 and 2015. Marcato Capital Management demanded in February of 2015 that Sotheby's, the large auction house, repurchase in the open market $500 million of its common stock shares. In 2014 activist investor Starboard Value LP tried to pressure Darden Restaurants Inc., owner of Olive Garden, not to automatically give more breadsticks to customers at Olive Garden restaurants, arguing that this practice cost the company too much money. In 2017 activist investor Nelson Peltz went after Procter & Gamble and waged a huge proxy war. He was appointed to the board in December of 2017. Mr. Peltz took his seat on the P&G board on March 8, 2018. He argued that P&G had been falling behind in product innovation and that it needs to improve its market share and profit margins. Actions of publicly traded corporations are increasingly being determined by a small number of very large institutional investors and their proxy advisory firms.

In this section, we investigated common stock characteristics, including classes of stock for stock issued by private and public corporations. We also looked at institutional ownership of common stock, proxy advisory companies, and activist investors. Next, we examine in greater detail the voting rights of common stockholders.

Voting Rights of Common Stockholders

Common stockholders have power to vote according to the number of shares they own. The general rule is "one vote per share." A stockholder or stockholder group holding more than 50 percent of the voting shares has a majority interest in the firm. The stockholder or group of stockholders that owns enough voting shares to control the board and operations of the firm has a controlling interest in the firm. The stockholder or stockholder group gains control when it elects a majority of its supporters to the board of directors.

In practice, a group can gain control with much less than 50 percent of the voting shares. This can happen if the remaining voting shares are widely distributed among many thousands of stockholders (each of whom owns a tiny percentage of the outstanding voting shares) who do not act in concert with each other. Many firms are controlled by groups of common stockholders owning as little as 5 percent or 10 percent of the voting shares, sometimes less.

Board of Directors Elections

Corporate elections typically use one of two different sets of voting rules to fill seats on the board of directors. These are majority voting and cumulative voting rules. Under majority voting rules, a given number of seats are to be filled in a given election. The number of voting shares held, plus proxy votes held, represents the number of votes a person may cast for a given candidate. If multiple seats are contested—say, for example, five—then the five candidates receiving the most votes are awarded seats on the board. The person receiving the greatest number of votes wins that seat. With majority voting, whoever controls the majority of the votes will get their candidates elected to every seat to be filled.

Under cumulative voting rules, the votes cast by a given stockholder may be allocated differently among different candidates for the board. If there are five seats to be filled in the election, the top five vote getters among all the candidates win those seats. Votes are cast—one vote per share times the number of seats being contested—for as many or as few candidates as a voter wishes. For example, if there were five seats to be filled with cumulative voting rules, and if a person were voting 100 shares, that shareholder would cast 500 votes that could be allocated to one, two, three, four, or five board candidates. This means that stockholders with shares and proxies for less than a majority of the number of voting shares can "accumulate" their votes by casting them all for only a few candidates (even casting all votes for one candidate).

Cumulative voting makes it more likely that those shareholders with less than a majority of the voting shares will get some representation on the board. With majority voting rules, minority stockholders would get outvoted by the majority stockholders in each of these separate elections.

Suppose Burgerworld Corporation has a ten-member board, and terms for three of the ten members are expiring. The firm uses cumulative voting rules. Seven candidates are competing for the right to fill these three seats. There are 100,000 voting shares of common stock outstanding for Burgerworld. This means that 300,000 total votes will be cast (100,000 shares × 3 contested seats = 300,000 total votes).

The stockholders are divided into two camps of differing corporate management philosophy. The majority group controls 60 percent of the voting shares, whereas the minority group of common stockholders controls the other 40 percent. One of the seven candidates was nominated by the minority group. The minority stockholder group knows that with only 40 percent of the votes, they have no hope of winning two or three of the three seats contested. Does the minority group of stockholders have enough voting power to get their one candidate on the board?

The majority stockholders would like to get three of their people elected to the three seats available. If they want to succeed, they will have to spread their 180,000 votes (60 percent of 300,000) among their three favorite candidates. Spreading the votes evenly among their preferred candidates, each candidate supported by the majority group would receive 60,000 votes (180,000 ÷ 3 = 60,000). If the minority stockholders cast all their votes for their candidate, that person will receive 120,000 (300,000 total − 180,000 majority votes = 120,000 minority votes) votes and win a seat on the board.

The formula for determining the number of directors that a stockholder group could elect, given the number of voting shares they control, is shown next in Equation 15-1.

The Number of Directors Who Can Be Elected under Cumulative Voting Rules

$$\text{NUM DIR} = \frac{(\text{SHARES CONTROLLED} - 1) \times (\text{TOT NUM DIR T.B.E.} + 1)}{\text{TOT NUM VOTING SHARES}} \qquad (15\text{-}1)$$

where: NUM DIR = Number of directors who can be elected by a given group

SHARES CONTROLLED = The number of voting shares controlled by a given group

TOT NUM DIR T.B.E. = Total number of directors to be elected

TOT NUM VOTING SHARES = Total number of voting shares in the election

Using the number of shares owned by the minority stockholders described in our Burgerworld example (40,000 of 100,000 shares outstanding), we can calculate the number of directors that this minority group could elect. Recall that the number of directors to be elected is three. The calculations follow:

$$\text{NUM DIR} = \frac{(40,000 - 1) \times (3 + 1)}{100,000}$$

$$= 1.60$$

This group can elect one of their people to the board out of the three to be elected. Note that we rounded down to get the answer. Because people cannot be divided, the minority group can't elect .6 (60 percent) of a person to the board.

The formula for determining the number of shares needed by a given group to elect a given number of directors is shown next in Equation 15-2.

The Number of Shares Needed to Elect a Given
Number of Directors under Cumulative Voting Rules

$$\text{NUM VOTING SHARES NEEDED} = \frac{\text{NUM DIR DESIRED} \times \text{TOT NUM VOTING SHARES}}{\text{TOT NUM DIR T.B.E.} + 1} + 1 \qquad (15\text{-}2)$$

where: NUM DIR DESIRED = Number of directors a given group of
                    stockholders desires to elect

TOT NUM VOTING SHARES = Total number of voting shares in the election

TOT NUM DIR T.B.E. = Total number of directors to be elected in the
                    election

For example, to calculate the number of voting shares needed to elect two of the three directors in the election described earlier, we could plug in the appropriate numbers into Equation 15-2. The calculation is shown next:

$$\text{NUM VOTING SHARES NEEDED} = \frac{2 \times 100{,}000}{3 + 1} + 1$$
$$= 50{,}001$$

We find that a group would need control of 50,001 voting shares to guarantee the election of two of the three directors in this election. This number is equivalent to 150,003 votes spread evenly between two director candidates. This would be 75,001.5 votes per candidate (50,001 voting shares × 3 total directors to be elected ÷ 2 directors sought to be elected). The other shareholders, holding 49,999 voting shares, would have the remaining 149,997 votes (49,999 voting shares × 3 total directors to be elected). If these 149,997 votes were divided between two candidates, that would be only 74,998.5 votes per candidate.

In this section, we reviewed the voting rights of common stockholders. We examine the advantages and disadvantages of equity financing next.

The Pros and Cons of Equity Financing

Selling new common stock has advantages and disadvantages for a corporation. Some disadvantages include dilution of power and earnings per share of existing stockholders, flotation costs, and possible unfavorable market perceptions about the firm's financial prospects. The advantages of a new stock issue include additional capital for the firm, lower risk, and the potential to borrow more in the future.

Disadvantages of Equity Financing

Selling new common stock is like taking in new partners (although we are referring to a corporation rather than to a partnership). When you sell new common stock, you must share the profits and the power with the new stockholders. When new common stock is issued, the ownership position of the existing common stockholders is diluted because the number of shares outstanding increases.

The dilution may result in a lower earnings per share for a profitable company. Losses, of course, would be shared, too, resulting in a lower negative earnings per share figure for a money-losing company. The voting power of the existing common stockholders would also be diluted. Firms concerned with losing control through diluted voting power, often avoid raising funds through a stock issue.

Also, when new common stock is sold, flotation costs are incurred. As we discussed in Chapter 9, **flotation costs** are fees paid to investment bankers, lawyers, and others when new securities are issued. The flotation costs associated with new common stock issues are normally much higher than those associated with debt.

Another reason that common stock issues are often a last resort for many corporations is because of signaling effects. **Signaling** is a message a firm sends, or investors infer, about a financial decision.

It is reasonable to suggest that the internal corporate managers have better insight about a firm's future business prospects than the average outside investor. If we accept this proposition as true, then we would not expect a company to sell additional shares of common stock to the general public unless its managers know that the future prospects for the company are worse than is generally believed. How do we know this? Equity financing is expensive and often used as a last resort. The inference drawn by investors who agree with this view is that a corporation issuing new stock wants more "partners" with whom to share future bad times. A company that expected good times would attempt to preserve the benefits for the current owners alone. Instead of issuing new stock, then, the firm would issue more debt securities.

Management may issue new common stock even though the future financial prospects for the firm are bright. However, if the market believes otherwise, the price of the common stock will drop when the new common stock is issued.

Advantages of Equity Financing

Why would any corporation issue new stock? One big reason is that corporations do not pay interest (and are not legally obligated to pay any dividends) to common stockholders. Unlike interest payments on debt, dividends can be skipped without incurring legal penalties. Interest payments on debt reduce a firm's earnings, whereas dividend payments to stockholders do not.

Some firms choose equity financing because they do not like borrowing. Some business people view being "in debt" as undesirable. They avoid it if possible and pay off unavoidable debts as soon as possible. Companies whose managers and owners hold this view will tend to favor equity financing.

A final reason that firms choose equity instead of debt financing is that the firm may have so much debt that borrowing more may be difficult or too expensive. Suppose, for example, that the "normal" ratio of debt to assets in your firm's industry is 20 percent, and your firm's debt to assets ratio is 40 percent. If this is the case, lenders may be reluctant to lend your firm any more money at an affordable interest rate; your firm might be forced to issue stock to raise funds. In this situation a new stock issue could bring the firm's debt ratios down to more normal industry levels. This would make it easier for the firm to borrow in the future.

In this section we described the pros and cons of a new stock issue. We turn to the process of issuing common stock next.

Issuing Common Stock

When a firm wishes to raise new equity capital, it must first decide whether to try to raise the capital from the firm's existing stockholders or to seek new investors. Private companies usually raise additional equity capital by selling new shares to existing common stockholders. This generally satisfies these stockholders because they continue to exercise complete control over the firm. However, when a large amount of equity capital must be raised, the existing stockholders may find that their only recourse is to sell shares of the firm's stock to the general public. A firm that sells its private shares of stock to the general public "goes public." The issuance of common stock to the public for the first time is known as an **initial public offering (IPO)**. Figure 15-2 describes the GoPro Corporation IPO.

flotation costs Fees that companies pay (to investment bankers and to others) when new securities are issued.

signaling The message sent by managers, or inferred by investors, when a financial decision is made.

initial public offering (IPO) The process whereby a private corporation issues new common stock to the general public, thus becoming a publicly traded corporation.

FIGURE 15-2
IPO of GoPro Corporation

On July 26, 2014, GoPro offered shares of its common stock to the general public for the first time at a price of $24 per share. The stock trades on the Nasdaq stock market with the ticker symbol GPRO. The lead underwriters were JP Morgan, Citigroup, and Barclays. The stock closed on that first trading day at $31.34 per share. GoPro ran into hard times after that and on March 8, 2018 its stock was trading at $5.74 per share.

Institutional investors are major buyers of new equity issues. Investment bankers who try to sell initial shares typically prefer to sell large blocks of shares to institutional investors, as opposed to selling many small blocks of shares to individual investors. The institutional investors do well because a new issue is generally sold for 10 percent to 20 percent below value to ensure that the new shares are sold.

The Function of Investment Bankers

When a corporation does decide to sell stock to the public, its first step is to contact an investment bank to handle the issue. Some of the names of investment banking firms that a corporation might contact would include J.P. Morgan, Morgan Stanley, Dean Witter, Merrill Lynch, Goldman Sachs, and Credit Suisse First Boston, to mention only a few. Investment bankers handle all the details associated with pricing the stock and marketing it to the public. A potential investor in a new security must be given a prospectus. A **prospectus** is a disclosure document that describes the security and the issuing company.

prospectus A disclosure document given to a potential investor when a new security is issued.

Investment bankers typically announce a new issue and the availability of the prospectus in a large boxed-in ad called a tombstone ad. It is so named because the large box with large print identifying the new issue looks like a tombstone. Figure 15-3 shows a tombstone ad for 5,462,500 shares of Geocities Corporation common stock.

Underwriting versus Best Efforts

Investment bankers take on the job of marketing a firm's stock to the public on one of two bases: underwriting or best efforts. When an investment banker underwrites a stock issue, it means the investment banker agrees to buy a certain number of shares from the issuing company at a certain price. Usually, a group of investment bankers will form a temporary alliance called a syndicate when underwriting a new security issue. The head of the investment banking syndicate is known as the manager. The manager has the primary responsibility for advising the security issuer. Extra fees are collected for this advice. It is up to the syndicate to sell the shares to the public at whatever price it can get. An underwriting poses the least risk to the firm whose stock is being issued. This is because the firm gets the stock issue proceeds from the investment bankers all at once, up front. However, because the investment bankers bear the risk that they might not be able to sell the firm's shares at the price they expect, they charge a rather substantial fee for underwriting.

A cheaper alternative to underwriting is called a *best efforts offering*. In this arrangement, the investment banker agrees to use its "best efforts" to sell the issuing company's shares at the desired price, but it makes no firm promises to do so. If the shares can only be sold at a lower price than was expected, then the issuing firm must either issue more shares to make up the difference or be satisfied with lower proceeds from the stock issue. Not surprisingly, the fees investment bankers charge for marketing stock on a best efforts basis are considerably less than those they charge for underwriting.

Pricing New Issues of Stock

When new shares of stock in a company are to be sold to the public, someone must decide at what price to offer them for sale. This is not a significant problem when

the company's shares are already publicly traded. The new shares are simply sold at the same price as the old shares, or perhaps a little lower.[1] However, if the company is going public, there is no previous market activity to establish what the shares are worth. In this situation the investment banker, in conjunction with the issuing company's managers, must put a price on the shares and hope that the market will agree that the price represents fair value. This is a daunting task indeed, and frequently investment bankers and firm managers miss the mark. Often an IPO stock will fluctuate wildly in price after it is issued. Table 15-1 shows three initial public offerings and stock prices after the IPO.

The figures in Table 15-1 show the differing fortunes of these three initial public offering stocks.

---

1. There is usually a little dilution (downward movement) in the price of a company's common stock when new shares are sold.

TABLE 15-1 Recent Prices of Four Initial Public Offerings (IPOs)

IPO Date	Stock	Initial Price	Price on March 8, 2018
May 2006	Vonage Holdings Corporation (VG)	$17	$ 10.89
Nov 2010	General Motors (GM)	$33	$ 37.84
May 2012	Facebook (FB)	$38	$ 182.34

Source: Yahoo.com (*http://finance.yahoo.com*).

Valuing the Stock of a Company That Is Not Publicly Traded

Before investment bankers offer a company's stock for sale to the public, they must have some idea of how the public will value the stock to predict the new issue market price. The trouble is, when a company's stock has not been sold to anyone before, it is perilously difficult to say how much it is worth.

Suppose you have been creating oil paintings for a few years and have become pretty good at it. One day the art club you belong to has a show, and one of your paintings is included. When you deliver the painting to the gallery, you are asked what sale price you wish posted on the painting. Now you face the same question firms and investment bankers face. How much is the painting worth? How much can you get for it?

Naturally, you want to sell the painting for as high a price as possible, but the potential buyers want to pay as low a price as possible. If you post too high an asking price, no one will buy your painting and you will leave empty handed. If you post too low a price, however, someone will snatch it up and may well resell it to someone else for a substantial profit. You can see that if you had previously sold a number of similar paintings you would have an idea of what to ask for this one. The first painting you try to sell is the one that presents the pricing problem.

In Chapter 12, we presented some of the methods that companies and investment bankers use to estimate the market value of a company's stock. These methods include calculating the present value of expected cash flows, multiplying earnings per share by the appropriate P/E ratio, the book value approach, and the liquidation value approach.

Rights and Warrants

Rights and warrants are securities issued by a corporation that allow investors to buy new common stock. They originate in different ways and have somewhat different characteristics, as explained in the following sections.

Preemptive Rights

When some companies plan to issue new stock, they establish procedures to protect the ownership interest of the original stockholders. The existing stockholders are given securities that allow them to preempt other investors in the purchase of new shares. This security is called a preemptive right. A **preemptive right**, sometimes referred to simply as a *right*, gives the holder the option to buy additional shares of common stock at a specified price (the *subscription price*) until a given expiration date. Current stockholders who do not wish to exercise their rights can sell them in the open market.

preemptive right A security given by some corporations to existing stockholders that gives them the right to buy new shares of common stock at a below-market price until a specified expiration date.

The Number of Rights Required to Buy a New Share

Suppose that Right Stuff Corporation has 100,000 shares of common stock currently outstanding. An additional 20,000 shares of common stock are to be sold to existing shareholders by means of a rights offering. Because one right is sent out to existing shareholders for each share held, 100,000 rights must be sent out. There are five shares of common stock outstanding for each new share to be sold (100,000/20,000 = 5). Five rights are therefore needed, along with the payment of the subscription price, to purchase a new share of common stock through the rights offering.

The Value of a Right

We know that five rights are required to buy a new share of Right Stuff Corporation's common stock through the rights offering. To determine the value of each right, we must also know the subscription price and the market price of Right Stuff's common stock.

This information, along with our knowledge of the number of rights required to buy a new share, will allow us to estimate the value of one of these rights.[2]

Suppose that the current market price of Right Stuff Corporation's common stock is $65 and that the subscription price is set at $50. This means that you are saving $15 ($65 − $50 = $15) when you send in your five rights to receive one of the new shares (known as "exercising your rights"). This means that each right would be worth $3 ($15 ÷ 5 = $3) before dilution effects are considered.

The approximate value of a right can be determined by two formulas. The formula used depends on the status of the stock as it trades in the marketplace, relative to the timing of the issuance of the rights. Timing is the key to determining which approximation formula to use.

Rights are generally sent out several weeks after the announcement of the rights offering is made. This initial period is called the **rights-on** period, and the stock is said to *trade rights-on* during this time. This means that if the common stock is purchased during the rights-on period, the investor will receive the forthcoming rights.

At the opening of trading on the day following the rights-on period, the stock is said to be trading **ex-rights**. This means that the purchaser buys the stock without (*ex* is Latin for "without") receiving the entitlement to the preemptive rights if the purchase is on or after the ex-rights date.

rights-on A characteristic of common stock such that it is trading with the entitlement to an upcoming right.

ex-rights A characteristic of common stock such that it is trading without the entitlement to an upcoming rights offering.

Trading Rights-On If the stock is trading rights-on, then we calculate the approximate market value of the right as depicted in Equation 15-3:

Approximate Value of a Right, Stock Trading Rights-On

$$R = \frac{M_0 - S}{N + 1}$$

(15-3)

where: R = Approximate market value of a right

M_0 = Market price of the common stock, selling rights-on

S = Subscription price

N = Number of rights needed to purchase one of the new shares of common stock

We call R the approximate market value of the right because rights are securities that can be traded just like stock and bonds. Once the rights are sent to the existing common stockholders (those who bought the stock before it "went ex-rights"), the rights can be traded in the marketplace at the option of the owner. The actual market price of the right may be slightly different than shown in the formulas presented here because of the option characteristics of the rights, which are discussed later.

Table 15-2 shows the calculation of the approximate market value of a Right Stuff Corporation right. This is the value of the right as determined by the rights-on formula, Equation 15-3.

---

2. The actual pricing of a right is somewhat more complicated than what we are presenting here. A right is an option to buy the new stock at the specified subscription price. Option pricing is discussed in the following section on warrants. The rights valuation presented here should be considered an approximation only.

TABLE 15-2 Right Valuation with Stock Selling Rights-On

M_0, Market Price of the Common Stock, Rights-On	$65
S, Subscription Price	$50
N, Number of Rights Required to Purchase One New Share	5
R, Approximate Market Price of One Right:	$R = \dfrac{\$65 - \$50}{5 + 1}$
	$= \dfrac{\$15}{6}$
	$= \$2.50$

We see from the calculations in Table 15-2 that the market value of the Right Stuff right is $2.50, given a market price of common stock of $65, a subscription price of $50, and five rights required to purchase one new share.

Selling Ex-Rights To find the approximate value of the right when the stock is selling ex-rights, the ex-rights formula must be used. This formula is presented as follows in Equation 15-4:

Approximate Value of a Right, Stock Trading Ex-Rights

$$R = \frac{M_x - S}{N}$$

(15-4)

where: R = Approximate market value of a right

M_x = Market price of the common stock, selling ex-rights

S = Subscription price

N = Number of rights needed to purchase one of the new shares of common stock

When the common stock begins trading ex-rights, the entitlement to the forthcoming rights is lost. Thus, the price of the common stock in the marketplace will drop by the value of the right now lost on the ex-rights date (other factors held constant).

Suppose Right Stuff Corporation common stock begins selling ex-rights today. When the opening bell rings on the exchange, the price of Right Stuff common stock will drop by the amount of the value of the right that has been lost. Holding other factors constant (no news overnight to otherwise affect the value of the common stock), the price of the common stock will drop by $2.50 from $65 to $62.50.

Table 15-3 shows the calculation of the approximate market value of the right when the common stock is selling ex-rights, using Equation 15-4.

When the common stock is selling ex-rights, Equation 15-4 gives the approximate market value of a right. The equation reflects the loss of the entitlement of the rights, $2.50 in our example.

Warrants

warrant A security that gives the holder the option to buy a certain number of shares of common stock of the issuing company, at a certain price, for a specified period of time.

A **warrant** is a security that gives its owner the option to buy a certain number of shares of common stock from the issuing company, at a certain exercise price, until a specified expiration date. The corporation benefits from issuing warrants because the issue raises funds. It also creates the possibility of a future increase in the company's number of common stock shares. The investor values warrants because of the option to buy the company's stock.

TABLE 15-3 Right Valuation with Stock Selling Ex-Rights

M$_x$, Market Price of the Common Stock, Ex-Rights	$62.50
S, Subscription Price	$50
N, Number of Rights Required to Purchase One New Share	5
R, Approximate Market Price of One Right:	

$$R = \frac{\$62.50 - \$50}{5}$$

$$= \frac{\$12.50}{5}$$

$$= \$2.50$$

Warrants are similar to rights except they are sold to investors instead of given away to existing shareholders. They typically have longer maturities than rights and are often issued with bonds as part of a security package.

Warrant Valuation

Warrants have value only until the expiration date, at which time they become worthless. Before a warrant expires, its value depends on how the price of the common stock compares to the warrant's exercise price—the price the firm sets for exercising the right to buy common stock shares—and on other factors, described next.

To value warrants, investors must be able to find the exercise value. The exercise value is the amount saved by purchasing the common stock by exercising the warrant rather than buying the common stock directly in the open market. If there is no saving, the exercise value is zero.

The formula for calculating the exercise value of a warrant is described in Equation 15-5 as follows:

The Exercise Value of a Warrant

$$XV = (M - XP) \times \# \tag{15-5}$$

where: XV = Exercise value of a warrant

M = Market price of the stock

XP = Exercise price of a warrant

$\#$ = Number of shares that may be purchased if the warrant is exercised

Suppose that the McGuffin Corporation warrant entitles the investor to purchase four shares of common stock, at an exercise price of $50 per share, during the next three years. If the current common stock price is $60, the exercise value according to Equation 15-5 follows:

$$XV = (M - XP) \times \#$$

$$= (\$60 - \$50) \times 4$$

$$= \$40$$

Our calculations show that the exercise value is $40.

If the market price of the common stock price were $50 or less, the exercise value of the warrant would be zero. This is because you would have an option to buy the common stock at a price that is no better than the regular market price of the stock. You would have no reason to exercise the warrant, and a rational investor would not do so.

Note that the time remaining until the expiration of the warrant does not affect the exercise value. For the McGuffin Corporation warrants, the investor saves $10/share on four shares of common stock, creating an exercise value of $40.

As long as there is still time remaining until expiration, the actual market price of a warrant will be greater than the exercise value. The difference between the market price and the exercise value is called the warrant's time value. Warrants have time value because if the price of the common stock goes up, the exercise value increases with leverage and without limit (because of the fixed exercise price). If, on the other hand, the price of the common stock falls, the exercise value cannot dip below zero. Once the common stock price is at or below the exercise price, no further damage can be done to the exercise value.

The exercise value is zero if the common stock price is at or below the exercise value, but it can never be negative. Table 15-4 shows the exercise value for a McGuffin Corporation warrant for different possible stock values.

No matter how much below $50 the market price of the common stock goes, the exercise value stays at zero. As the stock value goes above $50, however, the exercise value increases at a much faster rate than the corresponding increase in the stock price. The difference between the potential benefit if the stock price increases (unlimited and leveraged) and the potential loss (limited) is what gives a warrant its time value.

Because of this time value, warrants are seldom exercised until they near maturity, even when the exercise value is high. This is because if a warrant is exercised, only the exercise value is realized. If the warrant is sold to another investor, the seller realizes the exercise value plus the time value. The time value approaches zero as the expiration date nears. A warrant approaching its expiration date, having a positive exercise value, would be exercised by the investor before the value goes to zero on the expiration date.

The greater the volatility of the stock price, and the greater the time to expiration, the greater the market value of the warrant. If the stock price is volatile, the stock price could easily increase. This would give the warrant owner the benefit of an even greater increase due to leverage. If the common stock price decreases, no more than the price paid can be lost. The more time left before expiration, the better the chance for a major stock price change, up or down. Again, the warrant value upside is substantial if the stock price moves up, and the downside potential is limited if the stock price decreases. The asymmetry of the warrant's upside and downside potential gives the warrant greater value.

Option pricing has many applications in finance. We can apply the principles described here for warrant pricing to certain types of capital budgeting and even common stock valuation. What if a proposed capital budgeting project gives us an option to

TABLE 15-4 McGuffin Corporation Warrant Exercise Value

Market Price of Common Stock	Exercise Price	Number of Shares	Exercise Value
$100	$50	4	$200
$ 90	$50	4	$160
$ 80	$50	4	$120
$ 70	$50	4	$ 80
$ 60	$50	4	$ 40
$ 50	$50	4	$ 0
$ 40	$50	4	$ 0
$ 30	$50	4	$ 0
$ 20	$50	4	$ 0

undertake future projects that are tied to the first? Common stock has unlimited upside price potential, coupled with limited downside risk, just like a warrant. These are issues you may explore further in other finance courses.

What's Next

In this chapter, we examined types and traits of common stock, and the advantages and disadvantages of issuing common stock. We also explored rights and warrants. In Chapter 16, we will look at how a corporation determines the amount of cash dividends to pay and the timing of those dividend payments.

Summary

1. *Describe the characteristics of common stock.*
   Common stock is a security that represents an ownership claim on a corporation. The shareholders are entitled to the residual income of the firm, resulting in a high-risk position relative to other claimants and a relatively high-return potential. Common stock may come in different classes with different voting rights or dividend payments.

   The professional management team that handles the operations of the firm reports to the board of directors. The board of directors, in turn, is elected by the common stockholders to represent their interests. Because the stockholders have entrusted the board to represent their interests, board members have a fiduciary duty to act on stockholders' behalf. Stockholders usually vote according to the number of shares held. The two main types of voting rules are the majority voting rules, under which candidates run for specific seats, and the cumulative voting rules, under which all the candidates run against each other but do not run for a particular seat.

2. *Explain the disadvantages and advantages of equity financing.*
   Disadvantages of equity financing include the dilution of existing shareholder power and control, flotation costs incurred when new common stock is sold, and the negative signal investors often perceive (rightly or wrongly) when new common stock is sold. Equity financing has several advantages. It reduces the risk of a firm because common stockholders, as opposed to debtors, have no contractual entitlement to dividends. Equity financing can also increase the ability to borrow in the future.

3. *Explain the process of issuing new common stock.*
   Once a firm decides that the benefits outweigh the costs of issuing stock, the firm almost always seeks the help of an investment banking firm. The investment banker usually underwrites the new issue, which means that it purchases the entire issue for resale to investors. Sometimes the investment banker will try to find investors for the new common stock without a guarantee to the issuing company that the stock will be sold. This arrangement is known as a best efforts offering.

4. *Describe the features of rights and warrants.*
   Rights are securities given to existing common stockholders that allow them to purchase additional shares of stock at a price below market value. Corporations issue rights to safeguard the power and control of existing shareholders in the event of a new stock issue. Warrants are securities that give the holder the option to buy a certain number of shares of common stock of the issuing company at a certain price for a specified period of time. Warrants have high-return potential because if the stock price increases, the value of the warrant increases at a much higher rate due to leverage. The downside risk of a warrant is limited because the maximum loss potential is the price of the warrant. As a result of the high-return and low-risk potential, warrants have time value that is greatest when the stock price is volatile and the time to maturity is great.

Key Terms

activist investors Investors who buy a large number of shares of common stock of a target company with the goal of changing the direction of that company, often seeking a seat on the board.

board of directors A group of individuals elected by the common stockholders to oversee the management of the firm.

common stock A security that indicates ownership of a corporation.

ex-rights A characteristic of common stock such that it is trading without the entitlement to an upcoming rights offering.

fiduciary responsibility The legal requirement that those who are managing assets owned by someone else do so in a prudent manner and in accordance with the interests of the person(s) they represent.

flotation costs Fees that companies pay (to investment bankers and to others) when new securities are issued.

initial public offering (IPO) The process whereby a private corporation issues new common stock to the general public, thus becoming a publicly traded corporation.

preemptive right A security given by some corporations to existing stockholders that gives them the right to buy new shares of common stock at a below-market price until a specified expiration date.

private corporation A corporation that does not offer its shares to the general public and that can keep its financial statements confidential.

prospectus A disclosure document given to a potential investor when a new security is issued.

publicly traded corporations Corporations that have common stock that can be bought in the marketplace by any interested party and that must release audited financial statements to the public.

residual income Income left over, and available to common stockholders, after all other claimants have been paid.

rights-on A characteristic of common stock such that it is trading with the entitlement to an upcoming right.

signaling The message sent by managers, or inferred by investors, when a financial decision is made.

warrant A security that gives the holder the option to buy a certain number of shares of common stock of the issuing company, at a certain price, for a specified period of time.

Equations Introduced in This Chapter

Equation 15-1. The Number of Directors Who Can Be Elected under Cumulative Voting Rules:

$$\text{NUM DIR} = \frac{(\text{SHARES CONTROLLED} - 1) \times (\text{TOT NUM DIR T.B.E.} + 1)}{\text{TOT NUM VOTING SHARES}}$$

where: NUM DIR = Number of directors who can be elected by a given group

SHARES CONTROLLED = The number of voting shares controlled by a given group

TOT NUM DIR T.B.E. = Total number of directors to be elected

TOT NUM VOTING SHARES = Total number of voting shares in the election

Equation 15-2. The Number of Shares Needed to Elect a Given Number of Directors under Cumulative Voting Rules:

$$\text{NUM VOTING SHARES NEEDED} = \frac{\text{NUM DIR DESIRED} \times \text{TOT NUM VOTING SHARES}}{\text{TOT NUM DIR T.B.E.} + 1} + 1$$

where: NUM DIR DESIRED = Number of directors a given group of stockholders desires to elect

TOT NUM VOTING SHARES = Total number of voting shares in the election

TOT NUM DIR T.B.E. = Total number of directors to be elected in the election

Equation 15-3. Approximate Value of a Right, Stock Trading Rights-On:

$$R = \frac{M_0 - S}{N + 1}$$

where: R = Approximate market value of a right

M_0 = Market price of the common stock, selling rights-on

S = Subscription price

N = Number of rights needed to purchase one of the new shares of common stock

Equation 15-4. Approximate Value of a Right, Stock Trading Ex-Rights:

$$R = \frac{M_x - S}{N}$$

where: R = Approximate market value of a right

M_x = Market price of the common stock, selling ex-rights

S = Subscription price

N = Number of rights needed to purchase one of the new shares of common stock

Equation 15-5. The Exercise Value of a Warrant:

$$XV = (M - XP) \times \#$$

where:
XV = Exercise value of a warrant

M = Market price of the stock

XP = Exercise price of a warrant

$\#$ = Number of shares that may be purchased if the warrant is exercised

Self-Test

ST-1. What is residual income and who has a claim on it?

ST-2. Is a new common stock issue usually perceived as a good or bad signal by the market? Explain.

ST-3. What does it mean when a company's common stock is said to be trading ex-rights?

ST-4. If a company's common stock is selling at $80 per share and the exercise price is $60 per share, what would be the exercise value of a warrant that gives its holder the right to buy 10 shares at the exercise price?

Review Questions

1. What are some of the government requirements imposed on a public corporation that are not imposed on a private, closely held corporation?

2. How are the members of the board of directors of a corporation chosen and to whom do these board members owe their primary allegiance?

3. What are the advantages and the disadvantages of a new stock issue?

4. What does an investment banker do when underwriting a new security issue for a corporation?

5. How does a preemptive right protect the interests of existing stockholders?

6. Explain why warrants are rarely exercised unless the time to maturity is small.

7. Under what circumstances is a warrant's value high? Explain.

Build Your Communication Skills

CS-1. Review a financial publication, such as *The Wall Street Journal,* for a tombstone advertisement. Contact one of the investment banking firms you see listed in a tombstone ad announcing a new issue. Request a prospectus for that new issue. Once you receive the prospectus, write a report describing its key elements and what those elements reveal about the new security and its issuer.

CS-2. Research a company that is having a contested stockholder vote. You will find notice of such a vote in business publications, such as *The Wall Street Journal.* Different groups will typically run their own advertisements soliciting proxies so those groups can vote the shares of other stockholders. Analyze the positions of the opposing sides, break into small groups, and debate the direction the company should take on the issue in contention.

Problems

15-1. Sonny owns 20,000 shares of common stock in QuickFix Company. The company has 1 million shares of common stock outstanding at a market value of $50 per share. What percentage of the firm is owned by Sonny? If the company issues 500,000 new shares at $50 per share to new stockholders, how does Sonny's ownership change?

 Ownership Claim

Valuation of IPO **15-2.** Terence Mann is considering buying some shares of common stock of an initial public offering by NewAge Communications Corporation. The privately held company is going public by issuing 2 million new shares at $20 per share. Terence gathered the following information about NewAge:

Total assets:	$ 200 million (historical cost)
Total liabilities:	$ 150 million (market value)
Number of shares retained by pre-IPO owners outstanding	$ 3 million (5 million shares after IPO)
Estimated liquidation value:	$ 250 million
Estimated replacement value of assets:	$ 400 million
Expected dividend in one year:	$ 2 per share
Expected dividend growth rate:	8%

The required rate of return for Terence from a share of common stock for this type of company is 13 percent.

Compare the selling price of the stock with its value as obtained from different valuation methods. Would you recommend that Terence buy the stock?

Number of Directors **15-3.** Danali Corporation has 2,500,000 shares of common stock outstanding. Danali has a 15-member board, and five will leave at the end of this year. There are nine candidates for these five open seats. The minority group of stockholders controls 45 percent of the shares, and the majority group controls the other 55 percent. What is the maximum number of directors who definitely can be elected by each of the following under cumulative voting rules?

a. The minority group

b. The majority group

Number of Voting Shares Needed **15-4.** Using the information in the previous problem, how many voting shares would be needed to elect the specified directors?

a. 1 director

b. 3 directors

c. 5 directors

Number of Directors **15-5.** Alliances are shifting, and Danali Corporation (described in the previous two problems) now has 35 percent of the voting shares controlled by the minority group and 65 percent by the majority.

a. How many directors can now be elected for the minority group?

b. How many voting shares would be needed if the minority group wanted two directors under the revised group breakdown?

Term of Board Members **15-6.** Iowa Corn Corporation has nine board members. Three of these seats are up for election every three years. What is the length of the term served by each board member?

Cumulative Voting **15-7.** The stockholders of Blue Sky, Inc. are divided into two camps of different corporate management philosophy. The majority group controls 65 percent and the minority group controls 35 percent of the voting shares. The total number of shares of common stock outstanding is 1 million. The total number of directors to be elected in the near future is four. What is the maximum number of directors the minority group can possibly elect, assuming that the company follows cumulative voting procedures?

Cumulative Voting **15-8.** Ms. O'Niel owns 26,000 shares of Tri Star Corporation out of 200,000 shares of common stock outstanding. The board has seven members, and all seven seats are up for election now. Ms. O'Niel has long wanted to serve as a member of the board. Assuming that the company follows cumulative voting procedures, can Ms. O'Niel get herself elected to the board on the strength of her own votes?

15-9. The Rainbow Corporation had traditionally been a constant dollar-dividend paying company, with the board enjoying the support of retired investors holding 65 percent of the voting shares. A dissident group of high-salaried young investors holding 30 percent of the voting shares prefers reinvestment of earnings to save personal taxes and, hence, wants to elect board members supportive of its cause. The company has 600,000 shares of common stock outstanding and the board has 13 members—all to be reelected shortly.

Dissident Group and Cumulative Voting

   a. How many directors can the young stockholders elect under

   1. cumulative voting rules?

   2. majority voting rules?

   b. What percentage of voting shares and/or proxies must the dissident group have to be able to elect 7 out of the 13 board members?

15-10. Fargo Corporation has 500,000 shares of common stock currently outstanding. The company plans to sell 50,000 more shares of common stock to the existing shareholders through a rights offering. How many rights will it take to buy one share?

Rights Offering

15-11. A company with 2 million shares of common stock currently outstanding is planning to sell 500,000 new shares to its existing shareholders through a rights issue. Current market price of a share is $65, and the subscription price is $55. If the stock is selling rights-on, calculate the value of a right.

Value of Rights

15-12. Use the same information given in problem 15-11. Now calculate the value of a right if the stock is selling ex-rights.

Value of Rights

15-13. Fillsulate Products, a manufacturer of refractory powders, is about to declare a rights issue. The subscription price is $65. Seven rights in addition to the subscription price are required to buy one new share of stock. Rights on market price of the stock is $77. Calculate the value of one right. Also calculate the new stock price once it goes ex-rights.

Value of Rights

15-14. Johnny Rocco owns 700 shares of stock of East-West Tobacco Company, which is offering a rights issue to its existing shareholders. To buy one new share of stock, Johnny will need four rights plus $60. Rights-on market price of the stock is $72.

Rights Offering

   a. Calculate the value of a right.

   b. What is the maximum number of new shares Johnny can buy?

   c. How much would he have to spend if he decides to buy all the new stock he can?

   d. If he decides not to buy the new stock, how much would he be able to sell his rights for?

15-15. Kelsery Products is planning on selling 300,000 new shares to existing stockholders through a rights issue. The company currently has 1,500,000 outstanding shares at a market price of $40 and a subscription price of $25. The stock is selling rights-on. What is the value of one right?

Rights Value (Rights-On)

15-16. Using the data from problem 15-15, calculate the value of one right if the stock is selling ex-rights.

Rights Value (Ex-Rights)

15-17. Armand Goldman owns 60 shares of East Asia Shipping Company stock and has $750 in cash for investment. The company has offered a rights issue in which purchasing a new stock would require four rights plus $50 in cash. Current market value of the stock is $62.

Challenge Problem

   a. Calculate the value of a right if the stock is selling rights-on.

   b. Should Armand participate in the rights offering by buying as many shares as he can, or sell his rights and keep the shares he already owns at a diluted value?

15-18. The current market price of a share of common stock of SkyHigh, Inc. is $100. The company had issued warrants earlier to its new bond investors that gave the investors an option to buy five shares of common stock at an exercise price of $85. Calculate the exercise value of a warrant. What happens to the exercise value of the warrant if the stock price changes to:

Warrants

   a. $110?

   b. $80?

Comprehensive Problem **15-19.** The current market price of Digicomm's common stock is $40 per share. The company has 600,000 common shares outstanding. To finance its growing business, the company needs to raise $2 million. Due to its already high debt ratio, the only way to raise the funds is to sell new common stock. Alvin C. York, the vice president of finance of Digicomm, has decided to go ahead with a rights issue, but he is not sure at what price the existing shareholders would be willing to buy a share of new stock. Digicomm's investment banker has suggested that an analysis based on a wide range of possible prices be carried out, and the subscription prices agreed upon were $36, $33, $29, and $26 per share of new stock. Digicomm's net income for the year is $1 million.

Based on the preceding information, Mr. York has asked you to carry out the following analysis:

a. For each of the possible subscription prices, calculate the number of shares that would have to be issued and the number of rights required to buy one share of new stock.

b. For each of the possible subscription prices, calculate the earnings per share immediately before and immediately after the rights offering.

c. Guy Hamilton owns 10,000 shares of Digicomm stock. For each of the possible subscription prices, calculate the maximum number of new shares Guy would be able to buy. Under each of these cases, calculate Guy's total claim to earnings before and after the offering.

Answers to Self-Test

ST-1. Residual income is income that is left over after all claimants, except for common stockholders, have been paid. This leftover income belongs to the common stockholders, who receive this income either in the form of a dividend or by having it reinvested in the corporation that they own.

ST-2. The market usually infers bad news when new common stock is issued. Investors ask themselves why the current owners would want to share their profits with new owners if management expected good news ahead. The market often infers (rightly or wrongly) that there

must be bad news coming that the management of the firm wants to "share" with new stockholders. New stock issued is, therefore, usually perceived as a negative signal.

ST-3. A stock is selling ex-rights when the purchase of that stock no longer carries with it entitlement to the rights that are soon to be sent out to stockholders.

ST-4. ($80 stock price – $60 exercise price) × 10 shares purchased per warrant = $200 exercise value of the warrant

Dividend Policy

"Finance is the art of passing currency from hand to hand until it finally disappears."
—Robert W. Sarnoff

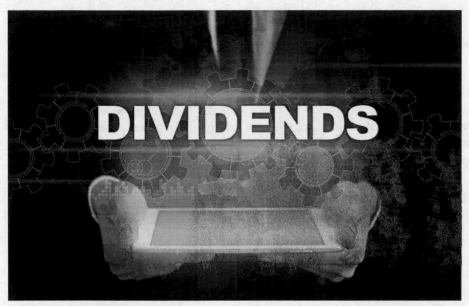

CHAPTER 16

Source: Wright Studio/Shutterstock

Learning Objectives

After reading this chapter, you should be able to:

1. Explain the importance of and identify the factors that influence the dividend decision.
2. Compare the major dividend theories.
3. Describe how a firm pays dividends.
4. Identify alternatives to paying cash dividends.

GE Cuts Its Dividend

General Electric (GE) cut its dividend in half in November, 2017. GE has long been considered an income stock for investors, which means it has consistently paid a healthy dividend to stockholders and has increased the amount of that dividend regularly over the years. This dividend cut of about 50% saved the company $4 billion in cash for the year.

GE is the ultimate "old school" company. The company was originally formed by the merger of Edison General Electric Company and Thompson-Houston Electric Company in 1892. Yes, the Edison in the name was for Thomas Alva Edison, the inventor of the incandescent light bulb. Younger, high-tech firms tend to pay little or no dividend to shareholders. Investors who like to receive dividends from their stock investments are attracted to companies like GE.

On the one hand investors like to receive cash. On the other hand, investors would like to think that the company they have invested in has productive things to invest in with its cash and receiving cash dividends triggers taxes owed by the investor on that dividend income. We will investigate these and other dividend issues in this chapter.

Chapter Overview

In this chapter, we explore the importance of dividends, the factors that determine a firm's dividend policy, and leading dividend policy theories. We then examine how a firm makes dividend payments to shareholders. We finish by identifying alternatives to paying cash dividends.

Dividends

Dividends are the cash payments that corporations make to their common stockholders. Dividends provide the return common stockholders receive from the firm for the equity capital they have supplied.[1] Companies that do not currently pay dividends reinvest in the firm the earnings they generate. In this way, they increase the ability of the firm to pay dividends in the future.

The board of directors decides what dividend policy best serves the common stockholders of the firm. Should a dividend be paid now, or should the earnings generated be reinvested for the future benefit of the common stockholders? If dividends are paid now, how much should be paid? These are some of the questions addressed in the following sections.

Although only corporations officially pay dividends to owners, sole proprietorships and partnerships also distribute profits to owners. Many of the same considerations examined in this chapter for corporate dividend policy can also be used to help make proper profit distribution decisions for these other forms of business organization.

Why a Dividend Policy Is Necessary

Why does a company need a strategic policy relating to dividend payments? Why not just "wing it" each year (or quarter, or other span of time) and pay the dividend that "feels right" at that time? Because market participants (current and potential stockholders) generally do not like surprises. An erratic dividend policy means that those stockholders who liked the last dividend cannot be sure that the next one will be to their liking. This uncertainty can result in a drop in the company's stock price. When stockholders do not get what they expect, they often show their displeasure by selling their stock. A well-planned policy, appropriate for the firm and its business strategy, can prevent unpleasant surprises for market participants and protect the stock price.

Factors Affecting Dividend Policy

Dividend policy is based on the company's need for funds, the firm's cash position, its future financial prospects, stockholder expectations, and contractual restrictions with which the firm may have to comply.

Need for Funds

Dividends paid to stockholders use funds that the firm could otherwise invest. Therefore, a company running short of cash or with ample capital investment opportunities may decide to pay little or no dividends. Alternatively, there may be an abundance of cash or a dearth of good capital budgeting projects available. This could lead to very large dividend payments.

Management Expectations and Dividend Policy

If a firm's managers perceive the future as relatively bright, on the one hand, they may begin paying large dividends in anticipation of being able to keep them up during the good times ahead. On the other hand, if managers believe that bad times are coming, they may decide to build up the firm's cash reserves for safety instead of paying dividends.

---

1. You may wonder about this statement because common stock investors can always receive a return by selling their stock. Remember, however, that when investors sell their stock, they are paid by other investors, not by the corporation. Except when a corporation buys back its own stock (which is a form of dividend payment), the only cash corporations pay to investors is a dividend payment.

Stockholders' Preferences

Reinvesting earnings internally, instead of paying dividends, would lead to higher stock prices and a greater percentage of the total return common stockholders receive coming from capital gains. *Capital gains* are profits earned by an investor when the price of a capital asset, such as common stock, increases.

Common stockholders may prefer to receive their return from the company in the form of capital gains and some may prefer to receive their return from the company in the form of dividends. In 2018 dividend income was tax-free for the first $38,600 of such qualified dividend and capital gains income for single tax filers. For dividend income to be considered "qualified" you must own the common stock for more than 60 days during the 121-day period that began 60 days before the ex-dividend date. Qualified dividend and capital gains income for individuals with such income from $38,601 to $425,800 for single filers is 15% and is 20% for those in the highest dividend income tax bracket. The 20% tax rate for qualified dividend and capital gains income is the highest rate applying to such income and it kicks in above $425,800 of this income. Capital gains are not taxed at all unless they are realized. That is, unless the stock is sold. The board of directors should consider stockholder preferences when establishing the firm's dividend policy. The Tax Cut and Jobs Act of 2017 created for the first time two different sets of tax brackets. One set, described here, is for dividend income. Ordinary income is taxed in brackets for individuals that have 10, 12, 22, 24, 32, 35, and 37 percent rates applied to them.

Restrictions on Dividend Payments

A firm may have dividend payment restrictions in its existing bond indentures or loan agreements. For example, a company's loan contract with a bank may specify that the company's current ratio cannot drop below 2.0 during the life of the loan. Because payment of a cash dividend draws down the company's cash account, the current ratio may fall below the minimum level required.[2] In such a case, the size of a dividend may have to be cut or omitted. In addition, many states prohibit dividend payments if they would create negative retained earnings on the balance sheet. This restriction is a prohibition against "raiding the initial capital." Figure 16-1 summarizes the factors that influence the dividend decision.

Cash versus Earnings

Dividends are often discussed in relation to a firm's earnings. The dividend payout ratio is often cited as an indicator of the generosity (or lack thereof) of the firm's dividend policy. The dividend payout ratio is calculated by dividing the total dollar amount of dividends paid by net income, as seen in Equation 16-1.

$$\text{Dividend Payout Ratio}$$
$$\text{Dividend Payout Ratio} = \frac{\text{Dividends Paid}}{\text{Net Income}}$$

$$(16\text{-}1)$$

If Calvin Corporation, for example, earns a net income of $10,000 and pays $3,000 in dividends, then its dividend payout ratio will be as follows:

$$\text{Dividend Payout Ratio} = \frac{\$3,000}{\$10,000}$$
$$= .30, \text{ or } 30\%$$

We see from our calculations that Calvin Corporation has a dividend payment ratio of 30 percent.

A caution, however: By focusing on reported earnings and the dividend payout ratio, we ignore the key to paying dividends. That key is *cash*. When a company generates earnings,

---

2. Recall that the current ratio is found by dividing current assets (of which cash is a part) by current liabilities. Thus, decreasing cash to pay a dividend will lower the ratio.

FIGURE 16-1

Dividend Decision Factors

This figure identifies key elements that make a dividend payment more or less likely.

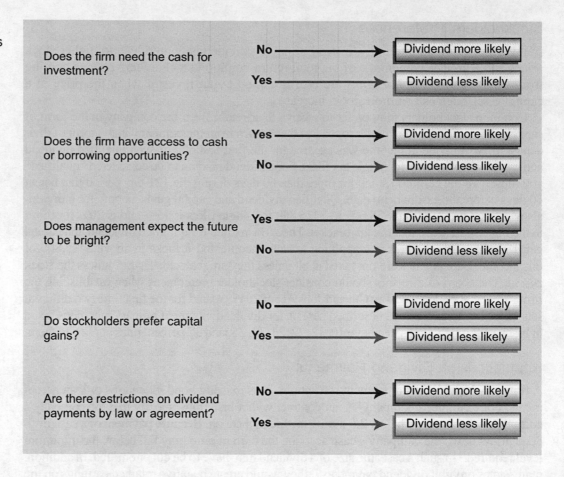

this usually results in cash flowing into the firm. The earnings and the cash flows do not necessarily occur at the same time, however. Table 16-1 illustrates these timing differences.

Table 16-1 shows us that Easy Credit Corporation reported $600,000 of earnings this year but did not receive any cash. Unless cash was acquired from previous earnings, the firm could not pay dividends.

Even if the company reported negative earnings, it could pay dividends if it had, or could raise, enough cash to do so. If a company believed that a certain dividend payment were critical to the preservation of the firm's value, it might even choose to borrow to obtain the cash needed for the dividend payment. Corporate borrowing to obtain cash for a dividend payment happens occasionally, when the dividend payment expected by the common stockholders is believed to be crucial.

Leading Dividend Theories

We've investigated how corporations consider many different factors when they decide what their dividend policies should be. Financial experts attempt to consolidate these factors into theories about how dividend policy affects the value of the firm. We turn to some of these theories next.

TABLE 16-1 Easy Credit Corporation Selected Financial Data for Current Year

Sales (all on credit, payments due in next year)	$ 1,000,000
Total expenses	400,000
Net income	600,000
Cash received this year	$ 0

The Residual Theory of Dividends

The residual dividend theory is widely known. The theory hypothesizes that the amount of dividends should not be the focus of the company. Instead, the primary issue should be to determine the amount of earnings the firm should retain within the firm for investment. The amount of earnings retained, according to this view, depends on the number and size of acceptable capital budgeting projects and the amount of earnings available to finance the equity portion of the funds needed to pay for these projects. Any earnings left after these projects have been funded are paid out in dividends. Because dividends arise from residual, or leftover, earnings, the theory is called the *residual theory*. Table 16-2 shows how to apply this theory.

We see in Table 16-2 that Residual Corporation needs $10 million to finance its acceptable capital budgeting projects. It has earnings of $12 million. It needs equity funds in the amount of 70 percent of the $10 million needed, or $7 million. This leaves residual earnings of $5 million for dividends.

If the earnings available had been $20 million instead of $12 million, then the dividend payment would have been $13 million ($20 million – $7 million). However, if earnings available had been $6 million instead of $12 million, then no dividends would have been paid at all. In fact, $1 million in additional equity funding would need to be raised by issuing new common stock. The amount of dividends to be paid is an afterthought, according to this theory. The important decision is to determine the amount of earnings to retain.

The residual dividend theory focuses on the optimal use of earnings generated from the perspective of the firm itself. This may appeal to some, but it ignores stockholders' preferences about the regularity of and the amount of dividend payments. If a firm follows the residual theory, when earnings are large and the acceptable capital budgeting projects small and few, dividends will be large. Conversely, when earnings are small and many large, acceptable projects are waiting to be financed, there may be no dividends if the residual theory is applied. The dividend payments will be erratic and the amounts will be unpredictable.

The Clientele Dividend Theory

The **clientele dividend theory** is based on the view that investors are attracted to a particular company in part because of its dividend policy. For example, young investors just starting out may want their portfolios to grow in value from capital gains rather than from dividends, so they seek out companies that retain earnings instead of paying dividends. Stock prices tend to increase as earnings are retained, and the resulting capital gain is not taxed until the stock is sold.

clientele dividend theory The theory that says that a company should attempt to determine the dividend wants of its stockholders and maintain a consistent policy of paying stockholders what they want.

Older investors, in contrast, may want to live off the income their portfolios provide. They would tend to seek out companies that pay high dividends rather than reinvesting for growth. According to the clientele dividend theory, each company, therefore, has its own clientele of investors who hold the stock in part because of its dividend policy.

If the clientele theory is valid, then it doesn't much matter what a company's dividend policy is so long as it has one and sticks to it. If the policy is changed, the clientele that liked the old policy will probably sell their stock. A new clientele will buy the stock based on the firm's new policy. When a dividend policy change is contemplated, managers must ask whether the effect of the new clientele's buying will outweigh the effect of the old clientele's selling. The new clientele cannot be sure that the most recent dividend policy implemented will be repeated in the future.

TABLE 16-2 Residual Corporation—Applying the Residual Dividend Theory

Investment Needed for New Projects	$10,000,000
Optimal Capital Structure	30% Debt – 70% Equity
Equity Funds Needed	70% x $10,000,000 = $ 7,000,000
Earnings Available	$12,000,000
Residual	$12,000,000 – $ 7,000,000 = $ 5,000,000
Amount of Dividends to Be Paid	$ 5,000,000

The Signaling Dividend Theory

signaling dividend theory
A theory that says that dividend payments often send a signal from the management of a firm to market participants.

The **signaling dividend theory** is based on the premise that the management of a company knows more about the future financial prospects of the firm than do the stockholders. According to this theory, if a company declares a dividend larger than that anticipated by the market, this will be interpreted as a signal that the future financial prospects of the firm are brighter than expected. Investors presume that management would not have raised the dividend if it did not think that this higher dividend could be maintained. As a result of this inferred signal of good times ahead, investors buy more stock, causing a jump in the stock price.

Conversely, if a company cuts its dividend, the market takes this as a signal that management expects poor earnings and does not believe that the current dividend can be maintained. In other words, a dividend cut signals bad times ahead for the business. The market price of the stock drops when the firm announces a lower dividend because investors sell their stock in anticipation of future financial trouble for the firm.

If a firm's managers believe in the signaling theory, they will always be wary of the message their dividend decision may send to investors. Even if the firm has some attractive investment opportunities that could be financed with retained earnings, management may seek alternative financing to avoid cutting the dividend that may send an unfavorable signal to the market.

The Bird-in-the-Hand Theory

bird-in-the-hand theory
A theory that says that investors value a dollar of dividends more highly than a dollar of reinvested earnings because uncertainty is resolved.

The **bird-in-the-hand theory** claims that stockholders prefer to receive dividends instead of having earnings reinvested in the firm on their behalf. Although stockholders should expect to receive benefits in the form of higher future stock prices when earnings are retained and reinvested in their company, there is uncertainty about whether the benefits will actually be realized. However, if the stockholders were to receive the earnings now, in the form of dividends, they could invest them now in whatever they desired. In other words, "a bird in the hand is worth two in the bush."

If the bird-in-the-hand theory is correct, then stocks of companies that pay relatively high dividends will be more popular—and, therefore, will have relatively higher stock prices—than stocks of companies that reinvest their earnings.

Modigliani and Miller's Dividend Theory

M&M dividend theory
A firm's dividend policy does not affect the value of the firm.

Franco Modigliani and Merton Miller (commonly referred to as M&M) theorized in 1961 that dividend policy is irrelevant.[3] Given some simplifying assumptions, M&M showed how the value of a company is determined by the income produced from its assets, not by its dividend policy. According to the **M&M dividend theory**, the way a firm's income is distributed (in the form of future capital gains or current dividends) doesn't affect the overall value of the firm. Stockholders are indifferent as to whether they receive their return on their investment in the firm's stock from capital gains or dividends—so dividends don't matter.

M&M's arguments have been critiqued for decades. Most often, financial theorists who disagree with M&M maintain that M&M's assumptions are unrealistic. The validity of a theory, however, lies with its ability to stand up to tests of its predictions. The results of these tests are mixed, and modern financial theorists continue to argue about what dividend policy a company should pursue.

The Mechanics of Paying Dividends

declaration date The date on which the board of directors announces a dividend is to be paid.

We've seen how the board of directors decides whether the firm will pay a dividend. Next, let's consider what happens when companies pay dividends and the timing of those payments.

The board's decision to pay a dividend is called *declaring* a dividend. This occurs on the **declaration date**. At that date a liability, called **dividends payable**, is created on the firm's balance sheet.

dividends payable
The liability item on a firm's balance sheet that reflects the amount of dividends declared but not yet paid.

---

3. Merton Miller and Franco Modigliani, "Dividend Policy, Growth, and the Valuation of Shares," *Journal of Business* (October 1961): 411–33.

Because the common stock of public corporations typically is traded every day in the marketplace, the board of directors must select a cutoff date, or **date of record**, to determine who will receive the dividend. At the end of business on this date, the company stockholder records are checked. All owners of the common stock at that time receive the forthcoming dividend.

When stock is traded on an exchange or in the over-the-counter market, it takes time to process the paperwork necessary to record the change of ownership that occurs when the stock changes hands. On the date of record, then, the company's transfer agent will not yet know of stock trading that occurred prior to the date of record.

The **transfer agent** is the party, usually a commercial bank, that keeps the records of stockholder ownership for a corporation. The transfer agent pays dividends to the appropriate stockholders of record after the company has deposited the required money with the transfer agent.

Because it takes time for news of a stock trade to reach the transfer agent, the rules of trading dictate that one day before the date of record, common stock that has an upcoming dividend payment will begin to trade **ex-dividend**. (The prefix *ex* is a Latin word meaning "without.") Investors who buy the stock on or after the ex-dividend date will be buying it "without" entitlement to the forthcoming dividend. The one-day period gives exchange officials enough time to notify the transfer agent of the last batch of stock trades that occurred before the ex-dividend period. The extra time ensures that the stockholder records will be correct on the date of record. In November of 2017 the ex-dividend date was changed from two business days before the date of record to one business day before. The speed at which stock trades are processed had increased so as to allow this change.

A few weeks after the date of record, the checks are mailed out to the common stockholders. The date of mailing is called the **payment date**.

Figure 16-2 shows a time line for the dividend payment sequence.

Table 16-3 summarizes the dividend payment sequence for the **General Dynamics Corp** first quarter 2018 dividend. The table shows the sequence of events that led to the payment of a 2018 first-quarter dividend of $0.93 per share.

Dividend Reinvestment Plans

Many corporations offer a **dividend reinvestment plan (DRIP)**, under which stockholders reinvest their dividends rather than receive them in cash. DRIPs are popular because they allow stockholders to purchase additional shares of stock without incurring the commission costs that accompany regular stock purchases made through a stockbroker. The new shares, including fractional shares, are purchased at the price prevailing in the market at that time. The amount of the dividend paid and reinvested is still taxable income to the stockholder.

Alternatives to Cash Dividends

Sometimes corporations want to give something to the stockholders even though there is insufficient cash available to pay a cash dividend. At other times, corporations don't want to pay a cash dividend because they want to build up their cash position. Let's look at some of the options available for giving stockholders something without using precious cash.

date of record The date on which stockholder records are checked for the purpose of determining who will receive the dividend that has been declared.

transfer agent A party, usually a commercial bank, that keeps track of changes in stock ownership, collects cash from a company, and pays dividends to its stockholders.

ex-dividend A characteristic of common stock such that it is trading without entitlement to an upcoming dividend.

payment date The date the transfer agent sends out a company's dividend checks.

dividend reinvestment plan (DRIP) An arrangement offered by some corporations where cash dividends are held by the company and used to purchase additional shares of stock for the investor.

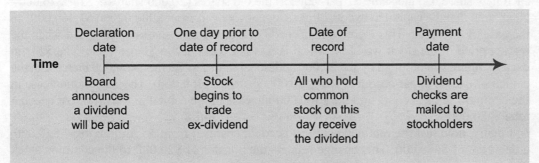

FIGURE 16-2
The Dividend Payment Time Line

This figure shows the sequence of events for a dividend payment.

TABLE 16-3 General Dynamics Corp Dividend Payment Sequence

General Dynamics announced on March 7, 2018 that it had declared a dividend of $0.93 per share to common stockholders of record on April 13, 2018.

Declaration Date	March 7, 2018
Ex-Dividend Date	April 12, 2018
Date of Record	April 13, 2018
Payment Date	May 11, 2018

Source: https://www.dividendinvestor.com/dividend-news/20180307/dividend-announcement-general-dynamics-corp-nyse-gd-today-declared-a-dividend-of-$0.9300-per-share/

Stock Dividends and Stock Splits

Instead of sending out checks to stockholders, the firm could issue additional shares. Many stockholders view the receipt of these extra shares as a positive event, similar to the receipt of a check. In the sections that follow, we will question the validity of this widely held view.

New shares of common stock can be distributed to existing shareholders with no cash payment in two different ways: stock dividends and stock splits. Both increase the number of shares of common stock outstanding, and neither raises additional equity capital. There is an accounting difference between them, however. Let's examine these two alternatives to cash dividends next.

Stock Dividends

stock dividend A firm sends out new shares of stock to existing stockholders and makes an accounting transfer from retained earnings to the common stock and capital in excess of par accounts of the balance sheet.

When a **stock dividend** is declared, the existing common stockholders receive new shares, proportionate to the number of shares currently held. This is usually expressed in terms of a percentage of the existing holdings, such as 5 percent, 10 percent, or 20 percent, but usually less than 25 percent. For example, if a 20 percent stock dividend were declared, one new share would be sent out to existing stockholders for every five currently owned. The following example illustrates how the process works and how the transaction would be accounted for on the firm's balance sheet.

Suppose that Bob and Bill own a chain of bed and breakfast lodges called BB Corporation. Now suppose the BB Corporation declares a 20 percent stock dividend so that each stockholder receives 20 new shares for every 100 shares they hold. This will increase the total number of shares outstanding from 100,000 to 120,000. Assume that the market price of BB's stock at the time of this stock dividend is $24. The equity section of BB's balance sheet, before and after the 20 percent stock dividend, is shown in Table 16-4.

First, note in Table 16-4 that after the 20 percent stock dividend the common stock account changed from $100,000 to $120,000, an increase of 20 percent or $20,000. This change occurred because as of January 1, 2019, the firm had 20,000 more shares outstanding and each new share had the same $1 par value as the old shares (20,000 shares × $1 = $20,000). Next, note that the capital in excess of par account changed from $900,000 to $1,360,000, an increase of $460,000. This increase happened because the new shares were issued when the market price of the stock was $24, which is $23 in excess of the $1 par value. The $23 "in excess" figure is multiplied by the 20,000 additional shares to get the $460,000 increase in the capital in excess of par account ($23 × 20,000 shares = $460,000). The $20,000 increase in the common stock account and the $460,000 increase in the capital in excess of par account total $480,000.

Finally, note that the retained earnings account changed from $5 million to $4,520,000, a decrease of $480,000. This change reflects the transfer of $20,000 to the common stock

TABLE 16-4 BB Corporation Capital Account as of 12/31/18 and 1/1/19

BB Corporation Capital Account as of December 31, 2018 (before a 20% stock dividend)	
Common Stock (100,000 shares, $1 par)	$ 100,000
Capital in Excess of Par	$ 900,000
Retained Earnings	$5,000,000
Total Common Stock Equity	$6,000,000
BB Corporation Capital Account as of January 1, 2019 (after a 20% stock dividend)	
Common Stock (120,000 shares, $1 par)	$ 120,000
Capital in Excess of Par	$1,360,000
Retained Earnings	$4,520,000
Total Common Stock Equity	$6,000,000

account and $460,000 to the capital in excess of par account ($20,000 + $460,000 = $480,000). Retained earnings must decrease because the 20 percent stock dividend did not alter the firm's total equity capital.

Thus, we see that a stock dividend is just an accounting transfer from retained earnings to the other capital accounts. The number of shares of common stock increased by 20,000 in this case, but the overall economic effect was zero. Neither profits nor cash flows changed, however, nor did the degree of risk in the firm. The firm's ownership "pie" was cut into more pieces, but the pie itself was the same size.

On receiving their new shares of stock in the mail, some stockholders may think they have received something of economic value because they have new stock certificates for which they did not pay. But who issued these new stock certificates? The corporation did. Who owns the corporation? The stockholders do. The stockholders have given themselves new shares of stock, but they continue to hold the same percentage of the firm as they held before the stock dividend.

The price per share of common stock will drop because of the increase in the number of shares outstanding. The price decrease happens or the total market value of the common stock will increase (price per share × number of shares outstanding) while no economically significant event has occurred.

Adjustment of a Stock's Market Price after a Stock Dividend

Investors in the stock market generally recognize that a stock dividend simply increases the number of shares of a firm and does not otherwise affect the total value of the firm. After a firm declares a stock dividend, then, the market price of the firm's stock will adjust accordingly. Table 16-5 illustrates the expected stock price adjustment for BB Corporation.

TABLE 16-5 BB Corporation Stock Price Adjustment in Response to a 20% Stock Dividend

	Number of Shares Outstanding	x	Price per Share	=	Total Value of the Firm's Stock
Before Stock Dividend	100,000	x	$24	=	$2,400,000
After Stock Dividend	120,000	x	?	=	$2,400,000

With the information from Table 16-5, we can find the new price of BB's stock as follows:

New number of shares: 120,000

Total value of firm's stock: $2,400,000

Now let X = the new stock price. We solve for the new stock price as shown:

$$120,000 \ X = \$2,400,000$$

$$X = \$20$$

Here's the key to solving for the new stock price after a stock dividend: Remember that the total value of all the firm's stock remains the same as it was before the stock dividend. There may be a positive effect on the stock price due to expectations about the cash dividend. We explore this effect later in the chapter.

Stock Splits

When an increase of more than 25 percent in the number of shares of common stock outstanding is desired, a corporation generally declares a stock split instead of a stock dividend. The firm's motivation for declaring a stock split is generally different from that for a stock dividend. A stock dividend appears to give stockholders something in place of a cash dividend. A **stock split** is an attempt to bring the firm's stock price into what management perceives to be a more popular trading range.

stock split A firm gives new shares of stock to existing shareholders; on the balance sheet, they decrease the par value of the common stock proportionately to the increase in the number of shares outstanding.

Stock splits are usually expressed as ratios. A *4–1 (four-for-one) stock split*, for example, indicates that new shares are issued such that there are four shares after the split for every one share before the split. In a 3–2 split, there would be three shares after the split for every two outstanding before the split.

The accounting treatment for a stock split is simpler than for a stock dividend. Table 16-6 shows how the BB Corporation would account for a 4–1 stock split.

Note in Table 16-6 that only the common stock entry in the equity section of the balance sheet is affected by the stock split. The entry indicates that after the stock split there are four times as many shares of common stock outstanding as before the split. It also indicates that the par value of each share is one-fourth the value it was before (100,000 shares × 4 = 400,000 shares and $1 par value ÷ 4 = $.25). The total dollar value of $100,000 remains the same. Capital in excess of par and retained earnings accounts are completely unaffected by a stock split.

TABLE 16-6 BB Corp. Capital Account as of Dec. 31, 2018

BB Corp. Capital Account as of Dec. 31, 2018 (before a 4–1 stock split)	
Common Stock (100,000 shares, $1 par)	$ 100,000
Capital in Excess of Par	$ 900,000
Retained Earnings	$5,000,000
Total Common Stock Equity	$6,000,000
BB Corp. Capital Account as of Jan. 1, 2019 (after a 4–1 stock split)	
Common Stock (400,000 shares, $.25 par)	$ 100,000
Capital in Excess of Par	$ 900,000
Retained Earnings	$5,000,000
Total Common Stock Equity	$6,000,000

Adjustment of a Stock's Market Price after a Stock Split

As with a stock dividend, investors in the stock market recognize that a stock split simply increases the number of shares of a firm and does not otherwise affect the total value of the firm. Therefore, the market price of the firm's stock will adjust accordingly following a stock split. Table 16-7 illustrates the stock price adjustment for the BB Corporation in response to the 4–1 stock split.

We see in Table 16-7 that, just as with the stock dividend, no economically significant event has occurred. The common stock ownership "pie" has been cut into four times as many pieces as before, but the size of the pie is the same. As Table 16-7 shows, after the 4–1 split, each share will trade in the market at approximately one-fourth the price it commanded before the split.

Sometimes the cash dividend is increased at the same time as a stock split or a stock dividend. In our 4–1 stock split example, if the cash dividend per share is decreased by less than three-fourths, stockholder cash dividends received would increase. A $1 per share cash dividend, for instance, could be cut to $0.30 instead of the $0.25 value that would leave total cash dividends unchanged. The market sometimes anticipates such an increase in the cash dividend, leading to a possible increase in the total market value of the common stock.

The Rationale for Stock Splits

Most companies split stock in an attempt to increase its value. Managers believe that as the market price per share of their common stock increases over time, it gets too expensive for some investors. Management perceives that a stock split will decrease the price per share, thereby increasing the number of potential investors who can afford to buy it. More potential investors might create additional buying pressure, which would result in an increase in stock price. This argument is less persuasive, however, as the percentage of stock ownership and trading activity by institutional investors (mutual funds, pension funds, insurance companies, and so on) continues to increase. These investors can afford to pay a very high price per share. Managers, however, continue to use stock splits to adjust the stock price to a lower level to make it more affordable. Berkshire Hathaway Inc., the company with Warren Buffett as its CEO, had its Class A shares trading at over $307,000 per share in early 2018. It's Class B shares have been split and they were trading in the low 200s in early 2018.

What's Next

In this chapter, we looked at how firms make their dividend decisions. This chapter ends Part 4 on long-term financing decisions. Part 5 focuses on short-term financing decisions. In Chapters 17 through 20, we will examine how firms manage the three primary current assets: cash, inventory, and accounts receivable.

TABLE 16-7 BB Corporation Stock Price Adjustment Due to a 4–1 Stock Split

	Number of Shares Outstanding	x	Price per Share	=	Total Value of the Firm's Stock
Before Stock Dividend	100,000	x	$24	=	$2,400,000
After Stock Dividend	400,000	x	$ 6	=	$2,400,000

Summary

1. *Explain the importance of and identify the factors that influence the dividend decision.*
   Stock prices often change dramatically when a dividend change is announced, indicating that the market believes dividends affect value. The dividend decision, then, must be carefully planned and implemented. Factors that influence dividend decisions are a company's need for funds, its future financial prospects, stockholder preferences and expectations, and the firm's contractual obligations.

   Although dividends are often discussed in the context of a firm's earnings, dividends are paid in cash. As a result, a firm's cash flow is a crucial factor affecting its dividend policy.

2. *Compare the major dividend theories.*
   The major dividend theories that help guide dividend policy include the residual theory of dividends, the clientele theory, the signaling theory, the bird-in-the-hand theory, and the Modigliani and Miller theory.

   The residual theory posits that the amount of dividends matters less than the amount of earnings retained. If a firm enacts a residual policy, its dividend payments are likely to be unpredictable and erratic.

   The clientele dividend theory assumes that one of the key reasons investors are attracted to a particular company is its dividend policy. Under this theory, it doesn't matter what the dividend policy is so long as the firm sticks to it.

   The signaling dividend theory is based on the premise that management knows more about the future finances of the firm than do stockholders, so dividends signal the firm's future prospects. A dividend decrease signals an expected downturn in earnings; a dividend increase signals a positive future is expected. Managers who believe the signaling theory will be conscious of the message their dividend decision may send to investors.

   The bird-in-the-hand theory assumes that stockholders prefer to receive dividends instead of having earnings reinvested in the firm on their behalf. If correct, stocks of companies that pay relatively high dividends will be more popular and, therefore, will have relatively higher stock prices than stocks of companies that reinvest their earnings.

   The Modigliani and Miller theory claims that earnings from assets, rather than dividend policy, affect firm value, so dividend policy is irrelevant.

3. *Describe how a firm pays dividends.*
   Dividends are declared by the corporate board of directors. Stockholders on the date of record are entitled to the declared dividend. Investors who buy the stock before the ex-dividend date (one day before the date of record) will receive the dividend declared by the board. Investors who buy the stock on or after the ex-dividend date have bought the stock too late to get the dividend.

4. *Identify alternatives to paying cash dividends.*
   Corporations often award stockholders stock dividends (additional shares of stock) and stock splits instead of cash dividends. Both stock splits and stock dividends increase the number of outstanding shares and decrease the price per share. Although neither of these actions is a real substitute for a cash dividend, many investors perceive these events as good news even though earnings do not increase nor does risk decrease.

Key Terms

bird-in-the-hand theory A theory that says that investors value a dollar of dividends more highly than a dollar of reinvested earnings because uncertainty is resolved.

clientele dividend theory The theory that says that a company should attempt to determine the dividend wants of its stockholders and maintain a consistent policy of paying stockholders what they want.

date of record The date on which stockholder records are checked for the purpose of determining who will receive the dividend that has been declared.

declaration date The date on which the board of directors announces a dividend is to be paid.

dividend reinvestment plan An arrangement offered by some corporations where cash dividends are held by the company and used to purchase additional shares of stock for the investor.

dividends payable The liability item on a firm's balance sheet that reflects the amount of dividends declared but not yet paid.

ex-dividend A characteristic of common stock such that it is trading without entitlement to an upcoming dividend.

M&M dividend theory A firm's dividend policy does not affect the value of the firm.

payment date The date the transfer agent sends out a company's dividend checks.

signaling dividend theory A theory that says that dividend payments often send a signal from the management of a firm to market participants.

stock dividend A firm sends out new shares of stock to existing stockholders and makes an accounting transfer from retained earnings to the common stock and capital in excess of par accounts of the balance sheet.

stock split A firm gives new shares of stock to existing shareholders; on the balance sheet, they decrease the par value of the common stock proportionately to the increase in the number of shares outstanding.

transfer agent A party, usually a commercial bank, that keeps track of changes in stock ownership, collects cash from a company, and pays dividends to its stockholders.

Equations Introduced in This Chapter

Equation 16-1. The Dividend Payout Ratio:

$$\text{Dividend Payout Ratio} = \frac{\text{Dividends Paid}}{\text{Net Income}}$$

Self-Test

ST-1. A company pays $4 per share in dividends and has 100,000 shares outstanding. The company has net income of $1 million. Its market price per share is $100. What is its dividend payout ratio?

ST-2. Is the amount of the dividend to be paid the primary focus of the board of directors if the board is guided by the residual theory of dividends? Explain.

ST-3. Does a company following the clientele theory of dividends pay high or low dividends? Explain.

ST-4. When paying dividends, what is the date of record?

ST-5. If a company stock has a $2 par value, what will be the accounting effect of a 4–1 stock split?

Review Questions

1. Explain the role of cash and of earnings when a corporation is deciding how much, if any, cash dividends to pay to common stockholders.

2. Are there any legal factors that could restrict a corporation in its attempt to pay cash dividends to common stockholders? Explain.

3. What are some of the factors that common stockholders consider when deciding how much, if any, cash dividends they desire from the corporation in which they have invested?

4. What is the Modigliani and Miller theory of dividends? Explain.

5. Do you believe an increased common stock cash dividend can send a signal to the common stockholders? If so, what signal might it send?

6. Explain the bird-in-the-hand theory of cash dividends.

7. What is the effect of stock (not cash) dividends and stock splits on the market price of common stock? Why do corporations declare stock splits and stock dividends?

Build Your Communication Skills

CS-1. Find a company that has recently cut its dividend. Write a report on the market's reaction to this decision and the timing of that reaction. What are some possible explanations for this market reaction?

CS-2. Many people perceive a stock split as a very positive event. Find a company that has gone through a stock split. Write a short report on the market's reaction to the stock split around the time it was announced and at the time the split actually occurred. Were they different? Were they what you would expect? Explain.

Problems

16-1. After discussion with the board of directors of the company, Lionel Mandrake, founder and chairman of Mandrake, Inc., decided to retain $600 million from its net income of $1 billion. Calculate the payout ratio. **Payout Ratio**

16-2. The net income of Harold Bissonette Resorts, Inc., was $50 million this past year. The company decided to have a 40 percent payout ratio. How much was paid in dividends and how much was added to the retained earnings? **Payout Ratio**

16-3. Charleston Industrial revised its dividend policy and decided that it wants to maintain a retained earnings account of $1 million. The company's retained earnings account at the end of 2017 was $750,000, and it had net income of $800,000 in 2018. What is Charleston Industrial's dividend payout ratio for 2018? **Payout Ratio**

Payout Ratio

⟹ **16-4.** Delenburk had net income of $4 million for 2018, and it has a policy of maintaining a dividend payout ratio of 35 percent. Calculate the amount that was paid to shareholders in 2018. If the company had a retained earnings account of $1.2 million at the end of 2017, what is the balance in the retained earnings account at the end of 2018?

Constant Payout Ratio and Retained Earnings

⟹ **16-5.** Hannah Brown International maintains a dividend policy with a constant payout ratio of 30 percent. In the last three years, the company has had the following earnings.

	Year 1	Year 2	Year 3
Net Income ($ million)	30	20	25

What is the total addition to retained earnings over the last three years?

Constant Dollar Dividend Policy

⟹ **16-6.** Use the same data given in problem 16-5. Now, if the company followed a constant dollar dividend policy and paid $10 million in dividends each year, compute the dividend payout ratios for each year and the total addition to retained earnings over the last three years.

Residual Dividend Theory

⟹ **16-7.** Eliza Doolittle, the chief financial officer of East West Communications Corporation, has identified $14 million worth of new capital projects that the company should invest in next year. The optimal capital structure for the company is 40 percent debt and 60 percent equity. If the expected earnings for this year are $10 million, what amount of dividend should she recommend according to residual theory?

Residual Dividend Theory

⟹ **16-8.** Use the same data given in problem 16-7. Now, what would be the amount of dividend that could be paid if East West's net income for this year is:

a. $16 million?

b. $6 million?

Residual Dividend Theory

⟹ **16-9.** DreamScapes Entertainment's financial managers have determined that the company needs $12 million to fund its new projects for next year. It has an optimal capital structure of 20 percent debt and the rest equity. This year the company has $24 million in earnings available to common stockholders and 20,000,000 shares outstanding. According to the residual theory, what is the dividend per share paid to common stockholders?

Stock Dividend

⟹ **16-10.** Jan Brady, chief accountant of Mulberry Silk Products, is trying to work out the feasibility of a 20 percent stock dividend. The equity section of the balance sheet follows:

	($ 000s)
Common Stock (2 million shares, $1 par)	2,000
Capital in Excess of Par	8,000
Retained Earnings	10,000
Total Common Equity	20,000

The current market price of the company's stock is $31 per share. Is it possible to pay a 20 percent stock dividend? Is it possible to pay a 10 percent stock dividend? Explain.

Stock Dividend

⟹ **16-11.** Use the same data given in problem 16-10. After payment of a 10 percent stock dividend, what will be the expected market price of the stock? Also, show how the equity section of the balance sheet will change.

Stock Dividend

⟹ **16-12.** Malea Liberty has 800,000 common stock shares outstanding. It has decided to declare a 30 percent stock dividend. The new par value is the same as the original par value, $3. Before the declared dividend, the retained earnings account was $60,000,000 and capital in excess of par was $13,600,000. The current stock price is $40 per share. Calculate the new values for the following items:

a. Number of shares of common stock

b. Capital in excess of par

c. Retained earnings

16-13. Malea Liberty's market price before the declared stock dividend was $40 per share. What would be the market price after the declared stock dividend described in the problem 16-12? (Assume the total value of the firm's stock remains the same.)

Stock Dividend

16-14. Wesley Crusher, chief accountant of Blue Sky Cruise Lines, is trying to figure out the effect of a 3–1 stock split. The equity section of the balance sheet follows:

Stock Split

	($ 000s)
Common Stock (3 million shares, $1.00 par)	3,000
Capital in Excess of Par	7,000
Retained Earnings	10,000
Total Common Equity	20,000

The current market price of the company's stock is $33 per share. If Blue Sky Cruise Lines decided to have a 3–1 stock split, how would the equity section change after the split? What would be the stock's market price?

16-15. Use the same information given in problem 16-14. If Blue Sky Cruise Lines' net income is $800,000, what is the earnings per share before and after the 3–1 stock split? Will there be any change in the price to earnings ratio before and after the stock split?

Stock Split

16-16. Sumner Outdoor Equipment Company decided to go for a 5–1 stock split. The common shareholders received a dividend of $1.33 per share after the split.

Stock Split

a. If the dollar amount of dividends paid after the split is the same as that paid last year before the split, what was the dividend per share last year?

b. If the dollar amount of dividends paid after the split is 10 percent higher than what was paid last year before the split, what was the dividend per share last year?

16-17. Market price of Linden Landscaping Company's stock is $30 the day before the stock goes ex-dividend. The earnings of the company are $10 million, and the company follows a dividend policy with constant payout ratio of 40 percent. There are 1 million shares of common stock outstanding. What would be the new ex-dividend price of the stock?

Challenge Problem

16-18. In its strategic plan for the next five years, Springfield Manufacturing Company has projected the following net income and capital investments (figures in $000s):

Long- Term Dividend (Residual Theory)

Year	Net Income	Investments
2019	1,000	800
2020	1,100	1,000
2021	1,200	2,000
2022	1,300	800
2023	1,400	1,000

For more, see 8e Spreadsheet Templates for *Microsoft Excel*.

The capital structure the company wishes to maintain is 40 percent debt and 60 percent equity. There are currently 500,000 shares of common stock outstanding.

If you own 500 shares of common stock, calculate the amounts you would receive in dividends over the next five years (2019 to 2023), assuming that the company uses the residual dividend theory each year to determine the dividend to be paid to its common stockholders.

16-19. Use the same data given in problem 16-18. Now assume that the company plans to issue 100,000 new shares of common stock in 2018 at $6 per share ($1 par plus $5 capital in excess of par). What will be the dividend that you receive in 2019 through 2023 assuming your common stock holding remains the same at 500 shares?

Long-Term Dividend (Residual Theory)

For more, see 8e Spreadsheet Templates for *Microsoft Excel*.

16-20. The equity section of the balance sheet of Cafe Vienna is given next:

	($ 000s)
Common Stock (500,000 shares, $3 par)	1,500
Capital in Excess of Par	3,500
Retained Earnings	5,000
Total Common Equity	10,000

The company earned a net income of $3 million this year. Historically, the company has paid dividends with a constant payout ratio of 50 percent. The stock will sell at $47 after the ex-dividend date.

William Riker, the vice president of finance for Cafe Vienna, is considering all possible ways to increase the company's earnings per share (EPS). One possibility he is weighing is to buy back some of the company's outstanding shares of common stock from the market using all the net income earned this year without paying any dividend to common stockholders.

a. Determine the repurchase price of the common stock.

b. Calculate the number of shares that could be repurchased using this year's net income.

c. Show the changes in the equity section of the balance sheet after the repurchase.

d. If net income next year is expected to be $4 million, what would be the EPS next year with and without the repurchase?

e. If you own 50 shares of the company's common stock, would you like the company's decision of buying back the stock instead of paying a dividend?

Stock Split   **16-21.** Blue Jays wants to bring its stock price down to a more attractive level. In order to do this, Blue Jays wants to implement a 4–1 stock split. Before the split, the company has 300,000 shares outstanding at $4 par that were issued at a market price of $9 per share; retained earnings are $10,000,000. Fill in the values before and after the split.

Before the Split		After the Split	
Number of shares	_____	Number of shares	_____
Common Stock	_____	Common Stock	_____
Par Value	_____	Par Value	_____
Capital in Excess of Par	_____	Capital in Excess of Par	_____
Retained Earnings	_____	Retained Earnings	_____
Total Common Stock Equity	_____	Total Common Stock Equity	_____

Answers to Self-Test

ST-1. Dividend Payout Ratio = Dividends Paid ÷ Net Income
= ($4/share × 100,000 shares) ÷ $1,000,000 =
$400,000 ÷ $1,000,000 = .40 = 40%

ST-2. No. According to the residual theory of dividends, the amount of earnings that should be retained is determined first. Whatever amount is not retained is paid out in dividends.

ST-3. A company following the clientele theory of dividends might have either high or low dividend payments. If the stockholders preferred high dividends, that is what would be paid. If they preferred low dividends, that would be the policy.

ST-4. The date of record is the date on which a company checks its stockholder records. Investors listed in the records on that date are entitled to receive the dividend that was recently declared.

ST-5. $2 original par value ÷ 4 (4 for 1 split) = $.50 new par value

Short-Term Financing Decisions

PART 5

Source: deepadesigns/Shutterstock

Chapter 17
Working Capital Policy

Chapter 18
Managing Cash

Chapter 19
Accounts Receivable
and Inventory

Chapter 20
Short-Term Financing

Whereas long-term financing decisions concern how the firm finances its assets over several years, short-term financing decisions concern how the firm can get the money it needs for daily, weekly, and monthly needs. Cash management is paramount, either by budgeting the amount on hand, buying supplies on credit, or borrowing it for short periods of time. Short-term funds are also often used for investments in accounts receivable and inventory. Chapter 17 begins this section with an examination of the trade-off that is at the heart of short-term financial management: liquidity versus profitability. Firms can either keep large balances of cash and inventory, which increases liquidity but decreases profitability, or they can keep low balances of cash and inventory, which helps profitability but decreases liquidity. Somewhere in-between is the proper balance for each individual firm. Chapters 18 through 20 take up the management of the individual current asset and current liability accounts. Chapter 18 explains cash management, including the process of developing a cash budget. Chapter 19 discusses the optimal levels of inventory and accounts receivable, including the decision process associated with offering credit to customers. Chapter 20 explores short-term financing alternatives and discusses how to calculate the effective interest rate for various types of short-term loans.

Working Capital Policy

"Having money isn't everything, not having it is."
—Kanye West

CHAPTER 17

Source: Zurainy Zain/Shutterstock

Learning Objectives

After reading this chapter, you should be able to:

1. Explain the importance of managing working capital.
2. Discuss how the trade-off between liquidity and profitability affects a firm's current asset management policy.
3. Describe how a firm reaches an optimal level of current assets.
4. Discuss the effects of the three approaches to working capital financing policy.

The Importance of Liquidity

People usually think about financial success in terms of profit and equity levels. Profit and equity do not pay the bills, however. Cash does. This is why a company's liquidity is so critical to its survival. If a company has adequate working capital, current assets, it can get the cash it needs to pay its bills. If bills are not paid, the company becomes insolvent. Having sufficient working capital to cover current liabilities is critical to a company's survival. A company may have a great product and a great strategic vision. Its long-run prospects might look excellent. It needs to survive in the short-run, however, if it is to realize its long-run potential. Many start-up companies have great ideas but never realize their potential because they have inadequate working capital to make it through the inevitable bumps a new company will face as it seeks to reach its goals. They go out of business before their potential can be realized. This chapter examines the primary issues related to working capital management.

Chapter Overview

In this chapter, we examine working capital policy—the management of a firm's current assets and its financing. First, we'll see why firms manage working capital carefully, why they accumulate it, and how to classify current assets. We then investigate what determines a firm's working capital policy and look at different types of policies.

Managing Working Capital

working capital Another name for the current assets on a firm's balance sheet.

Working capital refers to a firm's current assets. By "current," we mean those assets that the firm expects to convert into cash within a year. Current assets include cash; inventory, which generates cash when the items are sold; and accounts receivable, which produces cash when customers pay off their credit accounts. Current assets are considered liquid because they can be transformed into cash in a relatively short time.

net working capital The amount of current assets minus the amount of current liabilities of an economic unit.

Net working capital is the firm's current assets minus current liabilities. Current liabilities are business obligations (i.e., debts) that the firm is required to pay off or otherwise satisfy within a year. Examples include accounts payable—bills due soon—and notes payable—loans due to be paid in less than a year.

Table 17-1 shows the working capital and net working capital for Aspen Lawn and Garden Company, which manufactures lawn and gardening products and sells them to retailers.

In Table 17-1 we see that Aspen Lawn and Garden has $13,000 in current assets (working capital), $11,000 in current liabilities, and $2,000 in net working capital ($13,000 − $11,000 = $2,000). Net working capital is important to firms. It represents the amount of current assets remaining if they were liquidated to pay the company's short-term debts.

Working capital policy is the firm's policy about its working capital level and how its working capital should be financed. For instance, a firm needs to make decisions about how much to keep in its cash account, what level of inventory to maintain, and how much to allow accounts receivable to build up. The firm must also decide whether to finance current assets with short-term funds, long-term funds, or some mixture of the two. Together, the level and financing decisions make up the firm's working capital policy.

Why Businesses Accumulate Working Capital

Why do firms accumulate working capital, and why does its level vary over time? In this section, we examine the answers to these two questions.

Fluctuating Current Assets

Many factors affect a firm's working capital policy. For instance, a service firm may require a different level of current assets than a manufacturing firm. Or a business like Jason's Popcorn Wagon (from Chapter 13), which makes and sells popcorn during the summer months only, has different seasonal working capital needs than a firm that makes and sells products year-round.

To illustrate the principles of working capital policy, we focus on a manufacturing firm that has level production—that is, it produces the same amount of product every month, year-round. However, its sales are seasonal—the firm sells more in certain time periods

TABLE 17-1 Aspen Lawn and Garden Company Balance Sheet, as of December 31, 2018

Cash	$ 2,000	Accounts Payable	$ 7,000
Accounts Receivable	1,000	Notes Payable	4,000
Inventory	10,000	Total Current Liabilities	11,000
Total Current Assets	13,000	Other Liabilities	7,000
Other Assets	32,000	Common Stock	27,000
Total Assets	$ 45,000	Total Liabilities and Equity	$ 45,000

than in others. Many businesses are seasonal. (For instance, a swimwear manufacturer may sell many more swimsuits at the start of summer than it does in other months. A lawn care products manufacturer will probably have more sales at the start of the gardening season than it will in other months.)

If a business has level production but not level sales, inventory increases when production exceeds sales. Inventory then falls when sales exceed production. The firm's other current assets may fluctuate during the year as well. Accounts receivable, for example, will rise when new credit sales exceed customer payments and will fall when customer payments exceed new credit sales. Cash will accumulate as sales revenues are collected and will decline when bills are paid. Thus, the current assets of the business will fluctuate over time.

Permanent and Temporary Current Assets

Although the level of current assets in the firm may fluctuate, it rarely reaches zero. The firm will nearly always have some cash on hand, hold some inventory in stock, and be owed some amount of money. Current assets thus reach various temporary levels but will rarely fall below some minimal permanent level. This effect is illustrated for Aspen Lawn and Garden in Figure 17-1.

Figure 17-1 shows three categories of business assets that affect a firm's working capital policy:

1. Temporary current assets represent the level of inventory, cash, and accounts receivable that fluctuate seasonally.

2. Permanent current assets represent the base level of inventory, cash, and accounts receivable, which tends to be maintained.

3. Fixed assets represent the land, buildings, equipment, and other assets that would not normally be sold or otherwise disposed of for a long period of time.

Permanent current assets tend to build up on a firm's balance sheet year after year. Cash collections increase as the business grows, accounts receivable grow as the list of credit customers lengthens, inventory on hand rises as new facilities are opened, and so on. Figure 17-2 shows how Aspen Lawn and Garden's current assets might vary over several years.

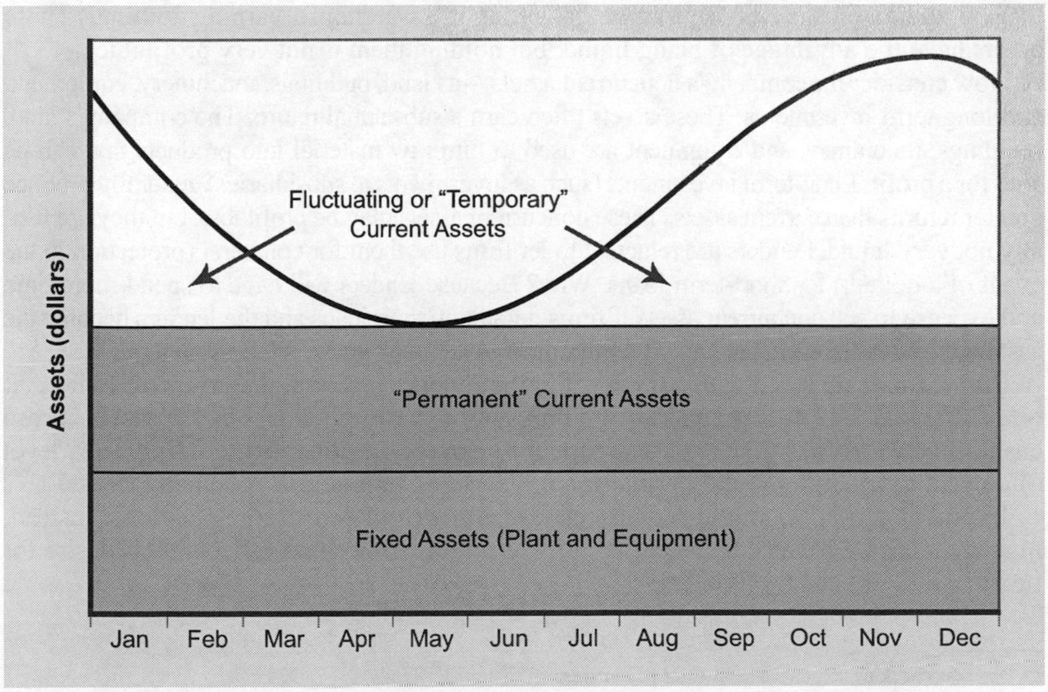

> **Take Note**
> The term *permanent current assets* may sound like an oxymoron (like "jumbo shrimp"), but it's not. A portion of a firm's current assets is likely to remain on a firm's balance sheet indefinitely.

FIGURE 17-1
The Variation in Current Assets over Time for Aspen Lawn and Garden

Figure 17-1 shows how the current assets of a company tend to fluctuate over time but never fall below a permanent level of current assets.

FIGURE 17-2

The Variation in Current Assets Over Several Years for Aspen Lawn and Garden

Figure 17-2 shows how a typical firm's current assets tend to build up from year to year, while fluctuating within each year. The effect occurs because as firms grow, they accumulate receivable, and inventory over time.

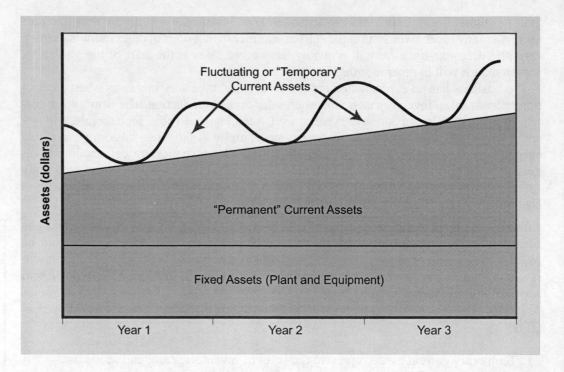

As Figure 17-2 shows, businesses have two tasks: First, they must contend with current assets that fluctuate through their business cycle. Second, they must manage permanent current asset growth due to long-term business growth over time. In the sections that follow, we discuss how firms do this.

Liquidity versus Profitability

Lenders would like a company to have a large excess of current assets over current liabilities. But the owners don't necessarily feel the same way. Think about it. Current assets—in the form of cash, accounts receivable, and inventory—do not earn the firm a very high return. Cash is usually held in a commercial bank checking account that pays no interest.[1] Accounts receivable earns no return because it represents money that customers owe to the firm that the firm doesn't have yet. Inventory earns no return until it's sold. (Inventory being held by the firm is just material sitting in a warehouse, earning nothing.) These assets have the advantage of being liquid, but holding them is not very profitable.

Now consider the company's noncurrent assets—its land, buildings, machinery, equipment, and long-term investments. These assets often earn a substantial return. The company's land, buildings, machinery, and equipment are used to turn raw material into products that can be sold for a profit. Long-term investments (such as investments in subsidiaries) generally produce greater returns than current assets. These noncurrent assets may be profitable, but they are usually not very liquid. Lenders are reluctant to let firms use them for collateral (protection in the event of a default) for short-term loans. Why? Because lenders will have to spend more time and expense to sell noncurrent assets if firms default on their loans and the lenders become the asset owners. As a result, lenders prefer that firms use liquid assets as loan collateral.

Firms, then, are faced with a trade-off in their working capital management policy. At one extreme, they can seek liquidity, holding a lot of cash and other current assets in case cash is needed soon. At the other extreme, they can seek profitability, holding a low level of current assets and investing primarily in long-term, high-return-producing assets.

In practice, no firm would actually choose either of these extreme positions. Instead, managers seek a balance between liquidity and profitability that reflects their desire for profit and their need for liquidity.

---

1. Business checking accounts almost never pay interest

Establishing the Optimal Level of Current Assets

The search for a balance between liquidity and profitability serves as a general guide for financial managers looking for an optimal level of current assets. However, the level managers eventually achieve is actually a result of their efforts to maintain optimal levels of each of the components of the current asset group. In other words, a firm's optimal level of current assets is reached when the optimal level of cash, of inventory, and of accounts receivable[2] is achieved. Each asset account is managed separately, and the combined results produce the actual level of current assets. Here's a description of the attempt to find the optimal level for each current asset account:

- *Cash:* Managers try to keep just enough cash on hand to conduct day-to-day business, while investing extra amounts in short-term marketable securities. We discuss cash in detail in Chapter 18.

- *Inventory:* Managers seek the level that reduces lost sales due to lack of inventory, while at the same time holding down inventory costs. We discuss inventory management in Chapter 19.

- *Accounts receivable:* Firms want to enhance sales but hold down bad debt and collection expenses through sound credit policies. We discuss credit policies in Chapter 19.

Once financial managers set policies to attain the optimal level of current assets, they must turn their attention to the flip side of working capital management: managing current liabilities.

Managing Current Liabilities: Risk and Return

A firm's current asset fluctuations and any long-term build-up of current assets (its working capital) must, of course, be financed. The question facing financial managers is whether to obtain the financing from short-term borrowing, long-term borrowing, contributions from the owners (equity financing), or some mixture of all three.

As is so often the case, the choice of the firm's working capital financing blend depends on managers' desire for profit versus their aversion to risk. Short-term debt financing is generally less expensive than long-term debt and always less expensive than equity financing. Recall from Chapter 2 that short-term interest rates are usually lower than long-term interest rates. Short-term loans, however, are more risky because a firm may not have enough cash to repay the loans (due to cash flow fluctuations) or interest rates may increase and increase the cost of short-term funds as loans are renewed. So relying on long-term debt and/or equity financing is less risky from the firm's perspective because it puts repayment off (forever, in the case of stock) and locks in an interest rate for a long time period in the case of long-term debt.

The balance between the risk and return of financing options depends on the firm, its financial managers, and its financing approaches. We discuss several financing approaches next.

> **Take Note**
> In our discussion, we assume that a firm has all available financing alternative options. In practice, however, some firms may have limited financing options. For example, small firms usually have limited access to long-term capital markets.

Three Working Capital Financing Approaches

The three primary working capital financing approaches are the aggressive approach, the conservative approach, and the moderate approach. A firm that takes an aggressive approach uses more short-term financing to finance current assets. Firm risk increases, due to the risk of fluctuating interest rates, but the potential for higher returns increases because of the generally low-cost financing. A firm that implements the conservative approach avoids short-term financing to reduce risk but decreases the potential for maximum value creation because of the high cost of long-term debt and equity financing. The moderate approach tries to balance risk and return concerns.

---

2. Along with any other current assets the firm possesses, of course. In this book, we concentrate on these three major categories of current assets.

The Aggressive Approach

We know that short-term interest rates are normally lower than long-term interest rates. We also know that borrowing short term is riskier than borrowing long term because the loan must be paid off or refinanced sooner rather than later.

The **aggressive working capital financing approach** involves the use of short-term debt to finance at least the firm's temporary assets, some or all of its permanent current assets, and possibly some of its long-term fixed assets. The aggressive approach is shown graphically in Figure 17-3.

If we compare current assets and current liabilities in Figure 17-3, we see that all the firm's temporary current assets and most of its permanent current assets are being financed with short-term debt (the current liabilities). As a result, the firm has very little net working capital. Depending on the nature of the firm's business, this small amount of net working capital can be risky. There isn't much cushion between the value of liquid assets and the amount of debt due in the short term.

Firms may be more aggressive than the firm depicted in Figure 17-3. If the firm's managers financed all working capital from short-term debt, then current assets would equal current liabilities and the firm would have zero net working capital—no cushion at all. Managers may go even further and finance a portion of the firm's long-term assets (plant and equipment) with short-term debt, creating a negative net working capital. However, such an approach is very risky. (Think what would happen to a firm using that approach if short-term interest rates rose unexpectedly.)

What tempts financial managers to take the aggressive approach and use a relatively large amount of short-term debt for working capital financing? Usually, lower interest rates tempt them. Managers will take a risk if the promise of return is high enough to justify it.

The Conservative Approach

Borrowing long term is considered less risky than borrowing short term. This is because the borrower has a longer time to use the loan proceeds before repayment is due. Furthermore, if interest rates should go up during the period of the loan, the long-term borrower has another advantage. The long-term borrower has locked in a fixed interest rate and may end up paying less total interest than the short-term borrower, who must renew the loan each time it comes due—at a new, higher interest rate. If market rates fall, the long-term borrower can usually refinance.

The **conservative working capital financing approach** involves the use of long-term debt and equity to finance all long-term fixed assets and permanent current assets, in

aggressive working capital financing approach The use of short-term funds to finance all temporary current assets, possibly all or some permanent current assets, and perhaps some fixed assets.

conservative working capital financing approach The use of long-term debt and equity to finance all long-term fixed assets and permanent current assets, in addition to some part of temporary current assets.

FIGURE 17-3
The Aggressive Working Capital Financing Approach

Figure 17-3 shows the firm's assets on the left and liabilities and equity on the right. Subtracting current liabilities from current assets shows that this firm's working capital financing strategy is to finance nearly all current assets with current liabilities, resulting in a small amount of net working capital.

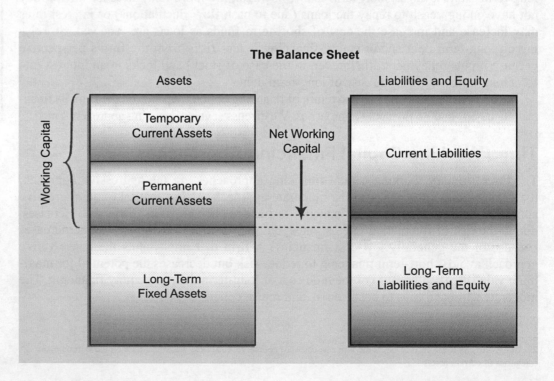

addition to some part of temporary current assets. The conservative approach is shown graphically in Figure 17-4.

Compare current assets with current liabilities in Figure 17-4. Note that all the firm's permanent current assets and most of its temporary current assets are being financed with long-term debt or equity. As a result, current assets exceed current liabilities by a wide margin and the firm has a large amount of net working capital. Having a large amount of net working capital is a relatively low-risk position because the firm has many assets that could be liquidated to satisfy short-term debts.

A financial manager who applies an ultra-conservative approach would use cash from the owners for all asset financing needs (high cash balance supported by equity) and incur no debt. By using only equity capital, the firm would also have the maximum amount of net working capital possible because it would have no current liabilities.

The safety of the conservative approach has a cost. Long-term financing is generally more expensive than short-term financing. Long-term interest rates are higher than short-term rates when there is an upward sloping yield curve, the normal yield curve described in Chapter 2. Also, the cost of equity is greater than the cost of either long-term or short-term debt, as described in Chapter 9. So relying on long-term debt and equity sources to finance working capital consumes funds that could otherwise be put to more productive use.

The Moderate Approach

An accounting concept known as the matching principle states that the cost of an asset should be recognized over the length of time that the asset provides revenue, or benefit, to the business.

The concept of the matching principle can be applied to define a moderate position between the aggressive and the conservative working capital financing approaches. According to the matching principle, temporary current assets that are only going to be on the balance sheet for a short time should be financed with short-term debt—that is, current liabilities. Permanent current assets and long-term fixed assets that are going to be on the balance sheet for a long time should be financed from long-term debt and equity sources. The **moderate working capital financing approach** is shown in Figure 17-5.

If we look at current assets and current liabilities in Figure 17-5, we see that the firm has matched its short-term temporary current assets to its current liabilities. It has also matched its long-term permanent current assets and fixed assets to its long-term financing sources. This policy gives the firm a moderate amount of net working capital. It calls for a

moderate working capital financing approach
An approach in which a firm finances temporary current assets with short-term funds and permanent current assets and fixed assets with long-term funds.

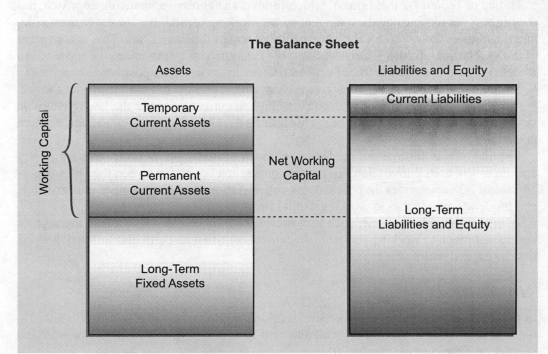

The Balance Sheet

Assets	Liabilities and Equity

Working Capital { Temporary Current Assets

Permanent Current Assets

Long-Term Fixed Assets

Net Working Capital

Current Liabilities

Long-Term Liabilities and Equity

FIGURE 17-4
The Conservative Working Capital Financing Approach

The relative size of the current asset and current liability accounts in Figure 17-4 reveals the firm's working capital financing strategy. The figure shows that this firm is financing nearly all current assets with long-term liabilities and equity, resulting in a high level of net working capital.

FIGURE 17-5

The Moderate Working Capital Financing Approach

In Figure 17-5, we see that this firm's approach to working capital financing policy is to finance its permanent current assets with long-term debt and equity and its temporary current assets with current liabilities. This results in a moderate level of net working capital.

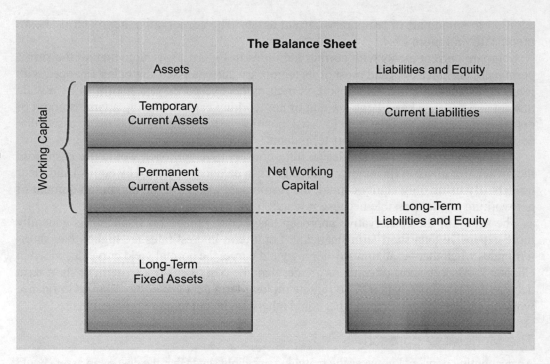

relatively moderate amount of risk balanced by a relatively moderate amount of expected return. We all have some feel for the rationale behind this approach. You would probably not be attracted to a 30-year car loan nor a 6-month mortgage.

Now that we have described three working capital financing policies, we turn to an analysis of the effect of such policies on a firm.

Working Capital Financing and Financial Ratios

The use of ratio analysis highlights how the three approaches to working capital financing policy can affect the risk and return potential of a firm. In Table 17-2, we compare selected financial ratios for three different firms that differ only in the manner in which they finance their working capital. Firm A takes the aggressive approach, Firm C takes the conservative approach, and Firm M takes the moderate approach.

Notice in Table 17-2 that Firm A, which follows an aggressive financing approach, has the highest net income, smallest amount of net working capital, the lowest current ratio, and the highest return on stockholders' equity of any of the three firms. This is consistent with the relationship between risk and return (the more risk a firm takes, the more return it earns). There is no guarantee, of course, that net income will be positive.

Firm C, which follows the conservative financing approach, has the lowest net income, the largest amount of net working capital, the highest current ratio, and the lowest return on stockholders' equity of the three firms. This reflects its relatively lower risk and lower return potential.

Firm M, which follows the moderate approach of matching its short-term temporary current assets to its current liabilities is, of course, in a position between the other two.

Table 17-3 summarizes the cost and risk considerations of the aggressive, conservative, and moderate approaches to working capital financing.

In the real world, of course, each firm must decide on its balance of financing sources and its approach to working capital management based on its particular industry and the firm's risk and return strategy.

What's Next

In this chapter, we examined the general working capital policy of a firm. In Chapter 18, we will look at cash. Accounts receivable and inventory will follow in Chapter 19 and short-term financing in Chapter 20.

TABLE 17-2 Ratio Analysis of Approaches to Working Capital Financing Policy (in thousands)

Data as of the End of the Last Fiscal Year	Firm A Aggressive	Firm C Conservative	Firm M Moderate
Temporary Current Assets	$ 200	$ 200	$ 200
Permanent Current Assets	$ 400	$ 400	$ 400
Fixed Assets	$ 600	$ 600	$ 600
Total Assets	$ 1,200	$ 1,200	$ 1,200
Current Liabilities	$ 300	$ 100	$ 200
Long-Term Debt	$ 300	$ 500	$ 400
Stockholders' Equity	$ 600	$ 600	$ 600
Total Liabilities and Equity	$ 1,200	$ 1,200	$ 1,200
Net Income for the Year	$ 126	$ 114	$ 120
Net Working Capital	$ 300	$ 500	$ 400
Current Ratio	2.0	6.0	3.0
Total Debt to Total Assets Ratio	50%	50%	50.0%
Return on Equity	21%	19%	20.0%

TABLE 17-3 The Three Approaches to Working Capital Financing Policy—Cost and Risk Factors

	Aggressive	Conservative	Moderate
Cost	Low	High	In-Between
Risk	High	Low	In-Between

Summary

1. *Explain the importance of managing working capital.*
   A firm's current assets—such as cash, inventory, and accounts receivable—are referred to as working capital. Managing the levels and financing of working capital effectively is necessary to keep the firm's costs and risk under control while maintaining a firm's returns and cash flow over the long term. Firms accumulate working capital because of fluctuations in sales, production, and cash or credit payments. For instance, cash accumulates as accounts are collected and declines when bills are paid. Inventory builds when production exceeds sales and falls when sales exceed production. Accounts receivable rises as credit sales are made and falls when customers pay off their accounts. The combined effect of changes in each current asset account causes working capital to fluctuate. Furthermore, working capital will gradually build up over time unless the firm takes some concrete action to either reinvest the funds in long-term assets or distribute them to the firm's owners.

   Temporary current assets represents the level of current assets that fluctuates, and permanent current assets represents the level of current assets a firm keeps regardless of periodic fluctuations.

2. *Discuss how the trade-off between liquidity and profitability affects a firm's current asset management policy.*
   Current asset management involves a trade-off between the need for liquidity and the desire for profitability. The more current assets a firm holds, the more liquid the firm, because the assets can be converted to cash relatively quickly. However, tying up funds to sustain a certain level of current assets prevents the funds from being invested in long-term, high-return-producing assets.

3. *Describe how a firm reaches an optimal level of current assets.*
   Firms reach an optimal level of current assets when the optimal level for each individual current asset account (mainly cash, inventory, and accounts receivable) is achieved. Separate techniques exist for managing each of the current asset accounts. The techniques for managing each current asset account are described in Chapters 18 and 19.

4. *Discuss the effects of the three approaches to working capital financing policy.*

Short-term interest rates are usually lower than long-term interest rates, so financing working capital with short-term debt generally lowers the firm's financing costs. However, using short-term debt increases the risk that cash won't be available to pay the loans back, and that the firm may have to renew its loans at higher interest rates. Relying on long-term debt and/or equity sources to finance working capital decreases risk because firms repay such obligations in the long term, and firms lock in an interest rate. A firm's return suffers, however, because long-term financing costs are normally higher than short-term costs.

The aggressive approach to working capital policy consists of financing all temporary current assets, and some or all long-term permanent current assets, and possibly a portion of fixed long-term assets with short-term debt. The conservative approach to working capital policy consists of financing all permanent current assets and some short-term temporary current assets with long-term debt and/or equity financing. The moderate approach consists of financing temporary current assets with short-term debt, and financing long-term permanent current assets with long-term debt and/or equity.

Key Terms

aggressive working capital financing approach The use of short-term funds to finance all temporary current assets, possibly all or some permanent current assets, and perhaps some fixed assets.

conservative working capital financing approach The use of long-term debt and equity to finance all long-term fixed assets and permanent current assets, in addition to some part of temporary current assets.

moderate working capital financing approach An approach in which a firm finances temporary current assets with short-term funds and permanent current assets and fixed assets with long-term funds.

net working capital The amount of current assets minus the amount of current liabilities of an economic unit.

working capital Another name for the current assets on a firm's balance sheet.

Self-Test

ST-1. Explain the liquidity–profitability trade-off associated with working capital management.

ST-2. How is the optimal level of working capital established?

ST-3. Using the following financial data, draw a diagram showing the company's temporary current assets, permanent current assets, and long-term fixed assets during this last year.

Selected Financial Data for Past Fiscal Year (in thousands)

	Jan 1	Mar 31	Jun 30	Oct 31	Dec 31
Total Assets	$580	$480	$280	$400	$ 58
Fixed Assets	$100	$100	$100	$100	$100

ST-4. As of today, a company has $100,000 of temporary current assets, $50,000 of permanent current assets, and $80,000 of long-term fixed assets. If the company follows the moderate approach to working capital financing, how much of its assets will be financed with short-term debt (current liabilities) and how much will be financed with long-term debt and/or equity as of today?

Review Questions

1. What is working capital?

2. What is the primary advantage to a corporation of investing some of its funds in working capital?

3. Can a corporation have too much working capital? Explain.

4. Explain how a firm determines the optimal level of current assets.

5. What are the risks associated with using a large amount of short-term financing for working capital?

6. What is the matching principle of working capital financing? What are the benefits of following this principle?

7. What are the advantages and disadvantages of the aggressive working capital financing approach?

8. What is the most conservative type of working capital financing plan a company could implement? Explain.

Build Your Communication Skills

CS-1. Research a business you find interesting. Prepare a short report outlining at least two ways that company could increase its liquidity. Consider both asset management and liability management.

CS-2. Choose any company for which you can locate balance sheet data for the last five years. Plot on a graph the company's total assets for each year and connect the data points with a line. Next, plot the company's net fixed assets for each year and connect the data points with a line. Finally, sketch a line that just touches the low points reached by the total asset line across the graph.

You should now have a graph similar to Figure 17-2. Label the appropriate areas of your graph as temporary current assets, permanent current assets, and fixed assets.

Refer to the company's latest balance sheet and note the amount of current liabilities and long-term debt and equity shown. Compare these amounts with the ending amount of current and fixed assets shown on your graph. The results will reveal the company's working capital financing policy. Explain your findings to the class.

Problems

17-1. WPS International has the following balance sheet. Twenty-five percent of its current assets are temporary, and the remainder are permanent current assets.

Working Capital

Cash	$ 150,000	Accounts Payable	$ 100,000
Inventory	120,000	Notes Payable	90,000
Accounts Receivable	80,000	Long-Term Debt	120,000
Fixed Assets	500,000	Common Equity	540,000
Total Assets	$ 850,000	Total Liabilities and Equity	$ 850,000

   a. What is WPS International's working capital?

   b. What is WPS International's net working capital?

   c. Calculate the temporary current assets.

   d. Calculate the permanent current assets.

17-2. Compare the following two firms and decide which has more liquidity. Explain why.

Liquidity

Firm 1		Firm 2	
Cash	$ 10,000	Cash	$ 8,000
Inventory	$ 3,000	Inventory	$ 6,000
Accounts Receivable	$ 2,500	Accounts Receivable	$ 3,500
Net Fixed Assets	$ 15,000	Net Fixed Assets	$ 13,000
Accounts Payable	$ 7,500	Accounts Payable	$ 3,500
Notes Payable	$ 4,000	Notes Payable	$ 11,000
Long-Term Debt	$ 7,000	Long-Term Debt	$ 9,000
Common Equity	$ 12,000	Common Equity	$ 7,000

17-3. Consider the following two companies:

Assessing Liquidity

	Company A	Company B
Cash	$ 1,000	$ 80
Accounts Receivable	400	880
Net Fixed Assets	1,500	1,620
	$ 2,900	$ 2,580
Accounts Payable	$ 900	$ 600
Long-Term Debt	800	1,100
Common Equity	1,200	880
	$ 2,900	$ 2,580

Which of the two firms is the more liquid? Why?

17-4. Capt. Louis Renault's Hikewell Outdoor Equipment Company has the following balance sheet accounts as of the end of last year. One-half current assets are permanent and one-half are temporary.

Cash	$ 30,000	Accounts Payable	$ 100,000
Accounts Receivable	15,000	Notes Payable	60,000
Inventory	130,000	Long-Term Debt	90,000
Fixed Assets	500,000	Common Equity	425,000
	$ 675,000		$ 675,000

a. What is the amount of the company's current assets, its working capital?

b. What is the amount of the company's current liabilities?

c. What is the amount of the company's net working capital?

d. What percentage of temporary current assets is financed by current liabilities? Would you consider this an aggressive approach or a conservative approach?

**Conservative
Working Capital
Financing Approach**

 17-5. Alexander Sebastian, the finance manager of Hikewell Outdoor Equipment Company of problem 17-4, thinks the way the company is financing its current assets is too risky. By the end of next year, he would like the *pro forma* balance sheet to look as follows:

Cash	$ 30,000	Accounts Payable	$ 30,000
Accounts Receivable	15,000	Notes Payable	20,000
Inventory	130,000	Long-Term Debt	150,000
Fixed Assets	500,000	Common Equity	475,000
	$ 675,000		$ 675,000

a. What is the amount of the company's projected current assets, its working capital?

b. What is the amount of the company's projected current liabilities?

c. What is the amount of the company's projected net working capital?

d. What percentage of temporary current assets is projected to be financed by current liabilities? Would you consider this an aggressive approach or a conservative approach?

**Assessing Working
Capital Policy**

17-6. Consider the following balance sheet for Lulu Belle's Killer Guard Dogs, Inc.:

Assets		Liabilities and Equity	
Cash	$ 50	Accounts Payable	$ 80
Marketable Securities	0	Short-Term Debt	90
Accounts Receivable	40	Long-Term Debt	210
Inventories	70	Common Equity	310
Net Fixed Assets	530		$ 690
	$ 690		

a. How much working capital does Lulu Belle have?

b. How much net working capital does Lulu Belle have?

c. What working capital financing policy (aggressive, moderate, or conservative) is Lulu Belle following?

d. Explain what actions Lulu Belle could take to increase the company's liquidity.

17-7. Laroux Products has the following balance sheet. Its temporary current assets are 30 percent of the current assets, and the remaining are permanent current assets.

Cash	$ 100,000	Accounts Payable	$ 600,000
Inventory	$ 200,000	Notes Payable	$ 200,000
Accounts Receivable	$ 150,000	Long-Term Debt	$ 150,000
Net Fixed Assets	$ 550,000	Common Equity	$ 50,000
Total Assets	$ 1,000,000	Total Liabilities and Equity	$ 1,000,000

The company would like to change its financing approach to a more conservative one. Create a new balance sheet using the conservative approach that the company could adopt. Laroux estimates the asset amounts will remain the same.

17-8. Tony Reynolds, CFO for Ridgeway Building Supplies, has determined that the company would run best if it used the moderate approach to financing. Recently, the company has thought about switching to this approach. The following is a partial balance sheet stating its assets. Permanent current assets are assumed to be 60 percent of the current assets.

Cash	$ 50,000	Accounts Payable	_____
Accounts Receivable	25,000	Notes Payable	_____
Inventory	150,000	Long-Term Debt	_____
Fixed Assets	475,000	Common Equity	_____
	$ 700,000		

What would the company's financing look like if Tony switched to the moderate approach? Calculate for the following scenarios:

a. Accounts payable is $40,000; common equity is $200,000.

b. Accounts payable is $30,000; common equity is $425,000.

17-9. Using the information given in problem 17-8, what would Ridgeway Building Supplies' financing look like if Tony decided to use an aggressive approach instead? Accounts payable is $180,000, and common equity is $200,000.

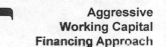

17-10. Marian Pardoo, the chief financial officer of Envirosafe Chemical Company, believes in a moderate approach of financing following the matching principle. Some of the projected balance sheet accounts of the company for the end of next year follow:

Current and Fixed Assets		Permanent Current Assets
Cash	$ 30,000	$ 15,000
Accounts Receivable	15,000	5,000
Inventory	130,000	80,000
Fixed Assets	500,000	
Total Assets	$ 675,000	

Liabilities and Equity	
Accounts Payable	$ 20,000
Short-Term Debt	?
Long-Term Debt	?
Common Equity	450,000
Total Liabilities and Equity	$ 675,000

How much should Marian finance by short-term debt and long-term debt to conform to the matching principle?

17-11. Use the same data given in problem 17-10. Marian's boss, Ann Lowell, is the vice president of finance of Envirosafe Chemical Company and she expects interest rates to decrease in the future and, hence, would like to follow a very aggressive policy using a large amount of short-term debt and a small amount of long-term debt. She would also like to decrease net working capital to $25,000. How much should Ann finance by short-term debt and how much by long-term debt to conform to her aggressive approach?

17-12. Comparative data at the end of this past year for three firms following aggressive, moderate, and conservative approaches to working capital policy follow (in thousands of dollars):

	Aggressive	Moderate	Conservative
Temporary Current Assets	$ 75	$ 75	$ 75
Permanent Current Assets	$ 100	$ 100	$ 100
Fixed Assets	$ 500	$ 500	$ 500
Total Assets	$ 675	$ 675	$ 675
Current Liabilities	$ 160	$ 75	$ 50
Long-Term Debt	$ 90	$ 150	$ 150
Stockholders' Equity	$ 425	$ 450	$ 475
Net Income	$ 70	$ 70	$ 70

Calculate, compare, and comment on the current ratios, total debt to asset ratios, and returns on equity of the three firms.

17-13. Greenplanet Recycling Company is considering buying an additional facility at a cost of $500,000. The facility will have an economic life of five years. The company's financial officer, Karen Holmes, can finance the project by:

a. A five-year loan at an annual interest rate of 13 percent

b. A one-year loan rolled over each year for five years

Compare the total interest expenses for both the preceding alternatives under the following assumptions, and calculate the savings in the interest expenses by choosing one of two alternatives:

1. The one-year loan has a constant interest rate of 11 percent per year over the next five years.

2. The one-year loan has an annual interest rate of 11 percent in the first two years, 14 percent in the third and fourth years, and 16 percent in the fifth year.

**The Matching
Principle**

17-14. To analyze your company's working capital financing policy, you have gathered the following balance sheet data for the past 12 months (in thousands):

Date	Total Assets	Fixed Assets
Jan 31	$45	$14
Feb 28	$46	$14
Mar 31	$34	$14
Apr 30	$48	$14
May 31	$40	$14
Jun 30	$30	$14
Jul 31	$28	$14
Aug 31	$39	$14
Sep 30	$45	$14
Oct 31	$39	$14
Nov 30	$52	$14
Dec 31	$50	$14

Plot these data on a trendline graph. Indicate the amount of your firm's current liabilities each month if you follow the matching principle.

For more, see 8e
Spreadsheet Templates
for *Microsoft Excel.*

17-15. Milton Warden, the finance manager of WinHeart Gift Company, is analyzing past data on the firm's fixed assets, permanent current assets, and temporary current assets for each month over the last five years. The company maintains level production, but its sales are seasonal. He found that the monthly level of the three types of assets over the last five years could be closely approximated by the following patterns (in thousands of dollars):

Comprehensive Problem

- Fixed assets remained constant at 39 each month over the last five years.

- Permanent current assets were equal to 2 in January of year 1 and had grown 0.16 per month each month over the last five years.

For more, see 8e Spreadsheet Templates for *Microsoft Excel.*

- Temporary current assets followed the same pattern each year, starting at 0 in January, then each year they increased by 1 monthly until July and reduced by 1 monthly until they reached 0 again in January of the next year.

  a. Plot these data on a graph similar to the one shown in Figure 17-2.

  b. Calculate and identify on the graph the level of temporary current assets, permanent current assets, and fixed assets in:

    1. The month of September of year 4

    2. The month of August of year 5

  c. Now calculate the levels of current liabilities in those months if the company followed:

    1. An aggressive working capital financing approach

    2. A moderate working capital financing approach

    3. A conservative working capital financing approach

  Assume that the stockholders' equity remained constant at 20 over those five years.

17-16. Buddy Love, a finance officer of Christmas Tree Ornaments and Gifts Company, is analyzing past data on the fixed assets, permanent current assets, and temporary current assets of the company each month over the last several years. The company maintains level production, but its sales peak at the end of the year. He found that the monthly level of the three types of assets over the last five years could be closely approximated by the following equations (in thousands of dollars):

Comprehensive Problem

- Fixed assets were equal to 55 and remained constant each month over the last five years.

- Permanent current assets were equal to 10 in January of year 1 and had grown 0.30 per month each month over the last five years.

For more, see 8e Spreadsheet Templates for *Microsoft Excel.*

- Temporary current assets = $m(m - 1)/4$, where m = 1, 2, . . . , 12 for Jan, Feb, . . . , Dec, respectively.

  a. Plot these data on a graph similar to the one shown in Figure 17-2.

  b. Calculate and identify on your graph the level of temporary current assets, permanent current assets, and fixed assets at the following times:

    1. The month of September of year 2

    2. The month of October of year 4

    3. Year 5's minimum and maximum levels of total assets and the months those levels occurred

  c. Now calculate the levels of current liabilities in the months described in part *b* of this problem if the company followed:

    1. An aggressive working capital financing approach

    2. A moderate working capital financing approach

    3. A conservative working capital financing approach

  Assume that the stockholders' equity remained constant at 30 over those five years.

Answers to Self-Test

ST-1. Working capital (i.e., current assets in the form of cash, accounts receivable, inventory, and so on) can normally be exchanged for cash, or liquidated, in a relatively short time. Therefore, the more working capital a company maintains, the easier it is to raise cash quickly. However, maintaining working capital costs money and it ties up funds that could otherwise be used to invest in long-term income-producing assets, so profits and returns suffer. For this reason, we say that managing working capital involves balancing liquidity and profitability.

ST-2. The optimal level of working capital is achieved when the optimal levels of each current asset account—cash, inventory, accounts receivable, and any others—are reached. Each current asset category is managed separately and the combined results produce the optimal level of current assets.

ST-4. Following the moderate approach, the company will finance its temporary current assets with short-term debt and the rest of its assets with long-term debt and equity. Therefore, as of today, the company will have on its balance sheet:

Current Liabilities	$100,000
Long-Term Debt and Equity	$130,000

ST-3.

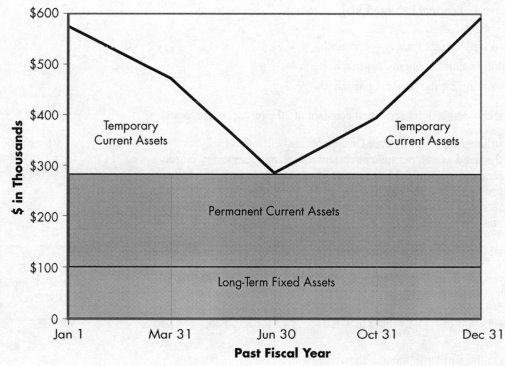

Managing Cash

"There's nothing wrong with cash. It gives you time to think."
—Robert Prechter Jr.

CHAPTER 18

Source: rvisoft/Shutterstock

Learning Objectives

After reading this chapter, you should be able to:

1. List the factors that affect a company's desired minimum cash balance.
2. List the factors that affect a company's desired maximum cash balance.
3. Apply the Miller–Orr model to establish a target optimal cash balance.
4. Prepare a cash budget.
5. Explain how firms manage their cash inflows and outflows to maximize value.

The Importance of Cash

Commercial banks provide a variety of cash management services to business customers. These banks create systems so that the customer can collect on receivables in a timely manner and pay obligations, but not too soon. These services may include credit checks on firms requesting purchases from the bank's customer on credit. This focuses on the quality of the bank customer's accounts receivable. Customer excess funds may be invested by the bank in appropriate short-term marketable securities. Payroll checks may be sent out to employees. There are electronic transfer services offered. Armored cars may be offered to companies that require them. These banks have many ways to help a business customer speed up collections and slow down disbursements.

Most companies of significant size outsource these cash management duties to commercial banks. Cash management is probably not a core competency of most firms. The time of their employees is probably better utilized in producing and selling the company's products. The commercial banks operating in this area provide expertise that has value to the company.

This chapter will focus on the management of that most important asset, cash.

Chapter Overview

In this chapter, we look at how firms manage cash. Cash flow management can even mean electronic cash, as shown in the chapter opening. Here we start by exploring factors that affect a company's optimal cash balance and learn how to estimate the optimal balance. Then we examine how firms forecast their cash needs, develop a cash budget, and manage cash inflows and outflows.

Cash Management Concepts

Whether they work in a large multinational corporation or a small business, financial managers need to know how much cash to keep on hand. Cash management may sound simple. Shouldn't businesses accumulate as much cash as possible? It's not that easy. Recall from Chapter 17 that cash earns no return for the business owners. In fact, a business that accumulated as much cash as possible and did not invest in any assets would fail because it would earn no return for the stockholders. Cash, then, should not be obtained for its own sake. Rather, it should be considered the "grease" that enables the machinery of the firm to run. Cash management is the process of controlling how much of this grease is needed and where and when to apply it.

Determining the Optimal Cash Balance

To determine how much cash a firm should keep on hand, financial managers must:

- Maintain enough in the cash account to make payments when needed (minimum balance)
- Keep just the needed amount in the cash account so that the firm can invest excess funds and earn returns (maximum balance)

Let's examine the factors that affect the desired minimum cash balance and the desired maximum cash balance.

The Desired Minimum Cash Balance

The size of a firm's desired minimum cash balance depends on three factors: (1) how quickly and cheaply a firm can raise cash when needed; (2) how accurately the firm's managers can predict when cash payment requirements will occur; and (3) how much precautionary cash the firm's managers want to keep to safeguard against emergencies. The effect of these three factors on the desired minimum cash balance is shown in Figure 18-1. We examine the three factors that affect a firm's desired minimum cash balance in the following sections.

FIGURE 18-1
Factors Affecting the Desired Minimum Cash Balance

Figure 18-1 shows the three factors that determine the minimum amount a firm will keep in its account.

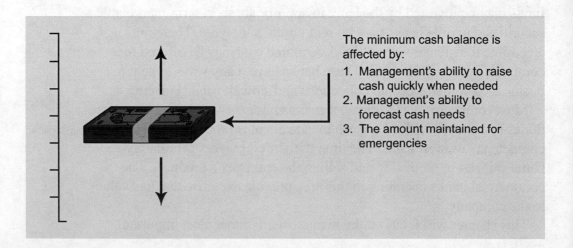

The minimum cash balance is affected by:
1. Management's ability to raise cash quickly when needed
2. Management's ability to forecast cash needs
3. The amount maintained for emergencies

Raising Cash Quickly When Needed

If a firm's managers could obtain cash instantly whenever they needed it, at zero cost, they wouldn't need to maintain any balance in the cash account at all. All the firm's funds could be invested in short-term income-producing securities as soon as received. In the real world, of course, neither firms nor anyone else can borrow or sell assets to raise all the cash they want anytime, instantly, at zero cost. In practice, obtaining cash usually takes time and has a positive cost. Therefore, businesses maintain at least some cash in their checking accounts.

The question is, how much cash is enough? The answer is, only experience will tell. The more difficult or expensive it is to get cash when needed, the more a firm needs to keep in its checking account. At most—if cash were very difficult to obtain because the firm had no liquid assets, or if short-term interest rates were very high—the firm would want to keep enough cash on hand to cover all foreseeable needs until the next time the firm expects to receive more cash.

Predicting Cash Needs

Cash flows can be volatile because of the business environment or the risk of the business. For instance, in a weak economy, people and firms pay bills more slowly. So even though sales may be strong, a firm may not have much cash. Also, in an economy with interest rate fluctuations or inflation, cash flow needs can vary suddenly because of economic factors. To protect against an uncertain business environment, firms may maintain extra cash to cover cash needs.

Similarly, the cash flows of a start-up or high-risk business may vary because the company grows at uneven, often unpredictable rates. Managers, then, may have a tough time estimating the firm's cash needs with certainty. Such firms often keep extra cash to act as a buffer against cash flow volatility.

How much extra cash a firm keeps in its coffers to protect against uncertainty depends on two factors: how difficult and expensive it is to raise cash when needed, and how volatile the firm's cash flow patterns are.

Coping with Emergencies

Most cash payments are expected and planned. But unforeseen emergencies may occur: storms, fires, strikes, riots, and, most often, failure of business plans to materialize. These emergencies can cause unexpected, sometimes large, drains on a firm's cash. Insurance can help, but there is no substitute for having cash ready when you need it. Managers, then, assess the likelihood of potential emergencies and how quickly and easily cash can be obtained in case of an emergency. They adjust their cash balances accordingly. The more *risk averse* managers are, the more precautionary cash they try to keep on hand for emergencies.

The Desired Maximum Cash Balance

Suppose that a firm's managers decide they wish to keep at least $20,000 in the firm's cash account. The next question is, how much should be allowed to accumulate in the cash account before the excess is withdrawn and invested in something that produces a return? If the balance in the cash account is $20,001, for example, should a dollar be withdrawn and invested? Should $30,000 be allowed to accumulate before any is withdrawn and invested? The answer depends on three factors: (1) the available investment opportunities, (2) the expected return from these opportunities, and (3) the transaction cost of withdrawing cash and making an investment. The factors that affect a firm's desired maximum cash balance are summarized in Figure 18-2. We describe the three factors affecting the desired maximum cash balance in detail next.

Available Investment Opportunities

All businesses have at least a few (and some have many) alternative short-term income-producing investments in which they could invest their cash. These range from money

FIGURE 18-2
Factors Affecting the
Desired Maximum Cash
Balance

Figure 18-2 shows the three
factors that affect a firm's
maximum cash balance.

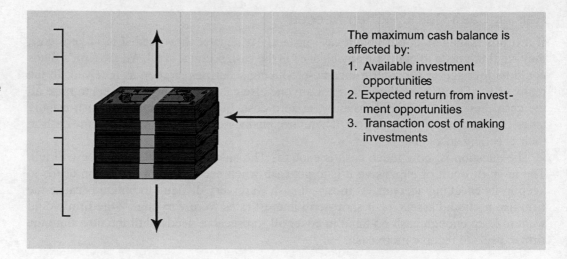

The maximum cash balance is
affected by:
1. Available investment
   opportunities
2. Expected return from investment opportunities
3. Transaction cost of making
   investments

market mutual funds and CDs to Eurodollars and commercial paper. The more opportunities a firm has, the sooner it will invest rather than allow cash to simply accumulate in the
firm's checking account.

Expected Return on Investments

The potential return on investments is just as important as the number of investments. If the
expected return is relatively high, firms will be quick to invest excess cash. If the expected
return is relatively low, however, firms might let more cash accumulate before investing.

Transaction Cost of Making Investments

Investing has costs. For instance, when you deposit money in a savings account, someone
must search for information about and arrange for the transfer of the funds to the savings
account. The search and implementation efforts take time. And that time has a cost.

Monetary and other costs of transferring cash into an investment are **transaction
costs**—the costs associated with the transaction. Managers are interested in transaction
costs because if the potential income from an investment does not exceed the cost of
making the investment, then the investment is not worthwhile. Transaction costs also
affect the frequency of a firm's investments. If transaction costs are relatively low, the
firm will invest often and will let only a small amount of excess cash accumulate in the
cash account. Conversely, if transaction costs are relatively high, the firm will make fewer
investments, letting a larger amount of cash accumulate in the meantime.

In this section, we have seen that firms determine some minimum and maximum amount
to keep in their cash accounts. The minimum amount is based on how quickly and cheaply
firms can raise cash when needed, how accurately cash needs can be predicted, and how
much precautionary cash a firm keeps for emergencies. The maximum amount depends
on available investment opportunities, the expected returns from the investments, and the
transaction costs of withdrawing the cash and making the investment.

The Optimal Cash Balance

Financial theorists have developed mathematical models to help firms find an optimal
"target" cash balance, between the minimum and maximum limits, that balances liquidity
and profitability concerns. In the following sections, we discuss one of these models, the
Miller–Orr model.

The Miller–Orr Cash Management Model

In 1966, Merton Miller and Daniel Orr developed a cash management model that solves
for an optimal target cash balance about which the cash balance fluctuates until it reaches
an upper or lower limit. If the upper limit is reached, investment securities are bought,

transaction cost The cost
of making a transaction,
usually the cost associated
with purchasing or selling a
security.

Take Note
The pattern of lottery
ticket sales illustrates
the principle of expected
return on investments.
When the jackpot is
relatively low, ticket sales
are sluggish. When the
jackpot is relatively high,
ticket sales increase.

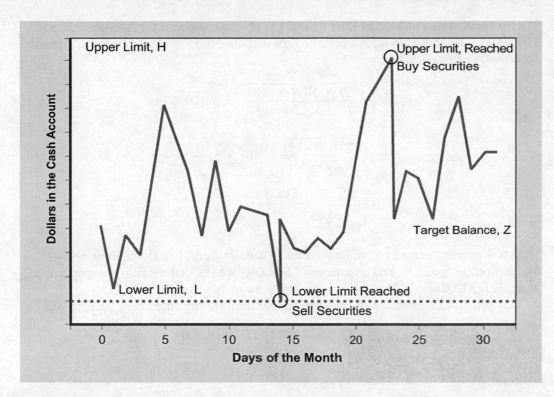

FIGURE 18-3

Cash Balances in a Typical Month Using the Miller–Orr Model

Figure 18-3 shows a firm's fluctuating cash flows, and its upper, lower, and optimal cash balances according to the Miller–Orr model.

bringing the cash balance down to the target again. If the lower limit is reached, investment securities are sold, bringing the cash balance up to the target. Figure 18-3 shows the operation of the model.

The formula for the target cash balance Z shown in Figure 18-3 follows:

Miller–Orr Model Formula for the Target Cash Balance (Z)

$$Z = \sqrt[3]{\frac{3 \times TC \times V}{4 \times r}} + L$$

(18-1)

where: TC = Transaction cost of buying or selling short-term investment securities

V = Variance of net daily cash flows

r = Daily rate of return on short-term investment securities

L = Lower limit to be maintained in the cash account

Remember that to take the cube root of a number you raise that number to the 1/3 power.

Notice in Figure 18-3 that the target cash balance, Z, is one-third of the way between the lower limit, L, and the upper limit, H. The Miller–Orr formula for the upper limit, H, is as follows:

Miller–Orr Model Formula for the Upper Limit on the Cash Account (H)

$$H = 3Z - 2L$$

(18-2)

In the Miller–Orr model, the lower limit, L, is set by management according to the desired minimum cash balance concerns discussed earlier.

To illustrate how the Miller–Orr model works, assume that short-term investment securities are yielding 4 percent per year and that it costs the firm $30 each time it buys or sells investment securities. Now assume that the firm's cash inflows and outflows occur irregularly and that the variance of the daily net cash flows has been found to be $90,846.

Management wants to keep at least $10,000 in the cash account for emergencies, so L = $10,000. Under these circumstances, the firm will have the following target cash balance, according to Equation 18-1:

$$Z = \sqrt[3]{\frac{3 \times 30 \times \$90,846}{4 \times (.04/365)}} + \$10,000$$

$$= \sqrt[3]{\frac{\$8,176,140}{.00043836}} + \$10,000$$

$$= \$2,652 + \$10,000$$

$$= \$12,652$$

With a 4 percent annual return (converted to a daily figure), a lower limit of $10,000, transaction costs of $30, and a variance of $90,846, we see that the firm's target cash balance, Z, is $12,652.

According to Equation 18-2, the firm's upper limit for the target cash balance will be

$$H = (3 \times \$12,652) - (2 \times \$10,000)$$

$$= \$37,956 - \$20,000$$

$$= \$17,956$$

According to the Miller–Orr model, then, the firm in this example will seek to maintain $12,652 in its cash account. If the cash balance increases to $17,956, the firm will buy $5,304 worth of investment securities to return the balance to $12,652. If the cash balance falls to $10,000, the firm will sell $2,652 worth of investment securities to raise the cash balance to $12,652. By finding the optimal cash balance, the firm seeks to accommodate its cash needs, given the volatility of cash inflows and outflows, and maximize its investment opportunities. We see, then, that the Miller–Orr model can help firms find their optimal cash balance.

Now that we have examined factors that affect a firm's minimum, maximum, and optimal cash balances and described how a firm may find its target cash balance, we next look at how a firm can forecast its cash needs.

Forecasting Cash Needs

Financial managers must frequently provide detailed estimates of their firm's future cash needs. The primary purpose of such estimates is to identify when excess cash will be available and when outside financing will be required to make up cash shortages.

Financial managers cannot base future cash estimates on *pro forma* income statements for the appropriate time period. Why? Because income and expenses are not always received and paid for in cash. Remember, if a firm is using an accrual-based accounting system, revenues and expenses may be recognized in one accounting period, but cash may not change hands until another period.

cash budget A detailed budget plan that shows the cash flows expected to occur during specific time periods.

One technique for estimating true future cash needs is to develop a cash budget. A **cash budget** is a detailed budget plan that shows where cash is expected to come from and where it is expected to go during a given period of time.

The best way to learn about cash budgets is to practice creating one. In the following sections, we will develop a cash budget for Bulldog Batteries that shows detailed cash flows from month to month throughout the upcoming year.

Developing a Cash Budget

The first step in developing a monthly cash budget is to identify sales revenue for each month of the period covered by the budget. Assume that it is the end of December 2018 and that Bulldog Batteries' 2019 sales are expected to occur as follows:

	Sales
Nov 2018 (reference)	$ 13,441
Dec 2018 (reference)	13,029
Jan 2019	12,945
Feb 2019	14,794
Mar 2019	16,643
Apr 2019	18,492
May 2019	20,341
Jun 2019	22,191
Jul 2019	24,040
Aug 2019	22,191
Sep 2019	20,341
Oct 2019	18,492
Nov 2019	16,643
Dec 2019	14,794
2019 Total	$ 221,907

Next, assume all of Bulldog's sales are on credit, so no cash is received immediately when a sale is made. Experience from past sales reveals that 30 percent of Bulldog's customers will pay off their accounts in the month of sale, 60 percent will pay off their accounts in the month following the sale, and the remaining 10 percent of the customers will pay off their accounts in the second month following the sale. Given this payment pattern, Bulldog's actual cash collections on sales throughout the year will follow the pattern shown in Table 18-1.

In Table 18-1, we computed January's cash collections as follows:

30% of January's 2019's Sales:	.30 × $12,945 = $	3,884
+ 60% of December 2018's Sales:	.60 × $13,029 =	7,817
+ 10% of November 2018's Sales:	.10 × $13,441 =	1,344
= Total Collections in January 2019:		$ 13,045

Collections for the other months are computed similarly.

The next step in developing the cash budget is to turn to cash outflows. Assume that Bulldog Batteries' cost of materials is 27 percent of sales. Bulldog manufactures batteries expected to be sold in February one month ahead of time in January, and it orders all the materials it needs for January's production schedule one month ahead of time in December. This schedule repeats for each month of the year. Bulldog makes all its purchases on credit and pays for them in cash during the month following the purchase. Therefore, December's purchase orders will be paid for in January, and so on. The situation is summarized in Figure 18-4.

> **Take Note**
> If Bulldog's managers expected other cash receipts during 2019, they would add them to sales collections in the appropriate month to obtain the total cash inflows for each month, as shown in Table 18-1.

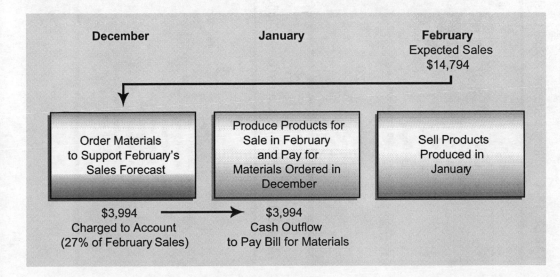

FIGURE 18-4
Timing for Bulldog Batteries' Cash Payments for Purchases

Figure 18-4 shows Bulldog Batteries' production and cash flow schedule.

TABLE 18-1 Bulldog Batteries, Actual Cash Collections

Cash Inflows	2018 Nov	2018 Dec	2019 Jan	Feb	Mar	Apr	May	Jun	Jul	Aug	Sep	Oct	Nov	Dec
Sales (reference only; not a cash flow)	$13,441	$13,029	$12,945	$14,794	$16,643	$18,492	$20,341	$22,191	$24,040	$22,191	$20,341	$18,492	$16,643	$14,794
Cash collections on sales:														
30% in month of sale			$3,884	$4,438	$4,993	$5,548	$6,102	$6,657	$7,212	$6,657	$6,102	$5,548	$4,993	$4,438
60% in first month after sale			$7,817	$7,767	$8,876	$9,986	$11,095	$12,205	$13,315	$14,424	$13,315	$12,205	$11,095	$9,986
10% in second month after sale			$1,344	$1,303	$1,295	$1,479	$1,664	$1,849	$2,034	$2,219	$2,404	$2,219	$2,034	$1,849
Total collections			$13,045	$13,508	$15,164	$17,013	$18,862	$20,711	$22,561	$23,300	$21,821	$19,971	$18,122	$16,273
Other cash receipts			$0	$0	$0	$0	$0	$0	$0	$0	$0	$0	$0	$0
Total Cash Inflows			$13,045	$13,508	$15,164	$17,013	$18,862	$20,711	$22,561	$23,300	$21,821	$19,971	$18,122	$16,273

TABLE 18-2 Bulldog Batteries, Cash Outflows for Materials Purchases

	2018 Nov	2018 Dec	2019 Jan	Feb	Mar	Apr	May	Jun	Jul	Aug	Sep	Oct	Nov	Dec
Sales (reference only; not a cash flow)	$13,441	$13,029	$12,945	$14,794	$16,643	$18,492	$20,341	$22,191	$24,040	$22,191	$20,341	$18,492	$16,643	$14,794
Materials purchases (27% of sales two months ahead—reference only, not a cash flow)		$3,994	$4,494	$4,993	$5,492	$5,992	$6,491	$5,992	$5,492	$4,993	$4,494	$3,994	$3,872	
Payments for materials purchases: 100% in month after purchase			$3,994	$4,494	$4,993	$5,492	$5,992	$6,491	$5,992	$5,492	$4,993	$4,494	$3,994	$3,872

TABLE 18-3 Bulldog Batteries, Total Cash Outflows

	2018	2019											
	Dec	Jan	Feb	Mar	Apr	May	Jun	Jul	Aug	Sep	Oct	Nov	Dec
Cash Outflows:													
Materials purchases (reference only; not a cash flow)	$3,994	$ 4,494	$ 4,993	$ 5,492	$ 5,992	$ 6,491	$ 5,992	$ 5,492	$ 4,993	$ 4,494	$ 3,994	$ 3,872	$ 3,872
Payments for materials purchases: 100% in month after purchase		$ 3,994	$ 4,494	$ 4,993	$ 5,492	$ 5,992	$ 6,491	$ 5,992	$ 5,492	$ 4,993	$ 4,494	$ 3,994	$ 3,872
Other cash payments:													
Production costs other than purchases		$ 3,994	$ 4,494	$ 4,993	$ 5,492	$ 5,992	$ 6,491	$ 5,992	$ 5,492	$ 4,993	$ 4,494	$ 3,994	$ 3,872
Selling and marketing expenses		$ 2,333	$ 2,667	$ 3,000	$ 3,333	$ 3,666	$ 4,000	$ 4,333	$ 4,000	$ 3,667	$ 3,333	$ 3,000	$ 2,667
General and administrative expenses		$ 903	$ 903	$ 903	$ 903	$ 903	$ 903	$ 903	$ 903	$ 903	$ 903	$ 903	$ 903
Interest payments													2,971
Tax payments					$ 4,995		$ 4,995			$ 4,995			$ 4,995
Dividend payments				$ 6,098			$ 6,098			$ 6,098			6,098
Total Cash Outflows		$ 11,225	$ 12,557	$ 19,987	$ 20,215	$ 16,553	$ 28,978	$ 17,219	$ 15,887	$ 25,649	$ 13,223	$ 11,892	$ 25,378

TABLE 18-4 Bulldog Batteries, Cash Inflows and Outflows and Net Cash Flows

	2019											
	Jan	Feb	Mar	Apr	May	Jun	Jul	Aug	Sep	Oct	Nov	Dec
Total Cash Inflows	$ 13,045	$ 13,508	$ 15,164	$ 17,013	$ 18,862	$ 20,711	$ 22,561	$ 23,300	$ 21,821	$ 19,971	$ 18,122	$ 16,273
Total Cash Outflows	$ 11,225	$ 12,557	$ 19,987	$ 20,215	$ 16,553	$ 28,978	$ 17,219	$ 15,887	$ 25,649	$ 13,223	$ 11,892	$ 25,378
Net Cash Gain (Loss)	$ 1,820	$ 951	($ 4,823)	($ 3,203)	$ 2,309	($ 8,267)	$ 5,342	$ 7,413	($ 3,828)	$ 6,748	$ 6,230	($ 9,105)

Take Note
If you are reading this on your computer screen using the Adobe Reader program, click on View/ Rotate View/Clockwise to read this table in proper orientation. When you are finished reading the table, click on View/ Rotate View/ Counterclockwise to return to the regular page orientation.

TABLE 18-5 Cash Flow and Financing Requirements Summary, January 2019

Cash Flow Summary	
1. Cash balance at start of month	$ 65,313
2. Net cash gain (loss) during month	1,820
3. Cash balance at end of month before financing	67,133
4. Desired minimum cash balance desired	65,000
5. Surplus cash (deficit) (line 3 – line 4)	$ 2,133
External Financing Summary	
6. External financing balance at start of month	$ 302
7. New financing required (negative amount on line 5)	0
8. Financing repayments (positive amount on line 5*)	302
9. External financing balance at end of month	0
10. Cash balance at end of month after financing (balance on line 3 + new financing on line 7 – repayments on line 8)	$ 66,831

*If the positive amount on line 5 exceeds the external financing balance on line 6, enter the external financing balance on line 6.

If Bulldog follows the production schedule illustrated in Figure 18-4 throughout 2019, its cash outflows for materials purchases will be as shown in Table 18-2. (Materials purchases for November and December of 2019 are based on sales forecasts for January and February 2020 of $14,342,000 and $14,794,000, respectively.)

For the sake of simplicity, assume Bulldog's remaining cash outflows are all direct expenses paid for in the month incurred as follows:

- Production expenses other than purchases are equal to purchases. (Bulldog's production costs are split evenly between materials cost and other production costs.)

- Sales and marketing expenses are 18.025 percent of sales each month.

- General and administrative expenses are $903,000 each month.

- Interest expense is expected to be $2,971 for the year. We assume that expense will be paid all at one time in December 2019.

- Bulldog's expected income tax bill for 2019 is $19,980. The bill will be paid in four installments in April, June, September, and December.

- Bulldog expects to declare four quarterly dividends of $6,098 in 2019. These will be paid in March, June, September, and December.

Bulldog's total cash outflows, including the preceding expenses and payments for materials purchases, are shown in Table 18-3.

After all the cash inflows and outflows for each month are accounted for (as we have done, see Tables 18-1, 18-2, and 18-3), the next step is to summarize the net gain (or loss) for each month in 2019. Table 18-4 contains the summary.

The final step in developing the cash budget is to summarize the effects of the monthly net cash flows on monthly cash balances and list any external financing required. The procedure for January 2019 is shown in Table 18-5. We assume a cash balance of $65,313 at the beginning of January, a desired target cash balance of $65,000, and short-term loans of $302 outstanding at the beginning of the month.

The procedure is repeated for February using January's cash balance at the end of the month after financing as the starting cash balance for February. Table 18-6 contains the 12-month summary for Bulldog Batteries.

TABLE 18-6 Bulldog Batteries, 12-Month Summary of Cash Flow and Financing Requirements

	2018	2019											
	Dec	Jan	Feb	Mar	Apr	May	Jun	Jul	Aug	Sep	Oct	Nov	Dec
Cash Flow Summary													
1. Cash balance at start of month		$ 65,313	$ 66,831	$ 67,782	$ 65,000	$ 65,000	$ 65,000	$ 65,000	$ 65,000	$ 66,554	$ 65,000	$ 69,473	$ 75,704
2. Net cash gain (loss) during month		$ 1,820	$ 951	($ 4,823)	($ 3,203)	$ 2,309	($ 8,267)	$ 5,341	$ 7,413	($ 3,828)	$ 6,748	$ 6,230	($ 9,105)
3. Cash balance at end of month before financing (line 1 plus line 2)		$ 67,133	$ 67,782	$ 62,959	$ 61,797	$ 67,309	$ 56,733	$ 70,341	$ 72,413	$ 62,725	$ 71,748	$ 75,704	$ 66,598
4. Minimum cash balance desired		$ 65,000	$ 65,000	$ 65,000	$ 65,000	$ 65,000	$ 65,000	$ 65,000	$ 65,000	$ 65,000	$ 65,000	$ 65,000	$ 65,000
5. Surplus cash (deficit) (line 3 minus line 4)		$ 2,133	$ 2,782	($ 2,041)	($ 3,203)	$ 2,309	($ 8,267)	$ 5,341	$ 7,413	($ 2,275)	$ 6,748	$ 10,704	$ 1,598
External Financing Summary													
6. External financing balance at start of month		$ 302	$ 0	$ 0	$ 2,041	$ 5,243	$ 2,934	$ 11,201	$ 5,860	$ 0	$ 2,275	$ 0	$ 0
7. New financing required (negative amount from line 5)		$ 0	$ 0	$ 2,041	$ 3,203	$ 0	$ 8,267	$ 0	$ 0	$ 2,275	$ 0	$ 0	$ 0
8. Financing repayments (positive amount from line 5 not to exceed line 6)		$ 302	$ 0	$ 0	$ 0	$ 2,309	$ 0	$ 5,341	$ 5,860	$ 0	$ 2,275	$ 0	$ 0
9. External financing balance at end of month	$302	$ 0	$ 0	$ 2,041	$ 5,243	$ 2,934	$ 11,201	$ 5,860	$ 0	$ 2,275	$ 0	$ 0	$ 0
10. Cash balance at end of month after financing (line 3 + line 7 – line 8)		$ 66,831	$ 67,782	$ 65,000	$ 65,000	$ 65,000	$ 65,000	$ 65,000	$ 66,554	$ 65,000	$ 69,473	$ 75,704	$ 66,598

TABLE 18-7 Bulldog Batteries, Complete Cash Budget

	2018 Nov	2018 Dec	2019 Jan	Feb	Mar	Apr	May	Jun	Jul	Aug	Sep	Oct	Nov	Dec
Cash Inflows:														
Sales (reference only; not a cash flow)	$13,441	$13,029	$12,945	$14,794	$16,643	$18,492	$20,341	$22,191	$24,040	$22,191	$20,341	$18,492	$16,643	$14,794
Cash collections on sales:														
30% in month of sale			3,884	4,438	4,993	5,548	6,102	6,657	7,212	6,657	6,102	5,548	4,993	4,438
60% in first month after sale			7,817	7,767	8,876	9,986	11,095	12,205	13,212	14,424	13,315	12,205	11,095	9,986
10% in second month after sale			1,344	1,303	1,295	1,479	1,664	1,849	2,034	2,219	2,404	2,219	2,034	1,849
Total collections			13,045	13,508	15,164	17,013	18,862	20,711	22,561	23,300	21,821	19,971	18,122	16,273
Other cash receipts			0	0	0	0	0	0	0	0	0	0	0	0
Total Cash Inflows			$13,045	$13,508	$15,164	$17,013	$18,862	$20,711	$22,561	$23,300	$21,821	$19,971	$18,122	$16,273
Cash Out flows:														
Materials purchases (reference only; not a cash flow)		$3,994	4,494	4,993	5,492	5,992	6,491	5,992	5,492	4,993	4,494	3,994	3,872	3,994
Payments for materials purchases:														
100% in month after purchase			3,994	4,494	4,993	5,492	5,992	6,491	5,992	5,492	4,993	4,494	3,994	3,872
Other cash payments:														
Production costs other than purchases			3,994	4,494	4,993	5,492	5,992	6,491	5,992	5,492	4,993	4,494	3,994	3,872
Selling and marketing expenses			2,333	2,667	3,000	3,333	3,666	4,000	4,333	4,000	3,667	3,333	3,000	2,667
General and administrative expenses			903	903	903	903	903	903	903	903	903	903	903	903
Interest payments														2,971
Tax payments						4,995		4,995			4,995			4,995
Dividend payments					6,098			6,098			6,098			6,098
Total Cash Outflows			$11,225	$12,557	$19,987	$20,215	$16,553	$28,978	$17,219	$15,887	$25,649	$13,223	$11,892	$25,378
Net Cash Gain (Loss)			$1,820	$951	($4,823)	($3,203)	$2,309	($8,267)	$5,341	$7,413	($3,828)	$6,748	$6,230	($9,105)
Cash Flow Summary														
1. Cash balance at start of month			$65,313	$66,831	$67,782	$65,000	$65,000	$65,000	$65,000	$65,000	$66,554	$65,000	$69,473	$75,704
2. Net cash gain (loss) during month (line 1 plus line 2)			$1,820	$951	($4,823)	($3,203)	$2,309	($8,267)	$5,341	$7,413	($3,828)	$6,748	$6,230	($9,105)
3. Cash balance at end of month before financing (line 1 plus line 2)			$67,133	$67,782	$62,959	$61,797	$67,309	$56,733	$70,341	$72,413	$62,725	$71,748	$75,704	$66,598
4. Minimum cash balance desired			$65,000	$65,000	$65,000	$65,000	$65,000	$65,000	$65,000	$65,000	$65,000	$65,000	$65,000	$65,000
5. Surplus cash (deficit) (line 3 minus line 4)			$2,133	$2,782	($2,041)	($3,203)	$2,309	($8,267)	$5,341	$7,413	($2,275)	$6,748	$10,704	$1,598
External Financing Summary														
6. External financing balance at start of month			$302	$0	$0	$2,041	$5,243	$2,934	$11,201	$5,860	$0	$2,275	$0	$0
7. New financing required (negative amount from line 5)			$0	$0	$2,041	$3,203	$0	$8,267	$0	$0	$2,275	$0	$0	$0
8. Financing repayments (positive amount from line 5, not to exceed line 6)			$302	$0	$0	$0	$2,309	$0	$5,341	$5,860	$0	$2,275	$0	$0
9. External financing balance at end of month		$302	$0	$0	$2,041	$5,243	$2,934	$11,201	$5,860	$0	$2,275	$0	$0	$0
10. Cash balance at end of month after financing (line 3 plus line 7 minus line 8)			$66,831	$67,782	$65,000	$65,000	$65,000	$65,000	$65,000	$66,554	$65,000	$69,473	$75,704	$66,598

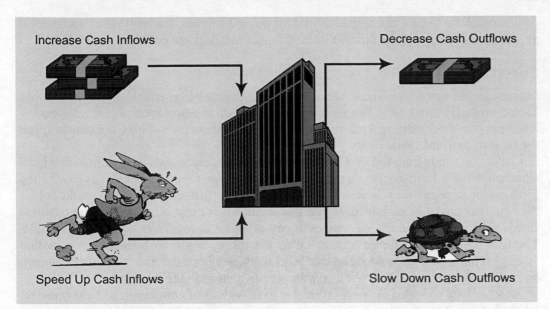

FIGURE 18-5

Managing the Cash Flowing In and Out of the Firm

Figure 18-5 shows the four objectives of cash flow management.

After filling out the cash budget through December 2019, Bulldog's managers can see that the firm will have surplus cash in January and February, but external financing will be needed in March, April, June, and September.

According to the budget, the loans can be fully paid off by October, and $66,598 will be in the cash account at the end of the year. Armed with this information, Bulldog's managers would approach their banker to establish a line of credit with a limit higher than $11,201—the largest anticipated loan balance.

For your convenience, Bulldog's complete cash budget for 2019 is shown in Table 18-7. We have described how to forecast a firm's short-term cash needs by constructing a cash budget. Next, we explore ways to manage a firm's short-term cash flow.

Take Note
Because the financing is only needed for a short time, it is typically obtained from a line of credit or short-term notes.

Managing the Cash Flowing In and Out of the Firm

People who manage a firm's cash should focus on four objectives: (1) to increase the flow of cash into the business; (2) to decrease the flow of cash out of the business; (3) to receive cash as quickly as possible; and (4) to pay cash out as slowly as possible, without missing the due date. This gives you more time to put cash to work earning a return. These four objectives are displayed in Figure 18-5. In the sections that follow, we discuss ways to accomplish the four objectives of cash flow management.

Increasing Cash Inflows

There are really only three ways to increase the amount of cash flowing into a business during any given time period. First, the firm can do more of whatever it is that makes money—that is, a manufacturing business can sell more products or a service business can serve more people. Of course, when sales increase, costs increase too. It is hoped, of course, that the sales revenue increase will be greater than the cost increase. Second, they can raise prices. This may or may not be practical depending on how resistant the market is to price increases. Third, firms can increase the return that the company's assets are earning—that is, find ways to produce more money with the same amount of assets.

Decreasing Cash Outflows

Managers can also increase the *net* amount of cash flowing into their firms during any given time period by decreasing the amount of cash flowing out. That is, by cutting costs.

A less obvious way to decrease cash outflows from the business is to decrease the *risk* of doing business. Risk in business equates to uncertainty, and a business that faces a lot of uncertainty must keep a lot of cash on hand to deal with unexpected events. If a firm

Take Note
Be wary of cost-cutting measures that hurt the business in the long term. For example, a drug company might boost profits now by cutting research and development spending (an expense). But that action will rob the company of new products that would generate extra value.

could somehow reduce the degree of risk of doing business, the number of unexpected events would drop, and the amount needed in the cash account could be reduced.

Speeding Up Cash Inflows

Most business managers would agree that, other things being equal, they would rather have cash earlier than later. This makes sense. The earlier a firm receives cash, the earlier it can put it to work earning a return. Accordingly, managers try to figure out how to speed the flow of cash into their firms.

Collecting funds from the firm's customers more quickly speeds cash inflow. The ideal situation, from a business firm's point of view, would be for all customers to pay for the products or services they buy immediately. However, the realities of the market-place demand that credit be extended. Given that credit often must be extended, the business firm's goal is to encourage customers to pay off their accounts as quickly as possible. The firm might even offer customers a discount if they pay their bills early, say, within 10 days. This technique works, and the firm's managers hope that the return they can earn by getting the cash early outweighs the amount lost through the discount.

Another way to speed up cash inflows is to make use of computerized fund transfers wherever possible. An electronic funds transfer is the act of crediting one account and debiting another automatically by a computer system. Electronic transfer is much faster than checks, which can take over a week to mail and clear.

lockbox A way station (typically a post office box) at which customers may send payments to a firm.

Another method of speeding cash collections is a lockbox system. A **lockbox** system allows customers to send checks to a nearby post office box. The firm arranges for these funds to be deposited in a bank in or near the customer's town for electronic transfer to the receiving firm's account. Here's how a lockbox system works. A San Francisco-based business that has customers nationwide rents post office boxes in major cities all around the country. The firm directs its customers to send payments for their bills to the post office box in the city nearest them. The firm arranges for a bank in each city to pick up the mail from the post office box at least once a day and to deposit any payments received in the firm's account at the bank. From that point on, the funds are immediately available for the firm's use, either from the individual banks directly or by having the banks electronically transfer the funds to the firm's bank in San Francisco. By using the lockbox system, the firm can receive cash two to five days faster than if customers mailed all their payments to San Francisco.

Slowing Down Cash Outflows

Just as speeding up the flow of cash into the firm gives managers more time to earn a return on the cash, so does slowing down the flow of cash out of the firm. Either way, the idea is to increase the amount of time that the firm has possession of the cash. One obvious way to slow down cash outflows is to delay paying bills as long as possible. However, the firm must take great care not to overstep the bounds of good sense and fair play in applying this principle. Imagine what would happen if a firm didn't pay its employees on time or delayed paying suppliers. Its business operations would suffer or it might not stay in business at all. Firms shouldn't pay bills that are due at the end of the month on the first of the month, but neither should they take unfair advantage of creditors by making late payments.

What's Next

This chapter examined how firms manage cash and the factors that determine how large a firm's cash balance will be. In Chapter 19 we study another component of working capital management: accounts receivable and inventory management.

Summary

1. *List the factors that affect a company's desired minimum cash balance.*

   Having a minimum balance ensures that enough money is maintained in the cash account to make payments when needed. The base level to be maintained is affected by: (1) how quickly and cheaply the firm can raise cash when needed; (2) how accurately the firm can predict cash needs; and (3) how much extra the firm wants to keep in the cash account for emergencies.

2. *List the factors that affect a company's desired maximum cash balance.*

   Having a maximum balance ensures that firms limit the cash balance so that the firms invest and earn a return on as much cash as possible. The maximum amount to be maintained is affected by three factors: (1) available investment opportunities; (2) expected returns from these opportunities; and (3) the transaction costs of withdrawing the cash and making the investments.

3. *Apply the Miller–Orr model to establish a target optimal cash balance.*

   The Miller–Orr model recognizes that a firm's cash balance might fluctuate up and down in an irregular fashion over time. The model solves for an optimal target cash balance about which the cash balance fluctuates until it reaches an upper or lower limit. If the upper limit is reached, short-term investment securities are bought, bringing the cash balance down to the target again. If the lower limit is reached, short-term investment securities are sold, bringing the cash balance up to the target.

4. *Prepare a cash budget.*

   Managers use a cash budget to estimate detailed cash needs for future periods. Cash budgets are necessary because *pro forma* income statements and balance sheets do not indicate the actual flow of cash in and out of the firm. A monthly cash budget shows detailed cash flows from month to month throughout the year and how much over or short the firm's cash account will be at the end of each month. By using a cash budget, managers can estimate when it will be necessary to obtain short-term loans from their bank.

5. *Explain how firms manage their cash inflows and outflows to maximize value.*

   The four objectives of cash management are to increase the flow of cash into the business, to decrease the flow of cash out of the business, to receive cash more quickly, and to pay cash out more slowly.

   Ways to increase the flow of cash into the firm include selling more products, serving more customers, and increasing the return earned by the firm's assets. Ways to reduce the flow of cash out of the business include cutting costs and decreasing the degree of risk in the business. Ways to speed up the flow of cash into the business include helping customers pay off their credit accounts more quickly and using electronic funds transfer or lockbox techniques. Ways to slow down the flow of cash out of the firm include taking advantage of credit terms whenever possible.

Key Terms

cash budget A detailed budget plan that shows the cash flows expected to occur during specific time periods.

lockbox A way station (typically a post office box) at which customers may send payments to a firm.

transaction cost The cost of making a transaction, usually the cost associated with purchasing or selling a security.

Equations Introduced in This Chapter

Equation 18-1. Formula for Miller–Orr Model Target Cash Balance:

$$Z = \sqrt[3]{\frac{3 \times TC \times V}{4 \times r}} + L$$

where: TC = Transaction cost of buying or selling short-term investment securities

V = Variance of net daily cash flows

r = Daily rate of return on short-term investment securities

L = Lower limit to be maintained in the cash account

Equation 18-2. Formula for the Upper Limit in the Miller–Orr Model:

$$H = 3Z - 2L$$

where: Z = The target cash balance

L = Lower limit to be maintained in the cash account

Self-Test

ST-1. Assume that short-term investment securities are yielding 5 percent, and it costs a firm $20 each time it buys or sells investment securities. The variance of the firm's daily net cash flows has been found to be $20,000. Management wants to keep at least $1,000 in the cash account for emergencies. Given these conditions, what is the firm's target cash balance?

ST-2. What is the maximum amount the firm in question ST-1 will let accumulate in its cash account before investing excess cash in marketable securities?

ST-3. Continuing with the firm in ST-1 and ST-2, how much will the firm invest in marketable securities if the upper limit in ST-2 is reached?

ST-4. Assume a company has $1,000 in its cash account at the beginning of a month and short-term loan balances of $3,500. If the company experiences a $14,000 net cash inflow during the month and its desired target cash balance is $3,000, how much of the outstanding loans can be paid off this month?

Review Questions

1. What are the primary reasons that companies hold cash?

2. Explain the factors affecting the choice of a desired minimum cash balance amount.

3. What are the negative consequences of a company holding too much cash?

4. Explain the factors affecting the choice of a desired maximum cash balance amount.

5. What is the difference between pro forma financial statements and a cash budget? Explain why *pro forma* financial statements are not used to forecast cash needs.

6. What are the benefits of "collecting early" and how do companies attempt to do this?

7. What are the benefits of "paying late" (but not too late) and how do companies attempt to do this?

8. Refer to the Bulldog Batteries Company's cash budget in Table 18-7. Explain why the company would probably not issue $1 million worth of new common stock in January to avoid all short-term borrowing during the year.

Build Your Communication Skills

CS-1. Assume the company you work for has $10,000 in its cash account on January 1, 2019 and short-term loans outstanding in the amount of $15,000. Net cash flows for January, February, and March 2019 are forecasted to be +$2,000, –5,000, and + $8,000, respectively. Prepare a report for your company's CEO showing any new borrowing required and any possible debt payoffs that may be made during the three-month period. Your company's minimum desired cash balance is $5,000. (Hint: Use the format in Table 18-5.)

CS-2. Assume you work for an electric utility that serves several western states and your boss is concerned that there is too much delay between the time the company's customers pay their bills and the time the cash is actually deposited in the corporation's cash account. Prepare a briefing for your boss outlining a method for streamlining cash collection procedures in such a way that the delay in making cash available is minimized.

Problems

Miller–Orr Model **18-1.** Your company wants to have a desired minimum cash balance of $3,000 and an upper-limit cash balance equal to $9,000. What would be your target cash balance?

Miller–Orr Model **18-2.** Selena Rogers, the financial analyst of Keep-Fit Health Equipment Company, has a short-term investment yield of 3 percent and transaction cost of $40 per transaction. The cash inflows and outflows have traditionally been irregular with a variance of daily net cash flows equal to $39,000. Management of the company wants a desired minimum cash balance of $2,200. Calculate:

   a. The target cash balance

   b. The upper limit of cash balance

18-3. Will Clark, the financial analyst of Get-Fit Health Equipment Company, a competitor of Keep-Fit of problem 18-2, has the same yield and transaction cost. However, the variance of daily net cash flows is equal to $52,000. Management of the company wants a desired minimum cash balance of $3,900. Calculate:

Miller–Orr Model

a. The target cash balance

b. The upper limit of cash balance

18-4. Nire Ltd. has determined that its short-term investments are yielding 5 percent annually, and the cost is $25 each time it buys and sells securities. Nire's total assets amount to $150,000, its variance of net daily cash flows is estimated to be $65,580, and it wants to keep a minimum 10 percent of total assets in a cash account. What is the firm's target cash balance according to the Miller–Orr model?

Miller–Orr Model

18-5. Using the information in problem 18-4, find Nire's upper limit for the cash account according to the Miller–Orr model.

Miller–Orr Model

18-6. Marion Crane, a financial analyst of Lifelong Appliances Company, is trying to develop a cash budget for each month of 2019. The sales are expected to occur as follows:

Cash Inflows

Month	Sales (in thousand dollars)
Nov 2018 (reference)	$131
Dec 2018 (reference)	$129
Jan 2019	$126
Feb 2019	$133
Mar 2019	$139
Apr 2019	$143
May 2019	$191
Jun 2019	$226
Jul 2019	$242
Aug 2019	$224
Sep 2019	$184
Oct 2019	$173
Nov 2019	$166
Dec 2019	$143
Jan 2020 (reference)	$136
Feb 2020 (reference)	$139

For more, see 8e Spreadsheet Templates for *Microsoft Excel.*

Assume all of Lifelong's sales are on credit, so no cash is received immediately when a sale is made. It is expected that 20 percent of Lifelong's customers will pay off their accounts in the month of sale, 70 percent will pay off their accounts in the month following the sale, and the remaining 10 percent of the customers will pay off their accounts in the second month following the sale. Given this payment pattern, help Marion in calculating Lifelong's actual monthly cash collections throughout 2019.

18-7. Use the same sales data given in problem 18-6. To improve the cash collections, Marion has decided to undertake stricter credit terms. With this change she expects that 40 percent of Lifelong's customers will pay off their accounts in the month of sale, 55 percent will pay off their accounts in the month following the sale, and the remaining 5 percent of the customers will pay off their accounts in the second month following the sale. Given this payment pattern, what would be Lifelong's actual monthly cash collections throughout 2019?

Cash Inflows

For more, see 8e Spreadsheet Templates for *Microsoft Excel.*

Cash Inflows

18-8. The following is an estimate of sales revenues for 2019 for Kcir, Inc.

	Sales		Sales		Sales
January	$17,956	May	$22,890	September	$21,650
February	$16,523	June	$22,980	October	$19,250
March	$18,366	July	$23,157	November	$18,920
April	$19,500	August	$23,000	December	$19,069

For more, see 8e Spreadsheet Templates for *Microsoft Excel.*

All purchases are made on credit. History shows that 45 percent of customers will pay off their accounts in the month the purchase is made, 40 percent of customers will pay off their accounts the month following the purchase month, and the remaining 15 percent will pay off their accounts in the second month following the purchase month. Find the cash collections for:

a. March

b. June

c. September

Cash Inflows

18-9. Kcir, Inc., has estimated expenses as follows: (Use the table in Problem 18-8 for sales figures needed to calculate expenses.)

For more, see 8e Spreadsheet Templates for *Microsoft Excel.*

- General and administrative: $2,000/month
- Material purchases: 5 percent of sales (paid the month following the purchase)
- Interest expense: $750.00/year (paid in monthly installments)
- Income tax: $4,500/year (paid in quarterly installments)

Find the cash outflows for the following months.

a. February

b. June

c. November

Challenge Problem ➡

18-10. Use the same sales data given in problem 18-6. Assume that Lifelong's cost of materials is 30 percent of sales. Appliances that are expected to be sold in February will be manufactured one month ahead of time in January, and all the materials needed for January's production schedule will be ordered one month ahead of time in December. This schedule repeats for each month of the year. Lifelong makes all of its purchases on credit and pays for them in cash during the month following the purchase. That is, December's purchase orders are paid for in January, and so on. Assume Lifelong's remaining cash outflows are all direct expenses paid for in the month incurred as follows:

For more, see 8e Spreadsheet Templates for *Microsoft Excel.*

- Production expenses other than purchases are equal to 80 percent of purchases.
- Sales and marketing expenses are 19 percent of sales each month.
- General and administrative expenses are $11,000 each month.
- Interest expense is expected to be $31,000 for the year. Assume it will be paid all at once in December 2019.
- Lifelong's income tax bill for 2019 is expected to be $100,000. The bill will be paid in four equal installments in April, June, September, and December.
- Two semiannual dividends of $50,000 each are expected to be declared in 2019. These will be paid in June and December.

Calculate Lifelong's total cash outflows, including the preceding expenses and payments for materials purchases.

Cash Outflows

18-11. Use the same data given in problem 18-10, except for the payment schedule for materials purchased. Now assume that Lifelong pays for the material purchased in the following manner: 30 percent is paid in cash in the month of purchase, and the remaining 70 percent is paid in cash during the month following the purchase. That is, 30 percent of December's purchase orders are paid for in December, and the balance of 70 percent is paid in January, and so on. With this change, calculate Lifelong's total cash outflows, including the preceding expenses, dividends, and payments for materials purchases.

For more, see 8e Spreadsheet Templates for *Microsoft Excel.*

18-12. Rose Sayer, a financial analyst of Fit-and-Forget Fittings Company, is trying to develop a cash budget for each month of 2019. The sales are expected to occur as follows:

◄ **Comprehensive Problem**

Month	Sales (in thousands dollars)	Month	Sales (in thousands dollars)
Nov 2018 (reference)	$2,266	Jul 2019	$4,164
Dec 2018 (reference)	$2,230	Aug 2019	$3,933
Jan 2019	$2,116	Sep 2019	$3,163
Feb 2019	$2,300	Oct 2019	$2,912
Mar 2019	$2,402	Nov 2019	$2,886
Apr 2019	$2,420	Dec 2019	$2,424
May 2019	$3,390	Jan 2020 (reference)	$2,353
Jun 2019	$3,909	Feb 2020 (reference)	$2,442

Assume all of Fit-and-Forget's sales are on credit, so no cash is received immediately when a sale is made. It is expected that 30 percent of Fit-and-Forget's customers will pay off their accounts in the month of sale, 65 percent will pay off their accounts in the month following the sale, and the remaining 5 percent of the customers will pay off their accounts in the second month following the sale.

Assume that Fit-and-Forget's cost of materials is 20 percent of sales. Fit-and-Forget manufactures fittings expected to be sold in February one month ahead of time, in January. They order all the materials they need for January's production schedule one month ahead of time, in December. This schedule repeats for each month of the year. Fit-and-Forget makes all purchases on credit and pays for the material purchased in the following manner: 20 percent is paid in cash in the month of ordering, and the balance of 80 percent is paid in cash during the month following the purchase. That is, 20 percent of December's purchase orders are paid for in December, and the balance of 80 percent is paid in January, and so on. Assume Fit-and-Forget's remaining cash outflows are all direct expenses paid for in the month incurred as follows:

For more, see 8e Spreadsheet Templates for *Microsoft Excel.*

- Production expenses other than purchases are equal to 14 percent of purchases.

- Sales and marketing expenses are 16 percent of sales each month.

- General and administrative expenses are $180,000 each month.

- Interest expense is expected to be $500,000 for the year. Assume it will be paid all at once in December 2019.

- Fit-and-Forget's income tax bill for 2019 is expected to be $1,600,000. The bill will be paid in four equal installments in April, June, September, and December.

- Two semiannual dividends of $855,000 each are expected to be declared in 2019. These will be paid in June and December.

Assuming a cash balance of $1,133,000 at the beginning of January, a desired target cash balance of $1,110,000, and short-term loans of $50,000 outstanding at the beginning of the month, calculate total cash inflows, total cash outflows, net cash gain (loss), cash flow summary, and external financing (if any) summary in the same format as in Table 18-7.

ST-1. Per Equation 18-1, the firm's target cash balance per the Miller–Orr model is

$$Z = \sqrt[3]{\frac{3 \times 20 \times \$20,000}{4 \times (.05 / 365)}} + \$1,000$$

$$= \sqrt[3]{\frac{\$1,200,000}{.000547945}} + \$1,000$$

$$= \$1,299 + \$1,000$$

$$= \$2,299$$

ST-2. Per Equation 18-2, the upper limit will be

$$H = (3 \times \$2,299) - (2 \times \$1,000)$$

$$= \$6,897 - \$2,000$$

$$= \$4,897$$

ST-3. If the upper limit is reached, the firm will invest the amount necessary to bring the cash balance back down to the target balance level. This amount is

$$\$4,897 - \$2,299 = \$2,598$$

ST-4. A summary of the company's cash flows and external financing is shown next:

Cash Flow Summary

1. Cash balance at start of month	$ 1,000
2. Net cash gain (loss) during month	14,000
3. Cash balance at end of month before financing	15,000
4. Desired minimum cash balance desired	3,000
5. Surplus cash (deficit) (line 3 minus line 4)	$ 12,000

External Financing Summary

6. External financing balance at start of month	$ 3,500
7. New financing required (negative amount on line 5)	0
8. Financing repayments (the entire loan balance)	3,500
9. External financing balance at end of month	0
10. Cash balance at end of month after financing (balance on line 3 plus new financing on line 7 minus repayments on line 8)	$ 11,500

As shown on line 8 of the preceding summary, the company can pay off the entire $3,500 short-term loan balance this month.

Accounts Receivable and Inventory

"If the money is coming in the front door at 100 miles per hour, and going out the back door at 110 miles per hour, that's not a good thing. Businesses don't fail because they are unprofitable; they fail because they get crushed on the accounts receivable side."
—Brian Hamilton

CHAPTER 19

Source: Andrey_Popoy/Shutterstock

Learning Objectives

After reading this chapter, you should be able to:

1. Describe how and why firms must manage accounts receivable and inventory as investments.
2. Compute the optimal levels of accounts receivable and inventory.
3. Describe alternative inventory management approaches.
4. Explain how firms make credit decisions and create collection policies.

Accounts Receivable and Inventory: Necessary Evils?

Have you ever driven by one of those large motor home dealerships? Some have hundreds of vehicles that sell from $250,000 to $2,000,000 sitting on the lot. Put yourself in the dealer's shoes. Wouldn't it be nice if customers came to your dealerships, sat down across from your desk, and looked at pictures of expensive motor homes? They could pick out the picture of the motor home they liked, put down a large deposit, sign the sales papers, and then wait patiently for months until that motor home was delivered by the manufacturer to your lot, where customers would pick it up.

The real world isn't like that, of course. Customers want to see, touch, and test drive lots of different motor homes before committing to a large purchase such as this. If you are going to be in the motor home business, you're going to have to maintain a large amount of expensive inventory.

Wouldn't it also be nice if every one of those customers came with cash to cover the full cost of these expensive motor homes? Your life as the dealer would be much easier if every potential customer had all the cash needed to purchase your product. This isn't the real world either. Buying on credit is the norm for certain kinds of products. Extending trade credit and carrying accounts receivable on your balance sheet come with the territory for many different types of businesses.

In this chapter, we look at how inventory and accounts receivable are managed. For some companies, a huge amount of capital is tied up in these assets. This capital needs to be invested wisely.

Chapter Overview

A key component of working capital policy is managing accounts receivable and inventory. In this chapter we see that accounts receivable and inventory are necessary investments that affect a firm's profitability and liquidity. Then we investigate how financial managers determine the optimal level of these current assets. Finally, we examine inventory management techniques and collection policies.

Why Firms Accumulate Accounts Receivable and Inventory

As we saw in Chapter 4, accounts receivable represent money that customers owe to the firm because they have purchased goods or services on credit. Accounts receivable, therefore, are assets that have value.[1] Nonetheless, any time a firm accumulates accounts receivable, it suffers opportunity costs because it is unable to invest or otherwise use the money owed until customers pay. A firm may also incur a direct cost when it grants credit because some customers may not pay their bills at all. The ideal situation, from a firm's point of view, is to have customers pay cash at the time of the purchase.[2]

In the real world, of course, it's unrealistic to expect customers always to pay cash for products and services. Who would buy lumber from a firm that insisted that all its customers pay cash if other lumber companies offered credit? Like it or not, for most firms, granting credit is an essential business practice. The real question managers must answer is, how much credit should the firm grant and to whom? Offering more credit enhances sales but also increases costs. At some point the cost of granting credit outweighs the benefits. Financial managers must manage accounts receivable carefully to make sure this asset adds to, rather than subtracts from, a firm's value.

The situation with inventory is similar. Inventory is costly to accumulate and maintain, so firms generally want to hold as few products in inventory as possible. For most firms, however, operating without any inventory is impractical—can you imagine a grocery store with no food on display? Most firms that sell products accumulate some inventory. Financial managers must find the best level of inventory. They do this by weighing the risk of losing sales due to unavailable products against the cost savings produced by reducing inventory.

Accounts receivable and inventory are investments because both tie up funds and have opportunity costs, but both can add to the firm's value. Be careful not to be confused by the term *investment*. Investment usually implies something desirable—a long-term venture specifically planned and implemented for profit. Instead, accounts receivable and inventory may be viewed as necessary evils. Most firms need accounts receivable and inventory to do business, but less is generally better. Managing accounts receivable and inventory, then, ought to be done with an eye toward reducing these assets to the lowest level possible consistent with the firm's goal of maximizing value.

---

1. In fact, firms sometimes sell their customers' "IOUs" to other businesses for cash. This process, known as factoring accounts receivable, is discussed later in this chapter.

2. Individuals are the same way. For example, if you sell your bicycle to another student, which would you prefer—to be paid in cash at the time of sale or to let the buyer pay you a little bit each month?

TABLE 19-1 Comparison of Accounts Receivable and Inventory Policies

Data as of December 31	Selected Financial Data for Firms A and B (in 000's)	
	Firm A **Sells Products** **for Cash and Holds** **No Inventory**	**Firm B** **Sells Products for** **Credit and Accumulates** **Inventory**
Cash	$ 100	$ 100
Accounts Receivable	0	200
Inventory	0	400
Fixed Assets	500	500
Total Assets	$ 600	$ 1,200
Current Liabilities	$ 50	$ 100
Long-Term Debt	200	400
Stockholders' Equity	350	700
Total Liabilities and Equity	$ 600	$ 1,200
Sales	$ 2,433	$ 2,433
Expenses	2,383	2,383
Net Income for the Year	$ 50	$ 50
Current Ratio	2.0	7.0
Quick Ratio	2.0	3.0
Return on Equity	14.3%	7.1%

How Accounts Receivable and Inventory Affect Profitability and Liquidity

Holding different levels of accounts receivable and inventory can affect a company's profitability and liquidity. To illustrate, consider Firms A and B in Table 19-1. Firm A sells all its products for cash and keeps no inventory. Firm B gives its customers 30 days to pay and maintains a large product inventory. Assuming every other factor is equal, including the firms' capital structures, Firm A can earn more than twice the return on its stockholders' equity as Firm B simply by eliminating accounts receivable and inventory (and any associated current liabilities and long-term debt).

The comparison between Firms A and B in Table 19-1 illustrates the liquidity, profitability, and risk of each firm. Observe that although Firm A is more *profitable* than Firm B as measured by return on equity (14.3 percent versus 7.1 percent), it is much less *liquid*, as measured by the current ratio[3] (2.0 versus 7.0). If the managers of Firm A needed to raise more than $100,000 cash in a hurry, they would have no recourse but to seek outside financing or sell some of their fixed assets. The managers of Firm B, however, could collect cash from customers, draw down inventory, or both.

However, Firm B's business practice of accumulating inventory adds risk to the firm if the inventory is hard to liquidate. Some inventory may not be sold, or it may be sold for a low value. Note how, when using the quick ratio[4] to compare firm liquidity, we see that Firm A's quick ratio is the same as its current ratio (2.0), but Firm B's quick ratio is 3.0 compared with its current ratio of 7.0. When using the quick ratio, then, we see that Firm A is less liquid than Firm B (2.0 versus 3.0), but how much less depends on the liquidity of the inventory.

---

3. The Current Ratio $= \dfrac{\text{Current Assets}}{\text{Current Liabilities}}$

4. The Quick Ratio $= \dfrac{\text{Current Assets less Inventory}}{\text{Current Liabilities}}$

Most firms accumulate some accounts receivable and inventory. Because these current assets can affect the profitability and liquidity of the firm, financial managers try to find the amounts of both assets that maximize firm value. In the following section, we examine how to find the optimal level of these current assets.

Finding Optimal Levels of Accounts Receivable and Inventory

The conclusions drawn from Table 19-1 assumed that sales for both firms were $2,433,000. That may not be a reasonable assumption. Firm B may have greater sales than Firm A because it grants credit and has inventory immediately available for purchase. Depending on how well customers respond to Firm B's decision to grant credit and maintain inventory, the resulting increase in sales and net income might boost Firm B's return on equity beyond that of Firm A.

However, bad debts and inventory costs are likely to drive up Firm B's expenses, possibly causing its net income to fall. The net result could be a decrease in Firm B's return on equity.

Conflicting forces make it more difficult to assess the situation. For accounts receivable, the forces are sales that increase as more generous credit terms are offered, versus costs that increase with collections, bad debts, and opportunity costs from foregone investments. For inventory, the conflicting forces are sales that increase as more products are made available, versus storage costs that increase as more inventory is accumulated and opportunity costs from foregone investments.

In the following sections, we discuss how to find a balance between these conflicting forces in order to determine the optimal levels of accounts receivable and inventory.

The Optimal Level of Accounts Receivable

To find the best level of accounts receivable, financial managers must review the firm's credit policies, any proposed changes in those policies, and the incremental cash flows of each proposed credit policy. We must then compute the net present value of each policy.

Credit Policy

A firm's credit terms and credit standards make up the firm's credit policy. Remember, accounts receivable are created by customers taking advantage of the firm's credit terms. These terms generally offer a discount to credit customers who pay off their accounts within a short time, and they specify a maximum number of days that credit customers have to pay off the total amount of their accounts. An example of such terms is "2/10, n30." This means that credit customers will receive a 2 percent discount if they pay off their accounts within 10 days of the invoice date, and the full net amount is due within 30 days if the discount is not taken.

For example, suppose you purchase $1,000 worth of camping supplies on credit July 1. If you pay the bill before July 11, you receive a 2 percent discount and the equipment will only cost you $980. If you pay the bill between July 11 and July 31, you'll owe the full amount—$1,000. The bill is past due if you don't pay it by July 31.

Some firms offer credit without a discount feature, simply giving their customers so many days to pay. An example would be "n90"—net 90, pay the invoice amount within 90 days.

Individual customers receive credit from the firm if they meet the firm's credit standards for character, payment history, and so on.[5] Taken together, the credit terms and credit standards constitute the firm's credit policy.

A firm that wishes to change its level of accounts receivable does so by changing its credit policy. *Relaxing* the credit policy—by adopting less stringent credit standards or extending the net due period—will tend to cause accounts receivable to increase. *Tightening* the credit policy—by adopting more stringent credit standards or shortening the net due period—will tend to cause accounts receivable to decrease.

---

5. Credit standards are discussed more fully later in this chapter.

The discount percent or time period could also be changed. This may either increase or decrease accounts receivable, depending on the reaction of customers to competing influences. Table 19-2 summarizes the effects of tightening credit policy on accounts receivable.

Analyzing Accounts Receivable Levels

To decide what level of accounts receivable is best for the firm, we follow this three-step process:

1. Develop *pro forma* financial statements for each credit policy under consideration.

2. Use the *pro forma* financial statements to estimate the incremental cash flows of the proposed credit policy and compare them to the current policy cash flows.

3. Use the incremental cash flows and calculate the net present value (NPV) of each policy change proposal. Select the credit policy with the highest NPV.

To demonstrate how the three-step credit policy evaluation works, let's analyze a proposed credit policy for a fictional firm, Bulldog Batteries. Assume Bulldog Batteries currently offers credit terms of 2/10, n30, and Jackie Russell, the vice president for marketing, thinks the terms should be changed to 2/10, n40. Doing so, she says, will result in a 10 percent increase in sales, but only a small increase in bad debts. Should Bulldog make the change?

After doing some research, we make the following assumptions:

- Ms. Russell is correct that sales will increase by 10 percent if the new credit policy is implemented.

- Cost of goods sold and other operating expenses on the firm's income statement, and all current accounts on the balance sheet, will vary directly with sales. Each of these accounts will increase by 10 percent with the change in credit policy.

- All of Bulldog's sales are made on credit.

> **Take Note**
> In real life, the firm's credit policy may be limited by marketplace constraints. A new, small firm attempting to sell to large, well-established customers may have to offer credit terms that match those of competitors in the industry.

TABLE 19-2 The Effects of Tightening Credit Policy

Action	Effect on Accounts Receivable
Raise standards for granting credit	Fewer credit customers
	Fewer people owing money to the firm at any given time
	Accounts receivable goes down
Shorten net due period	Accounts paid off sooner
	Less money owed to the firm at any given time
	Accounts receivable goes down
Reduce discount percent	Fewer credit customers, *but*
	Some customers who previously took discount now do not
	Net effect on accounts receivable depends on whether the number of customers lost will be more than the number of those now forgoing the discount and paying the higher net amount
Shorten discount	Same as above; some credit customers will leave, others will forgo the discount and pay the higher net amount; net effect on accounts receivable is indeterminate

Suppose further that Ms. Russell produced the following data on Bulldog's customers' historical payment patterns:

- 45 percent of Bulldog's customers take advantage of the discount and pay off their accounts in 10 days.

- 53 percent of Bulldog's customers forgo the discount, but pay off their accounts in 30 days.

- The remaining 2 percent of Bulldog's customers pay off their accounts in 100 days.[6]

Ms. Russell expects that under the new credit policy:

- 43 percent of Bulldog's customers will take advantage of the discount and pay off their accounts in 10 days. This percentage is expected to drop since a few customers who had paid during the discount period will not do so when an extra 10 days is offered in the net period.

- 53 percent of Bulldog's customers will forgo the discount and pay off their accounts in 40 days. Some existing customers who had paid within the discount period will no longer do so and will pay within the new more generous net period. Some sales will be made to new customers who are now attracted to Bulldog due to its more generous credit terms.

- 4 percent of Bulldog's customers will pay off their accounts in 100 days. With a longer net period, more customers will forget to pay on time.[7]

With this information, we calculate the weighted average of the customers' payment periods (average collection period, or ACP) under the old and new credit policies. We weight the averages for each scenario by multiplying the percentage of customers who pay times the number of days they take to pay. Then we total each scenario result, as follows:

Under the old credit policy:

$$ACP = (.45 \times 10 \text{ days}) + (.53 \times 30 \text{ days}) + (.02 \times 100 \text{ days})$$

$$= 22.4 \text{ days}$$

Under the new credit policy:

$$ACP = (.43 \times 10 \text{ days}) + (.53 \times 40 \text{ days}) + (.04 \times 100 \text{ days})$$

$$= 29.5 \text{ days}$$

Based on Ms. Russell's information, we know that under the current credit policy, bad debt expenses are 2 percent of sales; under the new policy, they will climb to 4 percent of sales. Bulldog's CFO has informed us that any increases in current assets resulting from the policy change will be financed from short-term notes at an interest rate of 6 percent. The CFO also tells us that the firm's effective tax rate is 25 percent, and that the cost of capital is 10 percent. The long-term interest rate is 8 percent.

Step 1: **Develop the *Pro forma* Financial Statements.** The first step is to develop the *pro forma* financial statements that reflect the effects of the proposed credit policy change. We begin by reviewing the firm's current income statement and balance sheet, and then we create new statements that incorporate the changes. The statements for Bulldog Batteries are shown in Figure 19-1. The left-hand column shows Bulldog's

---

6. In real life, many of these customers will never pay off their accounts, creating bad debts. Assume here, however, that they do pay off their accounts eventually. If we do not make that assumption, our mathematical average will include a certain percentage of customers taking an infinite amount of time to pay. As a result, we get an infinite average collection period (ACP), and that won't provide usable information.

7. It is difficult to generalize how current and new customers will react to credit terms changes. Each case is fact specific. The analyst would have to estimate the reaction of the customers of the specific company making the changes. An example of one possible set of reactions is presented here.

financial statements before the credit policy change, the middle column shows them after the change, and the right-hand column shows how the new figures were calculated, given our assumptions.

***Step 2*: Compute the Incremental Cash Flows.** Now it's time to compute the incremental cash flows that occur as a result of the credit policy change. Table 19-3 contains these cash flows. Table 19-3 shows that Bulldog's initial investment cash flow is $9,284, and its net annual incremental cash flows from t_1 through infinity are $2,329 per year.

***Step 3*: Compute the NPV of the Credit Policy Change.** Now that we have all the incremental cash flows, we can calculate the NPV of the proposed credit terms change. We learned in Chapter 10 that NPV is calculated by summing the present value (PV) of all a project's projected cash flows and then subtracting the amount of the initial investment.[8] In our example, we have a net incremental cash outflow (the initial investment) that occurs at time t_0 of $9,284, followed by net incremental cash inflows occurring from time t_1 through infinity of $2,329 per year. The PV of the $2,329 per year from time t_1 through infinity can be found using the formula in Chapter 8 for the present value of a perpetuity (PVP):

$$PVP = PMT \times \left(\frac{1}{k}\right)$$

where: PMT = Cash flow per period

k = Required rate of return

According to our assumptions, Bulldog Batteries' cost of capital is 10 percent. Applying Equation 8-5, we find the PV of an endless stream of payments of $2,329 discounted at 10 percent as follows:

$$PVP = PMT \times \left(\frac{1}{k}\right)$$

$$= \$2,329 \times \left(\frac{1}{.10}\right)$$

$$= \$23,290$$

We see that the present value of the $2,329 perpetuity with a 10 percent required rate of return is $23,290.

Take Note
Remember that this analysis depends on the accuracy of our assumptions. In this case, we assumed that sales would increase 10 percent, that bad debts would increase to 3 percent of sales, and that customers would pay according to the pattern described. If these assumptions are invalid, the credit policy analysis will also be invalid.

TABLE 19-3 Incremental Cash Flows Associated with Changing Bulldog Batteries' Credit Policy from 2/10, n30 to 2/10, n40

1. Net Incremental Cash Outflow at Time Zero (t_0)	
External Financing Required from the Projected Balance Sheet	$9,284
2. Incremental Cash Flows Occurring in the Future	
Incremental Cash Inflow:	
Increase in Sales	$20,173
Incremental Cash Outflows:	
Increase in Cost of Goods Sold	$10,728
Increase in Bad Debt Expenses	2,017
Increase in Other Operating Expenses	4,323
Increase in Taxes	776
Total Incremental Cash Outflows:	$17,844
Net Incremental Cash Flows Occurring from Time t_1 through Infinity: $20,173 − $17,844 =	$ 2,329 per year

---

8. See Equation 10-1a in Chapter 10.

	With old credit terms: 2/10, n30	With new credit terms: 2/10, n40	Remarks
Sales (all on credit)	$ 201,734	$ 221,907	10% increase assumed
Cost of Goods Sold	107,280	$ 118,008	Increase in proportion with sales (10%)
Gross Profit	94,454	103,899	
Bad Debt Expenses	4,035	6,052	Old: 2% of sales. New: 4% of sales
Other Operating Expenses	43,229	47,552	Increase in proportion with sales (10%)
Operating Income	47,190	50,295	
Interest Expense	1,221	1,221	(not including external financing)
Before-Tax Income	45,969	49,075	
Income Taxes (rate = 25%)	11,492	12,269	
Net Income and Cash Flow	$ 34,447	$ 36,806	

Balance Sheets, as of Dec. 31

	With old credit terms: 2/10, n30	With new credit terms: 2/10, n40	Remarks
Assets			
Current Assets:			
Cash and Marketable Securities	$ 65,313	$ 71,844	Increase in proportion with sales (10%)
Accounts Receivable	12,380	17,935	See Note 1
Inventory	21,453	23,598	Increase in proportion with sales (10%)
Total Current Assets	99,146	113,377	
Property, Plant and Equip, Net	92,983	92,983	No change
Total Assets	$ 192,129	$ 206,360	
Liabilities and Equity			
Current Liabilities:			
Accounts Payable	$ 26,186	$ 28,805	Increase in proportion with sales (10%)
Notes Payable	302	$ 302	No change
Total Current Liabilities	26,488	29,107	
Long-Term Debt	15,034	15,034	No change
Total Liabilities	41,522	44,141	
Common Stock	35,000	35,000	No change
Capital in Excess of Par	32,100	32,100	No change
Retained Earnings	83,507	85,836	Old RE + 2,329 net income difference
Total Stockholders' Equity	150,607	152,936	
Total Liabilities and Equity	$ 192,129	$ 197,077	
Additional Funds Needed		$ 9,284	See Notes 2 and 3
		$ 206,360	

Note 1: Accounts Receivable (AR) = Credit Sales per day × ACP

Under the old credit policy: AR = ($201,734/365) × 22.4 = $12,380
Under the new credit policy: AR = ($221,907/365) × 29.5 = $17,935

Note 2: $9,284 is the amount of additional financing needed (AFN) to balance the balance sheet. It is the amount that must be obtained from outside sources to undertake the proposed credit policy change. Therefore, $9,284 may be viewed as the net investment required at time zero for the project.

Note 3: If $9,284 is borrowed to make up for AFN, Bulldog will incur new interest charges. If included in the income statement these will reduce the net income and retained earnings—throwing the balance sheet off balance again and changing the amount of AFN. If the problem is solved using an electronic spreadsheet, the financial statements can be recast several times until the additional interest expense becomes negligible. Here, however, we will use the original interest rate to simplify the calculations.

FIGURE 19-1 Bulldog Batteries, Financial Statements before and after a Credit Policy Change

Figure 19-1 shows the *pro forma* financial statements for Bulldog Batteries with the current collection policy and with the proposed collection policy.

To complete the NPV calculation, we now need to subtract the $9,284 net cash outflow that occurs at time t_0—the initial investment—from the present value of the $2,329 perpetuity, as shown next:

$$NPV = \$23,290 - \$9,284$$
$$= \$14,006$$

We find that the net present value of the credit policy change is $14,006. Because the NPV is positive, the credit terms change proposal should be accepted. Doing so will increase the value of Bulldog Batteries by $14,006.[9]

Any credit policy change proposal can be evaluated using this framework. Managers may try any number of discount amounts, discount periods, and net due periods, until they discover that combination with the greatest NPV.

The Optimal Level of Inventory

Firms may be able to stimulate sales by maintaining more inventory, but they may drive up costs as well. The financial manager's task is to figure out what level of inventory produces the greatest benefit to the firm. Financial managers first estimate the costs that are associated with inventory.

The Costs of Maintaining Inventory

The two main costs associated with inventory are carrying costs and ordering costs. *Carrying costs* are those costs associated with keeping inventory on hand—warehouse rent, insurance, security expenses, utility bills, and so on. Carrying costs are generally expressed in dollars per unit per year.

Ordering costs are those costs incurred each time an order for inventory materials is placed—clerical expense, telephone calls, management time, and so on. Ordering costs tend to be fixed no matter what the size of the order, so they are generally expressed in dollars per order.

Although you would think financial managers would like to minimize these two costs, it's not so easy. Carrying costs tend to rise as the level of inventory rises, but ordering costs tend to fall as inventory rises (because less ordering is necessary). Firms that minimize carrying costs by keeping no inventory have to order materials every time they want to produce an item, so they actually maximize ordering costs. Likewise, firms that minimize ordering costs by ordering all materials at once have sky-high carrying costs.

Complicating the situation is the possibility that a larger stock of inventory might increase sales. More inventory on display means more opportunities to catch the customer's eye, and more inventory on hand means fewer sales lost due to not having the correct size or model available. The fact that more inventory might translate into more sales means the lowest-cost level of inventory might not be the optimal level of inventory. To find the optimal level, managers have to balance the costs and benefits of various inventory levels.

Analyzing Inventory Levels

To maximize the value created from the firm's investment in inventory, use a three-step process similar to the one used to find accounts receivable levels. First, generate *pro forma* income statements and balance sheets for each proposed inventory level. Second, observe the incremental cash flows that occur with the change. Third, compute the NPV of the incremental cash flows. The following example illustrates the three-step process.

---

9. Given all the information presented so far, we could also calculate the internal rate of return (IRR) of the credit terms proposal. We simply solve the PV of a perpetuity formula for k, which represents the IRR:

$$k, \text{ or } IRR = PMT / PVP$$

In our example: $IRR = \$2,329 / \$9,284$
$$= .2509, \text{ or } 25.09\%$$

Because 25.09 percent exceeds Bulldog's cost of capital of 10 percent, the credit terms change proposal should be accepted.

Dealin' Dan, the owner of Cream Puff Used Cars, wants to determine the optimal number of cars to display on his lot. Dan knows that increasing the number of cars on display will probably cause sales to increase, but it would also increase his inventory carrying costs. Dan also knows that decreasing the number of cars on display will save him inventory costs but might also cost him sales. As a result, Dan is not sure how a change in his planned average inventory level from 32 cars to 48 cars will affect the value of his firm.

We'll make the following assumptions about Cream Puff's financial condition:

1. Cream Puff's inventory ordering costs are $100 per order. (Each time Dealin' Dan takes action to obtain cars, whether from other dealers, or from trade-ins, he incurs $100 in processing costs.)

2. Inventory carrying costs are $500 per car per year.

3. Because Dealin' Dan does not expect to keep cars on the lot more than a few weeks, he finances all the firm's inventory with short-term debt. The short-term interest rate available to Cream Puff is 6 percent.

4. Cream Puff pays $5,000, on average, for each car it purchases for resale. The firm's average selling price per car is $6,000.

5. Cream Puff displays, on average, about 32 cars on its lot. Sales occur regularly throughout the year, and Dan expects to sell 200 cars this year.

6. Based on his business experience, Dan believes that the relationship between inventory and Cream Puff's car sales is direct, as shown in Figure 19-2. According to the graph, an increase in inventory from 32 to 48 cars should produce an increase in the number of cars sold per year from 200 to 232.

Dan uses the economic order quantity (EOQ) model to compute the number of cars to order from wholesale dealers when he replenishes his inventory.[10] According to the EOQ model, the optimal order size follows:

$$EOQ = \sqrt{\frac{2 \times S \times OC}{CC}}$$

$$(19\text{-}1)$$

where: OQ = Order quantity

S = Annual sales volume in units

OC = Ordering costs, per order

CC = Carrying costs, per unit per year

We may use the model to see what order size Cream Puff should have. We know that sales are 200 cars per year, ordering costs are $100 per order, and the carrying costs are $500 per year. According to Equation 19-1, the ordering quantity for Cream Puff is as follows:

$$EOQ = \sqrt{\frac{2 \times 200 \times 100}{500}}$$

$$= \sqrt{80}$$

$$= 8.94 \text{ (round to 9)}$$

We find that the ordering quantity that minimizes inventory costs is nine cars per order. Cream Puff's sales occur regularly, so Dan orders nine replacement cars at even intervals throughout the year. The sales forecast calls for 200 cars to be sold this year, so the number of

---

10. The EOQ model computes the inventory order size that, if certain other conditions are met, will minimize total inventory costs for the year. For a complete discussion of the model, refer to a production management text.

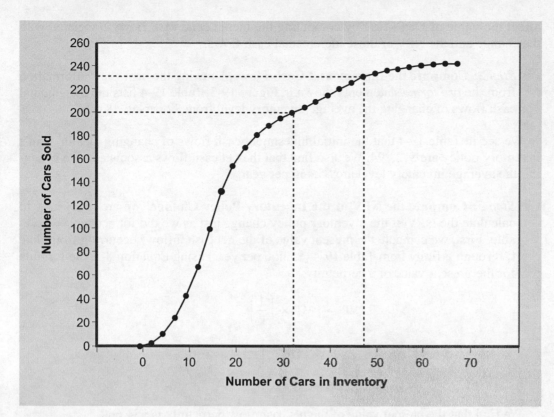

FIGURE 19-2
Cream Puff Used Cars
Inventory versus Number
of Cars Sold

Figure 19-2 shows the
direct relationship between
inventory and sales. As
inventory increases, sales
increase; as inventory
decreases, sales decrease.

orders for replacement cars will be 200/9 = 22.22 (round to 22).[11] Each order for replacement cars costs $100, so Cream Puff's total ordering cost—assuming 22 orders are made—is $2,200.

Under the current inventory policy, Cream Puff's average inventory level is 32 cars. Carrying costs are $500 per car per year, so total carrying costs are 32 × $500 = $16,000. We sum the ordering and carrying costs to find the total inventory costs for Cream Puff. The total costs are $2,200 + $16,000 = $18,200.

We assume in our example that other operating expenses on Cream Puff's income statement and all current accounts on the balance sheet vary directly with sales, so each of these accounts will increase (or decrease) proportionally with sales. We also assume that the interest rate on short-term debt is 6 percent and the rate on long-term debt is 8 percent. Finally, assume that Cream Puff's effective tax rate is 40 percent, and the firm's cost of capital is 10 percent.

Now we're ready to apply the three-step process to determine the optimal level of inventory for Cream Puff Used Cars.

Step 1: **Develop *Pro forma* Financial Statements.** Let's see how Dealin' Dan's proposed inventory change from 32 cars to 48 cars will affect the business. The left-hand column in Figure 19-3 shows Cream Puff's projected 2019 income statement and balance sheet. It also shows selected financial ratios, given our assumptions, current inventory policy of 32 cars, and the total inventory costs of $18,200. The right-hand column contains revised statements and ratios assuming average inventory is raised to 48 cars. The remarks column explains how the various numbers were computed.

If Dealin' Dan's assumptions are correct, increasing the number of cars on display at the Cream Puff used car lot to 48 will produce a $192,000 increase in sales (32 extra cars). Inventory costs and other expenses will increase too, of course, but only by a total of $186,534, so profits should rise by $5,466. On the surface it looks like Dan should go ahead with the inventory change, doesn't it? Perhaps, but let's see how the change will

---

11. Astute readers will note that, after rounding, 22 × 9 = 198. So Dealin' Dan will not actually order the exact number of cars he expects to sell this year. However, this small discrepancy will not materially affect our analysis.

affect the value of Dan's firm by computing the incremental cash flows associated with the change and the NPV of those incremental cash flows.

Step 2: Compute the Incremental Cash Flows. Drawing the necessary information from the *pro forma* statements shown in Figure 19-3, Table 19-4 lists the incremental cash flows of changing the average inventory level from 32 cars to 48 cars.

We see in Table 19-4 that the initial investment cash flows of changing Dealin' Dan's inventory policy are $72,294. We also find that the net cash flows associated with changing the average inventory level are $5,466 per year.

Step 3: Compute the NPV of the Inventory Policy Change. We are ready now to calculate the NPV of the inventory policy change just as we did for accounts receivable. First, we compute the present value of the net cash inflows occurring from time t_1 through infinity from Table 19-4 ($5,466 per year) using Equation 8-5, the formula for the present value of a perpetuity:

$$PVP = PMT \times \left(\frac{1}{k}\right)$$

$$= \$5,466 \times \left(\frac{1}{.10}\right)$$

$$= \$54,660$$

We find that the present value of the net cash flow perpetuity is $54,660.

Next, we subtract the present value of the net cash outflows at t_0 (the initial investment) to find the NPV of the inventory policy change. From Table 19-4 we see the net cash outflow that occurs at t_0 is $72,294. So, the NPV of Dealin' Dan's Cream Puff Used Cars inventory change proposal is as follows:

$$NPV = \$54,660 - \$72,294$$

$$= \$(17,634)$$

We find that the net present value of the inventory change proposal is –$17,634. Because the NPV is negative, the inventory change proposal should be rejected.

TABLE 19-4 Incremental Cash Flows If Cream Puff Changes Inventory Level from 32 to 48 Cars

1. Incremental Cash Outflows at t_0	
Additional Funds Needed from the Projected Balance Sheet	$ 72,294
2. Incremental Cash Flows Occurring in the Future	
Incremental Cash Inflows:	
Increase in Sales	$192,000
Incremental Cash Outflows:	
Increase in Cost of Goods Sold	$160,000
Increase in Inventory Costs	8,100
Increase in Other Operating Expenses	13,600
Increase in Interest Expense	1,190
Increase in Taxes	3,644
Total Incremental Cash Outflows:	$186,534
Net Incremental Cash Flows Occurring from Time t_1 through Infinity: $192,000 – $186,534 =	$ 5,466 per year

Income Statements

	Current Inventory Policy	New Inventory Policy	Remarks
Sales	$ 1,200,000	$ 1,392,000	32 car increase × $6,000 each
Cost of Goods Sold	1,000,000	1,160,000	32 car increase × $5,000 each
Gross Profit	200,000	232,000	
Inventory Costs	18,200	26,300	See Note 1
Other Operating Expenses	85,000	98,600	Change in proportion with sales (16% increase)
Operating Income	96,800	107,100	
Interest Expense	11,040	12,230	(CL × .06) + (LTD × .08)
Before-Tax Income	85,760	94,870	
Income Taxes (rate = 40%)	34,304	37,948	
Net Income	$ 51,456	$ 56,922	

Balance Sheets, as of Dec. 31

	Current Inventory Policy	New Inventory Policy	Remarks
Assets			
Current Assets:			
Cash and Marketable Securities	$ 47,000	54,520	Change in proportion with sales (16% increase)
Accounts Receivable	63,000	73,080	Change in proportion with sales (16% increase)
Inventory	160,000	240,000	16 car increase (48 – 32) × $5,000 each
Total Current Assets	270,000	367,600	
Property, Plant and Equip, Net	72,000	72,000	No change
Total Assets	$ 342,000	$ 439,600	
Liabilities and Equity			
Current Liabilities:			
Accounts Payable	$ 50,000	58,000	Change in proportion with sales (16% increase)
Notes Payable	74,000	85,840	Change in proportion with sales (16% increase)
Total Current Liabilities	124,000	143,840	
Long-Term Debt	45,000	45,000	No change
Total Liabilities	169,000	188,840	
Common Stock	35,000	35,000	No change
Capital in Excess of Par	34,000	34,000	No change
Retained Earnings	104,000	109,466	Old RE + $5,466 net income difference
Total Stockholders' Equity	173,000	178,466	
Total Liabilities and Equity	$ 342,000	367,306	
Additional Funds Needed		72,294	To be obtained from external sources
		$ 439,600	

Note 1: The new total inventory costs were computed as follows:

$$\text{New Order Quantity per the EOQ} = \sqrt{\frac{2 \times 232 \times 100}{500}}$$
$$= 9.63 \text{ (round to 10)}$$

Number of orders this year = 232/10 = 23.2 (round to 23)

New total ordering cost = 23 × $100 = $2,300

New average inventory level = 48

New total carrying cost = 48 × $500 = $24,000

New total inventory cost = $2,300 + $24,000 = $26,300 $8,100 increase

FIGURE 19-3 Dealin' Dan's Cream Puff Used Cars Inventory Analysis

Figure 19-3 shows the *pro forma* financial statements with Cream Puffs current average inventory policy of 32 cars and with the new inventory policy of 48 cars.

Accepting it would decrease the value of the Cream Puff Used Cars company by $17,634.12.[12]

In the preceding analysis, we used one possible inventory level and observed the effect on the value of the Cream Puff firm. By repeating this procedure a number of times, we could eventually find one inventory level, or a range of levels, at which the firm's value was maximized. We would then have found the true optimal level of inventory for the firm.

Inventory Management Approaches

Managing inventory is more than just determining the optimal level of items to keep on hand. Remember, the task is to hold down inventory costs without sacrificing sales too much. Techniques for doing this abound, but two approaches deserve special mention: the ABC classification system and the just-in-time (JIT) system.

The ABC Inventory Classification System

The ABC system of inventory classification is a tool used to lower inventory carrying costs. The system classifies inventory according to value. In many firms, inventory items may range in value from relatively expensive to relatively cheap. Generally, firms have fewer expensive items and more inexpensive items. In such a situation, it doesn't make sense to use one inventory control system to manage all inventory items because the firm would waste a lot of time and effort monitoring the relatively cheap items. For example, imagine the inventory system of a bicycle store. Its inventory would probably include several custom-designed racing bicycles; standard 10-speed and mountain bikes; and cycling helmets, water bottles, and other cycling equipment. Wouldn't it waste time and effort to assign serial numbers to all items in inventory and keep them all locked up in glass cases?

Under the ABC system, firm managers classify the relatively few, very expensive items as group A, the larger number of less expensive items as group B, and the rest of the relatively cheap items as group C.[13] Then different inventory control systems are designed for each group, appropriate for the value of that group. For example, the owner of a bicycle shop might assign custom-designed racing bikes to group A, less expensive standard bicycles to group B, and the rest of the inventory to group C. Then the owner could apply inventory control techniques appropriate for each group, as follows:

- Group A: Assign serial numbers to each item. Keep in secure storage. Check inventory daily. Keep fixed number on display, ordering replacements as each is sold.

- Group B: Assign serial numbers to each item. Keep in secure storage. Check inventory monthly. Manage levels of each type per the EOQ model.

- Group C: Check inventory annually. Reorder when visual checks of shelves indicate need.

This technique allows the bicycle storeowner to concentrate his or her time and effort on those items that deserve it. Unnecessary carrying costs on the rest of the inventory items are thus avoided.

---

12. The internal rate of return (IRR) of the inventory proposal is

k, or IRR = PMT/ PV (initial investment)
   IRR = 5,466 / 72,294
       = .0756, or 7.56%

Because 7.56 percent is less than Dealin' Dan's cost of capital of 10 percent, the inventory change proposal should be rejected.

13. Of course, the classifications are not limited to just A, B, and C. Depending on the firm's product lines, some companies might have D, E, and F as well. However, the guiding principle is the same.

Just-in-Time Inventory Control (JIT)

The **just-in-time (JIT)** inventory system, developed in Japan, is useful when storage space is limited and inventory carrying costs are high. The system attempts to operate the firm on little or no inventory.

just-in-time (JIT)
An inventory system in which inventory items are scheduled to be delivered "just in time" to be used as needed.

Here is an example of how JIT works. A firm that makes kitchen cabinets needs wood, brass handles and knobs, screws, and varnish. All these items constitute the firm's raw materials inventory. On the one hand, the firm could order these raw materials once a month and keep them in storage areas until needed in the manufacturing process (incurring inventory carrying costs as a result). On the other hand, the firm might strike a deal with its raw materials suppliers to deliver just the number of items needed immediately upon request. The items would thus arrive just in time to be used. The firm would not need to store materials, and inventory carrying costs would be eliminated.[14]

In addition to lowering inventory carrying costs, just-in-time systems tend to force quality into the manufacturing process. Any defect in materials will force the entire production line to shut down until the firm can obtain replacement materials.

Carrying little or no inventory can have drawbacks, however. Suppliers that are late or produce poor-quality products jeopardize the firm's customer relations. Little or no inventory means that the business does not have a buffer when a work slowdown occurs due to illness, natural disaster, or a labor dispute.

The JIT inventory system makes a company dependent on its suppliers to a much greater extent than traditional method of storing one's own inventory. As the economic crisis has taught us there are often ripple effects from one firm to another. If a key supplier were to fail, the company relying on that supplier as part of a JIT inventory system could find itself in serious trouble. Systematic risk factors could ripple from one company to another creating a domino effect. Economists call this contagion. These risks must be carefully considered before a company chooses to implement a JIT inventory system.

Making Credit Decisions

Earlier in this chapter, we said that individual customers receive credit from the firm if they meet the firm's credit standards. Credit standards are those requirements each individual customer must satisfy in order to receive credit from the firm. They are tests, in other words, of a person's creditworthiness.

Firms often base their credit standards on the Five Cs of Credit: character, capacity, capital, collateral, and conditions.

1. *Character:* the borrower's willingness to pay. Lenders evaluate character by looking at the borrower's past payment patterns. A good payment record in the past implies willingness to pay debts in the future.

2. *Capacity:* the borrower's ability to pay, as indicated by forecasts of future cash flows. The more confidence a lender has that a borrower is going to receive cash in the future, the more willing the lender will be to grant credit now.

3. *Capital:* how much wealth a borrower has to fall back on, in case the expected future cash flows with which the borrower plans to pay debts don't materialize. Lenders feel more comfortable if borrowers have something they could liquidate if necessary to pay their debts.

4. *Collateral:* what the lender gets if capacity and capital fail, and the borrower defaults on a loan. Collateral is usually some form of tangible asset, such as the firm's inventory, buildings, manufacturing equipment, and so on that has been pledged as security by the borrower.

---

14. You can see that, in effect, the requirement to store materials (and the attendant carrying costs) are passed on to the suppliers. Presumably, the suppliers would adopt such systems as well, until a closely coordinated chain from original suppliers to final customers developed.

5. *Conditions:* the business conditions the borrower is expected to face. The more favorable business conditions appear to be for the borrower, the more willing lenders are to grant credit.

To evaluate potential credit customers (in terms of the Five Cs of Credit, or any other criteria), firms find some way to quantify how well the customers compare to the measurement criteria. Some firms use a method known as credit scoring. Credit scoring works by assigning points according to how well customers meet indicators of creditworthiness. For example, statisticians have determined that established businesses tend to pay their debts more faithfully than new businesses. So, a credit applicant might be awarded points for each year that the applicant's firm has been in business. A sample of a simplified credit score sheet is shown in Figure 19-4 for Wishful Thinking Company.

We cannot overemphasize the importance of investigating creditworthiness carefully before granting credit. Not doing so is a quick way to end up with lots of accounts receivable and no cash!

Collection Policies to Handle Bad Debts

Sometimes, despite precautions, a firm ends up with customers who don't pay their bills. You thought your firm did a good job of scoring customers. But some of them are not paying their bills on time, and a few haven't paid at all. Now what?

Slow or no payment is bound to happen to any credit-granting business. Firms establish a collection policy to cope with the problem. For instance, what do you do if one of your long-time customers fails to pay a bill on the due date? Send it to a collection agency the next day? Ignore the situation and hope for the best? Send a reminder notice? Start charging interest? It helps to have a collection policy in place. That way, both the firm and its customers know what to expect once credit has been granted.

No one collection policy will be best for all firms and for all customers. The best policy depends on the business situation, the firm's tolerance for abuse, and the relationship it has with customers. However, most firms consider one or more of the following collection policies:

- *Send reminder letters.* Send one or more letters, each one becoming less friendly in tone. Certainly, the first letter should not sound threatening. (How often have you simply misplaced a bill and not realized it until you received a reminder notice?)

- *Make telephone calls.* If gentle reminders in the mail don't produce results, call the customer to see what the problem is. If there is a good reason why the customer hasn't paid the bill, you may choose to take no action or make accommodating arrangements. Make sure that any alternative payment plan is specific so that the firm can follow up early if the customer fails to pay again.

- *Hire collection agencies.* When all efforts to collect are unsuccessful, you may want to turn to professional collection agencies. This action should be used sparingly for two reasons. First, it will probably cost the firm any future business from this customer. Second, the price of the collection agency service may be very high, often 50 percent of the uncollected debt.

- *Sue the customer.* Legal action is a last resort. A lawsuit is even more expensive than using a collection agency, so firms should determine whether the court action is worth the trouble. Remember the "lawyers first" rule: Lawyers almost always get paid first.

- *Settle for a reduced amount.* A firm should keep in mind that trying too hard to collect from a customer may force the customer into bankruptcy. Once the client is in bankruptcy, the firm may not receive any money. In such a case, settling for a reduced amount, or a stretched-out payment schedule, may be the firm's best option.

- *Write off the bill as a loss.* In other words, forget it. This may be a firm's best alternative if the amount owed is relatively small or too costly to collect. Firms may have to write off all or part of the bill as a loss anyway, if efforts to collect are unsuccessful.

Take Note
A firm that frequently writes off uncollected amounts needs to tighten its standards for granting credit.

Criteria		Score
1. Length of time since missing a payment on any loan		_____
More than four years	4 points	
Three to four years	3 points	
Two to three years	2 points	
One to two years	1 point	
Less than one year	0 points	
2. Length of time in business		_____
More than four years	4 points	
Three to four years	3 points	
Two to three years	2 points	
One to two years	1 point	
Less than one year	0 points	
3. Net income		_____
More than $200,000	4 points	
100,000 to $200,000	3 points	
$50,000 to $100,000	2 points	
$25,000 to $50,000	1 point	
Less than $25,000	0 points	
4. Net worth		_____
More than $1,000,000	4 points	
$500,000 to $1,000,000	3 points	
$100,000 to $500,000	2 points	
$50,000 to $100,000	1 point	
Less than $50,000	0 points	
5. Market value of tangible assets		_____
More than $1,000,000	4 points	
$500,000 to $1,000,000	3 points	
$100,000 to $500,000	2 points	
$50,000 to $100,000	1 point	
Less than $50,000	0 points	
6. Expected business growth in next five years		_____
More than 20 percent	4 points	
15 to 20 percent	3 points	
10 to 15 percent	2 points	
5 to 10 percent	1 point	
Less than 5 percent	0 points	

Total Score: _____

Approved for credit if score = 12 or more

FIGURE 19-4
Sample Items on a Credit Scoring Worksheet for Wishful Thinking Company

- *Sell accounts receivable to factors.* Selling accounts receivable to some other person or business is known as factoring. Businesses that make money by buying accounts receivable from other firms, at less than their face value, are called factors. Suppose your firm had 100 customers who owed you a total of $10,000. Rather than wait for the customers to pay, you might sell the "IOUs" to a factor for $9,000 in cash. The factor discounts the accounts by an amount that both generates a return and compensates for the risk that some customers won't pay. Your firm no longer has to manage the accounts, plus it has cash to put to use elsewhere.

When granting credit to customers, it is best to remember the old saying, "An ounce of prevention is worth a pound of cure." In other words, crafting credit standards that avoid frequent collections can save a firm time and money.

What's Next

In this chapter we have explored how and why firms manage inventory and accounts receivable. We have examined methods for finding the optimal levels of both categories of current assets and have explored additional management techniques. In Chapter 20, we'll look at short-term financing.

Summary

1. *Describe how and why firms must manage accounts receivable and inventory as investments.*
   Granting credit and maintaining inventory are necessary business practices. Offering more credit and increasing inventory enhance sales. However, both accounts receivable and inventory tie up cash and incur opportunity costs—the cost of not having funds that could generate returns. The financial manager's task is to balance (1) the risk of losing sales due to not granting credit or having products available against (2) the savings produced by collecting cash immediately or maintaining inventory at a reduced level.

2. *Compute the optimal levels of accounts receivable and inventory.*
   The optimal level of accounts receivable or inventory may be found by using a three-step process: (1) create *pro forma* financial statements for alternative credit or inventory policies; (2) use the *pro forma* data to estimate the incremental cash flows associated with the proposed changes; and (3) compute the net present value of each alternative. When this process is complete, managers compare the NPVs of each alternative to see which policy produces the most favorable effect on the value of the firm.

3. *Describe alternative inventory management approaches.*
   Two popular inventory management approaches are the ABC and just-in-time (JIT) inventory systems. The ABC system classifies inventory items into categories according to their relative value. Management's time, money, and effort can then be directed to those inventory items in the proportions that they deserve.

   The JIT inventory system calls for close coordination between manufacturers and suppliers to ensure that parts and materials used in the manufacturing process arrive just in time to be used. If the coordination is close enough, raw materials inventories at the manufacturing firm can be eliminated.

4. *Explain how firms make credit decisions and create collection policies.*
   Firms evaluate the creditworthiness of their customers by applying the following Five Cs of Credit:
   • Character—a borrower's willingness to pay
   • Capacity—a borrower's ability to pay
   • Capital—how much wealth a borrower has to fall back on, in case the expected future cash flows with which the borrower plans to pay debts don't materialize
   • Collateral—what the lender gets if capacity and capital fail and the borrower defaults on a loan
   • Conditions—the business conditions a borrower is expected to face
   To evaluate potential credit customers, firms use a credit scoring procedure that assigns numerical values to the various indicators of creditworthiness.

   A firm's collection policy includes the actions the firm plans to take in the event that credit customers don't pay their bills on time. Policy actions include reminder letters, telephone calls, use of collection agencies, court action, settling for partial payment, factoring the accounts, and writing off the bills as a loss.

Key Term

just-in-time (JIT) An inventory system in which inventory items are scheduled to be delivered "just in time" to be used as needed.

Equations Introduced in This Chapter

Equation 19-1. The Economic Order Quantity for Inventory:

$$EOQ = \sqrt{\frac{2 \times S \times OC}{CC}}$$

where: OQ = Order quantity

S = Annual sales volume in units

OC = Ordering costs, per order

CC = Carrying costs, per unit per year

Self-Test

ST-1. Assume that Cash & Carry, Inc., is considering offering credit to its customers. Management estimates that if it does so, sales will increase 10 percent, expenses will increase 5 percent, accounts receivable will increase to $200,000, cash will decrease by $50,000, and current liabilities will increase to $300,000. No other accounts on the financial statements will be affected. Compute the company's return on equity (ROE) ratio and current ratio if it adopts the proposal. Base your calculations on Cash & Carry's latest financial statements, shown here.

Selected Financial Data for Cash & Carry, Inc.
(in 000's)

	Prior to Granting Credit	After Granting Credit
Cash	$ 100	
Accounts Receivable	0	
Total Current Assets	$ 100	
Current Liabilities	$ 50	
Total Equity	$ 2,000	
Sales	$ 2,500	
Expenses	2,300	
Net Income for the Year	$ 200	

ST-2. Your firm sells inventory at an even rate throughout the year. Sales volume this year is expected to be 100,000 units. Inventory ordering costs are $30 per order, and inventory carrying costs are $60 per unit per year. Given these conditions, what is the most economical inventory order quantity (EOQ)?

ST-3. Refer again to the Dealin' Dan's Cream Puff Used Cars example in the text. Continue with the assumptions given and compute the NPV of raising the company's average inventory level of cars to 60. Assume the inventory change would cause unit sales to increase to 240 per year.

ST-4. Your firm uses the credit scoring worksheet in Figure 19-4 to evaluate potential credit customers. If an applicant has never missed a loan payment, has been in business for two and a half years, has net income of $75,000, has a net worth of $90,000, has tangible assets worth $120,000, and has an expected business growth rate of 12 percent a year, will the applicant be granted credit?

Review Questions

1. Accounts receivable are sometimes not collected. Why do companies extend trade credit when they could insist on cash for all sales?

2. Inventory is sometimes thought of as a necessary evil. Explain.

3. What are the primary variables being balanced in the EOQ inventory model? Explain.

4. What are the benefits of the JIT inventory control system?

5. What are the primary requirements for a successful JIT inventory control system?

6. Can a company have a default rate on its accounts receivable that is too low? Explain.

7. How does accounts receivable factoring work? What are the benefits to the two parties involved? What are the risks?

Build Your Communication Skills

CS-1. The three-step process of evaluating the NPV of a proposed credit policy or inventory level change can intimidate some managers. Prepare an oral presentation to explain how to measure the value of the credit policy change analysis presented in this chapter. Lead a study group through the process.

CS-2. Evaluate the creditworthiness of a business in your local community using the credit scoring worksheet in Figure 19-4. To collect information, you may want to research local business publications, conduct interviews, or contact the local chamber of commerce. Prepare a brief written report of the results and include your credit scoring worksheet as an exhibit.

Problems

Accounts Receivable, ACP

19-1. Compu-Chip Co. had annual credit sales of $8,030,000 and an average collection period (ACP) of 22 days in 2018. What is the amount of the company's accounts receivable for the year? Assume 365 days in a year.

Accounts Receivable, ACP

19-2. If Compu-Chip Co. of problem 19-1 is expected to have annual credit sales of $7,600,000 and an average collection period of 26 days in 2019, what would be the company's accounts receivable? Do you think that the company is relaxing or tightening its credit policy in 2019, compared to its policy in 2018?

Accounts Receivable, ACP Credit Policy

19-3. Fitzgerald Company has credit terms of 2/15, n60. The historical payment patterns of its customers are as follows:
- 40 percent of customers pay in 15 days.
- 57 percent of customers pay in 60 days.
- 3 percent of customers pay in 100 days.

Annual sales are $730,000. Assume there are 365 days in a year.

a. Calculate the average collection period (ACP).

b. What is the accounts receivable (AR) assuming all goods are sold on credit?

Accounts Receivable, ACP Credit Policy

19-4. If Fitzgerald in problem 19-3 decides to adopt more stringent credit terms of 2/10, n30, sales are expected to drop by 10 percent, but the following improved payment pattern of its customers is expected:
- 40 percent of customers will pay in 10 days.
- 58 percent of customers will pay in 30 days.
- 2 percent of customers will pay in 100 days.

Calculate the new average collection period (ACP) and accounts receivable (AR) assuming all goods are sold on credit.

Accounts Receivable, ACP

19-5. Tuscany Style, a furniture company, has a current credit policy of 2/10, n20. It estimates under this policy that 25 percent of its customers will take advantage of the discount, 60 percent will pay within 20 days, and the remaining customers will pay within 30 days. What is its average collection period (ACP)?

Accounts Receivable, ACP

19-6. Tuscany Style, described in problem 19-5, is planning on revising its credit policy in an attempt to shorten its average collection period. Its new policy is 3/10, n30. Under this new policy, 32 percent of customers are expected to take advantage of the discount, 67 percent will pay within 30 days, and 1 percent will pay within 45 days. Calculate the new ACP. Should Tuscany Style adopt the new policy or keep the old one? Explain.

Effect of Change in Credit Policy

19-7. Elwood Blues, vice president of sales for East-West Trading, Inc., wants to change the firm's credit policy from 2/15, n40 to 2/15, n60, effective January 1, 2019. He is confident that the proposed relaxation will result in a 20 percent increase over the otherwise expected annual sales of $350,000 with the old policy. All sales are made on credit. The historical payment pattern under the present credit terms are as follows:

Under the old policy:
- 40 percent of the customers take advantage of the discount and pay in 15 days.
- 58 percent of the customers forgo the discount and pay in 40 days.
- The remaining 2 percent pay in 100 days.

Under the new credit policy, the payment pattern is expected to be as follows:
- 40 percent of the customers will take advantage of the discount and pay in 15 days.
- 57 percent of the customers will forgo the discount and pay in 60 days.
- The remaining 3 percent will pay in 100 days.

Bad debt expenses are expected to rise from 2 percent to 3 percent with the change in credit policy. Assume (i) any increase in current assets will be financed by short-term notes at an interest rate of 7 percent; (ii) long-term interest rate is 10 percent; (iii) income tax rate is 40 percent; (iv) cost of capital for East-West is 11 percent; (v) cost of goods sold is 80 percent of sales; (vi) other operating expenses is $10,000 under the old policy.

The *pro forma* balance sheet items of the company under the old policy would be as follows:

Cash and Securities	$ 15,000	Accounts Payable	$ 14,918
Inventory	50,000	Notes Payable	35,000
Plant and Equipment	120,000	Long-Term Debt	30,000
Common Stock	25,000	Capital in Excess of Par	60,000
Retained Earnings	50,000		

Also assume that the cost of goods sold and other operating expenses in the income statement and all current asset and current liability items, except accounts receivable, vary directly with sales.

a. Calculate average collection periods and accounts receivable under the old and the new policies.

b. Develop *pro forma* income statements and balance sheets under the old and the new policies.

c. Calculate the incremental cash flows for 2019 and the subsequent years.

d. Advise Mr. Blues if he should adopt the new policy.

For more, see 8e
Spreadsheet Templates
for *Microsoft Excel.*

19-8. Use the same information given in problem 19-7 with the following changes. Mr. Blues asked Mr. Scott Hayward, the general manager of sales of East-West, to recheck the payment patterns and credit history of East-West's customers to be absolutely sure that the change in credit policy would indeed be beneficial to the company. A strict scrutiny by Mr. Hayward resulted in the following changes in expected payment pattern and bad debts:

**Effect of Change in
Credit Policy**

Under the old policy:
- 40 percent of the customers take advantage of the discount and pay in 15 days.
- 58 percent of the customers forgo the discount and pay in 40 days.
- The remaining 2 percent pay in 100 days.

For more, see 8e
Spreadsheet Templates
for *Microsoft Excel.*

Under the new credit policy, the payment pattern is expected to be as follows:
- 30 percent of the customers will take advantage of the discount and pay in 15 days.
- 60 percent of the customers will forgo the discount and pay in 60 days.
- The remaining 10 percent will pay in 100 days.

Bad debt expenses are expected to rise from 2 percent to 4 percent with the change in credit policy. Under this changed scenario, is adoption of the new credit policy advisable?

19-9. Tom Jackson, the vice president of sales for A-Z Trading, Inc., wants to change the firm's credit policy from 3/10, n40 to 3/15, n30, effective January 1, 2019. He is confident that though the proposed tightening will result in a 10 percent decrease over the otherwise expected annual sales of $2 million with the old policy, it will increase profitability and value of the firm. All sales are made on credit. The historical payment pattern under the present credit terms is as follows:

Under the old policy:
- 30 percent of the customers take advantage of the discount and pay in 10 days.
- 60 percent of the customers forgo the discount and pay in 40 days.
- The remaining 10 percent pay in 100 days.

Under the new credit policy, the payment pattern is expected to be as follows:
- 42 percent of the customers will take advantage of the discount and pay in 15 days.
- 57 percent of the customers will forgo the discount and pay in 30 days.
- The remaining 1 percent will pay in 100 days.

Bad debt expenses are expected to decrease from 3 percent to 1 percent with the change in credit policy. Assume (i) any decrease in the current assets will be used to pay off short-term notes currently outstanding at an interest rate of 8 percent; (ii) long-term interest rate is 11 percent; (iii) income tax rate is 40 percent; (iv) cost of capital for A–Z is 13 percent; (v) cost of goods sold is 80 percent of sales; and (vi) other operating expenses is $60,000 under the old policy.

The *pro forma* balance sheet items of the company under the old policy would be as follows:

Cash and Securities	$ 86,000	Accounts Payable	$ 85,000
Inventory	285,000	Notes Payable	200,000
Plant and Equipment	652,000	Long-Term Debt	171,000
Common Stock	143,000	Capital in Excess of Par	342,000
Retained Earnings	285,000		

Also assume that the cost of goods sold and other operating expenses in the income statement and all current account items in the balance sheet vary directly with sales.

For more, see 8e Spreadsheet Templates for *Microsoft Excel.*

a. Calculate average collection periods and accounts receivable under the old and the new policies.

b. Develop *pro forma* income statements and balance sheets under the old and the new policies.

c. Calculate the incremental cash flows for 2019 and the subsequent years.

d. Advise Mr. Jackson if he should adopt the new policy.

19-10. Windhome and Drake Co., a dealer in building products, has the following costs associated with its business in 2018:

Ordering Cost	$250 per Order
Carrying Cost	$300 per Unit per Year
Annual Sales	500 Units

Calculate the EOQ and the number of orders placed per year.

19-11. Use the same data for problem 19-10, except that the carrying cost is expected to increase by 10 percent in 2019 due to increase in rentals of warehouse space. Recalculate the EOQ, number of orders placed per year, and total ordering cost for 2019.

19-12. TrailCrazer is updating its ordering strategy. Business has been increasing dramatically and it can't keep up with its current strategy. Executives have decided to implement the EOQ model to determine its ordering quantities and cycles. In 2018, TrailCrazer had the following costs:

Annual Sales	1,200 units
Carrying Costs	$100 per unit
Ordering Costs	$250 per unit per year

Calculate:

a. The EOQ

b. Number of orders to be placed each year

19-13. Jamison Electronics is forecasting next year's optimal order size. In 2018, annual sales are 200 units, with a carrying cost of $150 per unit and ordering costs of $50. However, its 2019 forecast is that annual unit sales will increase by 25 percent and that both ordering and carrying costs will increase by 10 percent. What will their optimal order size be for 2019, if these numbers are correct?

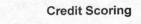

Economic Order Quantity

19-14. Mr. Danny Fisher's firm uses the credit scoring sheet in Figure 19-4 to evaluate the creditworthiness of its customers. An applicant missed a loan payment three and a half years back, has been in business for six years, has a net income of $143,000, a net worth of $1.5 million, a market value of $550,000 in tangible assets, and a business growth rate of 14 percent. Would Mr. Fisher approve credit to the applicant?

Credit Scoring

19-15. Kierna Jesup is the financial manager for Rummer International. She determines which customers are extended credit and how much. The following is a sample-scoring sheet that her company uses to grant credit:

Credit Scoring

Criteria	Points	Score
Length of time since last delinquent payment:		_____
Greater than 2.5 years	4	
2–2.5 years	3	
1.5–2 years	2	
1–1.5 years	1	
Less than 1 year	0	
Length of Time in Business		_____
Greater than 5 years	4	
4–5 years	3	
3–4 years	2	
2–3 years	1	
Less than 2 years	0	
Net Income		_____
Greater than $100,000	4	
$75,000–$100,000	3	
$50,000–$75,000	2	
$25,000–$50,000	1	
Less than $25,000	0	

For more, see 8e Spreadsheet Templates for *Microsoft Excel*.

Approved with a score above 8

Companies will receive the following credit with a score of

8 = 10% total assets

9 = 20% total assets

10 = 30% total assets

11 = 40% total assets

12 = 50% total assets

TWI has sent in an application for credit. It has been in business since 1992 and has never had a late payment. In 2018, its assets were $1.2 million, EBT was $100,000, and its tax rate was 40 percent. Will Kierna approve TWI for credit? If so, for how much?

19-16. Mr. Homer Smith is the vice president of sales for Sunrise Corporation, which buys and sells mobile homes. He is sure that increasing the number of homes on display will cause sales to increase. He thinks that an increase in inventory effective January 1, 2019, from the present level of 60 units to 100 units will boost sales from 350 units per year to 450 units per year. Assume ordering cost to be $200 per order, carrying cost to be $600 per unit per year, unit sales price to be $10,000, unit purchase price to be $8,000, and applicable income tax rate to be 40 percent. Also assume that any increase in the current assets will be financed by short-term notes at an interest rate of 7 percent, long-term interest rate is 10 percent, cost of capital for Sunrise is 11 percent, cost of goods sold is 80 percent of sales, and other operating expenses is $100,000 under the old policy. The *pro forma* balance sheet items of the company under the old policy would be as follows:

Cash and Securities	$ 55,000	Accounts Payable	$ 100,000
Accounts Receivable	105,000	Notes Payable	95,000
Plant and Equipment	100,000	Long-Term Debt	65,000
Common Stock	60,000	Capital in Excess of Par	220,000
Retained Earnings	200,000		

Also assume that the cost of goods sold and other operating expenses in the income statement and all current asset and current liability items vary directly with sales.

a. Calculate the EOQ, number of orders issued per year, and inventory cost.

b. Develop pro forma income statements and balance sheets under the old and the new policies.

c. Calculate the incremental cash flows for 2019 and the subsequent years.

d. Advise Mr. Smith if he should adopt the new policy.

19-17. Use the same information given in problem 19-16, except that Ms. Judy Benjamin, the general manager of sales for Sunrise, thinks that increasing the inventory level from 60 to 90 will increase sales from 350 to 390 units per year. With other assumptions remaining the same as in problem 19-16, evaluate this change in the inventory policy.

19-18. Ms. Terry McKay is the vice president of sales for Windermere Corporation, which sells hot air balloons. She is sure that increasing the number of balloons on display will cause sales to increase. She thinks that an increase in inventory effective January 1, 2019, from the present level will boost sales to higher levels in 2019 as shown:

Inventory Level (Units)			Sales (Units)
Present		70	340
Future (2019)	(1)	80	375
	(2)	90	390
	(3)	100	400

Assume ordering costs are $160 per order, carrying costs are $400 per unit per year, unit sales price is $16,000, unit purchase price is $12,800, and applicable income tax rate is 40 percent. Also assume that any increase in the current assets will be financed by short-term notes at an interest rate of 7 percent, the long-term interest rate is 11 percent, cost of capital for Windermere is 13 percent, cost of goods sold is 80 percent of sales, and other operating expenses are $130,000 under the present policy. The *pro forma* balance sheet items of the company under the present policy would be as follows:

Cash and Securities	$ 65,000	Accounts Payable	$ 110,000
Accounts Receivable	114,000	Notes Payable	95,000
Plant and Equipment	113,000	Long-Term Debt	65,000
Common Stock	80,000	Capital in Excess of Par	320,000
Retained Earnings	518,000		

Also assume that the cost of goods sold and other operating expenses in the income statement and all current account items in the balance sheet vary directly with sales.

Find out for Ms. McKay what level of inventory maximizes value of the firm by doing the following and comparing the net present values of the cash flows associated with each level of inventory:

a. Calculate the EOQ, number of orders issued per year, and inventory cost.

b. Develop *pro forma* income statements and balance sheets under the present and the future policies.

c. Calculate the incremental cash flows for 2019 and the subsequent years.

d. Advise Ms. McKay whether she should change the present inventory policy. If so, which inventory level should she adopt?

Answers to Self-Test

ST-1.

Selected Financial Data for Cash & Carry, Inc. (in 000's)

	Prior to Granting Credit	After Granting Credit
Cash	$ 100	$ 50
Accounts Receivable	0	20
Total Current Assets	$ 100	$ 250
Current Liabilities	$ 50	$ 300
Total Equity	$ 2,000	$ 2,000
Sales	$ 2,500	$ 2,750
Expenses	2,300	2,415
Net Income for the Year	$ 200	$ 335
Current Ratio	$100/$50 = 2.0	$250/$300 = .833
Return on Equity	$200/$2,000 = .10	$335/$2,000 = .1675

ST-2. Per Equation 19-1, the EOQ model:

$$EOQ = \sqrt{\frac{2 \times 100,000 \times 30}{60}}$$

$$= \sqrt{100,000}$$

$$= 316.228 \text{ (round to 316)}$$

ST-3. Use the three-step process to compute the NPV of raising the average inventory to 60 cars:

Step 1: Create *pro forma* financial statements for the new inventory policy:

Dealin' Dan's Cream Puff Used Cars Inventory Analysis
Income Statements

	Current Inventory Policy	New Inventory Policy	Remarks
Sales	$ 1,200,000	$ 1,440,000	Unit sales × price each, from assumptions
Cost of Goods Sold	1,000,000	1,200,000	Unit sales × cost each, from assumptions
Gross Profit	200,000	240,000	
Inventory Costs	18,200	32,400	See Note 1
Other Operating Expenses	85,000	102,000	Increase in proportion with sales
Operating Income	96,800	105,600	
Interest Expense	11,040	12,528	ST & LT Debt × Costs of Debt
Before-Tax Income	85,760	93,072	
Income Taxes (rate = 40%)	34,304	37,229	
Net Income	$ 51,456	$ 55,843	

Balance Sheets, as of Dec. 31

	Current Inventory Policy	New Inventory Policy	Remarks
Assets			
Current Assets:			
Cash and Securities	$ 47,000	$ 56,400	Change in proportion with sales
Accounts Receivable	63,000	75,600	Change in proportion with sales
Inventory	160,000	300,000	Average inventory × cost each, from assumptions
Total Current Assets	270,000	432,000	
Prop, Plant, and Equip, Net	72,000	72,000	No change
Total Assets	$ 342,000	$ 504,000	
Liabilities and Equity			
Current Liabilities:			
Accounts Payable	$ 50,000	$ 60,000	Change in proportion with sales
Notes Payable	74,000	88,800	Change in proportion with sales
Total Current Liabilities	124,000	148,800	
Long-Term Debt	45,000	45,000	No change
Total Liabilities	169,000	193,800	
Common Stock	35,000	35,000	No change
Capital in Excess of Par	34,000	34,000	No change
Retained Earnings	104,000	108,387	Old RE + net income change
Total Stockholders' Equity	173,000	177,387	
Total Liabilities and Equity	$ 342,000	$ 371,187	
Additional Funds Needed		132,813	Obtained from external sources
		$ 504,000	

Note 1: The new total inventory costs were computed as follows:

$$\text{New Order Quantity per the EOQ} = \sqrt{\frac{2 \times 240 \times 100}{500}}$$
$$= 9.8 \text{ (round to 10)}$$

Number of orders this year = 24/10 = 24
New total ordering cost = 24 × $100 = $2,400
New average inventory level = 60
New total carrying cost = 60 × $500 = $30,000
New total inventory cost = $2,400 + $30,000 = $32,400

Step 2: Compute the incremental cash flows:

Incremental Cash Flows Associated with Changing
Cream Puff Used Cars Inventory Level from 32 Cars to 60 Cars

1. Incremental Cash Outflows at Time Zero (t_0):

   Additional Funds Needed from the Projected
   Balance Sheet $ 132,813

2. Incremental Cash Flows Occurring in the Future

   Incremental Cash Inflows:

   Increase in Sales $ 240,000

   Incremental Cash Outflows:

   Increase in Cost of Goods Sold $ 200,000

   Increase in Inventory Costs   14,200

   Increase in Other Operating Expenses   17,000

   Increase in Interest Expense   1,488

   Increase in Taxes   2,925

   Total Incremental Cash Outflows: $ 235,613

   Net Incremental Cash Flows Occurring from Time
   t_1 through Infinity: $4,387 per year

Step 3: Compute the NPV of the inventory policy change:

PV of the net cash inflows occurring from time t_1 through infinity ($4,387 per year) using Equation 8-5:

$$PVP = PMT \times \left(\frac{1}{k} \right)$$

$$= \$4,387 \times \left(\frac{1}{.10} \right)$$

$$= \$43,870$$

Subtract the PV of the net cash outflows at t_0 ($132,813) to obtain the NPV of the inventory policy change:

$$NPV = \$43,870 - \$132,813$$

$$= (\$88,943)$$

Because the NPV is negative, the inventory change proposal should be rejected.

ST-4. The applicant's completed credit scoring worksheet from Figure 19-4 is shown next.

Credit Scoring Worksheet for		(applicant)
Criteria		**Score**

1. Length of time since missing a payment on any loan — 4

More than four years	4 points
Three to four years	3 points
Two to three years	2 points
One to two years	1 point
Less than one year	0 points

2. Length of time in business — 2

More than four years	4 points
Three to four years	3 points
Two to three years	2 points
One to two years	1 point
Less than one year	0 points

3. Net income — 2

More than $200,000	4 points
100,000 to $200,000	3 points
$50,000 to $100,000	2 points
$25,000 to $50,000	1 point
Less than $25,000	0 points

4. Net worth — 1

More than $1,000,000	4 points
$500,000 to $1,000,000	3 points
$100,000 to $500,000	2 points
$50,000 to $100,000	1 point
Less than $50,000	0 points

5. Market value of tangible assets — 2

More than $1,000,000	4 points
$500,000 to $1,000,000	3 points
$100,000 to $500,000	2 points
$50,000 to $100,000	1 point
Less than $50,000	0 points

6. Expected business growth in next five years — 2

More than 20 percent	4 points
15 to 20 percent	3 points
10 to 15 percent	2 points
5 to 10 percent	1 point
Less than 5 percent	0 points

Total Score: 13

Approved for credit if score = 12 or more

Result for applicant: Approved

Short-Term Financing

"A fool and his money are lucky enough to get together in the first place."
—Gordon Gekko in the movie Wall Street

Source: Supannee Hickman/Shutterstock

Cash 'Til Payday®

Loan Mart is one of the companies offering so-called payday loans. These loans are popular with some working people who need cash for a few weeks until payday.

In a typical transaction the borrower makes out a check to the lender dated two weeks hence. The lender then cashes the check on the specified date, which is typically after the borrower's payday. The lender provides cash to the borrower in exchange for this post-dated check.

Loan Mart charges the borrower a "fee" in the amount of $20 per $100 borrowed. This is for a loan that is repaid in two weeks.

If the $20 fee were considered to be interest, this would be an effective annual interest rate of 11,348% on a $100 loan. The interest rate on your Visa or Mastercard doesn't look too bad in comparison, does it? Read this chapter to see how the effective annual interest rate was calculated.

Source: Terms posted at Loan Mart, Fort Collins, Colorado.

CHAPTER 20

Learning Objectives

After reading this chapter, you should be able to:

1. Explain the need for short-term financing.
2. List the advantages and disadvantages of short-term financing.
3. Describe three types of short-term financing.
4. Compute the cost of trade credit and commercial paper.
5. Calculate the cost of a loan and explain how loan terms affect the effective interest rate.
6. Describe how accounts receivable and inventory can be used as collateral for short-term loans.

Chapter Overview

The credit card is perhaps the best-known source of short-term financing. However, businesses use many other types of short-term financing to sustain their business operations. In this chapter we discuss the advantages and disadvantages of short-term financing, sources of that financing, and methods for calculating the cost of each source. We also show how loan terms can affect a loan's effective interest rate, and how accounts receivable and inventory can be used as short-term loan collateral.

The Need for Short-Term Financing

Businesses rely on short-term financing from external sources for two reasons. The first is growth—profits may simply not be high enough to keep up with the rate at which the company is buying new assets. Imagine a convenience store chain that wished to open one new store a month. If each new store cost $100,000, the company would have to be very profitable to be able to do this without obtaining external financing.

The second reason that businesses rely on external short-term financing is choice. Rather than waiting to save enough money from net profits to make their desired purchases, many firms would rather borrow the money at the outset and make their purchases on time. People make the same choices in their personal lives. For example, you could save a little money each month until you saved enough to buy a car with cash. This might take a long time, however, and in the meantime you would be without transportation. Alternatively, you could borrow the money to buy the car and have it to drive around while you're paying off the loan. People—and businesses—often choose the latter alternative.

Clearly, the ability to obtain external financing is crucial for most businesses. Without it, most businesses could never even get started.

Short-Term Financing versus Long-Term Financing

Two factors influence the duration of external financing that businesses seek. The first, of course, is availability. A firm may want to take out a 10-year loan to finance its inventory purchases, but it may find no one willing to make such a loan. In general, businesses can usually find financing for short time periods. It is more difficult to find long-term financing.

The second factor influencing the length of time that firms finance for is the risk–return, or liquidity–profitability, trade-off discussed in Chapter 17.

In the context of financing alternatives, here is how the trade-off works:

- *Short-term financing* is usually cheaper than long-term financing because short-term interest rates are normally lower than long-term interest rates.[1] Therefore, the desire for profitability (return) pushes firms toward short-term financing.

- *Long-term financing* is regarded as less risky than short-term financing for the borrower because the borrower locks in the agreed-on interest rate for a long period of time. No matter how interest rates change during the life of the loan, the borrower's interest costs are certain. Furthermore, the borrower does not have to incur the transaction costs of obtaining new financing every few months. So, the desire to avoid risk encourages firms to use long-term financing.

The length of time that firms finance for depends on whether they want "to eat well or to sleep well."[2] Returns generally increase as financing maturities grow shorter, but so does risk. Risk decreases as financing maturities grow longer, but so do returns. The blend of financing maturities that a firm selects reflects how aggressive or conservative

---

1. Remember from Chapter 2 that a normal yield curve is upward sloping.

2. The phrase is adapted from a remark by J. Kenfield Morley, who said, "In investing money, the amount of interest you want should depend on whether you want to eat well or sleep well."

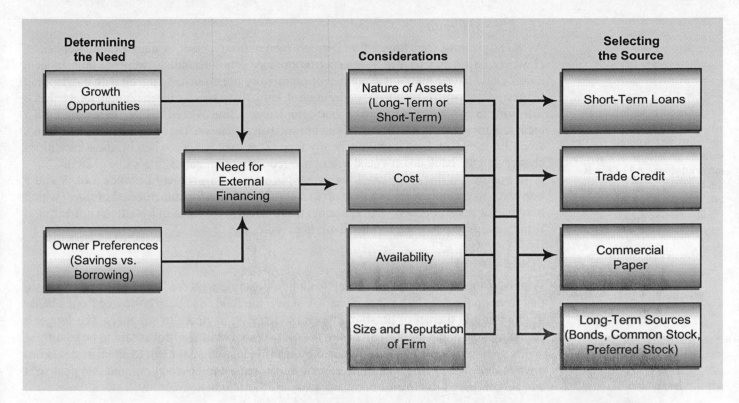

FIGURE 20-1
The External Financing
Source-Selection Process

The flowchart illustrates the
external financing source-
selection process. A firm
determines the need for
external financing, and then
considers several factors
before selecting the short-
term financing sources.

the firm's managers are. Figure 20-1 summarizes the factors that influence the sources of external financing. External financing can come from short-term or long-term sources. We discuss short-term financing sources next.

Short-Term Financing Alternatives

When most businesses need money for a short time—that is, for less than one year—they usually turn to two sources: short-term loans and trade credit (the process of delaying payments to suppliers). Large, well-established businesses may make use of a third financing source: commercial paper. In the sections that follow, we discuss the various aspects of obtaining money from these three sources.

Short-Term Loans from Banks and Other Institutions

Financial institutions offer businesses many types of short-term loans. No matter what the type of loan, however, the cost to a borrower is usually measured by the percent interest rate charged by the lender. The annual interest rate that reflects the dollars of interest paid divided by the dollars borrowed is the **effective interest rate**.

Often, the effective interest rate differs from the interest rate advertised by the bank, which is known as the **stated interest rate**.

Two common types of short-term loans are the *self-liquidating loan* and the *line of credit*. We examine these loan alternatives next. No matter what type of loan a firm uses, the firm must sign a promissory note. A **promissory note** is the legal instrument that the borrower signs and is the evidence of the lender's claim on the borrower.

Self-Liquidating Loans

Many of the short-term loans obtained from banks are self-liquidating. A **self-liquidating loan** is one in which the proceeds of the loan are used to acquire assets that will generate enough cash to repay the loan. An example is a loan used to finance a seasonal increase in inventory, such as the purchase of swimwear to sell during the summer months. The sale of the inventory generates enough cash to repay the loan.

effective interest rate
The annual interest rate that reflects the dollar interest paid divided by the dollar obtained for use.

stated interest rate
The interest rate advertised by the lender. Depending on the terms of the loan, the stated rate may or may not be the same as the effective interest rate.

promissory note A legal document the borrower signs indicating agreement to the terms of a loan.

self-liquidating loan A loan that is used to acquire assets that generate enough cash to pay off the loan.

The Line of Credit

As we now know, each time a firm borrows money from a bank, it signs a promissory note. However, a firm may have more than one promissory note outstanding at any one time. Indeed, a firm could have a substantial number of promissory notes outstanding, all with overlapping terms of payment. To keep loans under control, banks may specify the maximum total balance that firms may have in outstanding short-term loans. A **line of credit** is the borrowing limit a bank sets for a firm. A line of credit is an informal arrangement. The bank may change a firm's credit limit or withdraw it entirely at any time. This may happen when business conditions change, but the bank doesn't need a reason to reduce or eliminate a firm's line of credit.

In contrast, a *revolving credit agreement* is a formal agreement between a bank and a borrower to extend credit to a firm up to a certain amount for some period of time (which may be for several years). The agreements are usually set forth in a written contract, and firms generally pay a fee for the revolving credit.

Trade Credit

When a company purchases materials, supplies, or services on credit instead of paying cash, that frees up funds to be used elsewhere, just as if the funds had been borrowed from a bank. Trade credit is the act of obtaining funds by delaying payment to suppliers. The longer a company delays paying for purchases, the more trade credit the firm is said to be using.

Even though trade credit is obtained by simply delaying payment to suppliers, it is not always free. Next, we explain the cost of trade credit and how to compute that cost so it can be compared to the cost of a bank loan or other credit source.

Computing the Cost of Trade Credit

If a supplier charges a firm interest on credit balances, then computing the cost of trade credit is easy—simply read the interest rate charges on the supplier's account statements, much as we would read a credit card's interest charges.

Most wholesale suppliers, however, do not charge interest on credit balances. Instead, they simply give their customers so many days to pay and offer them a discount on the amount of the purchase if they pay early. A typical example of such credit terms is 2/10, n30—if customers pay their bills within 10 days of the invoice date, they will receive a 2 percent discount; if not, the net amount of the bill is due within 30 days.[3] Figure 20-2 diagrams a purchaser's payment deadlines for a $100 purchase on credit terms of 2/10, n30.

We see from Figure 20-2 that if a firm takes the discount, it can obtain the use of $98 for up to 10 days without any cost. In this case the trade credit the firm receives is free. But suppose a firm doesn't take the discount? Look at Figure 20-2 again and think of the situation this way: Instead of paying $98 on the tenth day, the firm can pay $98 anytime during the next 20 days as long as it pays a "fee" of $2 for delaying payment. In essence, the firm is "borrowing" $98 for 20 days at a cost of $2. Assuming the firm pays its bill on day 30, we can compute the effective annual interest rate of the trade credit using the following equation:

Trade Credit Effective Interest Rate Formula

$$k = \left(1 + \frac{\text{Discount \%}}{100 - \text{Discount \%}}\right)^{\left(\frac{365}{\text{Days to Pay} - \text{Discount Period}}\right)} - 1$$

$$(20\text{-}1)$$

where: k = Cost of trade credit expressed as an effective annual interest rate

Discount % = Percentage discount being offered

Days to Pay = Time between the day of the credit purchase and the day the firm must pay its bill

Discount Period = Number of days in the discount period

---

3. Credit terms of this type were introduced in Chapter 19 from the point of view of the supplier granting the credit. Here, we discuss the terms from the purchaser's point of view.

FIGURE 20-2
Payment Schedule with
2/10, n30 Credit Terms

Figure 20-2 shows the
purchaser's payment
schedule for a $100 purchase
from a supplier who offers
2/10, n30 credit terms.

The 365 in the equation represents the number of days in a year. We also multiply the result, k, by 100 to express it as a percentage.

In our example, the discount percentage is 2 percent, the total number of days to pay is 30, and the number of days in the discount period is 10. We use Equation 20-1 to solve for k as follows:

$$k = \left(1 + \frac{2}{100 - 2}\right)^{\left(\frac{365}{30 - 10}\right)} - 1$$

$$= \left(1 + .020408\right)^{(18.25)} - 1$$

$$= \left(1.020408\right)^{(18.25)} - 1$$

$$= 1.4458 - 1$$

$$= .4458, \text{ or } 44.58\%$$

As the calculation shows, the firm's trade credit—the use of $98 for an additional 20 days—costs the firm an effective annual percentage rate of interest of nearly 45 percent! Why would any reasonable financial manager pay such high rates? Most reasonable financial managers wouldn't, unless very unfavorable circumstances forced them to or they didn't realize they were doing it.

Instead, because bank loan rates are usually much lower than 45 percent, most reasonable financial managers would borrow $98 from the bank and use it to pay the supplier on the tenth day to take advantage of the discount. Twenty days later, the financial manager would repay the loan plus the interest charges, which would be considerably less than $2. Either way, a firm can obtain the use of $98 for 20 days, but borrowing from a bank is usually the much cheaper alternative.

Commercial Paper

Firms can sell **commercial paper**—unsecured notes issued by large, very creditworthy firms for up to 270 days—to obtain cash. Selling commercial paper is usually a cheaper alternative to getting a short-term loan from a bank. Remember that only large, creditworthy corporations sell commercial paper because only they can attract investors who will lend them money for lower rates than banks charge for short-term loans. In 2008 and 2009, the Financial Crisis hit the commercial paper market along with most of the rest of the financial system. Companies that had been considered very safe with ready access to the commercial paper market for funding found themselves having difficulty issuing new paper to refinance maturing issues. Investors had gotten very picky as to what they would buy. Commercial paper had been considered to be quite a safe investment but it is not as safe as U.S. Treasury securities. Investors were fleeing many investments that had previously been considered safe for those U.S. Treasury securities that have the backing of the full faith and credit of the United States.

commercial paper
A short-term, unsecured debt instrument issued by a large corporation or financial institution.

Calculating the Cost of Commercial Paper

Commercial paper is quoted on a *discount basis*. So, to compare the percent cost of a commercial paper issue to the percent cost of a bank loan, we first convert the commercial paper discount yield to an effective annual interest rate. We use the following three-step process to find this rate.

1. Compute the discount from face value using Equation 20-2, the formula for the dollar amount of the discount on a commercial paper note:

Dollar Amount of the Discount on a Commercial Paper Note

$$D = \frac{DY \times Par \times DTG}{360}$$

(20-2)

where: D = Dollar amount of the discount

DY = Discount yield

Par = Face value of the commercial paper issue; the amount to be paid at maturity

DTG = Days to go until maturity

2. Compute the price of the commercial paper issue by subtracting the discount (D) from par, as shown in Equation 20-3:

Price of a Commercial Paper Note

$$Price = Par - D$$

(20-3)

3. Compute the effective annual interest rate using the following formula, Equation 20-4:

Effective Annual Interest Rate of a Commercial Paper Note

$$k = \left(\frac{Par}{Price}\right)^{\left(\frac{365}{DTG}\right)} - 1$$

(20-4)

where: k = the effective annual interest rate

To illustrate the three-step process, imagine you are a financial analyst at Citigroup, Inc., and your commercial paper dealer has informed you that she is willing to pay 3.3 percent discount yield for a $1 million issue of 90-day Citigroup commercial paper notes. What effective annual interest rate does the 3.3 percent discount yield equate to?

Step 1: Compute the discount using Equation 20-2.

$$D = \frac{DY \times Par \times DTG}{360}$$

$$= \frac{.033 \times \$1,000,000 \times 90}{360}$$

$$= \frac{\$2,970,000}{360}$$

$$= \$8,250$$

We see that with a 3.3 percent discount rate, $1 million face value, and 90 days to go until maturity, the dollar amount of the discount on the commercial paper note is $8,250.

Step 2: Compute the price using Equation 20-3.

$$Price = Par - D$$

$$= \$1,000,000 - \$8,250$$

$$= \$991,750$$

Our calculations show that the price of the 90-day commercial paper note with a face value of $1 million at a discount price of $8,250 is $991,750.

Step 3: Compute the effective annual interest rate using Equation 20-4.

$$k = \left(\frac{Par}{Price}\right)^{\left(\frac{365}{DTG}\right)} - 1$$

$$= \left(\frac{\$1,000,000}{\$991,750}\right)^{\left(\frac{365}{90}\right)} - 1$$

$$= 1.00832^{4.056} - 1$$

$$= 1.0342 - 1$$

$$= .0342, \text{ or } 3.42\%$$

Applying Equation 20-4, we find that the effective annual interest rate of a $1 million, 90-day commercial paper note with a price of $991,750 is 3.42 percent. Now, you can compare the 3.42 percent effective annual interest rate Citigroup would pay for commercial paper to the various loan rates available and choose the best deal.

In the next section, we examine the effect of loan terms on the effective interest rate.

How Loan Terms Affect the Effective Interest Rate of a Loan

The effective interest rate of a bank loan may not be the same as the stated interest rate advertised by the bank because of a lender's loan terms. In the following sections, we describe how to find the effective interest rate and what terms affect the effective interest rate.

The Effective Interest Rate

Some loans have the same effective rate of interest as the stated rate of interest because the bank places no terms on the loan other than the amount of interest and the amount borrowed. In these cases, finding the effective interest rate per period is straightforward. We divide the interest paid on the loan by the amount of money borrowed during the period of the loan (and afterwards multiply the result by 100 to obtain a percent). Equation 20-5 shows the effective interest rate formula:

Effective Interest Rate of a Loan

$$k = \frac{\$ \text{ Interest You Pay}}{\$ \text{ You Get to Use}}$$

(20-5)

where: k = the effective interest rate

For example, suppose you borrow $10,000 from a bank for one year, and your promissory note specifies that you are to pay $1,000 in interest at the end of the year. We use Equation 20-5 to find the effective interest rate for the loan as follows:

$$k = \frac{\$1,000}{\$10,000}$$

$$= .10, \text{ or } 10\%$$

The calculations show that for a $10,000 loan with $1,000 in interest, the effective interest rate is 10 percent.

Effective interest rates are customarily expressed as annual rates. If a loan's maturity is for one year and there are no complicating factors, computing effective interest rates is quite simple, as we have just seen. Equation 20-5 gives the effective rate per period.

For many loans, however, things are not so simple. Lenders have a variety of terms and conditions that they apply to loans, and many of them affect the effective interest rate. Two of the more common loan terms, *discount loans* and *compensating balances*, are discussed next.

Discount Loans

discount loan A loan with terms that call for the loan interest to be deducted from the loan proceeds at the time the loan is granted.

Sometimes a lender's terms specify that interest is to be collected up front, at the time the loan is made, rather than at maturity. When this is the case, the loan is referred to as a **discount loan**. In a discount loan, the amount the borrower actually receives is the principal amount borrowed minus the interest owed. So the amount the borrower may use is lower than if the loan were a standard loan with interest paid annually at year's end. As a result, the borrower's effective interest rate is higher than it would be for a standard loan.

Let's return to our earlier one-year, $10,000 loan example to see what happens if it is a discount loan. Instead of paying $1,000 in interest at the end of the year (the equivalent of an effective interest rate of 10 percent), the $1,000 in interest must be paid at the beginning of the year. According to Equation 20-5, the effective interest rate is as follows:

$$k = \frac{\$ \text{ Interest You Pay}}{\$ \text{ You Get to Use}}$$

$$= \frac{\$1,000}{\$10,000 - \$1,000}$$

$$= \frac{\$1,000}{\$9,000}$$

$$= .1111, \text{ or } 11.11\%$$

Note that by collecting the $1,000 interest on the loan at the start of the year, the effective rate of interest rose from 10 percent to 11.11 percent, solely because of the timing of the interest payment. The stated interest rate, then, is lower than the borrower's effective rate of interest.

Compensating Balances

compensating balance A specified amount that a lender requires a borrower to maintain in a non-interest-paying account during the life of a loan.

Sometimes a lender's loan terms will specify that while a loan is outstanding the borrower must keep some minimum balance in a checking account at the lender's institution. The amount required is called a **compensating balance**. The lender would say that this minimum balance is its compensation for granting the borrower favorable loan terms (even though the terms may not be especially favorable). Because the borrower cannot allow the balance in the checking account to fall below the required minimum during the life of the loan, the borrower may not use these funds during the life of the loan. As a result, the borrower's effective interest rate is higher than it would be without a compensating balance requirement. This assumes that the borrower would not have kept the required compensating balance funds in the checking account if the loan were a standard loan.

Let's add a compensating balance requirement to our one-year, $10,000 loan with a year-end interest payment of $1,000. The stated rate of interest is 10 percent. Assume the bank requires a compensating balance of 12 percent of the amount borrowed in a checking account during the life of the loan. This compensating balance requirement would be referred to as a "12 percent compensating balance requirement." We quickly figure out that 12 percent of $10,000 is $1,200. Then we use Equation 20-5 to find the following effective interest rate:

$$k = \frac{\$ \text{ Interest You Pay}}{\$ \text{ You Get to Use}}$$

$$= \frac{\$1,000}{\$10,000 - \$1,200}$$

$$= \frac{\$1,000}{\$8,800}$$

$$= .1136, \text{ or } 11.36\%$$

Simple Interest	$\dfrac{\$ \text{ Interest You Pay}}{\$ \text{ You Get to Use}}$	$\dfrac{\$1,000}{\$10,000}$	= .10, or 10%
Discount Interest	$\dfrac{\$ \text{ Interest You Pay}}{\$ \text{ You Get to Use}}$	$\dfrac{\$1,000}{\$10,000 - \$1,000 = \$9,000}$	= .1111, or 11.11%
Compensating Balance (12%)	$\dfrac{\$ \text{ Interest You Pay}}{\$ \text{ You Get to Use}}$	$\dfrac{\$1,000}{\$10,000 - \$1,200 = \$8,800}$	= .1136, or 11.36%

We find that the effect of the bank's 12 percent compensating balance requirement is to raise the effective interest rate to the borrower by 1.36 percentage points. Instead of paying 10 percent, the borrower actually pays 11.36 percent. The effect of the compensating balance requirement is to increase the effective rate of interest, 11.36 percent, compared with the stated rate of interest of 10 percent. Compensating balances are getting less common although they are still used. Direct fees paid by the borrowing customer to the bank for services rendered are becoming more common.

Figure 20-3 shows how changing the terms of a one-year loan can affect the effective interest rate. The chart summarizes the effect of simple interest, discount interest, and compensating balances. Figure 20-3 demonstrates that loan terms such as discount interest and compensating balances reduce the amount the borrower gets to use, thus raising the effective interest rate.

Loan Maturities Shorter Than One Year

Another term that affects the effective interest rate is a loan maturity that is less than one year. In such cases we modify Equation 20-5 to convert the effective interest rate of the loan that is for less than a year into an annual rate. We find the annual rate so that we can compare that rate with those from other lenders, almost all of which are expressed as annual rates. Annualizing the rates allows a comparison of apples to apples, rather than apples to oranges. An example demonstrates this point.

Suppose you are borrowing $10,000 for one *month* and paying $1,000 in interest at the end of the *month* (with no other conditions). The effective interest rate of this loan is 10 percent, according to Equation 20-5. However, remember that the rate is 10 percent *per month*. It would be inaccurate to say that the interest rate on this loan was the same as a 10 percent loan from another financial institution. Why? Because the 10 percent stated rate from the other institution is an annual rate and you are comparing it to a monthly rate. For one month, the other institution's stated rate would be 10 percent divided by 12 months equals .83 percent, which is considerably less than the 10 percent monthly interest on your loan.

Annualizing Interest Rates

We can modify Equation 20-5 so that it annualizes interest rates that are not paid yearly. The modified formula, Equation 20-6, follows:

Effective Annual Interest Rate When the Loan Term Is Less Than One Year

$$k = \left(1 + \frac{\$ \text{ Interest You Pay}}{\$ \text{ You Get to Use}}\right)^{\left(\substack{\text{Loan Periods} \\ \text{in a Year}}\right)} - 1$$

(20-6)

where: k = the effective annual interest rate

We multiply the results of Equation 20-6 by 100 to find the percentage rate.

Now let's use Equation 20-6 to annualize the $10,000 loan with interest of $1,000 a month. Remember, the monthly interest rate for this loan is 10 percent, and there are 12 monthly loan periods in a year. The calculations follow:

$$k = \left(1 + \frac{\$1,000}{\$10,000}\right)^{(12)} - 1$$

$$= \left(1 + .10\right)^{(12)} - 1$$

$$= \left(1.10\right)^{(12)} - 1$$

$$= 3.1384 - 1$$

$$= 2.1384$$

$$\times 100 = 213.84\%$$

We find that the interest rate is more than 213 percent. Surely there is a cheaper alternative at another bank. Suppose you find one with a *stated* annual interest rate of 12 percent for a $10,000 one-month loan. What's the *effective* annual interest rate for this loan? In order to apply Equation 20-6 to find out, we first compute the dollar amount of interest to be paid:

- The stated rate for one year, or 12 months, is 12 percent, so the rate for one month is 12 percent/12 = 1 percent.[4]

- 1 percent of $10,000 is $10,000 × .01 = $100.

- So, the amount of "dollars you pay" to get this loan is $100.

Because the loan is for one month, we know that there are 12 loan periods in a year. Now we're ready to plug these numbers into Equation 20-6 as shown next:

$$k = \left(1 + \frac{\$ \text{ Interest You Pay}}{\$ \text{ You Get to Use}}\right)^{\left(\begin{smallmatrix} \text{Loan Periods} \\ \text{in a Year} \end{smallmatrix}\right)} - 1$$

$$= \left(1 + \frac{\$100}{\$10,000}\right)^{(12)} - 1$$

$$= \left(1 + .01\right)^{(12)} - 1$$

$$= \left(1.01\right)^{(12)} - 1$$

$$= 1.1268 - 1$$

$$= .1268$$

$$\times 100 = 12.68\%$$

The effective annual rate, 12.68 percent, is a little higher than the bank's stated rate of 12 percent because of the compounding effect of adding "interest on interest" for 12 months.

In the chapter opener, we described the payday loan terms of Loan Mart. If $100 were borrowed for the normal two-week period, a check for $120 dated two weeks hence would

---

4. If the loan's term is one week, divide by 52. If it is one day, divide by 365, and so on.

have to be turned over to Loan Mart by the borrower. This reflects the repayment of the $100 principal plus the $20 "fee" charged. Treating the fee as interest we get:

$$k = \left(1 + \frac{\$20}{\$100}\right)^{(26)} - 1$$

$$= 1.20^{26} - 1$$

$$= 114.47546 - 1$$

$$= 113.47546$$

$$\times 100 = 11,347.546\%$$

The exponent was 26, because there are 26 two-week periods per year (52 weeks per year divided by 2). The effective annual rate for this loan is 11,347.546 percent.

We have seen how discount loans, compensating balances, and loans that have maturities less than a year affect the effective annual interest rate. Next, we walk through an example of a loan with more than one complicating term.

A Comprehensive Example

Let's consider a loan that includes all the complicating factors discussed in the preceding sections. Suppose you want to borrow $5,000 for one week, and the bank's terms are 8 percent interest, collected on a discount basis, with a 10 percent compensating balance. What is the effective annual interest rate of this loan?

Computing the Interest Cost in Dollars

The bank's stated rate of interest for one year, or 52 weeks, is 8 percent, so the rate for one week is 8 percent/52 = 0.1538 percent.

.01538 percent of $5,000 is .001538 × $5,000 = $7.69

So, the amount of dollars in interest that you pay to obtain this loan is $7.69.

Computing the Net Amount Received

Because this is a discount loan, the interest will be collected up front. That means $7.69 will be deducted from the $5,000 loan.

The loan also has a 10 percent compensating balance requirement, so 10 percent of the $5,000, or $500, must remain in a checking account at the bank, denying you the use of it during the life of the loan.

The net amount of money that you will get to use during the life of the loan is $5,000 − $7.69 − $500 = $4,492.31.

Computing the Effective Annual Interest Rate

We use Equation 20-6, the formula for annualizing a loan with a term of interest payments less than a year, to find the effective annual interest rate for this loan. The calculations follow:

We see that the effective annual interest rate for a one-week, $5,000 discount loan with an interest rate of 8 percent and a 10 percent compensating balance requirement is 9.3 percent. The effective rate of interest, 9.3 percent, is higher than the 8 percent stated rate of interest.

$$k = \left(1 + \frac{\text{\$ Interest You Pay}}{\text{\$ You Get to Use}}\right)^{\left(\begin{array}{c}\text{Loan Periods} \\ \text{in a Year}\end{array}\right)} - 1$$

$$= \left(1 + \frac{\$7.69}{\$4,492.31}\right)^{(52)} - 1$$

$$= \left(1 + .001712\right)^{(52)} - 1$$

$$= \left(1.001712\right)^{(52)} - 1$$

$$= 1.093 - 1$$

$$= .093$$

$$\times 100 = 9.3\%$$

Computing the Amount to Borrow

In the preceding comprehensive example, you tried to borrow $5,000. Presumably that was the amount you needed to use for a week. But, as shown, if the bank collected $7.69 in interest up front and made you keep $500 in a checking account during the term of the loan, you would only receive $4,492.31. Clearly, given the bank's terms, you will have to borrow some amount greater than $5,000 to end up with the $5,000 you need. So the question is, how much do you have to borrow to walk out of the bank with $5,000?

We solve this question algebraically. Let X = the amount to borrow. Now, because the loan is a discount loan, the bank will collect one week's worth of interest, or (.08/52) times X at the beginning of the week. Furthermore, 10 percent of X must remain in a checking account at the bank as a compensating balance. When these two amounts are subtracted from X, the remainder must equal $5,000. Here is the equation describing the situation:

$$X - \left(\frac{.08}{52}\right)X - .10X = \$5,000$$

We then solve for X as follows:

$$X - \left(\frac{.08}{52}\right)X - .10X = \$5,000$$
$$X - .001538X - .10X = \$5,000$$
$$.8985X = \$5,000$$
$$X = \$5,564.83$$

We find that if you borrow $5,564.83 for one week at 8 percent, discount interest, with a 10 percent compensating balance requirement, you will leave the bank with $5,000.[5]

We have examined how loan terms can affect the effective interest rate. Now we turn to types of collateral that are used to secure short-term loans.

Collateral for Short-Term Loans

The promissory note that specifies the terms of the loan often includes the type of collateral used to secure the loan.

For secured short-term loans, lenders usually require that the assets pledged for collateral be short term in nature also. Lenders require short-term assets because they are

---

5. In case you're wondering, the effective annual interest rate for this loan, per Equation 20-2, is 9.3 percent.

generally more liquid than long-term assets and are easier to convert to cash if the borrower defaults on the loan. The major types of short-term assets used for short-term loan collateral are accounts receivable and inventory.

Accounts Receivable as Collateral

Accounts receivable are assets with value because they represent money owed to a firm. Because of their value, a lender might be willing to accept the accounts as collateral for a loan. If so, the borrowing firm may *pledge* its accounts receivable. The pledge is a promise that the firm will turn over the accounts receivable collateral to the lender in the case of default.

Loan agreements that use accounts receivable as collateral usually specify that the firm is responsible for the amount of the accounts receivable even if the firm's credit customers fail to pay. In short, the borrowing firm still has to pay even if its customers don't.

Lenders try to safeguard against accounts receivable that fluctuate so much that the value of the account becomes less than the value of the loan. Accounts receivable fluctuate because some credit customers may send in payments on their outstanding accounts receivable, others may make new charges, and some may be late with payments. If accounts receivable are pledged as short-term loan collateral, lenders usually require a loan payment plan that prevents the value of the accounts from dropping below the value of the loans. For instance, a bank may require a borrower to send payments received on pledged accounts to the lender to apply against the loan balance. Sending payments as received decreases the balance of the loan as the value of accounts receivable decreases, thereby protecting the lender.

Inventory as Collateral

Like accounts receivable, inventory represents assets that have value, so it can be used as collateral for loans. The practice of using inventory as collateral for a short-term loan is called **inventory financing**.

A major problem with inventory financing is valuing the inventory. If a borrowing firm defaults on a loan secured by inventory, the lender wants to know that the inventory can compensate for the remaining loan balance. To illustrate how important valuing inventory is, suppose you were a banker who lent a firm $200,000 for six months. As collateral, the firm put up its entire inventory of Alien Angels dolls, based on characters in a soon-to-be-released major motion picture. Unfortunately, the movie was a bust. The firm was unable to repay its loan, and you as the banker have ended up with 10,000 dolls no one wants. It is small comfort to you now that the firm said the angels were worth $20 each when they were offered as collateral.

inventory financing A type of financing that uses inventory as loan collateral.

To compensate for the difficulties in valuing inventory, lenders usually lend only a fraction of the stated value of the inventory. If the inventory consists of fairly standard items that can be resold easily, like 2 × 4s, then the lender might be willing to lend up to 80 percent of the inventory's stated value. In contrast, if the inventory consists of perishable or specialized items, like the Alien Angels in our example, then the lender will only lend a small fraction of their value, or might not be willing to accept them as collateral at all.

Inventory depletion is an additional concern for lenders who allow borrowers to use inventory as short-term loan collateral. The borrowing firm can sell the pledged inventory and use the cash received for other purposes, leaving the lender with nothing if the borrower defaults. This can happen when the lender has only a general claim, or *blanket lien*, on the borrower's inventory in the event of a default. Therefore, when inventory is used as collateral for a loan, the lender will often insist on some procedures to safeguard its interests.

One procedure to safeguard the interests of the lender is for the borrower to issue trust receipts to the lender. A *trust receipt* is a legal document in which specifically identified assets, inventory in this case, are pledged as collateral for the loan. Automobiles, railroad cars, and airplanes are often financed this way. The lender can make surprise visits to the borrower's business, checking to be sure that the pledged assets are on hand as they should be. There is often a unique identification number (a car's VIN, vehicle identification number, for example) on these assets.

Another procedure to control pledged inventory is to use a public warehouse where the inventory cannot be removed and sold without permission of the lender. When the inventory is sold (with the lender's permission), the proceeds are sent to the lender and used to reduce the outstanding loan balance. Although this arrangement gives the lender control, it is expensive for the borrowing firm. Usually the borrowing firm must pay for the warehouse and seek the lender's permission each time it wants to sell some inventory.

We have seen that short-term secured loans generally have short-term liquid assets pledged as collateral, such as accounts receivable or inventory. Lenders often add loan terms to protect against problems such as fluctuating accounts receivable and overvalued or depleted inventory.

What's Next

We discussed short-term financing in this chapter, the final chapter of Part 5 of the text. We turn next to Part 6, Finance in the Global Economy. In Chapter 21, we discuss international finance.

Summary

1. *Explain the need for short-term financing.*
   Firms rely on short-term financing from outside sources for two reasons:
   - *Growth:* Profits simply may not be high enough to keep up with the rate at which they are buying new assets.
   - *Choice:* Rather than save enough money to make desired purchases, many firms borrow money at the outset to make their purchases.

2. *List the advantages and disadvantages of short-term financing.*
   Short-term financing is usually a cheaper option than long-term financing because of its generally lower interest rates. However, short-term financing is riskier than long-term financing because, unlike long-term financing, the loans come due soon, the lender may not be willing to renew financing on favorable terms, and short-term interest rates may rise unexpectedly.

3. *Describe three types of short-term financing.*
   - *Loans from banks and other institutions:* When a bank or other institution agrees to lend money to a firm, the firm signs a promissory note that specifies the repayment terms. Two common types of short-term business loans are self-liquidating loans and a line of credit. A self-liquidating loan is a loan for an asset that will generate enough return to repay the loan balance. A line of credit is a maximum total balance that a bank sets for a firm's outstanding short-term loans.
   - *Trade credit:* Trade credit is obtained by purchasing materials, supplies, or services on credit. By buying on credit, the firm has use of the funds during the time of the purchase until the account is paid.
   - *Commercial paper:* Commercial paper consists of unsecured notes issued by large, creditworthy corporations for periods up to 270 days.

4. *Compute the cost of trade credit and commercial paper.*
   The cost of trade credit is calculated by dividing the amount of the discount offered by the supplier by the amount the buyer owes. The result is annualized for comparison with other financing sources.

   The cost of commercial paper is quoted as a discount yield. To compare the percent cost of a commercial paper issue to the percent cost of a bank loan, the commercial paper's discount yield must be converted to an effective annual interest rate.

5. *Calculate the cost of a loan and explain how loan terms affect the effective interest rate.*
   The cost of a loan is normally measured by dividing the amount paid to obtain the loan by the amount the borrower gets to use during the life of the loan. The result is converted to a percentage. The stated interest rate on a loan is not always the same as the loan's effective annual interest rate. If the lender collects interest up front (a discount interest loan) or requires the borrowing firm to keep a fraction of the loan in an account at the lending institution (a compensating balance), then the amount of money the borrower gets to use is reduced. As a result, the effective rate of interest the borrower is paying is increased.

6. *Describe how accounts receivable and inventory can be used as collateral for short-term loans.*
   Short-term loans are often secured by short-term, liquid assets, such as accounts receivable and inventory. When accounts receivable are used for collateral, the borrower pledges to turn over its accounts receivable to the lender if the borrower defaults. When inventory is used for collateral, the borrowing firm often sets aside the inventory that has been identified for collateral in a separate warehouse. When the inventory is sold, the cash received is forwarded to the lender in payment for the loan.

Key Terms

commercial paper A short-term, unsecured debt instrument issued by a large corporation or financial institution.

compensating balance A specified amount that a lender requires a borrower to maintain in a non-interest-paying account during the life of a loan.

discount loan A loan with terms that call for the loan interest to be deducted from the loan proceeds at the time the loan is granted.

effective interest rate The annual interest rate that reflects the dollar interest paid divided by the dollar obtained for use.

inventory financing A type of financing that uses inventory as loan collateral.

line of credit An informal arrangement between a lender and borrower wherein the lender sets a limit on the maximum amount of funds the borrower may use at any one time.

promissory note A legal document the borrower signs indicating agreement to the terms of a loan.

self-liquidating loan A loan that is used to acquire assets that generate enough cash to pay off the loan.

stated interest rate The interest rate advertised by the lender. Depending on the terms of the loan, the stated rate may or may not be the same as the effective interest rate.

Equations Introduced in This Chapter

Equation 20-1. Trade Credit Effective Annual Interest Rate Formula:

$$k = \left(1 + \frac{\text{Discount \%}}{100 - \text{Discount \%}}\right)^{\left(\frac{365}{\text{Days to Pay} - \text{Discount Period}}\right)} - 1$$

where: k = Cost of trade credit expressed as an effective annual interest rate

Discount % = Percentage discount being offered

Days to Pay = Time between the day of the credit purchase and the day the firm must pay its bill

Discount Period = Number of days in the discount period

Equation 20-2. Dollar Amount of the Discount on a Commercial Paper Note:

$$D = \frac{DY \times Par \times DTG}{360}$$

where: D = Dollar amount of the discount

DY = Discount yield

Par = Face value of the commercial paper issue; the amount to be paid at maturity

DTG = Days to go until maturity

Equation 20-3. Price of a Commercial Paper Note:

$$\text{Price} = Par - D$$

where: Par = Face value of the note at maturity

D = Dollar amount of the discount

Equation 20-4. Effective Annual Interest Rate of a Commercial Paper Note:

$$k = \left(\frac{Par}{\text{Price}}\right)^{\left(\frac{365}{DTG}\right)} - 1$$

where: k = The effective annual interest rate

Par = Face value of the note at maturity

Price = Price of the note when purchased

DTG = Number of days until the note matures

Equation 20-5. Effective Interest Rate of a Loan:

$$k = \frac{\$ \text{ Interest You Pay}}{\$ \text{ You Get to Use}}$$

where: k = The effective interest rate

Equation 20-6. Effective Annual Interest Rate:

$$k = \left(1 + \frac{\$ \text{ Interest You Pay}}{\$ \text{ You Get to Use}}\right)^{\left(\substack{\text{Loan Periods} \\ \text{in a Year}}\right)} - 1$$

where: k = The effective annual interest rate

Self-Test

ST-1. Your company's suppliers offer terms of 3/15, n40. What is the cost of forgoing the discount and delaying payment until the fortieth day?

ST-2. A commercial paper dealer is willing to pay 4 percent discount yield for a $1 million issue of Microsoft 60-day commercial paper notes. To what effective annual interest rate does the 4 percent discount yield equate?

ST-3. A bank is willing to lend your company $20,000 for six months at 8 percent interest, with a 10 percent compensating balance. What is the effective annual interest rate of this loan?

ST-4. Using the loan terms from ST-3, how much would your firm have to borrow in order to have $20,000 for use during the loan period?

Review Questions

1. Companies with rapidly growing levels of sales do not need to worry about raising funds from outside the firm. Do you agree or disagree with this statement? Explain.

2. Banks like to make short-term, self-liquidating loans to businesses. Why?

3. What are compensating balances and why do banks require them from some customers? Under what circumstances would banks be most likely to impose compensating balances?

4. What happens when a bank charges discount interest on a loan?

5. What is trustworthy collateral from the lender's perspective? Explain whether accounts receivable and inventory are trustworthy collateral.

6. Trade credit is free credit. Do you agree or disagree with this statement? Explain.

7. What are the pros and cons of commercial paper relative to bank loans for a company seeking short-term financing?

Build Your Communication Skills

CS-1. Your firm's request for a $50,000 loan for one month has been approved. The bank's terms are 10 percent annual discount interest with a 10 percent compensating balance. Prepare a one-page report for the CEO of your firm explaining how the effective interest rate of this loan is calculated.

CS-2. Imagine you are a loan officer for a bank. One of the town's businesses has applied for a loan of $200,000 for six months. The company has offered to put up the building in which its manufacturing operations are located as collateral for the loan. Local real estate agents estimate the building is worth at least $220,000. Write a letter to the company explaining why your bank does not wish to accept the building as collateral. Propose two alternative assets that your bank would accept.

Problems

20-1. Schoolboy Q is planning to borrow $20,000 for one year, paying interest in the amount of $1,600 to a bank. Calculate the effective annual interest rate if the interest is paid:

Simple and Discount Loans

a. At the end of the year

b. At the beginning of the year (discount loan)

20-2. Llewellyn Sinclair is planning to borrow $40,000 for one year, paying interest of $2,400 to a bank at the beginning of the year (discount loan). In addition, according to the terms of the loan, the bank requires Chad to keep 10 percent of the borrowed funds in a non-interest-bearing checking account at the bank during the life of the loan. Calculate the effective annual interest rate.

Loans with Compensating Balance

20-3. Hank Scorpio is considering borrowing $20,000 for a year from a bank that has offered the following alternatives:

Challenge Problem

a. An interest payment of $1,800 at the end of the year

b. An interest payment of 8 percent of $20,000 at the beginning of the year

c. An interest payment of 7.5 percent of $20,000 at the end of the year in addition to a compensating balance requirement of 10 percent

   1. Which alternative is best for Ralph from the effective-interest-rate point of view?

   2. If Ralph needs the entire amount of $20,000 at the beginning of the year and chooses the terms under part *c*, how much should he borrow? How much interest would he have to pay at the end of the year?

20-4. If Chester Lampwick borrows $14,000 for three months at an annual interest rate of 16 percent paid up-front with a compensating balance of 10 percent, compute the effective annual interest rate of the loan.

Loans with a Life of Less than a Year

20-5. You are planning to borrow $10,000 from a bank for two weeks. The bank's terms are 7 percent annual interest, collected on a discount basis, with a 10 percent compensating balance. Compute the effective annual interest rate of the loan.

Discount Loans with Compensating Balance for Less Than a Year

20-6. The company run by Bubbles, Ricky, and Julian is planning a $1 million issue of commercial paper to finance increased sales from easing the credit policy. The commercial paper note has a 60-day maturity and 6 percent discount yield. Calculate:

Commercial Paper

a. The dollar amount of the discount

b. The price

c. The effective annual interest rate for the issue

20-7. Carmen Velasco, an analyst at Smidgen Corporation, is trying to calculate the effective annual interest rate for a $2 million issue of a Smidgen 60-day commercial paper note. The commercial paper dealer is prepared to offer a 4 percent discount yield on the issue. Calculate the effective annual interest rate for Carmen.

Commercial Paper

20-8. Bathseba Everdene, the sales manager of Gordon's Bakery, Inc., wants to extend trade credit with terms of 2/15, n45 to your company to boost sales. Calculate the cost of forgoing the discount and paying on the forty-fifth day.

Trade Credit

20-9. Calculate the cost of forgoing the following trade credit discounts and paying on the last day allowed:

Trade Credit

a. 3/10, n60

b. 2/15, n30

Recalculate the costs assuming payments were made on the fortieth day in each of the preceding cases without any penalty. Compare your results.

20-10. Legacy Enterprises received an invoice from its supplier. The terms of credit were stated

Trade Credit

as 3/15, n45. Calculate the effective annual interest rate on the trade credit.

Commercial Paper ➡ **20-11.** Callaway Krugs issues $2,000,000 in commercial paper for 90 days at a 3.8 percent discount yield. Calculate each of the following.

    a. Dollar amount of the discount

    b. Price of the commercial paper

    c. Effective annual interest rate on the commercial paper

Effective Interest Rate ➡ **20-12.** Lugash wants to buy a new car. The bank has offered him a $20,000 discount interest loan at 6.5 percent. What is the effective interest rate?

Compensating Balance ➡ **20-13.** Third National Bank requires that all its borrowers have a compensating balance of 13 percent of the amount borrowed. If you need to take out a small-business expansion loan for $30,000 at 10 percent, what would be your effective interest rate on this one-year loan?

Annualizing Interest Rates ➡ **20-14.** You are the financial manager for Talc, Ltd., and the owner has just asked you to compute the effective annual interest rate on the loans the company currently has outstanding. The following is a list of these loans:

    a. $50,000; .5% monthly rate, maturity: 1 month

    b. $150,000, .6% monthly rate, maturity: 3 months

    c. $75,000, .75% monthly rate, maturity: 1 month

    d. $120,000; .8% monthly rate, maturity: 6 months

Comparing Costs of Alternative Short-Term Financing Sources ➡ **20-15.** To sustain its growth in sales, Monarch Machine Tools Company needs $100,000 in additional funds next year. The following alternatives for financing the growth are available:

    a. Forgoing a discount available on trade credit with terms of 1/10, n45 and, hence, increasing its accounts payable

    b. Obtaining a loan from a bank at 10 percent interest paid up front

    Calculate the cost of financing for each option and select the best source.

Comparing Costs of Alternative Short-Term Financing Sources ➡ **20-16.** If the bank imposes an additional requirement of a 12 percent compensating balance on Monarch in problem 20-15 and the company could negotiate more-liberal credit terms of 1/15, n60 from its supplier, would there be any change in Monarch's choice of short-term financing?

Amount to Borrow ➡ **20-17.** Stacy Lovell has just finished her company's *pro forma* financial statements and has concluded that $1.5 million in additional funds are needed. To cover this cash shortage, her company is going to take out a loan. HomeLand Bank has offered them a 9 percent discount interest loan with a 12 percent compensating balance. How much does Ms. Lovell's company need to borrow with these stated terms to leave the bank with $1.5 million in usable funds?

ST-1. The cost is found using Equation 20-1. The discount percentage is 3 percent, the discount period is 15 days, and payment is to be made on the fortieth day. The calculations follow:

$$k = \left(1 + \frac{3}{100 - 3}\right)^{\left(\frac{365}{40 - 15}\right)} - 1$$

$$= \left(1 + .0309278\right)^{(14.6)} - 1$$

$$= \left(1.0309278\right)^{(14.6)} - 1$$

$$= 1.56 - 1$$

$$= .56, \text{ or } 56\%$$

ST-2. Use the three-step process described in the text to find the effective annual interest rate as follows:

Step 1: Compute the discount using Equation 20-2.

$$D = \frac{DY \times Par \times DTG}{360}$$

$$= \frac{.04 \times \$1,000,000 \times 60}{360}$$

$$= \frac{\$2,400,000}{360}$$

$$= \$6,667$$

Step 2: Compute the price using Equation 20-3.

$$Price = Par - D$$

$$= \$1,000,000 - \$6,667$$

$$= \$993,333$$

Step 3: Compute the effective annual interest rate using Equation 20-4.

$$k = \left(\frac{Par}{Price}\right)^{\left(\frac{365}{DTG}\right)} - 1$$

$$= \left(\frac{\$1,000,000}{\$993,333}\right)^{\left(\frac{365}{60}\right)} - 1$$

$$= 1.00671^{6.083} - 1$$

$$= 1.0415 - 1$$

$$= .0415, \text{ or } 4.15\%$$

ST-3. The amount your firm would pay in interest with the loan is

$$.08 / 2 = .04 \text{ for six months}$$

$$.04 \times \$20,000 = \$800$$

The amount your firm would be able to use during the life of the loan is the principal less the compensating balance:

$$\$20,000 - (.10 \times \$20,000) = \$18,000$$

The loan is for six months, so we use Equation 20-6 to solve for the effective annual interest rate:

$$k = \left(1 + \frac{\$800}{\$18,000}\right)^{(2)} - 1$$

$$= \left(1 + .0444\right)^{(2)} - 1$$

$$= \left(1.044\right)^{(2)} - 1$$

$$= 1.0908 - 1$$

$$= .0908$$

$$\times 100 = 9.08\%$$

ST-4. Let X = the amount to borrow.

$$X - .10X = \$20,000$$

$$.9X = \$20,000$$

$$X = \$22,222$$

Finance in the Global Economy

PART 6

Source: canadastock/Shutterstock

It is abundantly clear that in today's world, financial management decisions cannot be made without considering their effects in international markets. U.S. financial markets lurch up and down as news from Europe, Asia, and other parts of the world alternates between good and bad, or perhaps between not so bad and very bad. The countries that adopted the euro as a common currency have centralized monetary policy but decentralized fiscal policy. Many companies not only have international sales, but also international divisions and subsidiaries (many Japanese cars are manufactured in the United States, for example). Will a trade war break out with companies imposing tariffs, quotas, and other barriers on goods imported from other countries? When one country imposes such trade barriers on imports from another country, that other country tends to retaliate by setting up its own barriers. This can escalate into a full-blown trade war involving many countries, harming national economies as costs rise and shortages of key goods develop. In short, the U.S. economy is connected to the rest of the world more closely than ever before. We are all interconnected whether we like it or not. Chapter 21 examines the issues in international finance in detail. Beginning with multinational corporations and how they work, the chapter proceeds through currency exchange rates, exchange rate theories, and the management of international risk, including political and cultural risks. The chapter concludes with a survey of the major international trade agreements governing how multinational firms do business.

International Finance

"It used to be said that when the U.S. sneezed, the world caught a cold. The opposite is equally true today."
—Lawrence Summers

Source: violetkaipa/Shutterstock

Cheering for a Weak Dollar—Is It Un-American?

Caterpillar is a United States–based corporation that sells heavy construction equipment. Its main competition comes from a Japan-based corporation named Komatsu. Building big machines that move tons of dirt around a construction site is something many people around the world would expect from an American company such as Caterpillar that has a long history in this business.

Many of the executives at Caterpillar are veterans of military service. This is a big, strong, American company that builds big, rugged equipment. As such, it is a foregone conclusion that executives at Caterpillar would be in favor of a strong dollar in the world currency markets. Isn't it?

Actually, no it isn't. Caterpillar likes to see the U.S. dollar weaken against the yen, euro, and other major world currencies. When the dollar weakens, people from those countries whose currencies are strengthening against the dollar can buy more dollars with a given amount of their currency. Products sold by U.S.-based companies such as Caterpillar become less expensive for these customers outside the United States when the dollar weakens. Products from competitors such as Japan's Komatsu become relatively more expensive to customers outside Japan when the yen strengthens in world currency markets.

In this chapter we examine the role of currency exchange rates in global business and a variety of other international business issues.

Learning Objectives

After reading this chapter, you should be able to:

1. Define a multinational corporation (MNC) and explain its importance.
2. Demonstrate how the law of comparative advantage leads to international trade that benefits individuals and firms.
3. Describe exchange rates and their effects on firms.
4. Show how firms manage the risks of fluctuating exchange rates.
5. Discuss exchange rate theories.
6. Describe the political and cultural risks that affect MNCs.
7. Explain how international trade agreements affect international business.

Chapter Overview

This chapter addresses the financial issues that companies face when they maintain operations in, or sell goods and services to, other countries. These issues include differences in currency, language, politics, and culture. We also explore the potential benefits and risks of doing business in other countries. We closely examine the risk of transacting business in either a domestic or foreign currency and how to manage that risk. Finally, we look at international trade agreements and their effect on business.

Multinational Corporations

multinational corporation (MNC) A corporation that has operations in more than one country.

A **multinational corporation (MNC)** is a corporation that has operations in more than one country. Most large corporations conduct at least some of their business in countries other than the one they call home. In fact, it is getting difficult to accurately describe whether companies are U.S., German, or Japanese, in spite of what their names might suggest.[1] What percent of their sales do you believe Samsung generates in its home country of South Korea, for example?

Financial Advantages of Foreign Operations

You may have read stories about McDonald's fast-food restaurants expanding into Russia and Japan, or Kentucky Fried Chicken (now known as KFC) opening a branch in the People's Republic of China. Coca-Cola and Pepsi-Cola executives count on the billion dollar growth potential of their popular products in overseas markets. Boeing, once a leading supplier for U.S. firms, is now primarily an exporter. Companies are always looking for growth opportunities, and many of these opportunities are in other countries.

In addition to the potential demand for products and services, operating abroad can decrease production costs. Labor may be less costly in other countries. For instance, much of the production of clothing by companies based in the United States is done in other countries where lower wages are paid to workers.

Companies can often obtain political advantages by shifting some operations away from home. For example, Toyota, Honda, and Nissan of Japan, and the German company BMW all produce some of their cars in the United States. This lessens the risk of the U.S. Congress passing laws that would restrict imports of, or increase the tax on, sales of these cars. Politicians generally approve of foreign-based companies opening plants in the United States, thus creating new U.S. jobs. Those politicians frequently appear at the ribbon-cutting ceremony when a new plant located in the U.S. and built by a foreign company opens for business. The same approval is not generally seen when U.S.-based companies open plants in foreign countries and create jobs for the citizens of those countries. Firms based in the United States often have the same import and tax reasons to open production plants in other countries.

Ethical Issues Facing Multinational Corporations

Using foreign labor may pose difficult ethical questions for U.S. companies. Are very poor people from other countries being exploited because they can be employed at lower wages than would be paid to U.S. workers? Are overseas plants as safe as U.S. plants, where OSHA inspectors check up on employers?[2] Does a corporation have the moral responsibility to meet the same health and safety standards for its workers in other countries as it applies to its U.S. workers, even if not legally required to do so? Calvin Klein, Liz Claiborne, The Gap, and other garment industry companies that manufacture clothing outside of the United States to control labor costs must balance the moral issues of human rights against their obligations to stockholders.

Another ethical issue arises when operations are moved to countries where environmental laws are less strict than the laws of the company's home country. Firms may lower costs by

---

1. Several years ago, the Volkswagen Rabbit, made by a German-based company, was the only car sold in the United States that was made in the United States, by U.S. workers, with all U.S.-made parts.

2. OSHA stands for Occupational Safety and Health Administration, a federal agency responsible for enforcing national laws intended to protect workers employed by U.S. companies.

disposing of waste products or emitting pollutants in a potentially dangerous manner. Even though the laws of the other country may not have pollution control or disposal guidelines, should a business harm the environment or create a danger that could harm future generations to lower current costs? How should managers weigh the morality of business procedures against their fiduciary duty to the owners of the company's common stock to maximize value?

Unfortunately, there are no clear-cut answers to many of these questions. Certainly, few people would condone worker exploitation and the destruction of the environment. But what if working conditions are only slightly less safe, or the environmental practices in that other country only slightly more offensive by the home country's standards? What if these slightly offensive environmental practices are commonplace and accepted in that other country? Where should we draw the line? Facing these questions, even when the answers are difficult to agree on, is an important first step in making ethical decisions.

Comparative Advantage

International trade creates significant financial benefits because not all countries can produce goods and services with the same degree of efficiency. The law of comparative advantage says that each country (and each person) should concentrate on producing those goods (or providing services) for which it has a lower opportunity cost than other countries (or people).

Having a comparative advantage at something is different than having an absolute advantage. For example, for the sake of this intellectual exercise let's assume that Lebron James is the world's best automobile mechanic. He has an absolute advantage at this activity over everyone else in the world. Will he fix his own car? No. Every hour he spends fixing his own car is an hour not spent on basketball and commercial endorsements. Playing basketball and doing commercial endorsements earn Lebron significantly more money than fixing cars ever could. It is in Lebron's interest to hire someone, whose skills at fixing cars may not be as great as his, to fix his car. The opportunity cost of spending time to fix his own car is too great. Although Lebron has an absolute advantage at fixing cars over the person he hires, the mechanic he hires has a comparative advantage over Lebron.

The same thing holds for countries and what they choose to produce for themselves and what they buy from other countries. The United States used to produce large amounts of athletic shoes. Today it produces almost none. China and Indonesia have developed a comparative advantage in the production of athletic shoes so the United States focuses on those things at which it has a comparative advantage, such as making motion pictures, and imports almost all its athletic shoes from countries such as China and Indonesia. The opportunity costs faced by China and Indonesia when they choose to produce athletic shoes are not as great as the opportunity costs faced by the United states were it to choose to make its own athletic shoes. This is why the United States has chosen to make almost none of the athletic shoes it uses.

People in China, Indonesia, and most every other country in the world seem to have a great preference of movies made by United States companies. This is not to say that U.S.-produced movies are better than those made in other countries. It does appear, however, that people from many countries are willing to pay to see blockbuster U.S.-made movies. The next James Bond, Despicable Me, Batman, Shrek, Star Wars, X-Men, or Transformers movies are almost certain to bring in large crowds around the world. Although many other countries make high quality movies, as a general rule the demand for them from people outside the country of origin doesn't tend to be as great as it is for U.S.-made movies.[3]

Exchange Rates and Their Effects

Given that countries can benefit from trading with each other, how do they overcome the problem of having different currencies? An **exchange rate** is an expression of the value of one country's currency in terms of another country's currency. It specifies how many units of one country's currency can be exchanged for one unit of the other country's currency. For example, the exchange rate between the U.S. dollar and the Mexican peso

exchange rate The number of units of one country's currency that is needed to purchase one unit of another country's currency.

---

3. The quality of U.S.-produced movies is a subjective judgment, but it is clear from film company revenues that the world seems to enjoy watching them.

might be 10 Mexican pesos per one U.S. dollar. The exchange rate between the U.S. dollar and the Japanese yen might be 100 Japanese yen per one U.S. dollar.

Exchange rates can be expressed as the number of units of the foreign currency per one unit of domestic currency, as in the previous paragraph, or as the number of units of the domestic currency per one unit of the foreign currency. For example, if 10 Mexican pesos can be exchanged for one U.S. dollar, then one Mexican peso is worth one-tenth of a U.S. dollar, or $0.10. The exchange rate can be expressed as 10 pesos per dollar or as one-tenth of a dollar per peso. The one exchange rate is the reciprocal of the other.

The International Organization for Standardization (ISO) has set standards for how exchange rates are to be expressed. (Yes, that's ISO and not IOS.) It labels the U.S. dollar USD, the euro EUR, the British pound GBP, and the Japanese yen JPY. When describing the exchange rate between two currencies, one of the currencies may be referred to as the home currency and the other as the foreign currency. In this text we take the U.S. perspective and refer to the U.S. dollar as the home currency and all other currencies as foreign. With a "direct quote," the number of units of the home currency per unit of the foreign currency is specified. Taking a U.S. perspective a direct quote would be the number of dollars it would take to buy one unit of a foreign (non-U.S.) currency. For example, in the financial press the exchange rate between the U.S. dollar and the euro would typically be described as EUR/USD = 1.23. The slash used in expressing this exchange rate does not mean "per." It is not the euros per dollar exchange rate. In fact it is the opposite. In March of 2018 it took 1.23 U.S. dollars to buy 1 euro. This is a direct quote. On the other hand the exchange rate between the U.S. dollar and the Japanese yen is usually given as an "indirect quote." The U.S. perspective for an indirect quote would be the number of units of a foreign (non-U.S) currency that could be obtained with a U.S. dollar. In March of 2018 the exchange rate between the U.S. dollar and Japanese yen was described as USD/JPY = 106. This indirect quote says that 1 U.S. dollar would buy 106 Japanese yen. The indirect quote is the inverse of the direct quote. For example if the direct quote of EUR/USD is 1.23 then the indirect quote is 1 divided by 1.23 or .81300813. If the indirect quote of USD/JPY is 106 then the direct quote is 1 divided by 106 or .009433962. Nine decimal places are being used here since that is the largest number the TI BAII Plus calculator featured in this book will display. Yahoo Finance provides four decimal places when displaying currency exchange rates. The financial press usually uses direct quotes for describing the exchange rates for the British pound and the euro relative to the U.S. dollar. The convention is to use indirect quote notation for describing the value of other non-U.S. currencies relative to the U.S. dollar.

In the rest of this chapter we will use the convention of describing the number of units of Currency A needed to buy 1 unit of Currency B and the inverse that describes the number of units of Currency B needed to buy 1 unit of Currency A.

A sampling of actual exchange rates as of March 19, 2018 is shown in Table 21-1. We see from Table 21-1 that the exchange rate is expressed as how many U.S. dollars (the number of units of the domestic currency) per one unit of the foreign currency. That is, one British pound would buy 1.4022 U.S. dollars. This indicates that one U.S. dollar would buy .7132 British pounds. Also on this day the U.S. dollar was worth 18.7056 Mexican pesos. This indicates that one Mexican peso was worth 5.35 U.S. cents (.0535 U.S. dollars).

Fluctuating Exchange Rates

Exchange rates fluctuate every day due to changing world conditions. Currency traders take advantage of these fluctuations by "buying" and "selling" currencies. This means they exchange a certain amount of one currency for a certain amount of another. The currency market is one of the largest financial markets in the world. Currency traders buy and sell the equivalent of over $1 trillion in an average trading day. The "price" of buying or selling a currency is its exchange rate. So, if a trader had wanted to sell U.S. dollars in exchange for British pounds on March 19, 2018, the trader would have paid about 1.40 dollars for each pound. If the value of one currency decreases relative to the value of another currency, the currency with the falling value is said to be weakening. For example, if the exchange rate between the U.S. dollar and the Mexican peso changes from 10 Mexican pesos per U.S. dollar to eight Mexican pesos per U.S. dollar, then the U.S. dollar weakened relative to the Mexican peso,

TABLE 21-1 Exchange Rates Relative to the U.S. Dollar

Currency	Rate in U.S. $ March 19, 2018
British Pound	1.4022
Canadian Dollar	0.7644
Mexican Peso	0.0535
Swiss Franc	1.0511
Japanese Yen	0.0094
Euro	1.2334
Bitcoin	8,400.0049

Sources: www.yahoo.finance.com/currency-investing

and it now takes more dollars to buy a given number of Mexican pesos. At the same time, of course, the Mexican peso is said to have strengthened relative to the U.S. dollar because the exchange rate would have changed from $0.10 dollar per peso to $0.125 dollar per peso. A given number of Mexican pesos now buys more U.S. dollars.

When a country's currency weakens relative to the currencies of other countries, imported goods become more expensive for citizens of the country with the weakened currency. Say that one pound of Mexican limes costs 10 pesos. If the exchange rate between Mexican pesos and U.S. dollars is 10 pesos per dollar, then one dollar (10 pesos) will buy a pound of Mexican limes. However, if the exchange rate changes from 10 pesos per dollar to 8 per dollar, then the importer could no longer buy the pound of limes with one dollar: The limes cost 10 pesos and the dollar is equivalent to 8 pesos. Each peso is now worth $0.125, so the importer would now need $1.25 ($0.125 × 10) to buy a pound of limes instead of the $1.00 that would have made this purchase earlier.

When the U.S. dollar weakens against the Mexican peso, U.S. importers of Mexican goods must pay more dollars to purchase Mexican goods that are sold in pesos. Similarly, people in the United States will find that Mexican goods and services are now more expensive in general. U.S. vacationers in Mexico learn this lesson quickly.

Conversely, a weakened dollar relative to the Mexican peso means that U.S. goods and services are less expensive for Mexican citizens to buy. This is why Mexican tourists tend to come to the United States in greater numbers when the dollar is weakening against the Mexican peso, and why business improves for U.S. companies exporting goods to Mexico. Generally, these same effects occur when the U.S. dollar weakens compared to any other given country's currency.

What happens when the U.S. dollar strengthens against the currency of another country? Using our Mexican peso example, if the dollar strengthens against the peso, more U.S. consumers would buy Mexican limes and other goods and vacation in greater numbers in Mexico. At the same time, Mexican people would buy fewer U.S. goods and take fewer U.S. vacations.[4]

These changes in spending patterns usually occur whenever the exchange rate fluctuates. The relative attractiveness of one country's goods and services abroad fluctuates with the relative value of the currency changes.

Cross Rates

If we know the exchange rate between the currencies of Country A and Country B, and also between the currencies of Country A and Country C, then we can determine the

---

4. In our running example, we assume that the domestic prices in the two countries stay the same.

exchange rate between the currencies of Country B and Country C. For example, if we know that one U.S. dollar is worth 10 Mexican pesos and that one U.S. dollar is worth 100 Japanese yen, we can determine how many Japanese yen a person would receive in exchange for each Mexican peso. An exchange rate of two currencies found by using a common third currency is known as a currency **cross rate**.

cross rate An exchange rate determined by examining how each of two currencies is valued in terms of a common third currency.

To calculate a currency cross rate, multiply the ratio of Currency A to Currency B exchange rate by the ratio of Currency B to Currency C exchange rate as shown in Equation 21-1.

Calculation of a Currency Cross Rate

$$\frac{\text{Currency A}}{\text{Currency B}} \times \frac{\text{Currency B}}{\text{Currency C}} = \frac{\text{Currency A}}{\text{Currency C}} \tag{21-1}$$

The calculation of the Japanese yen to the Mexican peso cross rate using the cross rate formula in Equation 21-1 is shown next.

$$\frac{\text{Japanese Yen}}{\text{U.S. Dollar}} \times \frac{\text{U.S. Dollar}}{\text{Mexican Peso}} = \frac{\text{Japanese Yen}}{\text{Mexican Peso}}$$

Suppose 100 Japanese yen are worth one dollar, as we said earlier. Then suppose one U.S. dollar is worth 10 Mexican pesos. Substituting these values into Equation 21-1 produces the following cross rate:

$$\frac{100 \text{ Japanese Yen}}{1 \text{ U.S. Dollar}} \times \frac{1 \text{ U.S. Dollar}}{10 \text{ Mexican Pesos}} = \frac{100 \text{ Japanese Yen}}{10 \text{ Mexican Pesos}} = \frac{10 \text{ Japanese Yen}}{1 \text{ Mexican Peso}}$$

We find that the U.S. dollar in the first term of the equation cancels out the U.S. dollar in the second term, leaving the yen-per-peso exchange rate, which in this case is 100 to 10, reduced to 10 to 1.

A sampling of currency cross rates is shown in Table 21-2.

Cross rates are a useful tool. If you were on a business trip in Europe but were managing a project for a U.S. firm that had a Japanese supplier, you might want to know the exchange rate between the dollar and yen but would only have information about the euro. The cross rate formula allows you to quickly calculate the dollar-to-euro exchange rate.

Exchange Rate Effects on MNCs

Fluctuating exchange rates present special risks and opportunities for multinational corporations. As the home currency of an MNC strengthens or weakens against currencies of other countries where the MNC has operations, the firm will feel a financial impact.

TABLE 21-2 Currency Cross Rates on March 19, 2018

	U.S. Dollar	British Pound	Canadian Dollar	Yen	Euro
U.S. Dollar	—	0.7132	1.3082	106.3829	0.8108
British Pound	1.4022	—	1.8348	148.7133	1.1369
Canadian Dollar	0.7644	0.5450	—	81.0700	0.6198
Japanese Yen	0.0094	0.0067	0.0123	—	0.0076
Euro	1.2334	0.8796	1.6134	130.8398	—

Sources: www.yahoo.finance.com/currency-investing

Suppose, for example, that McDonald's Corporation, a U.S.-based MNC, realized profits of 500 million euros from its operations in Germany during 2018. At some point, McDonald's Corporation is likely to convert its euro profits to U.S. dollars and bring the dollars to the United States. Converting foreign currency profits into domestic currency to send to the home country of the business is known as repatriating the profits. Why repatriate profits? McDonald's stockholders expect U.S. dollar dividends, not euro dividends.

To demonstrate how to report repatriated profits to shareholders, let's revisit the McDonald's example. Suppose the exchange rate is 1.50 U.S. dollars per euro at the start of the year. Also assume the exchange rate holds steady throughout the year. When McDonald's repatriates its profits at year's end, it will report on the income statement 500 million times 1.50 = 750 million in U.S. dollar profits from its German operations.

Now suppose that the exchange rate does not hold steady during the year. Suppose instead that the dollar per euro exchange rate falls from 1.50 dollars per euro to 1.10 dollar per euro by year's end. It now takes fewer dollars to buy a euro than it did at the start of the year, 1.10 instead of 1.50. The dollar has strengthened against the euro. The euro has weakened against the dollar. Now when the McDonalds profits are repatriated to the U.S., they are worth 500 million × 1.10 = 550 million U.S. dollars. Clearly, the strengthening of the U.S. dollar during the year hurt McDonald's Corporation. Its U.S. dollar profits were 200 million U.S. dollars lower ($750 million – $550 million) than they would have been had the dollar not strengthened.

A strengthening U.S. dollar has a negative effect on an MNC that repatriates its profits from the country whose currency is weakening. However, if the U.S. dollar weakens relative to the foreign currency, U.S. based company profits rise. Going back to our McDonald's example, suppose that the U.S. dollar had weakened relative to the euro during the year. McDonald's U.S. dollar profits would have been greater after converting the euros to dollars and repatriating the profits back to the United States.

Exchange Rate Effects on Foreign Stock and Bond Investments

A corporation does not have to have actual business operations in another country to be affected by exchange rate fluctuations. If a company holds stocks or bonds denominated in the currencies of other countries, the fluctuations in the value of these currencies will affect the dollar value of the stocks and bonds. This applies to individual investors' holdings as well.

If Betsy Ross, a U.S. investor, held 100 shares of Lufthansa common stock valued at 20 euros per share, a weakening of the euro (strengthening of the U.S. dollar) would hurt Ross just as it hurt McDonald's in our earlier example. If the exchange rate were, say, 1.10 dollars per euro, then Ross's investment would be worth 20 × 1.10 = 22 U.S. dollars per share.

However, if the exchange rate went from 1.10 to 1.00 dollars per euro, the U.S. dollar value of Ross's stock would decrease from $22 per share to $20 (20 euros × $1.00 per euro = $20). Ross experienced a loss of $2/$22 = .0909, or 9.09 percent, even though the stock's price on the German stock exchange did not change at all. Of course, if the dollar had weakened, there would have been a positive financial impact on Betsy. A strengthening dollar is one of the risks a U.S. citizen takes when investing in a country that uses a different currency.

Managing Risk

International operations provide not only special challenges and opportunities but also special risks. Exchange rate risk can be hedged. Investors and MNCs often find diversification benefits when foreign investments are added to an all-domestic portfolio. Risk of foreign securities held by U.S. citizens, caused by fluctuating exchange rates, can be managed by purchasing foreign claims on foreign securities denominated in U.S. dollars.

Hedging

The risk that a multinational corporation faces due to fluctuating exchange rates is one that can be managed. *Forward contracts*, *futures contracts*, and *currency swaps* are all available to help an MNC hedge currency risk. A **hedge** is a financial agreement used to

hedge A financial arrangement used to offset or protect against negative effects of something else, such as fluctuating exchange rates.

offset or guard against risk. A company may choose to hedge against adverse changes in interest rates, commodity prices, or currency exchange rates.

Forward contracts are contracts in which one party agrees to buy, and the other party agrees to sell, a certain amount of an asset (a currency for example) at a specified price (exchange rate) at a specified future time. *Futures contracts* are similar except they are standardized contracts and can be traded on organized exchanges. *Swaps* are directly negotiated contracts, like forward contracts, in which each party agrees to swap payments at specified points in time according to a predetermined formula. For instance, one party could pay U.S. dollars and the other Japanese yen, each according to the amounts called for in the swap contract. By agreeing to a forward, futures, or swap contract, an MNC can protect against a loss that will occur if the feared change in exchange rate occurs. The firm using these hedging instruments insulates itself from this risk.

Diversification Benefits of Foreign Investments

There are often significant diversification benefits to investing in a variety of countries, both for MNCs and for individual investors. Instead of putting all your money in one country, spreading your investment around several countries will often prove beneficial. If the economy or market is weak in one country, it may be stronger in another. If your money is spread around in several countries, the good news in one country will often cancel out the bad news from another.

The returns earned from investments in other countries often have low correlations with the returns earned from investments in the home country. Chapter 7 showed the risk-reducing potential of creating portfolios in which the individual assets have returns with low correlations relative to each other. Figure 21-1 shows how diversification benefits are greater with a portfolio that contains both domestic and foreign securities (average correlation of .4 in our example), rather than domestic securities alone (average correlation of .8 in our example).

If you review Chapter 7, you will see specifically how the correlation between the returns of assets affects the risk of a portfolio. Because the correlation of returns between a U.S. stock and a foreign stock tends to be lower than between two U.S. stocks, international diversification is often an important risk-management tool.

Figure 21-1 shows how the diversification effects differ for a portfolio with U.S. stock only compared to one with U.S. and foreign stock. The sample domestic portfolio has an average correlation coefficient of returns of .8. The sample portfolio containing both domestic and foreign securities has an average correlation coefficient of returns of .4. The mixed portfolio has a lower correlation coefficient, so the risk of that portfolio is lower than that of the domestic-only portfolio. The Financial Crisis of 2008 has taught us that the correlation of returns of a domestic security and a foreign security may not be as low as we originally thought. The contagion of the crisis seen across many countries including the U.S. caused security values across the board to go down together in close unison. Because so many investors tried to sell securities at the same time, prices on nearly all stocks fell and, hence, correlations among the stocks increased. The benefit normally observed from international diversification was reduced.

American Depository Receipts

The common stock of many major foreign companies is traded in the United States in a form that is denominated in U.S. dollars. Some examples include Alibaba (China), Nokia (Finland), Deutsche Telecom (Germany), Sony Corporation (Japan), and Unilever (United Kingdom).[5] Special trusts are created, and foreign stock is purchased and placed in these trusts. These trusts then issue their own securities, called **American Depository Receipts (ADRs)**. ADRs were established by JP Morgan in 1927 as a way for U.S. investors to make foreign investments. Many ADRs are traded on the New York Stock Exchange and the Nasdaq over-the-counter market, similar to stocks of U.S.-based companies. For example, ADRs listed on the NYSE must register with the SEC, comply with SEC regulations, and provide financial statements that comply with the U.S. GAAP. Investors like that ADRs offer the opportunity to own foreign securities through a mechanism that affords investors the advantages normally

American depository receipts (ADRs) Securities denominated in U.S. dollars that represent a claim on foreign currency-denominated stocks held in a trust.

---

5. *www.nyse.com*

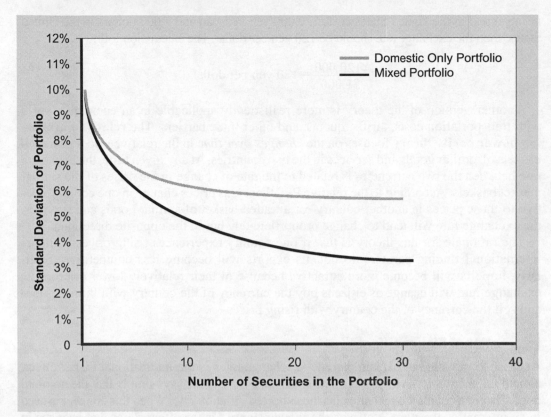

FIGURE 21-1
Portfolio Risk as Diversification Changes

Figure 21-1 shows the diversification effects for a sample domestic-only portfolio and a mixed (domestic and foreign) portfolio. The upper curve represents a domestic security-only portfolio. The lower curve represents a portfolio containing both domestic and foreign securities.

associated with ownership of securities of domestic U.S. issuers. For instance, while investors may be hesitant to invest directly in firms listed on the Brazilian stock market, they seem more willing to invest in Brazilian firms listed on the NYSE as ADRs.

There are over 3,000 ADRs available to U.S. investors. U.S. investors generally like to receive their dividends in dollars, not in a foreign currency. ADRs do this. U.S. investors probably also prefer to receive information about their foreign investments in English. ADRs do this too. Although ADRs are denominated in dollars, they still present the U.S. investor with exchange rate risk.[6]

In this section, we examined exchange-rate risk management tools, the diversification benefits of foreign investments, and American depository receipts. We turn to exchange rate theories next.

Exchange Rate Theories

To aid business decision makers, financial theorists try to explain exchange rate levels and fluctuations. Why is the current exchange rate between two currencies at the level it is? What causes that exchange rate to change? Among the most popular exchange rate theories are the purchasing power parity theory, the international Fisher effect, and the interest rate parity theory.

Purchasing Power Parity Theory

Economists have studied the question of how the financial market prices one country's currency in terms of another country's currency. One explanation, the *purchasing power parity (PPP) theory*, says that it is the relative prices in two countries that determine the exchange rate of their currencies. There are two versions of the PPP theory: the *absolute PPP* and the *relative PPP*.

The **absolute purchasing power parity theory** posits that exchange rates are determined by the differences in the prices of a given market basket of traded goods and services when there are no trade barriers. For instance, if a given basket of traded goods and services available

absolute purchasing power parity theory Theory that claims the current exchange rate is determined by the relative prices in two countries of a similar basket of traded goods and services.

---

6. *http://topforeignstocks.com/2016/11/29/ten-advantages-of-investing-in-adrs/*

in Japan and in the United States costs 120,000 yen in Japan and 1,000 dollars in the United States, then the exchange rate should be 120 yen per dollar. The calculation follows:

$$\frac{¥120,000}{\$1,000} = 120 \text{ yen per dollar}$$

relative purchasing power parity theory A theory that states that as prices change in one country relative to those prices in another country, for a given traded basket of similar goods and services, the exchange rate will tend to change proportionately but in the opposite direction.

Another version of the theory is more realistically applicable in an economic world with transportation costs, tariffs, quotas, and other trade barriers. The **relative purchasing power parity theory** focuses on the *changes over time* in the relative prices of traded baskets of similar goods and services in the two countries. At any given time, the exchange rate between the two currencies is related to the rate of change in the prices of the similar market baskets. According to the relative PPP theory, as prices change in one country relative to those prices in another country for a traded basket of similar goods and services, the exchange rate will tend to change proportionately but in the opposite direction.

The rationale for this theory is that if one country experiences rising prices while its international trading partners do not, its exports will become less competitive. Similarly, imports will become more attractive because of their relatively lower prices. The exchange rate will change as citizens buy the currency of the country with falling prices and sell the currency of the country with rising prices.

International Fisher Effect

international Fisher effect A theory developed by economist Irving Fisher that claims that changes in interest rates for two countries will be offset by equal changes, in the opposite direction, in the exchange rate.

Another theory used to explain currency exchange rates is the international Fisher effect, named for economist Irving Fisher. The *domestic Fisher effect* says simply that the nominal rate of interest equals the real rate plus the expected inflation rate. When this concept is used in an international setting, however, the **international Fisher effect** states that changes in the nominal interest rates for two countries will be offset by equal changes, in the opposite direction, in the exchange rate. The difference in nominal interest rates across countries reflects the difference in expected rates of inflation in those countries. According to Irving Fisher, the exchange rate would change by the same amount, but in the opposite direction, as the difference between the nominal interest rates of the two countries.

Changes in nominal interest rates are determined by changes in expected inflation, and exchange rates change for the same reason. The rationale is that investors must be compensated, or will offer compensation, to accommodate the expected change in the exchange rate.

Interest Rate Parity Theory

interest rate parity theory A theory that states that the difference between the exchange rate specified for future delivery and that for current delivery equals the difference in the interest rates for securities of the same maturity.

forward rate The exchange rate for future delivery.

spot rate The exchange rate for current delivery.

arbitrage The process whereby equivalent assets are bought in one place and simultaneously sold in another, making a risk-free profit.

The **interest rate parity theory** says that the percentage difference between the exchange rate specified for future delivery (the **forward rate**) and for current delivery (the **spot rate**) equals the difference in the interest rates for equal maturity securities in the two countries.

If the difference between the spot and forward rates for two countries' currencies did not equal the difference between the interest rates on equal maturity securities in those countries, an *arbitrage* opportunity would exist. **Arbitrage** is the process whereby equivalent assets are bought in one place and simultaneously sold in another, making a risk-free profit. Arbitragers buy in the spot market and sell in the forward market, or vice versa, depending on which was undervalued and which overvalued, until interest rate parity is achieved.

Other Factors Affecting Exchange Rates

Currency exchange rates fluctuate daily. Traders often buy and sell the dollar equivalent of trillions of dollars per day, continually reevaluating how many units of one country's currency should be exchanged for a given number of units of another country's currency.

The purchasing power parity theory, the international Fisher effect, and interest rate parity theory focus on rational economic explanations for exchange rates. But, like any market, the foreign exchange market is affected by both real economic factors and psychological factors.

If a country is experiencing political turmoil, for example, currency traders may fear that this will spill over to that country's economy. If investments in the foreign country are expected to suffer in the future because of the political turmoil, traders will dump that country's currency in the foreign exchange market. To liquidate investments in the troubled country, a firm must sell not only the investment but also the foreign currency it receives through the sale of the security. Currencies from other countries where the political climate is better will be preferred. These other currencies can then be invested in countries where the political climate is more hospitable.

The rationale seems to be that U.S. investments are safer because the United States has considerable military and economic power and secure location compared to countries with limited means to protect themselves from unfriendly neighbors. South Korea, for example, has a powerful economy that could crumble overnight if North Korea invaded. Similarly, Taiwan has a powerful economy that would be threatened if the People's Republic of China invaded. This "flight to the dollar" is not as reliable as it once was, however. The euro of the European Monetary Union has also been seen around the world as a safe haven in times of crisis. It remains to be seen whether the euro will continue to be seen as a safe haven currency given the economic and financial struggles in Europe. The U.S. dollar rose in value against most other currencies at the height of the Financial Crisis in 2008. When the next crisis comes it will have to be seen to which currency traders flock for protection.

Government Intervention in Foreign Exchange Markets

Sometimes the central banks of various countries will enter the foreign exchange market in an attempt to influence exchange rates. If the Fed (the central bank of the U.S.), for example, were unhappy with market conditions in which the U.S. dollar was weakening against other currencies, it could buy U.S. dollars, using its holdings of other currencies such as euros or British pounds, in an attempt to bid up (strengthen) the value of the dollar. Central banks of other countries can also buy or sell currencies in the foreign exchange market to further their own policy goals. Although the central banks of major countries have great market power, it is difficult to move a trillion-dollar-plus market when it doesn't want to be moved.

Sometimes central banks will act in concert with each other to pursue a common policy objective. The major economic powers of the world, known as the Group of Eight (G-8), have sometimes pursued a common effort to alter exchange rates. The Group of Eight countries are the United States, the United Kingdom, Germany, Japan, Canada, France, Russia, and Italy.

Psychological and political factors surely affect exchange rates. Like any other market, the foreign exchange market is influenced by logical and illogical factors alike, some of which are unidentifiable. The end result, however, is felt by multinational corporations and by individual consumers and investors alike.

In this section we explored exchange rate theories that help decision makers understand exchange rate risks and fluctuations. In the next section, we address the main political and cultural risks that multinational corporations may confront.

Political and Cultural Risks Facing MNCs

MNCs must deal with political and cultural factors when engaging in international business. Awareness and sensitivity to these factors are crucial to successful international business activities.

Political Risk

Political risk is the risk that a country's government may take some action that would harm a foreign-owned company doing business in that country. For example, a foreign government might expropriate (take) the assets of the company for its own reasons. Expropriation of assets is an extreme example of political risk. Sometimes funds are blocked by the host country, making it impossible for an MNC to repatriate profits earned in the foreign country.

Another political risk is the chance that a foreign government may impose a minimum number or minimum percentage of domestic workers that must be employed by foreign companies operating in that country. These workers may or may not have the same level of training and ability as the workers of the home country. In Bermuda, for instance, companies are not allowed to hire foreign workers unless they can demonstrate that they cannot obtain Bermudians for the job positions. If a Bermudian wants a job, then, he or she gets it even though there may be many more qualified foreigners willing to move to Bermuda to work.

Foreign governments may also impose a requirement for the use of a certain amount of raw materials or parts manufactured in the country where the foreign operation is located. Again, these materials and parts may or may not meet the standards of the home country.

These political risks must be weighed, along with other risks unique to international operations, against the special opportunities these international operations present.

Cultural Risk

When a company operates in another country, cultural issues often affect business. These differences include language barriers as well as differences in attitudes, values, and business protocol. Cultural risk is the risk that foreigners doing business in another country will fail to adapt to cultural differences, and this failure will affect the firm's success.

To offset cultural risk, companies that operate abroad often train their employees in cultural differences. A lack of awareness about differences in business practices could cause an unintentional insult or jeopardize a negotiation about a major project. For example, some hand gestures that have innocent connotations in one country are considered offensive or obscene in another country. What is considered a bribe in one country may be considered a routine gratuity in another country.

The risks of doing business in a foreign country include exchange rate fluctuations and political and cultural risk. Yet the return potential is high. Recognizing the risk and potential return, governments have forged trade agreements to promote and regulate international business. We look at trade agreements next.

International Trade Agreements

Groups of countries sometimes form alliances and agreements that both regulate and foster international trade. NAFTA, EU, and GATT are the major international agreements we discuss in this section. In early 2015 President Obama was trying to get approval for U.S. participation in the Trans-Pacific Partnership (TPP) trade accord. In 2017 President Trump withdrew the United States from the Trans-Pacific Partnership (TPP). China is widely seen as having benefited from this U.S. withdrawal. After the U.S. withdrew the other countries that had been part of the TPP trade agreement created a new agreement called the Comprehensive and Progressive Agreement for Trans-Pacific Partnership (CPTPP). The CPTPP was agreed to in 2018 by Australia, Brunei, Canada, Chile, Japan, Malaysia, Mexico, New Zealand, Peru, Singapore, and Vietnam. The main feature of this agreement is the reduction of tariffs on goods traded among the signing countries so as to encourage trade among them. U.S. labor unions were widely opposed to TPP, calling it a U.S. jobs killer. Pro-trade supporters of TPP argued that it would improve the world economy, including the U.S. economy and create new jobs in the U.S. and in other countries. Read on to learn the details of the alphabet soup of approved trade agreements. In early 2018 President Trump imposed tariffs on some imported steel and aluminum to protect U.S. producers in these industries. Companies that consume steel and aluminum, such as automobile and beverage companies, were against these tariffs since they increase costs for such companies.

NAFTA

Canada, Mexico, and the United States signed an agreement in 1994 called the *North American Free Trade Agreement (NAFTA)*. NAFTA breaks down some of the barriers to trade between these countries, such as tariffs and quotas.

Tariffs are taxes assessed by Country A on the goods of Country B that are sold in Country A. Mexico, for example, might impose a tariff on Canadian goods sold in Mexico. **Quotas** are quantity restrictions imposed by Country A on certain goods imported from Country B. Both are barriers to international trade. When Country A imposes tariffs and quotas on the goods of Country B, Country B is likely to impose tariffs and quotas on goods from

tariff A tax imposed by one country on imports from another country.

quota A quantity limit imposed by one country on the amount of a given good that can be imported from another country.

Country A. This can lead to a trade war wherein each country increases the barriers imposed on the goods of the other. Trade wars can lead to economic decline of both countries.

NAFTA is, in effect, a pact to end such wars. It should increase business for all three countries as tariffs, quotas, and other trade barriers are eliminated. NAFTA is politically controversial, however, because its opponents believe that U.S. jobs will be lost as U.S.-based companies shift some operations to Mexico, where labor costs tend to be lower. Proponents claim that jobs in exporting industries are likely to increase and create ripple-effect benefits for the economies of all three countries. In 2018 the Trump Administration was seeking to renegotiate key terms of the original NAFTA.

GATT and WTO

The *General Agreement on Tariffs and Trade (GATT)* was a treaty that provided for ongoing discussions among participating nations to find ways to minimize international trade barriers. The Uruguay round of GATT talks established the *World Trade Organization (WTO)* on April 15, 1994. GATT was replaced by the World Trade Organization (WTO) on January 1, 1995. The agreement to create the WTO was signed by 123 countries with the signing of the Marrakesh Agreement in 1994. When one WTO country has a trade complaint against another, the WTO court can hear the complaint and impose economic sanctions if the accused country is found guilty. In 2016 the United States accused Indonesia of imposing import restrictions on certain agricultural products. The WTO Panel that hears such cases ruled in favor of the U.S. position. These are the types of disputes that the WTO adjudicates.

European Union and the Euro

It is easy to understand why many countries in Europe sought to create a single currency. When the creation of the euro was enabled by the European Union at its meeting in Maastricht, Netherlands in 1992, there was much hope that this new currency would reduce trading barriers among the participating countries to the overall benefit of the entire group. Membership in this monetary union was not automatic. Countries applying for membership in the European Monetary Union had to meet certain requirements with regard to budget deficits, inflation, and other economic promises.[7] A country could be admitted to the Eurozone upon satisfaction of these requirements. It was never clear, however, what would happen to a country if it subsequently found itself out of compliance with the requirements it had met to gain admission to the Eurozone club. There was no clearly defined way to kick a participating country out of the Eurozone.

By agreeing to use a single currency, the participating countries gave up their right to control their own monetary policy. This would be handled on behalf of all the participating countries by the European Central Bank in Frankfurt, Germany. A country could no longer create its own money, as it was used to doing when the individual national central banks would use open market operations to increase or decrease the supply of drachmas, lira, marks, and guilders to name just a few of the national currencies that disappeared with the appearance of the euro.

Eurozone countries continued to conduct their fiscal policies as individual nations even though their monetary policy had been centralized and delegated to the European Central Bank. Some countries, such as Germany, were conservative in their spending habits and did not run up big debts. Other countries such as Greece and Spain had higher rates of government spending and ran up large deficits.

Those countries that ran up large deficits, and that then had to issue new government bonds to cover those deficits, found that the market was requiring higher interest rates on these increasingly risky bonds. If this government debt were to go into default this would create huge problems for the holders of this debt including many European banks. If there are significant problems at European banks this can lead to significant problems at banks outside Europe that do business with the European banks.

---

7. *http://www.bbc.co.uk/news/business-13856580*

In February of 2011, the Eurozone countries set up a bailout fund, called the European Stability Mechanism, initially funding it with €500 billion.[8] The stronger economies in the Eurozone, particularly Germany, have pressured the countries with struggling economies and mounting debt to impose austerity measures to get spending and debt under control. Such austerity measures, of course do not go over well in those countries where they are imposed. Elections in Greece in January 2012 saw the New Democracy Party, described as a center-right party, prevail. This kept Greece in the Eurozone. Many will be watching Greece, Italy, Spain, and Portugal to see if the Eurozone can hold together or whether some of these countries might default on their debts and perhaps return to their national currencies. Greece did receive a bailout in 2016 that allowed it to continue paying its bills. Whether Greece's creditors should grant the country debt relief has been a source of much controversy in Europe.

The EU encourages joint business ventures and coordinated economic policies. All EU members now have a common passport. Furthermore, each country recognizes professional and educational degrees of other member countries so that doctors, lawyers, and other licensed professionals can practice in any country within the EU. The European Union countries are Austria, Belgium, Bulgaria, Cyprus, Czech Republic, Denmark, Estonia, Finland, France, Germany, Greece, Hungary, Ireland, Italy, Latvia, Lithuania, Luxembourg, Malta, Netherlands, Poland, Portugal, Romania, Slovakia, Slovenia, Spain, Sweden, and United Kingdom (UK). However, after the May 2015 elections in the UK a ballot proposal was promised by the victorious Conservative Party (commonly referred to as the Tories) to allow the citizens of the UK to decide whether to stay in the European Union.

On January 1, 1999, 11 European countries fixed their exchange rates against each other and against the euro. The euro began trading against other currencies on January 4, 1999. In early 2018 the countries using the euro currency were Andorra, Austria, Belgium, Cyprus, Estonia, Finland, France, Germany, Greece, Ireland, Italy, Kosovo, Latvia, Lithuania, Luxembourg, Malta, Monaco, Montenegro, Netherlands, Portugal, San Marino, Slovakia, Slovenia, Spain, and Vatican City.

Free Trade versus Fair Trade

"Free trade" and "fair trade" differ. Free trade suggests an unconditional lowering of trade barriers. *Fair trade* suggests lowering trade barriers only if the other country lowers its barriers, and perhaps only if the other country meets additional conditions. Examples of other conditions include meeting minimum wage, worker safety, human rights, or environmental standards.

NAFTA, WTO, EMU, EU, and ECB are signs of an ever-increasing global economy. As the world moves into the twenty-first century, international business will become more significant for all countries. An understanding of the financial risks, potential returns, and basic rules of international business will hopefully lead to greater financial success.

---

8. *http://www.nytimes.com/2012/06/19/business/global/daily-euro-zone-watch.html?pagewanted=all*

Summary

1. *Define a multinational corporation (MNC) and explain its importance.*
A multinational corporation is a corporation that operates in more than one country. It is becoming increasingly difficult to accurately classify some corporations as U.S., Swedish, Canadian, and so forth because many large corporations operate worldwide. International concerns are a vital concern for many U.S. businesses because of the potential market for products in countries throughout the world.

Demonstrate how the law of comparative advantage leads to international trade that benefits individuals and firms.

The law of comparative advantage says that countries (and individuals) should do those things, or produce those items, for which they have a comparative advantage. This means that the person or country has a lower opportunity cost. Countries can export goods and services they produce well and import those goods and services that others develop better. By trading, both countries should see quality, quantity, or price benefits, or a combination of all three. Within the U.S. Minnesota has a comparative advantage in the production of wheat, while Florida as a comparative advantage in the production of oranges.

2. *Demonstrate how the law of comparative advantage leads to international trade that benefits individuals and firms.* The law of comparative advantage says that countries (and individuals) should do things, or produce those items, for which they have a comparative advantage. This means that the person or country has a lower opportunity cost. Countries can export goods and services for which they have a comparative advantage and import those goods and services for which others have a comparative advantage. By trading, both countries should see quality, quantity, or price benefits, or a combination of all three. Within the U.S., Minnesota has a comparative advantage in the production of wheat, while Florida has a comparative advantage in the production of oranges.

3. *Describe exchange rates and their effects on firms.* An exchange rate is an expression of the value of one country's currency relative to another country's currency. Fluctuating currency exchange rates affect the prices U.S. citizens pay for goods and services of other countries, and the prices that citizens of other countries pay for U.S. goods and services. When a country's currency weakens relative to the currencies of other countries, goods and services imported into that country become more expensive. That country's exported goods and services become cheaper to those countries that import them.

    MNCs are also affected when their profits are earned in one country, then converted to the currency of the home country. Converting foreign currency profits into domestic currency to send to the home country of the business is known as repatriating the profits. If the U.S. dollar weakens relative to the foreign currency, the U.S. company's profits increase due to the change in exchange rates. However, if the dollar strengthens, profits decrease.

4. *Show how firms manage the risks of fluctuating exchange rates.* Diversifying investments across several countries often reduces risk. Foreign securities can be bought in the United States by purchasing American depository receipts, which are U.S. dollar securities issued by a trust holding foreign-currency-denominated securities. Firms can also manage risk through hedging—entering into a financial agreement that offsets or guards against risk. Three common types of hedging instruments are forward contracts, futures contracts, and swaps. Forward contracts are contracts in which one party agrees to buy, and the other party agrees to sell, a certain amount of a currency at a specified exchange rate at a specified future time. Futures contracts are similar except they can be traded on organized exchanges. Swaps are negotiated contracts, like forward contracts, in which each party agrees to swap payments at specified points in time according to a predetermined formula.

5. *Discuss exchange rate theories.* Currency exchange rates fluctuate for a variety of reasons. Among the most popular theories seeking to explain these changes are those that focus on relative prices in the two countries (purchasing power parity), relative interest rates (international Fisher effect), and the difference between spot and forward rates relative to the exchange rate (interest rate parity).

6. *Describe the political and cultural risks that affect MNCs.* MNCs run the political risk of government trade restrictions, confiscation of assets by foreign governments, and even wars. Cultural risks include the risk of jeopardizing a deal or business due to insensitivity to differences in language, values, and attitudes. Training employees to recognize and respect cultural differences can reduce cultural risk.

7. *Explain how major international trade agreements affect international business.* International agreements such as NAFTA, GATT/WTO, and the Maastricht Treaty that created the EU can bring down trade barriers and potentially create wide-ranging benefits. Opponents of these agreements claim, however, that they can result in job loss or harm a country's identity and economy.

Key Terms

absolute purchasing power parity theory Theory that claims the current exchange rate is determined by the relative prices in two countries of a similar basket of traded goods and services.

American depository receipts (ADRs) Securities denominated in U.S. dollars that represent a claim on foreign currency-denominated stocks held in a trust.

arbitrage The process whereby equivalent assets are bought in one place and simultaneously sold in another, making a risk-free profit.

cross rate An exchange rate determined by examining how each of two currencies is valued in terms of a common third currency.

exchange rate The number of units of one country's currency that is needed to purchase one unit of another country's currency.

forward rate The exchange rate for future delivery.

hedge A financial arrangement used to offset or protect against negative effects of something else, such as fluctuating exchange rates.

interest rate parity theory A theory that states that the difference between the exchange rate specified for future delivery and that for current delivery equals the difference in the interest rates for securities of the same maturity.

international Fisher effect A theory developed by economist Irving Fisher that claims that changes in interest rates for two countries will be offset by equal changes, in the opposite direction, in the exchange rate.

quota A quantity limit imposed by one country on the amount of a given good that can be imported from another country.

relative purchasing power parity theory A theory that states that as prices change in one country relative to those prices in another country, for a given traded basket of similar goods and services, the exchange rate will tend to change proportionately but in the opposite direction.

spot rate The exchange rate for current delivery.

tariff A tax imposed by one country on imports from another country.

Equations Introduced in This Chapter

Equation 21-1. Calculation of a Currency Cross Rate:

$$\frac{\text{Currency A}}{\text{Currency B}} \times \frac{\text{Currency B}}{\text{Currency C}} = \frac{\text{Currency A}}{\text{Currency C}}$$

Self-Test

ST-1. What is the law of comparative advantage?

ST-2. What is the rationale given for trade agreements such as the North American Free Trade Agreement (NAFTA)?

ST-3. If you can get 1.20 Canadian dollars for one U.S. dollar and one U.S. dollar gets you 120 Japanese yen, how many Japanese yen do you get for one Canadian dollar?

ST-4. What are American Depository Receipts (ADRs)?

Review Questions

1. What does it mean when the U.S. dollar weakens in the foreign exchange market?

2. What kinds of U.S. companies would benefit most from a stronger dollar in the foreign exchange market? Explain.

3. Under what circumstance would the U.S. dollar and the Canadian dollar be said to have achieved purchasing power parity?

4. What are some of the primary advantages when a corporation has operations in countries other than its home country? What are some of the risks?

5. What is GATT, and what is its goal?

Build Your Communication Skills

CS-1. Form two groups to debate the issue of free trade versus fair trade. Some questions to address in the discussion include: (1) Should a country allow other countries to sell goods to its citizens with few or no restrictions (free trade)? (2) Should opening markets to companies from other countries be conditional on those other countries showing reciprocating openness (fair trade)? (3) Who decides which countries are engaging in fair trading practices?

CS-2. Write a short report on the current state of exchange rates. Which currencies are strengthening in foreign exchange markets and which are weakening? Why? Incorporate what you learned in this chapter in your analysis. What are the implications for international trade that can be drawn from the direction of the change in exchange rate values you observe?

Problems

Calculating Exchange Rates

21-1. Assume the foreign exchange selling rates shown below for a few selected currencies:

Country/(Currency)	U.S. $ Equivalent
Australia (dollar)	0.7716
Britain (pound)	1.4022
Canada (dollar)	0.7644
Hong Kong (dollar)	0.1275
India (rupee)	0.0153
Chile (peso)	0.0016
Japan (yen)	0.0094
Mexico (peso)	0.0538
Israel (shekel)	0.2878
Singapore (dollar)	0.7596
Thailand (baht)	0.0320
(Euro)	1.2334

Calculate the number of the following foreign currencies that can be bought with 1 million U.S. dollars.

a. British pounds

b. Indian rupees

c. Japanese yen

d. Australian dollars

e. Mexican pesos

f. Israeli shekels

21-2. Using the information given in problem 21-1, calculate the number of the following foreign currencies that can be bought with 1 million U.S. dollars.

Calculating Exchange Rates

a. Chilean pesos

b. Hong Kong dollars

c. Singaporean dollars

d. Euros

e. Indian rupees

f. Mexican pesos

g. Thai bahts

21-3. Using the information given in problem 21-1, calculate the number of U.S. dollars required to buy

Calculating Exchange Rates

a. 2 million Australian dollars

b. 1.6 million Singaporean dollars

c. 5 million euros

d. 2.6 million Mexican pesos

e. 2 million Japanese yen

f. 5 million Thai bahts

21-4. The following is a list of currency exchange rates for selected countries:

Calculating Exchange Rates

Country	U.S. $ Equivalent
Britain (pound)	1.4022
Mexico (peso)	0.0538
Canada (dollar)	0.7644
Japan (yen)	0.0094
Euro	1.2334

a. How many dollars would it take to buy one euro?

b. Calculate the amount of each of the following currencies you could have bought with $100,000 U.S. dollars.

1. Japan (yen)

2. Britain (pound)

3. Canada (dollar)

4. Mexico (peso)

21-5. Using the data from problem 21-4, find the cross rates for each of the following:

Cross Rates

a. Yen per peso

b. Pesos per pound

c. Euros per Canadian dollar

d. Yen per Canadian dollar

21-6. If the Canadian dollar is selling at U.S. $ 0.89 and the Israeli shekel at U.S. $0.25, how many shekels are equal to one Canadian dollar?

Cross Rates

Cross Rates	➡	**21-7.** If 58 rupees or 9.67 Hong Kong dollars could be purchased with one euro, how many rupees are equal to one Hong Kong dollar?
Cross Rates	➡	**21-8.** If one British pound is equivalent to 16.9 Mexican pesos or 2.8 Singapore dollars, how many Singapore dollars can one purchase with 10 million Mexican pesos?
Cross Rates	➡	**21-9.** If one British pound is equivalent to 1.5 euros and one euro can purchase 60 bahts, how many bahts can one purchase with 1 million British pounds?
Cross Rates	➡	**21-10.** If one British pound is equivalent to 1.5 euros, one euro can purchase .8 dinars, and one dinar is worth 160 yen, how many yen can one purchase with 1 million British pounds?
Exchange Rate	➡	**21-11.** Mrs. Pittner owns 100 shares of stock in Nokia valued at 16.5 euros per share. What is the value (in U.S. dollars) of Mrs. Pittner's shares of stock when the exchange rate is **a.** .90 = €/ $? **b.** .70 = €/ $? **c.** 1.2 = €/ $?
Exchange Rate	➡	**21-12.** John is planning on purchasing his dream car directly from the manufacturer in Germany. In order to do so, he must first convert his dollars to euros. His dream car has a price tag of 55,150 euros. How much does he need in U.S. dollars to purchase this car if the exchange rate is .9800 euros to the dollar?
Purchasing Power Parity	➡	**21-13.** Sony sells its 50-inch projection screen TVs in Japan for ¥230,000. In the United States, this same television sells for $2,000. What should the exchange rate be in order for purchasing power parity to exist?
Exchange Rate Effects	➡	**21-14.** Assume that you invested $100,000 in a Japanese security a year back when the exchange rate was 119 yen per one U.S. dollar. However, the U.S. dollar depreciated against the yen throughout the year, and the current exchange rate is 100 yen per U.S. dollar. Calculate your percentage return on the investment due to this depreciation of the dollar.
Challenge Problem	➡	**21-15.** A year ago an Indian investor bought 1,000 shares of General Motors at $37 per share when the exchange rate was 42 rupees per one U.S. dollar. A year later, the U.S. dollar had appreciated against the rupee and the present exchange rate is 44 rupees per one U.S. dollar. Calculate the annual rate of return on investment for the Indian investor assuming the stock price remained the same.

Answers to Self-Test

ST-1. The law of comparative advantage says that all will prosper when each party (or nation) does that for which it has a lower opportunity cost than other parties (or nations).

ST-2. NAFTA is a trade agreement between the United States, Canada, and Mexico that eliminated major barriers so the countries could freely trade goods and services to the benefit of the citizens of all three countries. Whether this has occurred is a matter of interpretation.

ST-3. $\dfrac{120\,¥}{\$1.00\ \text{U.S.}} \times \dfrac{\$1.00\ \text{U.S.}}{1.20\ \text{CD}} = 100.00\,¥$ per 1.00 CD

ST-4. American Depository Receipts (ADRs) are dollar-denominated securities traded in the United States that represent a claim on a special trust that is created to hold foreign stock.

Appendix
Future Value and Present Value Tables

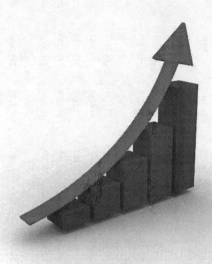

Source: KerdaZz/Shutterstock

TABLE I Future Value Interest Factors, FVIF, Compounded at k Percent per Period for n Periods:

$$FVIF_{k,n} = (1 + k)^n$$

Interest Rate, k

Number of Periods, n	1%	2%	3%	4%	5%	6%	7%	8%	9%	10%	12%	14%	16%	18%	20%	25%	30%	35%	40%	45%	50%
1	1.0100	1.0200	1.0300	1.0400	1.0500	1.0600	1.0700	1.0800	1.0900	1.1000	1.1200	1.1400	1.1600	1.1800	1.2000	1.2500	1.3000	1.3500	1.4000	1.4500	1.5000
2	1.0201	1.0404	1.0609	1.0816	1.1025	1.1236	1.1449	1.1664	1.1881	1.2100	1.2544	1.2996	1.3456	1.3924	1.4400	1.5625	1.6900	1.8225	1.9600	2.1025	2.2500
3	1.0303	1.0612	1.0927	1.1249	1.1576	1.1910	1.2250	1.2597	1.2950	1.3310	1.4049	1.4815	1.5609	1.6430	1.7280	1.9531	2.1970	2.4604	2.7440	3.0486	3.3750
4	1.0406	1.0824	1.1255	1.1699	1.2155	1.2625	1.3108	1.3605	1.4116	1.4641	1.5735	1.6890	1.8106	1.9388	2.0736	2.4414	2.8561	3.3215	3.8416	4.4205	5.0625
5	1.0510	1.1041	1.1593	1.2167	1.2763	1.3382	1.4026	1.4693	1.5386	1.6105	1.7623	1.9254	2.1003	2.2878	2.4883	3.0518	3.7129	4.4840	5.3782	6.4097	7.5938
6	1.0615	1.1262	1.1941	1.2653	1.3401	1.4185	1.5007	1.5869	1.6771	1.7716	1.9738	2.1950	2.4364	2.6996	2.9860	3.8147	4.8268	6.0534	7.5295	9.2941	11.3906
7	1.0721	1.1487	1.2299	1.3159	1.4071	1.5036	1.6058	1.7138	1.8280	1.9487	2.2107	2.5023	2.8262	3.1855	3.5832	4.7684	6.2749	8.1722	10.5414	13.4765	17.0859
8	1.0829	1.1717	1.2668	1.3686	1.4775	1.5938	1.7182	1.8509	1.9926	2.1436	2.4760	2.8526	3.2784	3.7589	4.2998	5.9605	8.1573	11.0324	14.7579	19.5409	25.6289
9	1.0937	1.1951	1.3048	1.4233	1.5513	1.6895	1.8385	1.9990	2.1719	2.3579	2.7731	3.2519	3.8030	4.4355	5.1598	7.4506	10.6045	14.8937	20.6610	28.3343	38.4434
10	1.1046	1.2190	1.3439	1.4802	1.6289	1.7908	1.9672	2.1589	2.3674	2.5937	3.1058	3.7072	4.4114	5.2338	6.1917	9.3132	13.7858	20.1066	28.9255	41.0847	57.6650
11	1.1157	1.2434	1.3842	1.5395	1.7103	1.8983	2.1049	2.3316	2.5804	2.8531	3.4785	4.2262	5.1173	6.1759	7.4301	11.6415	17.9216	27.1439	40.4957	59.5728	86.4976
12	1.1268	1.2682	1.4258	1.6010	1.7959	2.0122	2.2522	2.5182	2.8127	3.1384	3.8960	4.8179	5.9360	7.2876	8.9161	14.5519	23.2981	36.6442	56.6939	86.3806	129.7463
13	1.1381	1.2936	1.4685	1.6651	1.8856	2.1329	2.4098	2.7196	3.0658	3.4523	4.3635	5.4924	6.8858	8.5994	10.6993	18.1899	30.2875	49.4697	79.3715	125.2518	194.6195
14	1.1495	1.3195	1.5126	1.7317	1.9799	2.2609	2.5785	2.9372	3.3417	3.7975	4.8871	6.2613	7.9875	10.1472	12.8392	22.7374	39.3738	66.7841	111.1201	181.6151	291.9293
15	1.1610	1.3459	1.5580	1.8009	2.0789	2.3966	2.7590	3.1722	3.6425	4.1772	5.4736	7.1379	9.2655	11.9737	15.4070	28.4217	51.1859	90.1585	155.5681	263.3419	437.8939
16	1.1726	1.3728	1.6047	1.8730	2.1829	2.5404	2.9522	3.4259	3.9703	4.5950	6.1304	8.1372	10.7480	14.1290	18.4884	35.5271	66.5417	121.7139	217.7953	381.8458	656.8408
17	1.1843	1.4002	1.6528	1.9479	2.2920	2.6928	3.1588	3.7000	4.3276	5.0545	6.8660	9.2765	12.4677	16.6722	22.1861	44.4089	86.5042	164.3138	304.9135	553.6764	985.2613
18	1.1961	1.4282	1.7024	2.0258	2.4066	2.8543	3.3799	3.9960	4.7171	5.5599	7.6900	10.5752	14.4625	19.6733	26.6233	55.5112	112.4554	221.8236	426.8789	802.8308	1,477.8919
19	1.2081	1.4568	1.7535	2.1068	2.5270	3.0256	3.6165	4.3157	5.1417	6.1159	8.6128	12.0557	16.7765	23.2144	31.9480	69.3889	146.1920	299.4619	597.6304	1,164.1047	2,216.8378
20	1.2202	1.4859	1.8061	2.1911	2.6533	3.2071	3.8697	4.6610	5.6044	6.7275	9.6463	13.7435	19.4608	27.3930	38.3376	86.7362	190.0496	404.2736	836.6826	1,687.9518	3,325.2567
21	1.2324	1.5157	1.8603	2.2788	2.7860	3.3996	4.1406	5.0338	6.1088	7.4002	10.8038	15.6676	22.5745	32.3238	46.0051	108.4202	247.0645	545.7693	1,171.3556	2,447.5301	4,987.8851
22	1.2447	1.5460	1.9161	2.3699	2.9253	3.6035	4.4304	5.4365	6.6586	8.1403	12.1003	17.8610	26.1864	38.1421	55.2061	135.5253	321.1839	736.7886	1,639.8978	3,548.9187	7,481.8276
23	1.2572	1.5769	1.9736	2.4647	3.0715	3.8197	4.7405	5.8715	7.2579	8.9543	13.5523	20.3616	30.3762	45.0076	66.2474	169.4066	417.5391	994.6646	2,295.8569	5,145.9321	11,222.7415
24	1.2697	1.6084	2.0328	2.5633	3.2251	4.0489	5.0724	6.3412	7.9111	9.8497	15.1786	23.2122	35.2364	53.1090	79.4968	211.7582	542.8008	1,342.7973	3,214.1997	7,461.6015	16,834.1122
25	1.2824	1.6406	2.0938	2.6658	3.3864	4.2919	5.4274	6.8485	8.6231	10.8347	17.0001	26.4619	40.8742	62.6686	95.3962	264.6978	705.6410	1,812.7763	4,499.8796	10,819.3222	25,251.1683

TABLE I Future Value Interest Factors, FVIF, Compounded at k Percent per Period for n Periods: $FVIF_{k,n} = (1 + k)^n$ *(continued)*

Interest Rate, k

Number of Periods, n	1%	2%	3%	4%	5%	6%	7%	8%	9%	10%	12%	14%	16%	18%	20%	25%	30%	35%	40%	45%	50%
26	1.2953	1.6734	2.1566	2.7725	3.5557	4.5494	5.8074	7.3964	9.3992	11.9182	19.0401	30.1666	47.4141	73.9490	114.4755	330.8722	917.3333	2,447.2480	6,299.8314	15,688.0172	37,876.7524
27	1.3082	1.7069	2.2213	2.8834	3.7335	4.8223	6.2139	7.9881	10.2451	13.1100	21.3249	34.3899	55.0004	87.2598	137.3706	413.5903	1,192.5333	3,303.7848	8,819.7640	22,747.6250	56,815.1287
28	1.3213	1.7410	2.2879	2.9987	3.9201	5.1117	6.6488	8.6271	11.1671	14.4210	23.8839	39.2045	63.8004	102.9666	164.8447	516.9879	1,550.2933	4,460.1095	12,347.6696	32,984.0563	85,222.6930
29	1.3345	1.7758	2.3566	3.1187	4.1161	5.4184	7.1143	9.3173	12.1722	15.8631	26.7499	44.6931	74.0085	121.5005	197.8136	646.2349	2,015.3813	6,021.1478	17,286.7374	47,826.8816	127,834.0395
30	1.3478	1.8114	2.4273	3.2434	4.3219	5.7435	7.6123	10.0627	13.2677	17.4494	29.9599	50.9502	85.8499	143.3706	237.3763	807.7936	2,619.9956	8,128.5495	24,201.4324	69,348.9783	191,751.0592
31	1.3613	1.8476	2.5001	3.3731	4.5380	6.0881	8.1451	10.8677	14.4618	19.1943	33.5551	58.0832	99.5859	169.1774	284.8516	1,009.7420	3,405.9943	10,973.5418	33,882.0053	100,556.0185	287,626.5888
32	1.3749	1.8845	2.5751	3.5081	4.7649	6.4534	8.7153	11.7371	15.7633	21.1138	37.5817	66.2148	115.5196	199.6293	341.8219	1,262.1774	4,427.7926	14,814.2815	47,434.8074	145,806.2269	431,439.8833
33	1.3887	1.9222	2.6523	3.6484	5.0032	6.8406	9.3253	12.6760	17.1820	23.2252	42.0915	75.4849	134.0027	235.5625	410.1863	1,577.7218	5,756.1304	19,999.2800	66,408.7304	211,419.0289	647,159.8249
34	1.4026	1.9607	2.7319	3.7943	5.2533	7.2510	9.9781	13.6901	18.7284	25.5477	47.1425	86.0528	155.4432	277.9638	492.2235	1,972.1523	7,482.9696	26,999.0280	92,972.2225	306,557.5920	970,739.7374
35	1.4166	1.9999	2.8139	3.9461	5.5160	7.6861	10.6766	14.7853	20.4140	28.1024	52.7995	98.1002	180.3141	327.9973	590.6682	2,465.1903	9,727.8604	36,448.6878	130,161.1116	444,508.5083	1,456,109.606
36	1.4308	2.0399	2.8983	4.1039	5.7918	8.1473	11.4239	15.9682	22.2512	30.9127	59.1356	111.8342	209.1643	387.0368	708.8019	3,081.4879	12,646.2186	49,205.7285	182,225.5562	644,537.3371	2,184,164.409
37	1.4451	2.0807	2.9852	4.2681	6.0814	8.6361	12.2236	17.2456	24.2538	34.0039	66.2318	127.4910	242.6306	456.7034	850.5622	3,851.8599	16,440.0841	66,427.7334	255,115.7786	934,579.1388	3,276,246.614
38	1.4595	2.1223	3.0748	4.4388	6.3855	9.1543	13.0793	18.6253	26.4367	37.4043	74.1797	145.3397	281.4515	538.9100	1,020.6747	4,814.8249	21,372.1094	89,677.4402	357,162.0901	1,355,139.751	4,914,369.920
39	1.4741	2.1647	3.1670	4.6164	6.7048	9.7035	13.9948	20.1153	28.8160	41.1448	83.0812	165.6873	326.4838	635.9139	1,224.8096	6,018.5311	27,783.7422	121,064.5442	500,026.9261	1,964,952.639	7,371,554.881
40	1.4889	2.2080	3.2620	4.8010	7.0400	10.2857	14.9745	21.7245	31.4094	45.2593	93.0510	188.8835	378.7212	750.3783	1,469.7716	7,523.1638	36,118.8648	163,437.1347	700,037.6966	2,849,181.327	11,057,332.321
41	1.5038	2.2522	3.3599	4.9931	7.3920	10.9029	16.0227	23.4625	34.2363	49.7852	104.2171	215.3272	439.3165	885.4464	1,763.7259	9,403.9548	46,954.5243	220,640.1318	980,052.7752	4,131,312.924	16,585,998.481
42	1.5188	2.2972	3.4607	5.1928	7.7616	11.5570	17.1443	25.3395	37.3175	54.7637	116.7231	245.4730	509.6072	1,044.8268	2,116.4711	11,754.9435	61,040.8815	297,864.1780	1,372,073.885	5,990,403.740	24,878,997.722
43	1.5340	2.3432	3.5645	5.4005	8.1497	12.2505	18.3444	27.3666	40.6761	60.2401	130.7299	279.8392	591.1443	1,232.8956	2,539.7653	14,693.6794	79,353.1460	402,116.6402	1,920,903.439	8,686,085.423	37,318,496.583
44	1.5493	2.3901	3.6715	5.6165	8.5572	12.9855	19.6285	29.5560	44.3370	66.2641	146.4175	319.0167	685.7274	1,454.8168	3,047.7183	18,367.0992	103,159.0898	542,857.4643	2,689,264.815	12,594,823.863	55,977,744.875
45	1.5648	2.4379	3.7816	5.8412	8.9850	13.7646	21.0025	31.9204	48.3273	72.8905	163.9876	363.6791	795.4438	1,716.6839	3,657.2620	22,958.8740	134,106.8167	732,857.5768	3,764,970.741	18,262,494.602	83,966,617.312
46	1.5805	2.4866	3.8950	6.0748	9.4343	14.5905	22.4726	34.4741	52.6767	80.1795	183.6661	414.5941	922.7148	2,025.6870	4,388.7144	28,698.5925	174,338.8617	989,357.7287	5,270,959.038	26,480,617.173	125,949,925.968
47	1.5963	2.5363	4.0119	6.3178	9.9060	15.4659	24.0457	37.2320	57.4176	88.1975	205.7061	472.6373	1,070.3492	2,390.3106	5,266.4573	35,873.2407	226,640.5202	1,335,632.934	7,379,342.653	38,396,894.901	188,924,888.952
48	1.6122	2.5871	4.1323	6.5705	10.4013	16.3939	25.7289	40.2106	62.5852	97.0172	230.3908	538.8065	1,241.6051	2,820.5665	6,319.7487	44,841.5509	294,632.6763	1,803,104.461	10,331,079.714	55,675,497.606	283,387,333.428
49	1.6283	2.6388	4.2562	6.8333	10.9213	17.3775	27.5299	43.4274	68.2179	106.7190	258.0377	614.2395	1,440.2619	3,328.2685	7,583.6985	56,051.9386	383,022.4792	2,434,191.022	14,463,511.600	80,729,471.529	425,081,000.143
50	1.6446	2.6916	4.3839	7.1067	11.4674	18.4202	29.4570	46.9016	74.3575	117.3909	289.0022	700.2330	1,670.7038	3,927.3569	9,100.4382	70,064.9232	497,929.2230	3,286,157.879	20,248,916.240	117,057,733.717	637,621,500.214

TABLE II Present Value Factors, PVF, for a Single Amount, Discounted at k Percent Interest per Period for n Periods:

$$PVIF_{k,n} = \frac{1}{(1+k)^n} \quad \text{where } k = \text{the interest rate per period expressed as a decimal}$$

Interest Rate, k

Number of Periods, n	1%	2%	3%	4%	5%	6%	7%	8%	9%	10%	12%	14%	16%	18%	20%	25%	30%	35%	40%	45%	50%
1	0.9901	0.9804	0.9709	0.9615	0.9524	0.9434	0.9346	0.9259	0.9174	0.9091	0.8929	0.8772	0.8621	0.8475	0.8333	0.8000	0.7692	0.7407	0.7143	0.6897	0.6667
2	0.9803	0.9612	0.9426	0.9246	0.9070	0.8900	0.8734	0.8573	0.8417	0.8264	0.7972	0.7695	0.7432	0.7182	0.6944	0.6400	0.5917	0.5487	0.5102	0.4756	0.4444
3	0.9706	0.9423	0.9151	0.8890	0.8638	0.8396	0.8163	0.7938	0.7722	0.7513	0.7118	0.6750	0.6407	0.6086	0.5787	0.5120	0.4552	0.4064	0.3644	0.3280	0.2963
4	0.9610	0.9238	0.8885	0.8548	0.8227	0.7921	0.7629	0.7350	0.7084	0.6830	0.6355	0.5921	0.5523	0.5158	0.4823	0.4096	0.3501	0.3011	0.2603	0.2262	0.1975
5	0.9515	0.9057	0.8626	0.8219	0.7835	0.7473	0.7130	0.6806	0.6499	0.6209	0.5674	0.5194	0.4761	0.4371	0.4019	0.3277	0.2693	0.2230	0.1859	0.1560	0.1317
6	0.9420	0.8880	0.8375	0.7903	0.7462	0.7050	0.6663	0.6302	0.5963	0.5645	0.5066	0.4556	0.4104	0.3704	0.3349	0.2621	0.2072	0.1652	0.1328	0.1076	0.0878
7	0.9327	0.8706	0.8131	0.7599	0.7107	0.6651	0.6227	0.5835	0.5470	0.5132	0.4523	0.3996	0.3538	0.3139	0.2791	0.2097	0.1594	0.1224	0.0949	0.0742	0.0585
8	0.9235	0.8535	0.7894	0.7307	0.6768	0.6274	0.5820	0.5403	0.5019	0.4665	0.4039	0.3506	0.3050	0.2660	0.2326	0.1678	0.1226	0.0906	0.0678	0.0512	0.0390
9	0.9143	0.8368	0.7664	0.7026	0.6446	0.5919	0.5439	0.5002	0.4604	0.4241	0.3606	0.3075	0.2630	0.2255	0.1938	0.1342	0.0943	0.0671	0.0484	0.0353	0.0260
10	0.9053	0.8203	0.7441	0.6756	0.6139	0.5584	0.5083	0.4632	0.4224	0.3855	0.3220	0.2697	0.2267	0.1911	0.1615	0.1074	0.0725	0.0497	0.0346	0.0243	0.0173
11	0.8963	0.8043	0.7224	0.6496	0.5847	0.5268	0.4751	0.4289	0.3875	0.3505	0.2875	0.2366	0.1954	0.1619	0.1346	0.0859	0.0558	0.0368	0.0247	0.0168	0.0116
12	0.8874	0.7885	0.7014	0.6246	0.5568	0.4970	0.4440	0.3971	0.3555	0.3186	0.2567	0.2076	0.1685	0.1372	0.1122	0.0687	0.0429	0.0273	0.0176	0.0116	0.0077
13	0.8787	0.7730	0.6810	0.6006	0.5303	0.4688	0.4150	0.3677	0.3262	0.2897	0.2292	0.1821	0.1452	0.1163	0.0935	0.0550	0.0330	0.0202	0.0126	0.0080	0.0051
14	0.8700	0.7579	0.6611	0.5775	0.5051	0.4423	0.3878	0.3405	0.2992	0.2633	0.2046	0.1597	0.1252	0.0985	0.0779	0.0440	0.0254	0.0150	0.0090	0.0055	0.0034
15	0.8613	0.7430	0.6419	0.5553	0.4810	0.4173	0.3624	0.3152	0.2745	0.2394	0.1827	0.1401	0.1079	0.0835	0.0649	0.0352	0.0195	0.0111	0.0064	0.0038	0.0023
16	0.8528	0.7284	0.6232	0.5339	0.4581	0.3936	0.3387	0.2919	0.2519	0.2176	0.1631	0.1229	0.0930	0.0708	0.0541	0.0281	0.0150	0.0082	0.0046	0.0026	0.0015
17	0.8444	0.7142	0.6050	0.5134	0.4363	0.3714	0.3166	0.2703	0.2311	0.1978	0.1456	0.1078	0.0802	0.0600	0.0451	0.0225	0.0116	0.0061	0.0033	0.0018	0.0010
18	0.8360	0.7002	0.5874	0.4936	0.4155	0.3503	0.2959	0.2502	0.2120	0.1799	0.1300	0.0946	0.0691	0.0508	0.0376	0.0180	0.0089	0.0045	0.0023	0.0012	0.0007
19	0.8277	0.6864	0.5703	0.4746	0.3957	0.3305	0.2765	0.2317	0.1945	0.1635	0.1161	0.0829	0.0596	0.0431	0.0313	0.0144	0.0068	0.0033	0.0017	0.0009	0.0005
20	0.8195	0.6730	0.5537	0.4564	0.3769	0.3118	0.2584	0.2145	0.1784	0.1486	0.1037	0.0728	0.0514	0.0365	0.0261	0.0115	0.0053	0.0025	0.0012	0.0006	0.0003
21	0.8114	0.6598	0.5375	0.4388	0.3589	0.2942	0.2415	0.1987	0.1637	0.1351	0.0926	0.0638	0.0443	0.0309	0.0217	0.0092	0.0040	0.0018	0.0009	0.0004	0.0002
22	0.8034	0.6468	0.5219	0.4220	0.3418	0.2775	0.2257	0.1839	0.1502	0.1228	0.0826	0.0560	0.0382	0.0262	0.0181	0.0074	0.0031	0.0014	0.0006	0.0003	0.0001
23	0.7954	0.6342	0.5067	0.4057	0.3256	0.2618	0.2109	0.1703	0.1378	0.1117	0.0738	0.0491	0.0329	0.0222	0.0151	0.0059	0.0024	0.0010	0.0004	0.0002	0.0001
24	0.7876	0.6217	0.4919	0.3901	0.3101	0.2470	0.1971	0.1577	0.1264	0.1015	0.0659	0.0431	0.0284	0.0188	0.0126	0.0047	0.0018	0.0007	0.0003	0.0001	0.0001
25	0.7798	0.6095	0.4776	0.3751	0.2953	0.2330	0.1842	0.1460	0.1160	0.0923	0.0588	0.0378	0.0245	0.0160	0.0105	0.0038	0.0014	0.0006	0.0002	0.0001	0.0000

TABLE II Present Value Factors, PVF, for a Single Amount, Discounted at k Percent Interest per Period for n Periods:

$$PVIF_{k,n} = \frac{1}{(1+k)^n}$$ where k = the interest rate per period expressed as a decimal (continued)

Interest Rate, k

Number of Periods, n	1%	2%	3%	4%	5%	6%	7%	8%	9%	10%	12%	14%	16%	18%	20%	25%	30%	35%	40%	45%	50%
26	0.7720	0.5976	0.4637	0.3607	0.2812	0.2198	0.1722	0.1352	0.1064	0.0839	0.0525	0.0331	0.0211	0.0135	0.0087	0.0030	0.0011	0.0004	0.0002	0.0001	0.0000
27	0.7644	0.5859	0.4502	0.3468	0.2678	0.2074	0.1609	0.1252	0.0976	0.0763	0.0469	0.0291	0.0182	0.0115	0.0073	0.0024	0.0008	0.0003	0.0001	0.0000	0.0000
28	0.7568	0.5744	0.4371	0.3335	0.2551	0.1956	0.1504	0.1159	0.0895	0.0693	0.0419	0.0255	0.0157	0.0097	0.0061	0.0019	0.0006	0.0002	0.0001	0.0000	0.0000
29	0.7493	0.5631	0.4243	0.3207	0.2429	0.1846	0.1406	0.1073	0.0822	0.0630	0.0374	0.0224	0.0135	0.0082	0.0051	0.0015	0.0005	0.0002	0.0001	0.0000	0.0000
30	0.7419	0.5521	0.4120	0.3083	0.2314	0.1741	0.1314	0.0994	0.0754	0.0573	0.0334	0.0196	0.0116	0.0070	0.0042	0.0012	0.0004	0.0001	0.0000	0.0000	0.0000
31	0.7346	0.5412	0.4000	0.2965	0.2204	0.1643	0.1228	0.0920	0.0691	0.0521	0.0298	0.0172	0.0100	0.0059	0.0035	0.0010	0.0003	0.0001	0.0000	0.0000	0.0000
32	0.7273	0.5306	0.3883	0.2851	0.2099	0.1550	0.1147	0.0852	0.0634	0.0474	0.0266	0.0151	0.0087	0.0050	0.0029	0.0008	0.0002	0.0001	0.0000	0.0000	0.0000
33	0.7201	0.5202	0.3770	0.2741	0.1999	0.1462	0.1072	0.0789	0.0582	0.0431	0.0238	0.0132	0.0075	0.0042	0.0024	0.0006	0.0002	0.0001	0.0000	0.0000	0.0000
34	0.7130	0.5100	0.3660	0.2636	0.1904	0.1379	0.1002	0.0730	0.0534	0.0391	0.0212	0.0116	0.0064	0.0036	0.0020	0.0005	0.0001	0.0000	0.0000	0.0000	0.0000
35	0.7059	0.5000	0.3554	0.2534	0.1813	0.1301	0.0937	0.0676	0.0490	0.0356	0.0189	0.0102	0.0055	0.0030	0.0017	0.0004	0.0001	0.0000	0.0000	0.0000	0.0000
36	0.6989	0.4902	0.3450	0.2437	0.1727	0.1227	0.0875	0.0626	0.0449	0.0323	0.0169	0.0089	0.0048	0.0026	0.0014	0.0003	0.0001	0.0000	0.0000	0.0000	0.0000
37	0.6920	0.4806	0.3350	0.2343	0.1644	0.1158	0.0818	0.0580	0.0412	0.0294	0.0151	0.0078	0.0041	0.0022	0.0012	0.0003	0.0001	0.0000	0.0000	0.0000	0.0000
38	0.6852	0.4712	0.3252	0.2253	0.1566	0.1092	0.0765	0.0537	0.0378	0.0267	0.0135	0.0069	0.0036	0.0019	0.0010	0.0002	0.0000	0.0000	0.0000	0.0000	0.0000
39	0.6784	0.4619	0.3158	0.2166	0.1491	0.1031	0.0715	0.0497	0.0347	0.0243	0.0120	0.0060	0.0031	0.0016	0.0008	0.0002	0.0000	0.0000	0.0000	0.0000	0.0000
40	0.6717	0.4529	0.3066	0.2083	0.1420	0.0972	0.0668	0.0460	0.0318	0.0221	0.0107	0.0053	0.0026	0.0013	0.0007	0.0001	0.0000	0.0000	0.0000	0.0000	0.0000
41	0.6650	0.4440	0.2976	0.2003	0.1353	0.0917	0.0624	0.0426	0.0292	0.0201	0.0096	0.0046	0.0023	0.0011	0.0006	0.0001	0.0000	0.0000	0.0000	0.0000	0.0000
42	0.6584	0.4353	0.2890	0.1926	0.1288	0.0865	0.0583	0.0395	0.0268	0.0183	0.0086	0.0041	0.0020	0.0010	0.0005	0.0001	0.0000	0.0000	0.0000	0.0000	0.0000
43	0.6519	0.4268	0.2805	0.1852	0.1227	0.0816	0.0545	0.0365	0.0246	0.0166	0.0076	0.0036	0.0017	0.0008	0.0004	0.0001	0.0000	0.0000	0.0000	0.0000	0.0000
44	0.6454	0.4184	0.2724	0.1780	0.1169	0.0770	0.0509	0.0338	0.0226	0.0151	0.0068	0.0031	0.0015	0.0007	0.0003	0.0001	0.0000	0.0000	0.0000	0.0000	0.0000
45	0.6391	0.4102	0.2644	0.1712	0.1113	0.0727	0.0476	0.0313	0.0207	0.0137	0.0061	0.0027	0.0013	0.0006	0.0003	0.0000	0.0000	0.0000	0.0000	0.0000	0.0000
46	0.6327	0.4022	0.2567	0.1646	0.1060	0.0685	0.0445	0.0290	0.0190	0.0125	0.0054	0.0024	0.0011	0.0005	0.0002	0.0000	0.0000	0.0000	0.0000	0.0000	0.0000
47	0.6265	0.3943	0.2493	0.1583	0.1009	0.0647	0.0416	0.0269	0.0174	0.0113	0.0049	0.0021	0.0009	0.0004	0.0002	0.0000	0.0000	0.0000	0.0000	0.0000	0.0000
48	0.6203	0.3865	0.2420	0.1522	0.0961	0.0610	0.0389	0.0249	0.0160	0.0103	0.0043	0.0019	0.0008	0.0004	0.0002	0.0000	0.0000	0.0000	0.0000	0.0000	0.0000
49	0.6141	0.3790	0.2350	0.1463	0.0916	0.0575	0.0363	0.0230	0.0147	0.0094	0.0039	0.0016	0.0007	0.0003	0.0001	0.0000	0.0000	0.0000	0.0000	0.0000	0.0000
50	0.6080	0.3715	0.2281	0.1407	0.0872	0.0543	0.0339	0.0213	0.0134	0.0085	0.0035	0.0014	0.0006	0.0003	0.0001	0.0000	0.0000	0.0000	0.0000	0.0000	0.0000

TABLE III-A Future Value Factors for an Ordinary Annuity, FVFOA, Earning k Percent Interest per Period for n Periods:

$$FVFOA_{k,n} = \frac{(1+k)^n - 1}{k}$$ where k = the interest rate per period expressed as a decimal

Interest Rate, k

Number of Periods, n	1%	2%	3%	4%	5%	6%	7%	8%	9%	10%	12%	14%	16%	18%	20%	25%	30%	35%	40%	45%	50%
1	1.0000	1.0000	1.0000	1.0000	1.0000	1.0000	1.0000	1.0000	1.0000	1.0000	1.0000	1.0000	1.0000	1.0000	1.0000	1.0000	1.0000	1.0000	1.0000	1.0000	1.0000
2	2.0100	2.0200	2.0300	2.0400	2.0500	2.0600	2.0700	2.0800	2.0900	2.1000	2.1200	2.1400	2.1600	2.1800	2.2000	2.2500	2.3000	2.3500	2.4000	2.4500	2.5000
3	3.0301	3.0604	3.0909	3.1216	3.1525	3.1836	3.2149	3.2464	3.2781	3.3100	3.3744	3.4396	3.5056	3.5724	3.6400	3.8125	3.9900	4.1725	4.3600	4.5525	4.7500
4	4.0604	4.1216	4.1836	4.2465	4.3101	4.3746	4.4399	4.5061	4.5731	4.6410	4.7793	4.9211	5.0665	5.2154	5.3680	5.7656	6.1870	6.6329	7.1040	7.6011	8.1250
5	5.1010	5.2040	5.3091	5.4163	5.5256	5.6371	5.7507	5.8666	5.9847	6.1051	6.3528	6.6101	6.8771	7.1542	7.4416	8.2070	9.0431	9.9544	10.9456	12.0016	13.1875
6	6.1520	6.3081	6.4684	6.6330	6.8019	6.9753	7.1533	7.3359	7.5233	7.7156	8.1152	8.5355	8.9775	9.4420	9.9299	11.2588	12.7560	14.4384	16.3238	18.4314	20.7813
7	7.2135	7.4343	7.6625	7.8983	8.1420	8.3938	8.6540	8.9228	9.2004	9.4872	10.0890	10.7305	11.4139	12.1415	12.9159	15.0735	17.5828	20.4919	23.8534	27.7255	32.1719
8	8.2857	8.5830	8.8923	9.2142	9.5491	9.8975	10.2598	10.6366	11.0285	11.4359	12.2997	13.2328	14.2401	15.3270	16.4991	19.8419	23.8577	28.6640	34.3947	41.2019	49.2578
9	9.3685	9.7546	10.1591	10.5828	11.0266	11.4913	11.9780	12.4876	13.0210	13.5795	14.7757	16.0853	17.5185	19.0859	20.7989	25.8023	32.0150	39.6964	49.1526	60.7428	74.8867
10	10.4622	10.9497	11.4639	12.0061	12.5779	13.1808	13.8164	14.4866	15.1929	15.9374	17.5487	19.3373	21.3215	23.5213	25.9587	33.2529	42.6195	54.5902	69.8137	89.0771	113.3301
11	11.5668	12.1687	12.8078	13.4864	14.2068	14.9716	15.7836	16.6455	17.5603	18.5312	20.6546	23.0445	25.7329	28.7551	32.1504	42.5661	56.4053	74.6967	98.7391	130.1618	170.9951
12	12.6825	13.4121	14.1920	15.0258	15.9171	16.8699	17.8885	18.9771	20.1407	21.3843	24.1331	27.2707	30.8502	34.9311	39.5805	54.2077	74.3270	101.8406	139.2348	189.7346	257.4927
13	13.8093	14.6803	15.6178	16.6268	17.7130	18.8821	20.1406	21.4953	22.9534	24.5227	28.0291	32.0887	36.7862	42.2187	48.4966	68.7596	97.6250	138.4848	195.9287	276.1151	387.2390
14	14.9474	15.9739	17.0863	18.2919	19.5986	21.0151	22.5505	24.2149	26.0192	27.9750	32.3926	37.5811	43.6720	50.8180	59.1959	86.9495	127.9125	187.9544	275.3002	401.3670	581.8585
15	16.0969	17.2934	18.5989	20.0236	21.5786	23.2760	25.1290	27.1521	29.3609	31.7725	37.2797	43.8424	51.6595	60.9653	72.0351	109.6868	167.2863	254.7385	386.4202	582.9821	873.7878
16	17.2579	18.6393	20.1569	21.8245	23.6575	25.6725	27.8881	30.3243	33.0034	35.9497	42.7533	50.9804	60.9250	72.9390	87.4421	138.1085	218.4722	344.8970	541.9883	846.3240	1,311.6817
17	18.4304	20.0121	21.7616	23.6975	25.8404	28.2129	30.8402	33.7502	36.9737	40.5447	48.8837	59.1176	71.6730	87.0680	105.9306	173.6357	285.0139	466.6109	759.7837	1,228.1699	1,968.5225
18	19.6147	21.4123	23.4144	25.6454	28.1324	30.9057	33.9990	37.4502	41.3013	45.5992	55.7497	68.3941	84.1407	103.7403	128.1167	218.0446	371.5180	630.9247	1,064.6971	1,781.8463	2,953.7838
19	20.8109	22.8406	25.1169	27.6712	30.5390	33.7600	37.3790	41.4463	46.0185	51.1591	63.4397	78.9692	98.6032	123.4135	154.7400	273.5558	483.9734	852.7483	1,491.5760	2,584.6771	4,431.6756
20	22.0190	24.2974	26.8704	29.7781	33.0660	36.7856	40.9955	45.7620	51.1601	57.2750	72.0524	91.0249	115.3797	146.6280	186.6880	342.9447	630.1655	1,152.210	2,089.2064	3,748.7818	6,648.5135
21	23.2392	25.7833	28.6765	31.9692	35.7193	39.9927	44.8652	50.4229	56.7645	64.0025	81.6987	104.7684	134.8405	174.0210	225.0256	429.6809	820.2151	1,556.484	2,925.8889	5,436.7336	9,973.7702
22	24.4716	27.2990	30.5368	34.2480	38.5052	43.3923	49.0057	55.4568	62.8733	71.4027	92.5026	120.4360	157.4150	206.3448	271.0307	538.1011	1,067.280	2,102.253	4,097.2445	7,884.2638	14,961.655
23	25.7163	28.8450	32.4529	36.6179	41.4305	46.9958	53.4361	60.8933	69.5319	79.5430	104.6029	138.2970	183.6014	244.4868	326.2369	673.6264	1,388.464	2,839.042	5,737.1423	11,433.182	22,443.483
24	26.9735	30.4219	34.4265	39.0826	44.5020	50.8156	58.1767	66.7648	76.7898	88.4973	118.1552	158.6586	213.9776	289.4945	392.4842	843.0329	1,806.003	3,833.706	8,032.9993	16,579.115	33,666.224
25	28.2432	32.0303	36.4593	41.6459	47.7271	54.8645	63.2490	73.1059	84.7009	98.3471	133.3339	181.8708	249.2140	342.6035	471.9811	1,054.7912	2,348.803	5,176.504	11,247.199	24,040.716	50,500.337

TABLE III-A Future Value Factors for an Ordinary Annuity, FVFOA, Earning k Percent Interest per Period for n Periods:

$$FVFOA_{k,n} = \frac{(1+k)^n - 1}{k} \quad \text{where } k = \text{the interest rate per period expressed as a decimal } (continued)$$

Interest Rate, k

Number of Periods, n	1%	2%	3%	4%	5%	6%	7%	8%	9%	10%	12%	14%	16%	18%	20%	25%	30%	35%	40%	45%	50%
26	29.5256	33.6709	38.5530	44.3117	51.1135	59.1564	68.6765	79.9544	93.3240	109.1818	150.3339	208.3327	290.0883	405.2721	567.3773	1,319.4890	3,054.444	6,989.280	15,747.079	34,860.038	75,751.505
27	30.8209	35.3443	40.7096	47.0842	54.6691	63.7058	74.4838	87.3508	102.7231	121.0999	169.3740	238.4993	337.5024	479.2211	681.8528	1,650.3612	3,971.778	9,436.528	22,046.910	50,548.056	113,628.26
28	32.1291	37.0512	42.9309	49.9676	58.4026	68.5281	80.6977	95.3388	112.9682	134.2099	190.6989	272.8892	392.5028	566.4809	819.2233	2,063.9515	5,164.311	12,740.31	30,866.674	73,295.681	170,443.39
29	33.4504	38.7922	45.2189	52.9663	62.3227	73.6398	87.3465	103.9659	124.1354	148.6309	214.5828	312.0937	456.3032	669.4475	984.0680	2,580.9394	6,714.604	17,200.42	43,214.343	106,279.74	255,666.08
30	34.7849	40.5681	47.5754	56.0849	66.4388	79.0582	94.4608	113.2832	136.3075	164.4940	241.3327	356.7868	530.3117	790.9480	1,181.8816	3,227.1743	8,729.985	23,221.57	60,501.081	154,106.62	383,500.12
31	36.1327	42.3794	50.0027	59.3283	70.7608	84.8017	102.0730	123.3459	149.5752	181.9434	271.2926	407.7370	616.1616	934.3186	1,419.2579	4,034.9678	11,349.98	31,350.12	84,702.513	223,455.60	575,251.18
32	37.4941	44.2270	52.5028	62.7015	75.2988	90.8898	110.2182	134.2135	164.0370	201.1378	304.8477	465.8202	715.7475	1,103.4960	1,704.1095	5,044.7098	14,755.98	42,323.66	118,584.519	324,011.62	862,877.77
33	38.8690	46.1116	55.0778	66.2095	80.0638	97.3432	118.9334	145.9506	179.8003	222.2515	342.4294	532.0350	831.2671	1,303.1253	2,045.9314	6,306.8872	19,183.77	57,137.94	166,019.326	469,817.84	1,294,317.6
34	40.2577	48.0338	57.7302	69.8579	85.0670	104.1838	128.2588	158.6267	196.9823	245.4767	384.5210	607.5199	965.2698	1,538.6878	2,456.1176	7,884.6091	24,939.90	77,137.22	232,428.056	681,236.87	1,941,477.5
35	41.6603	49.9945	60.4621	73.6522	90.3203	111.4348	138.2369	172.3168	215.7108	271.0244	431.6635	693.5727	1,120.7130	1,816.6516	2,948.3411	9,856.7613	32,422.87	104,136.3	325,400.279	987,794.46	2,912,217.2
36	43.0769	51.9944	63.2759	77.5983	95.8363	119.1209	148.9135	187.1021	236.1247	299.1268	484.4631	791.6729	1,301.0270	2,144.6489	3,539.0094	12,321.952	42,150.73	140,584.9	455,561.390	1,432,303.0	4,368,326.8
37	44.5076	54.0343	66.1742	81.7022	101.6281	127.2681	160.3374	203.0703	258.3759	330.3395	543.5987	903.5071	1,510.1914	2,531.6857	4,247.8112	15,403.440	54,796.95	189,790.7	637,786.947	2,076,840.3	6,552,491.2
38	45.9527	56.1149	69.1594	85.9703	107.7095	135.9042	172.5610	220.3159	282.6298	364.0434	609.8305	1,030.9981	1,752.8220	2,988.3891	5,098.3735	19,255.299	71,237.03	256,218.4	892,902.725	3,011,419.4	9,828,737.8
39	47.4123	58.2372	72.2342	90.4091	114.0950	145.0585	185.6403	238.9412	309.0665	401.4478	684.0102	1,176.3378	2,034.2735	3,527.2992	6,119.0482	24,070.124	92,609.14	345,895.8	1,250,064.8	4,366,559.2	14,743,108
40	48.8864	60.4020	75.4013	95.0255	120.7998	154.7620	199.6351	259.0565	337.8824	442.5926	767.0914	1,342.0251	2,360.7572	4,163.2130	7,343.8578	30,088.655	120,392.9	466,960.4	1,750,091.7	6,331,511.8	22,114,663
41	50.3752	62.6100	78.6633	99.8265	127.8398	165.0477	214.6096	280.7810	369.2919	487.8518	860.1424	1,530.9086	2,739.4784	4,913.5914	8,813.6294	37,611.819	156,511.7	630,397.5	2,450,129.4	9,180,693.2	33,171,995
42	51.8790	64.8622	82.0232	104.8196	135.2318	175.9505	233.0322	304.2435	403.5281	537.6370	964.3595	1,746.2358	3,178.7949	5,799.0378	10,577.355	47,015.774	203,466.3	851,037.7	3,430,182.2	13,312,006	49,757,993
43	53.3978	67.1595	85.4839	110.0124	142.9933	187.5076	247.7765	329.5830	440.8457	592.4007	1,081.0826	1,991.7088	3,688.4021	6,843.8646	12,693.826	58,770.718	264,507.2	1,148,902	4,802,256.1	19,302,410	74,636,991
44	54.9318	69.5027	89.0484	115.4129	151.1430	199.7580	266.1209	356.9496	481.5218	652.6408	1,211.8125	2,271.5481	4,279.5465	8,076.7603	15,233.592	73,464.397	343,860.3	1,551,018	6,723,159.5	27,998,495	111,955,488
45	56.4811	71.8927	92.7199	121.0294	159.7002	212.7435	285.7493	386.5056	525.8587	718.9048	1,358.2300	2,590.5648	4,965.2739	9,531.5771	18,281.310	91,831.496	447,019.4	2,093,876	9,412,424.4	40,583,319	167,933,233
46	58.0459	74.3306	96.5015	126.8706	168.6852	226.5081	306.7518	418.4261	574.1860	791.7953	1,522.2176	2,954.2439	5,760.7177	11,248.261	21,938.572	114,790.370	581,126.2	2,826,734	13,177,395	58,845,814	251,899,850
47	59.6263	76.8172	100.3965	132.9454	178.1194	241.0986	329.2244	452.9002	626.8628	871.9749	1,705.8838	3,368.8380	6,683.4326	13,273.948	26,327.286	143,488.963	755,465.1	3,816,091	18,448,354	85,326,431	377,849,776
48	61.2226	79.3535	104.4084	139.2632	188.0254	256.5645	353.2701	490.1322	684.2804	960.1723	1,911.5898	3,841.4753	7,753.7818	15,664.259	31,593.744	179,362.203	982,105.6	5,151,724	25,827,697	123,723,326	566,774,665
49	62.8348	81.9406	108.5406	145.8337	198.4267	272.9584	378.9990	530.3427	746.8656	1,057.1896	2,141.9806	4,380.2819	8,995.3869	18,484.825	37,913.492	224,203.754	1,276,738	6,954,829	36,158,776	179,398,823	850,161,998
50	64.4632	84.5794	112.7969	152.6671	209.3480	290.3359	406.5289	573.7702	815.0836	1,163.9085	2,400.0182	4,994.5213	10,435.6488	21,813.094	45,497.191	280,255.693	1,659,761	9,389,020	50,622,288	260,128,295	1,275,242,998

TABLE III-B Future Value Factors for an Annuity Due, FVFAD, Earning k Percent Interest per Period for n Periods:

$$FVFAD_{k,n} = \frac{(1+k)^n - 1}{k} \times (1+k)$$ where k = the interest rate per period expressed as a decimal

Interest Rate, k

Number of Periods, n	1%	2%	3%	4%	5%	6%	7%	8%	9%	10%	12%	14%	16%	18%	20%	25%	30%	35%	40%	45%	50%
1	1.0100	1.0200	1.0300	1.0400	1.0500	1.0600	1.0700	1.0800	1.0900	1.1000	1.1200	1.1400	1.1600	1.1800	1.2000	1.2500	1.3000	1.3500	1.4000	1.4500	1.5000
2	2.0301	2.0604	2.0909	2.1216	2.1525	2.1836	2.2149	2.2464	2.2781	2.3100	2.3744	2.4396	2.5056	2.5724	2.6400	2.8125	2.9900	3.1725	3.3600	3.5525	3.7500
3	3.0604	3.1216	3.1836	3.2465	3.3101	3.3746	3.4399	3.5061	3.5731	3.6410	3.7793	3.9211	4.0665	4.2154	4.3680	4.7656	5.1870	5.6329	6.1040	6.6011	7.1250
4	4.1010	4.2040	4.3091	4.4163	4.5256	4.6371	4.7507	4.8666	4.9847	5.1051	5.3528	5.6101	5.8771	6.1542	6.4416	7.2070	8.0431	8.9544	9.9456	11.0216	12.1875
5	5.1520	5.3081	5.4684	5.6330	5.8019	5.9753	6.1533	6.3359	6.5233	6.7156	7.1152	7.5355	7.9775	8.4420	8.9299	10.2588	11.7560	13.4384	15.3238	17.4314	19.7813
6	6.2135	6.4343	6.6625	6.8983	7.1420	7.3938	7.6540	7.9228	8.2004	8.4872	9.0890	9.7305	10.4139	11.1415	11.9159	14.0735	16.5828	19.4919	22.8534	26.7255	31.1719
7	7.2857	7.5830	7.8923	8.2142	8.5491	8.8975	9.2598	9.6366	10.0285	10.4359	11.2997	12.2328	13.2401	14.3270	15.4991	18.8419	22.8577	27.6640	33.3947	40.2019	48.2578
8	8.3685	8.7546	9.1591	9.5828	10.0266	10.4913	10.9780	11.4876	12.0210	12.5795	13.7757	15.0853	16.5185	18.0859	19.7989	24.8023	31.0150	38.6964	48.1526	59.7428	73.8867
9	9.4622	9.9497	10.4639	11.0061	11.5779	12.1808	12.8164	13.4866	14.1929	14.9374	16.5487	18.3373	20.3215	22.5213	24.9587	32.2529	41.6195	53.5902	68.8137	88.0771	112.3301
10	10.5668	11.1687	11.8078	12.4864	13.2068	13.9716	14.7836	15.6455	16.5603	17.5312	19.6546	22.0445	24.7329	27.7551	31.1504	41.5661	55.4053	73.6967	97.7391	129.1618	169.9951
11	11.6825	12.4121	13.1920	14.0258	14.9171	15.8699	16.8885	17.9771	19.1407	20.3843	23.1331	26.2707	29.8502	33.9311	38.5805	53.2077	73.3270	100.8406	138.2348	188.7346	256.4927
12	12.8093	13.6803	14.6178	15.6268	16.7130	17.8821	19.1406	20.4953	21.9534	23.5227	27.0291	31.0887	35.7862	41.2187	47.4966	67.7596	96.6250	137.4848	194.9287	275.1151	386.2390
13	13.9474	14.9739	16.0863	17.2919	18.5986	20.0151	21.5505	23.2149	25.0192	26.9750	31.3926	36.5811	42.6720	49.8180	58.1959	85.9495	126.9125	186.9544	274.3002	400.3670	580.8585
14	15.0969	16.2934	17.5989	19.0236	20.5786	22.2760	24.1290	26.1521	28.3609	30.7725	36.2797	42.8424	50.6595	59.9653	71.0351	108.6868	166.2863	253.7385	385.4202	581.9821	872.7878
15	16.2579	17.6393	19.1569	20.8245	22.6575	24.6725	26.8881	29.3243	32.0034	34.9497	41.7533	49.9804	59.9250	71.9390	86.4421	137.1085	217.4722	343.8970	540.9883	845.3240	1,310.6817
16	17.4304	19.0121	20.7616	22.6975	24.8404	27.2129	29.8402	32.7502	35.9737	39.5447	47.8837	58.1176	70.6730	86.0680	104.9306	172.6357	284.0139	465.6109	758.7837	1,227.1699	1,967.5225
17	18.6147	20.4123	22.4144	24.6454	27.1324	29.9057	32.9990	36.4502	40.3013	44.5992	54.7497	67.3941	83.1407	102.7403	127.1167	217.0446	370.5180	629.9247	1,063.6971	1,780.8463	2,952.7838
18	19.8109	21.8406	24.1169	26.6712	29.5390	32.7600	36.3790	40.4463	45.0185	50.1591	62.4397	77.9692	97.6032	122.4135	153.7400	272.5558	482.9734	851.7483	1,490.5760	2,583.6771	4,430.6756
19	21.0190	23.2974	25.8704	28.7781	32.0660	35.7856	39.9955	44.7620	50.1601	56.2750	71.0524	90.0249	114.3797	145.6280	185.6880	341.9447	629.1655	1,151.2103	2,088.2064	3,747.7818	6,647.5135
20	22.2392	24.7833	27.6765	30.9692	34.7193	38.9927	43.8652	49.4229	55.7645	63.0025	80.6987	103.7684	133.8405	173.0210	224.0256	428.6809	819.2151	1,555.4838	2,924.8889	5,435.7336	9,972.7702
21	23.4716	26.2990	29.5368	33.2480	37.5052	42.3923	48.0057	54.4568	61.8733	70.4027	91.5026	119.4360	156.4150	205.3448	270.0307	537.1011	1,066.2796	2,101.2532	4,096.2445	7,883.2638	14,960.655
22	24.7163	27.8450	31.4529	35.6179	40.4305	45.9958	52.4361	59.8933	68.5319	78.5430	103.6029	137.2970	182.6014	243.4868	325.2369	672.6264	1,387.4635	2,838.0418	5,736.1423	11,432.182	22,442.483
23	25.9735	29.4219	33.4265	38.0826	43.5020	49.8156	57.1767	65.7648	75.7898	87.4973	117.1552	157.6586	212.9776	288.4945	391.4842	842.0329	1,805.0026	3,832.7064	8,031.9993	16,578.115	33,665.224
24	27.2432	31.0303	35.4593	40.6459	46.7271	53.8645	62.2490	72.1059	83.7009	97.3471	132.3339	180.8708	248.2140	341.6035	470.9811	1,053.7912	2,347.8033	5,175.5037	11,246.199	24,039.716	50,499.337
25	28.5256	32.6709	37.5530	43.3117	50.1135	58.1564	67.6765	78.9544	92.3240	108.1818	149.3339	207.3327	289.0883	404.2721	566.3773	1,318.4890	3,053.4443	6,988.2800	15,746.079	34,859.038	75,750.505

TABLE III-B Future Value Factors for an Annuity Due, FVFAD, Earning k Percent Interest per Period for n Periods:

$$FVFAD_{k,n} = \frac{(1+k)^n - 1}{k} \times (1+k)$$ where k = the interest rate per period expressed as a decimal *(continued)*

Interest Rate, k

Number of Periods, n	1%	2%	3%	4%	5%	6%	7%	8%	9%	10%	12%	14%	16%	18%	20%	25%	30%	35%	40%	45%	50%
26	29.8209	34.3443	39.7096	46.0842	53.6691	62.7058	73.4838	86.3508	101.7231	120.0999	168.3740	237.4993	336.5024	478.2211	680.8528	1,649.3612	3,970.7776	9,435.5280	22,045.910	50,547.056	113,627.26
27	31.1291	36.0512	41.9309	48.9676	57.4026	67.5281	79.6977	94.3388	111.9682	133.2099	189.6989	271.8892	391.5028	565.4809	818.2233	2,062.9515	5,163.3109	12,739.313	30,865.674	73,294.681	170,442.39
28	32.4504	37.7922	44.2189	51.9663	61.3227	72.6398	86.3465	102.9659	123.1354	147.6309	213.5828	311.0937	455.3032	668.4475	983.0680	2,579.9394	6,713.6042	17,199.422	43,213.343	106,278.74	255,665.08
29	33.7849	39.5681	46.5754	55.0849	65.4388	78.0582	93.4608	112.2832	135.3075	163.4940	240.3327	355.7868	529.3117	789.9480	1,180.8816	3,226.1743	8,728.9855	23,220.570	60,500.081	154,105.62	383,499.12
30	35.1327	41.3794	49.0027	58.3283	69.7608	83.8017	101.0730	122.3459	148.5752	180.9434	270.2926	406.7370	615.1616	933.3186	1,418.2579	4,033.9678	11,348.981	31,349.120	84,701.513	223,454.60	575,250.18
31	36.4941	43.2270	51.5028	61.7015	74.2988	89.8898	109.2182	133.2135	163.0370	200.1373	303.8477	464.8202	714.7475	1,102.4960	1,703.1095	5,043.7098	14,754.975	42,322.661	118,583.52	324,010.62	862,876.77
32	37.8690	45.1116	54.0778	65.2095	79.0638	96.3432	117.9334	144.9506	178.8003	221.2515	341.4294	531.0350	830.2671	1,302.1253	2,044.9314	6,305.8872	19,182.768	57,136.943	166,018.33	469,816.84	1,294,316.6
33	39.2577	47.0338	56.7302	68.8579	84.0670	103.1838	127.2588	157.6267	195.9823	244.4767	383.5210	606.5199	964.2698	1,537.6878	2,455.1176	7,883.6091	24,938.899	77,136.223	232,427.06	681,235.87	1,941,476.5
34	40.6603	48.9945	59.4621	72.6522	89.3203	110.4348	137.2369	171.3168	214.7108	270.0244	430.6635	692.5727	1,119.7130	1,815.6516	2,947.3411	9,855.7613	32,421.868	104,135.25	325,399.28	987,793.46	2,912,216.2
35	42.0769	50.9944	62.2759	76.5983	94.8363	118.1209	147.9135	186.1021	235.1247	298.1268	483.4631	790.6729	1,300.0270	2,143.6489	3,538.0094	12,320.952	42,149.729	140,583.94	455,560.39	1,432,302.0	4,368,325.8
36	43.5076	53.0343	65.1742	80.7022	100.6281	126.2681	159.3374	202.0703	257.3759	329.0395	542.5987	902.5071	1,509.1914	2,530.6857	4,246.8112	15,402.440	54,795.947	189,789.67	637,785.95	2,076,839.3	6,552,490.2
37	44.9527	55.1149	68.1594	84.9703	106.7095	134.9042	171.5610	219.3159	281.6298	363.0434	608.8305	1,029.9981	1,751.8220	2,987.3891	5,097.3735	19,254.299	71,236.031	256,217.40	892,901.73	3,011,418.4	9,828,736.8
38	46.4123	57.2372	71.2342	89.4091	113.0950	144.0585	184.6403	237.9412	308.0665	400.4478	683.0102	1,175.3378	2,033.2735	3,526.2992	6,118.0482	24,069.124	92,608.141	345,894.84	1,250,063.8	4,366,558.2	14,743,107
39	47.8864	59.4020	74.4013	94.0255	119.7998	153.7620	198.6351	258.0565	336.8824	441.5926	766.0914	1,341.0251	2,359.7572	4,162.2130	7,342.8578	30,087.655	120,391.88	466,959.38	1,750,090.7	6,331,510.8	22,114,662
40	49.3752	61.6100	77.6633	98.8265	126.8398	164.0477	213.6096	279.7810	368.2919	486.8518	859.1424	1,529.9086	2,738.4784	4,912.5914	8,812.6294	37,610.819	156,510.75	630,396.52	2,450,128.4	9,180,692.2	33,171,994
41	50.8790	63.8622	81.0232	103.8196	134.2318	174.9505	229.6322	303.2435	402.5281	536.6370	963.3595	1,745.2358	3,177.7949	5,798.0378	10,576.355	47,014.774	203,465.27	851,036.65	3,430,181.2	13,312,005	49,757,992
42	52.3978	66.1595	84.4839	109.0124	141.9933	186.5076	246.7765	328.5830	439.8457	591.4007	1,080.0826	1,990.7088	3,687.4021	6,842.8646	12,692.826	58,769.718	264,506.15	1,148,900.8	4,802,255.1	19,302,409	74,636,990
43	53.9318	68.5027	88.0484	114.4129	150.1430	198.7580	265.1209	355.9496	480.5218	651.6408	1,210.8125	2,270.5481	4,278.5465	8,075.7603	15,232.592	73,463.397	343,859.30	1,551,017.5	6,723,158.5	27,988,494	111,955,487
44	55.4811	70.8927	91.7199	120.0294	158.7002	211.7435	284.7493	385.5056	524.8587	717.9048	1,357.2300	2,589.5648	4,964.2739	9,530.5771	18,280.310	91,830.496	447,018.39	2,093,874.9	9,412,423.4	40,583,318	167,933,232
45	57.0459	73.3306	95.5015	125.8706	167.6852	225.5081	305.7518	417.4261	573.1860	790.7953	1,521.2176	2,953.2439	5,759.7177	11,247.261	21,937.572	114,789.37	581,125.21	2,826,732.5	13,177,394	58,845,813	251,899,849
46	58.6263	75.8172	99.3965	131.9454	177.1194	240.0986	328.2244	451.9002	625.8628	870.9749	1,704.8838	3,367.8380	6,682.4326	13,272.948	26,326.286	143,487.96	755,464.07	3,816,090.2	18,448,353	85,326,430	377,849,775
47	60.2226	78.3535	103.4084	138.2632	187.0254	255.5645	352.2701	489.1322	683.2804	959.1723	1,910.5898	3,840.4753	7,752.7818	15,663.259	31,592.744	179,361.20	982,104.59	5,151,723.2	25,827,696	123,723,325	566,774,664
48	61.8348	80.9406	107.5406	144.8337	197.4267	271.9584	377.9950	529.3427	745.8656	1,056.1896	2,140.9806	4,379.2819	8,994.3869	18,483.825	37,912.492	224,202.75	1,276,737.3	6,954,827.6	36,158,775	179,398,822	850,161,997
49	63.4632	83.5794	111.7969	151.6671	208.3480	289.3359	405.5289	572.7702	814.0836	1,162.9085	2,399.0182	4,993.5213	10,434.649	21,812.094	45,496.191	280,254.69	1,659,759.7	9,389,018.7	50,622,287	260,128,294	1,275,242,997
50	65.1078	86.2710	116.1808	158.7738	219.8154	307.7561	434.9860	619.6718	888.4411	1,280.2994	2,688.0204	5,693.7543	12,105.353	25,739.451	54,596.629	350,319.62	2,157,689.0	12,675,177	70,871,203	377,186,028	1,912,864,498

TABLE IV-A Present Value Factors for an Ordinary Annuity, PVFOA, Discounted at k Percent per Period for n Periods:

$$PVFOA_{k,n} = \frac{1 - \frac{1}{(1+k)^n}}{k}$$ where k = the interest rate per period expressed as a decimal

Discount Rate, k

Number of Periods, n	1%	2%	3%	4%	5%	6%	7%	8%	9%	10%	11%	12%	13%	14%	15%	16%	17%	18%	19%	20%	25%	30%	35%	40%	45%	50%
1	0.9901	0.9804	0.9709	0.9615	0.9524	0.9434	0.9346	0.9259	0.9174	0.9091	0.9009	0.8929	0.8850	0.8772	0.8696	0.8621	0.8547	0.8475	0.8403	0.8333	0.8000	0.7692	0.7407	0.7143	0.6897	0.6667
2	1.9704	1.9416	1.9135	1.8861	1.8594	1.8334	1.8080	1.7833	1.7591	1.7355	1.7125	1.6901	1.6681	1.6467	1.6257	1.6052	1.5852	1.5656	1.5465	1.5278	1.4400	1.3609	1.2894	1.2245	1.1653	1.1111
3	2.9410	2.8839	2.8286	2.7751	2.7232	2.6730	2.6243	2.5771	2.5313	2.4869	2.4437	2.4018	2.3612	2.3216	2.2832	2.2459	2.2096	2.1743	2.1399	2.1065	1.9520	1.8161	1.6959	1.5889	1.4933	1.4074
4	3.9020	3.8077	3.7171	3.6299	3.5460	3.4651	3.3872	3.3121	3.2397	3.1699	3.1024	3.0373	2.9745	2.9137	2.8550	2.7982	2.7432	2.6901	2.6386	2.5887	2.3616	2.1662	1.9969	1.8492	1.7195	1.6049
5	4.8534	4.7135	4.5797	4.4518	4.3295	4.2124	4.1002	3.9927	3.8897	3.7908	3.6959	3.6048	3.5172	3.4331	3.3522	3.2743	3.1993	3.1272	3.0576	2.9906	2.6893	2.4356	2.2200	2.0352	1.8755	1.7366
6	5.7955	5.6014	5.4172	5.2421	5.0757	4.9173	4.7665	4.6229	4.4859	4.3553	4.2305	4.1114	3.9975	3.8887	3.7845	3.6847	3.5892	3.4976	3.4098	3.3255	2.9514	2.6427	2.3852	2.1680	1.9831	1.8244
7	6.7282	6.4720	6.2303	6.0021	5.7864	5.5824	5.3893	5.2064	5.0330	4.8684	4.7122	4.5638	4.4226	4.2883	4.1604	4.0386	3.9224	3.8115	3.7057	3.6046	3.1611	2.8021	2.5075	2.2628	2.0573	1.8829
8	7.6517	7.3255	7.0197	6.7327	6.4632	6.2098	5.9713	5.7466	5.5348	5.3349	5.1461	4.9676	4.7988	4.6389	4.4873	4.3436	4.2072	4.0776	3.9544	3.8372	3.3289	2.9247	2.5982	2.3306	2.1085	1.9220
9	8.5660	8.1622	7.7861	7.4353	7.1078	6.8017	6.5152	6.2469	5.9952	5.7590	5.5370	5.3282	5.1317	4.9464	4.7716	4.6065	4.4506	4.3030	4.1633	4.0310	3.4631	3.0190	2.6653	2.3790	2.1438	1.9480
10	9.4713	8.9826	8.5302	8.1109	7.7217	7.3601	7.0236	6.7101	6.4177	6.1446	5.8892	5.6502	5.4262	5.2161	5.0188	4.8332	4.6586	4.4941	4.3389	4.1925	3.5705	3.0915	2.7150	2.4136	2.1681	1.9653
11	10.3676	9.7868	9.2526	8.7605	8.3064	7.8869	7.4987	7.1390	6.8052	6.4951	6.2065	5.9377	5.6869	5.4527	5.2337	5.0286	4.8364	4.6560	4.4865	4.3271	3.6564	3.1473	2.7519	2.4383	2.1849	1.9769
12	11.2551	10.5753	9.9540	9.3851	8.8633	8.3838	7.9427	7.5361	7.1607	6.8137	6.4924	6.1944	5.9176	5.6603	5.4206	5.1971	4.9884	4.7932	4.6105	4.4392	3.7251	3.1903	2.7792	2.4559	2.1965	1.9846
13	12.1337	11.3484	10.6350	9.9856	9.3936	8.8527	8.3577	7.9038	7.4869	7.1034	6.7499	6.4235	6.1218	5.8424	5.5831	5.3423	5.1183	4.9095	4.7147	4.5327	3.7801	3.2233	2.7994	2.4685	2.2045	1.9897
14	13.0037	12.1062	11.2961	10.5631	9.8986	9.2950	8.7455	8.2442	7.7862	7.3667	6.9819	6.6282	6.3025	6.0021	5.7245	5.4675	5.2293	5.0081	4.8023	4.6106	3.8241	3.2487	2.8144	2.4775	2.2100	1.9931
15	13.8651	12.8493	11.9379	11.1184	10.3797	9.7122	9.1079	8.5595	8.0607	7.6061	7.1909	6.8109	6.4624	6.1422	5.8474	5.5755	5.3242	5.0916	4.8759	4.6755	3.8593	3.2682	2.8255	2.4839	2.2138	1.9954
16	14.7179	13.5777	12.5611	11.6523	10.8378	10.1059	9.4466	8.8514	8.3126	7.8237	7.3792	6.9740	6.6039	6.2651	5.9542	5.6685	5.4053	5.1624	4.9377	4.7296	3.8874	3.2832	2.8337	2.4885	2.2164	1.9970
17	15.5623	14.2919	13.1661	12.1657	11.2741	10.4773	9.7632	9.1216	8.5436	8.0216	7.5488	7.1196	6.7291	6.3729	6.0472	5.7487	5.4746	5.2223	4.9897	4.7746	3.9099	3.2948	2.8398	2.4918	2.2182	1.9980
18	16.3983	14.9920	13.7535	12.6593	11.6896	10.8276	10.0591	9.3719	8.7556	8.2014	7.7016	7.2497	6.8399	6.4674	6.1280	5.8178	5.5339	5.2732	5.0333	4.8122	3.9279	3.3037	2.8443	2.4941	2.2195	1.9986
19	17.2260	15.6785	14.3238	13.1339	12.0853	11.1581	10.3356	9.6036	8.9501	8.3649	7.8393	7.3658	6.9380	6.5504	6.1982	5.8775	5.5845	5.3162	5.0700	4.8435	3.9424	3.3105	2.8476	2.4958	2.2203	1.9991
20	18.0456	16.3514	14.8775	13.5903	12.4622	11.4699	10.5940	9.8181	9.1285	8.5136	7.9633	7.4694	7.0248	6.6231	6.2593	5.9288	5.6278	5.3527	5.1009	4.8696	3.9539	3.3158	2.8501	2.4970	2.2209	1.9994
21	18.8570	17.0112	15.4150	14.0292	12.8212	11.7641	10.8355	10.0168	9.2922	8.6487	8.0751	7.5620	7.1016	6.6870	6.3125	5.9731	5.6648	5.3837	5.1268	4.8913	3.9631	3.3198	2.8519	2.4979	2.2213	1.9996
22	19.6604	17.6580	15.9369	14.4511	13.1630	12.0416	11.0612	10.2007	9.4424	8.7715	8.1757	7.6446	7.1695	6.7429	6.3587	6.0113	5.6964	5.4099	5.1486	4.9094	3.9705	3.3230	2.8533	2.4985	2.2216	1.9997
23	20.4558	18.2922	16.4436	14.8568	13.4886	12.3034	11.2722	10.3711	9.5802	8.8832	8.2664	7.7184	7.2297	6.7921	6.3988	6.0442	5.7234	5.4321	5.1668	4.9245	3.9764	3.3254	2.8543	2.4989	2.2218	1.9998
24	21.2434	18.9139	16.9355	15.2470	13.7986	12.5504	11.4693	10.5288	9.7066	8.9847	8.3481	7.7843	7.2829	6.8351	6.4338	6.0726	5.7465	5.4509	5.1822	4.9371	3.9811	3.3272	2.8550	2.4992	2.2219	1.9999
25	22.0232	19.5235	17.4131	15.6221	14.0939	12.7834	11.6536	10.6748	9.8226	9.0770	8.4217	7.8431	7.3300	6.8729	6.4641	6.0971	5.7662	5.4669	5.1951	4.9476	3.9849	3.3286	2.8556	2.4994	2.2220	1.9999

TABLE IV-A Present Value Factors for an Ordinary Annuity, PVFOA, Discounted at k Percent per Period for n Periods:

$$PVFOA_{k,n} = \frac{1 - \dfrac{1}{(1+k)^n}}{k} \quad \text{where } k = \text{the interest rate per period expressed as a decimal } (continued)$$

Discount Rate, k

Number of Periods, n	1%	2%	3%	4%	5%	6%	7%	8%	9%	10%	11%	12%	13%	14%	15%	16%	17%	18%	19%	20%	25%	30%	35%	40%	45%	50%
26	22.7952	20.1210	17.8768	15.9828	14.3752	13.0032	11.8258	10.8100	9.9290	9.1609	8.4881	7.8957	7.3717	6.9061	6.4906	6.1182	5.7831	5.4804	5.2060	4.9563	3.9879	3.3297	2.8560	2.4996	2.2221	1.9999
27	23.5596	20.7069	18.3270	16.3296	14.6430	13.2105	11.9867	10.9352	10.0266	9.2372	8.5478	7.9426	7.4086	6.9352	6.5135	6.1364	5.7975	5.4919	5.2151	4.9636	3.9903	3.3305	2.8563	2.4997	2.2221	2.0000
28	24.3164	21.2813	18.7641	16.6631	14.8981	13.4062	12.1371	11.0511	10.1161	9.3066	8.6015	7.9844	7.4412	6.9607	6.5335	6.1520	5.8099	5.5016	5.2228	4.9697	3.9923	3.3312	2.8565	2.4998	2.2222	2.0000
29	25.0658	21.8444	19.1885	16.9837	15.1411	13.5907	12.2777	11.1584	10.1983	9.3696	8.6501	8.0218	7.4701	6.9830	6.5509	6.1656	5.8204	5.5098	5.2292	4.9747	3.9938	3.3317	2.8567	2.4999	2.2222	2.0000
30	25.8077	22.3965	19.6004	17.2920	15.3725	13.7648	12.4090	11.2578	10.2737	9.4269	8.6938	8.0552	7.4957	7.0027	6.5660	6.1772	5.8294	5.5168	5.2347	4.9789	3.9950	3.3321	2.8568	2.4999	2.2222	2.0000
31	26.5423	22.9377	20.0004	17.5885	15.5928	13.9291	12.5318	11.3498	10.3428	9.4790	8.7331	8.0850	7.5183	7.0199	6.5791	6.1872	5.8371	5.5227	5.2392	4.9824	3.9960	3.3324	2.8569	2.4999	2.2222	2.0000
32	27.2696	23.4683	20.3888	17.8736	15.8027	14.0840	12.6466	11.4350	10.4062	9.5264	8.7686	8.1116	7.5383	7.0350	6.5905	6.1959	5.8437	5.5277	5.2430	4.9854	3.9968	3.3326	2.8569	2.4999	2.2222	2.0000
33	27.9897	23.9886	20.7658	18.1476	16.0025	14.2302	12.7538	11.5139	10.4644	9.5694	8.8005	8.1354	7.5560	7.0482	6.6005	6.2034	5.8493	5.5320	5.2462	4.9878	3.9975	3.3328	2.8570	2.5000	2.2222	2.0000
34	28.7027	24.4986	21.1318	18.4112	16.1929	14.3681	12.8540	11.5869	10.5178	9.6086	8.8293	8.1566	7.5717	7.0599	6.6091	6.2098	5.8541	5.5356	5.2489	4.9898	3.9980	3.3329	2.8570	2.5000	2.2222	2.0000
35	29.4086	24.9986	21.4872	18.6646	16.3742	14.4982	12.9477	11.6546	10.5668	9.6442	8.8552	8.1755	7.5856	7.0700	6.6166	6.2153	5.8582	5.5386	5.2512	4.9915	3.9984	3.3330	2.8571	2.5000	2.2222	2.0000
36	30.1075	25.4888	21.8323	18.9083	16.5469	14.6210	13.0352	11.7172	10.6118	9.6765	8.8786	8.1924	7.5979	7.0790	6.6231	6.2201	5.8617	5.5412	5.2531	4.9929	3.9987	3.3331	2.8571	2.5000	2.2222	2.0000
37	30.7995	25.9695	22.1672	19.1426	16.7113	14.7368	13.1170	11.7752	10.6530	9.7059	8.8996	8.2075	7.6087	7.0868	6.6288	6.2242	5.8647	5.5434	5.2547	4.9941	3.9990	3.3331	2.8571	2.5000	2.2222	2.0000
38	31.4847	26.4406	22.4925	19.3679	16.8679	14.8460	13.1935	11.8289	10.6908	9.7327	8.9186	8.2210	7.6183	7.0937	6.6338	6.2278	5.8673	5.5452	5.2561	4.9951	3.9992	3.3332	2.8571	2.5000	2.2222	2.0000
39	32.1630	26.9026	22.8082	19.5845	17.0170	14.9491	13.2649	11.8786	10.7255	9.7570	8.9357	8.2330	7.6268	7.0997	6.6380	6.2309	5.8695	5.5468	5.2572	4.9959	3.9993	3.3332	2.8571	2.5000	2.2222	2.0000
40	32.8347	27.3555	23.1148	19.7928	17.1591	15.0463	13.3317	11.9246	10.7574	9.7791	8.9511	8.2438	7.6344	7.1050	6.6418	6.2335	5.8713	5.5482	5.2582	4.9966	3.9995	3.3332	2.8571	2.5000	2.2222	2.0000
41	33.4997	27.7995	23.4124	19.9931	17.2944	15.1380	13.3941	11.9672	10.7866	9.7991	8.9649	8.2534	7.6410	7.1097	6.6450	6.2358	5.8729	5.5493	5.2590	4.9972	3.9996	3.3333	2.8571	2.5000	2.2222	2.0000
42	34.1581	28.2348	23.7014	20.1856	17.4232	15.2245	13.4524	12.0067	10.8134	9.8174	8.9774	8.2619	7.6469	7.1138	6.6478	6.2377	5.8743	5.5502	5.2596	4.9976	3.9997	3.3333	2.8571	2.5000	2.2222	2.0000
43	34.8100	28.6616	23.9819	20.3708	17.5459	15.3062	13.5070	12.0432	10.8380	9.8340	8.9886	8.2696	7.6522	7.1173	6.6503	6.2394	5.8755	5.5510	5.2602	4.9980	3.9997	3.3333	2.8571	2.5000	2.2222	2.0000
44	35.4555	29.0800	24.2543	20.5488	17.6628	15.3832	13.5579	12.0771	10.8605	9.8491	8.9988	8.2764	7.6568	7.1205	6.6524	6.2409	5.8765	5.5517	5.2607	4.9984	3.9998	3.3333	2.8571	2.5000	2.2222	2.0000
45	36.0945	29.4902	24.5187	20.7200	17.7741	15.4558	13.6055	12.1084	10.8812	9.8628	9.0079	8.2825	7.6609	7.1232	6.6543	6.2421	5.8773	5.5523	5.2611	4.9986	3.9998	3.3333	2.8571	2.5000	2.2222	2.0000
46	36.7272	29.8923	24.7754	20.8847	17.8801	15.5244	13.6500	12.1374	10.9002	9.8753	9.0161	8.2880	7.6645	7.1256	6.6559	6.2432	5.8781	5.5528	5.2614	4.9989	3.9999	3.3333	2.8571	2.5000	2.2222	2.0000
47	37.3537	30.2866	25.0247	21.0429	17.9810	15.5890	13.6916	12.1643	10.9176	9.8866	9.0235	8.2928	7.6677	7.1277	6.6573	6.2442	5.8787	5.5532	5.2617	4.9991	3.9999	3.3333	2.8571	2.5000	2.2222	2.0000
48	37.9740	30.6731	25.2667	21.1951	18.0772	15.6500	13.7305	12.1891	10.9336	9.8969	9.0302	8.2972	7.6705	7.1296	6.6585	6.2450	5.8792	5.5536	5.2619	4.9992	3.9999	3.3333	2.8571	2.5000	2.2222	2.0000
49	38.5881	31.0521	25.5017	21.3415	18.1687	15.7076	13.7668	12.2122	10.9482	9.9063	9.0362	8.3010	7.6730	7.1312	6.6596	6.2457	5.8797	5.5539	5.2621	4.9993	3.9999	3.3333	2.8571	2.5000	2.2222	2.0000
50	39.1961	31.4236	25.7298	21.4822	18.2559	15.7619	13.8007	12.2335	10.9617	9.9148	9.0417	8.3045	7.6752	7.1327	6.6605	6.2463	5.8801	5.5541	5.2623	4.9995	3.9999	3.3333	2.8571	2.5000	2.2222	2.0000

TABLE IV-B Present Value Factors for an Annuity Due, PVFAD, Discounted at k Percent per Period for n Periods: $PVFAD_{k,n} = \dfrac{1 - \dfrac{1}{(1+k)^n}}{k} \times (1+k)$

Discount Rate, k

Number of Periods, n	0%	1%	2%	3%	4%	5%	6%	7%	8%	9%	10%	11%	12%	13%	14%	15%	16%	17%	18%	19%	20%	25%	30%	35%	40%	45%	50%
1	1.0000	1.0000	1.0000	1.0000	1.0000	1.0000	1.0000	1.0000	1.0000	1.0000	1.0000	1.0000	1.0000	1.0000	1.0000	1.0000	1.0000	1.0000	1.0000	1.0000	1.0000	1.0000	1.0000	1.0000	1.0000	1.0000	1.0000
2	2.0000	1.9901	1.9804	1.9614	1.9430	1.9165	1.8911	1.8589	1.8285	1.7927	1.7593	1.7218	1.6871	1.6495	1.6150	1.5785	1.5452	1.5108	1.4794	1.4475	1.4185	1.3801	1.3466	1.3080	1.2752	1.2403	1.2112
3	3.0000	2.9704	2.9416	2.8860	2.8331	2.7582	2.6884	2.6022	2.5232	2.4330	2.3513	2.2627	2.1832	2.1001	2.0258	1.9501	1.8827	1.8151	1.7551	1.6958	1.6431	1.5752	1.5175	1.4530	1.3995	1.3443	1.2991
4	4.0000	3.9410	3.8839	3.7754	3.6736	3.5328	3.4044	3.2498	3.1116	2.9583	2.8230	2.6804	2.5554	2.4281	2.3170	2.2062	2.1097	2.0149	1.9322	1.8518	1.7815	1.6924	1.6179	1.5361	1.4693	1.4013	1.3466
5	5.0000	4.9020	4.8077	4.6312	4.4681	4.2472	4.0496	3.8177	3.6149	3.3954	3.2060	3.0108	2.8433	2.6761	2.5327	2.3922	2.2716	2.1550	2.0544	1.9580	1.8745	1.7699	1.6834	1.5894	1.5135	1.4371	1.3760
6	6.0000	5.8534	5.7135	5.4549	5.2196	4.9071	4.6329	4.3185	4.0489	3.7636	3.5218	3.2777	3.0715	2.8691	2.6979	2.5326	2.3922	2.2580	2.1434	2.0345	1.9409	1.8245	1.7291	1.6263	1.5439	1.4614	1.3958
7	7.0000	6.7955	6.6014	6.2479	5.9309	5.5179	5.1621	4.7625	4.4260	4.0769	3.7858	3.4969	3.2561	3.0230	2.8280	2.6419	2.4851	2.3367	2.2107	2.0919	1.9904	1.8650	1.7628	1.6532	1.5659	1.4789	1.4101
8	8.0000	7.7282	7.4720	7.0117	6.6045	6.0842	5.6434	5.1580	4.7560	4.3462	4.0092	3.6796	3.4080	3.1482	2.9328	2.7291	2.5587	2.3985	2.2633	2.1365	2.0286	1.8960	1.7884	1.6737	1.5825	1.4921	1.4207
9	9.0000	8.6517	8.3255	7.7474	7.2430	6.6101	6.0825	5.5121	5.0466	4.5795	4.2001	3.8338	3.5348	3.2518	3.0186	2.8000	2.6181	2.4481	2.3053	2.1720	2.0589	1.9205	1.8086	1.6896	1.5955	1.5023	1.4290
10	10.0000	9.5660	9.1622	8.4563	7.8486	7.0993	6.4842	5.8303	5.3039	4.7833	4.3648	3.9654	3.6421	3.3386	3.0901	2.8587	2.6670	2.4888	2.3395	2.2009	2.0834	1.9403	1.8248	1.7025	1.6058	1.5105	1.4356
11	11.0000	10.4713	9.9826	9.1395	8.4233	7.5551	6.8525	6.1174	5.5329	4.9623	4.5081	4.0789	3.7337	3.4123	3.1505	2.9080	2.7078	2.5227	2.3679	2.2247	2.1037	1.9565	1.8380	1.7129	1.6143	1.5172	1.4409
12	12.0000	11.3676	10.7868	9.7983	8.9691	7.9803	7.1910	6.3774	5.7378	5.1208	4.6337	4.1774	3.8128	3.4755	3.2019	2.9498	2.7424	2.5512	2.3918	2.2447	2.1206	1.9701	1.8491	1.7216	1.6213	1.5227	1.4454
13	13.0000	12.2551	11.5753	10.4335	9.4877	8.3776	7.5028	6.6137	5.9219	5.2617	4.7444	4.2638	3.8817	3.5303	3.2463	2.9858	2.7720	2.5756	2.4122	2.2617	2.1350	1.9815	1.8584	1.7290	1.6272	1.5273	1.4491
14	14.0000	13.1337	12.3484	11.0462	9.9809	8.7494	7.7907	6.8291	6.0879	5.3876	4.8426	4.3399	3.9420	3.5781	3.2849	3.0170	2.7975	2.5966	2.4297	2.2764	2.1473	1.9914	1.8664	1.7353	1.6322	1.5312	1.4522
15	15.0000	14.0037	13.1062	11.6374	10.4500	9.0977	8.0570	7.0261	6.2383	5.5008	4.9302	4.4074	3.9953	3.6201	3.3187	3.0442	2.8198	2.6149	2.4448	2.2890	2.1579	1.9999	1.8733	1.7407	1.6365	1.5346	1.4549
16	16.0000	14.8651	13.8493	12.2080	10.8966	9.4245	8.3039	7.2067	6.3750	5.6029	5.0088	4.4676	4.0426	3.6573	3.3485	3.0682	2.8394	2.6310	2.4581	2.3001	2.1672	2.0073	1.8793	1.7453	1.6403	1.5376	1.4573
17	17.0000	15.7179	14.5777	12.7588	11.3220	9.7314	8.5331	7.3727	6.4995	5.6953	5.0795	4.5216	4.0848	3.6904	3.3749	3.0894	2.8566	2.6451	2.4698	2.3098	2.1754	2.0138	1.8846	1.7495	1.6436	1.5401	1.4593
18	18.0000	16.5623	15.2919	13.2906	11.7274	10.0200	8.7463	7.5258	6.6135	5.7794	5.1434	4.5703	4.1227	3.7201	3.3986	3.1083	2.8720	2.6577	2.4802	2.3185	2.1826	2.0195	1.8892	1.7531	1.6465	1.5424	1.4612
19	19.0000	17.3983	15.9920	13.8042	12.1140	10.2918	8.9450	7.6671	6.7180	5.8561	5.2015	4.6142	4.1569	3.7467	3.4197	3.1253	2.8858	2.6689	2.4895	2.3262	2.1891	2.0246	1.8933	1.7563	1.6490	1.5444	1.4628
20	20.0000	18.2260	16.6785	14.3004	12.4829	10.5479	9.1305	7.7980	6.8141	5.9262	5.2544	4.6542	4.1878	3.7708	3.4388	3.1405	2.8981	2.6790	2.4978	2.3331	2.1948	2.0292	1.8970	1.7592	1.6513	1.5462	1.4642
21	21.0000	19.0456	17.3514	14.7799	12.8350	10.7896	9.3038	7.9194	6.9027	5.9906	5.3027	4.6906	4.2159	3.7927	3.4561	3.1543	2.9093	2.6881	2.5053	2.3393	2.2000	2.0333	1.9003	1.7618	1.6534	1.5478	1.4655
22	22.0000	19.8570	18.0112	15.2433	13.1713	11.0178	9.4661	8.0323	6.9846	6.0499	5.3470	4.7239	4.2416	3.8126	3.4718	3.1669	2.9194	2.6963	2.5120	2.3449	2.2047	2.0370	1.9033	1.7641	1.6552	1.5493	1.4666
23	23.0000	20.6604	18.6580	15.6913	13.4927	11.2336	9.6182	8.1375	7.0604	6.1045	5.3877	4.7544	4.2650	3.8307	3.4862	3.1783	2.9286	2.7038	2.5182	2.3500	2.2090	2.0404	1.9060	1.7663	1.6569	1.5506	1.4677
24	24.0000	21.4558	19.2922	16.1245	13.7999	11.4379	9.7611	8.2356	7.1308	6.1551	5.4252	4.7825	4.2865	3.8474	3.4993	3.1887	2.9370	2.7107	2.5238	2.3547	2.2128	2.0435	1.9085	1.7682	1.6584	1.5518	1.4686
25	25.0000	22.2434	19.9139	16.5435	14.0938	11.6314	9.8953	8.3273	7.1963	6.2020	5.4599	4.8084	4.3063	3.8627	3.5113	3.1983	2.9447	2.7169	2.5289	2.3589	2.2164	2.0463	1.9107	1.7699	1.6598	1.5529	1.4695

TABLE IV-B Present Value Factors for an Annuity Due, PVFAD, Discounted at k Percent per Period for n Periods:

$$PVFAD_{k,n} = \frac{1 - \dfrac{1}{(1+k)^n}}{k} \times (1+k) \quad \text{(continued)}$$

Discount Rate, k

Number of Periods, n	0%	1%	2%	3%	4%	5%	6%	7%	8%	9%	10%	11%	12%	13%	14%	15%	16%	17%	18%	19%	20%	25%	30%	35%	40%	45%	50%
26	26.0000	23.0232	20.5235	16.9488	14.3751	11.8149	10.0216	8.4131	7.2573	6.2455	5.4920	4.8324	4.3246	3.8768	3.5224	3.2071	2.9517	2.7227	2.5336	2.3628	2.2196	2.0489	1.9128	1.7716	1.6611	1.5539	1.4703
27	27.0000	23.7952	21.1210	17.3411	14.6444	11.9890	10.1406	8.4936	7.3142	6.2861	5.5218	4.8546	4.3414	3.8899	3.5326	3.2152	2.9582	2.7280	2.5380	2.3664	2.2226	2.0512	1.9147	1.7730	1.6623	1.5548	1.4710
28	28.0000	24.5596	21.7069	17.7207	14.9023	12.1543	10.2529	8.5692	7.3674	6.3239	5.5495	4.8752	4.3571	3.9020	3.5420	3.2228	2.9643	2.7329	2.5420	2.3697	2.2254	2.0534	1.9164	1.7744	1.6634	1.5556	1.4717
29	29.0000	25.3164	22.2813	18.0882	15.1495	12.3115	10.3589	8.6402	7.4173	6.3592	5.5753	4.8944	4.3716	3.9132	3.5508	3.2297	2.9698	2.7374	2.5457	2.3728	2.2279	2.0554	1.9181	1.7757	1.6644	1.5564	1.4723
30	30.0000	26.0658	22.8444	18.4441	15.3865	12.4611	10.4592	8.7071	7.4640	6.3923	5.5995	4.9123	4.3852	3.9236	3.5589	3.2362	2.9750	2.7416	2.5491	2.3757	2.2303	2.0573	1.9195	1.7768	1.6653	1.5572	1.4729
31	31.0000	26.8077	23.3965	18.7887	15.6139	12.6035	10.5540	8.7702	7.5079	6.4233	5.6220	4.9290	4.3978	3.9334	3.5665	3.2422	2.9798	2.7456	2.5523	2.3783	2.2325	2.0590	1.9209	1.7779	1.6661	1.5578	1.4734
32	32.0000	27.5423	23.9377	19.1226	15.8320	12.7392	10.6438	8.8297	7.5492	6.4524	5.6431	4.9447	4.4096	3.9425	3.5736	3.2478	2.9843	2.7492	2.5552	2.3808	2.2345	2.0607	1.9222	1.7789	1.6669	1.5584	1.4739
33	33.0000	28.2696	24.4683	19.4461	16.0415	12.8685	10.7290	8.8860	7.5881	6.4798	5.6629	4.9594	4.4207	3.9510	3.5802	3.2531	2.9885	2.7526	2.5580	2.3831	2.2364	2.0622	1.9234	1.7799	1.6677	1.5590	1.4743
34	34.0000	28.9897	24.9886	19.7597	16.2426	12.9920	10.8099	8.9392	7.6247	6.5055	5.6816	4.9732	4.4310	3.9590	3.5864	3.2580	2.9924	2.7558	2.5606	2.3852	2.2382	2.0636	1.9245	1.7807	1.6684	1.5596	1.4748
35	35.0000	29.7027	25.4986	20.0636	16.4358	13.1098	10.8866	8.9896	7.6593	6.5298	5.6991	4.9861	4.4407	3.9665	3.5922	3.2626	2.9960	2.7588	2.5630	2.3872	2.2398	2.0649	1.9256	1.7816	1.6690	1.5601	1.4752
36	36.0000	30.4086	25.9986	20.3583	16.6216	13.2225	10.9596	9.0374	7.6921	6.5528	5.7156	4.9983	4.4499	3.9735	3.5976	3.2670	2.9995	2.7616	2.5653	2.3891	2.2414	2.0661	1.9266	1.7823	1.6696	1.5606	1.4755
37	37.0000	31.1075	26.4888	20.6440	16.8002	13.3301	11.0291	9.0828	7.7230	6.5745	5.7311	5.0098	4.4585	3.9801	3.6027	3.2710	3.0027	2.7642	2.5674	2.3909	2.2428	2.0673	1.9275	1.7831	1.6702	1.5610	1.4759
38	38.0000	31.7995	26.9695	20.9212	16.9720	13.4332	11.0952	9.1259	7.7523	6.5950	5.7458	5.0207	4.4666	3.9864	3.6076	3.2749	3.0057	2.7667	2.5694	2.3926	2.2442	2.0684	1.9284	1.7837	1.6707	1.5614	1.4762
39	39.0000	32.4847	27.4406	21.1901	17.1373	13.5318	11.1582	9.1669	7.7801	6.6144	5.7597	5.0310	4.4743	3.9923	3.6121	3.2785	3.0086	2.7691	2.5713	2.3942	2.2455	2.0694	1.9292	1.7844	1.6712	1.5618	1.4765
40	40.0000	33.1630	27.9026	21.4510	17.2964	13.6263	11.2182	9.2058	7.8065	6.6329	5.7729	5.0407	4.4815	3.9979	3.6164	3.2819	3.0113	2.7713	2.5731	2.3956	2.2467	2.0704	1.9300	1.7850	1.6717	1.5622	1.4768
41	41.0000	33.8347	28.3555	21.7042	17.4496	13.7168	11.2756	9.2430	7.8316	6.6504	5.7854	5.0499	4.4884	4.0032	3.6205	3.2852	3.0139	2.7734	2.5748	2.3970	2.2479	2.0713	1.9307	1.7856	1.6721	1.5625	1.4771
42	42.0000	34.4997	28.7995	21.9501	17.5972	13.8036	11.3303	9.2784	7.8554	6.6670	5.7972	5.0587	4.4948	4.0082	3.6243	3.2882	3.0163	2.7753	2.5764	2.3984	2.2490	2.0722	1.9314	1.7861	1.6726	1.5629	1.4774
43	43.0000	35.1581	29.2348	22.1887	17.7395	13.8870	11.3826	9.3121	7.8781	6.6828	5.8084	5.0670	4.5010	4.0129	3.6280	3.2911	3.0186	2.7772	2.5779	2.3996	2.2500	2.0730	1.9320	1.7866	1.6730	1.5632	1.4776
44	44.0000	35.8100	29.6616	22.4205	17.8766	13.9669	11.4326	9.3444	7.8997	6.6979	5.8191	5.0749	4.5068	4.0174	3.6314	3.2939	3.0207	2.7790	2.5793	2.4008	2.2510	2.0738	1.9326	1.7871	1.6733	1.5635	1.4778
45	45.0000	36.4555	30.0800	22.6456	18.0088	14.0438	11.4804	9.3752	7.9203	6.7122	5.8293	5.0824	4.5124	4.0217	3.6347	3.2965	3.0228	2.7807	2.5807	2.4020	2.2519	2.0745	1.9332	1.7876	1.6737	1.5638	1.4781
46	46.0000	37.0945	30.4902	22.8643	18.1364	14.1176	11.5262	9.4046	7.9399	6.7259	5.8389	5.0895	4.5177	4.0258	3.6378	3.2990	3.0248	2.7823	2.5820	2.4030	2.2528	2.0752	1.9338	1.7880	1.6740	1.5640	1.4783
47	47.0000	37.7272	30.8923	23.0768	18.2594	14.1886	11.5701	9.4328	7.9586	6.7390	5.8481	5.0953	4.5227	4.0297	3.6408	3.3014	3.0266	2.7838	2.5832	2.4041	2.2536	2.0759	1.9343	1.7884	1.6744	1.5643	1.4785
48	48.0000	38.3537	31.2866	23.2834	18.3782	14.2569	11.6122	9.4598	7.9765	6.7515	5.8569	5.1028	4.5275	4.0334	3.6436	3.3036	3.0284	2.7853	2.5843	2.4050	2.2544	2.0765	1.9348	1.7888	1.6747	1.5645	1.4787
49	49.0000	38.9740	31.6731	23.4841	18.4929	14.3226	11.6525	9.4856	7.9936	6.7634	5.8653	5.1090	4.5320	4.0369	3.6463	3.3058	3.0301	2.7866	2.5854	2.4060	2.2552	2.0771	1.9353	1.7892	1.6750	1.5648	1.4788
50	50.0000	39.5881	32.0521	23.6793	18.6036	14.3859	11.6912	9.5104	8.0100	6.7748	5.8733	5.1149	4.5364	4.0403	3.6489	3.3078	3.0317	2.7880	2.5865	2.4069	2.2559	2.0777	1.9357	1.7895	1.6752	1.5650	1.4790

Glossary

A

ABC system An inventory system in which items are classified according to their value for inventory control purposes.

absolute purchasing power parity theory Theory that claims the current exchange rate is determined by the relative prices in two countries of a similar basket of traded goods and services.

actuaries People who use applied mathematics and statistics to predict claims on insurance companies and pension funds.

additional funds needed The additional external financing required to support asset growth when forecasted assets exceed forecasted liabilities and equity.

after-tax cost of debt (AT_{kd}) The after-tax cost to a company of obtaining debt funds.

agency costs Costs incurred to monitor agents to reduce the conflict of interest between agents and principals.

agency problem The possibility of conflict between the interests of a firm's managers and those of the firm's owners.

agent A person who has the implied or actual authority to act on behalf of another.

aggressive working capital financing approach The use of short-term funds to finance all temporary current assets, possibly all or some permanent current assets, and perhaps some fixed assets.

American depository receipts (ADRs) Securities denominated in U.S. dollars that represent a claim on foreign currency-denominated stocks held in a trust.

amortized loan A loan that is repaid in regularly spaced, equal installments, which cover all interest and principal owed.

annuitant A person who is entitled to receive annuity payments.

annuity A series of equal cash payments made at regular time intervals.

arbitrage The process whereby equivalent assets are bought in one place and simultaneously sold in another, making a risk-free profit.

B

B lab A non-profit organization that offers certification to companies that meet the organizations' standards for social and environmental activities.

balance sheet The financial statement that shows an economic unit's assets, liabilities, and equity at a given point in time.

banker's acceptance A security that represents a promise by a bank to pay a certain amount of money, if the original note maker doesn't pay.

bearer The owner of a security.

benefit corporation A corporation with a charter that allows the board of directors to take into account the interests of a wider range of stakeholders, not just the common stock shareholders, when making corporate decisions. Some states allow such a designation so that workers, suppliers, customers, and community members' interests are considered. Some corporations seek certification from B Lab, a nonprofit organization not affiliated with any state, that recognizes companies that have met its criteria for considering a similarly broad range of stakeholders when making company decisions.

best efforts basis An arrangement in which the investment banking firm tries its best to sell a firm's securities for the desired price, without guarantees. If the securities must be sold for a lower price, the issuer collects less money.

beta (β) The measure of nondiversifiable risk. The stock market has a beta of 1.0. Betas higher than 1.0 indicate more nondiversifiable risk than the market, and betas lower than 1.0 indicate less. Risk-free portfolios have betas of 0.0.

bird-in-the-hand theory A theory that says that investors value a dollar of dividends more highly than a dollar of reinvested earnings because uncertainty is resolved.

board of directors A group of individuals elected by the common stockholders to oversee the management of the firm.

bond maturity date The date on which the final payment is promised by the bond issuer.

bonds Securities that promise to pay the bearer a certain amount at a time in the future and may pay interest at regular intervals over the life of the security.

book value, net worth The total amount of common stockholders' equity on a company's balance sheet.

broker A person who brings buyers and sellers together.

business risk The uncertainty a company has due to fluctuations in its operating income.

C

call premium The premium the issuer pays to call in a bond before maturity. The excess of the call price over the face value.

call provision A bond indenture provision that allows the issuer to pay off a bond before the stated maturity date at a specified price.

capital Funds supplied to a firm.

capital asset pricing model (CAPM) A financial model that can be used to calculate the appropriate required payment of return for an investment project, given its degree of risk as measured by beta (β).

capital budget A document that shows planned expenditures for major asset acquisitions items, such as equipment or plant construction.

capital budgeting The process of evaluating proposed projects.

capital gains The profit made when an asset price is higher than the price paid.

capital market The market where long-term securities are traded.

capital rationing The process whereby management sets a limit on the amount of cash available for new capital budgeting projects.

capital structure The mixture of sources of capital that a firm uses (for example, debt, preferred stock, and common stock).

cash budget A detailed budget plan that shows the cash flows expected to occur during specific time periods.

C corporations Subchapter C corporations are large corporations that are taxed separately, via the corporate payment income tax, from their owners.

chief financial officer The manager who directs and coordinates the financial activities of the firm.

clientele dividend theory The theory that says that a company should attempt to determine the dividend wants of its stockholders and maintain a consistent policy of paying stockholders what they want.

coefficient of variation The standard deviation divided by the mean. A measure of the degree of risk used to compare alternatives with possible returns of different magnitudes.

collateral Assets a borrower agrees to give to a lender if the borrower defaults on the terms of a loan.

collection policy The firm's plans for getting delinquent credit customers to pay their bills.

combined leverage The phenomenon whereby a change in sales causes net income to change by a larger percentage because of fixed operating and financial costs.

commercial paper A short-term, unsecured debt instrument issued by a large corporation or financial institution.

common stock A security that indicates ownership of a corporation.

compensating balance A specified amount that a lender requires a borrower to maintain in a non-interest-paying account during the life of a loan.

component cost of capital The cost of raising funds from a particular source, such as bondholders or common stockholders.

compound interest Interest earned on interest in addition to interest earned on the original principal.

conservative working capital financing approach The use of long-term debt and equity to finance all long-term fixed assets and permanent current assets, in addition to some part of temporary current assets.

continuous compounding A process whereby interest is earned on interest every instant of time.

contribution margin Sales price per unit minus variable cost per unit.

controller The manager who is responsible for the financial and cost accounting activities of a firm.

conversion ratio The number of shares (usually of common stock) that the holder of a convertible bond would receive if he or she exercised the conversion option.

conversion value The value of the stock that would be received if the conversion option on a convertible bond were exercised.

convertible bond A bond that may be converted, at the option of the bond's owner, into a certain amount of a different type of security issued by the company.

corporate bond A security that represents a promise by the issuing corporation to make certain payments, according to a certain schedule, to the owner of the bond.

corporation A business chartered by the state that is a separate legal entity having some, but not all, of the rights and responsibilities of a natural person.

correlation The degree to which one variable is linearly related to another.

correlation coefficient The measurement of degree of correlation, represented by the letter r. Its values range from + 1.0 (perfect positive correlation) to –1.0 (perfect negative correlation).

cost of debt (k_d) The lender's required rate of return on a company's new bonds or other instrument of indebtedness.

cost of equity from new common stock (k_n) The cost of external equity, including the costs incurred to issue new common stock.

cost of internal equity (k_s) The required rate of return on funds supplied by existing common stockholders through earnings retained.

cost of preferred stock (k_p) Investors' required rate of return on a company's new preferred stock.

credit policy Credit standards a firm has established and the credit terms it offers.

credit scoring A process by which candidates for credit are compared against indicators of credit worthiness and scored accordingly.

credit standards Requirements customers must meet in order to be granted credit.

credit unions Financial institutions owned by members who receive interest on shares purchased and who obtain loans.

cross rate An exchange rate determined by examining how each of two currencies is valued in terms of a common third currency.

cross-sectional analysis Comparing variables for different entities (such as ratio values for different companies) for the same point in time or time period.

crowdfunding A means of raising funds, usually over the Internet, whereby a company sets a financing goal and suppliers of capital offer funds such that either the goal is met or no funds are raised.

current assets Liquid assets of an economic entity (e.g., cash, accounts receivable, inventory, etc.) usually converted into cash within one year.

current liabilities Liabilities that are coming due soon, usually within one year.

D

date of record The date on which stockholder records are checked for the purpose of determining who will receive the dividend that has been declared.

dealer A person who makes his or her living buying and selling assets.

debenture A bond that is unsecured.

declaration date The date on which the board of directors announces a dividend is to be paid.

default risk premium The extra interest lenders demand to compensate for assuming the risk that promised interest and principal payments may be made late or not at all.

deficit economic unit A government, business, or household unit with expenditures greater than its income.

degree of combined leverage (DCL) The percentage change in net income divided by the percentage change in sales.

degree of financial leverage (DFL) The percentage change in net income divided by the percentage change in operating income.

degree of operating leverage (DOL) The percentage change in operating income divided by the percentage change in sales.

depreciation basis The total value of an asset upon which depreciation expense will be calculated, a part at a time, over the life of the asset.

discounted cash flow (DCF) model A model that estimates the value of an asset by calculating the sum of the present values of all future cash flows.

discount loan A loan with terms that call for the loan interest to be deducted from the loan proceeds at the time the loan is granted.

discount rate The interest rate used when calculating a present value representing the required rate of return.

discount yield The return realized by an investor who purchases a security for less than face value and redeems it at maturity for face value.

diversification effect The effect of combining assets in a portfolio such that the fluctuations of the assets' returns tend to offset each other, reducing the overall volatility (risk) of the portfolio.

dividend reinvestment plan An arrangement offered by some corporations where cash dividends are held by the company and used to purchase additional shares of stock for the investor.

dividends Payments made to stockholders at the discretion of the board of directors of the corporation.

dividends payable The liability item on a firm's balance sheet that reflects the amount of dividends declared but not yet paid.

dividend yield A stock's annual dividend divided by its current market price.

E

economic value added (EVA) The amount of profit remaining after accounting for the return expected by the firm's investors.

effective interest rate The annual interest rate that reflects the dollar interest paid divided by the dollar obtained for use.

electronic funds transfers The act of crediting one account and simultaneously debiting another by a computer.

equity multiplier The total assets to total common stockholders' equity ratio.

euro The common currency used by the European Monetary Union countries.

excess financing The amount of excess funding available for expected asset growth when forecasted liabilities and equity exceed forecasted assets.

exchange rate The number of units of one country's currency that is needed to purchase one unit of another country's currency.

ex-dividend A characteristic of common stock such that it is trading without entitlement to an upcoming dividend.

ex-rights A characteristic of common stock such that it is trading without the entitlement to an upcoming rights offering.

externalities Positive or negative effects that will occur to existing projects if a new capital budgeting project is accepted.

F

face value, or par value, or principal The amount the bond issuer promises to pay to the investor when the bond matures. The terms *face value, par value,* and *principal* are often used interchangeably.

factoring The practice of selling accounts receivable to another firm.

factors Firms that buy and administer another firm's accounts receivable.

Federal Reserve System The government-sponsored entity that acts as the central bank of the United States and that examines and regulates banks and other financial institutions.

fiduciary responsibility The legal requirement that those who are managing assets owned by someone else do so in a prudent manner and in accordance with the interests of the person(s) they represent.

financial intermediaries Institutions that facilitate the exchange of cash and securities.

financial (capital) lease A lease that is generally long term and non-cancelable, with the lessee using up most of the economic value of the asset by the end of the lease's term.

financial leverage The phenomenon whereby a change in operating income causes net income to change by a larger percentage because of the presence of fixed financial costs.

financial markets Exchanges or over-the-counter mechanisms where securities are traded.

financial ratio A number that expresses the value of one financial variable relative to the value of another.

financial risk The additional volatility of a firm's net income caused by the presence of fixed financial costs.

financing cash flows Cash flows that occur as creditors are paid interest and principal, and stockholders are paid dividends.

first mortgage A mortgage bond (a bond secured by real property) that gives the holder first claim on the real property pledged as security if there is a foreclosure.

fixed assets Assets that would not normally be sold or otherwise disposed of for a long period of time.

fixed costs Costs that do not vary with the level of production.

flotation costs Fees that companies pay (to investment bankers and to others) when new securities are issued.

forward rate The exchange rate for future delivery.

future value The value money or another asset will have in the future.

future value factor (FVF) The factor, which when multiplied by a single amount present value, gives the future value. It equals $(1 + k)^n$ for given values of k and n.

future value factor for an annuity due (FVFAD) The factor, which when multiplied by an expected annuity payment, gives the sum of the future values of an annuity due stream. It equals

$$\left[\frac{(1+k)^n - 1}{k} \right] \times (1+k)$$

for given values of k and n.

future value factor for an ordinary annuity (FVFOA) The factor, which when multiplied by an expected annuity payment, gives the sum of the future values of an ordinary annuity stream. It equals

$$\left[\frac{(1+k)^n - 1}{k} \right]$$

for given values of k and n.

G

going concern value That value that comes from the future earnings and cash flows that can be generated by a company if it continues to operate.

H

hedge A financial arrangement used to offset or protect against negative effects of something else, such as fluctuating exchange rates.

hurdle rate The minimum rate of return that management demands from a proposed project before that project will be accepted.

I

income statement A financial statement that presents the revenues, expenses, and income of a business over a specific time period.

incremental cash flows Cash flows that will occur only if an investment is undertaken.

incremental depreciation expense The change in depreciation expense that a company will incur if a proposed capital budgeting project is accepted.

indenture The contract between the issuing corporation and the bond's purchaser.

independent projects A group of projects such that any or all could be accepted.

industry comparison The process whereby financial ratios of a firm are compared to those of similar firms to see if the firm under scrutiny compares favorably or unfavorably with the norm.

inflation premium The extra interest that compensates lenders for the expected erosion of purchasing power of funds due to inflation over the life of the loan.

initial public offering (IPO) The process whereby a private corporation issues new common stock to the general public, thus becoming a publicly traded corporation.

institutional investors Financial institutions that invest in the securities of other companies.

interest The compensation lenders demand and borrowers pay when money is lent.

interest rate parity A theory that states that the difference between the exchange rate specified for future delivery and that for current delivery equals the difference in the interest rates for securities of the same maturity.

interest rate spread The rate a bank charges for loans minus the rate it pays for deposits.

intermediation The process by which funds are channeled from surplus to deficit economic units through a financial institution.

internal rate of return (IRR) The estimated rate of return for a proposed project, given the size of the project's incremental cash flows and their timing.

international bonds Bonds that are sold in countries other than where the issuer is domiciled.

international Fisher effect A theory developed by economist Irving Fisher that claims that changes in interest rates for two countries will be offset by equal changes, in the opposite direction, in the exchange rate.

inventory financing A type of financing that uses inventory as loan collateral.

investment banking firm A firm that helps issuers sell their securities and that provides other financial services.

investment-grade bonds Bonds rated Baa3 or above by Moody's bond rating agency and BBB—or above by Standard & Poor's.

J

JIT An inventory system in which inventory items are scheduled to be delivered "just in time" to be used as needed.

junk bonds Bonds with lower than investment-grade ratings.

L

lease A contract between an asset owner (lessor) and another party who uses that asset (lessee) that allows the use of the asset for a specified period of time, specifies payment terms, and does not convey legal ownership.

lessee The party in a lease contract who uses the asset.

lessor The party in a lease contract who owns the asset.

leverage Something that creates a magnifying effect, such as when fixed operating or fixed financial costs cause a magnifying effect on the movements of operating income or net income.

leverage effect The result of one factor causing another factor to be magnified, such as when debt magnifies the return stockholders earn on their invested funds over the return on assets.

liability insurance Insurance that pays obligations that may be incurred by the insured as a result of negligence, slander, malpractice, and similar actions.

limited liability companies (LLCs) Hybrids between partnerships and corporations that are taxed like the former and have limited liability for the owners like the latter.

limited liability partnership (LLPs) Business entities that are usually formed by professionals such as doctors, lawyers, or accountants and that provide limited liability for the partners.

limited partnerships (LPs) Partnerships that include at least one partner whose liability is limited to the amount invested. They usually take a less active role in the running of the business than do general partners.

line of credit An informal arrangement between a lender and borrower wherein the lender sets a limit on the maximum amount of funds the borrower may use at any one time.

liquidation value The amount that would be received by the owners of a company that sold all its assets as market value, paid all its liabilities and preferred stock, and distributed what was left to the owners of the firm.

liquidity risk premium The extra interest lenders demand to compensate for holding a security that is not easy to sell at its fair value.

lockbox A way station (typically a post office box) at which customers may send payments to a firm.

M

MACRs, modified accelerated cost recovery system The depreciation rules established by the Tax Reform Act of 1986 that allow owners to take accelerated depreciation with greater deductions in earlier years than in later years.

managing investment banker The head of an investment banking underwriting syndicate.

marginal cost of capital (MCC) The weighted average cost of capital for the next dollar of funds raised.

marginal tax rate The tax rate applied to the next dollar of taxable income.

market efficiency The relative ease, speed, and cost of trading securities. In an efficient market, securities can be traded easily, quickly, and at low cost. In an inefficient market, one or more of these qualities is missing.

market risk premium The additional return above the risk-free rate demanded by investors for assuming the risk of investing in the market.

market value added (MVA) The market value of the firm, debt plus equity, minus the total amount of capital invested in the firm.

maturity date The date the bearer of a security is to be paid the principal, or face value, of a security.

maturity risk premium The extra (or sometimes lesser) interest that lenders demand on longer-term securities.

mixed ratio A financial ratio that includes variables from both the income statement and the balance sheet.

moderate working capital financing approach An approach in which a firm finances temporary current assets with short-term funds and permanent current assets and fixed assets with long-term funds.

Modified Internal Rate of Return (MIRR) The estimated rate of return for a proposed project for which the projected cash flows are assumed to be reinvested at the cost of capital rate.

Modigliani and Miller dividend theory A theory developed by financial theorists Franco Modigliani and Merton Miller that says the amount of dividends paid by a firm does not affect the firm's value.

money market The market where short-term securities are traded.

mortgage bond A bond secured by real property.

multinational corporation (MNC) A corporation that has operations in more than one country.

municipal bonds Bonds issued by a state, city, county, or other nonfederal government authority, including specially created municipal authorities such as a toll road or industrial development authority.

mutually exclusive projects A group of projects that compete against each other; only one of the mutually exclusive projects may be chosen.

mutuals Institutions (e.g., savings and loans or insurance companies) that are owned by their depositors or policy holders.

N

negotiable CDs A deposit security issued by financial institutions that comes in minimum denominations of $100,000 and can be traded in the money market.

net present value (NPV) The estimated change in the value of the firm that would occur if a project is accepted.

net working capital The amount of current assets minus the amount of current liabilities of an economic unit.

nominal interest rate The rate observed in the financial marketplace that includes the real rate of interest and various premiums.

nominal risk-free rate of interest The interest rate without any premiums for the uncertainties associated with lending.

nondiversifiable risk The portion of a portfolio's total risk that cannot be eliminated by diversifying. Factors shared to a greater or lesser degree by most assets in the market, such as inflation and interest rate risk, cause nondiversifiable risk.

nonsimple project A project that has a negative initial cash flow and also has one or more negative future cash flows.

NPV profile A graph that displays how a project's net present value changes as the discount rate, or required rate of return, changes.

O

open-market operations The buying and selling of U.S. Treasury securities or foreign currencies to achieve some economic objective.

operating lease A lease that has a term substantially shorter than the useful life of the asset and is usually cancelable by the lessee.

operating leverage The effect of fixed operating costs on operating income; because of fixed costs, any change in sales results in a larger percentage change in operating income.

opportunity cost The cost of forgoing the best alternative to make a competing choice.

optimal capital budget The list of all accepted projects and the total amount of their initial cash outlays.

over-the-counter market A network of dealers around the world who purchase securities and maintain inventories of securities for sale.

P

par value The stated value of a share of common stock.

partnership An unincorporated business owned by two or more people.

payback period The expected amount of time a capital budgeting project will take to generate cash flows that cover the project's initial cash outlay.

payment date The date the transfer agent sends out a company's dividend checks.

pension fund A financial institution that takes in funds for workers, invests those funds, and then provides for a retirement benefit.

permanent current assets The minimum level of current assets maintained.

perpetuity An annuity that has an infinite maturity.

portfolio A collection of assets that are managed as a group.

preemptive right A security given by some corporations to existing stockholders that gives them the right to buy new shares of common stock at a below-market price until a specified expiration date.

present value Today's value of promised or expected future value.

present value factor (PVF) The factor, which when multiplied by a single amount future value, gives the present value. It equals

$$\frac{1}{(1 + k)^n}$$

for given values of k and n.

present value factor for an annuity due (PVFAD) The factor, which when multiplied by an expected annuity payment, gives the sum of the present values of an annuity due stream. It equals

$$\left[\frac{1 - \dfrac{1}{(1 + k)^n}}{k} \right] \times (1 + k)$$

for given values of k and n.

present value factor for an ordinary annuity (PVFOA) The factor which, when multiplied by an expected ordinary annuity payment, gives you the sum of the present values of the ordinary annuity stream. It equals

$$\left[\frac{1 - \dfrac{1}{(1 + k)^n}}{k} \right]$$

for given values of k and n.

primary market The market in which newly issued securities are sold to the public.

primary reserves Vault cash and deposits at the Fed that go toward meeting a bank's reserve requirements.

principal A person who authorizes an agent to act for him or her.

private corporation A corporation that does not offer its shares to the general public and that can keep its financial statements confidential.

pro forma **financial statements** Projected financial statements.

progressive tax rate structure A tax structure under which the tax rate increases as taxable income increases, usually in a pattern of several steps.

promissory note A legal document the borrower signs indicating agreement to the terms of a loan.

proprietorship A business that is not incorporated and is owned by one person.

prospectus A disclosure document given to a potential investor when a new security is issued.

publicly traded corporations Corporations that have common stock that can be bought in the marketplace by any interested party and that must release audited financial statements to the public.

pure time value of money The value demanded by an investor to compensate for the postponement of consumption.

putable bonds Bonds that can be redeemed before the scheduled maturity date, at the option of the bondholder.

Q

quota A quantity limit imposed by one country on the amount of a given good that can be imported from another country.

R

real option A valuable characteristic of some projects where revisions to that project at a later date are possible.

real rate of interest The rate that the market offers to lenders to compensate for postponing consumption.

refunding Issuing new bonds to replace old bonds.

relative purchasing power parity theory A theory that states that as prices change in one country relative to those prices in another country, for a given traded basket of similar goods and services, the exchange rate will tend to change proportionately but in the opposite direction.

required reserve ratio The percentage of deposits that determines the amount of reserves a financial institution is required to hold.

residual income Income left over, and available to common stockholders, after all other claimants have been paid.

restrictive covenants Promises made by the issuer of a bond to the investor, to the benefit of the investor.

rights-on A characteristic of common stock such that it is trading with the entitlement to an upcoming right.

risk The potential for unexpected events to occur.

risk-adjusted discount rate (RADR) A required rate of return adjusted to compensate for the effect a project has on a firm's risk.

risk aversion A tendency to avoid risk that explains why most investors require a higher expected rate of return the more risk they assume.

risk-free rate of return The rate of return that investors demand in order to take on a project that contains no risk other than an inflation premium.

risk-return relationship The positive relationship between the risk of an investment and an investor's required rate of return.

S

sales breakeven point The level of sales that must be achieved such that operating income equals zero.

savings and loan associations (S&Ls) Financial institutions that take in deposits and make loans (primarily mortgage loans).

second mortgage A mortgage bond (a bond secured by real property) that gives the holder second claim (after the first-mortgage bond-holder) on the real property pledged as security.

secondary market The market in which previously issued securities are traded from one investor to another.

secondary reserves Marketable securities that can be readily sold to obtain cash.

secured bond A bond backed by specific assets that the investor may claim if there is a default.

security A document that establishes the bearer's claim to receive funds in the future.

self-liquidating loan A loan that is used to acquire assets that generate enough cash to pay off the loan.

senior debenture An unsecured bond having a superior claim on the earnings and assets of the issuing firm relative to other debentures.

serial payments A mode of payment in which the issuer pays off bonds according to a staggered maturity schedule.

short-term financing decisions Financial decisions relating to raising funds for a short period of time from sources such as bank loans, trade credit, and commercial paper.

signaling The message sent by managers, or inferred by investors, when a financial decision is made.

signaling dividend theory A theory that says that dividend payments often send a signal from the management of a firm to market participants.

simple project A project that has a negative initial cash flow, followed by positive cash flows only.

sinking fund A method for retiring bonds. The bond issuer makes regular contributions to a fund that the trustee uses to buy back outstanding bonds and retire them.

spot rate The exchange rate for current delivery.

stakeholder A party having an interest in a firm (for example, owners, workers, management, creditors, suppliers, customers, and the community as a whole).

standard deviation A statistic that indicates how widely dispersed actual or possible values are distributed around a mean.

stated interest rate The interest rate advertised by the lender. Depending on the terms of the loan, the stated rate may or may not be the same as the effective interest rate.

statement of retained earnings A financial statement that shows how the value of retained earnings changes from one point in time to another.

stock Certificates of ownership interest in a corporation.

stock dividend A firm sends out new shares of stock to existing stockholders and makes an accounting transfer from retained earnings to the common stock and capital in excess of par accounts of the balance sheet.

stock split A firm gives new shares of stock to existing shareholders; on the balance sheet, they decrease the par value of the common stock proportionately to the increase in the number of shares outstanding.

straight bond value The value a convertible bond would have if it did not offer the conversion option to the investor.

straight-line depreciation A depreciation rule that allows equal amounts of the cost of an asset to be allocated over the asset's life.

strengthening currency A currency that is now convertible into a larger number of units of another currency than previously.

Subchapter S corporation A small corporation whose income is taxed like a partnership.

subordinated debenture An unsecured bond having an inferior claim on the earnings and assets of the issuing firm relative to other debentures.

sunk cost A cost that must be borne whether a proposed capital budgeting project is accepted or rejected.

surplus economic unit A business, household, or government unit with income greater than its expenditures.

syndicate A temporary alliance of investment banking firms that is formed for the purpose of underwriting a new security issue.

T

tariff A tax imposed by one country on imports from another country.

temporary current assets The portion of current assets that fluctuates during the company's business cycle.

10-K reports An audited set of financial statements submitted annually by all public corporations to the Securities and Exchange Commission (SEC).

10-Q reports An unaudited set of financial statements submitted quarterly by all public corporations to the Securities and Exchange Commission (SEC).

terminal value The predicted value of a company's projected free cash flows at a specified future point in time from that point in time to perpetuity.

time value of money The phenomenon whereby money is valued more highly the sooner it is received.

trade credit Funds obtained by delaying payment to suppliers.

transaction cost The cost of making a transaction, usually the cost associated with purchasing or selling a security.

transfer agent A party, usually a commercial bank, that keeps track of changes in stock ownership, collects cash from a company, and pays dividends to its stockholders.

treasurer The manager responsible for financial planning, fund-raising, and allocation of money in a business.

Treasury bills Securities issued by the federal government in minimum denominations of $100 in maturities of 4, 13, 26, and 52 weeks.

Treasury bonds and notes Securities issued by the federal government that make semiannual coupon interest payments and pay the face value at maturity. Treasury notes come in maturities of one to ten years. Treasury bonds come in maturities of more than ten years.

trend analysis An analysis in which something (such as a financial ratio) is examined over time to discern any changes.

trustee The party that oversees a bond issue and makes sure all the provisions set forth in the indenture are carried out.

U

uncertainty The chance, or probability, that outcomes other than what is expected will occur.

underwriting The process by which investment banking firms purchase a new security issue in its entirety and resell it to investors. The risk of the new issue is transferred from the issuing company to the investment bankers.

V

variable costs Costs that vary with the level of production.

variable-rate bonds Bonds that have periodic changes in their coupon rates, usually tied to changes in market interest rates.

W

warrant A security that gives the holder the option to buy a certain number of shares of common stock of the issuing company, at a certain price, for a specified period of time.

weakening currency A currency that is now convertible into a smaller number of units of another currency than previously.

wealth Assets minus liabilities.

weighted average cost of capital (k_a) or (WACC) The average of all the component costs of capital, weighted according to the percentage of each component in the firm's optimal capital structure.

working capital Another name for the current assets on a firm's balance sheet.

Y

yield to maturity (YTM) The investor's return on a bond, assuming that all promised interest and principal payments are made on time and the interest payments are reinvested at the YTM rate.

Z

zero-coupon bonds Bonds that pay face value at maturity and that pay no coupon interest.

Index

Page numbers followed by *f* indicate figures; those followed by *t* indicate tables.

A

ABC system, 470
Abiomed Corporation, 312–316, 314f–315f
Absolute purchasing power parity theory, 515–516
Accelerated depreciation, 72–73
Accept/reject decision, 240, 246, 251
Accounting
　financial statements and, 63–71. *See also*
　　Financial statements fundamentals of, 62–63
Accounting depreciation, 71–72
Accounts payable
　on balance sheet, 67–68, 67f
　in business valuation, 300
　as current liability, 300, 422
　on *pro forma* balance sheet, 121
Accounts receivable
　accumulation of, 458
　on balance sheet, 66, 67f
　as collateral, 497
　collection policies for, 472–474, 473f
　credit policy and, 460–465, 461t, 463t, 464f
　as current asset, 423
　factoring of, 473
　as investment, 458
　liquidity and, 459–460, 459t
　optimal level of, 425, 460–465, 461t, 463t, 464t
　overview of, 457
　on *pro forma* balance sheet, 121
　profitability and, 459–460, 459t
Accrued expenses, 68, 67f
ACP. *See* Average collection period (ACP)
Actuaries, 52
Additional funds needed (AFN), 122
Addition to retained earnings, in *pro forma* income
　statement, 120
Adjusted taxable income, 64–65, 213–215
Administrative expenses, in *pro forma* income
　statement, 118–119
ADRs (American depository receipts), 514–515
AFN (additional funds needed), 122
After-tax cost of debt, 213–215, 363
Agency, 12–13
Agency costs, 13
Agency problem, 12–13
Agent
　defined, 12
　principal, 12
　transfer, 409
Aggressive working capital financing approach
　overview of, 426, 426f
　ratio analysis of, 428, 429t
AIG (American International Group Inc.), 3, 4, 12,
　13, 41, 136
Alibaba, 514

Alliances, trade, 518–520
Ally Financial, 52
Alternative minimum tax (AMT), 62
Amazon, 113–114
American depository receipts (ADRs), 514–515
American International Group Inc. (AIG), 3, 4, 12,
　13, 41, 136
Amortization, 64, 65, 72, 188, 192, 193t
Amortization table, 192, 193t
AMT (alternative minimum tax), 62
Annual percentage rate, 495
Annuitant, 54
Annuities
　compounding periods, 195–196
　equivalent annual, 275–276
　future value factor for, 174–176, A-6t–A-7t
　future value of, 173–176, 174f
　interest rate for, calculation of, 188–189
　overview of, 54
　perpetuities, 184
　present value factor for, 176–178, A-10t–A-11t
　present value of, 176–178
　time value of money and, 186–192
Annuities due
　future value factor for, 179–181, A-8t–A-9t
　future value of, 178–181, 180f
　overview of, 173
　present value factor for, 182–183, 188–189,
　　A-12t–A-13t
　present value of, 181–184, 183f
Apple, 9, 81–82, 239–240
Arbitrage, 516
Archer, Mary, 81
Articles of incorporation, 15
Articles of partnership, 15
Ask price, 25
Asset(s)
　on balance sheet, 66–67, 67f
　book value of, 311, 317–318
　current. *See* Current assets expropriation
　　of, 517
　fixed, 67, 67f, 423, 423f
　market value of, in business valuation, 318
　noncurrent, 424
　replacement value of, in business valuation, 318
　sale of, 281–282, 282t
　of savings and loan associations, 50
　Tax Cuts and Jobs Act of 2017 and, 61–62
Asset accounts, 66, 67f
Asset activity ratios. *See also* Financial ratios
　average collection period, 89–90, 99
　calculating, 89–90
　inventory turnover, 90, 99
　overview of, 83, 89–90

　in summary analysis, 99
　total asset turnover, 90, 99
Asset replacement, in capital budgeting, 287
Asset turnover, 90, 99
AT&T, 385
Average collection period (ACP)
　in accounts receivable analysis, 462
　calculating, 89–90
　in summary analysis, 99

B

Bad debts, collection of, 472–474, 473f
Bain Capital, 347
Balance sheets
　asset accounts on, 66–67, 67f
　changes in, 69–70, 69f, 70f
　liability and equity accounts on, 67, 67f, 69,
　　70, 70f, 71
　mixed financial ratios and, 87
　overview of, 66
　pro forma, 120–125, 123f, 124f
Balancing problem, 123
Bank(s)
　central, 23. *See also* Federal Reserve system
　commercial, 43–44
　vs. credit unions, 51
　operations of, 44–45, 44f
　regulation of, 44, 44f
Bank charter, 44
Bank of America, 3, 6–7, 136
Bank of Japan, 23
Banker's acceptance, 28
Bankruptcy, 3, 4, 15, 53–54, 114, 136
Barclays, 383, 390f
B Corp, 17
Bear Stearns, 3, 5, 41
Bearer, 24
Beatrice Company, 347
Benchmarking, 96
Benefit corporations, 13, 17
Berkshire Hathaway, 413
Best efforts basis, 25
Best efforts offering, vs. underwriting, 390
Beta, 149–150, 150f
Beta risk, 256
Bezos, Jeff, 113
Bid price, 25
Bill paying strategies, 450
Bird-in-the-hand theory, 408
B Lab, 17
Blackstone Group, 347
Blanket lien, 497
BMW, 508
Boeing, 508

Board of directors, 385, 386–388
Board of Governors, 45–46
Bond(s)
    call date for, 362
    call premium for, 362
    call provision for, 362
    convertible, 367–369, 368t
    corporate, 30, 360
    coupon interest, 29
    debentures, 361, 366, 367f
    deferred, 362
    downgraded, 369
    exchange rates and, 513
    face value of, 29
    general obligation, 30
    high-yield, 369
    indenture, 360–362
    international, 370
    investment-grade, 30, 360
    junk, 30, 360, 369
    in leveraged buyout, 346–347
    maturity date, 29
    mortgage, 366
    municipal, 30
    overview of, 28–29, 360
    par value of, 29
    payoff methods for, 361–362
    price of, 304–305, 305f
    principal, 29
    putable, 369
    rating of, 360, 361t
    refunding of, 362, 362–366, 363t, 364t
    restrictive covenants for, 365
    revenue, 30
    risk hierarchy for, 366, 367f
    secured, 361, 366
    staggered maturities for, 361
    super long-term, 370
    terminology for, 29
    Treasury, 29
    trustees for, 365–366
    types of, 366–370, 367f, 368t
    unsecured, 366, 367f
    valuation of, 301–305, 305f
    variable-rate, 369
    Yankee, 370
    yield to maturity of, 304, 304–305, 305f
Bond indenture, 360–362
Book value
    in common stock valuation, 311
    in complete business valuation, 316, 318
Book value per share (BPS) ratio, 91
Borg-Warner Corporation, 347
BPS (book value per share) ratio, 91
Break point
    debt, 222–223, 224f
    equity, 223–224, 225f
    identification of, 222–226, 224f, 225f, 341. See
        also Breakeven analysis MCC and, 222–226,
        224f, 225f
Breakeven analysis
    application of, 344–346, 346f
    breakeven chart in, 341–344, 342t, 343t, 344f,
        344t, 346f
    breakeven point in, 341

contribution margin in, 342
cost data in, 343, 344t
high/low tradeoff in, 341
leverage and, 341–346, 342t, 343t, 344f, 344t,
    346f, 346t
overview of, 341
profit/loss potential in, 344–346, 344f,
    345f, 346t
sales revenue in, 343, 343t
Breakeven chart, 341–344, 342t, 343t, 344f,
    344t, 346f
Brokers, 25
Budget(s)
    capital. See Capital budget; Capital budgeting
    cash, 116, 442–449, 443f, 444t, 445t, 446t,
        447t, 448t
    in forecasting, 116–117
Buffet, Warren, 113, 297, 413
Business interest expense deductibility, 61–62,
    64–65, 213–215, 347–348, 363–364
Business ownership, forms of, 14–17, 18t
Business risk. See also Risk
    operating leverage and, 337
    overview of, 142–144, 143t, 144t
Business valuation. See also Stock price; Value
    bonds in, 301–305, 305f
    capital structure changes and, 348–350, 349f
    common stock in, 307–317
    for complete business, 317–318
    current liabilities in, 300
    discounted cash flow model for, 299
    discount rate in, 299
    general valuation model for, 299–300, 300, 300f
    importance of, 298–301
    long-term debt in, 300–301
    market value of assets in, 318
    overview of, 298
    preferred stock in, 305–307
    present value of future cash flows in, 299
    replacement value of assets method for, 318
    terminal value in, 316
    total market value in, 300f, 316, 317f
Businesses. See also Corporations
    basic financial goal of, 8–11, 11t
    organization of, 7–8, 8f
    valuation of, 9–11, 11t
Buying, vs. leasing, 373–375, 374t

C

Call date, 362
Call premium, 362
Call price, 362
Call provision, 362
Calvin Klein, 508
Capital
    cost of. See Cost of capital
    in excess of par, 68
    overview of, 63
    sources of, 63, 212–222
    working. See Working capital
Capital asset pricing model (CAPM)
    for cost of internal common equity, 217,
        218–219
    overview of, 135–136, 152, 152–153, 153t, 154f

Capital budget
    optimal, 228, 228t
    overview of, 116–117
Capital budgeting
    accept/reject decision in, 240, 246
    asset replacement in, 287, 288f
    capital rationing in, 254–253, 255t
    decision practices in, 240
    decision trees in, 288, 289f
    equivalent annual annuity approach for,
        275–276
    financing cash flows in, 282, 283f
    incremental cash flows in, 241, 277–290.
        See also Incremental cash flows
    incremental depreciation expense in, 280–281,
        280t, 284
    for independent projects, 241
    internal rate of return method for, 248–251
    marginal cost of capital and, 227–229, 227f, 228t
    modified internal rate of return method for,
        252–254, 287
    for multiple internal rates of return, 272–273,
        272f, 273f
    for mutually exclusive projects, 241, 273–275,
        274f, 275f
    net present value method for, 243–248, 247f,
        248f, 251–252, 272–275, 273f, 274f
    for nonsimple projects, 272
    opportunity costs in, 281
    overview of, 239–240
    payback method for, 241–242
    process of, 240–241
    ranking decision in, 240, 246
    real options in, 287–290, 289f, 290t
    replacement chain approach for, 275, 275f
    risk adjustment in, 257–258, 258t
    risk measurement in, 256–257
    stages of, 241
    tax effects in, 280–281, 280t
Capital gains, 30, 281, 405
Capital in excess of par, 122
Capital leases, 372–373
Capital market
    overview of, 25–26, 26
    securities in, 28–31
Capital rationing, 254–255, 255t
Capital structure
    combined leverage and, 339–340
    debt break point and, 222–224, 224f
    financial leverage and, 334, 337–339, 338t
    operating leverage and, 334, 334–337,
        334t, 335t
    optimal, 348–350, 349f
    overview of, 334
    WACC and, 220–222
Capital structure theory, 347–350
CAPM. See Capital asset pricing model (CAPM)
Career paths, 7, 7t
Cargill, 16
Carlyle Group, 347
Carrying costs, 465
Cash
    as current asset, 423
    on pro forma balance sheet, 120–121
    raising quickly, 439

Cash balance
  calculation of, 440–441, 441f
  maximum, 439, 440f
  minimum, 438, 438f
  optimal, 438–442, 438f, 440f, 441f
Cash budget
  development of, 442–449, 443f, 444t, 445t,
    446t, 447t, 448t
  management of. *See* Cash management
  overview of, 116
  pro forma balance sheet, 120–121
Cash flow(s)
  in business valuation, 299–300
  changes in, 68–69, 70f
  financing, 282, 283f
  free, calculation of, 311–312. *See also* Free
    cash flow(s) future, present value of, 299
  vs. income, 68
  incremental. *See* Incremental cash flows
  initial investment, 279, 280t, 283, 283t
  management of, 449–450, 449f
  net, 68–69, 69f, 70f, 71
  operating, 280–281, 280t, 284, 284t
  shutdown, 281–282, 282t, 284–285, 285t
  statement of, 68–71, 69f, 70f
  stock price and, 10–11, 11t
  supernormal growth of, 308–310, 309f
  timing and, 10, 11t
  uneven, present value of, 184–186, 185t
  value and, 11, 11t
Cash management
  cash budget in, 442–449, 443f, 444t, 445t, 446t,
    447t, 448t
  cash flow in, 449–450, 449f
  coping with emergencies in, 439
  electronic funds transfer, 450
  forecasting cash needs in, 442–449, 443f, 444t,
    445t, 446t, 447t, 448t
  investment opportunities, 439–440
  lockbox system in, 450
  maximum cash balance and, 439, 440f
  Miller-Orr model for, 440–442, 441f
  optimal cash balance and, 438–442, 438f,
    440f, 441f
  overview of, 437, 438
  predicting cash needs in, 439
  risk considerations in, 449–450
Cash needs, forecasting of, 442–449, 443f, 444t,
  445t, 446t, 447t, 448t
Caterpillar, 507
Casualty insurance, 52–53
C corporations, 15–16
CDs (certificates of deposit), 28
Central banks, 23. *See also* Federal Reserve system
Central Jersey Bancorp, 384, 384f
Central Liquidity Facility (CLF), 51
CenturyLink, 369
Certificates of deposit (CDs), 28
Certified B Corporation, 17
Chapter 11 bankruptcy, 114
Charter
  bank, 44
  credit union, 51
  government-sponsored entities, 48
  savings and loan, 49

Chief financial offer, 8, 8f, 9f
Chrysler, 12
Citigroup, 13, 383, 390f
CLF (Central Liquidity Facility), 51
Clientele dividend theory, 407
Closely held corporations, 385
Coca-Cola, 370, 508
Coefficient of variation
  changes in, calculation of, 256–257
  in risk measurement, 140–141, 142f
COGS. *See* Cost of goods sold (COGS)
Collateral
  accounts receivable as, 497
  inventory as, 497–498
  overview of, 496–497
Collections policies, 472–474, 473f
Combined leverage, 339–340
Commercial banks
  operations of, 44–45
  overview of, 43–44
  regulation of, 44, 44f
  reserves of, 45, 45t
Commercial finance companies, 52
Commercial paper, 28, 489–491
Common bond requirement, 50
Common stock. *See also* Stock
  capital gains from, 405
  characteristics of, 384–386
  classes of, 384
  convertible bonds and, 367–369, 368t
  convertible preferred stock and, 371
  dividends from. *See* Dividends
  ex-dividend trading of, 409
  institutional ownership of, 385–386
  price of. *See* Stock price
  of private corporations, 385
  on *pro forma* balance sheet, 122
  of publicly traded corporations, 385
  valuation. *See* Common stock valuation
  voting rights and, 386–388
  yield on, 316–317
Common stock issues
  disadvantages of, 388–389
  flotation costs and, 389
  IPOs and, 389–390, 390f
  pricing of, 390, 392t
Common stock valuation
  book value in, 311
  constant growth dividend model for, 308
  discounted cash flow model in, 307
  free cash flow DCF model for, 317–318
  for individual shares, 307–310, 309f
  liquidation value in, 311
  nonconstant growth dividend model for,
    308–310, 309f
  overview of, 30
  P/E ratio in, 310
  for total stockholders' equity, 210–311
Companies. *See* Businesses; Corporations
Comparative advantage, 509
Compensating balance, 492–493
Component cost of capital, 212
Compound interest, 168–172, 172f

Compounding/compounding periods
  annual, 192
  annuity, 195–196
  calculation of, 189–191
  continuous, 196–197
  future value and, 168, 168f
  monthly, 195
  present value and, 171–172, 172f
  quarterly, 195
  semiannual, 193–194
Conforming mortgages, 48
Congress, federal tax rates, 61–62, 73
Conservative working capital financing approach
  overview of, 426–427, 427f
  ratio analysis of, 428, 429t
Constant growth dividend model, 217–218, 308
Constant growth free cash flow valuation model,
  313–316
Consumer finance companies, 51
Consumer Financial Protection Bureau, 54
Continuous compounding, 196–197
Continuous distribution, 137, 140,
Contracts
  forward, 513–514
  futures, 513–514
Contribution margin, 342
Controller, 8
Controlling interest, 386
Conversion ratio, 367
Conversion value, 367–368, 368t
Convertible bonds, 367–369, 368t
Corporate bonds, 30, 360. *See also* Bond(s)
Corporate stock, 30. *See also* Stocks
Corporations
  basic financial goal of, 8–11, 11t
  benefit, 17
  board of directors of, 385, 386–388
  C, 15–16
  closely held, 385
  federal tax law changes, 61–62, 73
  legal status of, 15–16
  marginal tax rates for, 214
  multinational, 508–509
  organization of, 8, 8f
  ownership forms, 14–17, 18t
  private, 16, 385
  professional, 16
  publicly traded, 16, 385
  S, 16
  tax rates for, 61–62, 73, 214, 239
  valuation of, 9–11, 11t. *See also* Stock price;
    Valuation; Value
Correlation, 147
Correlation coefficient, 147
Cost(s). *See also* Expense(s)
  agency, 13
  carrying, 465
  fixed. *See* Fixed costs
  flotation, 219–220, 389
  labor, fixed vs. variable, 341
  opportunity, 164
  ordering, 465
  sunk, 278
  transaction, 440
  variable, 341

Cost data, in breakeven analysis, 343, 343t
Cost of capital
    component, 220–221
    marginal, 222–226. *See also* Marginal cost of
      capital (MCC)
    overview of, 211–212
    weighted average. *See* Weighted average cost
      of capital (WACC)
Cost of common stock, 215–220
Cost of debt. *See also* Required rate of return
    after-tax, 213–215, 223
    break point for, 222–223, 224f
    business valuation and, 299
    in capital structure theory, 348–350, 349f
    impact of Tax Cuts and Jobs Act of 2017,
      213–215
    overview of, 212–213
Cost of equity from new common stock, 218–219
Cost of goods sold (COGS)
    on income statement, 64
    in inventory turnover ratio, 90
    in *pro forma* income statement, 118
Cost of internal common equity, 217
Cost of preferred stock, 215–220
Countrywide Financial, 41
Coupon interest payments
    annual, 301–302
    overview of, 29
    semiannual, 303
Coupon interest rate, 29
Credit
    five Cs of, 471–472
    necessity of, 450
    revolving, 488
    trade, 488–489, 489f
Credit default swap, 4
Credit line, 488
Credit policy
    accounts receivable and, 460–465, 461t,
      463t, 464f
    credit scoring in, 472–474, 473f
    credit standards in, 460, 472–474, 473f
    credit terms in, 460
    discount percentage/period in, 460–461,
      489, 489f
    loosening/tightening of, 460–461, 461t
    overview of, 460–461
Credit risk, 43
Credit scoring, 472–474, 473f
Credit standards, 460, 472–474, 473f
Credit Suisse First Boston, 390
Credit term, 460
Credit unions, 50–51
Cross rates, 511–512, 512t
Cross-sectional analysis, 96, 97t
Crowdfunding, 229
Cultural risks, facing multinational corporations, 518
Cumulative preferred stock, 370, 371
Cumulative voting, 386–388
Currency
    of European Union, 519–520
    exchange rates for, 509–513, 511t, 512t. *See*
     also Exchange rates
    strengthening, 511
    weakening, 511

Current assets. *See also* Working capital
    on balance sheet, 66, 67f
    in capital budgeting, 279
    components of, 423, 423f
    in current ratio, 87–88
    fluctuations in, 422–423
    net working capital and, 422, 422t
    optimal level of, 425
    permanent, 423–424, 423f, 424f
    in quick ratio, 99
    temporary, 423–424, 423f, 424f
Current liabilities
    on balance sheet, 67–68, 67f
    in business valuation, 300
    in capital budgeting, 279
    in current ratio, 87–88
    liquidity vs. profitability and, 424
    management of, 425
    net working capital and, 422, 422t
    in quick ratio, 88
    risk-return relationship and, 425
Current ratio, 87–88

D

Date of record, 409
DBP (defined benefit plan), 53
DCF model. *See* Discounted cash flow (DCF)
  model
DCL (degree of combined leverage), 339–340
Dealers, 25
Dean Witter, 390
Debentures
    overview of, 361
    senior, 366, 367f
    subordinated, 366, 367f
Debt
    benefits of, 347–350
    in capital structure theory, 347–350
    collection policies for, 472–474, 473f
    cost of, 212–215, 222–223, 224f, 347–350
    impact of Tax Cuts and Jobs Act of 2017,
      213–215
    leverage and, 334–340
    long-term. *See* Long-term debt
    restrictions on, 365
    short term. *See* Short-term financing
valuation of, 300–301, 300f
Debt break point, 222–223, 224f
Debt ratios. *See also* Financial ratios
    calculating, 88–89
    debt to equity, 88–89
    debt to total assets, 88–89
    overview of, 83, 88–89
    times interest earned, 89
Decision tree, 288, 289f
Declaration date, 408, 409f, 410t
Deductible expense
    depreciation as, 280
    interest as, 347–348
    overview of, 64
Default, 32
Default risk premium, 31f, 32
Deferred call provision, 362
Deficit economic units, 24, 42, 43f, 43, 52

Defined benefit plan (DBP), 53
Degree of combined leverage (DCL), 339–340
Degree of financial leverage (DFL), 337–339
Degree of operating leverage (DOL)
    calculation of, 334–335, 336–337
    fixed costs and, 335–336, 335t
Delivery, 279
Denomination matching, 42, 43f
Deposit maturities, vs. loan maturities, 49–50, 50t
Depreciation
    accelerated, 72–73
    accounting, 71–72
    economic, 72
    half-year convention, 72, 73t
    overview of, 72
    straight-line, 72
    Tax Cuts and Jobs Act of 2017 and, 61–62, 72
Depreciation basis, 72
Depreciation expense
    adjustment for, 69
    calculation of, 72–73, 284
    deductibility of, 280
    on income statement, 63f, 64
    incremental, in capital budgeting, 280–281,
      280t, 284
    in *pro forma* income statement, 119
Depreciation rules, 61–62, 72
Deutsche Telecom, 514
DFL. *See* Degree of financial leverage (DFL),
  337–339
Discounted cash flow (DCF) model
    in business valuation, 299
    in common stock valuation, 307
    free cash flow, 311–316, 341f–315f
    in preferred stock valuation, 305
Discount loan, 492
Discount percentage/period, 460–461, 489, 489f
Discount rate. *See also* Required rate of return
    in capital budgeting, 272–276, 274f
    in discounted cash flow model, 299
    present value and, 168–172
    risk-adjusted, 257–258, 258t
Discount window, 47
Discount yield, 489–490
Discrete distribution, 137
Disney corporation, 114, 370
Distributions
    continuous, 137, 140
    discrete, 137
    mean of, 137
    normal, 140, 141f
    probability, 137
    sales forecast, 137–140, 138f
    standard deviation of, 137–140, 138f
Diversification
    foreign investments and, 514, 515f
    risk reduction and, 151
Diversification effect, 146, 148, 149f
Dividend growth model
    in common stock valuation, 308
    constant growth, 217–218
    nonconstant growth, 308–310, 309f
Dividend payout ratio, 405–406, 406f, 406t
Dividend reinvestment plan (DRIP), 409
Dividend theories, 406–408, 407t

Dividend yield, 218, 317
Dividends
    alternatives to cash, 409–413, 410t, 411t, 412t, 413t
    bird-in-the-hand theory of, 408
    cash, 405–406, 406f, 406t
    cash vs. earnings and, 405–406, 406f, 406t
    clientele theory of, 407
    common stock, 65–66, 66f, 307–308, 365
    declaration of, 408
    double taxation of, 15–16, 17
    on income statement, 63f, 65–66, 66f
    M&M theory of, 408
    overview of, 403, 404
    payment of. See Dividends payment
    preferred stock, 305–306, 370, 371
    residual theory of, 407, 407t
    signaling theory of, 408
    stock, 410–413, 410t, 411t
    stockholders' preferences for, 404
    taxation of, 371, 409
Dividends paid, 120
Dividends payable, 408
Dividends payment
    date of record for, 409
    declaration date for, 408, 409f, 410t
    mechanics of, 408–409, 409f, 410t
    overview of, 30
    payment date for, 409, 409f, 410t
    restrictions on, 405, 406f
    time line for, 409f
    transfer agent for, 409
Dividends policy, 404–405, 406f
Dodd, Christopher, 54
Dodd-Frank Wall Street Reform and Consumer Protection Act, 4, 42, 54–55
DOL. See Degree of operating leverage (DOL)
Domestic Fisher effect, 517
Double taxation, 15–16, 17
Downgraded bonds, 369
DRIP (dividend reinvestment plan), 409
Du Pont equation, 94
    modified, 94–95
Du Point system, 94–95

E

EAA (equivalent annual annuity), 275–276
EAR (effective annual rate), 493–494
Earnings
    in P/E ratio, 91, 310
    retained, 63f, 65–66, 66f, 67f, 68
Earnings before interest, taxes, depreciation, and amortization (EBITDA), 65
Earnings before interest and taxes (EBIT), 64, 65
    financial leverage and, 337–339, 338t
    operating leverage and, 334, 334–337, 334t, 335t, 347
    overview of, 64, 65
Earnings before taxes (EBT), 64
Earnings per share, 63f, 65
EBIT. See Earnings before interest and taxes (EBIT)
EBITA (earnings before interest, taxes, depreciation, and amortization), 65

EBT (earnings before taxes), 64
ECB (European Central Bank), 519, 520
Economic depreciation, 72
Economic order quantity (EOQ) model, 466
Economic units, 24, 42, 43f, 43, 52
Economic value added (EVA), 92–93
Edison, Alva, Thomas, 403
Edison Electric Company, 403
Effective interest rate
    annualizing, 493–495
    calculation of, 488–489, 489f, 491–492
    with compensating balance, 492–493
    for discount loan, 492
    for loans with maturity of less than one year, 493–495, 493f
    loan terms affecting, 491–496
    overview of, 486
EGCs (emerging growth companies), 229
Elections, board of director, 386–388
Electronic funds transfer, 450
Emerging growth companies (EGCs), 229
EMU (European Monetary Union), 519, 520
Enterprise value, 316
Environmental regulations, 508–509
EOQ (economic order quantity) model, 466
Equity
    on balance sheet, 66, 67, 67f, 68, 70, 70f, 71
    in capital structure theory, 347–350
Equity break point, 223–224, 225f
Equity financing. See also Common stock
    in conservative working capital approach, 426–427, 427f
    vs. debt financing, 388–389
    in moderate working capital approach, 427–428, 428f
    pros and cons of, 388–389
Equity multiplier, 94–95
Equivalent annual annuity (EAA), in capital budgeting, 275–276
Effective annual rate (EAR), 493–494
Ethical issues
    financial management, 11–14
    multinational corporations, 508–509
EU (European Union), 519–520
Euro, 517, 519–520
Eurobonds, 370
European Central Bank (ECB), 23, 509, 520
European Monetary Union (EMU), 519, 520
European Stability Mechanism, 520
European Union (EU), 519–520
Eurozone, 519–520
EVA (economic value added), 92–93
Excess financing, 122
Exchange rates
    cross rates and, 511–512, 512t
    currency strength and, 511
    defined, 509
    factors affecting, 516–517
    foreign stock and bond investments and, 513
    fluctuation of, 510–511, 511t, 516–517
    government intervention for, 517
    hedging and, 513–514
    interest rate parity theory for, 515–516
    international Fisher effect and, 516

multinational corporations and, 512–513
    overview of, 509–510
    political instability and, 516–517
    purchasing power parity theory for, 515–516
    sample, 511t
Ex-dividend trade, 409
Exercise price, 394–395
Expense(s). See also Cost(s)
    accrued, 67f, 68
    administrative, 63f, 64, 118–119
    changes in, 68–69, 70f
    deductible, 64, 280, 347–348
    depreciation. See Depreciation expense
    fixed. See Fixed expenses
    on income statement, 63f, 64
    interest. See Interest expense
    marketing, 118
    prepaid, 66, 67f
    selling and administrative, 63f, 64
Expropriated assets, 517
Ex-rights, 393, 394
External financing
    long-term, 486–487, 487f
    short-term, 485–498. See also Short-term financing sources of, 486–477, 487f
Externalities, 281

F

Face value, 29
Facebook, 114, 151, 384
Factoring, 473
Factors, 473
Fair trade, vs. free trade, 520
Fair-value approach, 62
Fallen angels, 369
Fannie Mae, 3, 4, 13, 41, 48, 136
FASB (Financial Accounting Standards Board), 62, 65
FDIC (Federal Deposit Insurance Corporation), 34, 44
Federal debt, 29
Federal Deposit Insurance Corporation (FDIC), 34, 44
Federal funds market, 45
Federal Home Loan Mortgage Corporation (Freddie Mac), 3, 4, 13, 41, 48, 136
Federal Housing Administration (FHA), 48
Federal Housing Finance Agency (FHFA), 48
Federal National Mortgage Association (Fannie Mae), 3, 4, 13, 41, 48, 136
Federal Open Market Committee (FOMC), 45–46, 46–47
Federal Reserve Bank of New York, 46–47
Federal Reserve System
    bank regulation by, 44, 44f
    Board of Governors of, 45–46
    clearing services of, 47
    Consumer Financial Protection Bureau, 54
    discount window and, 47
    money supply regulation by, 46–47
    organization of, 45–46, 46f
    overview of, 45
    reserve requirements, 45, 45t
    yield curve and, 34–35

Ferrari, 370
FHA (Federal Housing Administration), 48
FHFA (Federal Housing Finance Agency), 48
Fidelity Investments, 53
Fiduciary responsibility, 385
Fiedler, Edgar R., 113
Finance
    career paths in, 7, 7t
    in firm's organization, 7–8, 8f
    overview of, 6–7
Finance companies, 51–52
Finance team, 8, 9f
Financial Accounting Standards Board (FASB),
    62, 65
Financial analysts, 83
Financial Crisis (of 2008)
    agency issues and, 12
    asset correlation and, 149
    central banks and, 23
    effect on commercial paper market, 489
    effect on global economy, 514, 517
    financial institutions and, 41–42
    legislation after, 3–4, 41–42, 54–55
    market risk premium and, 152
    partial cause of, 149
    review of, 4–6
    risk and return and, 135
Financial goal, primary, 8–11
Financial institutions, 41–55
Financial intermediaries, 24–25
Financial intermediation, 42–45
Financial leases, 372–373
Financial leverage
    calculation of, 337–339
    in combined leverage, 339–340
    degree of, 337–338
    interest expenses and, 339
    in leveraged buyouts, 346–347,
    risk of, 339
Financial management
    legal and ethical challenges in, 11–14
    overview of, 7–8
Financial managers
    influences on, 11–14, 14f
    responsibilities of, 7–8
Financial markets
    overview of, 25–27
    securities in, 27–31
Financial planning, forecasting for. See Forecasting
Financial ratios. See also Ratio analysis
    asset activity, 83, 89–90
    basic, 83–95
    as comparative measures, 83
    debt, 83, 88–89
    in industry comparisons, 96, 97t
    liquidity, 83, 87–88
    market value, 84, 90–92
    overview of, 83
    profitability, 83, 84–87
    relationships among, 94–95
    resources for, 99
    in summary analysis, 97–99, 98t
    in trend analysis, 96, 96t, 97f, 97t
Financial risk, 144–145, 145t

Financial Stability Council and Orderly Liquidation
    Authority, 4
Financial Stability Oversight Council, 4, 54
Financial statement analysis
    industry comparisons in, 96, 97t
    ratio analysis in, 83.–95. See also Financial
        ratios; Ratio analysis summary analysis in,
        97–99, 98t
    trend analysis in, 96, 96t, 97f, 97t
Financial statements
    analysis of, 81–99. See also Financial statement
        analysis balance sheet, 66–68, 67f
    forecasting of, 116–125. See also Forecasting;
        Pro forma financial statements
    income statements, 63–66, 63f, 66f
    pro forma, 116–127
    statement of cash flows, 68–71, 69f, 70f
    10-K and 10-Q reports, 62
Financial system, organization of, 24–25
Financing
    equity, 388–389. See also Common stock;
        Preferred stock excess, 122
    inventory, 497
    long-term, 331, 486–487, 478f
    short-term, 485–498. See also Loan(s)
Financing activities, on statement of cash flows,
    68–69, 69f, 71
Financing cash flows, 282, 283f
Firm risk, 256–257
Firms. See Businesses; Corporations
First-mortgage bond, 366
Fitch ratings, 5, 369
Five Cs of credit, 471–472
Fixed assets
    on balance sheet, 67, 67f
    depreciation of, 71
    in working capital management, 423, 423f
Fixed costs
    breakeven analysis and, 341–346, 342t, 343t,
        344f, 344t, 346f, 346t
    business risk and, 142–144, 143t, 144t
    combined leverage and, 339–340
    financial leverage and, 337
    labor costs as, 341
    leverage and, 341
    operating leverage and, 335–336, 335t
    overview of, 341
    reduction of, 144–145, 145t
Fixed expenses
    business risk and, 142–144, 143t, 144t
    operating leverage and, 334, 334–337,
        334t, 335t
    reduction of, 151
Flat tax rate, 61–62, 73, 214, 239
Flotation costs, 219–220, 389
FOMC (Federal Open Market Committee), 45–46,
    46–47
Ford, 12
Ford Motor Credit Corporation, 52
Forecasting
    analysis in, 123–125
    balancing problem in, 123
    budgets in, 116–117
    of cash needs, 442–449, 443f, 444t, 445t, 446t,
        447t, 448t

correlational approach to, 115
discounted free cash flow, 311–316, 314f–315f
distributions of, 137–140, 138f
experiential approach to, 115
financial statement, 116–125. See also Pro
    forma financial statements importance of,
    114–115
imprecision of, 115
overview of, 114
probability approach to, 115
sales, 115–116, 116f, 117f
Foreign stock. See also International finance/trade
    American depository receipts and, 514–515
    exchange rates and, 513
Forward contracts, 513–514
Forward rate, 516
Frank, Barney, 54
Franklin, Benjamin, 3
Freddie Mac, 3, 4, 13, 41, 48, 136
Free cash flow(s)
    in business valuation, 311–316, 314f–315f
    calculation of, 311–312
    DCF model, 311–316, 314f–315f, 317–318
Free trade, vs. fair trade, 520
Friedman, Milton, 14, 211
Futures contracts, 513–514
Future value
    of annuity due, 178–181, 180f
    compounding periods and, 168, 168f
    defined, 164–165
    interest rate changes and, 168, 168f
    of ordinary annuity, 173–176, 174f
    of single amount, 165–169
Future value factor (FVF), 166–167, 186–188, 190,
    194, A-2t–A-3t
Future value factor for an ordinary annuity
    (FVFOA), 174–176, A-6t–A-7t
Future value factor for an annuity due (FVFAD),
    179–181, A-8t–A-9t

G

GAAP (Generally Accepted Accounting
    Principles), 62, 514
Gap, The, 508
GATT (General Agreement on Tariffs and Trade),
    518, 519
GE (General Electric), 403
Gekko, Gordon, 485
General expenses, in pro forma income statement,
    118–119
Generally Accepted Accounting Principles
    (GAAP), 62, 514
General Electric (GE), 403
General Motors, 4, 12, 13, 370
General obligation (GO) bonds, 30
General partner, 15
General valuation model, 299–300, 300f
Geocities Corporation, 390, 391f
Getty, Jean Paul, 41
Ginnie Mae, 48
Glass, Lewis & Co LLC, 385
Globalization. See International finance/trade
GMAC, 52
GO (general obligation) bonds, 30

Going concern value, 91–92
Goldman Sachs, 390
GoPro, 383, 389, 390f
Gordon, Myron, 217, 308
Gordon growth model
    in common stock valuation, 308
    cost of capital and, 217–218
Government bailouts, 3–4, 12
Government National Mortgage Association
    (Ginnie Mae), 48
Government-sponsored enterprise (GSE)
    companies, 3, 4, 48
Great Depression, 48
Gross profit, 63t, 64
Gross profit margin, 84–85, 87, 97
Group of Eight, 517
Grupo Televisa SA, 347
GSE (government-sponsored enterprise)
    companies, 3, 4, 48

H

Half-year convention, 72, 73t
Hamilton, Brian, 457
Health insurance, 52
Hedge, 513–514
High/low tradeoff, in breakeven analysis, 341
High-yield bonds, 369
Home loans, 4–5, 48
Honda, 508
Human rights issues, 508, 520
Hurdle rate, 248
Hybrid securities, 370

I

IBM, 12, 370
IC (invested capital), 92–93
Icahn, Carl, 386
Illiquidity, 32
Illiquidity risk premium, 31f, 32–33
Income
    vs. cash flow, 68
    net. See Net income
    operating. See Operating income
    residual, 384
Income statement
    mixed financial ratios and, 87
    overview of, 63–66, 63f, 66f
    pro forma, 118–120, 120f, 123–125, 124f
Income taxes. See also Tax(es)
    in pro forma income statement, 120
    rates, 61–62, 73, 214–215, 239
Incremental cash flows
    in accounts receivable analysis, 460–465, 461t,
        463t, 464f
    asset replacement and, 287, 288f
    from bond refunding, 363–365, 363t, 364t
    capital budgeting and, 241. See also Capital
        budgeting of expansion project, 282–287
    initial investment, 279, 279t, 283, 283t
    in inventory analysis, 465–468, 468t, 469f
    operating, 280–281, 280t, 284, 284t
    shutdown, 281–282, 282t, 284–285, 285t
    types of, 278–287

Incremental depreciation expense, 280–281,
    280t, 284
Indenture, 360–362
Independent projects, 241
Individual income taxes, 61–62, 73
Industry comparisons
    in summary analysis, 97–99, 98t
    in trend analysis, 96, 97t
Inflation premium, 31f, 32
Initial investment cash flows, 279, 279t, 283, 283t
Initial public offerings (IPOs), 4, 113, 383,
    389–390, 390f, 391, 392t
Instagram, 114
Installation, 279
Institutional investors, 385–386
Institutional Shareholder Services (ISS), 385–386
Insurance
    health, 52
    liability, 52–53
    life, 52
    overview of, 52
    property and casualty, 52–53
    risk reduction and, 151
Insurance companies, 52–53
Interest
    compound, 168–172, 172f. See also
        Compounding/compounding periods coupon,
        29, 301–302, 303
    deductibility of, 61–62, 64–65, 213–215, 347–348,
        363–364
    overview of, 31–35
    simple, 165
    time value of money and, 164–169. See also Time
        value of money
    yield curve and, 34–35, 35f
Interest expense
    financial leverage and, 339
    financial risk and, 144–145, 145t
    fixed, financial leverage and, 339
    on income statement, 64–65
    in pro forma income statement, 119, 122–123
    Tax Cuts and Jobs Act of 2017 and, 61–62,
        64–65, 213–215, 347–348, 363–364
Interest rate(s)
    annual percentage rate for, 495
    for annuity, calculation of, 188–189
    calculation of, 186–189
    changes in, 171–172, 172f
    compounding periods for. See Compounding/
        compounding periods coupon, 29
    determinants of, 31–35
    effective. See Effective interest rate
    future value and, 164, 165–168, 168f
    inflation premium and, 31f, 32
    negative, 23, 359–360
    nominal, 31, 31f
    overview of, 43
    present value and, 165, 168–172, 172f
    real, 31–32, 31
    risk premiums and, 33
    of single-amount investment, calculation of,
        186–188
    stated, 487
    yield curve for, 34–35, 35f
Interest rate parity theory, 516

Interest rate spread, 43
Interest subsidy tax rate (ISTR), 214–215, 363
Intermediation, 42–45
Internal rate of return (IRR)
    calculation of, 248–250, 278
    in capital budgeting, 248–251
    decision rule, 251
    inventory levels and, 470
    multiple, capital budgeting for, 272–273,
        272f, 273f
    NPV and, 251–252
    overview of, 248
Internal rate of return reinvestment assumption, 253
Internal Revenue Service (IRS), 65, 73, 371–372
International bonds, 370
International finance/trade
    diversification benefits of, 514, 515f
    exchange rates and, 509–513, 511t, 512t. See
        also Exchange rates government intervention
        in, 517
    hedging in, 513–514
    international trade agreements and, 518–520
    law of comparative advantage and, 509
    multinational corporations and, 508–509,
        517–518. See also Multinational corporations
        (MNCs) overview of, 508
    political instability and, 516–517
    risk management in, 513–515, 515f
International Fisher effect, 516
International Organization for Standardization
    (ISO), 510
International trade agreements, 518–520
Inventory
    carrying costs of, 465
    as collateral, 497–498
    as current asset, 423
    as investment, 458
    liquidity and, 459–460, 459t
    optimal level of, 425, 465–470, 467f, 468t, 469f
    ordering costs of, 465
    on pro forma balance sheet, 121
    profitability and, 459–460, 459t
    valuation of, 497
Inventory financing, 497
Inventory management
    ABC system in, 470
    just-in-time system for, 471
    overview of, 470
Inventory turnover, 90
Invested capital (IC), 92–93
Investment activities, on statement of cash flows,
    70f, 71
Investment banking firms, 25
Investment-grade bonds, 30, 360
Investment opportunities, 439–440
Investment opportunity schedule (IOS),
    227–228, 227f
Investor's required rate of return, 299, 306
IOS (investment opportunity schedule),
    227–228, 227f
IPOs (initial public offerings), 4, 113, 383,
    389–390, 390f, 391, 392t
IRR. See Internal rate of return (IRR)
IRR reinvestment assumption, 253
IRS (Internal Revenue Service), 65, 73, 371–372

ISO (International Organization for Standardization), 510
ISS (Institutional Shareholder Services, 385–386
ISTR (interest subsidy tax rate), 214–215, 363

J

JIT (just-in-time inventory) system, 471
JOBS Act, 229
JPMorgan Chase, 4, 5, 13, 55, 136, 383, 390, 390f, 514
Jumpstart Our Business Startups (JOBS) Act, 229
Junk bonds, 30, 360, 369
Just-in-time inventory (JIT) system, 471

K

Kentucky Fried Chicken, 508
Keynes, John Maynard, 163
Kickstarter, 229
Koch Industries, 16
Kodak, 114, 369
Kohlberg, Kravis, & Roberts, 347
Komatsu, 507

L

Labor costs, fixed vs. variable, 341
Labor issues, multinational corporations and, 508, 517–518
Law of comparative advantage, 509
LBOs (leveraged buyouts), 213–214, 346–347
Leases
    accounting treatment of, 372–373
    financial (capital), 372–373
    genuine vs. fake, 371–372
    IRS standards for, 371–372
    operating, 372–373
    overview of, 371
    vs. purchases, 373–375, 374t
Legal considerations, 11–14
Lehman Brothers, 3, 5, 7, 41, 136
Lessee, 371
Lessor, 371
Leverage
    breakeven analysis and, 341–344, 342t, 343t, 344f, 344t, 346f, 346t
    combined, 339–340
    financial, 334, 337–339, 338t
    financial reporting and, 5
    operating, 334, 334–337, 334t, 335t
    overview of, 334
Leveraged buyouts (LBOs), 213–214, 346–347
Leverage effect, 95
Liabilities
    on balance sheet, 67–68, 67f, 70, 70f, 71
    changes in, 70, 70f
    current. See Current liabilities
    long-term, 68
    total, vs. total debt capital, 93
Liability
    of partnerships, 15
    of private corporations, 385
    of proprietorships, 14–15
Liability insurance, 52–53
LIBOR (London Interbank Offer Rate), 369

Lien, blanket, 497
Life insurance companies, 52
Limited liability companies (LLCs), 17, 18t
Limited liability partnerships (LLPs), 15
Limited partnerships (LPs), 15
Line of credit, 488
Lintner, John, 152
Liquidation value, 311
Liquidity
    accounts receivable and, 459–460, 459t
    fixed assets and, 67
    illiquidity risk premium and, 32
    inventory and, 459–460, 459t
    vs. profitability, 424
Liquidity function, 24
Liquidity ratios. See also Financial ratios
    calculating, 87–88
    current, 87–88, 98–99
    overview of, 83, 87
    quick, 88, 99
    in summary analysis, 98–99
Liz Claiborne, 508
LLCs (limited liability companies), 17, 18t
LLPs (limited liability partnerships), 15
Loan(s)
    amortized, 72, 188, 192
    amortization table for, 192, 193t
    collateral for, 496–498
    compensating balance for, 492–493
    cost of, calculation of, 488–489, 489f
    discount, 492
    effective interest rate of, 487, 491–496
    long-term, vs. short-term, 486–487, 487f
    maturity matching, 49–50, 49t, 50t
    with maturity of less than one year, 493–495, 493f
    mortgage, 4–5, 48
    payday, 485
    payments needed for, 191–192
    self-liquidating, 487
    short-term, 487–488. See also Short-term financing terms of, 491–496
Loan-deposit maturity matching, 49–50, 49t, 50t
Loan Mart, 485
Lockbox system, 450
Loeb, Dan, 386
London Interbank Offer Rate (LIBOR), 369
Long-term debt. See also Bond(s)
    in business valuation, 300–301
    in conservative working capital approach, 426–427, 427f
    in moderate working capital approach, 427–428, 428f
    on pro forma balance sheet, 122
    valuation of, 300–301, 300f, 301–305, 305f
Long-term financing, vs. short-term, 486–487, 487f
Long-term financing decisions, 331
Long-term liabilities, 68
LPs (limited partnerships), 15

M

MACRS (Modified Accelerated Cost Recovery System), 72–73, 73t
Maestri, Luca, 81
Majority interest, 386

Majority voting, for board of directors, 386–388
Manager, 390
Marcato Capital Management, 386
Marginal cost of capital (MCC)
    break points and, 222–226, 224f, 225f, 226f
    capital budgeting decisions and, 227–229, 227f, 228t
    change in, calculation of, 225
    overview of, 222
Marginal tax rate, 214
Mark-to-market approach, 62
Market efficiency, 27
Market risk, 135, 256
Market risk premium, 152
Market to book value (M/B) ratio, 91–92
Market value
    of bond, 301–305, 305f
    in business valuation, 312–316, 314f–315f
    calculation of. See Valuation
Market value added (MVA), 92, 93–94
Market value ratios. See also Financial ratios
    market to book value ratio, 91–92
    overview of, 84, 90
    price to earnings, 91
    in summary analysis, 99
Marketable securities
    on balance sheet, 66
    on pro forma balance sheet, 120–121
Marketing expenses, on pro forma income statement, 118
Matching principle, 72
Mattel, 369
Maturity dates, 24, 29
Maturity matching, 42–43, 49–50, 49t, 50t
Maturity risk premium, 31f, 33
Maximum cash balance, 439, 440f
M/B (market to book value) ratio, 91–92
MCC. See Marginal cost of capital (MCC)
McDonald's, 508, 513
McGuffin Corporation, 395–396, 396t
McGuire, Mick, 386
Mergent Online, 99
Merrill Lynch, 3, 5, 6–7, 136, 390
Miller, Merton, 23, 348, 408, 440
Miller-Orr cash management mode, 440–442, 441f
Minimum cash balance, 438, 438f
MIRR. See Modified internal rate of return (MIRR)
Mixed ratios, 87
M&M dividend theory, 408
MNCs. See Multinational corporations (MNCs)
Moderate working capital financing approach
    overview of, 427–428, 428f
    ratio analysis of, 428, 429t
Modified Accelerated Cost Recovery System (MACRS), 72–73, 73t
Modified Du Pont equation, 94–95
Modified internal rate of return (MIRR)
    calculation of, 287
    in capital budgeting, 252–254, 287
Modigliani, Franco, 348, 408
Modigliani and Miller dividend theory, 408
Money market
    overview of, 25, 26
    securities in, 27–28

Money supply, control of, 44, 45, 46–47
Montgomery Ward, 347
Monthly compounding, 195
Moody's bond rating, 4, 5, 360, 361t, 369
Morgan Stanley, 390
Morningstar, 99
Mortgage-backed securities, 4–5, 47, 48
Mortgage bonds, 366
Mortgage loans, 4–5, 48
Mossin, Jan, 152
Multinational corporations (MNCs)
    comparative advantage and, 509
    cultural risks facing, 518
    ethical issues facing, 508–509
    exchange rates and, 512–513
    financial advantages of, 508
    overview of, 508
    political risks facing, 517–518
Municipal bonds, 30
Mutually exclusive projects, 240, 273–275, 274f
Mutuals, 49
MVA (market value added), 92, 93–94

N

Nacional Electricidad SA, 370
NAFTA (North American Free Trade Agreement),
    518, 518–519, 520
Nasdaq, 16, 384, 390f
National Credit Union Administration (NCUA), 51
National Credit Union Share Insurance Fund
    (NCUSIF), 51
Negative interest rates, 359–360
Negotiable certificates of deposit, 28
Neiman Marcus, 347
Net cash flow, 68–69, 69f, 70f, 71
Net income
    coefficient of variation of, 140–141, 142f
    combined leverage and, 339–340
    in dividend payout ratio, 405
    financial leverage and, 337–339, 347
    on income statement, 63, 63f, 65
    operating income and, 337–339
Net present value (NPV)
    in accounts receivable analysis, 460–465, 461t,
        463t, 464f
    calculation of, 243–246
    decision rules, 246
    in inventory level analysis, 468–470, 469f
    for multiple internal rates of return, 272–273,
        273f, 274f
    overview of, 242
    problems in, 248
    real options and, 287–290, 289f, 290t
Net present value (NPV) profile
    in capital budgeting, 246–247, 247f, 248f
    internal rate of return and, 251–252
Net profit margin
    calculating, 86
    in Du Pont equation, 94
    in modified Du Point equation, 94–95
Net working capital
    changes in, 279, 279t
    overview of, 68
    in working capital management, 422, 422t

Net worth, common stock valuation, 311
New York Stock Exchange (NYSE), 26–27,
    514–515
Nissan, 508
Nokia, 514
Nominal interest rate, 31, 31f
Nominal risk-free rate of interest, 32
Nonconstant growth dividend model, for common
    stock valuation, 308–310, 309f
Noncumulative preferred stock, 370, 371
Nondiversifiable risk
    measurement of, 149–150
    overview of, 148–149, 149f
Nonsimple projects, capital budgeting, 272
Normal distribution, 140, 141f
North American Free Trade Agreement (NAFTA),
    518, 518–519, 520
Notes, 29
Notes payable
    on balance sheet, 68, 67f, 70f
    as current liability, 422
    on *pro forma* balance sheet, 121
NPV. *See* Net present value (NPV)
NPV profile. *See* Net present value (NPV) profile
NYSE (New York Stock Exchange), 26–27,
    514–515

O

Obama, Barack, 54, 229, 518
OCC (Office of the Comptroller of the Currency), 44
Occupational Safety and Health Administration
    (OSHA), 508
Offer price, 25
Office of the Comptroller of the Currency (OCC), 44
Office of Thrift Supervision, 49
Open-market operations, 46
Operating activities, on statement of cash flows,
    69, 69f, 70
Operating cash flows, 280–281, 280t, 284, 284t
Operating costs, 142–144, 143t, 144t. *See also*
    Expense(s)
Operating income
    business risk and, 142–144, 143t, 144t
    on income statement, 63f, 64–65, 65
    leverage and, 334, 334–337, 334t, 335t
    variability of, 142–144, 143t, 144t
    volatility of, 142–144, 143t, 144t
Operating leases, 372–373
Operating leverage
    breakeven analysis and, 341–346, 342t, 343t,
        344f, 344t, 346f, 346t
    in combined leverage, 339–340
    degree of, 334–335, 336–337
    risk of, 142–144, 143t, 144t, 337
Operating profit margin, 85
Operation Twist, 34
Opportunity costs, 164, 168–169, 281
Optimal capital budget, 228, 228t
Optimal cash balance, 438–442, 438f, 440f, 441f
Option pricing, 393, 395–397, 396t
Ordering costs, 465
Ordinary annuities
    future value factor for, 174–176, A-6t–A-7t
    future value of, 173–176, 174f

overview of, 173
    present value factor for, 176–178, A-10t–A-11t
    present value of, 176–178
Orr, Daniel, 440
OSHA (Occupational Safety and Health
    Administration), 508
OTS (Office of Thrift Supervision), 49
Over-the-counter (OTC) market, 27
Ownership, forms of, 14–17, 18t

P

Panasonic, 369
Partnerships
    limited, 15
    limited liability, 15
    overview of, 15, 18t
Par value, 29, 68
Patton, General George S., 135
Payback method, of capital budgeting, 241–242
Payback period, 241–242
Payday loans, 485
Payment date, 409, 409f, 410t
Pension Benefit Guaranty Corporation (PBGC), 53
Pension funds
    defined benefit plan, 53
    defined contribution plan, 53
    overview of, 53–54
P/E ratio, 90, 310
Pepsi-Cola, 508
Permanent current assets, 423–424, 423f, 424f
Perpetuity, 184
Personal income taxes, 61–62, 73
PetSmart, 346
Pinterest, 114
Pledge, of collateral, 497
Political instability, international trade and,
    516–517
Political risks, facing multinational corporations,
    517–518
Portfolio
    fluctuations in, beta and, 149–150, 150f
    standard deviation of, 148
Portfolio risks
    correlation and, 147, 147f
    diversification and, 146–148, 147f
    measurement of, 146, 147f
    nondiversifiable, 148–150, 149f, 150f
    overview of, 146
    standard deviation and, 148
Post, 26
PPP (purchasing power parity) theory, 515–516
Prechter, Robert, Jr. 437
Preemptive rights, 392–394, 394t, 395t
Preferred stock. *See also* Stock
    convertible, 371
    corporate investment in, 371
    cost of, 215–217
    cumulative, 370, 371
    dividends from, 65–66, 70, 371. *See also*
        Dividends noncumulative, 370, 371
    overview of, 31, 370
    participating, 370
    present value of, 305–306
    price of. *See* Stock price

valuation of, 305–307
yield on, 306–307
Premium
bond price at, 304, 305f
call, 362
inflation, 31f, 32
risk, 31f, 33, 152
Prepaid expenses, 66, 67f
Present value
of annuity due, 181–184, 183f
compounding periods and, 171–172, 172f
defined, 165
discount rate and, 168–171, 172f
of future cash flows, 305–306
interest rate changes and, 171–172, 172f
of investment with uneven cash flows,
184–186, 185t
of ordinary annuity, 176–178
of perpetuity, 184
of single amount, 168–172, 172f
Present value factor (PVF), 170, A-4t–A-5t
Present value factor for an ordinary annuity
(PVFOA), 176–178, A-10t–A-11t
Present value factor for an ordinary annuity due
(PVFAD), 182–183, 188–189, A-12t–A-13t
Present value interest factor for an annuity
(PVIFA), 176, 188, 243
Price
ask (offer), 25
bid, 25
call, 362
exercise, 395–397, 396t
stock. See Stock price
Price to earnings (P/E) ratio, 90, 310
Primary market, 25, 26
Primary reserves, 45
Principal, 12, 29
Private corporations
common stock of, 385
overview of, 16
Probability distribution
normal, 140, 141f
overview of, 137
Professional corporations, 16
Profit(s)
double taxation of, 15–16, 17
gross, 63f, 64
vs. stock value, 11
Profitability
accounts receivable and, 459–460, 459t
inventory and, 459–460, 459t
vs. liquidity, 424
Profitability ratios. See also Financial ratios
calculation of, 84–87
gross profit margin, 84–85, 87
mixed, 87
net profit margin, 86
operating profit margin, 85
overview of, 83, 84
return on assets, 86
return on equity, 86–87
Profit margin
gross, 84–85, 87
net. See Net profit margin
Pro forma balance sheets, 120–125, 123f, 124f

Pro forma financial statements
in accounts receivable analysis, 460–465, 461t,
463t, 464f
additional funds needed in, 122
analysis of, 123–125
balance sheet for, 120–125, 123f, 124f
budgets for, 116–117
excess financing in, 122
forecasting basis, for, 117
income statement for, 118–120, 120f,
123–125, 124f
in inventory analysis, 465–470, 467f, 468t, 469f
overview of, 116
production of, 117–123
Pro forma income statements, 118–120, 120f,
123–125, 124f
Progressive tax rate structure, 61–62, 73
Promissory note, 487
Property, plant, and equipment, on pro forma
balance sheet, 121
Property and casualty insurance companies, 52–53
Proprietary trading, 55
Proprietorship, 14–15, 18t
Prospectus, 390
Proxies, 385–386
Publicly traded corporations
common stock of, 385
overview of, 16
Public warehouse, collateral inventory storage
in, 498
Purchase price, 279
Purchasing, vs. leasing, 373–375, 374t
Purchasing power parity (PPP) theory, 515–516
Pure time value of money, 164
Putable bonds, 369
PVF (present value factor), 170, A-4t–A-5t
PVFAD (present value factor for an ordinary
annuity due), 182–183, 188–189, A-12t–A-13t
PVFOA (present value factor for an ordinary
annuity), 176–178, A-10t–A-11t
PVIFA (present value interest factor for an
annuity), 176, 188, 243

Q

Quantitative easing (QE), 47
Quarterly compounding, 195
Quick ratio, 88, 99
Quota, 519

R

RADRs (risk-adjusted discount rates),
257–258, 258t
Ranking decision, 240, 246
Ratio analysis
Du Pont system in, 94–95
industry comparisons in, 96, 97t
overview of, 83
ratios used in, 83–95. See also Financial ratios
resources for, 99
summary analysis and, 97–99, 98t
trend analysis and, 96, 96t, 97f, 97t
of working capital policy, 428, 429t
Real assets, 50

Real options, 287–290, 289f, 290t
Real rate of interest, 31–32, 31f
Refunding, 362, 362–365, 363t, 364t
Regency Centers Corporation, 26
Relative purchasing power parity theory, 516
Replacement chain approach
projects with unequal lives, 275, 275f
replacement value of assets method, 318
Required rate of return. See also Cost of debt
adjustment of, 151–152
in capital asset pricing model, 152–153,
153t, 154f
in discounted cash flow model, 299
investor's, 299, 306–307
risk and, 152–153, 153t, 154f
Required reserve ratio, 45, 45t
Reserves
commercial bank, 45, 45t
savings and loan, 49
Residual income, 384
Residual theory of dividends, 407, 407t
Restrictive covenants, 365
Retained earnings
on income statement, 63f, 65–66, 66f, 68
on pro forma balance sheet, 122
in residual theory of dividends, 407
statement of, 66, 66f
stock dividends and, 410–411
Retirement plans, 53–54
Return, risk and. See Risk-return relationship
Return on assets (ROA)
calculating, 86
in Du Pont equation, 94
Return on equity (ROE)
calculating, 86–87
in modified Du Point equation, 94–95
Return on investments, 440
Revco, 347
Revenue bonds, 30
Revenues, 63, 63f
Revolving credit agreement, 488
Rights, 392–394, 394t, 395t
Rights-on trading, 393–394, 394t
Risk
adjustment for, in capital budgeting,
257–258, 258t
beta, 149–150, 150f, 256
bond, 366, 367f
breakeven analysis and, 344–346
business, 142–144, 143t, 144t, 337
in business valuation, 299
compensation for, 151–152
diversification and, 146–148, 147f, 151,
514, 515f
financial, 144–145, 145t
firm, 256–257
hedging and, 513–514
in international finance and, 513–515, 515f
management of, 150–152, 513–515, 515f
market, 256
measurement of. See Risk measurement
nondiversifiable, 148–150, 149f, 150f
of operating leverage and, 337
overview of, 136
portfolio, 146–150

profit/loss potential and, 344–346, 344f, 346f, 346t
project-specific, 256
reduction of, 151
stock price and, 10–11, 11t
systematic, 5–6, 135–136
uncertainty and, 137
value and, 10–11, 11t
Risk-adjusted discount rates (RADRs), 257–258, 258t
Risk assessment, 52
Risk aversion, 136
Risk-free rate of return, 152
Risk measurement
  in capital budgeting, 255–258
  coefficient of variation in, 140–141, 142f, 256–257
  firm risk, 256–257
  standard deviation in, 137–140, 138f
Risk premium
  default, 32
  illiquidity, 32–33
  maturity, 33
Risk-return relationship
  capital asset pricing model and, 152–153, 153t, 154f
  current liabilities and, 425
  desirable, 151
  for leveraged buyouts, 347
  overview of, 136–137
  unsecured bonds, 366
Rite Aid, 369
RJR Nabisco, 347
ROA. See Return on assets (ROA)
ROE. See Return on equity (ROE)

S

S&Ls. See Savings and loan associations (S&Ls)
Safe storage premium, 33
Safeway, 346–347
SAIF (Savings Association Insurance Fund), 49
Sales breakeven analysis. See Breakeven analysis
Sales breakeven point, 341
Sales finance companies, 52
Sales forecasts, 115–116, 137–140. See also Forecasting Sales projection, in pro forma income statement, 118
Sales revenue, in breakeven analysis, 343, 343t
Sales volatility
  business risk and, 143
  leverage and, 337, 339
  operating income and, 334, 334–337, 334t, 335t
  reduction of, 151
Salvage value, 72
Sarbanes-Oxley Act, 5
Sarnoff, Robert W., 403
Savings and loan associations (S&Ls)
  loan-deposit matching by, 48–50, 49t, 50t
  mutual vs. stockholder owned, 49
  overview of, 48–49
  real assets of, 50
  regulation of, 49

Savings Association Insurance Fund (SAIF), 49
S corporations, 16
SEC (Securities and Exchange Commission), 16, 62, 229, 514
Second-mortgage bond, 366
Secondary market, 25, 26
Secondary reserves, 45
Section 179 deductions, 72
Secured bonds, 361
Securities
  in capital market, 28–31
  hybrid, 370
  marketable, 66, 120–121
  in money market, 27–28
  overview of, 24–25
  trading of, 27–31
  Treasury. See Treasury securities
Securities and Exchange Commission (SEC), 16, 62, 229, 514
Security exchanges, 26–27
Self-liquidating loan, 487
Selling and administrative expenses, 63f, 64
Selling expenses, in pro forma income statement, 118
Semiannual compounding, 193–194
Semiannual coupon interest payments, 303
Senior debentures, 366, 367f
Serial payments, 361
Share classes, 384
Shareholders, credit union, 51
Sharpe, William F., 152
Short-term financing. See also Loan(s)
  in aggressive working capital approach, 426, 426f
  alternatives for, 487–491
  amount to borrow, calculation of, 496
  bank loans in, 487–488
  collateral for, 496–498
  commercial paper in, 489–491
  cost of, calculation of, 495
  vs. long-term financing, 486–487, 487f
  in moderate working capital approach, 427–428, 428f
  need for, 486
  overview of, 419, 486
  pros and cons of, 486–487, 487f
  trade credit in, 488–489, 489f
Shutdown cash flows, 281–282, 282t, 284–285, 285t
Signaling, 389
Signaling dividend theory, 408
Simple interest, 165
Simple project, capital budgeting, 272
Sinking funds, 362
Small-loan companies, 51
Societal interests, 13–14, 14f, 508–509
Sole proprietorship, 14–15
Sony, 369, 514
Southland Corporation, 347
Spot rate, 516
Staggered maturities, 361
Stakeholders, 13

Standard deviation
  calculation of, 138–140
  coefficient of variation and, 140–141, 142f
  interpretation of, 140
  overview of, 137–138
  of two-asset portfolio, 148
Standard & Poor's, 4, 360, 361t, 369
Starboard Value, 386
Stated interest rate, 487
Statement of cash flows, 68–71, 69f, 70f
Statement of retained earnings, 66, 66f
Statistical independence, 147
Stern Stewart & Company, 92
Stock
  capital gains from, 30
  common. See Common stock
  controlling interest in, 386
  corporate, 30
  dividends from. See Dividends
  exchange-listed, 26
  ex-dividend trading of, 409
  foreign, 513, 514. See also International finance/trade
  overview of, 30
  preferred. See Preferred stock
Stock certificates, 384, 384f
Stock dividends, 410–413, 410t, 411t. See also Dividends Stock price
  cash flow and, 10–11, 11t
  determinants of, 10–11, 11t
  as indicator of firm's value, 9
  risk and, 10–11, 11t
  after stock dividend, 411–412
  after stock split, 413
  timing and, 10, 11, 11t
  vs. value, 11
Stock splits, 412–413, 412t, 413t
Stockholders
  common vs. preferred stock, 30
  overview of, 9, 30
  savings and loan associations, 49
  voting rights of, 386–388
Straight bond value, 368–369
Straight-line depreciation, 72
Strengthening currency, 511
Subordinated debentures, 366, 367f
Summary analysis, 97–99, 98t
Summers, Lawrence, 507
Sunk costs, 278
Super long-term bonds, 370
Supernormal growth dividend model, 308–310, 309f
Surplus economic units, 24, 42, 43f, 43, 52
Swaps, 135, 513–514
Syndicate, 390
Syrus, Publilius, 239
Systematic risk, 5–6, 135–136

T

Tariffs, 519
Tax(es)
  after-tax cost of debt and, 213–215, 363
  alternative minimum tax, 62

asset sale and, 281–282, 282t
capital gains, 281
corporations, 15–17
on dividends, 371, 409
double taxation and, 15–16
fake leases and, 371–372
income, 73, 120
on lease vs. purchase, 373–375, 374t
operating cash flows and, 280, 280t
partnerships, 15
on preferred stock dividends, 371
proprietorships, 14
Tax Cuts and Jobs Act of 2017 (TCJA)
after-tax cost of debt, 213–215, 363
business interest expense deductibility, 61–62,
64–65, 213–215, 347–348, 363–364
depreciation, 61–62, 72
leveraged buyouts, 213–214, 347
overview, 61–62
preferred stock investors, 371
tax rates, 61–62, 73, 214–215, 239
Tax-deductible expenses
on income statement, 64, 65
interest as, 61–62, 64–65, 213–215, 347–348,
363–364
Tax rates
capital gains, 281
flat, 61–62, 73, 214, 239
marginal, 214
overview of, 73
progressive, 61–62, 73
Tax Cuts and Jobs Act of 2017, 61–62, 73,
214–215, 239
Tax Reform Act of 1986, 61, 72
TCJA. See Tax Cuts and Jobs Act of 2017 (TCJA)
Temporary current assets, 423–244, 423f, 424f
10-K reports, 62
10-Q reports, 62
Terminal value, 253, 316
Thompson-Houston Electric Company, 403
TIAA–CREF, 53
Times interest earned, 89
Time value of money
annuities and, 186–192
deception and, bond example, 163–164
future value and, 164–168
measurement of, 164–165
problem solving, 186–192
present value and, 165, 168–172, 172f
pure, 164
Tombstone ad, 390, 391f
Toshiba, 241
Total asset turnover
calculating, 90
in Du Pont equation, 94
in modified Du Pont equation, 95
Total debt capital, vs. total liabilities, 93
Total market value, of business, 300f, 316, 317f
Total sales revenue, in breakeven analysis,
343, 343t
Total stockholders' equity, valuation of, 300, 300f,
310–311

Toyota, 508
Toys "R" Us, 347
TPP (Trans-Pacific Partnership) trade accord, 518
Trade, international, 507–520. See also
International finance/trade
Trade agreements, international, 518–520
Trade credit, 488–489, 489f
Transaction costs, 440
Transfer agent, 409
Trans-Pacific Partnership (TPP) trade accord, 51
Treasurer, 8
Treasury securities
commercial paper vs., 489
purchase of, 29
quantitative easing and, 47
Treasury bills (T-bills), 28, 360
Treasury bonds (T-bonds), 29
Treasury notes (T-notes), 29
yield curve, 34–35, 35f
Trend analysis
industry comparisons and, 96, 96t, 97f, 97t
in summary analysis, 97–99, 98t
Trump, Donald, 518, 519
Trustee, 365–366
Trust receipt, 497–498

U

Uncertainty, 137. See also Risk
Underwriting
vs. best efforts basis, 390
overview of, 25
Unlimited liability, 14–15
Unilever, 514
Univision Communications Inc., 347
Unsecured bonds, 366, 367f
U.S. Treasury, 3–4, 12, 23, 34, 35f, 48, 360

V

VA (Veterans Administration), 48
Valuation. See also Business valuation
of bonds, 301–305, 305f
of cash flow, 10, 11t
of common stock, 307–317. See also Common
stock valuation of inventory, 497
of preferred stock, 305–307
of total stockholders' equity, 310–311
of warrants, 395–396, 396t
Value
cash flow and, 10, 11, 11t
enterprise, 316, 318
overview of, 5–6
profits vs., 11
risk and, 10–11, 11t
terminal, 253, 316
timing and, 10, 11t
wealth and, 9
Variable costs, 341
Variable-rate bonds, 369
Venture capital (VC) firms, 229
Veterans Administration (VA), 48

Volcker, Paul, 55
Volcker Rule, 55
Voting rights, of common stockholders, 386–388

W

WACC. See Weighted average cost of capital
(WACC)
Wall Street, 3, 5
Warehouse, collateral inventory storage in, 498
Warrants, 394–397, 396t
Washington Mutual, 41
Weakening currency, 511
Wealth, 9
Weighted average cost of capital (WACC)
in capital structure theory, 348–349, 349f
cost of capital and, 220–222
cost of equity and, 348–349, 349f
economic value added and, 92
marginal cost of capital and, 222–226, 228
Wells Fargo Securities, 26
West, Kanye, 421
Working capital. See also Current assets
on balance sheet, 66, 68
bond-related restrictions on, 365
management of. See Working capital policy
net, 279, 279t, 422, 422t
overview of, 421, 422
Working capital policy
aggressive, 426, 426f
conservative, 426–427, 427f
liquidity vs. profitability and, 424
management of, 422, 422t, 425
moderate, 427–428, 428f
optimal level of current assets and, 425
ratio analysis of, 428, 429t
risk-return relationship and, 425
World Trade Organization (WTO), 519, 520

X

Xerox, 241

Y

Yahoo finance, 99
Yankee bond, 370
Yield
on common stock, 316–317
discount, 489–490
dividend, 218, 317
on preferred stock, 306–307
Yield curve, 34–35, 35f
Yield to maturity (YTM)
business valuation and, 304, 304–305, 305f
calculation of, 304–305
price and, 304–305, 305f

Z

Zero-coupon bonds, 29
Zuckerberg, Mark, 151, 384
Z value, in capital structure theory, 348–350, 349f